Textbook Trialware

Free 140-day Trial of Crystal Ball Software Compliments of the Crystal Ball Education Alliance

KEEP THIS CARD!!

See instructions below to download
Oracle Crystal Ball software

1 Visit http://www.oracle.com/technology/products/bi/crystalball (REGISTER)

2 Click on the Downloads Tab, accept license agreement

3 Download and install Oracle Crystal Ball software

4 Enter the information below when prompted during installation

username: Mantel 8th Edition 9780470533024
serial number: 72133FCE-3FAA13F5-420192E0-EBE202F5

Available Software

Crystal Ball® Trial Edition from Oracle: This software can be downloaded online by students by using the registration cards packaged with the text.

Microsoft Project®: Professors may get their students access to the full version of through Wiley's MSDN Academic Alliance

More Information

For more information about Microsoft Project®, *go to:*
http://www.microsoft.com/project

For information about a FREE 3-year membership to the MSDN Academic Alliance, *go to:*
http://msdn.microsoft.com/academic/

For more information about Crystal Ball®, *go to:*
http://www.crystalball.com/

Technical Support

Wiley technical support for Microsoft Project®
http://www.wiley.com/techsupport

Oracle tech support for Crystal Ball®
http://www.crystalball.com/support_center.html

Online Resources for Students

http://www.wiley.com/go/global/meredith
- Web Quizzes, PowerPoint® Slides
- Appendix A: Probability and Statistics
- Appendix B: Answers to Even-Numbered Problems
- Creativity and Idea Generation
- Technological Forecasting

Location of Materials for the Project Management Body of Knowledge (PMBOK) Areas

Area 1: Project Integration Management: Section 6.4
Area 2: Project Scope Management: Sections 4.3, 6.1, 11.3, 11.4
Area 3: Project Time Management: Chapters 6, 8, 10, 11
Area 4: Project Cost Management: Chapters 7, 9
Area 5: Project Quality Management: Chapters 6, 12
Area 6: Project Human Resource Management: Chapters 3, 4
Area 7: Project Communications Management: Sections 3.2, 3.4, 4.1, 4.2
Area 8: Project Risk Management: Sections 6.1, 6.5, 7.3, Chapters 10, 11
Area 9: Project Procurement Management: Sections 2.6, 6.4

EIGHTH EDITION

PROJECT MANAGEMENT

A Managerial Approach

EIGHTH EDITION

PROJECT MANAGEMENT
A Managerial Approach

International Student Version

Jack R. Meredith

Broyhill Distinguished Scholar and Chair in Operations
Wake Forest University

Samuel J. Mantel, Jr.

Joseph S. Stern Professor Emeritus of Operations Management
University of Cincinnati

John Wiley & Sons, Inc.

DEDICATION

To Avery and Mitchell, from "papajack."

J. R. M.

To Maggie and Patty for their help, support, and affection.

S. J. M.

Copyright © 2012 John Wiley & Sons Singapore Pte. Ltd.

Cover image from ©Niar/Shutterstock

Contributing Subject Matter Experts: Eric Woodcock and Ian Cammack

Founded in 1807, John Wiley & Sons, Inc. has been a valued source of knowledge and understanding for more than 200 years, helping people around the world meet their needs and fulfill their aspirations. Our company is built on a foundation of principles that include responsibility to the communities we serve and where we live and work. In 2008, we launched a Corporate Citizenship Initiative, a global effort to address the environmental, social, economic, and ethical challenges we face in our business. Among the issues we are addressing are carbon impact, paper specifications and procurement, ethical conduct within our business and among our vendors, and community and charitable support. For more information, please visit our website: www.wiley.com/go/citizenship.

ISBN: 978-1-118-09373-3

Printed in Asia

10 9 8 7 6 5 4 3

Preface

APPROACH

The use of projects and project management continues to grow in our society and its organizations. We are able to achieve goals through project organization that could be achieved only with the greatest of difficulty if organized in traditional ways. Though project management has existed since before the days of the great pyramids, its use has virtually exploded since the mid-1990s. Businesses regularly use project management to accomplish unique outcomes with limited resources under critical time constraints. In the service sector of the economy, the use of project management to achieve an organization's goals is even more common. Advertising campaigns, voter registration drives, political campaigns, a family's annual summer vacation, and even management seminars on the subject of project management are organized as projects. A relatively new growth area in the use of project management is the use of projects as a way of accomplishing organizational change. Indeed, there is a rapid increase in the number of firms that use projects as the preferred way of accomplishing almost everything they undertake.

As the field has grown, so has its literature. There are now professional books and booklets covering every imaginable aspect of project management: earned value calculations, team building, cost estimating, purchasing, project management software, scheduling, leadership, and so on. These are valuable for experienced project managers who can profit from advanced knowledge on specific topics. There are also handbooks—collections of articles written mainly by academics and consultants on selected topics of interest to project managers, somewhat akin to a summarized compilation of the books and booklets just noted.

When we wrote the first edition of this textbook in 1983, there weren't any textbooks for those interested in learning project management, only professional books. Now, however, there are a few, each using a different approach to learning the subject. One approach has been to take a behavioral orientation toward the subject, since teamwork is a key characteristic of projects. Another approach is to cover the basics, or tools, of project management in a straightforward and crisp manner. A third approach is to take a functional perspective, usually either engineering or information systems, since so many projects are engineering or IS endeavors. The approach we have used takes a *managerial* perspective. That is, it addresses project management from the perspective of what the project manager will encounter, both chronologically during the "life cycle" of the project as well as practically, in the sense of what the project manager needs to know and why. With this approach we hope that our educated future project managers understand not only the behaviors, tools, and topics of project management but also the context so they can apply, or change, the behaviors and tools for each unique situation they face in their projects.

This managerial perspective, we believe, addresses the basic nature of managing all types of projects—public, business, engineering, information systems, and so on—as well as the specific techniques and insights required to carry out this unique way of getting things done. It also deals with the problems of selecting projects, initiating and planning them, executing and controlling them, and finally evaluating and terminating them. It discusses the demands made on the project manager and the nature of the manager's interaction with the rest of the parent organization. And the book covers the difficult problems associated with conducting a project using people and organizations that represent different cultures and may be separated by considerable distances. Finally, it even covers the issues arising when the decision is made to terminate a project.

The book is primarily intended for use as a college textbook for teaching project management at the advanced undergraduate or master's level. The book is also intended for current and prospective project managers who wish to share our insights and ideas about the field. We have drawn freely on our personal experiences working with project managers and on the experience of friends and colleagues who have spent much of their working lives serving as project managers in what they like to call the "real world." Thus, in contrast to the books described earlier *about* project management, this book teaches students how to *do* project management. As well as being a text that is equally appropriate for classes on the management of service, product, or engineering projects, we have found that information systems (IS) students in our classes find the material particularly helpful for managing their IS projects. Thus, we have included some coverage of material concerning information systems and how IS projects differ from and are similar to regular business projects.

ORGANIZATION AND CONTENT

Given this managerial perspective, we have arranged the book to use the *project life cycle* as the primary organizational guideline. In this eighth edition we have altered the organization slightly to demark more clearly the activities that occur before the launch of the project, setting up those activities that have to do with the *context* (or *initiation*) of the project in the first part of the book, and those that have to do with the *planning* for the project in the second part. Actually *executing* the project to completion constitutes the third part of the book. Each part consists of four chapters, which seems to be a comfortable and easy framework for the reader.

Following an introductory chapter that comments on the role and importance of projects in our society and discusses project management as a potential career for aspiring managers, the book covers the context, events, and issues arising during the management of projects in the order in which they usually occur in the life of a project. *Part I, Project Initiation* concerns the context of the project, which is crucial for the project manager to understand if he or she is to be successful in executing the project. It begins with a description of how projects are selected for implementation, frequently based on their tie to the organization's strategy and goals. Part I also covers the many roles and responsibilities of the project manager, the skills the project manager needs for handling conflict, and the various ways of setting up the project within the organization's reporting structure (including how different ways of organizing projects tend to create different problems for project managers and their teams).

Part II, Project Planning then moves into the planning processes starting with the major tools used in project activity and risk planning. This is followed by project budgeting, project scheduling, and finally, resource allocation among the activities. *Part III, Project Execution* finally gets into the action, beginning with monitoring the activities, largely through information systems, and then controlling them to assure that the results meet expectations. Evaluating and possibly auditing the project at its major milestones or phase-gates is another, though separate, control action that senior management often employs, and last, the project must be terminated.

We have relegated the discussion of two important aspects of projects that usually occur very early in the project life cycle—creativity/idea generation and technological forecasting—to the book's Web site. Although few project managers engage in either of these tasks (typically being appointed to project leadership after these activities have taken place), we believe that a knowledge of these subjects will make the project manager more effective.

In writing this text we assume that all readers have taken an elementary course in management or have had equivalent experience, and are familiar with some basic principles of probability and statistics. (Appendix A on the Web site (http://www.wiley.com/go/global/meredith) can serve as an initial tutorial on the subject or as a refresher for rusty knowledge.)

Any approach chosen to organize knowledge carries with it an implication of neatness and order that rarely occurs in reality. We are quite aware that projects almost never proceed in an orderly, linear way through the stages and events we describe here. The need to deal with change and uncertainty is a constant task for the project manager. We have tried to reflect this in repeated references to the organizational, interpersonal, economic, and technical glitches that create crises in the life cycle of every project, and thus in the life of every project manager.

Finally, although we use a life-cycle approach to organization, the chapters include material concerning the major areas of the *Project Management Body of Knowledge* (PMBOK®) as defined by the Project Management Institute. (See Bibliography for Chapter 1.) Anyone wishing to prepare for PMI certification (see Chapter 1) in some of these areas may have to go beyond the information covered in this text.

PEDAGOGY

Because this book is primarily a textbook, we have included numerous pedagogical aids to foster this purpose. As in earlier editions, *short summaries* appear at the end of the text of each chapter, followed by *glossaries* defining key terms and concepts introduced in the chapter. End-of-chapter materials also include *review questions* and *problems* revisiting the materials covered in the chapter. The answers (though not the detailed solutions) to the even-numbered problems are on the book's Web site. There are also sets of conceptual *discussion questions* intended to broaden the students' perspectives and to force them to think beyond the chapter materials to its implications. To keep our attitude in perspective, we occasionally offer *Dilbert*® cartoons appropriate to the topic under discussion. Finally, there are questions covering the many Project Management in Practice application examples located throughout the chapters.

As in the past, we include *incidents for discussion*, which are brief "caselettes" oriented primarily toward the specific subjects covered in the chapter, but sometimes materials and concepts covered in earlier chapters. We also offer a *continuing integrative class project* for those users who prefer a running case throughout the chapters that builds on the chapter materials as students progress through the book. And at the very end of each chapter we typically offer a *reading* and/or a *case*, with potential discussion questions at the end of each.

WHAT'S NEW

In this edition, we have made many updates, additions, and changes.

- Continuing our effort to simplify and shorten the writing, we have eliminated many of the historical explanations of the derivation of particular tools and subjects, as well as descriptions of equivalent topics in other fields, particularly systems engineering.

- One of the authors' sons, an Intel Corp. engineer, upon reading this book, had vociferous complaints about obscure Latin words and historical references, so we eliminated most (though not quite all) of these.

- Equally irritating to him, and to some of the reviewers as well, was our habit of constantly referring to locations where a topic would be again discussed in upcoming chapters, most of which we also eliminated.

We have also put a major effort into aligning the book with the 4th edition (2008) of PMBOK® in multiple ways.

- First, we combined most of the risk techniques and discussion throughout the book into Chapter 6, now called "Project Activity and Risk Planning," although we still discuss risk when talking about project selection, budgeting, and control. In the risk discussion we now include examples of FMEA, cause-effect diagrams, risk matrices, and decision trees.

- We moved the risk technique of simulating costs with Crystal Ball® from Chapter 2 to Chapter 7: "Budgeting: Estimating Costs and Risks." Reviewers were concerned that introducing simulation so early in Chapter 2 not only was tackling a difficult subject too early but also made the chapter too long—moving it to Chapter 7 not only gives the student more time to digest the subject but also puts it where it belongs in the costs chapter, which was short to begin with.

- We also followed PMBOK in dropping the concept of the Action Plan in Chapter 6 and instead use the work breakdown structure (WBS) to lay the foundation for project planning.

- We also dropped the concepts of a "master schedule" as well as that of a "project plan," instead referring to the project "charter."

- Last, we refer to the PMBOK more frequently in our discussions, and when we do, we identify where in PMBOK that topic is covered.

- Similar to our aggregating most of the risk topics in one chapter, we also aggregated most of the discussion of "scope creep" in Chapter 11: Project Control. We do mention scope creep in many places throughout the book but the major discussion, including how it arises and how to control it, now is aggregated in Chapter 11.

- Last, we have added a lot more Project Management in Practice examples (sidebars) from the very recent literature (mostly 2010), and deleted some older ones. As well, we have slimmed down some of the lengthy older ones to focus more directly on their message. New discussion questions have been added for the new PMIP examples also, of course.

As before, a student version of Crystal Ball®, an Excel® add-in, again comes with the book. This software makes simulation reasonably straightforward and not particularly complicated. The use of simulation as a technique for risk analysis is demonstrated in several ways in different chapters. (Because relatively few students are familiar with simulation software, step-by-step instruction is included in the text.)

Microsoft Project® has become the dominant application software in the field, outselling its closest competitor about 4 to 1. Our coverage of software tends, therefore, to be centered on Microsoft Project® (and on Crystal Ball®), but includes a brief discussion of the many "add-ons" that are now available to supplement Microsoft Project® and its competitors. Because the various versions of Microsoft Project® are quite similar in the way that they perform most of the basic tasks of project management, we generally do not differentiate between the versions, referring to any and all simply as Microsoft Project (MSP). We have also added some exercises to the end-of-chapter material that can utilize computer software. Similar materials are also available on the Web site.

A new option now available to educational institutions adopting this Wiley textbook is a free 3-year membership to the MSDN Academic Alliance. The MSDN AA is designed to provide the easiest and most inexpensive way for academic departments to make the latest Microsoft software available in labs, classrooms, and on student PCs.

Microsoft Project 2007 software is available through this Wiley and Microsoft publishing partnership, free of charge with the adoption of any qualified Wiley textbook. Each copy of Microsoft Project is the full version of the software, with no time limitations, and can be used indefinitely for educational purposes. Contact your Wiley sales rep for details. For more information about the MSDN AA program, go to http://msdn.microsoft .com/academic/.

There is, of course, the danger that human nature, operating in its normal discreet mode, will shift the task of learning project management to that of learning project management *software*. Projects have often failed because the project manager started managing the software instead of the project. Instructors need to be aware of the problem and must caution students not to fall into this trap.

ONLINE SUPPLEMENTS

The *Instructor's Resource Guide* on the Web site www.wiley.com/go/global/meredith provides additional assistance to the project management instructor. In addition to the answers/ solutions to the problems, questions, readings, and cases, this edition includes teaching tips, a computerized test bank, additional cases, and PowerPoint slides. All of these valuable resources are available online (http://www.wiley.com/go/global/meredith). In addition, the student Web site contains Web quizzes, PowerPoint® slides, Appendix A: Probability and Statistics, Appendix B: Answers to the Even-Numbered Problems, Creativity and Idea Generation, Technological Forecasting, a Glossary, and a Microsoft Project Manual.

ACKNOWLEDGMENTS

We owe a debt of gratitude to all those who have helped us with this book, especially the staff at Wiley. First, we thank the managers and students who helped us solidify our ideas about proper methods for managing projects and proper ways of teaching the subject. Second, we thank the project teams and leaders in all of our project management classes. We are especially grateful to Margaret Sutton and Scott Shafer whose creative ideas, extensive skills with software, and ability to sniff out inconsistencies saved us countless hours of fumbling and potential embarrassment. Last, but never least, we thank Suzanne Ingrao/Ingrao Associates, editor nonpareil, and Ramya Srinivasan/MPS Limited, a MacMillan Company for seemingly effortless production.

Special thanks are due those who have significantly influenced our thinking about project management or supplied materials to help us write this book: Jeffrey Camm, James Evans, Martin Levy, John McKinney, and William Meyers, all of the Univ. of Cincinnati; S. J. Mantel III, PMP; Jeffrey Pinto, Pennsylvania State Univ. at Erie; Stephen Wearne, Univ. of Manchester; and the Staff of the Project Management Institute.

We owe a massive debt of gratitude to the reviewers for previous editions: Nicholas Aquilano, Univ. of Arizona; Steve Allen, Truman State Univ.; Bob Ash, Indiana Univ., Southeast; Bud Baker, Wright State Univ.; Robert J. Berger, Univ. of Maryland; Robert Bergman, Univ. of Houston; William Brauer, Bemidji State Univ.; Maj. Mark D. Camdle, Air Force Inst. of Tech.; Howard Chamberlin, Texas A&M Univ.; Chin-Sheng Chen, Florida International Univ.; Susan Cholette, San Francisco Univ.; Denis Cioffi, George Washington Univ.; Desmond Cook, Ohio State Univ.; Edward Davis, Univ. of Virginia; Burton Dean, San Jose State Univ.; Michael H. Ensby, Clarkson Univ.; Abel Fernandez, Univ. of the Pacific; Richard E. Gunther, California State Univ., Northridge; William Hayden, Jr., SUNY, Buffalo; Jane E. Humble, Arizona State Univ.; Richard H. Irving, York Univ.; Roderick V. James, DeVry Univ.; Homayoun Kahmooshi, George Washington Univ.; David L. Keeney, Stevens Inst. of Tech.; Ted Klastorin, Univ. of Washington; David Kukulka, Buffalo State Univ.; Young Hoon Kway, George Washington Univ.; William Leban, DeVry Univ.; Ardeshir Lohrasbi, Univ. of Illinois, Springfield; Bil Matthews, William Patterson University; Sara McComb, Univ. of Massachusetts, Amherst; Abe Meilich, Walden Univ.; Mary Meixell, Quinnipiac Univ.; Jaindeep Motwani, Grand Valley State Univ.; Barin Nag, Towson Univ.; John E. Nicolay, Jr., Univ. of Minnesota; David L. Overbye, DeVry Univ.; Pat Penfield, Syracuse Univ.; Ed Pohl, Univ. of Arkansas; Michael Poli, Stevens Inst. of Tech.; Amit Raturi, Univ. of Cincinnati; David J. Robb, Univ. of Calgary; Arthur C. Rogers, City Univ., Washington; David Russo, Univ. of Texas, Dallas; Boong-Yeol Ryoo, Florida International Univ.; Thomas Schuppe, Milwaukee School of Engineering; Ruth Seiple, Univ. of Cincinnati; John Shanfi, DeVry Inst. of Tech., Irving, TX; Wade Shaw, Florida Inst. of Tech.; Richard V. Sheng, DeVry Inst. of Tech., San Marino, CA; Bill Sherrard, San Diego State Univ.; Joyce T. Shirazi, Univ. of Maryland, Univ. College; Chris Simber, Stevens Inst. of Tech.; Gene Simons, Rensselaer Polytech. Inst.; Herbert Spirer, Univ. of Connecticut; Eric Sprouls, Univ. of Southern Indiana; Peter Strunk, Univ. of Cincinnati; Samuel Taylor, Univ. of Wyoming; Tony Trippe, Rochester Inst. of Tech.; Jerome Weist, Univ. of Utah; William G. Wells, Jr., The George Washington Univ.; Susan Williams, Northern Arizona State Univ.; James Willman, Univ. of Bridgeport, and Charles I. Zigelman, San Diego State Univ.

For this edition, we thank the following reviewers: Kwasi Amoako-Gyampah, Univ. of North Carolina at Greensboro; the late Larry Crowley, Auburn Univ.; Catherine Crummett, James Madison Univ.; Bertie M. Geer, Northern Kentucky Univ.; Kimberlee Snyder, Winona State Univ. Thanks for the preparation of additional material for this International Student Version go to Eric Woodcock and Ian Cammack.

Jack Meredith
Broyhill Distinguished Scholar and Chair in
   Operations
Wake Forest University, P.O. Box 7659
Winston-Salem, NC 27109
jack.meredith@mba.wfu.edu
www.mba.wfu.edu

Samuel J. Mantel, Jr.,
Joseph S. Stern Professor Emeritus of Operations
   Management
University of Cincinnati
608 Flagstaff Drive
Cincinnati, OH 45215
mantelsj@earthlink.net

Contents

*Please visit http://www.wiley.com/go/global/meredith for Appendices.
A: Probability and Statistics and Appendix B: Answers to the Even-
Numbered Problems.*

Projects in Contemporary Organizations

The past several decades have been marked by rapid growth in the use of project management as a means by which organizations achieve their objectives. In the past, most projects were external to the organization—building a new skyscraper, designing a commercial ad campaign, launching a rocket—but the growth in the use of projects lately has primarily been in the area of projects internal to organizations: developing a new product, opening a new branch, improving the services provided to customers, and achieving strategic objectives. As exhilarating as outside projects are, successfully executing internal projects is even more satisfying in that the organization has substantially improved its ability to execute more efficiently, effectively, or quickly, resulting in an agency or business that can even better contribute to society while simultaneously enhancing its own competitive strength. Project management provides an organization with powerful tools that improve its ability to plan, implement, and control its activities as well as the ways in which it utilizes its people and resources.

It is popular to ask, "Why can't they run government the way I run my business?" In the case of project management, however, business and other organizations learned from government, not the other way around. A lion's share of the credit for the development of the techniques and practices of project management belongs to the military, which faced a series of major tasks that simply were not achievable by traditional organizations operating in traditional ways. The United States Navy's Polaris program, NASA's Apollo space program, and more recently, the space shuttle and the development of "smart" bombs and missiles are a few of the many instances of the application of these specially developed management approaches to extraordinarily complex projects. Following such examples, nonmilitary government sectors, private industry, public service agencies, and volunteer organizations have all used project management to increase their effectiveness. Most firms in the computer software business routinely develop their output as projects or groups of projects.

Project management has emerged because the characteristics of our contemporary society demand the development of new methods of management. Of the many forces involved, three are paramount: (1) the exponential expansion of human knowledge; (2) the growing demand for a broad range of complex, sophisticated, customized goods and services; and (3) the evolution of worldwide competitive markets for the production and consumption of goods and services. All three forces combine to mandate the use of teams to solve problems that used to be solvable by individuals. These three forces combine to increase greatly the complexity of goods and services produced plus the complexity of the processes used to produce them. This, in turn, leads to the need for more sophisticated systems to control both outcomes and processes.

Forces Fostering Project Management

First, the expansion of knowledge allows an increasing number of academic disciplines to be used in solving problems associated with the development, production, and distribution of goods and services. Second, satisfying the continuing demand for more complex and customized products and services depends on our ability to make product design an integrated and inherent part of our production and distribution systems. Third, worldwide markets force us to include cultural and environmental differences in our managerial decisions about what, where, when, and how to produce and distribute output. The requisite knowledge does not reside in any one individual, no matter how well educated or knowledgeable. Thus, under these conditions, teams are used for making decisions and taking action. This calls for a high level of coordination and cooperation between groups of people not particularly used to such interaction. Largely geared to the mass production of simpler goods, traditional organizational structures and management systems are simply not adequate to the task. Project management is.

The organizational response to the forces noted above cannot take the form of an instantaneous transformation from the old to the new. To be successful, the transition must be systematic, but it tends to be slow and tortuous for most enterprises. Accomplishing organizational change is a natural application of project management, and many firms have set up projects to implement their goals for strategic and tactical change.

Another important societal force is the intense competition among institutions, both profit and not-for-profit, fostered by our economic system resulting in organizational "crusades" such as "total quality control," "supply chain management," and particularly prominent these days: "Six Sigma*." The competition that all of these crusades engender puts extreme pressure on organizations to make their complex, customized outputs available as quickly as possible. "Time-to-market" is critical. Responses must come faster, decisions must be made sooner, and results must occur more quickly. Imagine the communications problems alone. Information and knowledge are growing explosively, but the time permissible to locate and use the appropriate knowledge is decreasing.

In addition, these forces operate in a society that assumes that technology can do anything. The fact is, this assumption is reasonably true, within the bounds of nature's fundamental laws. The problem lies not in this assumption so much as in a concomitant assumption that allows society to ignore both the economic and noneconomic costs associated with technological progress until some dramatic event focuses our attention on the costs (e.g., the global financial crisis, the Gulf oil spill). At times, our faith in technology is disturbed by difficulties and threats arising from its careless implementation, as in the case of industrial waste, but on the whole we seem remarkably tolerant of technological change. For a case in point, consider California farm workers who waited more than 20 years to challenge a University of California research program devoted to the development of labor-saving farm machinery (Sun, 1984). The acceptance of technological advancement is so strong it took more than two decades to muster the legal attack. Consider also the easy acceptance of communication by e-mail and shopping on the Internet.

---

*Six Sigma (see Pande et al., 2000; Pyzdek, 2003) itself involves projects, usually of a process improvement type that involves the use of many project management tools (Chapter 8), teamwork (Chapters 5 and 12), quality tools such as "benchmarking" (Chapter 11), and even audits (Chapter 12).

Finally, the projects we undertake are large and getting larger. The modern advertising company, for example, advances from blanket print ads to regionally focused television ads to personally focused Internet ads. As each new capability extends our grasp, it serves as the base for new demands that force us to extend our reach even farther. Projects increase in size and complexity because the more we can do, the more we try to do.

The projects that command the most public attention tend to be large, complex, multi-disciplinary endeavors. Often, such endeavors are both similar to and different from previous projects with which we may be more or less familiar. Similarities with the past provide a base from which to start, but the differences imbue every project with considerable risk. The complexities and multidisciplinary aspects of projects require that many parts be put together so that the project's objectives—deliverables, time (or schedule), and cost—are met.

Three Project Objectives: The "Triple Constraint"

While multimillion-dollar, five-year projects capture public attention, the overwhelming majority of all projects are comparatively small—though nonetheless important to doer and user alike. They involve outcomes, or deliverables, such as a new floor for a professional basketball team, a new insurance policy to protect against a specific casualty loss, a new Web site, a new casing for a four-wheel-drive minivan transmission, a new industrial floor cleanser, the installation of a new method for peer-review of patient care in a hospital, even the development of new software to help manage projects. The list could be extended almost without limit. These undertakings have much in common with their larger counterparts. They are complex, multidisciplinary, and have the same general objectives—specified deliverables (also commonly known as *scope**), time, and cost. We refer to these as "direct" project objectives or goals.

There is a tendency to think of a project solely in terms of its outcome—that is, its scope. But the time at which the outcome is available is itself a part of the outcome, as is the cost entailed in achieving the outcome. The completion of a building on time and on budget is quite a different outcome from the completion of the same physical structure a year late or 20 percent over budget, or both.

Indeed, even the concept of scope is more complex than is apparent. Much has been written in recent years arguing that, in addition to time, cost, and specifications, there is a fourth dimension to be considered. This fourth dimension is the expectations of the client (see Darnell, 1997), which sometimes tend to increase as the project progresses, known as "scope creep" (see Chapter 11). However, it seems that the expectations of the client are not an additional target, *but an inherent part of the project specifications*. To consider the client's desires as different from the project specifications is to court conflict between client and project team because client and team rarely act in concert. The client specifies a desired outcome. *Then* the project team designs and implements the project. *Then* the client views the result of the team's ideas.

Despite this logic, differences between the client's expectations and the project team's designs commonly develop as a project proceeds. As a result, meeting the client's desires may *not* be well reflected by the initially specified scope of the project. The expectations of client and project team should therefore be realigned and integrated throughout the entire project,

PMBOK Guide
Glossary

*The term "scope" is typically used when differentiating between what is included and what is excluded in something, but in project management the term has come to mean the specified deliverables. The Project Management Institute's Project Management Body of Knowledge ("PMBOK®") defines Scope as: "The sum of the products, services, and results to be provided as a project." We will refer to the PMBOK guide frequently throughout this book and use the icon seen here in the margin to draw the student's attention to this important reference (see the PMI reference in the chapter Bibliography). If particular PMBOK Figures, Tables, Sections, or Chapters are relevant to the discussion, we note this under the icon as, for example, 3.2, which means Chapter 3, Section 2.

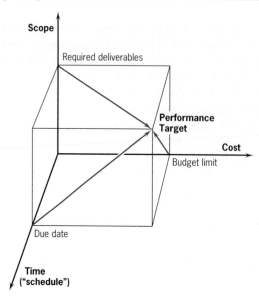

Figure 1-1   Direct project goals—scope, cost, time.

but they frequently are not. As a result, we believe the nebulous elements of the client's evolving expectations and desires, along with the "specified" scope stated in the project proposal, in reality constitute the total "required deliverables" objective for the project.

The three direct project objectives are shown in Figure 1-1, with the specified project objectives on the axes. This illustration implies that there is some "function" that relates them, one to another—and so there is! Although the functions vary from project to project, and from time to time for a given project, we will refer to these relationships, or trade-offs, throughout this book. The primary task of the project manager is to manage these trade-offs, along with a fourth trade-off that always exists: trading off between the direct project objectives/goals and a set of *ancillary* (frequently process, as noted below) objectives/goals.

In a more basic sense, those with a stake in the project (the project manager, project team, senior management, the client, and other project stakeholders) have an interest in making the project a success. Shenhar et al. (1997) have concluded that project success has four dimensions: (1) project efficiency, (2) impact on the customer, (3) the business impact on the organization, and (4) opening new opportunities for the future. The first two are clearly part of what we have defined as the project's direct objectives; the latter two are typical of what are frequently unspecified ancillary goals. Ancillary goals include improving the organization's project management competency and methods, increasing individuals' managerial experience through project management, gaining a foothold in a new market, and similar goals.

One other crucial, but unstated, trade-off that a PM must consider is the health of the project team as well as the rest of the organization. The PM cannot burn out the team in an attempt to achieve the direct objectives, nor destroy the organization's functional departments in an attempt to meet the project's goals. Another factor in making project trade-offs is the project's *environment,* that is, those things or persons outside the project, and often outside the sponsoring organization, that affect the project or are affected by it. Examples of this environment might be antipollution groups, trade unions, competitive firms, and the like. We will deal with these issues in more detail in Chapter 12.

From the early days of project management, the direct project objectives of time, cost, and scope (as generally agreed to by the client and the organization actually doing the project) have been accepted as the primary determinants of project success or failure. In the past 25 years or so, other direct and ancillary objectives have been suggested. These did not replace the traditional time, cost, and scope, but were added as also relevant. For the most part, however, Chapters 1–11 will focus mainly on the traditional direct objectives.

The Project Manager and Project Management Organizations

While managing the trade-offs, the project manager (PM) is expected to integrate all aspects of the project, ensure that the proper knowledge and resources are available when and where needed, and above all, ensure that the expected results are produced in a timely, cost-effective manner.

The complexity of the problems faced by the PM, taken together with the rapid growth in the number of project-oriented organizations, has contributed to the professionalization of project management. In the early days of projects, being a project manager was known as the "Accidental Profession." As pointed out in the reading "Lessons for an Accidental Profession" at the end of this chapter, there was no training or career path in project management; you just became one by accident. That has now all changed and the role has become "professionalized." One of the major international organizations dedicated to this professionalization is the Project Management Institute (PMI®, www.pmi.org), established in the United States of America in 1969. By 1990, the PMI had 7,500 members, and by 2010 it had exploded to over 320,000 members in more than 170 countries (see Figure 1-2). This exponential growth is indicative of the rapid growth in the use of projects, but also reflects the importance of the PMI as a force in the development of project management as a profession. Its mission is to foster the growth of project management as well as "building professionalism" in the field through its many worldwide chapters, its meetings and seminars around the globe, and its journals, books, and other publications. However, there are many other project management organizations as well, such as the Association for Project Management (APM; www.apm.org.uk) headquartered in the United Kingdom, which started in the early 1970s and serves all of Europe. As well, there

Figure 1-2 Project Management Institute growth history.

PMBOK Guide

is the International Project Management Association (IPMA; www.ipma.ch) headquartered in Switzerland, which began in 1965 and serves a global constituency.

Another major objective of these organizations is to codify the areas of knowledge required for competent project management. As a result, the APM has its APM Body of Knowledge, PMI has its project management body of knowledge, PMBOK® (Project Management Institute, 2008), and other groups have similar project management bodies of knowledge, as well as credentials (see below), such as PRINCE2 (**PR**ojects **IN** **C**ontrolled **E**nvironments) used primarily in the information systems industry and employed extensively by the UK government. Table 1-1 illustrates the difference between the APM BOK and PMBOK®.

Table 1-1   Comparison of APM's BOK (5th ed., ©2006) and PMI's PMBOK® (4th ed., ©2008)

APM's BOK: *This 179 page book consists of 1½ page introductions, definitions, and references for 52 major project management areas of knowledge divided among 7 sections.*	**PMI's PMBOK®:** *This 479 page book tries to capture the basic knowledge of project management, consisting of 9 knowledge areas (Chapters 4–12) and 5 process groups: initiating, planning, executing, monitoring/controlling, and closing. It aims to describe the norms, methods, processes, and practices of PM.*	
Section 1: Project Mgt. in Context—projects, programs, portfolios, sponsors, PMO, project context	**Chapter 1: Introduction**—projects, programs, portfolios, role of the project manager, environment, PMBOK	**Chapter 8: Project Quality Management**—plan quality, perform quality assurance, control quality
Section 2: Planning the Strategy—success, stakeholders, value, risk, quality, environment, health, safety	**Chapter 2: Project Life Cycle and Organization**—life cycle, routine work, stakeholders, organization	**Chapter 9: Project Human Resource Management**—develop HRM plan, acquire & develop team
Section 3: Executing the Strategy—scope, schedule, resources, budgets/cost, changes, earned value, information	**Chapter 3: Project Management Processes**—interactions, process groups: initiating, planning, executing, monitor/controlling, closing	**Chapter 10: Project Communications Management**—identify stakeholders, plan communications, distribute information, manage expectations, report performance
Section 4: Techniques—Requirements, development, estimates, technology, value engr., modeling, testing, configuration management	**Chapter 4: Project Integration Management**—charter, plan, execution, monitor/control, change, close	**Chapter 11: Project Risk Management**—identify, qualitative risk analysis (RA), quantitative RA, plan response, monitor/control risks
Section 5: Business and Commercial—business case, marketing, sales, financing, procurement, legal	**Chapter 5: Project Scope Management**—collect requirements, define scope, create WBS, verify scope, control scope	**Chapter 12: Project Procurement Management**—plan, conduct, administer, close procurements
Section 6: Organisation and Governance—life cycles, implementation, handover, closeout, reviews, org. structure, org. roles, methods, procedures, governance	**Chapter 6: Project Time Management**—define activities, sequence, resources, durations, schedule, control schedule	
Section 7: People & the Profession—communication, teamwork, leadership, conflicts, negotiation, HRM, behavior, learning, development, professionalism, ethics.	**Chapter 7: Project Cost Management**—estimate costs, determine budget, control costs	

All these compilations of knowledge are meant to serve as the fundamental basis for education for project managers. To certify that active project managers understand and can competently apply these bodies of knowledge, various associations offer credentials certifying to this proficiency. For example, PMI offers a certificate called the Project Management Professional (PMP®) that includes a group of education, experience, and testing requirements to obtain. More recently, PMI has added four more certificates, one for advanced program managers, called the Program Management Professional (PgMP®), another for developing project managers, the Certified Associate in Project Management (CAPM®), which has less educational and experience requirements, and two more specialized certificates: PMI Risk Management Professional and PMI Scheduling Professional. (More information on these certificates is contained in the Appendix to this chapter.) As a result of all this activity, the profession has flourished, with the result that many colleges and universities offer education and training in project management, and some offer specialized degree programs in the area.

Although obtaining more education in the field is always desirable, and being certified or credentialed verifies that knowledge to a potential employer, the recipient of such proof must avoid preaching the "body of knowledge" bible excessively lest they find themselves again seeking employment. As one employer stated (Starkweather, 2011, p. 37): "It is useful background info, but fresh PMPs® want to ram that knowledge down clients' throats and clients are not willing to pay for it." Others added (pp. 36, 38, 39): "There is no correlation between a good project manager and certification based on my 15 years of experience," and "Would like the PMP® program to more rigorously measure understanding of the *methodology* rather than *memorization*. I've seen very little correlation between having a PMP® and having a deep understanding of *how to apply the methodology,* how to tailor it *for a specific situation.*"

Clearly, rapid growth in the number of project managers and the membership in these project management associations were the result, not the cause, of tremendous growth in the number of projects being carried out. The software industry alone has been responsible for a significant percentage of the growth. Another major source of growth has been the need to control project activity in large organizations. As the number of nonroutine activities increases in an organization, there is an increased need in senior management to understand and control the system. Project management, with its schedules, budgets, due dates, risk assessments, statements of expected outcomes, and people who take responsibility, is a way to meet this need. These forces have combined and led to the creation of a project-organized firm. Much more will be said about project-oriented organizations in Chapter 4.

As we note in the coming chapters, the project manager's job is not without problems. There is the ever-present frustration of being responsible for outcomes while lacking full authority to command the requisite resources or personnel. There are the constant problems of dealing with the parties involved in any project—senior management, client, project team, and public—all of whom seem to speak different languages and have different objectives. There are the ceaseless organizational and technical "fires to be fought." There are vendors who cannot seem to keep "lightning-strike-me-dead" promises about delivery dates. This list of troubles only scratches the surface.

Difficult as the job may be, most project managers take a considerable amount of pleasure and job satisfaction from their occupation. The challenges are many and the risks significant, but so are the rewards of success. Project managers usually enjoy organizational visibility, considerable variety in their day-to-day duties, and often have the prestige associated with work on the enterprise's high-priority objectives. The profession, however, is not one for the timid. Risk and conflict avoiders do not make happy project managers. Those who can stomach the risks and enjoy practicing the art of conflict resolution, however, can take substantial monetary and psychological rewards from their work.

Trends in Project Management

Many new developments and interests in project management are being driven by quickly changing global markets, technology, and education. Global competition is putting pressure on prices, response times, and product/service innovation. Computer and telecommunications technologies along with greater education are allowing companies to respond to these pressures, pushing the boundaries of project management into regions where new tools are being developed for types of projects that have never been considered before. In addition, the pressure for more and more products and services has led to initiating more projects, but with faster life cycles. We consider a variety of trends in turn.

Achieving Strategic Goals (Chapter 2, especially Section 2.5). There has been a greater push to use projects to achieve more strategic goals, and filtering existing major projects to make sure that their objectives support the organization's strategy and mission. Projects that do not have clear ties to the strategy and mission are terminated and their resources are redirected to those that do. An example of this is given in Section 2.5 where the Project Portfolio Process is described.

Achieving Routine Goals (Section 1.1). On the other hand, there has also been a push to use project management to accomplish routine departmental tasks that would previously have been handled as a functional effort. This is because lower level management has become aware that projects accomplish their scope objectives within their budget and deadline, and hope to employ this new tool to improve management of their functions. As a result, artificial deadlines and budgets are created to accomplish specific, though routine, tasks within the functional departments, a process called "projectizing." However, as reported by Jared Sandberg (Sandberg, 2007) in the *Wall Street Journal*, there is an important danger with this new tactic. If the deadline isn't really important and the workers find out it is only artificial (e.g., either by meeting it but getting no appreciation or missing it but with no penalty), this will destroy the credibility of any future deadlines or budgets, much like "the boy who cried wolf."

Improving Project Effectiveness (Sections 2.1, 2.7, 5.6, 6.1, 6.5, 11.2, 11.3). A variety of efforts are being pursued to improve the results of project management, whether strategic or routine. One well-known effort is the creation of a formal *Project Management Office* (PMO, see Section 5.6) in many organizations, which is responsible for the successful initiation and completion of projects throughout the organization. Another effort is the evaluation of an organization's project management "*maturity*," or skill and experience in managing projects (discussed in Section 2.1). This is often one of the responsibilities of the PMO. Another responsibility of the PMO is to educate project managers about the *ancillary goals* of the organization (mentioned earlier in this chapter), which automatically become a part of the goals of every project whether the project manager knows it or not. Achieving better control over each project through the use of phase gates (Sections 6.1, 6.5, 11.2), earned value (Section 10.3), critical ratios (Section 11.3), and other such techniques is also a current trend.

Virtual Projects (Sections 5.3, 10.2). With the rapid increase in globalization, many projects now involve global teams with team members operating in different countries and different time zones, each bringing a unique set of talents to the project. These are known as virtual projects because the team members may never physically meet before the team is disbanded and another team reconstituted. Advanced telecommunications and computer technologies allow such virtual projects to be created, conduct their work, and complete their project successfully.

Dynamic and Quasi-Projects (Section 1.1). Led by the demands of the information technology/systems departments, project management is now being extended into areas where the final scope requirements may not be understood, the time deadline unknown, and/or the budget undetermined. When any one or all of the three project objectives are ill-defined, we call this a "quasi-project." Such projects are extremely difficult to manage and are often initiated by setting an artificial due date and budget, and then completed by "de-scoping" the required deliverables as the project progresses, to meet those limits. However, new tools for these kinds of quasi-projects are now being developed—prototyping, phase-gating, agile project management, and others—to help these teams achieve results that satisfy the customer in spite of all the unknowns. Similarly, when change happens so rapidly that the project is under constant variation, other approaches are developed such as "emergent planning" (also known as "rolling wave"), environmental manipulation, alternate controls, competing experiments, and collaborative leadership (Collyer et al., 2010).

Recent Changes in Managing Organizations

In the two decades since the first edition of this book was published, the process of managing organizations has been impacted by three revolutionary changes. First, we have seen an accelerating replacement of traditional, hierarchical management by consensual management. Second, we are currently witnessing the adoption of the "systems approach" to deal with organizational or technological problems because it is abundantly clear that when we act on one part of an organization or system, we are certain to affect other parts. Third, we have seen organizations establishing projects as the preferred way to accomplish their goals. Examples vary from the hundreds of projects required to accomplish the "globalization" of a multi-billion dollar household products firm to the incremental tailoring of products and services for individual customers. We elaborate on this tie between the organization's goals and the projects it selects for implementation in the following chapter. And as we will note in Chapter 5 and elsewhere, there has been a rapid and sustained growth in the number of organizations that use projects to accomplish almost all of the nonroutine tasks they undertake. While all three of these phenomena have been known for many years, it is comparatively recent that they have been widely recognized and practiced.

In his fascinating book, *Rescuing Prometheus* (Hughes, 1998), technology historian Thomas Hughes examines four large-scale projects that required the use of a nontraditional management style, a nontraditional organizational design, and a nontraditional approach to problem solving in order to achieve their objectives. These huge projects—the Semiautomatic Ground Environment (SAGE) air defense system, the Atlas Intercontinental Ballistic Missile, the Boston Central Artery/Tunnel, and the Department of Defense Advanced Research Projects Agency's Internet (ARPANET)—are all characterized by extraordinarily diverse knowledge and information input requirements.* The size and technological complexity of these projects required input from a large number of autonomous organizations—governmental, industrial, and academic—that usually did not work cooperatively with other organizations, were sometimes competitors, and could be philosophical and/or political opponents. Further, any actions taken to deal with parts of the total project often had disturbing impacts on many other parts of the system.

Obviously, these projects were not the first complex, large-scale projects carried out in this country or elsewhere. For example, the Manhattan Project—devoted to the development of the atomic bomb—was such a project. The Manhattan Project, however, was the sole and full-time work for a large majority of the individuals and organizations working on it. The organizations contributing to the projects Hughes describes were, for the most part, working on many other tasks. For example, Massachusetts Institute of Technology (MIT), the Pentagon, IBM, Bell Labs (now Lucent Technologies), RAND Corporation, the Massachusetts Department of Highways, and a great many other organizations were all highly involved in one or more of these projects while still carrying on their usual work. The use of multiple

---

*Hughes's term for this is "transdisciplinary" (across disciplines), which is rather more accurate than the usual "interdisciplinary" (between disciplines).

organizations (both within and outside of the sponsoring firm) as contributors to a project is no longer remarkable. Transdisciplinary projects are more the rule than the exception.

These revolutions and modifications in the style of management and organization of projects will be reflected throughout this book. For example, we have come to believe that the use of a traditional, hierarchical management style rather than a consensual style to manage multiorganizational projects is a major generator of conflict between members of the project team. We have long felt, and are now certain, that staffing multidisciplinary projects with individuals whose primary focus is on a specific discipline rather than on the problem(s) embodied in the project will also lead to high levels of interpersonal conflict between project team members. In Chapter 5 we will discuss some issues involved in the widespread use of projects to accomplish organizational change. As in earlier editions, we adopt a systems approach to dealing with the problems of managing projects.

This book identifies the specific tasks facing PMs. We investigate the nature of the projects for which the PM is responsible, the skills that must be used to manage projects, and the means by which the manager can bring the project to a successful conclusion in terms of the three primary criteria: scope, time, and cost. Before delving into the details of this analysis, however, we clarify the nature of a project and determine how it differs from the other activities that are conducted in organizations. We also note a few of the major advantages, disadvantages, strengths, and limitations of project management. At this end of this chapter, we describe the approach followed throughout the rest of the book.

1.1   THE DEFINITION OF A "PROJECT"

PMBOK Guide
Glossary

The PMBOK® has defined a project as "A temporary endeavor undertaken to create a unique product, service, or result" (Project Management Institute, 2008, p. 442). There is a rich variety of projects to be found in our society. Although some may argue that the construction of the Tower of Babel or the Egyptian pyramids were some of the first "projects," it is probable that cavemen formed a project to gather the raw material for mammoth stew. It is certainly true that the construction of Boulder Dam and Edison's invention of the light bulb were projects by any sensible definition. Modern project management, however, is usually said to have begun with the Manhattan Project. In its early days, project management was used mainly for very large, complex research and development (R & D) projects like the development of the Atlas Intercontinental Ballistic Missile and similar military weapon systems. Massive construction programs were also organized as projects—the construction of dams, ships, refineries, and freeways, among others.

As the techniques of project management were developed, mostly by the military, the use of project organization began to spread. Private construction firms found that project organization was helpful on smaller projects, such as the building of a warehouse or an apartment complex. Automotive companies used project organization to develop new automobile models. Both General Electric and Pratt & Whitney used project organization to develop new jet aircraft engines for airlines, as well as the Air Force. Project management has even been used to develop new models of shoes and ships (though possibly not sealing wax). More recently, the use of project management by international organizations, and especially organizations producing services rather than products, has grown rapidly. Advertising campaigns, global mergers, and capital acquisitions are often handled as projects, and the methods have spread to the nonprofit sector. Weddings, scout-o-ramas, fund drives, election campaigns, parties, and recitals have all made use of project management. Most striking has been the widespread adoption of project management techniques for the development of computer software.

In discussions of project management, it is sometimes useful to make a distinction between terms such as *project, program, task,* and *work packages*. The military, source of most of these terms, generally uses the term *program* to refer to an exceptionally large, long-range objective that is broken down into a set of projects. These projects are divided further into *tasks*, which are, in turn, split into *work packages* that are themselves composed of *work units*. But exceptions to this hierarchical nomenclature abound. The Manhattan Project was a huge "program," but a "task force" was created to investigate the many potential futures of a large steel company. In the broadest sense, a project is a specific, finite task to be accomplished. Whether large- or small-scale or whether long- or short-run is not particularly relevant. What is relevant is that the project be seen as a unit. There are, however, some attributes that characterize projects.

Importance

The most crucial attribute of a project is that it must be important enough in the eyes of senior management to justify setting up a special organizational unit outside the routine structure of the organization. If the rest of the organization senses, or even suspects, that it is not really that important, the project is generally doomed to fail. The symptoms of lack of importance are numerous and subtle: no mention of it by top management, assigning the project to someone of low stature or rank, adding the project to the responsibilities of someone who is already too overworked, failing to monitor its progress, failing to see to its resource needs, and so on.

Scope

A project is usually a one-time activity with a well-defined set of desired end results. (We discuss poorly defined, or "quasi-" projects a bit later.) It can be divided into subtasks that must be accomplished in order to achieve the project goals. The project is complex enough that the subtasks require careful coordination and control in terms of timing, precedence, cost, and scope. Often, the project itself must be coordinated with other projects being carried out by the same parent organization.

Life Cycle with a Finite Due Date

Like organic entities, projects have life cycles. From a slow beginning they progress to a buildup of size, then peak, begin a decline, and finally must be terminated by some due date. (Also like organic entities, they often resist termination.) Some projects end by being phased into the normal, ongoing operations of the parent organization. The life cycle is discussed further in Section 1.3 where an important exception to the usual description of the growth curve is mentioned. There are several different ways in which to view project life cycles. These will be discussed in more detail later.

Interdependencies

Projects often interact with other projects being carried out simultaneously by their parent organization. Typically, these interactions take the form of competition for scarce resources between projects, and much of Chapter 9 is devoted to dealing with these issues. While such interproject interactions are common, projects always interact with the parent organization's standard, ongoing operations. Although the functional departments of an organization (marketing, finance, manufacturing, and the like) interact with one another in regular, patterned ways, the patterns of interaction between projects and these departments tend to be changeable. Marketing may be involved at the beginning and end of a project, but not in the middle. Manufacturing may have major involvement throughout. Finance is often involved at the beginning and accounting (the controller) at the end, as well as at periodic reporting times. The PM must keep all these interactions clear and maintain the appropriate interrelationships with all external groups.

Uniqueness

Though the desired end results may have been achieved elsewhere, they are at least unique to this organization. Moreover, every project has some elements that are unique. No two construction or R & D projects are precisely alike. Though it is clear that construction projects are usually more routine than R & D projects, some degree of customization is a characteristic of projects. In addition to the presence of risk, as noted earlier, this characteristic means that projects, by their nature, cannot be completely reduced to routine. The PM's importance is emphasized because, as a devotee of *management by exception*, the PM will find there are a great many exceptions to manage by.

Project Management in Practice
A Unique Method for Traveler-Tracking at Copenhagen Airport

IT University of Copenhagen, Denmark, was working with Copenhagen Airport to improve the management of their airport through traveler-tracking, without invading people's privacy. The 3-year project focused on a unique, low-cost approach—capturing the Bluetooth signals from passengers' phones with two electronic readers that cost only $30 each. Not everyone has a smartphone that emits signals, of course, but about 7 percent of the passengers do, enough to provide a completely random sample for tracking. To ensure privacy, they collected only a portion of each signal and deleted the addresses. They also informed the public about the project on the airport's website and on-site as well. To encourage positive traveler response to the project, they provided alerts to passengers willing to synchronize their Bluetooth to receive information regarding when their plane was boarding and a map to the gate.

Knowing when people were entering and leaving Security allowed the airport to balance the staff at Security so lines didn't build up, thereby shortening the time passengers must wait, while also reducing over- and under-staffing of screeners. In addition, the information allows them to also post wait times at the check-in gates. The data also lets the airport determine which shops and areas are getting the most traffic so they can shift usage of facility space to better serve the travelers and the friends and families accompanying them. And when construction and rerouting changes traffic flows, they can determine the impact on passengers and take action to reduce the inconvenience.

Source: S. F. Gale, "Data on the Go," *PM Network*, Vol. 24.

Resources

Projects have limited budgets, both for personnel as well as other resources. Often the budget is implied rather than detailed, particularly concerning personnel, but it is strictly limited. The attempt to obtain additional resources (or *any* resources) leads to the next attribute—conflict.

Conflict

More than most managers, the PM lives in a world characterized by conflict. Projects compete with functional departments for resources and personnel. More serious, with the growing proliferation of projects, is the project-versus-project conflict for resources within multiproject organizations. The members of the project team are in almost constant conflict for the project's resources and for leadership roles in solving project problems. The PM must be expert in conflict resolution, but we will see later that there are helpful types of conflict. The PM must recognize the difference.

The four parties-at-interest or "stakeholders" (client, parent organization, project team, and the public) in any project even define success and failure in different ways. The client wants changes, and the parent organization wants profits, which may be reduced if those changes are made. Individuals working on projects are often responsible to two bosses at the same time; these bosses may have different priorities and objectives. Project management is no place for the timid.

Project Management in Practice
The Smart-Grid Revolution Starts in Boulder, Colorado

Boulder's utility company, Xcel Energy, decided that it was time to create a roadmap for a 3-year, $100 million "smart-grid" electrical system that would span the entire city. There were no standards, benchmarks, or tested procedures for converting a city from a conventional electric-grid system to a fully integrated smart one, though it was known that if customers can monitor the true cost of their energy, they will automatically reduce their usage, by up to 30 percent in some cases. Of course, the smart grid would also allow Xcel to reroute power around bottlenecked lines, detect power outages, identify service risks, cut its use of road crews, read customer meters remotely, reduce outages, and identify false alarms more quickly.

Xcel brought in a mass of partners on the project, such as Accenture consulting for engineering, energy industry consultants, leading technologists, business leaders, IT experts, and of course, Boulder city managers, leaders, and user-citizens. The public and private partners were divided into eight teams, all led by a senior project manager working with a Project Management Office. With all these different stakeholders, with different objectives and interests, it was crucial to have steady, reliable communication to keep everyone up to date and the project on track. Security and privacy were high-priority items on the project, and communication with the community was facilitated through town-hall meetings, the local media, tours of project sites, and even a touring trailer allowing citizens to get a hands-on demonstration of the smart-grid technology. With the completion of the project, Xcel is now measuring its many benefits and expects it will take a year to collect and analyze all the data across all the seasons. The project partners have also created an industry consortium to establish industry standards for future, larger smart-grid projects. They now see Boulder as a living laboratory from which they can continue to learn and thereby successfully deploy smart grids across the entire country.

Source: S. F. Gale, "A Closer Look," *PM Network*, Vol. 24.

Nonprojects and Quasi-Projects

If the characteristics listed above define a project, it is appropriate to ask if there are nonprojects. There are. The use of a manufacturing line to produce a flow of standard products is a nonproject. The production of weekly employment reports, the preparation of school lunches, the delivery of mail, the flight of Delta-1288 from Dallas to Dulles, checking your e-mail, all are nonprojects. While one might argue that each of these activities is, to some degree, unique, it is not their uniqueness that characterizes them. They are all *routine*. They are tasks that are performed over and over again. This is not true of projects. Each project is a one-time event. Even the construction of a section of interstate highway is a project. No two miles are alike and constructing them demands constant adaptation to the differences in terrain and substructure of the earth on which the roadbed is to be laid. Projects cannot be managed adequately by the managerial routines used for routine work.

In addition to projects and nonprojects, there are also quasi-projects: "Bill, would you look into this?" "Judy, we need to finish this by Friday's meeting." "Can you find out about this before we meet with the customer?" Most people would consider that they have just been assigned a project, depending on who "we" and "you" is supposed to include. Yet there may be no specific task identified, no specific budget given, and no specific deadline defined. Are they still projects, and if so, can project management methods be used to manage them? Certainly! The scope, schedule, and budget have been implied rather than carefully delineated by the words "this," "meet," and "we" (meaning "you") or "you" (which may mean a group or team). In such cases, it is best to try to quickly nail down the scope, schedule, and budget as precisely as possible, but without antagonizing the manager who assigned the project. You may need to ask for additional help or other resources if the work is needed soon—is it needed soon? How accurate/thorough/detailed does it need to be? And other such questions.

One common quasi-project in the information systems area is where the project includes discovery of the scope or requirements of the task itself (and possibly also the budget and deadline). How can you plan a project when you don't know the scope requirements? In this case, the project is, in fact, determining the scope requirements (and possibly the budget and deadline also). If the entire set of work (including the discovery) has been assigned to you as a project, then the best approach is to set this determination as the first "milestone" in the project, at which point the resources, budget, deadline, capabilities, personnel, and any other matters will be reviewed to determine if they are sufficient to the new project requirements. Alternatively, the customer may be willing to pay for the project on a "cost-plus" basis, and call a halt to the effort when the benefits no longer justify the cost.

Project Management in Practice
The Australian Pavilion at the World Expo 2010

© Australian Department of Foreign trade and Affairs. Used with permission.

The World Expo has been referred to as the "economic Olympics" and the scale of this project is quite staggering. Costing US$58 billion with 246 participating countries and international organisations, the Expo attracted 73,000,000 visitors to the 22,000 events that were managed by a staff of 80,000 volunteers.

The Expo was in effect thousands of projects that came together to create the big picture. These projects covered the relocation of thousands of families and hundreds of factories to provide a suitable venue, the creation of six new metro lines and the construction of over 200 spectacular pavilions that individual countries built to represent their nation's brand.

These infrastructure projects provided a venue for literally tens of thousands of other smaller projects. The spectacular opening gala saw over 2,000 performers, including action star Jackie Chan and the opera singer Andrea Bocelli, perform to an audience of global leaders. However, beneath these major projects there were literally thousands of other projects happening as individual participants sought to promote their own countries and organisations.

The Australian pavilion is just one of the 246 pavilions created and it illustrates some of the dynamics of this project. Its key purpose was to shift perceptions so Australia was seen as dynamic and innovative and thereby to strengthen trade, investment and institutional links with other nations. To satisfy this objective, a consortium of government, regional and business partners created a visually impressive pavilion inspired by Uluru (Ayers Rock). This pavilion was the host to over 200 business events and 2,500 cultural performances. In what has been called the largest ever single pubic diplomacy project undertaken by the Australian government, the pavilion attracted over 8,000,000 visitors including 32 senior international ministerial visits.

Whilst it is relatively easy to identify the costs of the Australian pavilion (Au$83m), the official report on this project identifies that it is hard to place a monetary value on the benefits from this project. The indicators of a positive outcome include the impact it made in the media (over 7,900 newspaper articles), the volume of visitors (over 8,000,000) and their satisfaction (95% of visitors rating the pavilion as 'good' or 'very good'). However, it is harder to make the direct link between these 'soft' measures and future value for Australia.

What is certain, though, is that the creation of a successful pavilion (one that came in on schedule, under budget and was rated among the top 5 pavilions by its visitors) required the application of excellent project management skills. Identifying the critical success factors at the front end of the project (maximise value for money, meet stakeholder expectations, achieve performance targets and meet national Audit Office requirements) allowed for a clear picture of 'what good looks like'. This vision was then broken down into specific contracts for 4 distinct phases (design, construction, operations, decommissioning) and 2 processes (cultural programming and communications) of the project. This breakdown, supported by clear definitions of the quality benchmarks, provided a framework for success.

However, as with all projects the key to success lies in the quality of the people you have doing the work. The enthusiasm, motivation and flexibility of the team working on the Expo site was crucial to the success of this project. Their ability to work with higher than anticipated visitor numbers and in gruelling weather conditions and yet be rated as the 'most friendly' pavilion says a lot about the Australian spirit as well as the exceptional project leadership displayed by all of the team members.

Sources: www.dfat.gov.au/publications/shanghai-expo-final-report.pdf accessed 7th April 2011
http://en.expo2010.cn/ accessed 7th April 2011
http://news.bbc.co.uk/1/hi/world/asia-pacific/8653426.stm accessed 7th April 2011

1.2 WHY PROJECT MANAGEMENT?

The basic purpose for initiating a project is to accomplish specific goals. The reason for organizing the task as a project is to focus the responsibility and authority for the attainment of the goals on an individual or small group. In spite of the fact that the PM often lacks authority at a level consistent with his or her responsibility, the manager is expected to coordinate and integrate all activities needed to reach the project's goals. In particular, the project form of organization allows the manager to be responsive to: (1) the client and the environment, (2) identify and correct problems at an early date, (3) make timely decisions about trade-offs between conflicting project goals, and (4) ensure that managers of the separate tasks that comprise the project do not optimize the performance of their individual tasks at the expense of the total project—that is, that they do not suboptimize.

Actual experience with project management (such as through the currently popular Six-Sigma projects) indicates that the majority of organizations using it experience better control and better customer relations (Davis, 1974), and probably an increase in their project's return on investment (Ibbs et al., 1997). A significant proportion of users also report shorter development times, lower costs, higher quality and reliability, and higher profit margins. Other reported advantages include a sharper orientation toward results, better interdepartmental coordination, and higher worker morale.

On the negative side, most organizations report that project management results in greater organizational complexity. Many also report that project organization increases the likelihood that organizational policy will be violated—not a surprising outcome, considering the degree of autonomy required for the PM. A few firms reported higher costs, more management difficulties, and low personnel utilization. As we will see in Chapter 5, the disadvantages of project management stem from exactly the same sources as its advantages. The disadvantages seem to be the price one pays for the advantages. On the whole, the balance weighs in favor of project organization if the work to be done is appropriate for a project.

The tremendous diversity of uses to which project management can be put has had an interesting, and generally unfortunate, side-effect. While we assert that all projects are to some extent unique, there is an almost universal tendency for those working on some specific types of projects to argue, "Software (or construction, or R & D, or marketing, or machine maintenance, or . . .) projects are different and you can't expect us to schedule (or budget, or organize, or manage, or . . .) in the same way that other kinds of projects do." Disagreement with such pleas for special treatment is central to the philosophy of this book. The fundamental similarities between the processes involved in carrying out all sorts of projects, be they long or short, product- or service-oriented, parts of all-encompassing programs or stand-alone, are far more pervasive than are their differences.

There are also real limitations on project management. For example, the mere creation of a project may be an admission that the parent organization and its managers cannot accomplish the desired outcomes through the functional organization. Further, conflict seems to be a necessary side-effect. As we noted, the PM often lacks the authority-of-position that is consistent with the assigned level of responsibility. Therefore, the PM must depend on the goodwill of managers in the parent organization for some of the necessary resources. Of course, if the goodwill is not forthcoming, the PM may ask senior officials in the parent organization for their assistance. But to use such power often reflects poorly on the skills of the PM and, while it may get cooperation in the instance at hand, it may backfire in the long run.

We return to the subject of the advantages, disadvantages, and limitations of the project form of organization later. For the moment, it is sufficient to point out that project management is difficult even when everything goes well. When things go badly, PMs have been known to turn gray overnight and take to hard drink! The trouble is that project organization is the only feasible way to accomplish certain goals. It is literally not possible to design and build a major weapon system, for example, in a timely and economically acceptable manner, except by project organization. The stronger the emphasis on achievement of results in an organization, the more likely it will be to adopt some form of project management. The stake or risks in using project management may be high, but no more so than in any other form of management. And for projects, it is less so. Tough as it may be, it is all we have—and it works!

All in all, the life of a PM is exciting, rewarding, at times frustrating, and tends to be at the center of things in most organizations. Project management is now being recognized as a "career path" in a growing number of firms, particularly those conducting projects with lives extending more than a year or two. In such organizations, PMs may have to function for several years, and it is important to provide promotion potential for them. It is also common for large firms to put their more promising young managers through a "tour of duty" during which they manage one or more projects (or parts of projects). This serves as a good test of the aspiring manager's ability to coordinate and manage complex tasks and to achieve results in a politically challenging environment where negotiation skills are required.

1.3   THE PROJECT LIFE CYCLE

Most projects go through similar stages on the path from origin to completion. We define these stages, shown in Figure 1-3, as the project's *life cycle*. The project is born (its start-up phase) and a manager is selected, the project team and initial resources are assembled, and the work program is organized. Then work gets under way and momentum quickly builds. Progress is made. This continues until the end is in sight. But completing the final tasks seems to take an inordinate amount of time, partly because there are often a number of parts that must come together and partly because team members "drag their feet" for various reasons and avoid the final steps.

This "stretched-S" pattern of slow-rapid-slow progress toward the project goal is common. Anyone who has watched the construction of a home or building has observed this phenomenon. For the most part, it is a result of the changing levels of resources used during the successive stages of the life cycle. Figure 1-4 shows project effort, usually in terms of person-hours or resources expended per unit of time (or number of people working on the project) plotted against time, where time is broken up into the several phases of project life. Minimal effort is required at the beginning, when the project concept is being developed and subjected to project selection processes. (Later, we will argue that increasing effort in the early stages of the life cycle will improve the chance of project success.) Normally there is a strong cor-

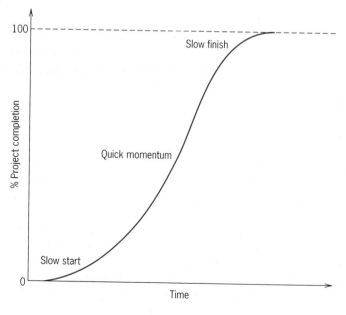

Figure   1-3   The   common stretched-S project life cycle.

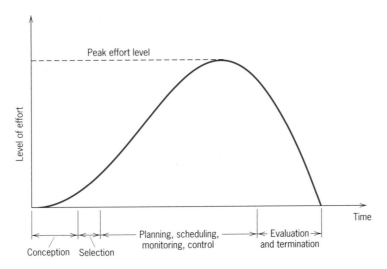

Figure 1-4 Time distribution of project effort.

relation between the life-cycle progress curve of Figure 1-3 and the effort curve of Figure 1-4 because effort usually results in corresponding progress (although not always). Hence the mathematical derivative of the former tends to resemble the latter (Cioffi, 2004). Moreover, since the effort curve is generally nonsymmetrical, the progress curve will in general not be symmetrical either.

Activity increases as planning is completed and the real work of the project gets underway. This rises to a peak and then begins to taper off as the project nears completion, finally ceasing when evaluation is complete and the project is terminated. While this rise and fall of effort always occurs, there is no particular pattern that seems to typify all projects, nor any reason for the slow-down at the end of the project to resemble the buildup at its beginning. Some projects end without being dragged out, as is shown in Figure 1-4. Others, however, may be like T. S. Eliot's world, and end "not with a bang but a whimper," gradually slowing down until one is almost surprised to discover that project activity has ceased. In some cases, the effort may never fall to zero because the project team, or at least a cadre group, may be maintained for the next appropriate project that comes along. The new project will then rise, phoenix-like, from the ashes of the old.

The ever-present goals of meeting scope, time, and cost are the major considerations throughout the project's life cycle. It was generally thought that scope took precedence early in the project's life cycle. This is the time when planners focus on finding the specific methods required to meet the project's scope goals. We refer to these methods as the project's *technology* because they require the application of a science or art.

When the major "how" problems are solved, project workers sometimes become preoccupied with improving scope, often beyond the levels required by the original specifications. This search for better scope delays the schedule and pushes up the costs.

At the same time that the technology of the project is defined, the project schedule is designed and project costs are estimated. Just as it was thought that scope took precedence over schedule and cost early in the life cycle, cost was thought to be of prime importance during the periods of high activity, and then schedule became paramount during the final stages, when the client demanded delivery. This conventional wisdom turns out to be untrue. Recent research indicates that scope and schedule are more important than cost during *all* stages. The reality of time-cost-scope trade-offs will be discussed in greater detail in Chapter 3.

Figure 1-3 presents the conventional view of the project life cycle. There are, however, many projects that have a life cycle quite different from the S-shaped Figure 1-3, conventional wisdom to the contrary. Remember that Figure 1-3 shows "percent project completion" as a function of "time." The life-cycle function is essentially unchanged if, for the horizontal axis, we use "resources" instead. In effect, the life cycle shows what an economist might call "return on input," that is, the amount of project completion resulting from inputs of time or resources. While the S-shaped return curve reflects reality on many projects, it is seriously misleading for others.

For example, consider your progress toward getting a degree, which is usually specified, in large part, by the number of credit hours for courses successfully passed. For smooth progress toward the degree, the life-cycle "curve" would probably resemble a stairstep, each level portion representing a term of study and the step up representing completion of credit toward the degree. Summer vacation would, of course, be a longer horizontal stair continuing into the fall term. Passing a crucial licensing exam, such as the Certified Public Accountant (CPA), the bar exam for attorneys, or even an electrician's or plumber's certification, might appear as a long flat line along the horizontal axis with a spike at the time of passing the exam; of course, the effort curve of Figure 1-4 would look completely different.

Another type of life-cycle curve might be the installation of a new technology consisting of multiple parts, where each independent part resulted in different incremental benefits. In these cases, organizations prefer to install those parts resulting in "the biggest bang for the buck" first, so the resulting life-cycle curve would show great progress at first, and slightly less next, and continual dwindling off as the remaining parts were installed, essentially concave with "decreasing returns to scale," as the economists call it. And there might even be an "inverse S-curve" representing fast progress at first, a slowdown in the middle, and then speeding up again at the end.

A particularly important alternative life cycle shape can be captured by the analogy of baking a cake. Once the ingredients are mixed, we are instructed to bake the cake in a 350° (F) oven for 35 minutes. At what point in the baking process do we have "cake"? Experienced bakers know that the mixture changes from "goop" (a technical term well known to bakers and cooks) to "cake" quite rapidly in the last few minutes of the baking process. The life cycle of this process looks like the stretched-J curve shown in Figure 1-5. A number of actual projects have a similar life cycle, for example, some computer software projects, or chemistry and chemical engineering projects. In general, this life cycle often exists for projects in which the output is composed or constructed of several *subunits* (or subroutines) that have little use in and of themselves, but are quite useful when put together. This life-cycle curve would also be typical for projects where a chemical-type reaction occurs that rapidly transforms the output from useless to useful—from goop to cake. Another example is the preparation of the manuscript for the current edition of this book. A great deal of information must be collected, a great deal of rewriting must be done and new materials gathered, but there is no visible result until everything is assembled.

Figure 1-3 shows that, as the project nears completion, continued inputs of time or resources result in successively smaller increments of completion—diminishing marginal returns. Figure 1-5 shows the opposite. As these projects near completion, additional inputs result in successively larger increments of progress—increasing marginal returns, obviously bounded at 100 percent completion. In Chapter 7, we will see that the distinction between

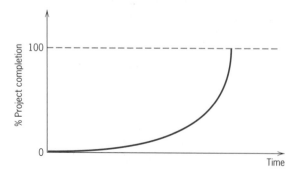

Figure 1-5 The stretched-J project life cycle.

Project Management in Practice
Turning London's Waste Dump into the 2012 Olympic Stadium

Back in 2006, the 2012 Olympic Delivery Authority (ODA) chose a river-surrounded, 1-square-mile East London disposal site loaded with discarded appliances, tons of waste, shanties, and soil polluted with petrol, oil, lead, tar, and arsenic as the site for their 2012 Olympic Stadium to seat 80,000 visitors. To meet a mid-2011 completion due date, the ODA project manager Ian Crockford quickly assembled a project team of over 1,000 including governmental employees and other stakeholders, such as the London Development Agency as landowner, politicians, utility firms, community councils, miscellaneous local governmental groups, and of course, the athletes, all of whom wanted a voice in the site design. To clean up the site, the team created a "Soil Hospital" on-site with 60 scientists and technicians who processed and cleaned 800,000 tons of soil. To use the surrounding river for transporting equipment and materials to the site, others on the team dredged 30,000 tons of silt, gravel, garbage, and one car from 2.2 kilometers of the river, which hadn't seen commercial use in over 35 years.

When they were ready to design the stadium, they referred to plans and schedules for London's 90,000-seat Wembley Stadium (but that took 10 years to build) and Sydney's 2000 Olympics 80,000-seat stadium (but that would have stretched halfway across the surrounding rivers on the London site). Moreover, the scope for this stadium was that 25,000 seats would be permanent but the other 55,000 would be temporary, built solely for the 2012 Olympics. To respond, the design team planned a highly compact field of play that was acceptable to everyone, including the athletes. Construction started in May 2008 with the pouring of concrete, but soon they found that the steel-beamed roof as designed would create turbulence on the compact field. The team redesigned a lighter, more flexible roof made, in part, with 52 tons of scrap metal from old keys, knives, and guns confiscated by the London police, fitting with the ODA's goals of using recycled materials. The entire stadium uses only one-quarter the amount of steel used in the 2008 Olympic Stadium in Beijing. Construction is on-track to be completed by the mid-2011 deadline at a price of £537 million.

Source: J. Danko, "Serious Conditioning," *PM Network*, Vol. 24.

these types of life cycles plays a critical role in developing budgets and schedules for projects. It is not necessary for the PM to estimate the precise shape of the life-cycle curve, but the PM must know which type of project life cycle applies to the project at hand.

There is another comparison between the two types of project life cycles that is instructive. For the stretched-S life cycle in Figure 1-3, percentage of project completion is closely correlated with cost, or the use of resources. In fact, this is the basis for the use of "earned value," a technique for monitoring project progress that we will describe in more detail in Chapter 10. However, for the stretched-J progress curve in Figure 1-5, the expenditure of resources has little correlation with progress, at least in terms of final benefit.

Finally, not only does the shape of the project life-cycle curve fail to conform to a neat, single shape—there are also several different ways in which a project life cycle can be *viewed and understood*. We might view the project life cycle as a mechanism to control quality, as a way of organizing the management of risk, or as a collection of small projects within larger projects within still larger projects. Each of these views of a project's life is useful to the project manager.

Risk During the Life Cycle

It would be a great source of comfort if one could predict with certainty, at the start of a project, how the scope, time, and cost goals would be met. In a few cases, routine construction projects, for instance, we can generate reasonably accurate predictions, but often we cannot. There may be considerable uncertainty about our ability to meet project goals. The shaded portion of Figure 1-6 illustrates that uncertainty.

Figure 1-6 shows the uncertainty as seen at the beginning of the project. Figure 1-7 shows how the uncertainty decreases as the project moves toward completion. From project start time,

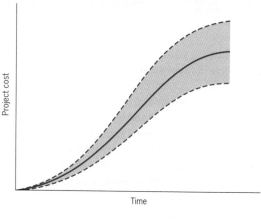

Figure 1-6 Estimate of project cost: estimate made at project start.

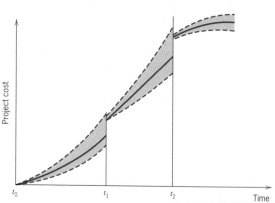

Figure 1-7 Estimates of project cost: estimates made at time t_0, t_1, and t_2.

t_0, the band of uncertainty grows until it is quite wide by the estimated end of the project. As the project actually develops, the degree of uncertainty about the final outcome is reduced. (See the estimate made at t_1, for example.) A later forecast, made at t_2, reduces the uncertainty further. It is common to make new forecasts about project scope, time, and cost either at fixed intervals in the life of the project or when specific technological milestones are reached. In any event, the more progress made on the project, the less uncertainty there is about achieving the final goal.

Note that the focus in Figures 1-6 and 1-7 is on the uncertainty associated with project cost—precisely, the uncertainty of project cost at specific points in time. Without significantly altering the shapes of the curves, we could exchange titles on the axes. The figures would then show the uncertainty associated with estimates of the project schedule, given specific levels of expenditure. The relationship between time and cost (and scope) is emphasized throughout this book. Dealing with the uncertainty surrounding this relationship is a major responsibility of the PM. PMBOK® devotes an entire chapter to the subject of risk and uncertainty.

PMBOK Guide
Chapter 11

1.4   THE STRUCTURE OF THIS TEXT

This book, a project in itself, has been organized to follow the life cycle of all projects. It begins with the creative idea that launches most projects and ends with termination of the project. This approach is consistent with our belief that it is helpful to understand the entire process of project management in order to understand and manage its parts. Another characteristic of the book also relates to the process of project management: some topics, such as "procurement," can largely be treated as stand-alone issues, discussed in a single appropriate place in the book, and then dispensed with. Other topics, however, such as "risk," or "planning," arise throughout the book and are treated wherever they are relevant, which may be quite often. To attempt to treat them in a single section, or chapter, would be misleading. In addition, although this book is intended primarily for the student who wants to study project management, we feel it can also be of value to the prospective or acting PM, and to senior managers who initiate projects and select, work with, or manage PMs. Therefore, our interests often go beyond the issues of primary concern to beginning students.

Most actual projects will not be of the size and complexity addressed in many of our discussions. Though our intent was not to confine our remarks only to large engineering-oriented projects, these are typically the most complex and place the greatest demands on project management. Smaller, simpler projects may therefore not require the depth of tools and techniques we will present, but the student or manager should be aware that such tools exist.

Project management actually begins with the initial concept for the project. We feel that this aspect of project management is so important, yet so universally ignored in books on project management, that we included two appendices covering this area in previous editions of this book. In one paper we discussed *creativity* and *idea generation*. In another, we described some of the techniques of *technological forecasting*. While our notion about the importance of these subjects is unchanged, the location of the two appendices has been moved from the end of this work to the Internet. The complete text of both appendices now appears in *www.wiley.com/go/global/meredith/* (along with other items noted in the preface to this edition). We realize that these topics may be of more direct interest to the senior manager than the PM. Though a PM may prefer to skip this material, since what is past is past, we believe that history holds lessons for the future. Wise PMs will wish to know the reasons for, and the history behind, the initiation of their project.

In years past, there were arguments between those who insisted that project management was primarily a quantitative science and those who maintained that it was a behavioral science. It has become clear that one cannot adequately manage a project without depending heavily on both mathematics and the science of human behavior. To contend that mathematics is exact and that behavioral science is "mushy" is to ignore the high level of subjectivity in most of the numeric estimates made about the time, costs, and risks associated with projects. On the other hand, to assert that "people don't really use that stuff" (mathematical models) is to substitute wishful thinking for reality. For nonmathematicians, we have computers to help with the requisite arithmetic. For the nonbehaviorists, there is no help except hard work and an accepting attitude toward the subject.

Before undertaking a journey, it is useful to know what roads are to be traveled. While each individual chapter begins with a more detailed account of its contents, what follows is a brief description of chapter contents along with their organization (Figure 1-8) into three general areas: project initiation, project planning, and project execution.

Part I: Project Initiation.   Following this current introductory chapter, the material in Part I focuses on the *context* for initiating the project. We realize that many instructors (and students) would rather get right to the basics of managing projects, and that can be done by moving directly to Part II of the text. However, we believe that without understanding the context of the project—why it was selected and approved, what project managers are responsible for and their many roles (such as running a team and negotiating for resources), the importance of the Project Management Office, and where (and why) the project resides in the organization's hierarchy—a PM is courting disaster. Chapter 2 starts with a description of the concept of project management "maturity," or sophistication, and how firms can evaluate their own competence in project management. It then details the problems of evaluating and selecting projects, as well as the information needed for project selection, the consideration of risk, and some technical details of proposals. The chapter concludes by expanding the concept of project selection to strategic management through judicious selection of the organization's projects by means of a procedure called the "project portfolio process." Chapter 3, "The Project Manager," concerns the PM's roles, responsibilities, and some personal characteristics a project manager should possess. It also discusses problems a PM faces when operating in a multicultural environment. Next, Chapter 4 covers a subject of critical importance to the PM that is almost universally ignored in project management texts: the art of negotiating for resources.

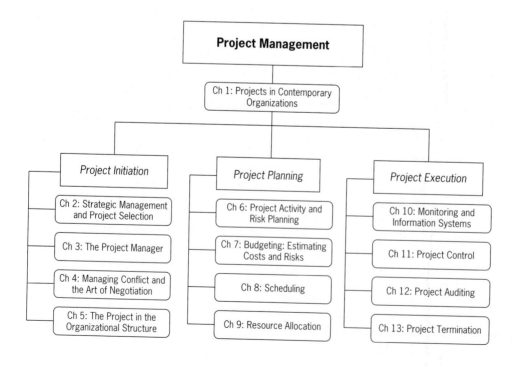

Figure 1-8 Organization chart of the parts and chapters of the text.

The chapter also includes some major sources of interpersonal conflict among members of the project team. Concluding Part I of the book, Chapter 5 concentrates on establishing the project organization. Different project organizational forms are described, as well as their respective advantages and disadvantages. The staffing of the project team is also discussed.

Part II Project Planning.   This part of the text discusses the essentials of planning the project in terms of activities, costs, risks, and schedule. Chapter 6 deals with project activity and risk planning and presents tools useful in organizing and staffing the various project tasks and assessing and prioritizing risks to the project. It also contains a short discussion of phase-gate management systems and other ways of dealing with the problems that arise when multidisciplinary teams work on complex projects. Because costs are an important element of project planning, the topic of budgeting, including techniques such as simulation to estimate costs and risks, is addressed next in Chapter 7. Scheduling, a crucial aspect of project planning, is then described in Chapter 8, along with the most common scheduling models such as the Program Evaluation and Review Technique (PERT), and precedence diagramming. Concluding Part II, resource allocation is covered in Chapter 9, where the Critical Path Method (CPM) of applying resources to speed up projects is explained. For single projects, we also discuss how the resource allocation problem can be addressed through resource *leveling* to minimize the cost of the resources; but for multiple projects, we learn that the issue is how to allocate limited resources among several projects in order to achieve the objectives of each.

Part III: Project Execution.   Finally, we can address how to actually run a project. Chapter 10 examines the information requirements of a project and the need for monitoring critical activities, particularly through the concepts of time and cost variances and "earned value." Included in this chapter is a description of some common Project Management Information Systems (PMIS). In general, it is not possible to manage adequately any but the smallest of projects without the use of a computerized PMIS. There are many such systems available and several are briefly discussed, but here we only demonstrate *Microsoft Project*® (as well as *Excel*® and other software made to interact easily with *Microsoft Project*® and *Excel*®), by far the most popular project management software. *(A note of caution:* To use any project management software wisely, the user must understand the principles of project management.) Chapter 11 then describes the control process in project management. This chapter covers standards for comparison and tools to help the manager keep the project in control. Chapter 12 deals with methods for both ongoing and terminal audits and evaluations of a project, as well as identifying factors associated with project success and failure. Chapter 13 describes the different forms of project termination, such as outright shutdown, integration into the regular organization, or extension into a new project. Each of these forms presents unique problems for the PM to solve.

With this introduction, let us begin our study, a project in itself, and, we hope, an interesting and productive one.

 SUMMARY

This chapter introduced the subject of project management and discussed its importance in our society. It defined what we mean by a "project," discussed the need for project management, and described the project life cycle. The final section explained the structure of this text and gave an overview of the material to be described in coming chapters.

The following specific points were made in the chapter.

- The Project Management Institute (PMI) was founded in 1969 to foster the growth and professionalism of project management.

- Project management is now being recognized as a valuable "career path" in many organizations, as well as a way to gain valuable experience within the organization.

- Project management, initiated by the military, provides managers with powerful planning and control tools.

- The three primary forces behind project management are (1) the growing demand for complex, customized goods and services; (2) the exponential expansion of human knowledge; and (3) the global production–consumption environment.

- The three prime objectives of project management are to meet specified scope within cost and on schedule.

- Our terminology follows in this order: program, project, task, work package, work unit.

- Projects are characterized by their importance, specific end results, a definite life cycle, complex interdependencies, some or all unique elements, limited resources, and an environment of conflict.

- Project management, though not problem-free, is the best way to accomplish certain goals.

- Projects often start slowly, build up speed while using considerable resources, and then slow down as completion nears.

- This text is organized along the project life cycle concept, starting with project initiation in Chapters 2 to 5, where selection of the project and project manager occurs and project organization begins. Project planning, Chapters 6 to 9, is concerned with activity planning, budgeting, scheduling, and resource allocation. Project execution, covered in Chapters 10 to 13, relates to actually running the project and includes activity monitoring and control, auditing and evaluation, and finally, project termination.

 ## GLOSSARY

Deliverables   The desired elements of value, outcomes, or results that must be delivered for a project to be considered complete.

Interdependencies   Relations between organizational functions where one function or task is dependent on others.

Life Cycle   A standard concept of a product or project wherein it goes through a start-up phase, a building phase, a maturing phase, and a termination phase.

Parties-at-Interest   Individuals or groups (the stakeholders) with a special interest in a project, usually the project team, client, senior management, and specific public interest groups.

Program   Often not distinguished from a project, but frequently meant to encompass a group of projects oriented toward a specific goal.

Project Management   The means, techniques, and concepts used to run a project and achieve its objectives.

Risk   The chance that project processes or outcomes will not occur as planned.

Stakeholder   see "Parties-at-Interest."

Suboptimize   Doing the best within a function or area but at a cost to the larger whole.

Task   A subset of a project, consisting of work packages.

Technology   The means for accomplishing a task.

Trade-off   Taking less on one measure, such as scope, in order to do better on another, such as schedule or cost.

Uncertainty   Having only partial or no information about the situation or outcomes, often due to ambiguity or complexity.

Work Package   A subelement of a task at the lowest level in the Work Breakdown Structure, used to assign costs and values.

 ## QUESTIONS

Material Review Questions

1. Name and briefly describe the societal forces that have contributed to the need for project management.

2. Describe the life cycle of a project in terms of (1) the degree of project completion, and (2) the required effort.

3. Describe the limitations of project management.

4. List the seven main characteristics of a project and briefly describe the important features of each.

5. Name and briefly describe the three primary goals of a project.

6. Discuss the advantages and disadvantages of project management.

7. How do projects, programs, tasks, and work packages differ?

8. How would you define a project?

9. What are some of the interdependencies related to a project?

10. What are some sources of conflict the project manager must deal with?

11. Differentiate between direct and ancillary project goals. Would learning a new skill through the project be a direct or ancillary goal? Entering a new market?

12. Describe the characteristics of quasi-projects.

Class Discussion Questions

13. Give several examples of projects found in our society, avoiding those already discussed in the chapter.

14. Describe some situations in which project management would probably not be effective.

15. How does the rate-of-project-progress chart (Fig. 1-3) help a manager make decisions?

16. Expound on the adage, "Projects proceed smoothly until 90 percent complete, and then remain at 90 percent forever."

17. Discuss the duties and responsibilities of the project manager. How critical is the project manager to the success of the project?

18. Would you like to be a project manager? Why, or why not?

19. Discuss why there are trade-offs among the three prime objectives of project management.

20. Why is the life cycle curve often "S" shaped?

21. How might project management be used when doing a major schoolwork assignment?

22. Why is there such a pronounced bend in the curve of Figure 1-2?

23. Which of the identified project attributes in Section 1.1 are *always* present? Which are simply *frequently* present?

24. Describe a project whose life cycle would be a straight line from start to finish. Describe a project with an inverse-S life cycle.

A Unique Method for Traveler Tracking at Copenhagen Airport

25. What was unique about this project? What was the main conflict?

26. What additional benefits can the Copenhagen Airport reap from this passenger data?

27. How widespread will this technology become? What uses will be garnered from it? Do any of them concern you?

The Smart-Grid Revolution Starts in Boulder, Colorado

28. What other benefits will accrue with smart grids?

29. Why do you imagine Xcel agreed to invest $100 million in this risky experiment?

30. What conflicts do you suspect might have occurred between all the different stakeholders in this project?

The Australian Pavilion at the World Expo 2010

31. Projects are delivered for diverse communities of stakeholders. Who do you think the stakeholders were in this project?

32. How was the performance of the Australian Pavilion measured?

Turning London's Waste Dump into the 2012 Olympic Stadium

33. Which of the "triple constraints" seems to be uppermost here? Which constraints was Crockford trading between?

34. Was the life cycle for this project S-shaped, J-shaped, or something else? Considering just the purpose of the river dredging as a project itself, what was the shape of its life cycle?

35. Were there any ancillary goals for this project? What might they have been?

36. Which of the project-defining factors in Section 1.1 were active here?

INCIDENTS FOR DISCUSSION

Bloomfield Transport, Inc.

After several years of driving long-haul trucks, Joe Bloomfield founded his own trucking company, Bloomfield Transport Inc. (BTI), which specialized in less-than-carload shipments in the United Kingdom. Joe developed a successful method for scheduling BTI's runs that met or exceeded the delivery expectations of its customers. As a result, BTI shipments were growing at a rate between 15 and 20 percent per year. The growth, however, was not evenly distributed across BTI's territory. On some routes, capacity was overloaded in one direction and underloaded in the other.

Joe noticed that the imbalance problem was not stable across time. In some months capacity was short in one direction, and in other months it was short in another direction. He thought that one way of solving the problem would be through marketing, by offering incentives to customers whose shipments would improve load balance. Another approach to the problem was to analyze and restructure the route–equipment combinations. He also thought that it might be possible to warehouse some less-urgent shipments for short periods in order to help the balance.

Joe's son, the first member of the Bloomfield family to attend university, was in his third year of an engineering degree. He had just completed a course in project management, and after briefly describing some of the basic concepts to his father, he suggested that a project might be a good way to deal with the balance problem. He thought that the Marketing Manager and the Route Manager could serve as project co-managers. He also felt that some of the older, more experienced drivers might be helpful. The objective of the project would be to decrease the size of the route imbalances by 75 percent in a 1-year period.

Questions: Is this a proper approach to the problem? What, if any, helpful suggestions would you make to Joe?

Groenlo Cosmetics Company

The plant manager of the Groenlo Cosmetics Company must replace several of her filling machines that have become obsolete. She is about to take delivery of six machines at a total cost of €4 million. These machines must be installed and fully tested in time to be used on a new production line scheduled to begin operation in six months. Because this project is important, the plant manager would like to devote as much time as possible to the job, but she is currently handling several other projects. She thinks she has three basic choices: (1) she can handle the project informally out of her office; (2) she can assign the project to a member of her staff; or (3) the company that manufactures the machines can handle the installation project for a fee close to what the installation would cost Maladroit.

Questions: Which of the three choices do you recommend, and why? If the project was one small machine at a total cost of €4,000, would your answer be different? Discuss the relative importance of the capital investment required versus the role of the investment in machinery.

CONTINUING INTEGRATIVE CLASS PROJECT

It often helps in communicating the process, difficulties, and satisfactions of project management if the class can do a team project together during the term of the course. The instructor may have a pre-chosen project for the class to work on, perhaps in a local organization, or the school itself (where there are many excellent projects: the cafeteria, parking, library, counseling, class scheduling, etc.), but if not, the following project is offered as an alternative.

The project is to prepare a "Student Study Guide" for this course, due (time requirement) on the last day of the course *before* the final examination. The purpose of the guide is to help the students learn the material of the course, both by preparing the guide as well as using it to study for the final examination. The requirements (scope) for the guide are as follows:

- a professional-looking appearance
- a consistent approach throughout the chapters
- a copy for every student, as well as the Instructor
- presented in either hard copy CD, flash memory, or electronic (e.g., web) form (check with your Instructor)
- everyone in class must participate, with one exception noted further below.
- if subteams are used, they must not be organized to operate independently of each other (for example, by doing all the work on one of the chapters).
- the project plans can be constructed manually or in Microsoft Project® or another software program (check with your Instructor)

In addition, one student will be appointed as "Historian," whose job is to monitor and prepare a written report on the progress of the project over its duration. This includes both the tasks to be accomplished, but also the attitude and spirit of the Project Manager (PM), the project team and/or subteams, and the various stakeholders in the project (team members, Instructor, future students who may use the Guide) as well as the culture and environment of the project. The main task of the Historian is to compare the reality of the class project to that described in the textbook and point out in the written report similarities and differences that will be recognizable by the PM and team members. The Historian will have no work to do on the project itself, but will need to sit in on meetings, confer with the PM and subteam heads, talk to team members occasionally, confer with the Instructor, and other such activities as needed to properly monitor task progress. The role of this person is especially critical for the class to learn how closely their project followed the typical path of a normal project, what problems arose and how they should have been handled, and so forth. As a result, this person should probably be selected by the Instructor right at the beginning of the course.

There may also be some expenses (budget requirement), such as photocopying costs and travel expenses, that may require assistance from the Instructor. Usually these costs are minor, but it depends on the project. Of course, in a real project the major cost would be the labor/personnel costs of the team members doing the work, a cost that is essentially "free" here.

In future chapters we will continue to develop the various elements of the project, such as selecting the PM, organizing the team, scheduling the deliverables, and monitoring progress. However, executing the requisite tasks of the project takes the most time in a real project but is a topic that is outside the scope of this text, which concerns only the generic tasks of project *management.* (Every project will have different tasks associated with it, many with very technical requirements.) Therefore, it will be necessary to forge ahead and do all the preparatory project elements, particularly in Parts I and II of the book, so that progress on the project tasks can begin right away. It would, of course, be best if the class could read all the material up to Chapter 10, which initiates Part III: Project Execution, where the work begins, before actually starting the project. Unfortunately, the course would be almost over by then and it would be too late to start a project. As a result, the PM and the class will have to skip ahead and read the Continuing Integrative Class Project assignments, at least for Chapters 2–10 now; hopefully, they will discover in retrospect how they could have conducted each of the various elements of the project better.

But for right now, it is most important to cover the project elements in Chapters 2 and 3—what the project will be and who will be the PM, respectively, so the project can get underway ASAP. It is best to do these two elements in the very first class, the first one in consultation with the Instructor, and the second one with the Instructor ABSENT from the room but with instructions for where to find him or her once the class has selected the PM, hopefully within 20 minutes but most certainly by the end of the class. Good luck!

 # BIBLIOGRAPHY

Cioffi, D. F. Personal communication, 2004.

Collyer, S., C. Warren, B. Hemsley, and C. Stevens. "Aim, Fire, Aim—Project Planning Styles in Dynamic Environments." *Project Management Journal,* September 2010.

Darnell, R. "The Emerging Role of the Project Manager." *PM Network*, July 1997.

Davis, E. W. "CPM Use in Top 400 Construction Firms." *Journal of the Construction Division*, American Society of Civil Engineers, 1974.

Davis, E. W. *Project Management: Techniques, Applications, and Managerial Issues*, 2nd ed. Norcross, GA: AIIE Monograph, 1983.

Gido, J., and J. P. Clements. *Successful Project Management, with Microsoft Project 2003 CD-ROM*. Cincinnati: Thompson/South-Western, 2004.

Grey, C. F., and E. W. Larson. *Project Management: The Managerial Process*. New York: McGraw-Hill/Irwin, 2005.

Hughes, T. P. *Rescuing Prometheus*. New York, Pantheon, 1998.

Ibbs, C. W., and Y. H. Kwak. "Measuring Project Management's Return on Investment." *PM Network*, November 1997.

Ibbs, C. W., and Y. H. Kwak. "Assessing Project Management Maturity." *Project Management Journal*, March 2000.

Kerzner, H. *Project Management: A Systems Approach to Planning, Scheduling, and Controlling*, 8th ed. New Jersey: Wiley, 2003.

Pande, P. S., R. P. Newman, and R. R. Cavanagh. *The Six Sigma Way*, New York: McGraw-Hill, 2000.

Project Management Institute. *A Guide to the Project Management Body of Knowledge*, 4th ed. Newtown Square, PA: Project Management Institute, 2008.

Pyzdek, T. *The Six Sigma Handbook*, rev. ed., New York: McGraw-Hill, 2003.

Sandberg, J. "Rise of False Deadline Means Truly Urgent Often Gets Done Late." *Wall Street Journal*, January 24, 2007.

Shenhar, A. J., O. Levy, and D. Dvir. "Mapping the Dimensions of Project Success." *Project Management Journal*, June 1997.

Starkweather, J. A., and D. H. Stevens. "PMP® Certification as a Core Competency: Necessary but Not Sufficient." *Project Management Journal*, February 2011.

Sun, M. "Weighing the Social Costs of Innovation." *Science*, March 30, 1984.

 # APPENDIX: PMI CERTIFICATIONS

We discuss here only the CAPM® and PMP® certifications. For information on the other credentials, please visit the PMI website at www.pmi.org.

Certified Associate in Project Management (CAPM®):

This is the "entry level" credential which typically leads to qualifying for the full Project Management Professional (PMP®) credential, although a candidate can maintain their CAPM® certification by retaking the exam every 5 years. It is mainly for project team members with 1,500 hours of documented experience or for those who can verify they have taken 23 face-to-face hours of project management classroom education or training. The exam is 3 hours to complete 150 questions and costs $225 to sit for the exam.

Project Management Professional (PMP®):

This is the longstanding standard certification that a person is fully competent in project management and regularly lead and direct project teams. The credential is maintained by gaining 60 PDUs every three years. To sit for the exam, a candidate must have a high school education plus five years of documented project management experience and can verify they have taken 35 hours of face-to-face project management classroom education or training. Alternatively, a candidate can demonstrate that they have a bachelor's degree (or global equivalent) plus three years of documented project management experience and can verify they have taken 35 hours of project management classroom education or training. The exam is 4 hours to complete 200 questions and costs $405 to sit for the exam.

The following reading describes the common occurrence of someone suddenly being appointed a project manager and finding he or she has been inadequately trained for the task. Based on the authors' own experiences and interviews with dozens of senior project managers, they distill 12 guidelines for new project managers. The guidelines run the gamut from project initiation, through planning, to execution and close-out. Some are technical, some are uncommon sense, and many are philosophical, and sometimes political. But they are sage advice, not only for the novice but for the experienced project manager as well.

DIRECTED READING

LESSONS FOR AN ACCIDENTAL PROFESSION*
J. K. Pinto and O. P. Kharbanda

Projects and project management are the wave of the future in global business. Increasingly technically complex products and processes, vastly shortened time-to-market windows, and the need for cross-functional expertise make project management an important and powerful tool in the hands of organizations that understand its use. But the expanded use of such techniques is not always being met by a concomitant increase in the pool of competent project managers. Unfortunately, and perhaps ironically, it is the very popularity of project management that presents many organizations with their most severe challenges. They often belatedly discover that they simply do not have sufficient numbers of the sorts of competent project managers who are often the key driving force behind successful product or service development. Senior managers in many companies readily acknowledge the ad hoc manner in which most project managers acquire their skills, but they are unsure how to better develop and provide for a supply of well-trained project leaders for the future.

In this article, we seek to offer a unique perspective on this neglected species. Though much has been written on how to improve the process of project management, less is known about the sorts of skills and challenges that specifically characterize project managers. What we do know tends to offer a portrait of successful project managers as strong leaders, possessing a variety of problem-solving, communication, motivational, visionary, and team-building skills. Authors such as Posner (1987), Einsiedel (1987), and Petterson (1991) are correct. Project managers are a special breed. Managing projects is a unique challenge that requires a strategy and methodology all its own. Perhaps most important, it requires people willing to function as leaders in every sense of the term. They must not only chart the appropriate course, but provide the means, the support, and the confidence for their teams to attain these goals. Effective project managers often operate less as directive and autocratic decision makers than as facilitators, team members, and cheerleaders. In effect, the characteristics we look for in project managers are varied and difficult to pin down. Our goal is to offer some guidelines for an accidental profession, based on our own experiences and interviews with a number of senior project managers—most of whom had to learn their own lessons the hard way.

"Accidental" Project Managers

Project managers occupy a unique and often precarious position within many firms. Possessing little formal authority and forced to operate outside the traditional organizational hierarchy, they quickly and often belatedly learn the real limits of their power. It has been said that an effective project manager is the kingpin, but not the king. They are the bosses, it is true, but often in a loosely defined way. Indeed, in most firms they may lack the authority to conduct performance appraisals and offer incentives and rewards to their subordinates. As a result, their management styles must be those of persuasion and influence, rather than coercion and command.

Because of these and other limitations on the flexibility and power of project managers, project management has rightly been termed the "accidental profession" by more than one writer. There are two primary reasons for this sobriquet. First, few formal or systematic programs exist for selecting and training project managers, even within firms that specialize in project management work. This results at best in ad hoc training that may or may not teach these people the skills they need to succeed. Most project managers fall into their responsibilities by happenstance rather than by calculation. Second, as Frame (1987) cogently observed, few individuals grow up with the dream of one day becoming a project manager. It is neither a well-defined nor a well-understood career path within most modern organizations. Generally, the role is thrust upon people, rather than being sought.

Consider the typical experiences of project managers within many corporations. Novice managers, new to the company and its culture, are given a project to complete with the directive to operate within a set of narrowly defined constraints. These constraints most commonly include a specified time frame for completion, a budget, and a set of performance characteristics. Those who are able to quickly master the nature of their myriad duties succeed; those who do not generally fail. This "fly or die" mentality goes far toward creating an attitude of fear among potential project managers. Generation after generation of them learn their duties the hard way, often after having either failed completely or stumbled along from one crisis to another. The predictable result is wasteful: failed projects; managers battling entrenched bureaucracy and powerful factions; money, market opportunities, and other resources irretrievably lost to the company.

The amazing part of this scenario is that it is repeated again and again in company after company. Rather than treating project management as the unique and valuable discipline it is, necessitating formal training and selection policies, many companies continue to repeat their past mistakes. This almost leads one to believe they implicitly view experience and failure as the best teacher.

We need to shed light on the wide range of demands, opportunities, travails, challenges, and vexations that are part of becoming a better project manager. Many of the problems these individuals struggle with every day are far more managerial or behavioral in nature than technical. Such behavioral challenges are frequently vexing, and though they can sometimes seem inconsequential, they have a tremendous impact on the successful implementation of projects. For example, it does not take long for many project managers to discover exactly how far their personal power and status will take them in interacting with the rest of the organization. Hence, an understanding of influence tactics and political behavior is absolutely essential. Unfortunately, novice project managers are rarely clued into this important bit of information until it is too late—until, perhaps, they have appealed through formal channels for extra resources and been denied.

Consider the following examples:

- A long-distance telephone company whose CEO became so enamored of the concept of high-profile project teams—or "skunkworks," as they have come to be called—that he assigned that title to the few most highly visible, strategically important projects. Quickly, both senior and middle managers in departments across the organization came to realize that the only way to get their pet projects the resources necessary to succeed was to redesignate all new projects as "skunkworks." At last report, there were more than 75 high-profile skunkworks projects whose managers report directly to the CEO. The company now has severe difficulties in making research allocation decisions among its projects and routinely underfunds some vital projects while overfunding other, less important ones.

- A large computer hardware manufacturer has been dominated by the members of the hardware engineering department to such an extent that practically all new product ideas originate internally, within the department. By the time marketing personnel (sneeringly called "order takers" by the engineering department) are brought on board, they are presented with a fait accompli: a finished product they are instructed to sell. Marketing managers are now so cynical about new projects that they usually do not even bother sending a representative to new product development team meetings.

- A medium-sized manufacturing firm made it a policy to reward and punish project managers on the basis of their ability to bring projects in on time and under budget. These project managers were never held to any requirement that the project be accepted by its clients or become commercially successful. They quickly learned that their rewards were simply tied to satisfying the cost accountants, so they began to cut corners and make decisions that seriously undermined product quality.

- Projects in one division of a large, multinational corporation are routinely assigned to new managers who often have less than one year of experience with the company. Given a project scheduling software package and the telephone number of a senior project manager to be used "only in emergencies," they are instructed to form their project teams and begin the development process without any formal training or channels of communication to important clients and functional groups. Not surprisingly, senior managers at this company estimate that fewer than 30 percent of new product development efforts are profitable. Most take so long to develop, or incur such high cost overruns, that they are either abandoned before scheduled introduction or never live up to their potential in the marketplace.

This ad hoc approach to project management—coupled, as it frequently is, with an on-the-job training philosophy—is pervasive. It is also pernicious. Under the best of circumstances, project managers are called upon to lead, coordinate, plan, and control a diverse and complex set of processes and people in the pursuit of achieving project objectives. To hamper them with inadequate training and unrealistic expectations is to unnecessarily penalize them before they can begin to operate with any degree of confidence or effectiveness. The successful management of projects is simultaneously a human and technical challenge, requiring a far-sighted, strategic outlook coupled with the flexibility to react to conflicts and trouble areas as they arise on a daily basis. The project managers who are ultimately successful at their profession must learn to deal with and anticipate the constraints on their project team and personal freedom of action while consistently keeping their eyes on the ultimate prize.

From Whence Comes the Challenge?

One of the most intriguing and challenging aspects of project management lies in the relationship of project teams to the rest of the parent organization. With the exception of companies that are set up with matrix or project structures, most firms using project management techniques employ some form of standard functional structure. When project teams are added to an organization, the structural rules change dramatically. The vast majority of personnel who serve on project teams do so while maintaining links back to their functional departments. In fact, they typically split their time between the project and their functional duties.

The temporary nature of projects, combined with the very real limitations on power and discretion most project managers face, constitutes the core challenge of managing projects effectively. Clearly the very issues that characterize projects as distinct from functional work also illustrate the added complexity and difficulties they create for project managers. For example, within a functional department it is common to find people with more homogeneous backgrounds. This means that the finance department is staffed with finance people, the marketing department is made up of marketers, and so on. On the other hand, most projects are constructed from special, cross-functional teams composed of representatives from each of the relevant functional departments, who bring their own attitudes, time frames, learning, past experiences, and biases to the team. Creating a cohesive and potent team out of this level of heterogeneity presents a challenge for even the most seasoned and skilled of project managers.

But what is the ultimate objective? What determines a successful project and how does it differ from projects we may rightfully consider to have failed? Any seasoned project manager will usually tell you that a successful project is

one that has come in on time, has remained under budget, and performs as expected (that is, it conforms to specifications). Recently, though, there has been a reassessment of this traditional model for project success. The old triple constraint is rapidly being replaced by a new model, invoking a fourth hurdle for project success: client satisfaction. This means that a project is only successful if it satisfies the needs of its intended user. As a result, client satisfaction places a new and important constraint on project managers. No wonder, then, that there is a growing interest in the project manager's role within the corporation.

The Vital Dozen for Project Managers

Over the last several years, we have conducted interviews with dozens of senior project managers in which we asked them a simple question: "What information were you never given as a novice project manager that, in retrospect, could have made your job easier?" From the data gathered in these interviews, we have synthesized some of the more salient issues, outlined in Figure 1 and detailed below, that managers need to keep in mind when undertaking a project implementation effort. While not intended to appear in any particular order, these 12 rules offer a useful way to understand the challenge project managers face and some ways to address these concerns.

1. *Understand the context of project management.* Much of the difficulty in becoming an effective project manager lies in understanding the particular challenges project management presents in most corporations. Projects are a unique form of organizational work, playing an important role within many public and private organizations today. They act as mechanisms for the effective introduction of new products and services. They offer a level of intraorganizational efficiency that all companies seek but few find. But they also

---

1. **Understand** the context of project management.
2. **Recognize** project team conflict as progress.
3. **Understand** who the stakeholders are and what they want.
4. **Accept** and use the political nature of organizations.
5. **Lead** from the front.
6. **Understand** what "success" means.
7. **Build** and maintain a cohesive team.
8. **Enthusiasm** and despair are both infectious.
9. **One look** forward is worth two looks back.
10. **Remember** what you are trying to do.
11. **Use time** carefully or it will use you.
12. **Above all,** plan, plan, plan.

Figure 1 Twelve points to remember.

force managers to operate in a temporary environment outside the traditional functional lines of authority, relying upon influence and other informal methods of power. In essence, it is not simply the management of a project per se that presents such a unique challenge; it is also the atmosphere within which the manager operates that adds an extra dimension of difficulty. Projects exist outside the established hierarchy. They threaten, rather than support, the status quo because they represent change. So it is important for project managers to walk into their assigned role with their eyes wide open to the monumental nature of the tasks they are likely to face.

2. *Recognize project team conflict as progress.* One of the common responses of project managers to team conflict is panic. This reaction is understandable in that project managers perceive—usually correctly—that their reputation and careers are on the line if the project fails. Consequently, any evidence they interpret as damaging to the prospects of project success, such as team conflict, represents a very real source of anxiety. In reality, however, these interpersonal tensions are a natural result of putting individuals from diverse backgrounds together and requiring them to coordinate their activities. Conflict, as evidenced by the stages of group development, is more often a sign of healthy maturation in the group.

The result of differentiation among functional departments demonstrates that conflict under these circumstances is not only possible but unavoidable. One of the worst mistakes a project manager can make when conflicts emerge is to immediately force them below the surface without first analyzing the nature of the conflict. Although many interpersonal conflicts are based on personality differences, others are of a professional nature and should be addressed head-on.

Once a project manager has analyzed the nature of the conflict among team members, a variety of conflict handling approaches may be warranted, including avoidance, defusion, or problem-solving. On the other hand, whatever approach is selected should not be the result of a knee-jerk reaction to suppress conflict. In our experience, we have found many examples that show that even though a conflict is pushed below the surface, it will continue to fester if left unaddressed. The resulting eruption, which will inevitably occur later in the project development cycle, will have a far stronger effect than would the original conflict if it had been handled initially.

3. *Understand who the stakeholders are and what they want.* Project management is a balancing act. It requires managers to juggle the various and often conflicting demands of a number of powerful project stakeholders. One of the best tools a project manager can use is to develop a realistic assessment early in the project identifying the principal stakeholders and their agendas. In some projects, particularly those with important external clients or constituent groups, the number of stakeholders may be quite large, particularly when "intervenor" groups are included. Intervenors, according to Cleland (1983), may include any external group that can drastically affect the potential for project success, such as environmental activists in a nuclear plant construction project. Project managers who acknowledge the impact of stakeholders and work to minimize their effect by fostering good relations with them are often more successful than those who operate in a reactive mode, continually surprised by unexpected demands from groups that were not initially considered.

As a final point about stakeholders, it is important for a project manager's morale to remember that it is essentially impossible to please all the stakeholders all the time. The conflicting nature of their demands suggests that when one group is happy, another is probably upset. Project managers need to forget the idea of maximizing everyone's happiness and concentrate instead on maintaining satisfactory relations that allow them to do their job with a minimum of external interference.

4. *Accept the political nature of organizations and use it to your advantage.* Like it or not, we exist in a politicized world. Unfortunately, our corporations are no different. Important decisions involving resources are made through bargaining and deal-making. So project managers who wish to succeed must learn to use the political system to their advantage. This involves becoming adept at negotiation as well as using influence tactics to further the goals of the project.

At the same time, it is important to remember that any project representing possible organizational change is threatening, often because of its potential to reshuffle the power relationships among the key units and actors. Playing the political system acknowledges this reality. Successful project managers are those who can use their personal reputations, power, and influence to ensure cordial relations with important stakeholders and secure the resources necessary to smooth the client's adoption of the project.

Pursuing a middle ground of political sensibility is the key to project implementation success. There are two alternative and equally inappropriate approaches to navigating a firm's political waters: becoming overly political and predatory—we call these people "sharks"—and refusing to engage in politics to any degree—the politically "naive." Political sharks and the politically naive are at equal disadvantage in managing their projects: sharks because they pursue predatory and self-interested tactics that arouse distrust, and the naive because they insist on remaining above the fray, even at the cost of failing to attain and keep necessary resources for their projects.

Figure 2 illustrates some of the philosophical differences among the three types of political actors. The process of developing and applying appropriate political tactics means using politics as it can most effectively be used: as a basis for negotiation and bargaining. "Politically sensible" implies being politically sensitive to the concerns (real or

Characteristics	*Naive*	*Sensible*	*Sharks*
Underlying Attitude	Politics is unpleasant	Politics is necessary	Politics is an opportunity
Intent	Avoid at all costs	Further departmental goals	Self-serving and predatory
Techniques	Tell it like it is	Network; expand connections; use system to give and receive favors	Manipulate; use fraud and deceit when necessary
Favorite Tactics	None—the truth will win out	Negotiate, bargain	Bully; misuse information; cultivate and use "friends" and other contacts

Figure 2   Characteristics of political behaviors.

imagined) of powerful stakeholder groups. Legitimate or not, their concerns over a new project are real and must be addressed. Politically sensible managers understand that initiating any sort of organizational disruption or change by developing a new project is bound to reshuffle the distribution of power within the firm. That effect is likely to make many departments and managers very nervous as they begin to wonder how the future power relationships will be rearranged.

Appropriate political tactics and behavior include making alliances with powerful members of other stakeholder departments, networking, negotiating mutually acceptable solutions to seemingly insoluble problems, and recognizing that most organizational activities are predicated on the give-and-take of negotiation and compromise. It is through these uses of political behavior that managers of project implementation efforts put themselves in the position to most effectively influence the successful introduction of their systems.

5. *Lead from the front; the view is better.*   One message that comes through loud and clear is that project management is a "leader intensive" undertaking. Strong, effective leaders can go a long way toward helping a project succeed even in the face of a number of external or unforeseen problems. Conversely, a poor, inflexible leader can often ruin the chances of many important projects ever succeeding. Leaders are the focal point of their projects. They serve as a rallying point for the team and are usually the major source of information and communication for external stakeholders. Because their role is so central and so vital, it is important to recognize and cultivate the attributes project "leaders" must work to develop.

The essence of leadership lies in our ability to use it flexibly. This means that not all subordinates or situations merit the same response. Under some circumstances an autocratic approach is appropriate; other situations will be far better served by adopting a consensual style. Effective project leaders seem to understand this idea intuitively. Their approach must be tailored to the situation; it is self-defeating to attempt to tailor the situation to a preferred approach. The

worst leaders are those who are unaware of or indifferent to the freedom they have to vary their leadership styles. And they see any situation in which they must involve subordinates as inherently threatening to their authority. As a result, they usually operate under what is called the "Mushroom" Principle of Management." That is, they treat their subordinates the same way they would raise a crop of mushrooms—by keeping them in the dark and feeding them a steady diet of manure.

Flexible leadership behavior consists of a realistic assessment of personal strengths and weaknesses. It goes without saying that no one person, including the project manager, possesses all necessary information, knowledge, or expertise to perform the project tasks on his own. Rather, successful project managers usually acknowledge their limitations and work through subordinates' strengths. In serving as a facilitator, one of the essential abilities of an exceptional project manager is knowing where to go to seek the right help and how to ask the right questions. Obviously, the act of effective questioning is easier said than done. However, bear in mind that questioning is not interrogation. Good questions challenge subordinates without putting them on the spot; they encourage definite answers rather than vague responses, and they discourage guessing. The leader's job is to probe, to require subordinates to consider all angles and options, and to support them in making reasoned decisions. Direct involvement is a key component of a leader's ability to perform these tasks.

6. *Understand what "success" means.*   Successful project implementation is no longer subject to the traditional "triple constraint." That is, the days when projects were evaluated solely on adherence to budget, schedule, and performance criteria are past. In modern business, with its increased emphasis on customer satisfaction, we have to retrain project managers to expand their criteria for project success to include a fourth item: client use and satisfaction. What this suggests is that project "success" is a far more comprehensive word than some managers may have initially thought. The implication for rewards is also important. Within some organizations that regularly implement projects, it is common practice to reward the implementation manager when, in reality, only half the job has been accomplished. In other words, giving managers promotions and commendations before the project has been successfully transferred to clients, is being used, and is affecting organizational effectiveness is seriously jumping the gun.

Any project is only as good as it is used. In the final analysis, nothing else matters if a system is not productively employed. Consequently, every effort must be bent toward ensuring that the system fits in with client needs, that their concerns and opinions are solicited and listened to, and that they have final sign-off approval on the transferred project. In other words, the intended user of the project is the major determinant of its success. Traditionally, the bulk of the team's efforts are centered internally, mainly on their own concerns: budgets, timetables, and so forth. Certainly, these aspects of the project implementation process are necessary, but they should not be confused with the ultimate determinant of success: the client.

7. *Build and maintain a cohesive team.*   Many projects are implemented through the use of cross-functional teams. Developing and maintaining cordial team relations and fostering a healthy intergroup atmosphere often seems like a full-time job for most project managers. However, the resultant payoff from a cohesive project team cannot be overestimated. When a team is charged to work toward project development and implementation, the healthier the atmosphere within that team, the greater the likelihood the team will perform effectively. The project manager's job is to do whatever is necessary to build and maintain the health (cohesion) of the team. Sometimes that support can be accomplished by periodically checking with team members to determine their attitudes and satisfaction with the process. Other times the project manager may have to resort to less conventional methods, such as throwing parties or organizing field trips. To effectively intervene and support a team, project managers play a variety of roles—motivator, coach, cheerleader, peacemaker, conflict resolver. All these duties are appropriate for creating and maintaining an effective team.

8. *Enthusiasm and despair are both infectious.*   One of the more interesting aspects of project leaders is that they often function like miniaturized billboards, projecting an image and attitude that signals the current status of the project and its likelihood for success. The team takes its cue from the attitudes and emotions the manager exhibits. So one of the most important roles of the leader is that of motivator and encourager. The worst project managers are those who play their cards close to their chests, revealing little or nothing about the status of the project (again, the "Mushroom Manager"). Team members want and deserve to be kept abreast of what is happening. It is important to remember that the success or failure of the project affects the team as well as the manager. Rather than allowing the rumor mill to churn out disinformation, team leaders need to function as honest sources of information. When team members come to the project manager for advice or project updates, it is important to be honest. If the manager does not know the answer to the questions, he should tell them that. Truth in all forms is recognizable, and most project team members are much more appreciative of honesty than of eyewash.

9. *One look forward is worth two looks back.*   A recent series of commercials from a large computer manufacturer had as their slogan the dictum that the company never stop asking "What if?" Asking "What if?" questions is another way of saying we should never become comfortable with the status of the project under development. One large-scale study found that the leading determinant of project failure was the absence of any troubleshooting mechanisms—that is, no one was asking the "What if?" questions. Projecting a skeptical eye toward the future may seem gloomy to some managers. But in our opinion, it makes good sense. We cannot control the future but we can actively control our response to it.

A good example of the failure to apply this philosophy is evidenced by the progress of the "Chunnel" intended to link Great Britain with France. Although now in full operation, it was not ready for substantial traffic until some 15 months later than originally scheduled. As a result, Chunnel traffic missed the major summer vacation season with a concomitant loss in revenue. At the same time, the final cost (£15 billion) is likely to be six times the original estimate of £2.3 billion (O'Connor, 1993). It is instructive to take note of a recent statement by one of the project's somewhat harassed directors who, when pressed to state when the Chunnel would be ready, replied, "Now it will be ready when it's ready and not before!" Clearly, the failure to apply adequate contingency planning has led to the predictable result: a belief that the project will simply end when it ends.

10. *Remember what you are trying to do.*   Do not lose sight of the purpose behind the project. Sometimes it is easy to get bogged down in the minutiae of the development process, fighting fires on a daily basis and dealing with thousands of immediate concerns. The danger is that in doing so, project managers may fail to maintain a view of what the end product is supposed to be. This point reemphasizes the need to keep the mission in the forefront—and not just the project manager, but the team as well. The goal of the implementation serves as a large banner the leader can wave as needed to keep attitudes and motives focused in the right direction. Sometimes a superordinate goal can serve as a rallying point. Whatever technique project managers use, it is important that they understand the importance of keeping the mission in focus for all team members. A simple way to discover whether team members understand the project is to intermittently ask for their assessment of its status. They should know how their contributions fit into the overall installation plan. Are they aware of the specific contributions of other team members? If no, more attention needs to be paid to reestablishing a community sense of mission.

11. *Use time carefully or it will use you.*   Time is a precious commodity. Yet when we talk to project managers, it seems that no matter how hard they work to budget it, they never have enough. They need to make a realistic assessment of the "time killers" in their daily schedule: How are they spending their time and what are they doing profitably or unprofitably? We have found that the simple practice of keeping a daily time log for a short time can be an eye-opening experience. Many project managers discover that they spend far too much of their time in unproductive ways: project team meetings without agendas that grind on and on, unexpected telephone calls in the middle of planning sessions, quick "chats" with other managers that end up taking hours, and so forth. Efficient time management—one of the keys to successful project development—starts with project managers. When they actively plan their days and stick to a time budget, they usually find they are operating efficiently. On the other hand, when they take each problem as it comes and function in an ad hoc, reactive mode, they are likely to remain prisoners of their own schedules.

A sure recipe for finding the time and resources needed to get everything done without spending an inordinate amount of time on the job or construction site is provided by Gosselin (1993). The author lists six practical suggestions to help project managers control their tasks and projects without feeling constantly behind schedule:

- Create a realistic time estimate without overextending yourself.
- Be absolutely clear about what the boss or client requires.
- Provide for contingencies (schedule slippage, loss of key team member).
- Revise original time estimate and provide a set of options as required.
- Be clear about factors that are fixed (specifications, resources, and so on).
- Learn to say "Yes, and . . ." rather than "No, but . . ." Negotiation is the key.

12. *Above all, plan, plan, plan.*   The essence of efficient project management is to take the time to get it as right as possible the first time. "It" includes the schedule, the team composition, the project specifications, and the budget. There is a truism that those who fail to plan are planning to fail. One of the practical difficulties with planning is that so many of us distinguish it from other aspects of the project development, such as doing the work. Top managers are often particularly guilty of this offense as they wait impatiently for the project manager to begin doing the work.

Of course, too much planning is guaranteed to elicit repeated and pointed questions from top management and other stakeholders as they seek to discover the reason why "nothing is being done." Experienced project managers, though, know that it is vital not to rush this stage by reacting too quickly to top management inquiries. The planning stage must be managed carefully to allow the project manager and team the time necessary to formulate appropriate and workable plans that will form the basis for the development process. Dividing up the tasks and starting the "work" of the project too quickly is often ultimately wasteful. Steps that were poorly done are often steps that must be redone.

A complete and full investigation of any proposed project does take significant time and effort. However, bear in mind that overly elaborate or intricate planning can be detrimental to a project; by the time an opportunity is fully investigated, it may no longer exist. Time and again we have emphasized the importance of planning, but it is also apparent that there comes a limit, both to the extent and the time frame of the planning cycle. A survey among entrepreneurs, for example, revealed that only 28 percent of them drew up a full-scale plan (Sweet, 1994). A lesson here for project managers is that, like entrepreneurs, they must plan, but they must also be smart enough to recognize mistakes and change their strategy accordingly. As is noted in an old military slogan, "No plan ever survives its first contact with the enemy."

Project Managers in the Twenty-First Century

In our research and consulting experiences, we constantly interact with project managers, some with many years of experience, who express their frustration with their organizations because of the lack of detailed explication of their assigned tasks and responsibilities. Year after year, manager after manager, companies continue to make the same mistakes in "training" their project managers, usually through an almost ritualized baptism of fire. Project managers deserve better. According to Rodney Turner (1993), editor of the *International Journal of Project Management*:

> Through the 90's and into the 21st century, project-based management will sweep aside traditional functional line management and (almost) all organizations will adopt flat, flexible organizational structures in place of the old bureaucratic hierarchies . . . [N]ew organizational structures are replacing the old . . . [M]anagers will use project-based management as a vehicle for introducing strategic planning and for winning and maintaining competitive advantage.

Turner presents quite a rosy future, one that is predicated on organizations recognizing the changes they are currently undergoing and are likely to continue to see in the years ahead. In this challenging environment, project management is emerging as a technique that can provide the competitive edge necessary to succeed, given the right manager.

At the same time, there seems to have been a sea change in recent years regarding the image of project managers. The old view of the project manager as essentially that of a decision maker, expert, boss, and director seems to be giving way to a newer ideal: that of a leader, coach, and facilitator. Lest the reader assume these duties are any easier, we would assert that anyone who has attempted to perform these roles knows from personal experience just how difficult they can be. As part of this metamorphosis, says Clarke (1993), the new breed of project manager must be a natural salesperson who can establish harmonious customer (client) relations and develop trusting relationships with stakeholders. In addition to some of the obvious keys to project managers' success—personal commitment, energy, and enthusiasm—it appears that, most of all, successful project managers must manifest an obvious desire to see others succeed.

For successful project managers, there will always be a dynamic tension between the twin demands of technical training and an understanding of human resource needs. It must be clearly understood, however, that in assessing the relative importance of each challenge, the focus must clearly be on managing the human side of the process. As research and practice consistently demonstrate, project management is primarily a challenge in managing people. This point was recently brought to light in an excellent review of a book on managing the "human side" of projects (Horner, 1993):

> There must be many project managers like me who come from a technological background, and who suffered an education which left them singularly ill-prepared to manage people.

Leading researchers and scholars perceive the twenty-first century as the upcoming age of project management. The globalization of markets, the merging of many European economies, the enhanced expenditures of money on capital improvement both in the United States and abroad, the rapidly opening borders of Eastern European and Pacific Rim countries, with their goals of rapid infrastructure expansion—all of this offers an eloquent argument for the enhanced popularity of project management as a technique for improving the efficiency and effectiveness of organizational operations. With so much at stake, it is vital that we immediately begin to address some of the deficiencies in our project management theory and practice.

Project management techniques are well known. But until we are able to take further steps toward formalizing training by teaching the necessary skill set, the problems with efficiently developing, implementing, and gaining client acceptance for these projects are likely to continue growing. There is currently a true window of opportunity in the field of project management. Too often in the past, project managers have been forced to learn their skills the hard way, through practical experience coupled with all the problems of trial and error. Certainly, experience is a valuable component of learning to become an effective project manager, but it is by no means the best.

What conclusions are to be drawn here? If nothing else, it is certain that we have painted a portrait of project management as a complex, time-consuming, often exasperating process. At the same time, it is equally clear that successful project managers are a breed apart. To answer the various calls they continually receive, balance the conflicting demands of a diverse set of stakeholders, navigate tricky corporate political waters, understand the fundamental process of subordinate motivation, develop and constantly refine their leadership skills, and engage in the thousands of pieces of detailed minutiae while keeping their eyes fixed firmly on project goals requires individuals with special skills and personalities. Given the nature of their duties, is it any wonder successful project managers are in such short supply and, once identified, so valued by their organizations?

There is good news, however. Many of these skills, though difficult to master, can be learned. Project management is a challenge, not a mystery. Indeed, it is our special purpose to demystify much of the human side of project management, starting with the role played by the linchpin in the process: the project manager. The problem in the past has been too few sources for either seasoned or novice project managers to turn to in attempting to better understand the nature of their unique challenge and methods for performing more effectively. Too many organizations pay far too little attention to the process of selecting, training, and encouraging those people charged to run project teams. The predictable result is to continually compound the mistake of creating wave after wave of accidental project managers, forcing them to learn through trial and error with minimal guidance in how to perform their roles.

Managing a project is a challenge that requires a strategy and methodology all its own. Perhaps most important, it requires a project manager willing to function as a leader in every sense of the term. We have addressed a wide range of challenges, both contextual and personal, that form the basis under which projects are managed in today's organizations. It is hoped that readers will find something of themselves as well as something of use contained in these pages.

References

B. N. Baker, P. C. Murphy, and D. Fisher, "Factors Affecting Project Success," in D. I. Cleland and W. R. King, eds., *Project Management Handbook* (New York: Van Nostrand Reinhold, 1983): 778–801.

K. Clarke, "Survival Skills for a New Breed," *Management Today*, December 1993, p. 5.

D. I. Cleland, "Project Stakeholder Management," in D. I. Cleland and W. R. King, eds., *Project Management Handbook* (New York: Van Nostrand Reinhold, 1983): 275–301.

J. C. Davis, "The Accidental Profession," *Project Management Journal, 15*, 3 (1984): 6.

A. A. Einsiedel, "Profile of Effective Project Managers," *Project Management Journal, 18*, 5 (1987): 51–56.

J. Davidson Frame, *Managing Projects in Organizations* (San Francisco: Jossey-Bass, 1987).

T. Gosselin, "What to Do with Last-Minute Jobs," *World Executive Digest*, December 1993, p. 70.

R. J. Graham, "A Survival Guide for the Accidental Project Manager," *Proceedings of the Annual Project Management Institute Symposium* (Drexel Hill, PA: Project Management Institute, 1992), pp. 355–361.

M. Horner, "Review of 'Managing People for Project Success,'" *International Journal of Project Management, 11* (1993): 125–126.

P. R. Lawrence and J. W. Lorsch, "Differentiation and Integration in Complex Organizations," *Administrative Science Quarterly, 11* (1967):147.

M. Nichols, "Does New Age Business Have a Message for Managers?" *Harvard Business Review*, March–April 1994, pp. 52–60.

L. O'Connor, "Tunnelling Under the Channel," *Mechanical Engineering*, December 1993, pp. 60–66.

N. Pettersen, "What Do We Know about the Effective Project Manager?" *International Journal of Project Management,* 9 (1991): 99–104.

J. K. Pinto and O. P. Kharbanda, *Successful Project Managers: Leading Your Team to Success* (New York: Van Nostrand Reinhold, 1995).

J. K. Pinto and D. P. Slevin, "Critical Factors in Successful Project Implementation," *IEEE Transactions on Engineering Management*, EM-34, 1987, pp. 22–27.

B. Z. Posner, "What It Takes to Be a Good Project Manager," *Project Management Journal, 18*, 1 (1987): 51–54.

W. A. Randolph and B. Z. Posner, "What Every Manager Needs to Know about Project Management," *Sloan Management Review, 29*, 4 (1988): 65–73.

P. Sweet, "A Planner's Best Friend," *Accountancy, 113* (1994): 56–58.

H. J. Thamhain, "Developing Project Management Skills," *Project Management Journal, 22*, 3 (1991): 39–53.

R. Turner, "Editorial," *International Journal of Project Management, 11* (1993): 195.

Questions

1. What are the reasons the author advances for project management to be considered an "accidental profession"? The 12 guidelines are presented in no particular order. Order them by level of importance and explain your reasoning.

2. Where would you place yourself in Figure 2?

3. A few of the guidelines are related to the need to understand the reason for the project in the first place. Which guidelines would you place in this category? Why is this so crucial?

4. Why, in lesson 9, is always thinking about "what if" so important?

5. Lesson 12 warns about not planning enough, but also about spending too much time planning. How do you draw the line?

P A R T

I

PROJECT INITIATION

As noted earlier, the material in Part I of this text (highlighted in the figure) focuses on *project initiation*, which relates to the *context* of the project. Although this material may not appear germane to someone who wants to learn about how to actually run a project, having only the planning and execution tools and being ignorant of the context of the project is a recipe for disaster. It's like knowing how to sail a ship but not understanding your role as the captain and the purpose of the trip.

Project initiation begins with the judicious selection of the organization's projects to align them with the organization's overall strategy.

Chapter 2 describes how to evaluate and select projects that contribute to the organization's strategy and discusses the information needed as well as the

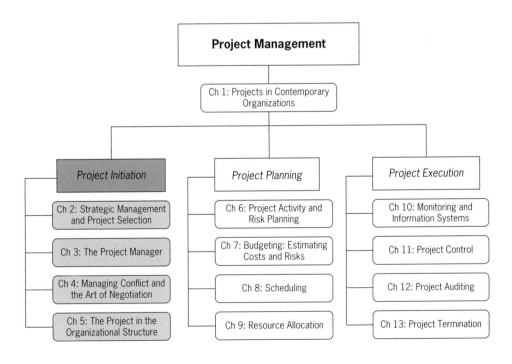

management of risk during this process. The chapter concludes with a description of an eight-step procedure called the "project portfolio process" that aligns project selection with the strategy.

Chapter 3, "The Project Manager," concerns the many roles of the project manager (PM), the multiple responsibilities, and some personal characteristics a project manager should possess. It also discusses the problems a PM faces when operating in a multicultural environment.

Next, Chapter 4 covers a subject of critical importance to the PM that is almost universally ignored in project management texts: the art of negotiating for resources. The chapter also describes some major sources of interpersonal conflict among members of the project team.

Concluding Part I of the book, Chapter 5 discusses various ways to establish the project organization. Different organizational forms are described, as well as their respective advantages and disadvantages. The staffing of the project team is also discussed.

CHAPTER

2

Strategic Management and Project Selection

More and more, the accomplishment of important tasks and goals in organizations today is being achieved through the use of projects. The phrases we hear and read about daily at our work and in conversations with our colleagues, such as "management by projects" and "project management maturity," reflect this increasing trend in our society. The explosively rapid adoption of such a powerful tool as project management to help organizations achieve their goals and objectives is certainly awesome. In addition to project management's great utility when correctly used, however, its utility has also led to many misapplications. As noted by one set of scholars (Cleland et al., 1983, p. 155), the rapid adoption of project management means:

- there are many projects that fall outside the organization's stated mission;
- there are many projects being conducted that are completely unrelated to the strategy and goals of the organization; and
- there are many projects with funding levels that are excessive relative to their expected benefits.

What was true 30 years ago, is still true today.

In addition to the growth in the number of organizations adopting project management, there is also accelerating growth in the number of multiple, simultaneous, and often interrelated projects in organizations. Thus, the issue naturally arises as to how one manages all these projects. Are they all really projects? (It has been suggested that perhaps up to 80 percent of all "projects" are not actually projects at all, since they do not include the three project requirements for objectives, budget, and due date.) Should we be undertaking all of them? Of those we should implement, what should be their priorities?

It is not unusual these days for organizations to be wrestling with hundreds of new projects. With so many ongoing projects it becomes difficult for smaller projects to get adequate support, or even the attention of senior management. Three particularly common problems in organizations trying to manage multiple projects are:

1. Delays in one project cause delays in other projects because of common resource needs or technological dependencies.

2. The inefficient use of corporate resources results in peaks and valleys of resource utilization.

3. Bottlenecks in resource availability or lack of required technological inputs result in project delays that depend on those scarce resources or technology.

As might be expected, the report card on organizational success with management by projects is not stellar. For example, one research study (Thomas et al., 2001) has found that 30 percent of all projects are canceled midstream, and over half of completed projects came in up to 190 percent over budget and 220 percent late. This same study found that the primary motivation of organizations to improve and expand their project management processes was due to major troubled or failed projects, new upcoming mega-projects, or to meet competition or maintain their market share. Those firms that "bought" project management skills from consultants tended to see it as a "commodity." These firms also commonly relied on outsourcing difficult activities, or even entire projects. Those who developed the skills internally, however, saw project management as offering a proprietary competitive advantage. The latter firms also moved toward recognizing project management as a viable career path in their organization, leading to senior management positions.

A major development among those choosing to develop project management expertise in house, particularly those interested in using projects to accomplish organizational goals and strategies, is the initiation of a Project Management Office (PMO), described in detail in Chapter 5. This office strives to develop multi-project management expertise throughout the organization, to evaluate the interrelationships between projects (e.g., such as resource and skill requirements), and to ensure that projects are clearly related to the organization's goals. It is expected that the PMO will promote those projects that capitalize on the organization's strengths, offer a competitive advantage, and mutually support each other, while avoiding those with resource or technology needs in areas where the organization has no desire for development.

The challenges thus facing the contemporary organization are how to make sure that projects are closely tied to the organization's goals and strategy, how to handle the growing number of ongoing projects, and how to make these projects more successful, topics we discuss more fully in Section 2.7. The latter two of these objectives concern "project management maturity"—the development of project and multiproject management expertise. Following a discussion of project management maturity, we launch into a major aspect of multiproject management: selecting projects for implementation and then briefly discuss the uncertainty, or risk, involved.

Given that the organization has an appropriate mission statement and strategy, projects must be selected that are consistent with the strategic goals of the organization. *Project selection* is the process of evaluating individual projects or groups of projects and then choosing to implement some set of them so that the objectives of the parent organization will be achieved. Because considerable uncertainty may surround one's initial notions of precisely how most projects will be carried out, what resources will be required, and how long it will take to complete the project, we will introduce *risk analysis* into the selection process. Following this, we illustrate the process of selecting for implementation the set of projects that best meets the strategic goals of the organization, the Project Portfolio Process. Last, the chapter closes with a short discussion of *project proposals*.

Before proceeding, a final comment is pertinent. It is not common to discuss project selection, the construction of a project portfolio, and similar matters in any detail in elementary texts on project management. The project manager typically has little or no say in the project funding decision, nor is he or she usually asked for input concerning the development of organizational strategy. Why then discuss these matters? The answer is simple, yet persuasive. *The project manager who does not understand what a given project is expected to contribute to the parent organization lacks critical information needed to manage the project in order to optimize its contribution.*

2.1   PROJECT MANAGEMENT MATURITY

As organizations have employed more and more projects for accomplishing their objectives (often referred to as "managing organizations by projects"), it has become natural for senior managers—as well as scholars—to wonder if the organization's project managers have a mastery of the skills required to manage projects competently. For a great many organizations, the answer appears to be "NO!" The record of IT/software projects is particularly poor with less than 15 percent reaching "planned expectations" (KPMG, 2005; Cicmil et al., 2006; and elsewhere). A recent survey by PMI (2011) indicated that one of the key factors for improving the success rate of projects was the organization's project management competency, now known as "maturity," including the standardization of project management techniques which increased project success rates by over 25 percent. For more on this topic, see the Afterword in Section 13.5.

Dinsmore (1998) describes one such "project management maturity" measure that scores firms on five successive levels of maturity. In the first level, "Initial," there is no formal process for managing projects. The second level, "Repeatable," has procedures in place for planning, scheduling, tracking, and estimating. The data are not integrated even if the firm has PM software available. The third level is "Defined." On this level, the firm has integrated systems for tracking and managing projects, but are not routinely understood and used for controlling projects. At level four, "Managed," systems are installed and used to manage and control projects. The project success rate is high. Level five, "Optimizing," has integrated databases used to generate information on the senior-management level as well as for managers of single projects or portfolios of several projects. The database also contains historical information to allow continued improvement of the project management system.

PMBOK Guide

1.7

In the last few years, a number of different ways to measure "project management maturity" have been suggested (Pennypacker et al., 2003), such as basing the evaluation on PMI's *PMBOK Guide* (Lubianiker, 2000), PMI's Organizational Project Management Maturity Model (OPM3; see www.pmi.org/opm3/), or the ISO 9001 standards (contact the American Society for Quality). We will refer to project management maturity models again in Chapter 11 on Project Control and we will also urge that historical information on how to improve project management be maintained and utilized to allow continued improvement of project management systems.

Project Management in Practice
Implementing Strategy through Project Management Tools

Since strategic plans are usually developed at the executive level, implementation by middle level managers is often a problem due to poor understanding of the organisation's capabilities and top management's expectations. However, bottom-up development of departmental goals and future plans invariably lacks the vision of the overall market and competitive environment. At one of the largest software project organisations in India, this problem is avoided by closely tying project management tools to the organisational strategy. The resulting system provides a set of checks and balances for both top management executives and project managers.

Overseeing the system is the Software Engineering Process Group (SEPG) that helps senior management translate their strategic goals and objectives into project management performance, budget, and schedule targets. These may include new product development, upgrading information systems, or identifying best practices, lessons learned, and areas of further improvement. SEPG also works with the project teams to develop their plans, monitoring activities, and reports to ensure they are aligned to the organisations overall strategic intentions.

The primary benefit of this system has been the organisation's ability to translate and implement senior management strategic goals into tasks and activities. There is constant review and re-evaluation of organisational initiatives and resources in terms of the overall strategic plans, and enables senior management to further plan, track and adjust strategy through feedback provided by the system.

Source: Pankaj Jalote, *CMM in Practice*, pp. 22–26, Pearson Education, 2000.

Printed and Electronically reproduced by permission of Pearson Education, Inc., Upper Saddle River, New Jersey.

Quite a few consulting firms, as well as scholars, have devised formal maturity measures. One of these measures, PM3®, is described by R. Remy (1997). In this system, the final project management "maturity" of an organization is assessed as being at one of five levels: ad-hoc (disorganized, accidental successes and failures); abbreviated (some processes exist, inconsistent management, unpredictable results); organized (standardized processes, more predictable results); managed (controlled and measured processes, results in line with plans); and adaptive (continuous improvement in processes, success is normal, performance keeps improving).

PMBOK Guide
Table 3-1

Another maturity model has been devised and applied to 38 organizations in four different industries (Ibbs et al., 2000). This model consists of 148 questions divided into six processes/life-cycle phases (initiating, planning, executing, controlling, closing, and organizational environment), and the nine PMBOK knowledge areas (integration, scope, time, cost, quality, human resources, communication, risk, and procurement). The model assesses an organization's project management maturity in terms of five stages of maturity: ad-hoc, planned, managed, integrated, and sustained (the highest level).

Regardless of model form, it appears that most organizations do not score very well in terms of maturity. On one form, about three-quarters are no higher than level 2 (planned) and fewer than 6 percent are above level 3 (managed). On another perspective, the average of the 38 organizations was only slightly over 3, though individual firms ranged between 1.8 and 4.6 on the five-point scale.

Next we detail the project selection process, discussing the various types of selection models commonly used, some criteria for selection, and the role of risk in the process.

2.2   PROJECT SELECTION CRITERIA AND MODELS

Project selection is the process of evaluating proposed projects or groups of projects, and then choosing to implement some set of them so that the objectives of the parent organization will be achieved. This same systematic process can be applied to any area of the organization's business in which choices must be made between competing alternatives. For example, a manufacturing firm can use evaluation/selection techniques to choose which machine to adopt in a part-fabrication process; a TV station can select which of several syndicated comedy shows to rerun in its 7:30 P.M. weekday time-slot; a construction firm can select the best subset of a large group of potential projects on which to bid; or a hospital can find the best mix of psychiatric, orthopedic, obstetric, and other beds for a new wing. Each project will have different costs, benefits, and risks. Rarely are these known with certainty. In the face of such differences, the selection of one project out of a set is a difficult task. Choosing a number of different projects, a *portfolio*, is even more complex (discussed in Section 2.5).

In the paragraph just above, all firms except the hypothetical construction firm are considering projects that are "inside" the organization; that is, they are for "clients" within the organization funding the projects. The construction firm is considering a set of potential projects to perform for clients outside of the construction firm itself. Whether for inside or outside clients, the projects will use the organization's own resources, and both types of projects are usually dealt with as "competing" for the same pool of resources.

Only rarely will a project manager be involved in the process by which projects are selected for inclusion in the set of projects the parent organization adopts for investment. It is, however, critically important to the success of the PM that he or she fully understands the parent organization's objectives in undertaking a project that the PM is expected to lead. As we will see, most of the decisions that the PM is forced to make will have an impact on the degree to which the project contributes to those objectives the parent organization expected from the project. This is not the last time we will note the importance for the PM to understand why his or her project was selected for investment.

In the following sections, we discuss several techniques that can be used to help senior managers select projects. Project selection is only one of many decisions associated with project management. To deal with all of these problems, we use models. We need such models because they abstract the relevant issues about a problem from the mass of detail in which the problem is embedded—reality is far too complex to deal with in its entirety. The model allows us to strip away almost all the reality from a problem, leaving only the relevant aspects of the "real" situation for us to deal with. This process of carving away the unwanted reality from the bones of a problem is called *modeling the problem.*

The proper choice of investment projects is crucial to the long-run survival of every firm. Daily we witness the results of both good and bad investment choices. In our daily newspapers we read of Cisco System's decision to purchase firms that have developed valuable communication network software rather than to develop its own software. We read of Procter and Gamble's decision to invest heavily in marketing its products on the Internet and through social media; or problems faced by school systems when they update student computer labs—should they invest in Microsoft®-based systems or stick with their traditional choice, Apple®? But can such important choices be made rationally? Once made, do they ever change, and if so, how? These questions reflect the need for effective selection models.

Within the limits of their capabilities, such models can be used to increase profits, select investments competing for limited capital resources, or improve the market position of an organization. They can be used for ongoing evaluation as well as initial selection, and thus are a key to the allocation and reallocation of the organization's scarce resources.

When a firm chooses a project selection model, the following criteria, based on Souder (1973), are most important.

1. *Realism* The model should reflect the reality of the firm's decision situation, especially the multiple objectives of both the firm and its managers, bearing in mind that without a common measurement system, direct comparison of different projects is impossible. The model should also take into account the realities of the firm's limitations on facilities, capital, personnel, and so forth, and include factors that reflect project technical and market risks: performance, cost, time, customer rejection, and implementation.

2. *Capability* The model should be sophisticated enough to deal with the relevant factors: multiple time periods, situations both internal and external to the project (e.g., strikes, interest rate changes), and so on.

3. *Flexibility* The model should give valid results within the range of conditions that the firm might experience. It should be easy to modify in response to changes in the firm's

environment; for example, tax law changes, new technological advancements that alter risk levels, and, above all, organizational goal changes.

4. *Ease of use*   The model should be reasonably convenient, not take a long time to execute, and be easy to use and understand. It should not require special interpretation, data that are difficult to acquire, excessive personnel, or unavailable equipment.

5. *Cost*   Data-gathering and modeling costs should be low relative to the cost of the project and less than the potential benefits of the project. All costs should be considered, including the costs of data management and of running the model.

We would add the following sixth criterion.

6. *Easy computerization*   It should be easy and convenient to gather and store the information in a computer database, and to manipulate data in the model through use of a widely available, standard computer package such as Excel®.

Since the development of computers and the establishment of operations research as an academic subject in the mid-1950s, the use of formal, numeric models to assist in decision making has expanded. Many of these models use financial metrics such as profits and/or cash flow to measure the "correctness" of a managerial decision. Project selection decisions are no exception, being based primarily on the degree to which the financial goals of the organization are met. As we will see later, this stress on financial goals, largely to the exclusion of other criteria, raises some serious problems for the firm, irrespective of whether the firm is for-profit or not-for-profit.

There are two basic types of project selection models, *numeric* and *nonnumeric*. Both are widely used. Many organizations use both at the same time, or they use models that are combinations of the two. Nonnumeric models, as the name implies, do not use numbers as inputs. Numeric models do, but the criteria being measured may be either objective or subjective. It is important to remember that the *qualities* of a project may be represented by numbers, and that *subjective* measures are not necessarily less useful or reliable than *objective* measures.

Before examining specific kinds of models within the two basic types, let us consider just what we wish the model to do for us, never forgetting two critically important, but often overlooked, facts.

- Models do not make decisions—people do. The manager, not the model, bears responsibility for the decision. The manager may "delegate" the task of making the decision to a model, but the responsibility cannot be abdicated.

- All models, however sophisticated, are only partial representations of the reality they are meant to reflect. Reality is far too complex for us to capture more than a small fraction of it in any model. Therefore, no model can yield an optimal decision except within its own, possibly inadequate, framework.

We seek a model to assist us in making project selection decisions. This model should possess the characteristics discussed previously and, above all, it should evaluate potential projects by the degree to which they will meet the firm's objectives. To construct a selection/ evaluation model, therefore, it is necessary to develop a list of the firm's objectives. This list of objectives should be generated by top management and might include maintenance of specific market shares, development of an improved image with specific clients or competitors, or expansion into a new line of business, just to mention a few.

When the list of objectives has been developed, an additional refinement is recommended. The elements in the list should be *weighted*. Each item is added to the list because it represents a contribution to the success of the organization, but each item does not make an equal contribution. The weights reflect different degrees of contribution each element makes in accomplishing a set of goals.

Once the list of weighted goals has been developed, one more task remains. The probable contribution of each project to each goal should be estimated. A project is selected or rejected because it is predicted to have certain outcomes, if implemented, which contribute to goal achievement. If the estimated level of goal achievement is sufficiently large, the project is selected.

A paper by Åstebro (2004) reports on a study of more than 500 R & D projects. He found that four project characteristics were excellent predictors of a project's commercial success: (1) expected profitability, (2) technological opportunity, (3) development risk, and (4) appropriability, the degree to which a project is appropriate for the organization undertaking it. This finding is particularly important because the experimental design was free of the hindsight bias that is so common in studies of project success and failure. The model correctly predicted almost 80 percent of the project failures and almost 75 percent of the project successes.

A major consulting firm (Booz, Allen, and Hamilton, 1966) has argued that the primary cause for the failure of R & D projects is insufficient care in evaluating the proposal before the expenditure of funds. What is true for R & D projects also appears to be true for other kinds of projects, and it is clear that product development projects are more successful if they incorporate user needs and satisfaction in the design process (Matzler et al., 1998). Careful analysis of a potential project is mandatory for profitability in the construction business. There are many horror stories (Meredith, 1981) about firms that undertook projects for the installation of a computer information system without sufficient analysis of the time, cost, and disruption involved.

Once again, we must emphasize that the tendency of many organizations to depend on profitability models to the exclusion of nonfinancial costs and benefits is a serious mistake. It is not uncommon for the "minor side-effects" of a new product or process to have major impacts on the parent organization. Often, projects intended to alter the organization's infrastructure—extending engineering software to include new analytic methods or installing a day-care facility for preschool children of employees—can have significant positive effects on worker morale and productivity. On the other hand, replacing workers with new technology may make financial sense but could hurt morale and productivity so much that the change substantially reduces profitability.

2.3 TYPES OF PROJECT SELECTION MODELS

Of the two basic types of selection models (numeric and nonnumeric), nonnumeric models are older and simpler, and have only a few subtypes to consider. We examine them first.

Nonnumeric Models

The Sacred Cow In this case the project is suggested by a senior and powerful official in the organization. Often the project is initiated with a simple comment such as, "If you have a chance, why don't you look into…," and there follows an undeveloped idea for a new product, for the development of a new market, for the design and adoption of a global database and information system, or for some other project requiring an investment of the firm's resources. The immediate result of this bland statement is the creation of a "project" to investigate whatever the boss has suggested. The project is "sacred" in the sense that it will be maintained until successfully concluded, or until the boss, personally, recognizes the idea as a failure and terminates it.

The Operating Necessity If a flood is threatening the plant, a project to build a protective dike does not require much formal evaluation. XYZ Steel Corporation has used this criterion (and the following criterion also) in evaluating potential projects. If the project is required in order to keep the system operating, the primary question becomes: Is the system worth saving at the estimated cost of the project? If the answer is yes, project costs will be examined to make sure they are kept as low as is consistent with project success, but the project will be funded.

The Competitive Necessity   Using this criterion, XYZ Steel undertook a major plant rebuilding project in the late 1960s in its steel-bar-manufacturing facilities near Chicago. It had become apparent to XYZ's management that the company's bar mill needed modernization if the firm was to maintain its competitive position in the Chicago market area. Although the planning process for the project was quite sophisticated, the decision to undertake the project was based on a desire to maintain the company's competitive position in that market.

In a similar manner, many business schools are restructuring their undergraduate and MBA programs to stay competitive with the more forward-looking schools. In large part, this action is driven by declining numbers of tuition-paying students and the need to develop stronger programs to attract them.

Investment in an *operating necessity* project takes precedence over a *competitive necessity* project, but both types of projects may bypass the more careful numeric analysis used for projects deemed to be less urgent or less important to the survival of the firm.

The Product Line Extension   In this case, a project to develop and distribute new products would be judged on the degree to which it fits the firm's existing product line, fills a gap, strengthens a weak link, or extends the line in a new, desirable direction. Sometimes careful calculations of profitability are not required. Decision makers can act on their beliefs about what will be the likely impact on the total system performance if the new product is added to the line.

Comparative Benefit Model   For this situation, assume that an organization has many projects to consider, perhaps several dozen. Senior management would like to select a subset of the projects that would most benefit the firm, but the projects do not seem to be easily comparable. For example, some projects concern potential new products, some require the conduct of a research and development project for a government agency, some concern changes in production methods, others concern computerization of certain records, and still others cover a variety of subjects not easily categorized (e.g., a proposal to create a daycare center for employees with small children). The organization has no formal method of selecting projects, but members of the Selection Committee think that some projects will benefit the firm more than others, even if they have no precise way to define or measure "benefit."

The concept of comparative benefits, if not a formal model, is widely adopted for selection decisions on all sorts of projects. Most United Way organizations use the concept to make decisions about which of several social programs to fund. Senior management of the funding organization then examines all projects with positive recommendations and attempts to construct a portfolio that best fits the organization's aims and its budget.

Of the several techniques for ordering projects, the Q-Sort (Helin et al., 1974) is one of the most straightforward. First, the projects are divided into three groups—*good, fair*, and *poor*—according to their relative merits. If any group has more than eight members, it is subdivided into two categories, such as *fair-plus* and *fair-minus*. When all categories have eight or fewer members, the projects within each category are ordered from best to worst. Again, the order is determined on the basis of relative merit. The rater may use specific criteria to rank each project, or may simply use general overall judgment. (See Figure 2-1 for an example of a Q-Sort.)

The process described may be carried out by one person who is responsible for evaluation and selection, or it may be performed by a committee charged with the responsibility. If a committee handles the task, the individual rankings can be developed anonymously, and the set of anonymous rankings can be examined by the committee itself for consensus. It is common for such rankings to differ somewhat from rater to rater, but they do not often vary

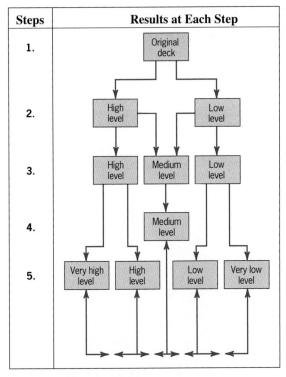

Steps	Results at Each Step
1.	
2.	
3.	
4.	
5.	

Figure 2-1 The Q-sort method. *Source: Souder 1983.*

strikingly because the individuals chosen for such committees rarely differ widely on what they feel to be appropriate for the parent organization. Projects can then be selected in the order of preference, though they are usually evaluated financially before final selection.

There are other, similar nonnumeric models for accepting or rejecting projects. Although it is easy to dismiss such models as unscientific, they should not be discounted casually. These models are clearly goal-oriented and directly reflect the primary concerns of the organization. The sacred cow model, in particular, has an added feature; sacred cow projects are visibly supported by "the powers that be." Full support by top management is certainly an important contributor to project success (Meredith, 1981). Without such support, the probability of project success is sharply lowered.

Sustainability   The December 2009 issue of *PM Network* is devoted to "sustainability." The discussion begins with the following (Gale, 2009): "Somewhere along the line, sustainability became interchangeable with that *other* buzzword; green. There's just one small problem. It's not really accurate. Sustainability does, of course, call for incorporating environmental concerns into project decision-making, but it also covers social issues—and the bottom line."

More and more organizations are building sustainability into the set of criteria that must be met for proposed projects to be selected for funding. Jewelry companies avoid the use of "blood diamonds," and manufacturing firms avoid purchasing inputs from suppliers that use child labor. The sale of a pharmaceutical of questionable purity or serious side-effects is commonly far more costly in the long run than the cost of better quality control or the research needed for better drug design. In other words, sustainability focuses on long-run profitability rather than short-run payoff. To integrate sustainability into the organization's decision-making requires the appointment of a senior manager with responsibility for the task. Metrics must be developed to measure the results of policy changes to increase sustainability, and this often requires developing the "soft" measures we will discuss later in this chapter.

Project Management in Practice
Taipei 101: Refitted as World's Tallest Sustainable Building

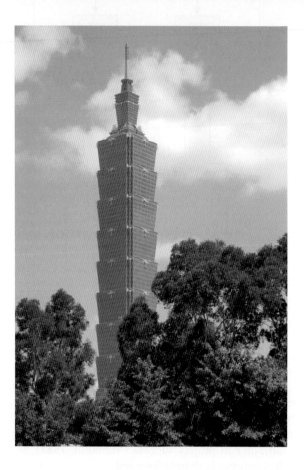

The owners of Taiwan's Taipei 101 tower, the tallest building in East Asia, wanted to show the world that it is possible to make an existing building sustainable by winning a LEED (Leadership in Energy and Environmental Design) certification. When the building was constructed in 1998, advanced elements of sustainability were included, such as low-emissivity windows, energy-efficient HVAC systems, and smart controls on its double-deck elevators. The new $1.8 million effort will extend these green elements to include eco-friendly processes (cleaning, solid-waste management, purchasing), healthy office environments (air-quality testing, environmental inspections), energy consumption (optimizing operating and maintenance programs, automatic turnoff of lighting in unoccupied restrooms), water usage (replacing toilet and urinal flush valves, reducing washbasin faucet flow rates), and tenant recycling, waste management, and office fit-outs.

However, the engineering aspects of the tower refitting were the easy parts of the project. More difficult was getting all 85 organizations occupying the tower, comprising over 10,000 people, on board with the recycling (including purchase of recycled supplies) and other sustainability routines. The project manager notes that changing people's attitudes is by far the greatest challenge for sustainability.

Source: S. A. Swanson. "The Sky's the Limit," *PM Network,* Vol. 24.

Numeric Models: Profit/Profitability

PMBOK Guide
Chapter 7

As noted earlier, a large majority of all firms using project evaluation and selection models use profitability as the sole measure of acceptability. We will consider these models first, and then discuss more comprehensive models. Cost aspects of profitability are covered in area 4 of the PMBOK®.

Payback Period   The payback period for a project is the initial fixed investment in the project divided by the estimated annual net cash inflows from the project. The ratio of these quantities is the number of years required for the project to repay its initial fixed investment. For example, assume a project costs $100,000 to implement and has annual net cash inflows of $25,000. Then

$$\text{Payback period} = \$100,000/\$25,000 = 4 \text{ years}$$

This method assumes that the cash inflows will persist at least long enough to pay back the investment, and it ignores any cash inflows beyond the payback period. The method also serves as an (inadequate) proxy for risk. The faster the investment is recovered, the less the risk (discussed further in Section 2.4) to which the firm is exposed.

Discounted Cash Flow   Also referred to as the net present value (NPV) method, the discounted cash flow method determines the net present value of all cash flows by discounting them by the required rate of return (also known as the *hurdle rate, cutoff rate,* and similar terms) as follows:

$$\text{NPV (project)} = A_0 + \sum_{t=1}^{n} \frac{F_t}{(1+k)^t}$$

where

F_t = the net cash flow in period t,

k = the required rate of return, and

A_0 = initial cash investment (because this is an outflow, it will be negative).

To include the impact of inflation (or deflation) where p_t is the predicted rate of inflation during period t, we have

$$\text{NPV (project)} = A_0 + \sum_{t=1}^{n} \frac{F_t}{(1+k+p_t)^t}$$

Early in the life of a project, net cash flow is likely to be negative, the major outflow being the initial investment in the project, A_0. If the project is successful, however, cash flows will become positive. The project is *acceptable* if the sum of the net present values of all estimated cash flows over the life of the project is positive. A simple example will suffice. Using our $100,000 investment with a net cash inflow of $25,000 per year for a period of eight years, a required rate of return of 15 percent, and an inflation rate of 3 percent per year, we have

$$\text{NPV (project)} = -\$100,000 + \sum_{t=1}^{8} \frac{\$25,000}{(1+0.15+0.03)^t}$$

$$= \$1,939$$

Because the present value of the inflows is greater than the present value of the outflow—that is, the net present value is positive—the project is deemed acceptable.

PsychoCeramic Sciences, Inc.

PsychoCeramic Sciences, Inc. (PSI), a large producer of cracked pots and other cracked items, is considering the installation of a new marketing software package that will, it is hoped, allow more accurate sales information concerning the inventory, sales, and deliveries of its pots as well as its vases designed to hold artificial flowers.

The information systems (IS) department has submitted a project proposal that estimates the investment requirements as follows: an initial investment of $125,000 to be paid upfront to the Pottery Software Corporation; an additional investment of $100,000 to modify and install the software; and another $90,000 to integrate the new software into the overall information system. Delivery and installation is estimated to take one year; integrating the entire system should require an additional year. Thereafter, the IS department predicts that scheduled software updates will require further expenditures of about $15,000 every second year, beginning in the fourth year. They will not, however, update the software in the last year of its expected useful life.

The project schedule calls for benefits to begin in the third year, and to be up-to-speed by the end of that year. Projected additional profits resulting from better and more timely sales information are estimated to be $50,000 in the first year of operation and are expected to peak at $120,000 in the second year of operation, and then to follow the gradually declining pattern shown in the table at the end of this box.

Project life is expected to be 10 years from project inception, at which time the proposed system will be obsolete for this division and will have to be replaced. It is estimated, however, that the software can be sold to a smaller division of PSI and will thus have a salvage value of $35,000. PSI has a 12 percent hurdle rate for capital investments and expects the rate of inflation to be about 3 percent over the life of the project. Assuming that the initial expenditure occurs at the beginning of the year and that all other receipts and expenditures occur as lump sums at the end of the year, we can prepare the Net Present Value analysis for the project as shown in the table below.

The Net Present Value of the project is positive and, thus, the project can be accepted. (The project would have been rejected if the hurdle rate were 14 percent.)

Just for the intellectual exercise, note that the total inflow for the project is $759,000, or $75,900 per year on average for the 10-year project. The required investment is $315,000 (ignoring the biennial overhaul charges). Assuming 10-year, straight line depreciation, or $31,500 per year, the payback period would be:

$$PB = \frac{\$315,000}{\$75,900 + 31,500} = 2.9$$

A project with this payback period would probably be considered quite desirable.

Year A	Inflow B	Outflow C	Net Flow D = (B − C)	Discount Factor $1/(1 + k + p)^t$	Net Present Value D × (Disc. Fact.)
2006*	$ 0	$125,000	−$125,000	1.0000	−$125,000
2006	0	100,000	−100,000	0.8696	−86,957
2007	0	90,000	−90,000	0.7561	−68,053
2008	50,000	0	50,000	0.6575	32,876
2009	120,000	15,000	105,000	0.5718	60,034
2010	115,000	0	115,000	0.4972	57,175
2011	105,000	15,000	90,000	0.4323	38,909
2012	97,000	0	97,000	0.3759	36,466
2013	90,000	15,000	75,000	0.3269	24,518
2014	82,000	0	82,000	0.2843	23,310
2015	65,000	0	65,000	0.2472	16,067
2015	35,000		35,000	0.2472	8,651
Total	$759,000	$360,000	$399,000		$ 17,997

*$t = 0$ at the beginning of 2006.

Internal Rate of Return   If we have a set of expected cash inflows and cash outflows, the internal rate of return is the discount rate that equates the present values of the two sets of flows. If A_t is an expected cash outflow in the period t and R_t is the expected inflow for the period t, the internal rate of return is the value of k that satisfies the following equation (note that the A_0 will be positive in this formulation of the problem):

$$A_0 + A_1 / (1+k) + A_2 / (1+k)^2 + \ldots + A_n / (1+k)^n = R_1 / (1+k) + R_2 / (1+k)^2$$
$$+ \ldots + R_n / (1+k)^n$$

The value of k is found by trial and error.

Profitability Index   Also known as the benefit–cost ratio, the profitability index is the net present value of all future expected cash flows divided by the initial cash investment. (Some firms do not discount the cash flows in making this calculation.) If this ratio is greater than 1.0, the project may be accepted.

Other Profitability Models   There are a great many variations of the models just described. These variations fall into three general categories: (1) those that subdivide net cash flow into the elements that comprise the net flow; (2) those that include specific terms to introduce risk (or uncertainty, which is treated as risk) into the evaluation; and (3) those that extend the analysis to consider effects that the project might have on other projects or activities in the organization.

Several comments are in order about all the profit/profitability numeric models. First, let us consider their advantages:

1. The undiscounted models are simple to use and understand.
2. All use readily available accounting data to determine the cash flows.
3. Model output is in terms familiar to business decision makers.
4. With a few exceptions, model output is on an "absolute" profit/profitability scale and allows "absolute" go/no-go decisions.
5. Some profit models can be amended to account for project risk.

The disadvantages of these models are the following:

1. These models ignore all nonmonetary factors except risk.
2. Models that do not include discounting ignore the timing of the cash flows and the time–value of money.
3. Models that reduce cash flows to their present value are strongly biased toward the short run.
4. Payback-type models ignore cash flows beyond the payback period.
5. The internal rate of return model can result in multiple solutions.
6. All are sensitive to errors in the input data for the early years of the project.
7. All discounting models are nonlinear, and the effects of changes (or errors) in the variables or parameters are generally not obvious to most decision makers.
8. All these models depend for input on a determination of cash flows, but it is not clear exactly how the concept of cash flow is properly defined for the purpose of evaluating projects.

A complete discussion of profit/profitability models can be found in any standard work on financial management—see Ross et al. (2008), for example. In general, the net present value models are preferred to the internal rate of return models. Despite wide use, financial models rarely include nonfinancial outcomes in their benefits and costs. In a discussion of the financial value of adopting project management (that is, selecting as a project the use of project management) in a firm, Githens (1998) notes that traditional financial models "simply cannot capture the complexity and value-added of today's process-oriented firm."

The commonly seen phrase "return on investment," or ROI, does not denote any *specific* method of calculation. It usually involves NPV or internal rate of return (IRR) calculations, but we have seen it used in reference to undiscounted rate of return models and (incorrectly) payback period models.

In our experience, the payback period model, occasionally using discounted cash flows, is one of the most commonly used models for evaluating projects and other investment opportunities. Managers generally feel that insistence on short payout periods tends to minimize the *risks* associated with outstanding monies over the passage of time. While this is certainly logical, we prefer evaluation methods that discount cash flows and deal with uncertainty more directly by considering specific risks. Using the payback period as a cash-budgeting tool aside, *its primary virtue is its simplicity.*

Numeric Models: Real Options

The real options project selection model was developed based on a notion well known in financial markets. When a firm invests in something, such as conducting a joint venture with another firm, it forgoes the value of alternative future investments. Economists refer to the value of an opportunity forgone as the "opportunity cost" of the investment made. But making such an investment often gives the firm the *option* to do something in the future that it could not have done without making the investment, like buying out the other firm's share of the business if the venture is profitable, or selling out to the other firm. The concept of a real option is that the investment leads to opportunities that would not have been available otherwise. It is not unknown for firms and other organizations to invest in an alternative that, in and of itself, is not profitable or beneficial, but opens options for the future that may have great promise, such as:

- Learning about a new technology
- Gaining access to potential new customers
- Obtaining the right to bid on a lucrative follow-on contract
- Improving the firm's competitive strength
- Being able to offer profitable maintenance, repair, or service on new equipment

During the computerization boom of the 1980s and 1990s, many firms ignored the value of real options in investing in advanced technology. Their project selection evaluation process compared the costs, risks, and supposed benefits of these technologies against the value of waiting a bit longer for less risky (or more advanced) technology at a possibly reduced price (from higher volumes). This seemed to make sense—they could use the money now for other investments and avoid the risk of investing in new technologies that might not pay off. But within months their knowledge of advanced technologies was obsolete, while their sales and profits had collapsed because all their competitors had invested in the technology. They made two errors in their thinking: (1) that they could stay on the leading knowledge edge of technology without gaining experience using these technologies, and (2) that the market environment would continue as it had. It is always imperative to consider the real options of an investment and never assume that things will continue as they have in the past if you don't make the investment.

The real options approach acts to reduce both technological and commercial risk. For a full explanation of the method and its use as a strategic selection tool, see Luehrman (1998a and 1998b). An interesting application of real options as a project selection tool for pharmaceutical R & D projects is described by Jacob et al. (2003). Real options combined with Monte Carlo simulation is compared with alternative selection/assessment methods by Doctor et al. (2001).

Project Management in Practice
Virtual Project Team Strategy

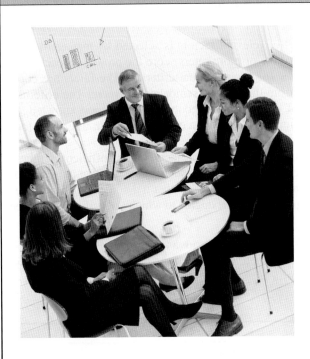

To support software development globalisation, organisations are increasingly implementing virtual project team strategies. However, these project teams have to work within the confines of the factors which distance introduces, thus not always allowing effective coordination, visibility, communication and cooperation to take place. The successful implementation and management of such project teams must be done differently to those at single-site locations.

The advent of the Internet, e-mail and improved and low cost international telecommunications has facilitated the development of virtual project teams, resulting in the global distribution of software development. This has led to organisations either outsourcing application development and maintenance to third party organisations, or setting up their own subsidiaries in low cost economies.

However, due to the level of complexity involved in software development, outsourcing is not a straightforward task. Some of the difficulties encountered include such factors as the problem of understanding requirements and the testing of systems. These difficulties are compounded by cultural and language differences, lack of communication, distance from the customer, different process maturity levels, testing tools, standards, technical ability and experience. The management of global software development is therefore a difficult and complex task.

To address the difficulty and complexity of globally distributed software development, virtual project teams need to practice effective project management, knowledge management and software development processes, in addition to the use of communication tools and collaboration technology. Virtual project teams need to be always in tune with the organisation's strategic business goals. Therefore virtual project teams need to assess if they:

- address the strategic notion of delivering the benefits of globally distributed software development
- are taking into consideration the human-centric notion of software development knowledge in relation to the activity context of the organisation, and defining the levels of task performance
- provide for incorporation of the creative capabilities of team members needed for developing quality software products that deliver the required specifications and functionality

Source: Valentine Casey & Ita Richardson, *Uncovering the Reality within Virtual Software Teams*, Proceedings of the International Workshop on Global Software Development for the Practitioner, Shanghai China, pp. 66–72, 2006, and, Marcus Goncalves, *Managing Virtual Projects*, McGraw-Hill, 2005.

Numeric Models: Scoring

In an attempt to overcome some of the disadvantages of profitability models, particularly their focus on a single decision criterion, a number of evaluation/selection models that use multiple criteria to evaluate a project have been developed. Such models vary widely in their complexity and information requirements. The examples discussed illustrate some of the different types of numeric scoring models.

Unweighted 0–1 Factor Model A set of relevant factors is selected by management and then usually listed in a preprinted form. One or more raters score the project on each factor, depending on whether or not it qualifies for an individual criterion. The raters are chosen by senior managers, for the most part from the rolls of senior management. The criteria for choice are (1) a clear understanding of organizational goals and (2) a good knowledge of the firm's potential project *portfolio.* Figure 2-2 shows an example of the rating sheet for an unweighted, 0–1 factor model.

The columns of Figure 2-2 are summed and those projects with a sufficient number of qualifying factors may be selected. The main advantage of such a model is that it uses several criteria in the decision process. The major disadvantages are that it assumes all criteria are of equal importance and it allows for no gradation of the degree to which a specific project meets the various criteria.

Unweighted Factor Scoring Model The second disadvantage of the 0–1 factor model can be dealt with by constructing a simple linear measure of the degree to which the project being evaluated meets each of the criteria contained in the list. The x marks in Figure 2-2

Project _____

Rater _____ Date _____

	Qualifies	Does Not Qualify
No increase in energy requirements	x	
Potential market size, dollars	x	
Potential market share, percent	x	
No new facility required	x	
No new technical expertise required		x
No decrease in quality of final product	x	
Ability to manage project with current personnel		x
No requirement for reorganization	x	
Impact on work force safety	x	
Impact on environmental standards	x	
Profitability		
Rate of return more than 15% after tax	x	
Estimated annual profits more than $250,000	x	
Time to break-even less than 3 years	x	
Need for external consultants		x
Consistency with current line of business		x
Inpact on company image		
With customers	x	
With our industry		x
Totals	12	5

Figure 2-2 Sample project evaluation form.

would be replaced by numbers. Often a five-point scale is used, where 5 is very good, 4 is good, 3 is fair, 2 is poor, 1 is very poor. (Three-, seven-, and 10-point scales are also common.) The second column of Figure 2-2 would not be needed. The column of scores is summed, and those projects with a total score exceeding some critical value are selected. A variant of this selection process might choose the highest-scoring projects (still assuming they are all above some critical score) until the estimated costs of the set of projects equaled the resource limit. However, the criticism that the criteria are all assumed to be of equal importance still holds.

The use of a discrete numeric scale to represent the degree to which a criterion is satisfied is widely accepted. To construct such measures for project evaluation, we proceed in the following manner. Select a criterion, say, "estimated annual profits in dollars." For this criterion, determine five ranges of performance so that a typical project, chosen at random, would have a roughly equal chance of being in any one of the five performance ranges. (Another way of describing this condition is: Take a large number of projects that were selected for support in the past, regardless of whether they were actually successful or not, and create five levels of predicted performance so that about one-fifth of the projects fall into each level.) This procedure will usually create unequal ranges, which may offend our sense of symmetry but need not concern us otherwise. It ensures that each criterion performance measure utilizes the full scale of possible values, a desirable characteristic for performance measures.

Consider the following two simple examples. Using the criterion just mentioned, "estimated annual profits in dollars," we might construct the following scale:

Score	Performance Level
5	Above $1,100,000
4	$750,001 to $1,100,000
3	$500,001 to $750,000
2	$200,000 to $500,000
1	Less than $200,000

As suggested, these ranges might have been chosen so that about 20 percent of the projects considered for funding would fall into each of the five ranges.

The criterion "no decrease in quality of the final product" would have to be restated to be scored on a five-point scale, perhaps as follows:

Score	Performance Level
	The quality of the final product is:
5	significantly and visibly improved
4	significantly improved, but not visible to buyer
3	not significantly changed
2	significantly lowered, but not visible to buyer
1	significantly and visibly lowered

This scale is an example of scoring cells that represent opinion rather than objective (even if "estimated") fact, as was the case in the profit scale.

Weighted Factor Scoring Model   When numeric weights reflecting the relative importance of each individual factor are added, we have a weighted factor scoring model. In general, it takes the form

$$S_i = \sum_{j=1}^{n} s_{ij} w_j$$

where

S_i = the total score of the *i*th project,

s_{ij} = the score of the *i*th project on the *j*th criterion, and

w_j = the weight of the *j*th criterion.

The weights, w_j, may be generated by any technique that is acceptable to the organization's policy makers. There are several techniques available to generate such numbers, but the most effective and most widely used is the Delphi technique. The Delphi technique was developed by Brown and Dalkey of the Rand Corporation during the 1950s and 1960s (Dalkey, 1969). It is a technique for developing numeric values that are equivalent to subjective, verbal measures of relative value.

Another popular and quite similar approach is the Analytic Hierarchy Process, developed by Saaty (1990). For an extensive example involving finance, sales, and purchasing, see pages 306–316 of Turban et al. (1994). This example also illustrates the use of Expert Choice®, a software package to facilitate the application of the Analytic Hierarchy Process. Meade et al. (2002) developed a more general form of Saaty's AHP. They call it the Analytic Network Process, and their paper includes an example of its application to evaluation of multiple R & D projects. (Which reminds us, once more, to caution those who include "technological risk" when evaluating projects. The probability of technical success for any project is 1.0 if there is no limit on time and/or budget. Any estimate of technical success should be accompanied by time and cost constraints, or it is meaningless.)

Finally, the use of experts to develop weightings is nicely demonstrated by Jolly (2003) who applies the technique to the development of weights to a technology portfolio.

When numeric weights have been generated, it is helpful (but not necessary) to scale the weights so that

$$0 \leq w_j \leq 1 \quad j = 1, 2, 3, \ldots, n$$

$$\sum_{j=1}^{n} w_j = 1$$

The weight of each criterion can be interpreted as the "percent of the total weight accorded to that particular criterion."

A special caveat is in order. It is quite possible with this type of model to include a large number of criteria. It is not particularly difficult to develop scoring scales and weights, and the ease of gathering and processing the required information makes it tempting to include marginally relevant criteria along with the obviously important items. Resist this temptation! After the important factors have been weighted, there usually is little residual weight to be distributed among the remaining elements. The result is that the evaluation is simply insensitive to major differences in the scores on trivial criteria. A good rule of thumb is to discard elements with weights less than 0.02 or 0.03. (If elements are discarded, and if you wish $\Sigma w_j = 1$, the weights must be rescaled to 1.0.) As with any linear model, the user should be aware that the elements in the model are assumed to be independent. This presents no particular problems for these scoring models because they are used to make estimates in a "steady-state" system, and we are not concerned with transitions between states.

Gettin' Wheels

Rather than using an example in which actual projects are selected for funding with a weighted factor scoring model (hereafter "scoring model") that would require tediously long descriptions of the projects, we can demonstrate the use of the model in a simple, common problem that many readers will have faced—the choice of an automobile for purchase. This problem is nicely suited to use of the scoring model because the purchaser is trying to satisfy multiple objectives in making the purchase and is typically faced with several different cars from which to choose.

Our model must have the following elements:

1. A set of criteria on which to judge the value of any alternative;

2. A numeric estimate of the relative importance (i.e., the "weight") of each criterion in the set; and

3. Scales by which to measure or score the performance or contribution–to–value of each alternative on each criterion.

The criteria weights and measures of performance must be numeric in form, but this does not mean that they must be either "objective" or "quantitative." Criteria weights, obviously, are subjective by their nature, being an expression of what the decision maker thinks is important. The development of performance scales is more easily dealt with in the context of our example, and we will develop them shortly.

Assume that we have chosen the criteria and weights shown in Table A to be used in our evaluations.* The weights represent the relative importance of the criteria measured on a 10-point scale. The numbers in parentheses show the proportion of the total weight carried by each criterion. (They add to only .99 due to rounding.) Raw weights work just as well for decision making as their percentage counterparts, but the latter are usually preferred because they are a constant reminder to the decision maker of the impact of each of the criteria.

Prior to consideration of performance standards and sources of information for the criteria we have chosen,

---

*The criteria and weights were picked arbitrarily for this example. Because this is typically an individual or family decision, techniques like Delphi or the analytic hierarchy process are not required.

Table A Criteria and Weights for Automobile Purchase

Appearance	4	(.10)
Braking	3	(.07)
Comfort	7	(.17)
Cost, operating	5	(.12)
Cost, original	10	(.24)
Handling	7	(.17)
Reliability	5	(.12)
Total	41	.99

Table B Automobile Selection Criteria, Measures and Data Sources

Appearance	Subjective judgment, personal
Braking	Distance in feet, 60–0 mph, automotive magazine [a]
Comfort	Subjective judgment, 30 min. road test
Cost, operating	Annual insurance cost plus fuel cost [b]
Cost, original	Dealer cost, auto-cost service [c]
Handling	Average speed through standard slalom, automotive magazine [a]
Reliability	Score on *Consumer Reports*, "Frequency-of-Repair" data (average of 2 previous years)

[a] Many automotive periodicals conduct standardized performance tests of new cars.

[b] Annual fuel cost is calculated as (17,500 mi/DOE ave. mpg) $4.259/gal.

[c] There are several sources for dealer-cost data (e.g., AAA, which provides a stable database on which to estimate the price of each alternative).

we must ask, "Are there any characteristics that must be present (or absent) in a candidate automobile for it to be acceptable?" Assume, for this example, that to be acceptable, an alternative must not be painted green, must have air conditioning, must be able to carry at least four adults, must have at least 10 cubic feet of luggage space, and must be priced less than $34,000. If an alternative violates any of these conditions, it is immediately rejected.

For each criterion, we need some way of measuring the estimated performance of each alternative. In this case, we might adopt the measures shown in Table B.

Criteria	**Scores**				
Criteria	**1**	**2**	**3**	**4**	**5**
Appearance	Ugh	Poor	Adequate	Good	WOW
Braking	>165	165–150	150–140	140–130	<130
Comfort	Bad	Poor	Adequate	Good	Excellent
Cost, operating*	>$2.5	$2.1–2.5	$1.9–2.1	$1.6–1.9	<$1.6
Cost, original*	>$32.5	$26–32.5	$21–26	$17–21	<$17
Handling	<45	45–49.5	49.5–55	55–59	>59
Reliability	Worst	Poor	Adequate	Good	Excellent

*Cost data in $1,000s

Figure A Performance measures and equivalent scores for selection of an automobile.

Our purpose is to transform a measure of the degree to which an alternative meets a criterion into a score, the s_{ij}, that is a general measure of the utility or value of the alternative with respect to that criterion. Note that this requires us to define the criterion precisely, as well as to specify a source for the information.

Figure A shows the scores for each criterion transformed to a 5-point scale, which will suffice for our ratings.

Using the performance scores shown in Figure A, we can evaluate the cars we have identified as our alternatives: the Leviathan 8, the NuevoEcon, the Maxivan, the Sporticar 100, and the Ritzy 300. Each car is scored on each criterion according to the categories shown in Figure A. Then each score is multiplied by the criterion weight and the result is entered into the appropriate box in Figure B. Last, the results for each alternative are summed to represent the weighted score.

According to this set of measures, we prefer the Ritzy 300, but while it is a clear winner over the Leviathan 8 and the Maxivan, and scores about 8 percent better than the Sporticar 100, it rates only about 0.13 points or 4 percent above the NuevoEcon. Note that if we overrated the Ritzy by one point on comfort or handling, or if we underrated the NuevoEcon by one point on either of these criteria, the result would have been reversed. (We assume that the original cost data are accurate.) With the scores this close, we might want to evaluate these two cars by additional criteria (e.g., ease of carrying children, status, safety features like dual airbags or ABS) prior to making a firm decision.

All in all, if the decision maker has well-delineated objectives, and can determine how specific kinds of performance contribute to those criteria, and finally, can measure those kinds of performance for each of the alternative courses of action, then the scoring model is a powerful and flexible tool. To the extent that criteria are not carefully defined, performance is not well linked to the criteria, and is carelessly or wrongly measured, the scoring model rests on a faulty foundation and is merely a convenient path to error.

	Criteria and Weights							
Alternatives	**Appearance (0.10)**	**Braking (0.07)**	**Comfort (0.17)**	**Cost, operating (0.12)**	**Cost, original (0.24)**	**Handling (0.17)**	**Reliability (0.12)**	$\Sigma s_{ij} w_j$
Leviathan 8	3 × 0.10 = 0.30	1 × 0.07 = 0.07	4 × 0.17 = 0.68	2 × 0.12 = 0.24	1 × 0.24 = 0.24	2 × 0.17 = 0.34	3 × 0.12 = 0.36	2.23
NuevoEcon	3 × 0.10 = 0.30	3 × 0.07 = 0.21	2 × 0.17 = 0.34	5 × 0.12 = 0.60	4 × 0.24 = 0.96	2 × 0.17 = 0.34	4 × 0.12 = 0.48	3.23
Maxivan	2 × 0.10 = 0.20	1 × 0.07 = 0.07	4 × 0.17 = 0.68	4 × 0.12 = 0.48	3 × 0.24 = 0.72	1 × 0.17 = 0.17	3 × 0.12 = 0.36	2.68
Sporticar 100	5 × 0.10 = 0.50	4 × 0.07 = 0.28	3 × 0.17 = 0.51	2 × 0.12 = 0.24	2 × 0.24 = 0.48	5 × 0.17 = 0.85	2 × 0.12 = 0.24	3.10
Ritzy 300	4 × 0.10 = 0.40	5 × 0.07 = 0.35	5 × 0.17 = 0.85	2 × 0.12 = 0.24	1 × 0.24 = 0.24	4 × 0.17 = 0.68	5 × 0.12 = 0.60	3.36

Figure B Scores for alternative cars on selection criteria.

It is useful to note that if one uses a weighted scoring model to aid in project selection, the model can also serve as an aid to project *improvement*. For any given criterion, the difference between the criterion's score and the highest possible score on that criterion, multiplied by the weight of the criterion, is a measure of the potential improvement in the project score that would result were the project's performance on that criterion sufficiently improved. It may be that such improvement is not feasible or is more costly than the improvement warrants. On the other hand, such an analysis of each project yields a valuable statement of the comparative benefits of project improvements. Viewing a project in this way is a type of sensitivity analysis. We examine the degree to which a project's score is sensitive to attempts to improve it—usually by adding resources. We will use sensitivity analysis several times in this book. It is a powerful managerial technique.

It is not particularly difficult to computerize a weighted scoring model by creating a template on Excel® or one of the other standard computer spreadsheets. In Chapter 13 we discuss an example of a computerized scoring model used for the project termination decision. The model is, in fact, a project selection model. The logic of using a "selection" model for the termination decision is straightforward: Given the time and resources required to take a project from its current state to completion, should we make the investment? A "Yes" answer to that question "selects" for funding the partially completed project from the set of all partially finished and not-yet-started projects.

As was the case with profitability models, scoring models have their own characteristic advantages and disadvantages. The advantages are:

1. These models allow multiple criteria to be used for evaluation and decision making, including profit/profitability models and both tangible and intangible criteria.
2. They are structurally simple and therefore easy to understand and use.
3. They are a direct reflection of managerial policy.
4. They are easily altered to accommodate changes in the environment or managerial policy.
5. Weighted scoring models allow for the fact that some criteria are more important than others.
6. These models allow easy sensitivity analysis. The trade-offs between the several criteria are readily observable.

The disadvantages are the following:

1. The output of a scoring model is strictly a relative measure. Project scores do not represent the value or "utility" associated with a project and thus do not directly indicate whether or not the project should be supported.
2. In general, scoring models are linear in form and the elements of such models are assumed to be independent.
3. The ease of use of these models is conducive to the inclusion of a large number of criteria, most of which have such small weights that they have little impact on the total project score.
4. Unweighted scoring models assume all criteria are of equal importance, which is almost certainly contrary to fact.
5. To the extent that profit/profitability is included as an element in the scoring model, this element has the advantages and disadvantages noted earlier for the profitability models themselves.

Numeric Models: Window-of-Opportunity Analysis

In the early stages of new product development, one may know little more than the fact that the potential product seems technically feasible. Just because one can develop and/or install a new technology does not necessarily imply that the new technology is worth implementing, or will be economically profitable. Fundamentally, the decision to invest in the development of a new process or product depends on an estimate of cash flows and other benefits expected to result if the innovation is successful—a difficult problem at best. The traditional approach has been to implement the technology in question (or a pilot version of it) and then test it to see if it qualifies as useful and economic. This is often a wasteful process because it assumes the innovation will be successful—a condition only occasionally met in practice.

Given some idea for a new product or process, we can invert this traditional approach by attempting to determine the cost, timing, and performance specifications that must be met by this new technology *before* any R & D is undertaken. (This is called the *window-of-opportunity* for the innovation.) The method for conducting such an analysis is as follows. Given a potential production process innovation, for example, the current production process is analyzed in detail and any element of that process that might be affected by the innovation is noted. Baseline data on the current process are collected (e.g., its cycle time, its cost) and the effect of the innovation is estimated relative to (usually some fraction or multiple of) the baseline system. Having thus estimated the economic impact of the innovation, the decision of whether or not to undertake the development project is much simpler. For examples of such an approach see Evans et al. (1985) and Mantel et al. (1985).

Numeric Models: Discovery-Driven Planning

Like the window-of-opportunity analysis, discovery-driven planning (McGrath et al., 1995; Rice et al., 2008) also reverses the expensive and risky traditional approach of trying out the technology to determine its benefits. This approach funds enough of the project to determine if the initial assumptions concerning costs, benefits, etc., were accurate. When the funds are gone, the assumptions are reevaluated to determine what to do next.

The idea isn't to implement the project but rather to *learn* about the project. The assumptions about the project are written down and analyzed carefully to determine two aspects about them: (1) which are the critical assumptions that will make or break the desirability of the project, and (2) how much it will cost to test each of the assumptions. The high-priority, deal-killer assumptions that will cost the least then are ranked at the top, with the lesser and more expensive assumptions following. If a critical assumption proves to be invalid, management must rethink its strategy and the project. This process is not just a one-time exercise, however; the process continues as the stages of the project are executed so that at any point in the project, management can step in and terminate it if conditions change and the project looks less promising. And conditions are always changing: the economy gets worse, the market moves toward or away from the promise of the project, a key team member of the project leaves the company, the strategy of the organization changes with a new executive, a new government regulation impacts the project, and so on. Project failure is more often management's failure to consider an important problem or question than it is a technical failure within the project.

Choosing a Project Selection Model

Selecting the type of model to aid the evaluation/selection process depends on the philosophy and wishes of management. Liberatore et al. (1983) conducted a survey of 40 high-level staff persons from 29 *Fortune 500* firms. Eighty percent of their respondents report the use of one or more financial models for R & D project decision making. Although their sample is small and nonrandom, their findings are quite consistent with the present authors' experience. Swanson (2011) reports on an airline that previously considered only ROI in prioritizing projects but now also considers strategic contributions, resource limitations, and non-numeric factors such as regulatory mandates and operating necessities. Other organizations are considering the real options their projects offer.

We strongly favor weighted scoring models for three fundamental reasons. First, they allow the multiple objectives of all organizations to be reflected in the important decision about which projects will be supported and which will be rejected. Second, scoring models are easily adapted to changes in managerial philosophy or changes in the environment. Third, they do not suffer from the bias toward the short run that is inherent in profitability models that discount future cash flows. This is not a prejudice against discounting and most certainly does not argue against the inclusion of profits/profitability as an important factor in selection, but rather *it is an argument against the exclusion of nonfinancial factors* that may require a longer-run view of the costs and benefits of a project. For a powerful statement of this point, see Hayes et al. (1980).

It is also interesting to note that Liberatore et al. (1983, p. 969) found that firms with a significant amount of contract research funded from outside the organization used scoring models for project screening much more frequently than firms with negligible levels of outside funding. It was also found that firms with significant levels of outside funding were much less likely to use a payback period model, presumably to reduce their risk.

The structure of a weighted scoring model is quite straightforward. Its virtues are many. Nonetheless, the actual use of scoring models is not as easy as it might seem. Decision makers are forced to make difficult choices and they are not always comfortable doing so. They are forced to reduce often vague feelings to quite specific words or numbers. Multiattribute, multiperson decision making is not simple. [For an interesting discussion of this process, see Irving et al. (1988).]

The use of any project selection model assumes that the decision-making procedure takes place in a reasonably rational organizational environment. Such is not always the case. In some organizations, project selection seems to be the result of a political process, and sometimes involves questionable ethics, complete with winners and losers (Baker et al., 1995). In others, the organization is so rigid in its approach to decision making that it attempts to reduce all decisions to an algorithmic proceeding in which predetermined programs make choices so that humans have minimal involvement—and responsibility. Here too, Saaty's (1990) Analytic Hierarchy Process can lend rationality to a sometimes irrational process.

Whether managers are familiar with accounting systems or not, it is useful to reflect on the methods and assumptions used in the preparation of accounting data. Among the most crucial are the following:

1. Accountants live in a linear world. With few exceptions, cost and revenue data are assumed to vary linearly with associated changes in inputs and outputs.

2. The accounting system often provides cost-revenue information that is derived from standard cost analyses and equally standardized assumptions regarding revenues. These standards may or may not accurately represent the cost-revenue structure of the physical system they purport to represent.

3. The data furnished by the accounting system may or may not include overhead costs. In most cases, the decision maker is concerned solely with cost-revenue elements that will be changed as a result of the project under consideration. Incremental analysis is called for, and great care should be exercised when using pro forma data in decision problems. Remember that the assignment of overhead cost is always arbitrary. The accounting system is the richest source of information in the organization, and it should be used—but with great care and understanding.

4. **Warning!** A great many organizations utilize project cost data as the primary, *and the only* routine measure of project performance. In Chapter 1 we emphasized that projects should be measured on three dimensions: time, cost, and scope. Without including information on the schedule and the physical completion of work, cost measurements have no useful meaning. We will repeat this warning throughout this book.

Finally, no matter what method is used for project selection, as time goes by the selection model's inputs must be constantly updated. The world does not stand still—things change! What was a promising project yesterday may be a loser today—and yesterday's loser may be today's winner.

2.4 RISK CONSIDERATIONS IN PROJECT SELECTION

In our previous discussion of factors to consider when selecting projects, we emphasized costs and benefits, with only a side reference to the inherent uncertainty associated with both of these, though benefits are usually more uncertain than costs. However, both are uncertain, and can be greater or less than expected. In the case of being worse than expected, the organization is exposed to some, perhaps substantial, level of risk. There are many more ways of dealing with project risk besides using a shorter payback period. Although our major discussion of techniques to handle risk will come in Chapters 6 and 7 when we discuss project activity and budget planning, the topic is highly relevant to project selection as well, and we will briefly comment on it here. PMI (2011) reports that risk management is used significantly more by high-performing project organizations than low-performing organizations.

PMBOK Guide

Chapter 11

During the past several years, increasing attention has been paid to the subject of managing some of the risks inherent in most projects. The subject first appeared in PMI's 1987 edition of PMBOK (PMI, 2008). For the most part, risk has been interpreted as being unsure about project task durations and/or costs, but uncertainty plagues all aspects of the work on projects and is present in all stages of project life cycles. The impact of imperfect knowledge on the way a project is organized and on its budget and schedule will be discussed in the chapters devoted to those subjects.

In the real world of project management, it has been common to deal with estimates of task durations, costs, etc., as if the information were known with certainty. In fact, a great majority of all decisions made in the course of managing a project are actually made under conditions of uncertainty. However, we can still make some estimates about the *probabilities* of various outcomes. If we use appropriate methods for doing this, we can apply what knowledge we have to solving project decision problems. We will not always be correct, but we will be doing the best we can. Such estimates are called "subjective probabilities," and are dealt with in most elementary courses on probability and statistics. While such probabilities are no more than guesses, they can be processed just as empirically determined probabilities are. In the world of project management, a best guess is always better than no information at all. Then it is possible to examine some of the effects of uncertainty on project selection.

At times, an organization may wish to evaluate a project about which there is little information. R & D projects sometimes fall into this general class. But even in the comparative mysteries of R & D activities, the level of uncertainty about the outcomes of R & D is not beyond analysis. As we noted earlier, there is actually not much uncertainty about whether a product, process, or service can be developed, but there can be considerable uncertainty about *when* it will be developed and at *what* cost.

As they are with R & D projects, time and cost are also often uncertain in other types of projects. When the organization undertakes projects in which it has little or no recent experience—for example, investment in an unfamiliar business, engaging in international trade, and a myriad of other projects common enough to organizations, in general, but uncommon to any single organization—there are three distinct areas of uncertainty. First, there is uncertainty about the timing of the project and the cash flows it is expected to generate. Second, though not as common as generally believed, there may be uncertainty about the direct outcomes of the project—that is, what it will accomplish. Third, there is uncertainty about the side effects of the project—its unforeseen consequences.

Typically, we try to reduce such uncertainty by the preparation of *pro forma* documents. *Pro forma* profit and loss statements and break-even charts are examples of such documents. The results, however, are not very satisfactory unless the amount of uncertainty is reflected in the data that go into the documents. When relationships between inputs and outputs in the projects are complex, Monte Carlo simulation (Meredith et al., 2002) can handle such uncertainty by exposing the many possible consequences of embarking on a project. With the great availability of microcomputers and user-friendly software (e.g., Crystal Ball®), simulation for assessing risk is becoming very common. A thorough discussion of methods for handling risk is coming in Chapter 6, and some simulation examples will be given in Chapters 7 and 8.

2.5   THE PROJECT PORTFOLIO PROCESS (PPP)

Although up to now we have primarily talked about the selection of a project in competition with other projects, in reality organizations typically maintain a *portfolio* of projects, and trying to keep a proper balance among this portfolio is the real task of upper management. With limited resources, management must choose between long-term and short-term projects, safe and risky projects, manufacturing and marketing projects, and so on. To help choose between the myriad of project proposals, in competition with ongoing projects as well as each other, management needs some overarching measures to evaluate each of the projects, and those measures are commonly related to the organization's mission, goals, and strategy. Project portfolio management is briefly defined and compared to project and program management in Chapter 1 of PMBOK®.

PMBOK Guide
1.4.1

We will assume here that the organization has already identified its mission, goals, and strategy—by using some formal analytic method such as SWOT analysis (strengths, weaknesses, opportunities, threats), and that these are well known throughout the organization. If this is not the case, then any attempt to tie the organization's projects to its goals is folly and the PPP will have little value. Deloitte Consulting (McIntyre, 2006) found that only 30 percent of surveyed organizations insisted on knowing the value a project would add to the organization's strategy before granting approval. Deloitte also identified the following eight symptoms of a misaligned portfolio:

- Many more projects than management expected
- Inconsistent determination of benefits, including double-counting
- Competing projects; no cross-comparison of projects
- "Interesting" projects that don't contribute to the strategy
- Projects whose costs exceed their benefits
- Projects with much higher risks than others in the portfolio; no risk analysis of projects
- Lack of tracking against the plan, at least quarterly
- No identified "client" for many projects

If the goals and strategies have been well articulated, however, then the PPP can serve many purposes, as articulated by Swanson (2011):

- To identify proposed projects that are not really projects and should be handled through other processes
- To prioritize the list of available projects
- To intentionally limit the number of overall projects being managed so the important projects get the resources and attention they need

- To identify the real options that each project offers
- To identify projects that best fit the organization's goals and strategy
- To identify projects that support multiple organizational goals and cross-reinforce other important projects
- To identify co-dependent projects
- To eliminate projects that incur excessive risk and/or cost
- To eliminate projects that bypassed a formal selection process and may not provide benefits corresponding to their risks and/or costs
- To keep from overloading the organization's resource availability
- To balance the resources with the needs
- To balance short-, medium-, and long-term returns

Project Management in Practice
Using a Project Portfolio to Achieve 100% On-Time Delivery at Decor Cabinet Company

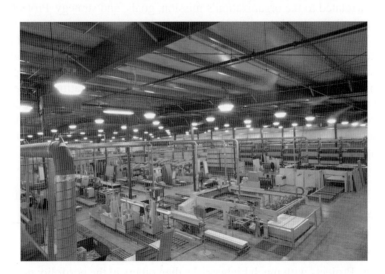

Décor Cabinet Company, a custom cabinet maker in Canada, adopted the strategic goal of 100 percent on-time delivery of their cabinets to achieve long-term customer loyalty and create added value that enhances their profitability. Having such a clear objective helped them assemble a project portfolio uniquely focused on their goal, although it also meant declining some seemingly profitable project ideas requested by customers. However, if demand increased for the requested products, it could have had a serious negative impact on their delivery goals. It was difficult to resist pressure from different areas of the company to support these kinds of projects: "You can easily lose focus," the CEO admitted. "Sometimes when ROI drives all decision-making you miss the bigger picture."

Source: S. F. Gale, "The Bottom Line," *PM Network*, Vol. 21.

The PPP attempts to link the organization's projects directly to the goals and strategy of the organization. This occurs not only in the project's initiation and planning phases, but also throughout the life cycle of the projects as they are managed and eventually brought to completion. In the reading "From Experience: Linking Projects to Strategy" at the end of this chapter, Hewlett-Packard, a firm that is highly dependent on successful new-product projects, found that through their version of PPP they could reduce their portfolio of projects by about two-thirds. This resulted in better funding and executing only those projects that were most strategically important to the company, thereby substantially improving the chances of project success.

Thus, the PPP is also a means for monitoring and controlling the organization's strategic projects. On occasion, and particularly during recessions and difficult economic times, this will mean shutting down projects prior to their completion because their risks have become excessive, their costs have escalated out of line with their expected benefits, another (or a new) project does a better job of supporting the goals, or any variety of similar reasons. It should be noted that a significant portion of the administration of this process could be managed by the Project Management Office, a concept to be discussed in Chapter 5.

The steps in this process generally follow those described in Longman et al. (1999) and Englund et al. (1999).

Step 1: Establish a Project Council

The main purpose of the project council is to establish and articulate a strategic direction for those projects spanning internal or external boundaries of the organization, such as cross-departmental or joint venture. Thus, senior managers must play a major role in this council. Without the commitment of senior management, the PPP will be incapable of achieving its main objectives. The council will also be responsible for allocating funds to those projects that support the organization's goals and controlling the allocation of resources and skills to the projects.

In addition to senior management, others who should be members of the project council are:

- the project managers of major projects
- the head of the Project Management Office, if one exists
- particularly relevant general managers
- those who can identify key opportunities and risks facing the organization
- anyone who can derail the progress of the PPP later on in the process

Step 2: Identify Project Categories and Criteria

In this step, various project categories are identified so the mix of projects funded by the organization will be spread appropriately across those areas making major contributions to the organization's goals. In addition, within each category, criteria are established to discriminate between very good and even better projects. The criteria are also weighted to reflect their relative importance. Identifying separate categories not only facilitates achievement of multiple organizational goals (e.g., long term, short term, internal, external, tactical, strategic) but also keeps projects from competing with each other on inappropriate categories.

The first task in this step is to list the goals of each existing and proposed project: What is the mission, or purpose, of this project? Relating these to the organization's goals and strategies should allow the council to identify a variety of categories that are important to achieving the organization's goals. Some of these were noted above, but another way to position some of the projects (particularly product/service development projects) is in terms of their extent of product and process changes.

Wheelwright et al. (1992) have developed a matrix called the *aggregate project plan* illustrating these changes, as shown in Figure 2-3. Based on the extent of product change and process change, they identified four separate categories of projects:

1. *Derivative projects.* These are projects with objectives or deliverables that are only incrementally different in both product and process from existing offerings. They are often meant to replace current offerings or add an extension to current offerings (lower priced version, upscale version).

2. *Platform projects.* The planned outputs of these projects represent major departures from existing offerings in terms of either the product/service itself or the process used to make and deliver it, or both. As such, they become "platforms" for the next generation of organizational offerings, such as a new model of automobile or a new type of insurance plan. They thus form the basis for follow-on derivative projects that attempt to extend the platform in various dimensions.

3. *Breakthrough projects.* Breakthrough projects typically involve a newer technology than platform projects. It may be a "disruptive" technology that is known to the industry or something proprietary that the organization has been developing over time. Examples here include the use of fiber-optic cables for data transmission, cash-balance pension plans, and hybrid gasoline-electric automobiles.

4. *R&D projects.* These projects are "blue-sky," visionary endeavors oriented toward using newly developed technologies, or existing technologies in a new manner. They may also be for acquiring new knowledge, or developing new technologies themselves.

The size of the projects plotted on the array indicates the size/resource needs of the project and the shape may indicate another aspect of the project, e.g., internal/external, long/medium/

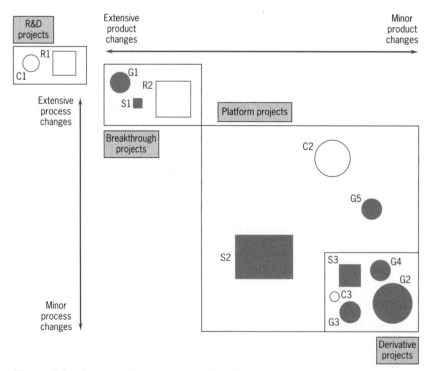

Figure 2-3   An example aggregate project plan.

short term, or whatever aspect needs to be shown. The numbers indicate the order, or time frame, in which the projects are to be (or were) implemented, separated by category, if desired. The aggregate project plan can be used for many purposes:

- To view the mix of projects within each illustrated aspect (shape)
- To analyze and adjust the mix of projects within each category or aspect
- To assess the resource demands on the organization, indicated by the size, timing, and number of projects shown
- To identify and adjust the gaps in the categories, aspects, sizes, and timing of the projects
- To identify potential career paths for developing project managers, such as team member of a derivative project, then team member of a platform project, manager of a derivative project, member of a breakthrough project, and so on

Next, the council should develop separate criteria and cost ranges for each category that determine those projects that will support the organizational strategy and goals. Example criteria might include alignment with the organization's goals/strategy, riskiness of the project, financial return, probability of success, likelihood of achieving a breakthrough in a critical offering, appeal to a large (or new) market, impact on customer satisfaction, contribution to employee development, knowledge acquisition, and availability of staff/resources.

Scales also need to be determined for each criterion to measure how different projects score on each of them. The scales on which these criteria are measured should be challenging so that the scores separate the best projects from those that are merely good. The scales should also serve as an initial screen, to start the process of winnowing out the weakest projects. Thus, they should include limits on their extremes, such as minimum rate of return (if a financial criterion is appropriate), maximum probability of technical failure given proposed budget and schedule, or minimum acceptable potential market share.

Finally, the council needs to set an importance weighting for the various criteria in each category. Note that even if the same criteria apply to multiple categories, their weights might be different. For example, if a firm needs to develop high-level, skilled project managers for their strategic projects, employee development might be more important for breakthrough projects but less important for derivative projects. Also, the weights might change depending on the life cycle stage of the project. For example, early in a project's life, strategic considerations are often most important while in the midpoint of a project, tactical considerations might be more important.

The model we have described above is a "weighted, factor scoring model," as described earlier. As noted then, there are some standard, well-known tools to help develop the weights, scales, and criteria such as the Delphi method (Dalkey, 1969), the analytic hierarchy process (AHP), (Saaty, 1980), a simplified version of AHP by Frame (1997), and even software such as *Expert Choice*®. For more complex situations, with large numbers of projects and/or large councils, the more sophisticated approaches are often more helpful, particularly if used with software that automatically calculates the scores and ranks the projects.

Step 3: Collect Project Data

For each existing and proposed project, assemble the data appropriate to that category's criteria. Be sure to update the data for ongoing projects and not just use the data from the previous evaluation. For cost data, use "activity based costs" (see Section 7.1) rather than incremental costs. Challenge and try to verify all data; get other people involved in validating the data, perhaps even customers (e.g., market benefit). Include the timing, both date and duration, for expected benefits and resource needs. Use the project plan, a schedule of project activities, past experience, expert opinion, whatever is available to get a good estimate of the data. Then document any assumptions made so that they can be checked in the future as the project progresses. If the project is new, you may want to fund only enough work on the project to verify the assumptions or determine the window-of-opportunity for the proposed product or process, holding off full funding until later. Similarly, identify any projects that can be deferred to a later time period, those that must precede or follow other projects, those that support other projects or should be done in conjunction with them, those that can be outsourced, and other such special aspects of the projects.

Next, use the criteria score limits to screen out the weaker projects: Have costs on existing projects escalated beyond the project's expected benefits? Has the benefit of a project lessened because the organization's goals have changed? Does a competitor's new entry obviate the advantages of a project? Does a new (or old) project dominate an existing or proposed project in terms of its benefits, furtherance of organizational goals, reduced costs? Also, screen *in* any projects that do not require deliberation, such as projects mandated by regulations or laws, projects that are operating or competitive necessities, projects required for environmental or personnel reasons, and so on. The fewer projects that need to be compared and analyzed, the easier the work of the council.

Step 4: Assess Resource Availability

Next, assess the availability of both internal and external resources, by type, department, and timing. Note that labor availability should be estimated conservatively, leaving time for vacations, personal needs, illness, holidays, and most importantly, regular functional (nonproject) work. After allowing for all of these things that limit labor availability, add a bit more, perhaps 10 percent, to allow for the well-known fact that human beings need occasional short breaks to rest or meet other human needs. Timing is particularly important, since project resource needs by type typically vary up to 100 percent over the life cycle of projects. Needing a normally plentiful resource at the same moment it is fully utilized elsewhere may doom an otherwise promising project. Eventually, the council will be trying to balance aggregate project resource needs over future periods with resource availabilities so timing is as important as the amount of maximum demand and availability. This is the major subject of Chapter 9.

Step 5: Reduce the Project and Criteria Set

In this step, multiple screens are employed to try to narrow down the number of competing projects. As noted earlier, the first screen is each project's support of the organization's goals. Other possible screens might be criteria such as:

- Whether the required competence exists in the organization
- Whether there is a market for the offering
- How profitable the offering is likely to be
- How risky the project is
- If there is a potential partner to help with the project
- If the right resources are available at the right times
- If the project is a good technological/knowledge fit with the organization
- If the project uses the organization's strengths, or depends on its weaknesses
- If the project is synergistic with other important projects
- If the project is dominated by another existing or proposed project
- If the project has slipped in its desirability since the last evaluation

One way to evaluate the dominance of some projects over others, and at the same time eliminate nondifferentiating criteria, is by comparing the coefficients of variation of each of the criteria across the projects. This technique allows an analyst to maximize the variation within the project set across relevant criteria, eliminating similar projects that are dominated, and identifying criteria that, at least in this evaluation round, do not differentiate among the projects. See Raz (1997) for an example of this approach.

The result of this step may involve canceling some ongoing projects or replacing them with new, more promising projects. Beware, however, of the tendency to look more favorably upon new, untested concepts than on current projects experiencing the natural problems and hurdles of any promising project.

Step 6: Prioritize the Projects within Categories

Apply the scores and criterion weights to rank the projects within each category. It is acceptable to hold some hard-to-measure criteria out for subjective evaluation, such as riskiness, or development of new knowledge. Subjective evaluations can be translated from verbal to numeric terms easily by the Delphi or other methods and used in the weighted factor scoring model. It should be remembered that such criteria as riskiness are usually composite measures of a set of "risks" in different areas. The same is true of criteria like "development of new knowledge."

When checking the results of this step, however, reconsider the projects in terms of their benefits first and their resource costs second. The former are commonly more difficult to assess and a reconsideration based on more familiarity with the project profiling process and other project evaluations may suggest interchanging the priority of neighboring projects. This could be especially critical around the project cutoff point. Because the projects competing around the cutoff point are typically quite close in benefit/cost scores, there are usually no serious consequences resulting from "errors." This is, however, an excellent problem on which to use *sensitivity analysis*.

It is also possible at this time for the council to summarize the "returns" from the projects to the organization. However, this should be done by category, not for each project individually since different projects are offering different packages of benefits that are not comparable. For example, R & D projects will not have the expected monetary return of derivative projects; yet it would be foolish to eliminate them simply because they do not measure up on this (irrelevant, for this category) criterion.

Step 7: Select the Projects to Be Funded and Held in Reserve

The first task in this step is an important one: determining the mix of projects across the various categories (and aspects, if used) and time periods. Next, be sure to leave some percent (often 10–15 percent) of the organization's resource capacity free for new opportunities, crises in existing projects, errors in estimates, and so on. Then allocate the categorized projects in rank order to the categories according to the mix desired. It is usually a good practice to include some speculative projects in each category to allow future options, knowledge improvement, additional experience in new areas, and such.

Overall, the focus should be on committing to fewer projects but with sufficient funding to allow project completion. Document why late projects were delayed and why some, if any, were defunded. One special type of delayed project mentioned earlier is sometimes called an "out-plan" project (in contrast to the selected "in-plan" projects) (Englund et al., 1999). Out-plan projects are those that appear promising but are awaiting further investigation before a final decision is made about their funding, which could occur in the next PPP cycle or sooner, if they warrant the use of some of the 10–15 percent funding holdout.

The result of this step (and most of the project portfolio process) is illustrated in the Plan of Record shown in Figure 2-4. Here, the mix across categories is listed, the priorities and resource needs of each project are given, the timing (schedule) of each project over the PPP cycle (6 months assumed here) is shown (to match resource availability), the out-plan projects, if any, are shown, and the total resource needs and availabilities are listed.

Step 8: Implement the Process

The first task in this final step is to make the results of the PPP widely known, including the documented reasons for project cancellations, deferrals, and non-selection as was mentioned earlier. Top management must now make their commitment to this project portfolio process totally clear by supporting the process and the results. This may require a PPP champion near the top of the organization. As project proposers come to understand the workings and importance of the PPP, their proposals will more closely fit the profile of the kinds of projects the organization wishes to fund. As this happens, it is important to note

Category	Priority	Project	Resources	May	June	July	Aug	Sept	Oct
Derivative									
50% of mix	1	R	500	▬	▬				
	2	K	800	▬	▬	▬			
	3	M	300		▬	▬			
Total			1600						
Available			(1800)						
External									
20% of mix	1	S	500		▬	▬	▬		
	2	V	150				▬		
	out-plan	LT							
Total			650						
Available			(720)						
Strategic									
30% of mix	1	A	600					▬	▬
	2	W	370						▬
	out-plan	SB							
Total			970						
Available			(1080)						
Aggregate Total			3220						
Unspent			380						
10% reserve			400						
Total Available			4000						

Figure 2-4   Plan of Record.

that the council will have to concern itself with the reliability and accuracy of proposals competing for limited funds.

Senior management must fully fund the selected projects. It is neither appropriate nor ethical for senior management to undermine PPP and the council, as well as strategically important projects by playing a game of arbitrarily cutting X percent from project budgets. The council needs to be wary of interpersonal or interdepartmental competition entering the scene at this point also. In some organizations, individuals with their own particular agenda will ignore committees and processes (they may be heard to argue that committees never affect anything anyway) until implementation time rolls around, and then they attempt to exercise their political power to undermine the results of others' long labors. If this does occur, it is indicative of serious organizational problems and the PPP process will fail until the problems are corrected.

Of course, the process will need to be repeated on a regular basis. The council should determine how often this should be, and to some extent it depends on the speed of change in the industry the organization is in. For some industries, quarterly analysis may be best while in slow-moving industries, yearly may be fine. Swanson (2011) warns, however, that too-frequent reprioritizing of projects can result in confusion and frustration, particularly if resources suddenly are unavailable.

Finally, the process should be flexible and improved continuously. Instinct may suggest ways that the process may be altered to better match the competitive environment, or to reflect more closely the organization's goals. The process should be changed when it is found appropriate to do so, including categories, criteria, steps, the order of tasks, and so on.

We offer a final note on this subject of creating and managing a portfolio of projects. In the preceding description of portfolio building it was tacitly assumed that the projects were independent and could be dealt with individually. At times, the projects in a portfolio are not independent. Dickinson et al. (2001) describe a model developed for the Boeing Company that optimizes a portfolio of interdependent product improvement projects. The model includes risk as well as cost/benefit analysis.

Before leaving the subject of project portfolios, it is important to consider the problem of decreasing the size of the organization's investment in projects. The sharp economic downturn of 2008–09 required a great many firms to do just that, and many were simply not prepared to handle the problem. Senior management, or the project council, or the Enterprise Project Management Office, or whatever group is in charge of selecting projects for inclusion in the organization's portfolio of project should also develop a set of criteria for removing projects from the portfolio.

In an interesting short paper, Wheatley (2009) discusses this issue. He notes that such issues as the size of the expected ROI may be of less importance than the timing of cash in-and-outflows. He also notes that risk should be included as a factor in all decisions. The organization's tolerance for risk is very likely to change during downturns. Some projects are luxuries. Others may be major drivers of future profits and growth. Some may be oriented to cost savings that could have almost immediate benefits. Even projects aimed at meeting legal mandates may have a cost that is significantly higher than the possible legal penalties if the mandates are ignored for a time. Many firms are choosing to pay the penalty instead of implementing costly federal mandates. Competitive necessity projects with low immediate returns may well outrank projects with higher returns—or they may not. Some projects can be stopped midway without doing much damage to the project's expected success. Others cannot, and if delayed must start from scratch, or be cancelled.

Developing a list of possible criteria for cutting or eliminating the funding for a project is complicated. To be useful, each item in the list should be prioritized. This is a job that demands close attention from senior management.

2.6 PROJECT BIDS AND RFPS (REQUESTS FOR PROPOSALS)*

PMBOK Guide
Chapter 12

The topic of bidding on requests for proposals is highly relevant to the PMBOK knowledge area (9) of *Procurement*. Further discussion of procurement is included in Sections 5.2 and 6.5.

Now that project selection methods have been discussed, it is appropriate to consider what documentation is needed to evaluate a project that is being considered. We have spoken about costs, benefits, risks, profits, timing, and other such matters in general terms but now we are looking at the specifics that need to be documented in response to a requested bid. The set of documents submitted for evaluation is called the *project proposal*, whether it is brief (a page or two) or extensive, and regardless of the formality with which it is presented. Several issues face firms preparing bid proposals, particularly firms in the aerospace, construction, defense, and consulting industries. These are:

1. Which projects should be bid on?
2. How should the proposal-preparation process be organized and staffed?
3. How much should be spent on preparing proposals for bids?
4. How should the bid prices be set? What is the bidding strategy? Is it ethical?

Generally, these decisions are made on the basis of their overall expected values, perhaps as reflected in a scoring model. In-house proposals submitted by a firm's personnel to that firm's top management do not usually require the extensive treatment given to proposals submitted to outside clients or agencies such as the Department of Defense. For the Department of Defense, a proposal must be precisely structured to meet the requirements contained in the official Request for Proposal (RFP) or Request for Quotation (RFQ)—more specifically, in the Technical Proposal Requirements (TPR) that is part of the RFP or RFQ.

The details of the construction and preparation of a proposal to be submitted to the government or other outside funder are beyond the scope of this book. Fortunately, the subject has been well treated by Knutson (1996a, 1996b, and 1996c), but it should be noted that customs, practices, rules, and laws concerning proposals vary from nation to nation (e.g., see Jergeas et al., 1997). We comment only on the general approach below.

All bid proposals should begin with a short summary statement (an "Executive Summary") covering the fundamental nature of the proposal in *minimally technical language*, as well as the general benefits that are expected. All proposals should be accompanied by a "cover letter." Roman (1986, pp. 67–68) emphasizes that the cover letter is a key marketing document and is worthy of careful attention. In addition to the Executive Summary and the cover letter, every proposal should deal with four distinct issues: (1) the nature of the technical problem and how it is to be approached; (2) the plan for implementing the project once it has been accepted; (3) the plan for logistic support and administration of the project; and (4) a description of the group proposing to do the work, plus its past experience in similar work.

The precise way in which the contents of a proposal are organized usually follows the directions found in the TPR or RFP, the stated requirements of a specific potential funder, the traditional form used by the organization issuing the proposal, or, occasionally, the whim of the writer. As is the case with most products, the highest probability of acceptance will occur when the proposal meets the expectations of the "buyer," as to form and content. At times there is a tendency to feel that "nontechnical" projects (which usually means projects not concerned with the physical sciences or a physical product) are somehow exempt from the need to describe how the problem will

---

*Occasionally, particular sections will be shaded, meaning that they can be skipped without loss of continuity.

be approached and how the project will be implemented—including details such as milestones, schedules, and budgets. To deal with nontechnical projects casually is folly and casts considerable doubt on the proposer's ability to deliver on promises. (It is all too common for projects concerned with the development of art, music, drama, and computer software, among other "nontechnical" areas, to be quite vague as to deliverables, deadlines, and costs.) On the other hand, when the proposal is aimed at another division or department of the same parent organization, the technical requirements of the proposal may be greatly relaxed, but the technical approach and implementation plan are still required—even if presented in an informal manner.

The Technical Approach

The proposal begins with a general description of the problem to be addressed or project to be undertaken. If the problem is complex, the major subsystems of the problem or project are noted, together with the organization's approach to each. The presentation is in sufficient detail that a knowledgeable reader can understand what the proposer intends to do. The general method of resolving critical problems is outlined. If there are several subsystems, the proposed methods for interfacing them are covered.

In addition, any special client requirements are listed along with proposed ways of meeting them. All test and inspection procedures to assure performance, quality, reliability, and compliance with specifications are noted.

The Implementation Plan

The implementation plan for the project contains estimates of the time required, the cost, and the materials used. Each major subsystem of the project is listed along with estimates of its cost. These costs are aggregated for the whole project, and totals are shown for each cost category. Hours of work and quantities of material used are shown (along with the wage rates and unit material costs). A list of all equipment costs is added, as is a list of all overhead and administrative costs.

Depending on the wishes of the parent organization and the needs of the project, project task schedules (e.g., time charts, network diagrams, Gantt charts) are given for each subsystem and for the system as a whole. (See Chapter 8 for more about time charts, network diagrams, and Gantt charts.) Personnel, equipment, and resource usages are estimated on a period-by-period basis in order to ensure that resource constraints are not violated. Major milestones are indicated on the time charts. Contingency plans are specifically noted. For any facility that might be critical, load charts are prepared to make sure that the facility will be available when needed.

The Plan for Logistic Support and Administration

The proposal includes a description of the ability of the proposer to supply the routine facilities, equipment, and skills needed during any project. Having the means to furnish artist's renderings, special signs, meeting rooms, stenographic assistance, reproduction of oversized documents, computer graphics, word processing, video teleconferencing, and many other occasionally required capabilities provides a "touch of class." Indeed, their unavailability can be irritating. Attention to detail in all aspects of project planning increases the probability of success for the project—and impresses the potential funder.

It is important that the proposal contain a section explaining how the project will be administered. Of particular interest will be an explanation of how control over subcontractors will be administered, including an explanation of how proper subcontractor performance is to be insured and evaluated. The nature and timing of all progress reports, budgetary reports, audits, and evaluations are covered, together with a description of the final documentation to be prepared for users of the proposed deliverables. Termination procedures are described, clearly indicating the disposition of project personnel, materials, and equipment at project end.

A critical issue, often overlooked, that should be addressed in the administrative section of the proposal is a reasonably detailed description of how *change orders* will be handled and how their costs will be estimated. Change orders are a significant source of friction (and lawsuits) between the organization doing the project and the client. The client rarely understands the chaos that can be created in a project by the introduction of a seemingly simple change. To make matters worse, the group proposing the project seems to have a penchant for misleading the potential client about the ease with which "minor" changes can be adopted during the process of implementing the project. Control of change orders is covered in Chapter 11.

Past Experience

All proposals are strengthened by including a section that describes the past experience of the proposing group. It contains a list of key project personnel together with their titles and qualifications. For outside clients, a full résumé for each principal should be attached to the proposal. When preparing this and the other sections of a proposal, the proposing group should remember that the basic purpose of the document is to convince a potential funder that the group and the project are worthy of support. The proposal should be written accordingly.

SUMMARY

This chapter initiated our discussion of the project management process by describing procedures for strategically evaluating and selecting projects. We first described the strategic objective of using projects to help achieve the organization's goals and strategy, and a project portfolio process to help achieve this. We then outlined some criteria for project selection models and discussed the general nature of these models. The chapter described the types of models in use and their advantages and disadvantages. Considering the degree of uncertainty associated with many projects, a section was devoted to evaluating the impact of risk and uncertainty. Concluding the discussion, some general comments were made about data requirements, the use of these models, and how to implement the project portfolio process. The final section discussed the documentation required to bid on RFPs (requests for proposals).

The following specific points were made in this chapter:

- The role of projects in achieving the organization's goals and strategy is critical.

- The eight-step project portfolio process is an effective way to select and manage projects that are tied to the organization's goals.

- Primary model selection criteria are realism, capability, flexibility, ease of use, and cost.

- Preparatory steps in using a model include: (1) identifying the firm's objectives; (2) weighting them relative to each other; and (3) determining the probable impacts of the project on the firm's competitive abilities.

- Project selection models can generally be classified as either numeric or nonnumeric; numeric models are further subdivided into profitability and scoring categories.

- Nonnumeric models include: (1) the sacred cow; (2) the operating necessity; (3) the competitive necessity; and (4) comparative benefit.

- Profitability models include standard forms such as: (1) payback period; (2) average rate of return; (3) discounted cash flow; (4) internal rate of return; and (5) profitability index.

- Project management maturity measurement is a way of assessing an organization's ability to conduct projects successfully.

- Scoring models—the authors' preference—include: (1) the unweighted 0–1 factor model; (2) the unweighted factor scoring model; (3) the weighted factor scoring model; and (4) the constrained weighted factor scoring model.

- Project proposals generally consist of a number of sections: (1) the technical approach; (2) the implementation plan; (3) the plan for logistic support and administration; and (4) past experience.

In the next chapter we consider the selection of the appropriate manager for a project and what characteristics are most helpful for such a position. We also address the issue of the project manager's special role, and the demands and responsibilities of this critical position.

GLOSSARY

Decision Support System   A computer package and database to aid managers in making decisions. It may include simulation programs, mathematical programming routines, and decision rules.

Delphi   A formalized method for transforming the opinions of a group of individuals into quantitative measures that can be aggregated to use in decision making.

Expert System   A computer package that captures the knowledge of recognized experts in an area and can make inferences about a problem based on decision rules and data input to the package.

Maturity   The sophistication and experience of an organization in managing multiple projects.

Model   A way of looking at reality, usually for the purpose of abstracting and simplifying it, to make it understandable in a particular context.

Network   A group of items connected by some common mechanism.

Portfolio   A group or set of projects with varying characteristics.

Pro forma   Projected or anticipated, usually applied to financial data such as balance sheets and income statements.

Programming   An algorithmic methodology for solving a particular type of complex problem, usually conducted on a computer.

Project portfolio process   An eight-step procedure for selecting, implementing, and reviewing projects that will help an organization achieve its strategic goals.

Simulation   A technique for emulating a process, usually conducted a considerable number of times to understand the process better and measure its outcomes under different policies.

QUESTIONS

Material Review Questions

1. What are the four parts of a technical proposal?

2. By what criteria do you think managers judge selection models? What criteria *should* they use?

3. Contrast the competitive necessity model with the operating necessity model. What are the advantages and disadvantages of each?

4. What is a sacred cow? Give some examples.

5. Give an example of a Q-Sort process for project selection.

6. What are some of the limitations of project selection models?

7. Contrast the real options selection approach with profitability models.

8. How does the discounted cash flow method answer some of the criticisms of the payback period and average rate of return methods?

9. What are some advantages and disadvantages of the profit/profitability numeric models?

10. What is the desired result of applying the project portfolio process? What do firms usually find happens?

11. Describe the discovery-driven planning approach.

12. Describe the eight-step project portfolio process.

13. What does the term "project management maturity" mean?

14. Where do most firms fall on the maturity scale?

Class Discussion Questions

15. Which of the many purposes of the project portfolio process are most important to a firm with a low project management maturity? Which to a firm with high maturity?

16. On what basis does the real options model select projects?

17. What is the real difference between profitability and scoring models? Describe a model that could fit both categories.

18. Contrast the window-of-opportunity approach with discovery-driven planning.

19. Discuss how the following project selection models are used in real-world applications. (a) Capital investment with discounted cash flow. (b) Simulation models.

20. Why do you think managers underutilize project selection models?

21. Would uncertainty models be classified as profitability models, scoring models, or some other type of model?

22. Is project management maturity focused on doing better on multiple projects or single projects?

23. Are there certain types of projects that are better suited for nonnumeric selection methods as opposed to numeric ones?

24. Identify some of the ethical issues that can arise in a bid response to an RFP.

25. What important comparisons does the aggregate project plan in Figure 2-3 allow?

26. What does the plan of record illustrate that the aggregate project plan does not?

27. If sustainability focuses on long-run profitability, why is it classified as a "non-numeric" model?

Implementing Strategy through Project Management Tools

28. Is the new project management approach to implementing strategy bottom-up or top-down?

29. What is the role of projects and their management in this new process? That is, wouldn't a functional approach have worked just as well?

30. What other benefits might you expect from a system such as this?

Taipei 101: Refitted as World's Tallest Sustainable Building

31. Why did the owners pick such a big building for sustainability refitting?

32. What aspect of the tenant's habits and routines relates to sustainability, as opposed to "green"?

Virtual Project Team Strategy

33. What is strategic benefit of virtual teams for project management?

34. Why is global software development a difficult and complex task?

35. How can virtual project teams deliver value and benefit for project management?

36. What other factors do virtual project teams need to assess and re-evaluate while implementing distributed projects?

Using a Project Portfolio to Achieve 100% On-Time Delivery at Décor Cabinet Company

37. Might it not make sense to include a least a few of the more promising new product projects in their portfolio?

38. If ROI isn't the big picture, what do you think is?

PROBLEMS

1. Two new Internet site projects are proposed to a young start-up company. Project A will cost $250,000 to implement and is expected to have annual net cash flows of $75,000. Project B will cost $150,000 to implement and should generate annual net cash flows of $52,000. The company is very concerned about their cash flow. Using the payback period, which project is better, from a cash flow standpoint?

2. Sean, a new graduate at a telecommunications firm, faces the following problem his first day at the firm: What is the average rate of return for a project that costs $200,000 to implement and has an average annual profit of $30,000?

3. A four-year financial project has net cash flows of $20,000, $25,000, $30,000, and $50,000 in the next four years. It will cost $75,000 to implement the project. If the required rate of return is 0.2, conduct a discounted cash flow calculation to determine the NPV.

4. What would happen to the NPV of the above project if the inflation rate was expected to be 4 percent in each of the next four years?

5. Calculate the profitability index for Problem 3 and Problem 4.

6. A four-year financial project has estimates of net cash flows shown in the following table:

Year	Net Cash Flow
1	$20,000
2	25,000
3	30,000
4	35,000

It will cost $65,000 to implement the project, all of which must be invested at the beginning of the project. After the fourth year, the project will have no residual value.

Using the most likely estimates of cash flows, conduct a discounted cash flow calculation assuming a 20 percent hurdle rate with no inflation. (You may use either Excel® or a paper-and-pencil calculation.) What is the discounted profitability index of the project?

7. Use a weighted score model to choose between three methods (A, B, C) of financing the acquisition of a major competitor. The relative weights for each criterion are shown in the following table as are the scores for each location on each criterion. A score of 1 represents unfavorable, 2 satisfactory, and 3 favorable.

Category	Weight	*Method* A	*Method* B	*Method* C
Consulting costs	20	1	2	3
Acquisition time	20	2	3	1
Disruption	10	2	1	3
Cultural differences	10	3	3	2
Skill redundancies	10	2	1	1
Implementation risks	25	1	2	3
Infrastructure	10	2	2	2

8. Develop a spreadsheet for Problem 7.
 (a) What would your recommendation be if the weight for the implementation risks went down to 10 and the weight of cultural differences went up to 25?
 (b) Suppose instead that method A received a score of 3 for implementation risks. Would your recommendation change under these circumstances?
 (c) The vice president of finance has looked at your original scoring model and feels that tax considerations should be included in the model with a weight of 15. In addition, the VP has scored the methods on tax considerations as follows: method A received a score of 3, method B received a score of 2, and method C received a score of 1. How would this additional information affect your recommendation?

9. Nina is trying to decide in which of four shopping centers to locate her new boutique. Some locations attract a higher class of clientele than others, some are in an indoor mall, some have a much greater customer traffic volume than others, and, of course, rent varies considerably from one location to another. Because of the nature of her store, she has decided that the class of clientele is the most important consideration, the higher the better. Following this, however, she must pay attention to her expenses and rent is a major item, probably 90 percent as important as clientele. An indoor, temperature-controlled mall is a big help, however, for stores such as hers where 70 percent of sales are from passersby slowly strolling and window shopping. Thus, she rates this as about 95 percent as important as rent. Lastly, a higher traffic volume of shoppers means more potential sales; she thus rates this factor as 80 percent as important as rent.

As an aid in visualizing her location alternatives, she has constructed the following table. A "good" is scored as 3, "fair" as 2, and "poor" as 1. Use a weighted score model to help Nina come to a decision.

	Location 1	*Location* 2	*Location* 3	*Location* 4
Class of clientele	Fair	Good	Poor	Good
Rent	Good	Fair	Poor	Good
Indoor mall	Good	Poor	Good	Poor
Traffic volume	Good	Fair	Good	Poor

10. Referring to Problem 11, develop a spreadsheet to help Nina select a location for her boutique. Suppose Nina is able to negotiate a lower rent at location 3 and thus raise its ranking to "good." How does this affect the overall rankings of the four locations?

INCIDENTS FOR DISCUSSION

Portillo, Inc.

Portillo, Inc. is a manufacturer of small household appliances and cooking utensils. Working with Johanna Portillo, the CEO of the firm, her executive team has developed a scoring model to analyze and select new items to be added to the product line. The model is also used to select old items to be dropped from the line. It employs both objective and subjective estimates of scores for the financial and nonfinancial elements that make up the model. The model is used by a Drop/Add Committee she appointed.

Ms. Portillo is pleased with the construct of the model and feels that it includes all of the factors relevant to the drop/add decision. She is also comfortable with the factor weights developed by her executives.

Following a review of the past year's meetings of the Drop/Add Committee, Ms. Portillo discovered that several managers made significant errors when estimating costs and benefits of many projects. After a careful study of the estimates, she noticed that the sponsors of a product seemed to overestimate its benefits and underestimate its costs. It also appeared that other managers might be underestimating benefits and overestimating costs.

She was not sure about her suspicions and wondered how to find out if her notions were correct. Even if they were correct, she wondered what to do about it.

Questions: How can Ms. Portillo find out if her suspicions are correct? What are her options if her idea is supported?

L & M Power

In the next two years, a large municipal gas company must begin constructing new gas storage facilities to accommodate the Federal Energy Regulatory Commission's Order

636 deregulating the gas industry. The vice president in charge of the new project believes there are two options. One option is an underground deep storage facility (UDSF) and the other is a liquified natural gas facility (LNGF). The vice president has developed a project selection model and will use it in presenting the project to the president. For the models she has gathered the following information:

	Initial Cost	Operating Cost/ Cu. Ft.	Expected Life	Salvage Value
UDSF	$10,000,000	$0.004	20 years	10%
LNGF	25,000,000	0.002	15	5

Since the vice president's background is in finance, she believes the best model to use is a financial one, net present value analysis.

Questions: Would you use this model? Why or why not? Base your answer on the five criteria developed by Souder and evaluate this model in terms of the criteria.

 ## CONTINUING INTEGRATIVE CLASS PROJECT

The task for the class here is to select an appropriate project for the course. Consideration should be given to the fixed end-of-term deadline, the limited monetary but large personnel resources available, the irrelevance of financial returns, and the availability of contacts and good project possibilities outside the classroom. As indicated in Chapter 1, there are often many excellent projects on a college campus, such as in the residence halls, the library, the cafeteria, the medical care office, and so on. When evaluating these situations for potential projects, consider factors such as whether the class has a good inside contact to sponsor the project, whether data will be easily accessible for the class, how many students the organization or department can handle at a time, how extensive the project is, how clear the problem/opportunity is, when they will need an answer, and other such important issues.

 ## BIBLIOGRAPHY

Åstebro, T. "Key Success Factors for Technological Entrepreneurs' R & D Projects." *IEEE Transactions on Engineering Management*, August 2004.

Baker, B. "The Fall of the Firefly: An Assessment of a Failed Project Strategy." *Project Management Journal*, September 2002.

Baker, B., and R. Menon. "Politics and Project Performance: The Fourth Dimension of Project Management." *PM Network*, November 1995.

Booz, Allen, and Hamilton, Inc. *Management of New Products*. New York: Booz, Allen, and Hamilton, Inc., 1966.

Cicmil, S., and D. Hodgson. "New Possibilities for Project Management Theory: A Critical Judgement." *Project Management Journal,* December 2006.

Cleland, D. I., and W. R. King. *Project Management Handbook*. New York: Van Nostrand-Reinhold, 1983.

Dalkey, N. C. *The Delphi Method: An Experimental Study of Group Opinion* (RM-5888-PR). Santa Monica, CA: The Rand Corporation, June 1969.

Dickinson, M. W., A. C. Thornton, and S. Graves. "Technology Portfolio Management: Optimizing Interdependent Projects over Multiple Time Periods." *IEEE Transactions on Engineering Management*, November 2001.

Dinsmore, P. C., "How Grown-Up Is Your Organization?" *PM Network,* June 1998.

Doctor, R. N., D. P. Newton, and A. Pearson. "Managing Uncertainty in Research and Development." *Technovation*, February 2001.

Englund, R. L., and R. J. Graham. "From Experience: Linking Projects to Strategy." *Journal of Product Innovation Management*, Vol. 16, No. 1, 1999.

Evans, J. R., and S. J. Mantel, Jr. "A New Approach to the Evaluation of Process Innovations." *Technovation*, October 1985.

Frame, J. D. *The New Project Management: Tools for an Age of Rapid Change, Corporate Reengineering, and Other Business Realities*. San Francisco: Jossey-Bass, 1997.

Gale, S. F. "The Real Deal." *PM Network,* December 2009.

Githens, G. "Financial Models, Right Questions, Good Decision." *PM Network*, July 1998.

Hayes, R., and W. J. Abernathy. "Managing Our Way to Economic Decline." *Harvard Business Review*, July–August 1980.

Helin, A. F., and W. E. Souder. "Experimental Test of a Q-Sort Procedure for Prioritizing R & D Projects."

IEEE Transactions on Engineering Management, November 1974.

Ibbs, C. W., and Y. H. Kwak. "Assessing Project Management Maturity." *Project Management Journal*, March 2000.

Irving, R. H., and D. W. Conrath. "The Social Context of Multiperson, Multiattribute Decision-making." *IEEE Transactions on Systems, Man, and Cybernetics*, May–June 1988.

Jacob, W. F., and Y. H. Kwak. "In Search of Innovative Techniques to Evaluate Pharmaceutical R & D Projects." *Technovation*, April 2003.

Jergeas, G. F., and V. G. Cooke. "Law of Tender Applied to Request for Proposal Process." *Project Management Journal*, December 1997.

Jolly, D. "The Issue of Weightings in Technology Portfolio Management." *Technovation*, May 2003.

Knutson, J. "Proposal Management: Analyzing Business Opportunities." *PM Network*, January 1996a.

Knutson, J. "Proposal Management: Generating Winning Proposals, Part 1." *PM Network*, February 1996b.

Knutson, J. "Proposal Management: Generating Winning Proposals, Part 2." *PM Network*, March 1996c.

KPMG, "Global IT Project Management." <http://www.kpmg.com/>, 2005.

Liberatore, M. J., and G. J. Titus. "The Practice of Management Science in R & D Project Management." *Management Science*, August 1983.

Longman, A., D. Sandahl, and W. Speir. "Preventing Project Proliferation." *PM Network*, July 1999.

Lubianiker, S. "Opening the Book on the Open Maturity Model." *PM Network*, March 2000.

Luehrman, T. A. "Investment Opportunities as Real Options: Getting Started on the Numbers." *Harvard Business Review*, July–August 1998a.

Luehrman, T. A. "Strategy as a Portfolio of Real Options." *Harvard Business Review*, September–October 1998b.

Mantel, S. J., Jr., J. R. Evans, and V. A. Tipnis. "Decision Analysis for New Process Technology," in B. V. Dean, ed., *Project Management: Methods and Studies*. Amsterdam: North-Holland, 1985.

Matzler, K., and H. H. Hinterhuber. "How to Make Product Development Projects More Successful by Integrating Kano's Model of Customer Satisfaction into Quality Function Deployment." *Technovation*, January 1998.

McGrath, R. G., and I. MacMillan. "Discovery-Driven Planning." *Harvard Business Review,* July–August 1995.

McIntyre, J. "The Right Fit," *PM Network*, November. 2006.

Meade, L. M., and A. Presley. "R & D Project Selection Using the Analytic Network Process." *IEEE Transactions on Engineering Management*, February 2002.

Meredith, J. "The Implementation of Computer Based Systems." *Journal of Operations Management*, October 1981.

Meredith, J. R., S. M. Shafer, and E. Turban. *Quantitative Business Modeling.* Cincinnati, OH: Southwestern, 2002.

Pennypacker, J. S., and K. P. Grant. "Project Management Maturity: An Industry Benchmark." *Project Management Journal*, March 2003.

Project Management Institute. *A Guide to the Project Management Body of Knowledge,* 4th ed. Newtown Square, PA: Project Management Institute, 2008.

Project Management Institute. "Survey Reveals How Organizations Succeed." *PMI Today*, February 2011.

Remy, R. "Adding Focus to Improvement Efforts with PM[3]." *PM Network*, July 1997.

Rice, M. P., G. C. O'Connor, and R. Pierantozzi. "Implementing a Learning Plan to Counter Project Uncertainty." *Sloan Management Review,* Winter 2008.

Roman, D. D. *Managing Projects: A Systems Approach.* New York: Elsevier, 1986.

Ross, S. A., R. W. Westerfield, and B. D. Jordan. *Fundamentals of Corporate Finance,* 8th ed. New York: Irwin/McGraw-Hill, 2008.

Saaty, T. S. *Decision for Leaders: The Analytic Hierarchy Process.* Pittsburgh: University of Pittsburgh, 1990.

Simon, H. *The New Science of Management Decisions*, rev. ed. Englewood Cliffs, NJ: Prentice Hall, 1977.

Souder, W. E. "Utility and Perceived Acceptability of R & D Project Selection Models." *Management Science*, August 1973.

Souder, W. E. "Project Evaluation and Selection," in D. I. Cleland and W. R. King, eds., *Project Management Handbook.* New York: Van Nostrand Reinhold, 1983.

Swanson, S. A. "All Things Considered." *PM Network,* February 2011.

Thomas, J., C. L. Delisle, K. Jugdev, and P. Buckle. "Mission Possible: Selling Project Management to Senior Executives." *PM Network*, January 2001.

Turban, E., and J. R. Meredith. *Fundamentals of Management Science,* 6th ed. Homewood, IL: Irwin, 1994.

Wheatley, M., "Making the Cut." *PM Network*, June 2009.

Wheelwright, S. C., and K. B. Clark. "Creating Project Plans to Focus Product Development." *Harvard Business Review*, March–April 1992.

The following case concerns a European firm trying to choose between almost a dozen capital investment projects being championed by different executives in the firm. However, there are many more projects available for funding than there are funds available to implement them, so the set must be narrowed down to the most valuable and important to the firm. Financial, strategic, and other data are given concerning the projects in order to facilitate the analysis needed to make a final investment recommendation to the Board of Directors.

C A S E

PAN-EUROPA FOODS S.A.*
C. Opitz and R. F. Bruner

It was early January, and the senior-management committee of Pan-Europa Foods was to meet to draw up the firm's capital budget for the new year. Up for consideration were 11 major projects that totaled over €208 million (euros). Unfortunately, the board of directors had imposed a spending limit of only €80 million; even so, investment at that rate would represent a major increase in the firm's asset base of €656 million. Thus the challenge for the senior managers of Pan-Europa was to allocate funds among a range of compelling projects: new-product introduction, acquisition, market expansion, efficiency improvements, preventive maintenance, safety, and pollution control.

The Company

Pan-Europa Foods, headquartered in Brussels, Belgium, was a multinational producer of high-quality ice cream, yogurt, bottled water, and fruit juices. Its products were sold throughout Scandinavia, Britain, Belgium, the Netherlands, Luxembourg, western Germany, and northern France. (See Exhibit 1 for a map of the company's marketing region.)

The company was founded in 1924 by Theo Verdin, a Belgian farmer, as an offshoot of his dairy business. Through keen attention to product development, and shrewd marketing, the business grew steadily over the years. The company went public in 1979 and by 1993 was listed for trading on the London, Frankfurt, and Brussels exchanges. Last year Pan-Europa had sales of almost €1.1 billion.

Ice cream accounted for 60 percent of the company's revenues; yogurt, which was introduced in 1982,

contributed about 20 percent. The remaining 20 percent of sales was divided equally between bottled water and fruit juices. Pan-Europa's flagship brand name was "Rolly," which was represented by a fat, dancing bear in farmers' clothing. Ice cream, the company's leading product, had a loyal base of customers who sought out its high butterfat content, large chunks of chocolate, fruit, nuts, and wide range of original flavors.

Recently, Pan-Europa sales had been static (see Exhibit 2), which management attributed to low population growth in northern Europe and market saturation in some areas. Outside observers, however, faulted recent failures in new-product introductions. Most members of management wanted to expand the company's market presence and introduce more new products to boost sales. These managers hoped that increased market presence and sales would improve the company's market value. Pan-Europa's stock was currently at eight times earnings, just below book value. This price/earnings ratio was below the trading multiples of comparable companies, but it gave little value to the company's brands.

Resource Allocation

The capital budget at Pan-Europa was prepared annually by a committee of senior managers who then presented it for approval by the board of directors. The committee consisted of five managing directors, the *président directeur-général* (PDG), and the finance director. Typically, the PDG solicited investment proposals from the managing directors. The proposals included a brief project description, a financial analysis, and a discussion of strategic or other qualitative considerations.

As a matter of policy, investment proposals at Pan-Europa were subjected to two financial tests, payback

---

EXHIBIT 1 Pan-Europa Foods S. A. Nations Where Pan-Europa Competed

Note: The shaded area in this map reveals the principal distribution region of Pan-Europa's products. Important facilities are indicated by the following figures:

1. Headquarters, Brussels, Belgium
2. Plant, Antwerp, Belgium
3. Plant, Strasbourg, France
4. Plant, Nuremberg, Germany
5. Plant, Hamburg, Germany

6. Plant, Copenhagen, Denmark
7. Plant, Svald, Sweden
8. Plant, Nelly-on-Mersey, England
9. Plant, Caen, France
10. Plant, Melun, France

and internal rate of return (IRR). The tests, or hurdles, had been established by the management committee and varied according to the type of project:

Type of Project	Minimum Acceptable IRR	Maximum Acceptable Payback Years
1. New product or new markets	12%	6 years
2. Product or market extension	10%	5 years
3. Efficiency improvements	8%	4 years
4. Safety or environmental	No test	No test

The most recent estimated weighted-average cost of capital (WACC) for Pan-Europa was 10.5 percent. In describing the capital-budgeting process, the finance director,

EXHIBIT 2 Summary of Financial Results (all values in € millions except per-share amounts)

Fiscal Years Ending December 31			
	Previous Year	Last Year	This Year
Gross sales	1,076	1,072	1,074
Net income	51	49	37
Earnings per share	0.75	0.72	0.54
Dividends	20	20	20
Total assets	477	580	656
Shareholders' equity (book value)	182	206	235
Shareholders' equity (market value)	453	400	229

Trudi Lauf, said, "We use the sliding scale of IRR tests as a way of recognizing differences in risk among the various types of projects. Where the company takes more risk, we should earn more return. The payback test signals that we are not prepared to wait for long to achieve that return."

Ownership and the Sentiment of Creditors and Investors

Pan-Europa's 12-member board of directors included three members of the Verdin family, four members of management, and five outside directors who were prominent managers or public figures in northern Europe. Members of the Verdin family combined owned 20 percent of Pan-Europa's shares outstanding, and company executives owned 10 percent of the shares. Venus Asset Management, a mutual-fund management company in London, held 12 percent. Banque du Bruges et des Pays Bas held 9 percent and had one representative on the board of directors. The remaining 49 percent of the firm's shares were widely held. The firm's shares traded in London, Brussels, and Frankfurt.

At a debt-to-equity ratio of 125 percent, Pan-Europa was leveraged much more highly than its peers in the European consumer-foods industry. Management had relied on debt financing significantly in the past few years to sustain the firm's capital spending and dividends during a period of price wars initiated by Pan-Europa. Now, with the price wars finished, Pan-Europa's bankers (led by Banque du Bruges) strongly urged an aggressive program of debt reduction. In any event, they were not prepared to finance increases in leverage beyond the current level. The president of Banque du Bruges had remarked at a recent board meeting,

> Restoring some strength to the right-hand side of the balance sheet should now be a first priority. Any expansion of assets should be financed from the cash flow after debt amortization until the debt ratio returns to a more prudent level. If there are crucial investments that cannot be funded this way, then we should cut the dividend!

At a price-to-earnings ratio of eight times, shares of Pan-Europa common stock were priced below the average multiples of peer companies and the average multiples of all companies on the exchanges where Pan-Europa was traded. This was attributable to the recent price wars, which had suppressed the company's profitability, and to the well-known recent failure of the company to seize significant market share with a new product line of flavored mineral water. Since last year, all of the major securities houses had been

issuing "sell" recommendations to investors in Pan-Europa shares. Venus Asset Management in London had quietly accumulated shares during this period, however, in the expectation of a turnaround in the firm's performance. At the most recent board meeting, the senior managing director of Venus gave a presentation in which he said,

> Cutting the dividend is unthinkable, as it would signal a lack of faith in your own future. Selling new shares of stock at this depressed price level is also unthinkable, as it would impose unacceptable dilution on your current shareholders. Your equity investors expect an improvement in performance. If that improvement is not forthcoming, or worse, if investors' hopes are dashed, your shares might fall into the hands of raiders like Carlo de Benedetti or the Flick brothers.[1]

At the conclusion of the most recent meeting of the directors, the board voted unanimously to limit capital spending in the next year to €80 million.

Members of the Senior Management Committee

The capital budget would be prepared by seven senior managers of Pan-Europa. For consideration, each project had to be sponsored by one of the managers present. Usually the decision process included a period of discussion followed by a vote on two to four alternative capital budgets. The various executives were well known to each other:

Wilhelmina Verdin (Belgian), PDG, age 57. Granddaughter of the founder and spokesperson on the board of directors for the Verdin family's interests. Worked for the company her entire career, with significant experience in brand management. Elected "European Marketer of the Year" in 1982 for successfully introducing low-fat yogurt and ice cream, the first major roll-out of this type of product. Eager to position the company for long-term growth but cautious in the wake of recent difficulties.

Trudi Lauf (Swiss), finance director, age 51. Hired from Nestlé to modernize financial controls and systems. Had been a vocal proponent of reducing

---

[1]De Benedetti of Milan and the Flick brothers of Munich were leaders of prominent hostile-takeover attempts in recent years.

leverage on the balance sheet. Also had voiced the concerns and frustrations of stockholders.

Heinz Klink (German), managing director for Distribution, age 49. Oversaw the transportation, warehousing, and order-fulfillment activities in the company. Spoilage, transport costs, stock-outs, and control systems were perennial challenges.

Maarten Leyden (Dutch), managing director for Production and Purchasing, age 59. Managed production operations at the company's 14 plants. Engineer by training. Tough negotiator, especially with unions and suppliers. A fanatic about production-cost control. Had voiced doubts about the sincerity of creditors' and investors' commitment to the firm.

Marco Ponti (Italian), managing director for Sales, age 45. Oversaw the field sales force of 250 representatives and planned changes in geographical sales coverage. The most vocal proponent of rapid expansion on the senior-management committee. Saw several opportunities for ways to improve geographical positioning. Hired from Unilever to revitalize the sales organization, which he successfully accomplished.

Fabienne Morin (French), managing director for Marketing, age 41. Responsible for marketing research, new-product development, advertising, and, in general, brand management. The primary advocate of the recent price war, which, although financially difficult, realized solid gains in market share. Perceived a "window of opportunity" for product and market expansion and tended to support growth-oriented projects.

Nigel Humbolt (British), managing director for Strategic Planning, age 47. Hired two years previously from a well-known consulting firm to set up a strategic-planning staff for Pan-Europa. Known for asking difficult and challenging questions about Pan-Europa's core business, its maturity, and profitability. Supported initiatives aimed at growth and market share. Had presented the most aggressive proposals in 1992, none of which were accepted. Becoming frustrated with what he perceived to be his lack of influence in the organization.

The Expenditure Proposals

The forthcoming meeting would entertain the following proposals (see summary table also):

1. *Replacement and expansion of the truck fleet.* Heinz Klink proposed to purchase 100 new refrigerated tractor-trailer trucks, 50 this year and another 50 next year. By doing so, the company could sell 60 old, fully depreciated trucks over the two years for a total of €1.2 million. The purchase would expand the fleet by 40 trucks within two years. Each of the new trailers would be larger than the old trailers and afford a 15 percent increase in cubic meters of goods hauled on each trip. The new tractors would also be more fuel and maintenance efficient. The increase in number of trucks would permit more flexible scheduling and more efficient routing and servicing of the fleet than at present and would cut delivery times and, therefore, possibly inventories. It would also allow more frequent deliveries to the company's major markets, which would reduce the loss of sales caused by stock-outs. Finally, expanding the fleet would support geographical expansion over the long term. As shown in Exhibit 3, the total net investment in trucks of €20 million and the

Project	Expenditure (€ millions)	Sponsoring Manager
1. Replacement and expansion of the truck fleet	22	Klink, Distribution
2. A new plant	30	Leyden, Production
3. Expansion of a plant	10	Leyden, Production
4. Development and introduction of new artificially sweetened yogurt and ice cream	15	Morin, Marketing
5. Plant automation and conveyor systems	14	Leyden, Production
6. Effluent water treatment at four plants	4	Leyden, Production
7. Market expansion eastward	20	Ponti, Sales
8. Market expansion southward	20	Ponti, Sales
9. Development and roll-out of snack foods	18	Morin, Marketing
10. Networked, computer-based inventory-control system for warehouses and field representatives	15	Klink, Distribution
11. Acquisition of a leading schnapps brand and associated facilities	40	Humbolt, Strategic Planning

EXHIBIT 3 Free Cash Flows and Analysis of Proposed Projects [1] (all values in € millions)

Project	1 Expand Truck Fleet (note 3)	2 New Plant	3 Expanded Plant	4 Artificial Sweetener	5 Automation and Conveyer Systems	7 Eastward Expansion (note 5)	8 Southward Expansion (note 5)	9 Snack Foods	10 Inventory-Control System	11 Strategic Acquisition (note 6)
Investment										
Property	20.00	25.00	10.00	15.00	14.00	20.00	20.00	15.00	15.00	30.00
Working Capital	2.00	5.00						3.00		10.00
Year				**EXPECTED FREE CASH FLOWS (note 4)**						
0	(11.40)	(30.00)	(10.00)	(5.00)	(14.00)	(20.00)	(20.00)	(18.00)	(12.00)	(15.00)
1	(7.90)	2.00	1.25	(5.00)	2.75	3.50	3.00	3.00	5.50	(20.00)
2	3.00	5.00	1.50	(5.00)	2.75	4.00	3.50	4.00	5.50	5.00
3	3.50	5.50	1.75	3.00	2.75	4.50	4.00	4.50	5.00	9.00
4	4.00	6.00	2.00	3.00	2.75	5.00	4.50	5.00		11.00
5	4.50	6.25	2.25	4.00	2.75	5.50	5.00	5.00		13.00
6	5.00	6.50	2.50	4.50	2.75	6.00	5.50	5.00		15.00
7	7.00	6.75	1.50	5.00		6.50	6.00	5.00		17.00
8		5.00	1.50	5.50		7.00	6.50	5.00		19.00
9		5.25	1.50	6.00		7.50	7.00	5.00		21.00
10		5.50	1.50	6.50		8.00	7.50	5.00		59.00
Undiscounted Sum	7.70	23.75	7.25	22.50	5.25	37.50	32.50	28.50	4.00	134.00
Payback (years)	6	6	6	7	6	5	6	5	3	5
Maximum Payback Accepted	4	5	5	6	4	6	6	6	4	6
IRR	7.8%	11.3%	11.2%	17.3%	8.7%	21.4%	18.8%	20.5%	16.2%	28.7%
Minimum Accepted ROR	8.0%	10.0%	10.0%	12.0%	8.0%	12.0%	12.0%	12.0%	8.0%	12.0%
Spread	−0.2%	1.3%	1.2%	5.3%	0.7%	9.4%	6.8%	8.5%	8.2%	16.7%
NPV at Corp. WACC (10.5%)	−1.92	0.99	0.28	5.21	−0.87	11.99	9.00	8.95	1.16	47.97
NPV at Minimum ROR	−0.13	1.87	0.55	3.88	0.32	9.90	7.08	7.31	1.78	41.43
Equivalent Annuity (note 2)	−0.02	0.30	0.09	0.69	0.06	1.75	1.25	1.29	0.69	7.33

[1]The effluent treatment program is not included in this exhibit.

[2]The equivalent annuity of a project is that level annual payment over 10 years that yields a net present value equal to the NPV at the minimum required rate of return for that project. Annuity corrects for differences in duration among various projects. For instance, project 5 lasts only 7 years and has an NPV of 0.32 million; a 10-year stream of annual cash flows of 0.05 million, discounted at 8.0 percent (the required rate of return) also yields an NPV of 0.32 million. In ranking projects on the basis of equivalent annuity, bigger annuities create more investor wealth than smaller annuities.

[3]This reflects €11 million spent both initially and at the end of year 1.

[4]Free cash flow = incremental profit or cost savings after taxes + depreciation − investment in fixed assets and working capital.

[5]Franchisees would gradually take over the burden of carrying receivables and inventory.

[6]€15 million would be spent in the first year, 20 million in the second, and 5 million in the third.

increase in working capital to support added maintenance, fuel, payroll, and inventories of €2 million was expected to yield total cost savings and added sales potential of €7.7 million over the next seven years. The resulting IRR was estimated to be 7.8 percent, marginally below the minimum 8 percent required return on efficiency projects. Some of the managers wondered if this project would be more properly classified as "efficiency" than "expansion."

2. *A new plant.* Maarten Leyden noted that Pan-Europa's yogurt and ice-cream sales in the southeastern region of the company's market were about to exceed the capacity of its Melun, France, manufacturing and packaging plant. At present, some of the demand was being met by shipments from the company's newest, most efficient facility, located in Strasbourg, France. Shipping costs over that distance were high, however, and some sales were undoubtedly being lost when the marketing effort could not be supported by delivery. Leyden proposed that a new manufacturing and packaging plant be built in Dijon, France, just at the current southern edge of Pan-Europa's marketing region, to take the burden off the Melun and Strasbourg plants.

The cost of this plant would be €25 million and would entail €5 million for working capital. The €14 million worth of equipment would be amortized over seven years, and the plant over 10 years. Through an increase in sales and depreciation, and the decrease in delivery costs, the plant was expected to yield after-tax cash flows totaling €23.75 million and an IRR of 11.3 percent over the next 10 years. This project would be classified as a market extension.

3. *Expansion of a plant.* In addition to the need for greater production capacity in Pan-Europa's southeastern region, its Nuremberg, Germany, plant had reached full capacity. This situation made the scheduling of routine equipment maintenance difficult, which, in turn, created production-scheduling and deadline problems. This plant was one of two highly automated facilities that produced Pan-Europa's entire line of bottled water, mineral water, and fruit juices. The Nuremberg plant supplied central and western Europe. (The other plant, near Copenhagen, Denmark, supplied Pan-Europa's northern European markets.)

The Nuremberg plant's capacity could be expanded by 20 percent for €10 million. The equipment (€7 million) would be depreciated over seven years, and the plant over 10 years. The increased capacity was expected to result in additional production of up to €1.5 million per year, yielding an IRR of 11.2 percent. This project would be classified as a market extension.

4. *Development and introduction of new artificially sweetened yogurt and ice cream.* Fabienne Morin noted that recent developments in the synthesis of artificial sweeteners were showing promise of significant cost savings to food and beverage producers as well as stimulating growing demand for low-calorie products. The challenge was to create the right flavor to complement or enhance the other ingredients. For ice-cream manufacturers, the difficulty lay in creating a balance that would result in the same flavor as was obtained when using natural sweeteners; artificial sweeteners might, of course, create a superior taste.

€15 million would be needed to commercialize a yogurt line that had received promising results in laboratory tests. This cost included acquiring specialized production facilities, working capital, and the cost of the initial product introduction. The overall IRR was estimated to be 17.3 percent.

Morin stressed that the proposal, although highly uncertain in terms of actual results, could be viewed as a means of protecting present market share, because other high-quality ice-cream producers carrying out the same research might introduce these products; if the Rolly brand did not carry an artificially sweetened line and its competitors did, the Rolly brand might suffer. Morin also noted the parallels between innovating with artificial sweeteners and the company's past success in introducing low-fat products. This project would be classed in the new-product category of investments.

5. *Plant automation and conveyor systems.* Maarten Leyden also requested €14 million to increase automation of the production lines at six of the company's older plants. The result would be improved throughput speed and reduced accidents, spillage, and production tie-ups. The last two plants the company had built included conveyer systems that eliminated the need for any heavy lifting by employees. The systems reduced the chance of injury to employees; at the six older plants, the company had sustained an average of 75 missed worker-days per year per plant in the last two years because of muscle injuries sustained in heavy lifting. At an average hourly wage of €14.00 per hour, over €150,000 per year was thus lost, and the possibility always existed of more serious injuries and lawsuits. Overall cost savings and depreciation totaling €2.75 million per year for the project were expected to yield an IRR of 8.7 percent. This project would be classed in the efficiency category.

6. *Effluent water treatment at four plants.* Pan-Europa preprocessed a variety of fresh fruits at its Melun and Strasbourg plants. One of the first stages of processing involved cleaning the fruit to remove dirt and pesticides. The dirty water was simply sent down the drain and into the Seine or Rhine rivers. Recent European Community directives called for any waste water containing even slight traces of poisonous chemicals to be treated at the sources and gave companies four years to comply. As an environmentally oriented project, this proposal fell outside the normal financial tests of project attractiveness. Leyden noted, however, that the water-treatment equipment could be purchased today for €4 million; he speculated that the same equipment would cost €10 million in four years when immediate conversion became mandatory. In the intervening time, the company would run the risks that European Community regulators would shorten the compliance time or that the company's pollution record would become public and impair the image of the company in the eyes of the consumer. This project would be classed in the environmental category.

7. and **8.** *Market expansions eastward and southward.* Marco Ponti recommended that the company expand its market eastward to include eastern Germany, Poland, Czechoslovakia, and Austria and/or southward to include southern France, Switzerland, Italy, and Spain. He believed the time was right to expand sales of ice cream, and perhaps yogurt, geographically. In theory, the company could sustain expansions in both directions simultaneously, but practically, Ponti doubted that the sales and distribution organizations could sustain both expansions at once.

Each alternative geographical expansion had its benefits and risks. If the company expanded eastward, it could reach a large population with a great appetite for frozen dairy products, but it would also face more competition from local and regional ice cream manufacturers. Moreover, consumers in eastern Germany, Poland, and Czechoslovakia did not have the purchasing power that consumers did to the south. The eastward expansion would have to be supplied from plants in Nuremberg, Strasbourg, and Hamburg.

Looking southward, the tables were turned: more purchasing power and less competition but also a smaller consumer appetite for ice cream and yogurt. A southward expansion would require building consumer demand for premium-quality yogurt and ice cream. If neither of the plant proposals (i.e., proposals 2 and 3) were accepted, then the southward expansion would need to be supplied from plants in Melun, Strasbourg, and Rouen.

The initial cost of either proposal was €20 million of working capital. The bulk of this project's costs was expected to involve the financing of distributorships, but over the 10-year forecast period, the distributors would gradually take over the burden of carrying receivables and inventory. Both expansion proposals assumed the rental of suitable warehouse and distribution facilities. The after-tax cash flows were expected to total €37.5 million for eastward expansion and €32.5 million for southward expansion.

Marco Ponti pointed out that eastward expansion meant a higher possible IRR but that moving southward was a less risky proposition. The projected IRRs were 21.4 percent and 18.8 percent for eastern and southern expansion, respectively. These projects would be classed in the new market category.

9. *Development and roll-out of snack foods.* Fabienne Morin suggested that the company use the excess capacity at its Antwerp spice- and nut-processing facility to produce a line of dried fruits to be test-marketed in Belgium, Britain, and the Netherlands. She noted the strength of the Rolly brand in those countries and the success of other food and beverage companies that had expanded into snack-food production. She argued that Pan-Europa's reputation for wholesome, quality products would be enhanced by a line of dried fruits and that name association with the new product would probably even lead to increased sales of the company's other products among health-conscious consumers.

Equipment and working-capital investments were expected to total €15 million and €3 million, respectively, for this project. The equipment would be depreciated over seven years. Assuming the test market was successful, cash flows from the project would be able to support further plant expansions in other strategic locations. The IRR was expected to be 20.5 percent, well above the required return of 12 percent for new-product projects.

10. *Networked, computer-based inventory-control system for warehouses and field representatives.* Heinz Klink had pressed for three years unsuccessfully for a state-of-the-art computer-based inventory-control system that would link field sales representatives, distributors, drivers, warehouses, and even possibly retailers. The benefits of such a system would be shortening delays in ordering and order processing, better control of inventory, reduction of spoilage, and faster recognition of changes in demand at the customer level. Klink was reluctant to quantify these benefits, because they could range between modest and quite large amounts. This year, for the first time, he presented a cash-flow forecast, however, that reflected an initial outlay of

€12 million for the system, followed by €3 million in the next year for ancillary equipment. The inflows reflected depreciation tax shields, tax credits, cost reductions in warehousing, and reduced inventory. He forecasted these benefits to last for only three years. Even so, the project's IRR was estimated to be 16.2 percent. This project would be classed in the efficiency category of proposals.

11. *Acquisition of a leading schnapps brand and associated facilities.* Nigel Humbolt had advocated making diversifying acquisitions in an effort to move beyond the company's mature core business but doing so in a way that exploited the company's skills in brand management. He had explored six possible related industries, in the general field of consumer packaged goods, and determined that cordials and liqueurs offered unusual opportunities for real growth and, at the same time, market protection through branding. He had identified four small producers of well-established brands of liqueurs as acquisition candidates. Following

exploratory talks with each, he had determined that only one company could be purchased in the near future, namely, the leading private European manufacturer of schnapps, located in Munich.

The proposal was expensive: €15 million to buy the company and €25 million to renovate the company's facilities completely while simultaneously expanding distribution to new geographical markets.[2] The expected returns were high: after-tax cash flows were projected to be €134 million, yielding an IRR of 28.7 percent. This project would be classed in the new-product category of proposals.

Conclusion

Each member of the management committee was expected to come to the meeting prepared to present and defend a proposal for the allocation of Pan-Europa's capital budget of €80 million. Exhibit 3 summarizes the various projects in terms of their free cash flows and the investment-performance criteria.

 QUESTIONS

1. Strategically, what must Pan-Europa do to keep from becoming the victim of a hostile takeover? What rows/categories in Exhibit 2 will thus become critically important this coming year? What should Pan-Europa do now that they have won the price war? Who should lead the way for Pan-Europa?

2. Using NPV, conduct a straight financial analysis of the investment alternatives and rank the projects. Which NPV of the three should be used? Why? Suggest a way to evaluate the effluent project.

3. What aspects of the projects might invalidate the ranking you just derived? How should we correct for each investment's time value of money, unequal lifetimes, riskiness, and size?

4. Reconsider the projects in terms of:
   • are any "must do" projects of the nonnumeric type?
   • what elements of the projects might imply greater or lesser riskiness?

   • might there be any synergies or conflicts between the projects?
   • do any of the projects have nonquantitative benefits or costs that should be considered in an evaluation?

5. Considering all the above, what screens/factors might you suggest to narrow down the set of most desirable projects? What criteria would you use to evaluate the projects on these various factors? Do any of the projects fail to pass these screens due to their extreme values on some of the factors?

6. Divide the projects into the four Project Profile Process categories of incremental, platform, breakthrough, and R&D. Draw an aggregate project plan and array the projects on the chart.

7. Based on all the above, which projects should the management committee recommend to the Board of Directors?

 The following reading describes the approach Hewlett-Packard uses to select and monitor its projects for relevance to the firm's strategic goals. The article describes the behavioral aspects of the process as well as many of the technical tools, such as the aggregate project plan, the plan of record, and the software aids they employed. In addition, the authors give tips and identify pitfalls in the process so anyone else implementing their approach will know what problems to watch out for.

---

[2]Exhibit 3 shows negative cash flows amounting to only €35 million. The difference between this amount and the €40 million requested is a positive operating cash flow of €5 million in year 1 expected from the normal course of business.

DIRECTED READING

FROM EXPERIENCE: LINKING PROJECTS TO STRATEGY*
R. L. Englund and R. J. Graham

Growth in organizations typically results from successful projects that generate new products, services, or procedures. Managers are increasingly concerned about getting better results from the projects under way in their organizations and in getting better cross-organizational cooperation. One of the most vocal complaints of project managers is that projects appear almost randomly. The projects seem unlinked to a coherent strategy, and people are unaware of the total number and scope of projects. As a result, people feel they are working at cross-purposes, on too many unneeded projects, and on too many projects generally. Selecting projects for their strategic emphasis helps resolve such feelings and is a corner anchor in putting together the pieces of a puzzle that create an environment for successful projects [6].

This article covers a series of steps for linking projects to strategy. These steps constitute a process that can be applied to any endeavor. Included throughout are suggestions for action as well as guidelines to navigate many pitfalls along the path. Process tools help illustrate ways to prioritize projects. The lessons learned are from consulting with many firms over a long time period and from personal experiences in applying the lessons within Hewlett-Packard Company (HP), a $40 billion plus company where two thirds of its revenue derives from products introduced within the past 2 years.

The Importance of Upper Management Teamwork

Developing cooperation across an organization requires that upper managers take a systems approach to projects. That means they look at projects as a system of interrelated activities that combine to achieve a common goal. The common goal is to fulfill the overall strategy of the organization. Usually all projects draw from one resource pool, so they interrelate as they share the same resources. Thus, the system of projects is itself a project, with the smaller projects being the activities that lead to the larger project (organizational) goal.

Any lack of upper management teamwork reverberates throughout the organization. If upper managers do not model desired behaviors, there is little hope that the rest of the organization can do it for them. Any lack of upper management cooperation will surely be reflected in the behavior of project teams, and there is little chance that project managers alone can resolve the problems that arise.

A council concept is one mechanism used at HP to establish a strategic direction for projects spanning organizational boundaries. A council may be permanent or temporary, assembled to solve strategic issues. As a result, a council typically will involve upper managers. Usually its role is to set directions, manage multiple projects or a set of projects, and aid in cross-organizational issue resolution. Several of these council-like activities become evident through the examples in this article.

Employing a comprehensive and systematic approach illustrates the vast and important influence of upper management teamwork on project success. Increasingly evident are companies who initiate portfolio selection committees. We suggest that organizations begin by developing councils to work with project managers and to implement strategy. These councils exercise leadership by articulating a vision, discussing it with the project managers, asking them their concerns about and needs for implementing the strategy, listening carefully to them, and showing them respect so they become engaged in the process. In this way, upper managers and project managers develop the joint vision that is so necessary for implementation of strategy.

Process for Project Selection and Prioritization

Once the upper management team is established, they can follow a process to select sets of projects that achieve organizational goals. They are then ideally positioned to implement consistent priorities across all departments. Figure 1 represents a mental model of a way to structure this process. Outputs from the four steps interrelate in a true systems approach. This model comes from experience in researching and applying a thorough approach to all the issues encountered in a complex organization. It is both simple in concept and complex in richness. The authors use the model both as an educational tool and to facilitate management teams through the process.

What the Organization Should Do and How to Know When You Are Doing It.   First, identify who is leading the

---

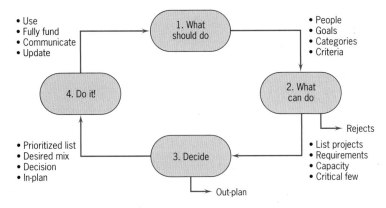

- Use
- Fully fund
- Communicate
- Update

1. What should do

- People
- Goals
- Categories
- Criteria

4. Do it!

2. What can do

→ Rejects

- Prioritized list
- Desired mix
- Decision
- In-plan

3. Decide

- List projects
- Requirements
- Capacity
- Critical few

→ Out-plan

Figure 1   A systematic approach to selecting projects.

process and who should be on the management team. More time spent here putting together a "mission impossible" team pays dividends later by getting up-front involvement of the people who will be affected by the decisions that will be made. Take care not to overlook any key-but-not-so-visible players who later may speak up and jeopardize the plan. This team may consist solely of upper managers or may include project managers, a general manager, and possibly a customer. Include representation of those who can best address the key opportunities and risks facing the organization. Ideally they control the resources and are empowered to make decisions on all projects. The leader needs to get explicit commitment from all these people to participate actively in the process and to use the resulting plan when making related decisions. Be aware that behavioral issues become super urgent. This process hits close to home and may have a severe impact on projects that people care personally about. Uncertainty and doubt are created if management does not tread carefully and pay attention to people concerns.

The team begins by listing all projects proposed and under way in the organization. Many times this step is a revelation in itself. A usual reaction is, "I didn't realize we had so many projects going on." The intent is to survey the field of work and begin the organizing effort, so avoid going into detailed discussion about specific projects at this point.

The team clarifies or develops the goals expected from projects. Be careful not to get constrained through considering only current capabilities. Many teams get sidetracked by statements such as "We don't know how to do that," effectively curtailing discussion on whether the organization ought to pursue the goal and develop or acquire the capability. Rather, the discussions at this stage center around organizational purpose, vision, and mission. This is a crucial step that determines if the rest of the project selection process can be successful. In the authors' experience, those organizations with clear, convincing, and compelling visions about what they should be doing move ahead rapidly. Any lack of understanding or commitment to the vision by a member

of the team leads to frustration, wheel spinning, and eventual disintegration of the whole process. This pattern is so prevalent that clarity of the goal or strategy is applied as a filter before agreeing to facilitate teams through the process.

Organize the projects into categories that will later make it easier to facilitate a decision-making process. Wheelwright and Clark [14] suggest using grids where the axes are the extent of product change and the extent of process change. Some organizations use market segments. The benefit to this effort is that seeing all projects and possible projects on a continuum allows checking for completeness, gaps, opportunities, and compliance with strategy. This might also be a good time to encourage "out-of-the-box" thinking about new ways to organize the work. Use creative discussion sessions to capture ideas about core competences, competitive advantage, and the like to determine a set of categories most effective for the organization. For example, the categories might be:

Evolutionary or derivative—sustaining, incremental, enhancing.

Platform—next generation, highly leveraged; and

Revolutionary or breakthrough—new core product, process, or business.

The actual products in Figure 2 were introduced to the market over time in alphabetical order and positioning shown. Although the figure represents a retrospective view, it illustrates a successful strategy of sequencing projects and products. There is a balanced mix of breakthrough products, such as A, followed by enhancements, B through E, before moving on to new platforms, F through H, and eventually developing a new architecture and product family with L. At the time, this strategy was improvisational [1]; it now represents a learning opportunity for planning new portfolios. No one area of the grid is overpopulated, and where large projects exist there are not too many of them.

Another reason to organize projects into these "strategic buckets" is to better realize what business(es) the organization is in. Almost every group the authors work with get

Figure 2   Bubble diagram of a product grid for one HP division. Size of bubble = size of project.

caught in the "tyranny of the OR" instead of embracing the "genius of the AND" [2]. In trying to do too many projects and facing the need to make tradeoffs among them, the decision becomes *this* OR *that*. In reality, most organizations need a balanced portfolio that creates complete solutions for their customers. They need to do *this* AND *that*. The way to achieve this goal is to set limits on the size of each category and then focus efforts on selecting the best set of projects within each category. The collective set of categories becomes the desired mix, a way of framing the work of the organization. The ideal percentage that constitutes the size of each category can be determined from the collective wisdom of the team or perhaps through experimentation. The organization can learn the right mix over time but only if it makes a concerted effort to do so.

Within each category, determine criteria that can assess the "goodness"—quality or best fit—of choices for the plan. A criterion is a standard on which a comparative judgment or decision may be based. Because the types of projects and the objectives within categories may be quite different, develop unique criteria for each category or have a core set of criteria that can be modified. Many teams never get to the point of developing or clarifying criteria, and they usually want to discuss projects before agreeing on criteria; reversing the order is much more effective.

Several works on research and development project selection [8, 9, 12] provide a robust set of criteria for consideration. Examples include strategic positioning, probability of success, market size, and availability of staff. Most important is to identify the criteria that are of greatest significance to the organization; fewer are better. However, teams usually need to brainstorm many criteria before focusing on the few.

The role of each criterion is to help compare projects, not specify them. Select criteria that can measurably compare how projects support the organizational strategy. For example, one criterion may be degree of impact on HP business as interpreted by a general manager. On a scaling

model from 1 to 10, small impact scores a 2, strong a 6, critical to the success of one business an 8, and critical to the success of multiple businesses a 10. Most likely all proposed projects meet meaningful specifications and provide value to the organization. The task is to develop tough criteria to select the best of the best.

Some organizations use narratives to describe how each project contributes to the vision; others use numerical scores on whether one project is equal, moderate, or strongly better than another. It is also helpful to set thresholds or limits for projects that will be considered for the plan. These help to screen out projects so that later prioritization efforts can focus on fewer projects.

Writing a thorough description of each criterion helps ensure understanding of the intent and expectations of data that must be supplied to fulfill it. One team of three or four people at HP spent 5 days working only on the criteria they were to use for decision making. And this was only the beginning; they next involved customers in the same discussion before reaching consensus and beginning to evaluate choices. An "Aha" occurred when people found they were wrong to assume that everyone meant the same thing by terms such as packaging; some used wider definitions than others did, and the misunderstanding only surfaced through group discussion. Asked if the selection process ever failed the team, its leader replied, "If the results didn't make sense, it was usually because the criteria weren't well defined." Unfortunately, most teams do not exhibit the same patience and discipline that allowed this team to be successful.

Before moving to the next step, the team should establish relative importance among criteria. Assign a weighting factor for each criterion. All criteria are important but some more so than others. The example in Figure 3 is the result of one team's brainstorming session that ultimately led to selecting four criteria. Breakout groups subsequently defined each criterion with subcriteria. They also devised scoring methods to apply the criteria. Collectively they then determined the respective weighting or importance of each

Customer Satisfaction (28%)	Employee Satisfaction (7%)
• Improves service levels • Results in more consistent and accurate information/transactions • Helps ensure services are delivered as expected	• Improves employee knowledge • Increases employee efficiency or effectiveness • Improves work/life balance promised • Positive impact to employee survey • Helps balance workload
Business Value (46%)	**Process Effectiveness (19%)**
• Achieves results that are critical for a specific window of opportunity • Minimizes risk for implementation and ongoing sustainability • Improves integration and relationships with partners • Provides a positive ROI in < 2 yrs • Aligns with business goals	• Enables employees to do things right the first time • Increases the use of technology for service delivery • Reduces manual work and non-value added activities • Increases employee self-sufficiency

Figure 3   Sample criteria and weighting, plus subcriteria, developed by one HP team.

criterion (see the Process Tools section for how they did this). Unlike threshold criteria that "gate" whether a project is go or no-go, all projects have to satisfy selection criteria to some extent. Weighting of criteria is the technique that can optimize and determine the best of the best. Another "Aha" that helped teams get through the hurdle to develop effective criteria is when they realized the task at this point is "weighting, not gating."

It is the authors' experience that criteria, while universally desired, are usually lacking or not formalized. One benefit of effective criteria is the shaping effect it has on behavior in the organization. When people know how projects will be scored, they tend to shape proposals in positive ways to meet the criteria better. A pitfall is when people play games to establish criteria that support personal agendas. Then it is up to the leader to identify and question these tactics. Remind people to support the greater good of the organization. Significant effort could be devoted to the behavioral aspects that become relevant when deciding upon criteria; suffice to say, be warned that this is a touchy area to approach with sensitivity and persuasiveness.

What the Organization Can Do.   The next step for the team is to gather data on all projects. Use similar factors when describing each project in order to ease the evaluation process. Engage people in extensive analysis and debate to get agreement on the major characteristics for each project. This is a time to ask basic questions about product and project types and how they contribute to a diversified set of projects. Reexamine customer needs, future trends, commercial opportunities, and new markets. The person consolidating the data should challenge assertions about benefits

and costs instead of accepting assumptions that may have been put together casually. It is important for each member of the team to assess the quality of the data, looking closely at sources and the techniques for gathering the data. When putting cost figures together, consider using activity-based costing models instead of traditional models based on parts, direct labor, and overhead. Activity-based costing includes the communications, relationship building, and indirect labor costs that usually are required to make a project successful.

The team needs to constantly apply screening criteria to reduce the number of projects that will be analyzed in detail. Identify existing projects that can be canceled, downscaled, or reconceived because their resource consumption exceeds initial expectations, costs of materials are higher than expected, or a competitive entry to the market changed the rules of the game. The screening process helps eliminate projects that require extensive resources but are not justified by current business strategies; maybe the projects were conceived based on old paradigms about the business. The team can save discussion time by identifying must-do projects or ones that require simple go/no-go decisions, such as legal, personnel, or environmental projects. These fall right through the screens and into the allocation process. Determine if some projects can be postponed until others are complete or until new resources or funding become available. Can project deliverables be obtained from a supplier or subcontractor rather than internally? Involve customers in discussions. The team constantly tests project proposals for alignment with organizational goals.

It is not necessary to constrain the process by using the same criteria across all categories of projects. In fact, some teams found that different criteria for each category of projects was more effective. Also, consider adjusting the weighting of criteria as projects move through their life cycles. Kumar et al. [7] documented research showing that the most significant variable for initial screening of projects is the extent to which "project objectives fit the organization's global corporate philosophy and strategy." Other factors, such as available science and technology, become significant later during the commercial evaluation stage. A big "Aha" experienced by some teams when confronted with this data is that they usually did it the other way around. That explains why they got into trouble—by focusing on technology or financial factors before determining the link to strategic goals.

Cooper (and others before him) report that top-performing companies do not use financial methods for portfolio planning. Rather, they use strategic portfolio management methods where strategy decides project selection [3]. This lesson is still a hotly debated one, especially for those who cling to net present value as the single most important criterion. The difficulty lies in relying upon forecast numbers that are inherently fictitious. The authors' experience is that teams get much better results tapping their collective wisdom about the merits of each project based upon tangible assessments against strategic goals. Using computed financial numbers more often leads to arguments about computation methods and reliability of the data, resulting in unproductive team dynamics.

The next part of gathering data is to estimate the time and resources required for each potential and existing project. Get the data from past projects, statistical projections, or simulations. The HP Project Management Initiative particularly stresses in its organizational initiatives to get accurate bottom-up project data from work breakdown structures and schedules. Reconcile this data with top-down project goals. Document assumptions so that resource requirements can be revisited if there are changes to the basis for an assumption. For new or unknown projects, make a best estimate, focusing first on the investigation phase with the intent to fund only enough work to determine feasibility. The team can revisit the estimates when more information becomes available. Constantly improve estimation accuracy over time by tracking actuals with estimated task durations.

Next, the team identifies the resource capacity both within and outside the organization that will be available to do projects. Balance project with nonproject work by using realistic numbers for resource availability, taking into account other projects, vacations, meetings, personal appointments, and other interruptions. Tip: a wise planner consumes no more than about 50% of a person's available time.

One assessment about the quality of projects in a portfolio is to look at the rejects. In a story attributed to HP founder Bill Hewlett, he once established a single metric for how he would evaluate a portfolio manager's performance. He asked to see only the rejects. He reasoned that if the rejects looked good, then the projects that were accepted must be excellent.

All the actions in this step of the process are intended to screen many possible projects to find the critical few. The team may take a path through multiple screens or take multiple passes through screens with different criteria to come up with a short list of viable projects. Figure 4 represents one scenario where Screen 1 is a coarse screen that checks for impact on the strategic goal. Subsequent screens apply other criteria when more data are available. Any number of screens may be applied, up to the number n, until the team is satisfied that the remaining projects relate to compelling business needs. These steps actually save time because the next section on analysis can get quite extensive if all possible projects go through it.

It usually is necessary to go through several validation cycles before finishing the next step: the upper management team proposes project objectives, project teams provide preliminary estimates based on scope, schedule, and resources back to management, management is not happy with this response and makes adjustments, and so on. This exercise in due diligence is a healthy negotiation process that results in more realistic projects getting through the funnel.

Analyze and Decide on Projects.   The next step is to compare estimated resource requirements with available resources. A spreadsheet is useful to depict allocation of resources according to project priority.

Part of the analysis is qualitative: Consider the opportunity costs of committing to short-term, opportunistic, or poorly conceived projects that take resources away from

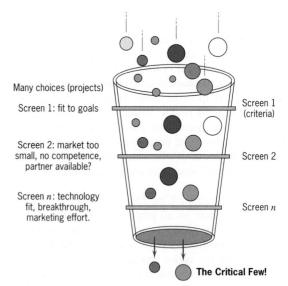

Figure 4 Application of criteria screens during a funneling process eliminates the *trivial many projects* from the *critical few* that the organization can realistically complete.

future prospects that may be a better fit strategically. Also, avoid selecting "glamorous" new ideas over addressing the tough issues from ongoing projects. Some people lack the stamina to deal with the details of implementation and so are ready to jump to a new solution at the slightest glimmer of hope from the latest technology. This is a recipe for disaster. Also, be careful to balance the important projects rather than giving in to urgent, but not so important, demands.

Documenting all the findings and supportive data using a common set of descriptive factors makes it easier to compare similar factors across projects. Use a "project charter" form or a template where all information about each project, its sponsors, and key characteristics is recorded.

The team can now prioritize the remaining projects. Focus on project benefits before costs; that way the merits of each project get full consideration. Later include costs to determine the greatest value for the money. Compute overall return from the set of projects, not from individual projects, because some projects may have greater strategic than monetary value. Requiring each and every project to promise a high financial return actually diminishes cooperation across an organization. Also, optimize return over time and continuity or uniformity of revenue from the projects. Some future projects must be funded early to ensure a revenue stream when current projects taper off.

Using previously agreed-upon criteria and weighting factors, the team compares each project with every other one within a category. Repeat the process for each criterion. See the discussion and example later in this article about using an analytical hierarchy process (AHP) to facilitate this step. Consider using software to compute results—an ordered list of projects within each category. A pitfall to avoid that engenders fear among the team is showing one list that prioritizes all projects from top to bottom. People get concerned when their project is on the line. It is not fair to compare internal development projects with high grossing products; keep them separated and within their respective categories.

Finally, the team is ready to decide which projects to pursue. Be prepared to do fewer projects and to commit complete resources required by projects that are selected. Decide on a mix of projects consistent with business strategy, such as 50% platform projects, 20% derivative projects, 10% breakthrough projects, and 10% partnerships. Note that these total only 90%; taking some lessons from financial portfolio management, diversify the set of projects by investing in some speculative projects. The team may not be sure which markets or technologies will grow, so buy an "option" and make a small investment to investigate the possibilities. Include experimental projects. It is also important to leave a small percent of development capacity uncommitted to take advantage of unexpected opportunities and to deal with crises when they arise.

Wheelwright and Clark [14] cite an organization that reduced the number of its development projects from 30 to 11: "The changes led to some impressive gains...as commercial development productivity improved by a factor of three. Fewer products meant more actual work got done, and more work meant more products." Addressing an internal project management conference, an HP Executive Vice President emphasized the need to focus on doing fewer projects, especially those that are large and complex: "We have to be very selective. You can manage cross-organizational complex programs if you don't have very many. If you have a lot of them with our culture, it just won't work. First of all, we need to pick those opportunities very, very selectively. We need to then manage them aggressively across the company. That means have joint teams work together, strong project management and leadership, constant reviews, a framework, a vision, a strong owner—all those things that make a program and project successful." Subsequently, a number of organizations sought help from the HP Project Management Initiative to systematically reduce 120 projects down to 30. Another organization went from 50 projects down to 17. It appears counter-intuitive, but by prioritizing and more carefully selecting projects, organizations actually get more projects completed.

Figure 5 illustrates a document that captures the output of this process. Record projects that are fully funded in an aggregate project plan (*in-plan*). In a separate section or another document, list projects for future consideration (*out-plan*); also capture and communicate reasons for delaying or not funding projects. The *plan of record* (POR) is both a process and a tool used by some organizations at HP to keep track of the total list of projects. It lists all projects under way or under consideration by the entity. If a project is funded and has resources assigned, it has achieved *in-plan status*. Projects below the cutoff line of available resources or that have not yet achieved priority status are on the *out-plan*. The figure also categorizes the projects and specifies the desired mix.

Project managers at HP describe one benefit of the POR process as identifying gaps between required and actual resources. For flexible changes, the process gets all people into the communications loop. If people want to add something, the management team has to decide what should be deleted. The process helps two divisions that work together agree on one prioritized list instead of two. They utilize direct electronic connections for bottom-up entry of projects and resources by all project managers into a centralized administration point.

Implement the Plan.   No job is complete until it is acted upon. The team needs to "evangelize" all others in the organization to use the aggregate project plan or POR to guide people who plan work, make decisions, and execute projects. Although it may be countercultural to do so, do not starve

ID	Strategic Category	Priority	Project	Head Ct	Feb Mar Apr May Jun Jul Aug Sep
1	**Platform (Mix = 40%)**				
2	In Plan	1	Proj F	2	
3		2	Proj G	2	
4		3	Proj H	4	
5		4	Proj J	5	
6		5	Proj K	3	
7	Out Plan		Next Step		
8					
9	**Enhance (Mix = 20%)**				
10	In Plan	1	Proj B	2	
11		2	Proj C	1	
12		3	Proj D	1	
13		4	Proj E	2	
14		5	Proj I	1	
15	Out Plan		Fat City		
16					
17	**R & D (Mix = 30%)**				
18	In Plan	1	Proj A	7	
19		2	Proj L	5	
20					
21					
22					
23	Out Plan		Blue Sky		
24					
25	**Infrastructure (Mix = 10%)**				
26	In Plan	1	Bus. Plan	1	
27		2	Portfolio	1	
28		3	Update plan	1	
29					
30					
31	Out Plan		Corner Office		

Figure 5   An example plan of record showing the mix of projects in priority order and the time line for each project.

committed projects of the resources they need. The team or the responsible upper managers need to enforce the plan by fully staffing committed projects; that now becomes possible because fewer projects are happening simultaneously. Also, use the plan to identify opportunities for leverage across projects or for process reengineering. Match people skills to project categories to tap their strengths and areas for contribution.

The team or a program management office needs to maintain the plan in a central place, such as a project office or online. Make it known to, and accessible by, all people in the organization doing projects, subject to confidentiality requirements. All the work to this point may go for naught if the process, the steps, and the results are not widely communicated.

The same people who develop the plan are also the ones who can best update it periodically, perhaps quarterly or as changes occur. Use tools such as an online shared database to gather data directly from project managers about resources needed for each project. This system can be used both to gather data when developing the plan and to update it. View the plan as a "living document" that accurately reflects current realities.

The challenge for HP and many companies is to "master both adaptive innovation and consistent execution... again and again and again...in the context of relentless change....Staying on top means remaining poised on the edges of chaos and time...These edges are places of adaptive behavior. They are also unstable. This instability means that managers have to work at staying on the edge" [1]. The advice is clear: the plan is indispensable as a strategic guideline, but don't fall in love with it! Be prepared to adapt it and to communicate the changes.

Process Tools

One tool that can assist in the decision-making process is the AHP [10]. Because of the interactions among many factors affecting a complex decision, it is essential to identify the important factors and the degree that they affect each other before a clear decision can be made. The AHP helps structure a complex situation, identify its criteria and other intangible or concrete factors, measure the interactions among them in a simple way, and synthesize all the information to obtain priorities. The priorities then can be used in a benefit-to-cost determination to decide which projects to select. The AHP organizes feelings and intuition alongside logic in a structured approach to decision making—helpful in complex situations where it is difficult to comprehend multiple variables together. An individual or team focuses on one criterion at a time and applies it step by step across alternatives. A number of sites across HP find value in using AHP.

In another example, a team got together to choose among a set of services they will offer to customers. More choices were available than the organization had capacity to support. After defining organizational strategy or product goals, the first task was to identify which criteria to enter into the decision-making process. After give-and-take discussion, they decided that the criteria were customer satisfaction, business value, process effectiveness, and employee satisfaction.

Next, the criteria were ranked according to priority by making pairwise comparisons between them. Which is the more desirable criterion and by how much, customer satisfaction or business value? Process effectiveness or employee satisfaction? Business value or process effectiveness? These questions were asked about all possible pairs.

Each potential project or service then was scored underneath each criterion, and decisions were made about which projects to include in the portfolio, based upon existing resources. This team went on to create a POR similar to Figure 5.

A detailed explanation for computing the priority scores and the final rank ordering list can be quite complex, involving eigenvalues and eigenvectors, so it is much easier to get a software package (Expert Choice [4]) that does the computations. As an alternative, a spreadsheet could be constructed to normalize the numbers.

This process appears complex and analytical but is easy when the software handles the computations, and the management team concentrates on the comparisons. It is thorough in guiding the team to consider all criteria, both emotional and logical, and to apply them to all projects. One team rejected the process as too analytical, so be aware that it does not work for everyone.

The key benefit in doing this process is the improved quality of dialogue that occurs among the management team members. In facilitating a number of teams at HP through this process, each one achieved far more progress than they thought possible. People admit that they become addicted to the AHP process. They immediately buy the software. The systematic approach is feasible whether selecting products for a product line, projects that comprise a portfolio, or the best supplier or candidate for a job. In reality, the discussions are more valuable than the analysis. The process in this case provides the discipline that makes the dialogue happen.

Frame [5] offers an alternative "poor man's hierarchy." He puts selection criteria along the side as well as across the top of a grid. If the criterion on the side is preferred to the one on the top, put a 1 in the cell. If the criterion on top is preferred, put a 0 in the cell. Diagonals are blanked out where criteria would be compared to themselves. Below the diagonal, put the opposite value from corresponding cells above the diagonal. Then add up the numbers across the rows to get total scores, which provide a rank order. One team at HP modified this process to replace the 1s and 0s with an actual count of how 18 people voted in each pairwise comparison of alternatives. Again, they added up the rows and normalized the results for a priority order and weighted ranking (Figure 6).

	Business	Customer	Technology	Employee		Total Votes	%
Business	***	16	16	18	=	50	46
Customer	2	***	13	15	=	30	28
Technology	2	5	***	14	=	21	19
Employee	0	3	4	***	=	7	7

Figure 6   A simplified hierarchy used by one HP team to weight criteria.

This simplified hierarchy is especially helpful for weighting criteria. It can be used for prioritizing projects when applied to one criterion at a time. It becomes bulky and less useful when applied to multiple projects over multiple criteria.

Barriers to Implementation

Now for a reality check. The model depicted in this article is thorough, and it integrates objective and subjective data. When all is said and done, however, people may throw out the results and make a different decision. Sometimes the reason is a hunch, an instinct, or simply a desire to try something different. Sometimes people have a pet project and use the process to justify its existence, or a hidden agenda may be at play—perhaps the need to maneuver among colleagues, trading projects for favors. Politics at this stage cannot be ignored, nor are they likely to disappear. It is imperative for leaders to become skilled in the political process. Any attempt at leading change in how an organization links projects to strategy is bound to meet resistance. The concept receives almost unanimous intellectual support. Implementing it into the heart and soul of all people in the organization is another story. It goes against the cultural norms in many organizations and conjures up all kinds of resistance if the values it espouses are not the norm in that organization. The path is full of pitfalls, especially if information is presented carelessly or perceived as final when it is work in process.

Some people resist because the process is too analytical. Some want decision making to be purely interactive, intuitive, or the purview of a few people. A complete process cannot be forced upon people if the organization has more immediate concerns or unresolved issues. Resistance occurs when there is no strategy, the strategy is unclear, or people are uncomfortable with the strategy. Work on the process may come to a standstill when people realize how much work is involved to fully link projects to strategy. If the pain is not great enough with the status quo, people are not going to be ready to change.

And if people sense that the leader does not authentically believe in the elements, such as the goals, the process, or the tools, they are hesitant to follow with any enthusiasm. When the leader lacks integrity and exhibits incongruity between words and actions, people may go through the motions but do not exert an effort that achieves meaningful results.

Enablers for Effective Implementation

It is possible to lead people through this change process if the leader asks many questions, listens to the concerns of all people involved, and seeks to build support so that people feel they have an active role in developing the process [9]. A flexible process works better than a rigid one. Cultivate "champions" who have the credibility and fortitude to carry the process across the organization. Believe that change is possible.

When the effort appears too massive, one approach is to go after the low-hanging fruit. Start with one of the more pressing issues and use the general concepts of this model to address it. Still have a vision for what the organization ultimately can achieve but understand that patience and pacing are necessary to get there. Consider also that this process is hierarchical—it can be applied singularly or collectively, up or down the organization.

For people who get frustrated when all linkages are not present, the authors urge teams and individuals to "just do it." Small changes in initial conditions have enormous consequences. Eventually successes or small wins are noticed. The practices start to permeate an organization. This can happen in the middle, move up, and then over to other organizations. Incidentally, a corporate group like HP's Project Management Initiative helps facilitate this transformation. We do this by acting as a conduit for success stories and best practices.

Over the long run, we believe that organizations that follow a process similar to the one described increase their odds for greater success. This happens because teams of people following a systematic process and using convincing data to support their arguments more often produce better results than individuals. Their projects have more visibility, and the quality of dialogue and decision making improve. The power of using criteria that are tightly linked with strategy and known by everyone in the organization is the mitigating effect it has to guide behavior in constructive ways. Having a process means it can be replicated and improved over time until it is optimized. It also means other people can learn the process and coach others, thereby creating a learning organization.

References

1. Brown, S. L., and K. M. Eisenhardt. *Competing on the Edge: Strategy as Structured Chaos*. Boston: Harvard Business School Press, 1998.

2. Collins, J. C. and J. I. Porras. *Built to Last: Successful Habits of Visionary Companies*. New York: Harper-Collins, 1994.

3. Cooper, R. G., S. J. Edgett, and E. J. Kleinschmidt. *Portfolio Management for New Products*. Reading, MA: Addison-Wesley, 1998.

4. "Expert Choice," Pittsburgh, PA: Expert Choice Inc. (see *www.expertchoice.com*).

5. Frame, J. D. *The New Project Management: Tools for an Age of Rapid Change, Corporate Reengineering, and Other Business Realities*. San Francisco: Jossey-Bass Publishers, 1994.

6. Graham, Robert J. and Randall L. Englund. *Creating an Environment for Successful Projects: The Quest to Manage Project Management*. San Francisco: Jossey-Bass Publishers, 1997.

7. Kumar, V., et al. "To Terminate or Not an Ongoing R&D Project: A Managerial Dilemma." *IEEE Transactions on Engineering Management* 279 (1996).

8. Martino, J. *R & D Project Selection*. New York: Wiley, 1995.

9. O'Toole, J. *Leading Change: Overcoming the Ideology of Comfort and the Tyranny of Custom*. San Francisco: Jossey-Bass Publishers, 1995.

10. Saaty, T. L. *Decision Making for Leaders*. Pittsburgh, PA: RWS, 1990.

11. Stacey, R. D. *Managing the Unknowable: Strategic Boundaries Between Order and Chaos in Organizations*. San Francisco: Jossey-Bass Publishers, 1992, p. 62.

12. Turtle, Q. C. *Implementing Concurrent Project Management*. Englewood Cliffs, NJ: Prentice Hall, 1994.

13. Westney, R. E. *Computerized Management of Multiple Small Projects*. New York: Dekker, 1992.

14. Wheelwright, S., and K. Clark. "Creating Project Plans to Focus Product Development." *Harvard Business Review*, March–April (1992).

Questions

1. Why are successful projects so important to Hewlett-Packard?

2. How far should an evaluation team go in trying to quantify project contributions to the firm's mission or goals? What is the role of financial selection criteria in HP's project selection process?

3. Considerable attention is paid to the measures HP uses to evaluate its projects. Is the aim of carefully defining these measures to simplify the project selection process or something else?

4. What do the aggregate project plan and the plan of record illustrate to upper management?

5. When should out-plan projects be reconsidered for inclusion?

6. What was your impression of the impact that HP's project selection process had on the number of projects underway? How do you expect HP would score on project management maturity?

7. How did the new project selection process handle non-numeric type projects? Risk? How did this new process alter new project proposals at HP?

CHAPTER

3

The Project Manager

PMBOK Guide
1.6, 4.3, 9

Chapters 3 and 4 discuss topics relevant to PMBOK knowledge area 6, *Human Resource Management*. In the last chapter, we described how projects are evaluated and selected for development. Before more progress can be made, a project manager (PM) must be appointed. Not only is the appointment of a PM (the project "leader") important to initiate any project, but the PM is probably the major resource input to the project compared to the team, the capital, the materials, and any other inputs—hence our extensive discussion here. As the leader, this person will take responsibility for planning, implementing, and completing the project, beginning with the job of getting things started. Actually, the way to get things started is to hold a meeting. We will delay discussion of the initial project meeting, however, until Chapter 5 because it is the first step in the process of planning the project.

The PM can be chosen and installed as soon as the project is selected for funding or at any earlier point that seems desirable to senior management. If the PM is appointed prior to project selection or if the PM originated the project, several of the usual start-up tasks are simplified. On occasion, a PM is chosen late in the project life cycle, usually to replace another PM who is leaving the project for other work. For example, a large agricultural products firm regularly uses a senior scientist as PM until the project's technical problems are solved and the product has been tested. Then it replaces the scientist with a middle manager from the marketing side of the firm as marketing becomes the focal point of the project. (The transition is difficult and, according to firm spokespeople, the results are sometimes unsatisfactory.)

Usually, a senior manager briefs the PM on the project so that the PM can understand where it fits in the general scheme of things in the parent organization, and its priority relative to other projects in the system and to the routine work of the organization. The PM's first set of tasks is typically to prepare a preliminary budget and schedule, to help select people to serve on the project team, to get to know the client (either internal or external), to make sure that the proper facilities are available, to ensure that any supplies required early in the project life are available when needed, and to take care of the routine details necessary to get the project moving.

As people are added to the project, plans and schedules are refined. The details of managing the project through its entire life cycle are spelled out, even to the point of planning for project termination when the work is finally completed.

Mechanisms are developed to facilitate communication between the PM and top management, the functional areas, and the client. As plans develop still further, the PM holds meetings and briefings to ensure that all those who will affect or be affected by the project are prepared in advance for the demands they will have to meet as the project is implemented.

In this chapter we discuss the unique nature of project management and some of the ways project management differs from *functional* management. Our emphasis is on the role and responsibilities of the PM. We concentrate on the demands placed on the PM, particularly on those unique to project management. For example, consider the differences in the challenges faced by the project manager who must add a security/privacy segment in a software program, and those faced by the PM who must design and implement a global database for an international chemical firm. We then identify the skills required by the project manager and link them to the nature of the task faced by the PM.

It is best to describe the PM's job relative to some assumptions about the nature of projects and the organization within which the project must function. We assume that the parent firm is functionally organized and is conducting many projects simultaneously with its ongoing, routine operations. We also assume a fairly large firm, a project that has some technical components, with an output to be delivered to an "arms-length" customer. Clearly, not all, and possibly even not most, projects operate under these circumstances, but these are the most demanding and we address the most difficult problems a PM might have to face. Smaller, simpler projects may not require the tools we will present here, but the PM for these projects should be aware that such tools exist.

Thus far, we have had in mind a PM with reasonably normal skills, and operating under reasonably normal circumstances. In the last sections of this chapter, we will discuss a major complication for project managers—managing a project being carried out in a *multicultural* environment. We emphasize the word multicultural, a word that is not synonymous with (but includes) projects whose member organizations and geographical locations may transcend national boundaries. In fact, it is not the differences in national boundaries that matter; it is differences in *cultures*. Moreover, it is not merely the differences in cultures that matter, it is also differences between the *environments* within which the projects are conducted—economic, political, legal, and sociotechnical environments.

In this chapter, two conditions receive special attention. Both have a profound effect on the outcome of the project, and neither is under the complete control of the PM—though the PM can greatly influence both by dealing with the conditions early in the project life. The first of these concerns the degree to which the project has the support of top management. If that support is strong and reasonably unqualified, the project has a much better chance of success (Pinto et al., 1989; Zimmerer et al., 1998).

The second condition concerns the general orientation of the project team members. If they are highly oriented toward their individual, functional disciplines, as opposed to the project itself, project success is threatened. If, on the other hand, they are oriented toward the project (that is, problem oriented rather than discipline oriented), the likelihood of success is much greater. As Thomas Hughes (1998) writes about the SAGE and Atlas projects:

"Teams of engineers, technicians, and scientists polarized around problems rather than disciplines. As a result, new discipline-transcending organizational forms...presided over system-building projects rather than discipline-bound departments. The transdisciplinary team approach is still considered front-edge management almost half a century later."

3.1 PROJECT MANAGEMENT AND THE PROJECT MANAGER

The Functional Manager versus the Project Manager

The best way to explain the unique role of the PM is to contrast it with that of a functional manager in charge of one of a firm's functional departments such as marketing, engineering, or finance (see Figure 3-1). Such department heads are usually specialists in the areas they manage. Being specialists, they are analytically oriented and they know something of the details of each operation for which they are responsible. When a technically difficult task is required of their departments, they know how to analyze and attack it. As functional managers, they are administratively responsible for deciding how something will be done, who will do it, and what resources will be devoted to accomplish the task.

A PM generally starts his or her career as a specialist in some field who is blithely informed by a senior manager that he or she is being promoted to the position of Project Manager on the Whizbang Project. The PM must now metamorphose from technical caterpillar into generalist butterfly. (For an excellent set of instructions for the transformation, see Matson (1998).) The PM, new or experienced, must oversee many functional areas, each with its own specialists (see Figure 3-2). Therefore, what is required is an ability to put many pieces of a task together to form a coherent whole—that is, the project manager should be more skilled at synthesis, whereas the functional manager should be more skilled at analysis. The functional manager uses the *analytic approach* and the PM uses the *systems approach.*

The analytic method focuses on breaking the components of a system into smaller and smaller elements. We are not saying that this is wrong, it is merely inadequate for understanding a complex system. Regardless of the dissector's skill or the degree to which, say, a frog is dissected, the dissection allows only a partial understanding of the total animal "frog." The systems approach maintains that to understand a component, we must understand the system of which the component is a part. And to understand the system, we must understand the environment (or larger system) of which it is a part.

Adoption of the systems approach is crucial for the project manager. Consider, if you will, the problem of managing a project devoted to the development of software that will create and maintain a database, and to undertake this task without knowing anything about the decision support system in which the database will be used, or the operating system of the computers

Figure 3-1 Functional management organization chart: marketing department of an insurance company.

Figure 3-2 Project management organization showing typical responsibilities of a project manager.

that will contain the DSS, or the purposes for which the information in the database will be used, and so forth.

Our comparison between the PM and the functional manager reveals another crucial difference between the two. The functional manager is a direct, technical supervisor. The project manager is a facilitator and generalist. These simple statements, while true, are misleading. Both require specialized technical knowledge. The functional manager's knowledge must be in the technology of the process being managed. The PM should be competent in the science of project management (Sahlin, 1998; Zimmerer et al., 1998), but this is not sufficient. In our opinion, there is strong evidence that the PM should be both generalist and facilitator and have a reasonably high level of technical competence in the science of the project.

Three major questions face PMs in their task of synthesis: What needs to be done, when must it be done (if the project is not to be late), and how are the resources required to do the job to be obtained? In spite of the fact that the PM is responsible for the project, the functional managers will probably make some of the fundamental and critical project decisions. For example, they usually select the people who will actually do the work required to carry out the project. They may also develop the technological design detailing how some tasks will be accomplished. And they frequently influence the precise deployment of the project's resources.

This separation of powers between functional and project managers, which may aid in the successful completion of the project, is also a source of considerable "discomfort" for both. Note here that the PM is responsible for organizing, staffing, budgeting, directing, planning, and controlling the project. In other words, the PM "manages" it, but the functional managers may affect the choice of technology to be used by the project and the specific individuals who will do the work. (It is not uncommon, however, for the PM to negotiate with functional managers about the assignment of special individuals to carry out certain project work.) Arguments about the logic or illogic of such an arrangement will fall on deaf ears. The PM cannot allow the functional manager to usurp control of the project. If this happens, work on the project is likely to become secondary to the work of the functional group and the project will suffer. But the functional manager cannot allow the PM to take over authority for technical decisions in the functional area or to control the assignment of functional area personnel.

At times, a senior manager (often the PM's immediate superior) will, in effect, take over the PM's job by exercising extremely close supervision over every action the PM takes, or will actually tell the PM precisely what to do. All of the powers normally delegated to the PM are withdrawn and the PM's boss runs the project. This condition is known as *micromanagement*. It stamps out any creativity or initiative from the PM or project workers, frustrates almost everyone connected with the project, and generally ensures mediocre performance, if not failure. To be frank, we do not know how to cure or prevent micromanagement. It is practiced by individuals who have so little trust in their co-workers that they must control everything. Our considered advice to PMs who are micromanaged is to request a transfer.

At the other end of the spectrum, the relationship between the PM, the functional managers, the project team, and the PM's superior may be characterized as "collegial," and the organization may be populated by talented people. In such organizations conflict is minimized, cooperation is the norm, no one is terribly concerned with who gets the credit, and the likelihood of success is high. We will have more to say later in this chapter and in other chapters about building and maintaining teams. Effective teams tend to operate in a collegial mode. It is worth noting, however, that collegiality without talent leads to failure—even if the project team smiles a lot while failing.

The Project Manager's Responsibilities

The PM's responsibilities are broad and fall primarily into three separate areas: responsibility to the parent organization, responsibility to the project and the client, and responsibility to the members of the project team. Responsibilities to the firm itself include proper conservation of resources, timely and accurate project communications, and the careful, competent management of the project. It is very important to keep senior management of the parent organization fully informed about the project's status, cost, timing, and prospects. Senior managers should be warned about likely future problems. The PM should note the chances of running over budget or being late, as well as methods available to reduce the likelihood of these dreaded events. Reports must be accurate and timely if the PM is to maintain credibility, protect the parent firm from high risk, and allow senior management to intercede where needed. *Above all, the PM must never allow senior management to be surprised!*

The PM's responsibility to the project and client is met by ensuring that the integrity of the project is preserved in spite of the conflicting demands made by the many parties who have legitimate interests in the project. The manager must deal with the engineering department when it resists a change advised by marketing, which is responding to a suggestion that emanated from the client. In the meantime, contract administration says the client has no right to request changes without the submission of a formal Request for Change order. Manufacturing says that the argument is irrelevant because marketing's suggestion cannot be incorporated into the project without a complete redesign.

The PM is in the middle of this turmoil. The PM must sort out understanding from misunderstanding, soothe ruffled feathers, balance petty rivalries, and cater to the demands of the client. One should, of course, remember that none of these strenuous activities relieves the PM of the responsibility of keeping the project on time, within budget, and up to specifications.

In Chapter 5 it will become evident that it is very common for the PM to have no direct subordinates in spite of the fact that several, perhaps many, people "work for him/her" on the project. These people form what we have been referring to as the "project team." In spite of the strange circumstance where people are said to work for someone who is not their boss, the PM's relationship to the team may be considerably closer than one might expect, particularly when individuals are assigned to spend much or all of their time working on the project.

The project manager's responsibilities to members of the project team are dictated by the finite nature of the project itself and the specialized nature of the team. Because the project is, by definition, a temporary entity and must come to an end, the PM must be concerned with the future of the people who serve on the team. If the PM does not get involved in helping project workers with the transition back to their functional homes or to new projects, then as the project nears completion, project workers will pay more and more attention to protecting their own future careers and less to completing the project on time.

One final note on this subject. If we have made the process of project management seem orderly and rational, we apologize. If any single descriptor could be used to characterize project management, the adjective would be "messy." In an excellent article that should be read by anyone interested in understanding the reality of management, Kotter (1982) has shown that general managers are less organized, less formal, and less structured than college students are led to believe. The same is undoubtedly true of project managers. This fundamental lack of organization and structure makes it all the more important that PMs implement good planning and organizational skills where possible, or the chaos becomes unmanageable.

PM Career Paths

Many firms have a wide variety of types and sizes of projects in progress simultaneously. Of these, it is typical to find that many are not large enough or sufficiently complex to require a full-time manager. Quite a few project managers are in charge of several projects simultaneously. The firm may be planning and building a new factory (three years), undertaking several dozen R & D projects (one to seven years), improving the landscape surrounding its factory in Mussent Point (two months), considering the acquisition of another firm (six months), upgrading the equipment in its thiotimolene plant (two years), buying art works produced by artists in each city in which the firm operates for display in corporate offices (one year), planning the annual stockholders' meeting (three months), and doing a large number of other things, many of which are organized as projects.

PMBOK Guide

Who manages these projects? Where does the company find people competent to manage such a wide variety of projects? In Chapter 1, we referred to the professionalization and rapid growth of project management, to PMBOK (the project management body of knowledge), as well as to the development of college and university-level courses and degree programs available in the field. Although the percentage of PMs who are academically trained is increasing rapidly, many current project managers have no college-level training in the field. A rapidly growing number of private consulting firms offer instruction in project management as well as programs preparing individuals for the PMI's examination for certification as Project Management Professionals (PMPs–see Chapter 1 Appendix).

The great number of fairly small, short-term projects being carried out, when managed by an experienced PM, serve a purpose beyond the output of the projects themselves. They provide an excellent training ground for new project managers who frequently begin their preparation with involvement in some major aspect of a small project. A number of firms, Procter & Gamble for one, often take management trainees and give them some project-management responsibility; for instance, the guidance of a new cosmetic through test procedures to ensure that it is not toxic to users. Such experience serves to teach trainees many things, not the least of which are the importance of an organized plan for reaching an objective, of "follow-through," of negotiation with one's co-workers, and of sensitivity to the political realities of organizational life. The skills and experiences gained from managing a project, even a small one, are a scaled-down version of what it is like to run a full-sized organization. Thus, projects provide an excellent growth environment for future executives and for developing managerial skills.

The career path of a PM often starts with participation in small projects, and later in larger projects, until the person is given command over small and then larger projects. For example, the path could be tooling manager for small Project U, project engineer for larger Project V, manufacturing manager for large Project W, deputy project manager for large Project X, project manager for small Project Y, and project manager for large Project Z.

The actual establishment of multiple career paths to the top of organizations is more talked about than acted on. Wishful thinking aside, with a very few notable exceptions,* we know of no *specific* career paths that can take project managers to CEO positions. In a great many firms, however, experience as a PM is seen as a desirable (sometimes mandatory) step on the way up the corporate ladder. The logic of such a view is obvious. The capability of a PM to meet the demands of senior management positions is clearly evidenced by the PM's ability to achieve the project's goals without the need for explicit authority while operating in an environment typified by uncertainty, if not chaos.

The recent global recession and accompanying unemployment has put pressure on the project management profession as much as any other profession. Recent comments in the media (e.g., Zupek, 2010) seem to indicate that "the days of a 'generic' project manager are numbered" and that firms are now looking for PMs who have "specific experience and understand the nuts and bolts" of the technology or project being implemented. As a result, it's important that PMs not only continue to develop their project management skills and gain their PMP® certifications, but keep themselves trained in the latest technologies. If true, then

---

*For example, Eli Lilly and Co., the pharmaceutical firm, finds that projects involving new drugs often last 8–12 years. No PM would be willing to manage a project that long without the opportunity for promotion. Lilly, therefore, has established a career path for their PMs that potentially leads to the top of the firm. They already had career paths progressing through "administration" or "R & D" to the top and have clearly demonstrated the reality of both paths.

it would appear that gaining a wide range of experience would also be more likely to win a job or promotion than gaining depth in one particular area.

Project Management in Practice
Churchill as a Project Manager

Winston Churchill is widely regarded as one of the greatest leaders of the 20th century. But as he became British Prime Minister in May 1940, in a period of calamitous change during World War II, what did he actually do? How did he transform his organisation to turn his perilous situation around? Both Churchill in 1940 and business people today grapple with an unprecedented level of change adversely impacting their organisations at the enterprise, business unit, or project level.

A project manager needs experience in projects relative to their selection, initiation, definition, planning, risk management, resource management, budgeting, communication, tracking issues and status, and evaluating performance. Churchill had experience with large scale projects in abundance. His experience included preparing the Navy for war, to planning the Gallipoli campaign, to coordinating the economy for the production of war materials and tanks, to running the finances of the country.

As well as experience, project managers require strong traits in business, technology, and behaviour, and of course leadership skills. In Churchill's situation:

- He understood the challenges the country faced better than anyone. He had learned many lessons from the First World War which guided his priorities in May 1940. Foremost on his agenda was overcoming the lack of a central policy, which undermined resource coordination and prolonged Britain's response.

- He was very aware of technology and could see its application providing a clear advantage. For example, in 1915 even though he was the Lord of Admiralty he sponsored the initial tank design. In 1938 he supported the development of Radar. Although he would be involved in technical discussions, he would leave decisions to trusted Lieutenants—people he knew could do the job.

- He was very savvy at understanding human behaviour and motivating teams around him. Communication management was a cornerstone of his strategy in 1940, communicating in all directions (cabinet, government, people) to avoid any surprises.

When Churchill became PM at the age of 65 in 1940, he had to find the strength to lead his nation out of the darkest and most dangerous of times, towards the defeat of a tenacious enemy. But Churchill was ready for this and he had always believed he had a fate with destiny that would require him to lead his nation.

When he took over as Prime Minister, he had a very good idea of what he was undertaking, with the background he had, and could draw from his experience in tough international negotiations and fierce political battles. In many ways, he was so well prepared that he wasted little time in taking action.

During the Second World War, Churchill, as a historian, understood early on what was happening and he was astute enough to maximise the impact of valuable information he had collected, and build up his case. He recognised that one of the chief goals of a project manager was to rally people to a cause, and to do this required considerable credibility gained through self-belief, steadfastness, courage, and integrity to the cause.

Organisations today need to pay close attention to events and changes in the business environment, and prepare for worst case situations. Techniques like future scenario planning, better prepare poten-tial options available to organisations which then have the ability to react and respond through a project if a series of events take a turn for the worse. In today's world, changing events initiate projects. But the response needs to be very rapid and so the project, vision, and scope need to be thought through, already in place, and well understood in relation to the planned response scenarios. This also requires a project team in position to enact the project according to available options. Churchill was viewed as someone with moral conviction who could pick up a cause and stay true to it, and his stature grew as he provided leadership to a project he inherited.

Source: Mark Kozak-Holland, "Churchill as Project Manager", series published in PM World Today, Vol VIII, Connecting the World of Project Management. Also Mark Kozak-Holland's website: www.lessons-from-history.com, accessed 2008-09-13.

3.2   SPECIAL DEMANDS ON THE PROJECT MANAGER

A number of demands are unique to the management of projects, and the success of the PM depends to a large extent on how capably they are handled. These special demands can be categorized under the following headings.

Acquiring Adequate Resources

It was noted earlier that the resources initially budgeted for a project are frequently insufficient to the task. In part, this is due to the natural optimism of the project proposers about how much can be accomplished with relatively few resources. Sometimes, it is caused by a deliberate, unethical understatement of resource requirements to ensure that a project is accepted for funding. At times it is caused by the great uncertainty associated with a project. Many details of resource purchase and usage are deferred until the project manager knows specifically what resources will be required and when. For instance, there is no point in purchasing a centrifuge now if in nine months we will know exactly what type of centrifuge will be most useful.

The good PM knows there are resource trade-offs that need to be taken into consideration. A skilled machinist can make do with unsophisticated machinery to construct needed parts, but a beginning machinist cannot. Subcontracting can make up for an inadequate number of computer programmers, but subcontractors will have to be carefully instructed in the needs of the contractor, which is costly and may cause delays. Crises occur that require special resources not usually provided to the project manager.

All these problems produce glitches in the otherwise smooth progress of the project. To deal with these glitches, the PM must scramble, elicit aid, work late, wheedle, threaten, or do whatever seems necessary to keep the project on schedule. On occasion, the additional required resources simply alter the project's cost-benefit ratio to the point that the project is no longer cost-effective. Obviously, the PM attempts to avoid these situations, but some of what happens is beyond the PM's control.

Project Management in Practice
A Surprise "Director of Storm Logistics" for Katrina

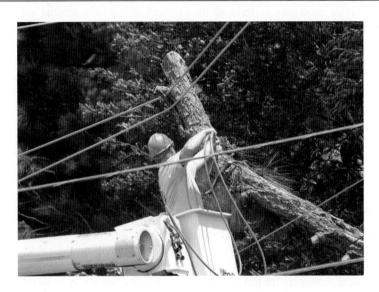

One day, Melvin Wilson was simply a marketing manager for the small 1,250-employee Mississippi Power in Gulfport, Mississippi. But the next day, after Hurricane Katrina hit New Orleans and Gulfport, he was suddenly the firm's "Director of Storm Logistics," responsible for restoring power to 195,000 customers within 12 days. Although Mississippi Power's primary storm center at headquarters was knocked out, they had a backup storm center 5 miles inland. However, when Wilson got there, the cars were floating in the parking lot, so he moved his small group in charge to a third location, an old service office without electricity or running water. In spite of the phone lines being down, the group managed to get word of their needs to the outside world and within days, 11,000 repairmen from 24 states and Canada came to help. To support the 11,000 workers, the group needed housing, beds, food, clean water, showers, laundry, bulldozers, 5,000 trucks, 140,000 gallons of fuel each day, 8,000 tetanus shots, and hundreds of other such items. Directing such a massive project as the restoration of power was far beyond the experience of little Mississippi Power's group, but they succeeded, and the power was restored to every building that could handle it within 12 days.

Source: D. Cauchon, "The Little Company That Could," *USA Today*, 2005.

The problems of time and budget are aggravated in the presence of a phenomenon that has been long suspected but only proven in the mid-1980s (Gagnon, 1982; Gagnon et al., 1987). The individual who has the responsibility for performing and completing a task sometimes overestimates the time and cost required. That individual's immediate supervisor often discounts the worker's pessimism but, in so doing, may underestimate the time and cost. Moving up the management hierarchy, each successive level frequently lowers the time and cost estimates again, becoming more optimistic about the ability of those working for them to do with less— or, perhaps, more forgetful about what things were like when they worked at such jobs. The authors have informally observed—and listened to complaints about—such doings in a variety of organizations. We suspect they reflect the superior's natural tendency to provide challenging work for subordinates and the desire to have it completed efficiently. The mere recognition of this phenomenon does not prevent it. Complaints to upper-level managers are usually met with a hearty laugh, a pat on the back, and a verbal comment such as, "I know you can do it. You're my best project manager, and you can...." We will consider the doubtful ethics in over/understating resource requirements and project schedules along with other ethical problems in Section 3.3.

Another issue may complicate the problem of resource acquisition for the PM. Project and functional managers alike perceive the availability of resources to be strictly limited and thus a strict "win-lose" proposition. Under these conditions, the "winners" may be those managers who have solid political connections with top management. Often, there are times in the life of any project when success or survival may depend on the PM's "friendship" with a champion or "sponsor" high in the parent organization (Pinto et al., 1989). For example (PMI, 2005), in 1994 a Chicago-based Commemoration Committee was formed to build a four-story, $1 million monument memorializing the 150th anniversary of the Irish potato famine. However, the project manager selected depended on a church sponsor to support the project, but in 1999 the church sponsor who championed the project had moved on to another city and the church thus stopped supporting the project. This illustrates the difficulty of a long, multiyear effort when the sponsor leaves.

Acquiring and Motivating Personnel

A major problem for the PM is the fact that most of the people needed for a project must be "borrowed" from elsewhere in the organization conducting the project. With few exceptions, they are borrowed from the functional departments. The PM must negotiate with the functional department managers for the desired personnel, and then, if successful, negotiate with the people themselves to convince them to take on these challenging temporary project assignments.

Most functional managers cooperate when the PM comes seeking good people for the project, but the cooperative spirit has its limits. The PM will be asking for the services of the two types of people most needed and prized by the functional manager: first, individuals with scarce but necessary skills and, second, top producers. Both the PM and functional manager are fully aware that the PM does not want a "has-been," a "never-was," or a "never-will-be." Perceptions about the capabilities of individuals may differ, but the PM is usually trying to borrow precisely those people the functional manager would most like to keep.

A second issue may reduce the willingness of the functional manager to cooperate with the PM's quest for quality people. At times, the functional manager may perceive the project as more glamorous than his or her function and hence a potent source of managerial glory. The functional manager may thus be a bit jealous or suspicious of the PM, a person who may have little interest in the routine work of the functional area even if it is the bread and butter of the organization.

On its surface, the task of motivating good people to join the project does not appear to be difficult, because the kind of people who are most desired as members of a project team are those naturally attracted by the challenge and variety inherent in project work. The subordinate who is being seduced to leave the steady life of the functional area for the glamour of a project can be gently reminded that the functional manager retains control of personnel evaluation, salary, and promotion for those people lent out to projects. (A few exceptions to these general rules will be discussed in Chapter 5.) There may even be comments about how easy it is to lose favor or be forgotten when one is "out of sight."

Unless the PM can hire outsiders with proven ability, it is not easy to gather competent people; but having gathered them, they must be motivated to work. Because the functional manager controls pay and promotion, the PM cannot promise much beyond the challenge of the work itself. Fortunately, as Herzberg (1968) has argued, that is often sufficient (also see Pinto et al., 1989) since many of the project personnel are professionals and experts in their respective specialties.

A story has it that when asked "How do you motivate astronauts?" a representative of NASA responded, "We don't motivate them, but, boy, are we careful about whom we select."

The issue of motivating people to join and work creatively for a project is closely related to the kind of people who are invited to join. The most effective team members have some common characteristics. A list of the most important of these follows, but only the first is typically considered during the usual selection process.

1. *High-quality technical skills* Team members should be able to solve most of the technical problems of a project without recourse to outside assistance. Even if the relevant functional department has furnished technical specialists to the project, the exact way technology is applied usually requires adaptation by the project team.

2. *Political, and general, sensitivity* It is obvious that the PM requires political skills of a high order. Though it is less obvious, project team members also need to be sensitive to organizational politics and similar matters outside their realm of normal interaction. Project success is dependent on support from senior management in the parent organization. This support depends on the preservation of a delicate balance of power between projects and functional units, and between the projects themselves. The balance can be upset by individuals who demand their own way or are otherwise insensitive to political and organization needs and constraints external to the project.

3. *Strong problem orientation* Research conducted by Pill (1971), more than 25 years before Hughes's (1998) work, has shown that the chances for successful completion of a multidisciplinary project are greatly increased if project team members are *problem-oriented* rather than *discipline-oriented*, as noted earlier. Pill indicates that problem-oriented people tend to learn and adopt whatever problem-solving techniques appear helpful, but discipline-oriented individuals tend to view the problem through the eyes of their discipline, ignoring aspects of the problem that do not lie within the narrow confines of their educational expertise.

4. *Strong goal orientation* Projects do not provide a comfortable work environment for individuals whose focus is on activity rather than on results. Work flow is rarely even, and for professionals a 60-hour week is common, as are periods when there seems to be little to do. "Clock watchers" will not be successful team members.

5. *High self-esteem* As we noted earlier, a prime law for projects (and one that applies equally well to the entire organization) is: *Never let the boss be surprised*. Projects can rapidly get into deep trouble if team members hide their failures, or even a significant risk of failure, from the PM. Of course, the PM must be aware that "shooting the messenger who brings bad news" will immediately stop the flow of any negative information. Individuals on the team should have sufficiently high levels of self-esteem that they are not threatened by acknowledgment of their own errors, or by pointing out possible problems caused by the work of others.

Dealing with Obstacles

> "What I need is a list of specific unknown problems that we will encounter."*
>
> Anonymous manager

---

*The authors received this and several other "Management Quotes" in an e-mail communication. They were reported to be entries in a magazine contest and supposedly came from "real-life managers." They have been set in a distinctive box so they will be easy to recognize. We list other such quotes in similar boxes, but without credit and without repeating this footnote.

One characteristic of any project is its uniqueness, and this characteristic means that the PM will have to face and overcome a series of crises. These crises, such as changes in the required project scope (better known as "scope creep"), affect not only the project but the PM as well, and his or her ability to make trade-offs to keep the project on track, a topic discussed further below. From the beginning of the project to its termination, crises appear without warning. The better the planning, the fewer the crises, but no amount of planning can take account of the myriad changes that can and do occur in the project's environment. The successful PM is a firefighter by avocation.

At the inception of the project, the "fires" tend to be associated with resources. The technical plans to accomplish the project have been translated into a budget and schedule, and forwarded up the managerial hierarchy or sent to the client for approval. In an earlier section we noted that some of the budget and schedule is pared away at each successive step up the hierarchy. Each time this happens, the budget and schedule cuts must be translated into changes in the technical plans. Test procedures may be shortened, suppliers' lead times may be cut. The required cost and schedule adjustments are made, a nip here and a tuck there. To the people affected, these may well be crises. As we will note in Chapter 7, an obvious cure for these crises is to "pad" the budget when it is originally submitted. This is unethical, a bad idea, and generally creates more serious problems than it solves.

To be useful, experience must be generalized and organized. Managing a project is much like managing a business. Business firms often develop special routines for dealing with various types of fires. Human resource departments help put out "people fires" just as engineering helps deal with "mechanical fires." Firefighting, to be optimally effective, should be organized so that fires are detected and recognized as early as possible. As the Reading at the end of this chapter emphatically notes, what clearly differentiates successful PMs from their counterparts is their problem *finding* ability. This allows the fires to be assigned to project team members who specialize in dealing with specific types of fires. Although this procedure does not eliminate crises, it does reduce the pain of dealing with them.

This emphasis on the need for fire-fighting raises another issue worth a brief comment. Some individuals thrive on dealing with crises. They have been referred to as "adrenaline junkies." If a PM finds such people fighting fires in her or his project, the PM should be aware that she or he may have found an arsonist. The wise PM will keep a careful eye on those who appear to be addicted to the excitement of crises.

As the project nears completion, obstacles tend to be clustered around two issues: first, last-minute schedule and technical changes, and second, a series of problems that have as their source the uncertainty surrounding what happens to members of the project team when the project is completed. These two types of problems are very different from one another, as well as from the problems that faced the PM earlier in the life cycle of the project. The way to deal with last-minute schedule and technical changes is "the best you can." Beyond knowing that such changes will occur and will be disruptive to the project, there is little the PM can do except be prepared to "scramble." Coping with the uncertainty surrounding what happens at the end of a project is a different matter. The issue will be covered at greater length in Chapter 13, but it deserves mention here because it is certainly an obstacle that the PM must overcome. The key to solving such problems is communication. The PM should make open communications between the PM and team members first priority. The notion of "open communications" requires that emotions, feelings, worries, and anxieties be communicated, as well as factual messages.

Making Project Goal Trade-offs

The PM must make trade-offs between the project goals of cost, time, and scope and, of course, the ancillary goals. The PM must also make trade-offs between project progress and process—that is, between the technical and managerial functions. The first set of trade-offs is required by the need to preserve some balance between the project time, cost, and scope goals. Conventional wisdom had it that the precise nature of the trade-offs varied depending on the stage of the project life cycle. At the beginning of the life cycle, when the project is being planned, scope was felt to be the most important of the goals, with cost and schedule sacrificed to the technical requirements of the project. Following the design phase, the project builds momentum, grows, and operates at peak levels. Because it accumulates costs at the maximum rate during this period, cost was felt to take precedence over scope and schedule. Finally, as the project nears completion, schedule becomes the high-priority goal, and cost (and perhaps scope) suffers. Research (Kalu 1993) has shown that these assumptions, sensible as they seem, are not true.

During the design or formation stage of the project life cycle, there is no significant difference in the importance project managers place on the three goals. It appears that the logic of this finding is based on the assumption that the project should be designed to meet all the client-set goals. If compromises must be made, each of the objectives is vulnerable.

Schedule is the dominant goal during the buildup stage, being significantly more important than scope, which is in turn significantly more important than cost. Kloppenborg et al. (1990, p. 127) conjectures that this is so because scheduling commitments are made during the buildup stage. Scheduling and scope are approximately tied for primacy during the main stage of the life cycle when both are significantly more important than cost. During the final stage, phaseout, scope is significantly more important than schedule, which is significantly more important than cost. Table 3-1 shows the relative importance of each objective for each stage of the project life cycle.

The second set of trade-offs concerns sacrificing smoothness of running the project team for technical progress. Near the end of the project it may be necessary to insist that various team members work on aspects of the project for which they are not well trained or which they do not enjoy, such as copying or collating the final report. The PM can get a fairly good reading on team morale by paying attention to the response to such requests.

The PM also has responsibility for other types of trade-offs, ones rarely discussed in the literature of project management. If the PM directs more than one project, he or she must make trade-offs between the several projects. As noted earlier, it is critical to avoid the appearance of favoritism in such cases. Thus, we strongly recommend that when a project manager is directing two or more projects, care should be taken to ensure that the life cycles of the projects are sufficiently different that the projects will not demand the same constrained resources at the same time, thereby avoiding forced choices between projects.

In addition to the trade-offs between the goals of a project, and in addition to trade-offs between projects, the PM will also be involved in making choices that require balancing the goals of the project with the goals of the firm. Such choices are common. Indeed, the necessity

Table 3-1 Relative Importance of Project Objectives during Different Stages of the Project Life Cycle

Life Cycle Stage	Cost	Schedule	Scope
Formation	1	1	1
Buildup	3	1	2
Main	3	1	1
Phaseout	3	2	1

Note: 1 = high importance.

Source: Kloppenborg et al., 1990, p. 78.

for such choices is inherent in the nature of project management. The PM's enthusiasm about a project—a prime requirement for successful project management—can easily lead him or her to unethical decisions: (1) overstate the benefits of a project, (2) understate the probable costs of project completion, (3) ignore technical difficulties in achieving the required level of performance, and (4) make trade-off decisions that are clearly biased in favor of the project and antithetical to the goals of the parent organization. Similarly, this enthusiasm can lead the PM to take risks not justified by the likely outcomes.

Finally, the PM must make trade-off decisions between the project, the firm, and his or her own career goals. Depending on the PM's attitudes toward risk, career considerations might lead the PM to take inappropriate risks or avoid appropriate ones.

Maintaining a Balanced Outlook

Sometimes it is difficult to distinguish whether a project is heading for failure or success. Indeed, what appears to be a failure at one point in the life of a project may look like success at another. The reality is that projects often run into technical problems or snags. More serious than the snags themselves can be the psychic consequences of such technical snags. The occurrence and solution of technical problems tend to cause waves of pessimism and optimism to sweep over the project staff.

There is little doubt that these swings of mood can have a destructive effect on performance. The PM must cope with these alternating periods of elation and despair, and the task is not simple. Performance will be strongest when project team members are "turned on," but not so much that they blandly assume that "everything will turn out all right in the end," no matter what. Despair is even worse because the project is permeated with an attitude that says, "Why try when we are destined to fail?"

Maintaining a balanced, positive outlook among team members is a delicate job. Setting budgets and schedules with sufficient slack to allow for Murphy's law, but not sufficient to arouse suspicion in cost and time-conscious senior management, is also a delicate job.

Breadth of Communication

PMBOK Guide
Chapter 10

Communication is considered a specific knowledge area (7) in PMBOK. The topic will be discussed further in the later sections of this chapter as well as Chapter 4. As pointed out clearly in the Reading at the end of this chapter, communication skills, especially listening and persuading, are the most important skills in successfully managing projects.

As is the case with any manager, most of the PM's time is spent communicating with the many groups interested in the project (Mintzberg, 1973). Running a project requires constant selling, reselling, and explaining the project to outsiders, top management, functional departments, clients, and a number of other such parties-at-interest to the project, as well as to members of the project team itself. The PM is the project's liaison with the outside world, but the manager must also be available for problem solving in the lab, for crises in the field, for threatening or cajoling subcontractors, and for reducing interpersonal conflict between project team members. And all these demands may occur within the span of one day—a typical day, cynics would say.

To some extent, every manager must deal with these special demands; but for a PM such demands are far more frequent and critical. As if this were not enough, there are also certain fundamental issues that the manager must understand and deal with so that the demands noted can be handled successfully. First, the PM must know *why* the project exists; that is, the PM must fully understand the project's intent. The PM must have a clear definition of how *success* or *failure* is to be determined. When making trade-offs, it is easy to get off the track and strive to meet goals that were really never intended by top management.

Second, any PM with extensive experience has managed projects that failed. As is true in every area of business we know, competent managers are rarely ruined by a single failure, but repeated failure is usually interpreted as a sign of incompetence. On occasion a PM is asked to take over an ongoing project that appears to be heading for failure. Whether or not the PM will be able to decline such a doubtful honor depends on factors unique to each situation: the PM's relationship with the program manager, the degree of organizational desperation about the project, the PM's seniority and track record in dealing with projects like the one in question, and other matters, not excluding the PM's being engaged elsewhere when the "opportunity" arises. Managing successful projects is difficult enough that the PM is, in general, well advised not to volunteer for undertakings with a high probability of failure.

Third, it is critical to have the support of top management (Pinto et al., 1989). If support is weak, the future of the project is clouded with uncertainty, and if it is an R & D project, it is more likely to be terminated (Green, 1995). Suppose, for example, that the marketing vice-president is not fully in support of the basic project concept. Even after all the engineering and manufacturing work has been completed, sales may not go all out to push the product. In such a case, only the chief executive officer (CEO) can force the issue, and it is very risky for a PM to seek the CEO's assistance to override a lukewarm vice-president. If the VP acquiesces and the product fails (and what are the chances for success in such a case?), the project manager looks like a fool. If the CEO does not force the issue, then the VP has won and the project manager may be out of a job. As noted earlier, political sensitivity and acumen are mandatory attributes for the project manager. The job description for a PM should include the "construction and maintenance of alliances with the leaders of functional areas."

Fourth, the PM should build and maintain a solid information network. It is critical to know what is happening both inside and outside the project in order to head off potential problems, a major skill of successful PMs, as noted earlier. The PM must be aware of customer complaints and department head criticism, who is favorably inclined toward the project, when vendors are planning to change prices, or if a strike is looming in a supplier industry. Inadequate information can blind the PM to an incipient crisis just as excessive information can desensitize the PM to early warnings of trouble.

Finally, the PM must be flexible in as many ways, with as many people, and about as many activities as possible throughout the entire life of the project. The PM's primary mode of operation is to trade off resources and criteria accomplishment against one another. Every decision the PM makes limits the scope of future decisions, but failure to decide can stop the project in its tracks.

Project Management in Practice
Channel Tunnel

The Channel Tunnel was one of the largest privately financed engineering projects in history. The tunnel was a dream for about two centuries. The 50.45 km long tunnel fulfilled this old dream by linking Britain and the rest of Europe when it became operational in mid-1995, and is a crucial link in the European high-speed rail system.

The Channel Tunnel consists of three tunnels. Trains enter the tunnels at terminals located at Folkestone in the county of Kent in Southeast England and at Calais in the Nord-Pas-de-Calais region of France. The tunnels contain a railway system which takes shuttle trains between the terminals, and through-trains which link with the national rail networks of France and Great Britain. Through two of the tubes rush the broadest trains ever built — double-decker behemoths 4.2 m across — travelling at close to 160 km/h.

The project involved installing huge infrastructure containing massive machinery and control systems in an underwater tunnel system. The tunnels connect England and France 50 m below the seabed of the English Channel and 38 km of the 50.45 km are under sea. Three concrete tubes, each 1.5 m thick, plunge into the earth at Coquelles, France, and burrow through the chalky basement of the English Channel. They re-emerge at Folkstone, behind the white cliffs of Dover. The tunnels are 30 m apart and were bored in the rock strata under the Channel at an average depth of 45 m (50 m maximum) below the seabed. The two larger tunnels (7.6 m in diameter) each contain a single-track railway line. The smaller service tunnel, for ventilation, maintenance and safety access, (4.8 m in diameter) is located between the two rail tunnels and is equipped with a wire guidance system for specially designed service tunnel vehicles. All three tunnels are connected every 375 m by a cross-passage which gives access to the service tunnel in case of emergency. The cross-passages are also used for ventilation and maintenance service access. Every 200 m, the two rail tunnels are linked by piston relief ducts to allow the passage of air through the tunnels, thereby reducing the aerodynamic resistance of the trains passing through at speeds of up to 160 km/h. All three tunnels are lined with concrete linings. The rail track consists of continuously welded rails set on rubber pads fixed to individual pairs of concrete blocks. The blocks are cast into a concrete track bed to provide firm, smooth running.

Nearly 13,000 engineers, technicians and workers constructed the tunnel. Engineering geological investigations were carried out on Shakespeare Cliff in England and on Sangatte in France. The geology of undersea crossovers were characterised as sedimentary rock layers of chalk, chalk marl and gault clay type down to a depth of 50 m beneath seabed. The data from geophysical surveys provided information about the geology and helped to determine the alignment and route of the tunnel. To maximise the favourable ground conditions, the tunnels were excavated in the layer of chalk marl except for a 3 km section on the French side. Special tunnel boring machines (TBMs) were designed for excavating the chalk marl rock. The ground conditions were expected to be generally

favourable in the dry and stable chalk marl, except for the section to be bored in the layer of upper chalk between Sangatte and the terminal site at Coquelles. It was a challenge for those 11 TBMs because the considerable length of tunnel would be driven under the sea, a high advance rate was required in construction programme, and there was a high probability of facing unexpected ground conditions. The facts below give an indication of the performance of TBMs, and the achievement of all the engineers and workers involved in this remarkable engineering task.

Number of drives: (tunnels excavated): 12-6 undersea, 6 underland

Number of TBMs: 11-6 undersea, 5 underland (a French machine bored 2 underland tunnels)

Rate of advance (UK TBMS): Best day 75.5 m; best week 428 m; best month 1,719.1 m

Rate of advance (FRENCH TBMS): Best day 56 m; best week 292.6 m; best month 1,105.7 m

Dates of breakthroughs: Undersea service tunnel 1 December 1990; undersea rail tunnel north 22 May 1991; undersea rail tunnel south 28 June 1991

Date tunnelling commenced: 1 December 1987

Finished tunnel diameter: Rail tunnels 7.6 m, service tunnel 4.8 m

In France, the construction of the Channel Tunnel began at Sangatte on the Nord-Pas-de-Calais coastline at a location just over 3 km away from the French terminal site at Coquelles. A circular access shaft, 70 m deep and 55 m in diameter, was excavated and lined with concrete. A shed was built to shelter the shaft in the centre of the large construction site, which also contained offices and a lining segment manufacturing factory.

All materials, workers and equipment were lowered down the shaft to the working platform at 47 m, where the tunnel boring machines could be assembled in dry conditions. From this point, 3 machines excavated the undersea rail tunnels and service tunnel beneath the seabed towards Kent and two boring machines began the drive underground and inland towards the terminal site. One of these machines was then re-assembled to excavate the second running tunnel, thus only 5 machines were used on the French side.

Construction work began on the British side at a platform located at the foot of Shakespeare Cliff. The site, situated between Folkestone and Dover on the Kent coast, had been used for the previous tunnel attempt in 1974. The earlier tunnel workings were used as one of the two access shafts to the underground workings. The equipment and material were transported via a rack-and-pinion railway system to the marshalling area underground. The 6 TBMs were each assembled in a large cavern area (over 20 m high and equipped with overhead cranes for lifting the TBM sections) which had first been excavated to accommodate the 8.6 m diameter machines. From this point under the platform at Shakespeare Cliff, 3 undersea tunnels were bored towards France, and 3 underground tunnels towards the terminal site at Folkestone.

The service tunnel machines at both ends bored in advance of the two running tunnel machines. Probes on the service tunnel machines provided advance warning of difficult ground conditions and the data obtained provided information on alignment and conditions for the larger tunnel drives.

Work on the Folkestone terminal started in 1988 with a major land-fill engineering project in order to provide the level area needed for the railway transport system. The site chosen for the terminal at Coquelles, near Calais, required a major drainage exercise and millions of tonnes of earth were spread and compacted to lay the foundations for the 480 hectare terminal complex.

The Channel Tunnel was opened for business around mid-1995 and cost in excess of £10 billion. However, the Channel Tunnel project itself had been beset, since its inception, by financial and technical woes, lagging schedules, and highly public battles between the Anglo-French company managing the project (Eurotunnel) and its contractors. During the project there were major cost and time overruns. The total cost of the project had been estimated at £4.9 billion in 1987 yet cost more than £10 billion when completed, while the expected date of completion for the tunnel was delayed several times. Private funding for such a complex infrastructure project was at an unprecedented scale. An initial equity of £45 million was raised by Channel Tunnel Group/France–Manche (CTG/F-M), increased by £206 million in private institutional placement; £770 million was raised in a public share offer that included press and television advertisements; a syndicated bank load and letter of credit arranged £5 billion. Privately financed, the total investment costs at 1985 prices were £2,600 million. At the 1994 completion, actual costs were, in 1985 prices, £4,650 million: an 80% cost overrun. The cost overrun was partly due to enhanced safety, security, and environmental demands. Financing costs were 140% higher than forecast.

The Channel Tunnel Group consisted of 2 banks and 5 construction companies, and the French equivalent, France–Manche, consisted of 3 banks and 5 construction companies. The role of the banks was to advise on financing and secure loan commitments. The design and construction was done by the 10 construction companies in the CTG/F-M group. The French terminal and boring from Sangatte was undertaken by the 5 French construction companies in the joint venture group GIE Transmanche Construction. The English Terminal and boring from Shakespeare Cliff was undertaken by 5 English construction companies in the Trankslink Joint Venture. The 2 partnerships were linked by TransManche Link (TML), a binational project organisation. The Maître d'Oeuvre was a supervisory engineering body employed by Eurotunnel under the terms of the concession that monitored project activity and reported back to the governments and banks.

Source: http://www.itc.nl/~ingeokri/newsletter/summer98/new page1.html.

Negotiation

In order to meet the demands of the job of project manager—acquiring adequate resources, acquiring and motivating personnel, dealing with obstacles, making project goal trade-offs, maintaining a balanced outlook, and establishing a broad network of communication—the project manager must be a highly skilled negotiator. There is almost no aspect of the PM's job that does not depend directly on this skill. We have noted the need for negotiation at several points in the previous pages, and we will note the need again and again in the pages that follow. The subject is so important, Chapter 4 is devoted to a discussion of the matter.

3.3   ATTRIBUTES OF EFFECTIVE PROJECT MANAGERS

Selection of the project manager is one of the two or three most important decisions concerning the project. In this section, we note a few of the many skills the PM should possess in order to have a reasonable chance of success.

The following is a list of some of the most popular attributes, skills, and qualities that have been sought when selecting project managers:

- A strong technical background
- A hard-nosed manager
- A mature individual
- Someone who is currently available
- Someone on good terms with senior executives
- A person who can keep the project team happy
- One who has worked in several different departments
- A person who can walk on (or part) the waters

These reasons for choosing a PM are not so much wrong as they are "not right." They miss the key criterion. Above all, the best PM is *the one who can get the job done*! As any senior manager knows, hard workers are easy to find. What is rare is the individual whose focus is on the completion of a difficult job, a "closer." Of all the characteristics desirable in a PM, this *drive to complete the task* is the most important.

If we consider the earlier sections of this chapter, we can conclude that there are four major categories of skills that are required of the PM and serve as the key criteria for selection, given that the candidate has a powerful bias toward task completion. Moreover, it is not sufficient for the PM simply to possess these skills; they must also be perceived by others. The fact and the perception are both important.

Credibility

The PM needs two kinds of credibility. First is *technical credibility*. The PM must be perceived by the client, senior executives, the functional departments, and the project team as possessing sufficient technical knowledge to direct the project. A PM with reasonable technical competence seems to be associated with project success and is seen by project team members to be a "positive" leadership characteristic (Ford et al., 1992; Zimmerer et al., 1998). (We remind the reader that "technical credibility" includes technical knowledge in such arcane fields as accounting, law, psychology, anthropology, religion, history, playwriting,

Greek, and a host of other nonhard sciences.) The PM does not need to have a high level of expertise, know more than any individual team members (or all of them), or be able to stand toe-to-toe and intellectually slug it out with experts in the various functional areas. Quite simply, the PM has to have a reasonable understanding of the base technologies on which the project rests, must be able to explain project technology to senior management, and must be able to interpret the technical needs and wants of the client (and senior management) to the project team. Similarly, the PM must be able to hear the problems of the project team and understand them sufficiently to address them, possibly by communicating them to upper management.

Second, the PM must be *administratively credible*. The PM has several key administrative responsibilities that must be performed with apparently effortless skill. One of these responsibilities is to the client and senior management—to keep the project on schedule and within cost and to make sure that project reports are accurate and timely. This can place the PM in an ethically awkward situation sometimes. Another responsibility is to the project team—to make sure that material, equipment, and labor are available when and where needed. Still another responsibility is to represent the interests of all stakeholders (team, management, functional departments, community, and client) to one another. The PM is truly the "person in the middle." Finally, the PM is responsible for making the tough trade-off decisions for the project, and must be perceived as a person who has the mature judgment and courage to do so consistently.

Sensitivity

The preceding pages contain many references to the PM's need for political sensitivity. There is no point in belaboring the issue further. In addition to a good, working set of political antennae, the PM needs to sense interpersonal conflict on the project team or between team members and outsiders. Successful PMs are not conflict avoiders. Quite the opposite, they sense conflict early, then confront and deal with it before the conflict escalates into interdepartmental and intradepartmental warfare.

The PM must keep project team members "cool." This is not easy. As with any group of humans, rivalries, jealousies, friendships, and hostilities are sure to exist. The PM must persuade people to cooperate irrespective of personal feelings, to set aside personal likes and dislikes, and to focus on achieving project goals.

Finally, the PM needs a sensitive set of technical sensors. It is common, unfortunately, for otherwise competent and honest team members to try to hide their failures. Individuals who cannot work under stress would be well advised to avoid project organizations. In the pressure-cooker life of the project, failure is particularly threatening. Remember that we staffed the team with people who are task-oriented. Team members with this orientation may not be able to tolerate their own failures (though they are rarely as intolerant of failure in others), and may hide failure rather than admit to it. The PM must be able to sense when things are being "swept under the rug" and are not progressing properly.

Leadership, Ethics, and Management Style

Leadership has been defined (Tannenbaum et al., 1957) as "interpersonal influence, exercised in situations and directed through the communication process, toward the attainment of a specified goal or goals." Much has been written about how interpersonal influence is generated and the impact of leadership characteristics on team performance. Examples are Jiang et al. (1998); Scott et al. (1998); see also the bibliography.

The following discussion is based on Müller and Turner (2010). Many approaches have been postulated to develop a coherent leadership theory: the trait school, the behavioral school, and the contingency school, to mention only the first three of several. Recently, the competency school has combined parts of all earlier "schools" by defining various leadership qualities with three major areas of competence; intellectual (IQ), managerial (MQ), and emotional (EQ). The leadership competencies associated with the three areas are shown in Table 3-2.

It has been well established that for different types of projects to be successful, project managers need different types of skills. Müller and Turner (2010) showed that engineering (and construction) projects, IT projects, and organizational change projects all required different levels of the 15 competencies to be successful. Further, they showed that the competency levels required varied with the complexity of the project, the importance of the project, and with the type of contract under which the project was carried out. We will return to the relationship between leadership competencies, level of complexity, and project success, including project type, in later chapters.

Another aspect of leadership that is important in a project manager is a strong sense of ethics. There is a considerable amount of attention to this topic in the news media these days, both good and bad, such as Enron, Lehman Brothers' use of Repo 105 (to get debt off their balance sheet), and of course, Bernie Madoff. Though less clear, some situations raise serious ethical questions such as:

- BP's subcontracting and safety procedures before the Gulf oil spill
- Goldman Sachs betting both ways on the synthetic CDO (collateralized debt obligation) it created for John Paulson to bet against the housing market
- protection payments made to terrorists by firms
- mining companies' safety procedures

Table 3-2   Three Styles of Leadership and Fifteen Leadership Competencies. (Dulewicz et al., 2003)

Area of Competence	*Competency*
Intellectual (IQ)	1. Critical analysis and judgment
	2. Vision and imagination
	3. Strategic perspective
Managerial (MQ)	4. Engaging communication
	5. Managing resources
	6. Empowering
	7. Developing
	8. Achieving
Emotional (EQ)	9. Self-awareness
	10. Emotional resilience
	11. Motivation
	12. Sensitivity
	13. Influence
	14. Intuitiveness
	15. Conscientiousness

Nixon (1987) has identified some ethical missteps that are relatively common in business:

- "wired" bids and contracts (the winner has been predetermined)
- "buy-in" (bidding low with the intent of cutting corners or forcing subsequent contract changes)
- kickbacks
- "covering" for team members (group cohesiveness)
- taking "shortcuts" (to meet deadlines or budgets)
- using marginal (substandard) materials
- compromising on safety
- violating standards
- consultant (e.g., auditors) loyalties (to employer or to client or to public)

A project manager, particularly in the public sector, may easily become embroiled in the ethics concerning such issues as pollution, public safety, industrial plant locations, the use of public lands, and so on. A Code of Ethics for project managers was created at the PMI 1982 symposium on Project Management (Ireland et al., 1982), updated and approved in 1989, again in 1995, and once more in 2006. The 2006 version of the Code resulted from extended discussions and is roughly 8 times the length of earlier versions—including appendices. It is available to anyone at the PMI website, *www.PMI.org*. The issue is receiving an increasing amount of attention.

Anyone seriously considering a career in project management should study the new code. It focuses on behavior that will lead to a high trust level between the PM, project team members, senior management, the client, and other stakeholders. The section entitled "Honesty" should be read, reread, and read once again. We will revisit the subjects of honesty and trust in almost every chapter of this book.

An "ethics audit" has also been recommended for nonprofit organizations (Schaefer et al., 1998), and we would recommend a similar audit for any firm. The extent of this subject is far beyond what we can cover here, but, fortunately, there are a number of excellent books on the topic (Barry, 1979; Blanchard et al., 1988; Pastin, 1986). A concise bibliography on business ethics is included in Robb (1996).

While a great deal has been written about the leadership attributes required or desirable in a project manager, comparatively little has been written about the proper management style for a PM. Shenhar (1998) classifies projects across two dimensions and concludes that management style should be adapted to certain differences in the type of project. His dimensions are: (1) the level of technological uncertainty; and (2) the level of system complexity. As the uncertainty increases from "low tech" to "high tech," the appropriate management style progresses from "firm, rigid, and formal" to "highly flexible." As the system complexity increases from simple to highly complex, the style progresses from "in-house informal" to "remote and highly formal."

Ability to Handle Stress

Throughout this chapter and elsewhere in this book, we have noted that the life of the project manager is rarely serene. The PM is surrounded by conflict, often caught in an irrational management structure (described further in Chapter 5), and trapped in a high-stress occupation.

Kent (2008) identifies six signs of excessive stress in the workplace: (1) inability to switch-off work issues, (2) disturbed sleep, (3) lack of pleasure in non-work related leisure activities,

(4) difficulty concentrating or making decisions, (5) tendency to anger quickly, and (6) lack of energy. There are ways to deal with excessive stress. It is best if the organization is attuned to the problem and monitors their PMs and employees for work overload. Also, the PM should be self-aware and spot the danger signals early. Kent suggests several ways to control stress:

1. Keep a journal, taking time to reflect on the events of the day.

2. Prioritize all tasks facing you, eliminating tasks that do not really need to be done, transferring or delegating what you can, delaying low priority items, and minimizing the scope of any subtask that is not crucial to your overall task.

3. Give yourself time to unwind from high stress meetings, perhaps by taking a short walk or doing 15 minutes of exercise or meditation. Avoid meditating on the high-stress meeting.

4. Engage in after-work physical activities that take your mind off the tasks.

5. Improve your physical surroundings so they are pleasant, enjoyable, and comfortable, helping you to relax.

6. Become aware of the control you do or do not have over events. One of the great laws of living is "Do not develop anxiety about things over which you have no control!"

One way PMs try to handle excess work is by "multitasking." But as Hunsberger (2008) points out, this does not work. In fact, multitasking is a misnomer. What you are doing is switching back and forth between tasks. You lose time whenever you do this. Her advice is to divide your tasks into small steps, prioritize them on a to-do list, be proactive by tackling and completing tasks as soon as possible, and then cross them off the list. If you can't finish in one sitting, leave notes that trigger your memory about where you were when you were interrupted.

There are numerous factors in life that cause stress, and project managers are as prone to them as other humans. There do, however, appear to be four major causes of stress often associated with the management of projects. First, some PMs never develop a reasonably consistent set of procedures and techniques with which to manage their work. Second, many simply have "too much on their plates." Third, some have a high need to achieve that is consistently frustrated. Fourth, the parent organization is in the throes of major change.

This book is primarily devoted to helping the PM deal with the first cause of stress. As for the second cause, we would remind the PM to include him/herself as a "resource" when planning a project. Almost all project management software packages will signal the planner when a project plan calls for a resource to be used beyond its capacity (see Chapters 9 and 10). Such signals, at least, provide PMs with some evidence with which to discuss the work load with the appropriate senior manager.

Concerning the third cause of stress, Slevin (1989) points out that stress results when the demands made on an individual are greater than the person's ability to cope with them, particularly when the person has a high need for achievement. It is axiomatic that senior managers give the toughest projects to their best project managers. It is the toughest projects that are most apt to be beset with unsolvable problems. The cure for such stress is obvious, except to the senior managers who continue the practice.

Finally, in this era of restructuring and downsizing, stress from worry about one's future is a common condition in modern organizations. Dealing with and reducing these stresses as well as the stress resulting from everyday life is beyond the scope of this book as well as the expertise of its authors. Fortunately, any bookstore will have entire sections devoted to the subject of stress and its relief.

Project Management in Practice
Why Project Managers Need to Have Local Knowledge

Despite globalisation many different calendars and clocks coexist and will most likely continue to do so in the future. It is very improbable that centuries of history will be completely changed by the pressures of current commerce. Project managers need to aware of such local knowledge and nuances while scheduling projects. For example, the beginning of the lunar New Year is the same for many people from the Indian states of Karnataka and Andhra Pradesh, but it is different from the days for those from the states of Tamil Nadu and Gujarat. Hence, even when a person is located in a different state, he or she may celebrate the New Year on the day it is celebrated in that person's state of origin.

In India, where large construction projects are undertaken in cities, most of the workers come from villages in different parts of the country. Many of these workers have very strong cultural ties with their villages. Accordingly, the construction workers return to their village to attend to a village festival or to help during the harvesting. This time is specific to the region from where the person comes. Most of these festivals are based on the lunar calendar and hence do not fall on the same day of the Gregorian calendar each year. One has to consult the local almanac to determine their date. Other local nuances to be taken into account while determining project delivery include the following examples:

- Most workers will not commence work at an inauspicious period of day called *rau kala*. This period varies by the day of the week and the geographical location and can be found by consulting a local almanac. Similarly, no important work is started on a Tuesday because it is considered inauspicious.

- Carpenters from Rajasthan take off only once a fortnight. They do not work on a new moon or full moon day.

- Plastering masons from the states of Bihar and Rajasthan are known for their long working hours and high productivity. Starting with the Ayudha Puja day during Dussher, a the workers may not use their tools for nearly a week, depending upon the region from which they come. On this day people decorate and worship the tools of their trade.

Similarly, while a project's events may be marked on the Gregorian calendar, many social, personal, and even professional events are likely to be marked on or driven by the local calendar. Some of these latter events embody deep-rooted beliefs and traditions, as illustrated in the examples above. Violating them would be a taboo; complying with them, on the other hand, would require local knowledge, some of which may be elusive even to a native.

While the multitude of calendars and clocks may appear to pose an unbearable burden on a project manager if one has to accommodate all of them, there is a brighter side to the same picture. Adherence to a clock or calendar, albeit different from the western ones, often reflects a social discipline and a deep commitment to core values critical for project management. A worker not wanting to start a project on a particular day or at a particular time of day may be an inconvenience. At the same time underlying that behaviour may be an implicit commitment to finishing the project on time by beginning at a propitious time. Would it be worthwhile to sacrifice the start date and time for the sake of psychological commitment from, and satisfaction of, the employee? Could a project manager elicit such cooperation by harmonising with the local context but yet not compromising on the overall goals?

Source: Arkalgud Ramaprasad and A N Praksah, *Emergent Project Management: How Foreign Project Managers can Leverage Local Knowledge,* International Journal of Project Management, Vol. 21, pp. 199–205, 2003.

3.4 PROBLEMS OF CULTURAL DIFFERENCES*

In this section, we raise a number of issues that plague certain projects. Sometimes these projects require cooperation by individuals and groups from different countries. Sometimes they require cooperation by individuals or groups in one country, but from different industries or even from different divisions of the same firm. It is not, however, the geographical or organizational differences that matter, it is the differences in *cultures*. Moreover, it is not merely the differences in culture that matter, it is also differences in the *environments* within which projects are conducted, as we mentioned at the start of this chapter, the economic, political, legal, and sociotechnical environments. While the impacts of these dissimilarities are greatest and most visible in the case of international projects, they exist, to some extent, any time different organizations (including different parts of one organization) are asked to work together on a project. Throughout this book we emphasize that the PM must manage and reduce conflict between the parties-at-interest or stakeholders in a project: the project team, client, senior management, and the public. If the parties-at-interest represent different nations, industries, and firms, the conflicts and problems besetting the project are greater by an order of magnitude.

"Culture" refers to the entire way of life for a group of people. It encompasses every aspect of living and has four elements that are common to all cultures: technology, institutions, language, and arts (*The World Book*, 1997). The *technology* of a culture includes such things as the tools used by people, the material things they produce and use, the way they prepare food, their skills, and their attitudes toward work. It embraces all aspects of their material lives. The *institutions* of a culture make up the structure of the society: the organization of the government, the nature of the family, the way in which religion is organized, the division of labor, the kind of economic system adopted, the system of education, and the way in which voluntary associations are formed and maintained.

Language, another ingredient of all cultures, is always unique because it is developed in ways that meet the express needs of the culture. The translation of one culture's language into another's is rarely precise because words carry connotative meanings as well as denotative meanings. The English word "apple" may denote a fruit, but it also connotes health ("keeps the doctor away"), bribery ("for the teacher"), New York city, a color, a computer, a dance (late 1930s), favoritism ("of my eye"), as well as several other things. Finally, the *arts* or aesthetic values of a culture are as important to communication as the culture's language. Aesthetic values dictate what is found beautiful and satisfying. If a society can be said to have "style," it is from the culture's aesthetic values that style has its source.

Culture and the Project

A nation's culture affects projects in many ways. One of the most obvious ways is in how people of different cultures regard time. In the United States and several other Western industrialized nations, time is highly valued as a resource (Smith et al., 1993). We say, "Time is money." It isn't, of course, but the expression is one way of expressing impatience with delay and lateness. Latin Americans, on the other hand, hold quite different views of time. The pace of life differs from one culture to another, just as do the values that people place on family or success. The PM conducting a construction project in South America will learn that to be half-an-hour late to a project meeting is to be "on time." In Japan, lateness causes loss of face. In some cultures, the quality of the work is seen to be considerably more important than on-time delivery. The great value placed on time in the United States and the distaste for tardiness leads to a common perception that U.S. managers are "impatient."

---

*Occasionally, particular sections will be shaded, meaning that they can be skipped without loss of continuity.

The fundamental philosophy of staffing projects varies greatly in different cultures. In Latin America, for example, the *compadre* system leads a manager to give preference to relatives and friends when hiring.* U.S. managers feel that such practices are a major source of inefficiency in Latin American firms. In fact, there appears to be scant evidence that this is so. One private study of several firms in the U.S. and Latin American chemical industries indicates that the differences in management practices between U.S. and Latin American chemical firms were, in general, significantly less than the differences between the U.S. chemical firms and U.S. clothing manufacturers.

The United States is, by far, the most litigious society on this planet. This does not mean that there are fewer disagreements in other societies, but rather that there is less recourse to courts of law, and, therefore, more recourse to trust and negotiation as a means of resolving conflict. Many authors have noted that trust plays an important role in business relationships (Gogal et al., 1988, for example). The impact of trust on project management, with its dependence on the ability and willingness of others to meet commitments, is clear. The importance of trust is also demonstrated by the critical role played by the *compadre* system in Latin America. Use of a general agreement with the extended family, as trusted suppliers to a project, for example, is a substitute for the detailed and highly explicit contracts usually required for dealing with "arms-length" suppliers in the United States.

In recent years, certain types of collaboration between competitors have grown rapidly, even in the United States (Rosegger et al., 1990). In the United States, SEMATECH is a consortium of semiconductor manufacturers conducting joint research projects in the field, one example among many of collaborative efforts allowed by the National Cooperative Research Act passed in 1984. European nations have also backed research consortia; for example, between 1961 and 1983, Japan initiated more than 60 research consortia, some with more than 40 members (Lynn et al., 1988).

The move to collaborative projects has also been transnational. Airbus Industries, the British-French-German-Spanish venture, operating with financial support from its several governments, has achieved outstanding success in commercial aircraft development and production. Other examples are CFM International composed of GE (USA) and Snecma (France), and International Aero Engines composed of Pratt & Whitney (USA), Rolls Royce (UK), Japan Aero Engines, MTU (Germany), and Fiat (Italy).

A view almost uniformly held by other societies is that U.S. managers understand everything about technology and nothing about people (e.g., Smith et al., 1993). This view apparently originates in the desire to "get down to business," while many foreign cultures—certainly Asian, Middle Eastern, Latin American, and southern European—value "getting to know you" as a precursor to the trust required to have satisfying business relationships. In many cultures, the manager is expected to take a personal interest in his or her subordinates' lives, to pay calls on them, to take an interest in the successes of family members, and to hold a caring attitude. On the other hand, it is clear that U.S. project managers are being urged to value cultural diversity in ways that are often not shared by their foreign cohorts.

For at least three-quarters of the world's population, relationship comes above all else: above time, above budget, above specification. The savvy project manager knows this and knows that he or she will always be balancing, for instance, the needs of the Japanese for meeting deadlines against the Latin American tendency toward a more relaxed approach to dealing with others (Dodson, 1998). We will have much more to say about negotiation in the next chapter.

---

*We are quite aware that the *compadre* system is a system of networks of extended family members, and is far more complex than is implied in this simple example.

For some years, management theorists have been writing about "corporate culture." We call these "microcultures" to differentiate them from the broader national or regional cultures about which we have been writing. It is just as true, though less obvious, to observe that microcultures vary from industry to industry and from firm to firm, just as cultures do from nation to nation. Sales techniques perfectly permissible in one industry, the wholesale automobile industry, for instance, would cause outrage and lawsuits in the business-machine industry. Promises have very different meanings in different areas of business. No one takes seriously the "promised" date of completion of a software application project, any more than a finish-date promise made by a home-remodeling contractor.

The impact of interindustry, interfirm, and intrafirm microcultural diversity on the project manager is significant. Perhaps more than any other type of manager, the PM is dependent on commitments made by people, both inside and outside the parent organization, who owe little allegiance to the project, have little cause for loyalty to the PM, and over whom the PM has little or no *de jure* authority. Hence, the PM must know whose promises can be relied upon and whose cannot. In a major study of 50 transnational projects, Hauptman et al. (1996) found that the accomplishment of product development teams depended on the skill with which they handled two-way communication and cultural differences. On the positive side, Levinson et al. (1995) spell out several steps that allow "interorganizational learning" for groups that form international alliances (see also, Fedor et al., 1996).

Project Management in Practice
Success at Energo by Integrating Two Diverse Cultures

A major project involving some hundreds of millions of dollars was stymied due to the cultural differences between the owner/client, a state-run Middle Eastern developer, and the contractor, a state-run European international designer and builder of industrial and construction projects. As can be imagined, the difference in the cultures is extreme and includes religion, the role of women in society, the difference in power between managers and workers, and the style of management itself. These differences were exacerbated by the conditions surrounding the project: an isolated desert, poor communication, extremely harsh living/ working conditions, and a highly unstable legal/ political environment (taxes, regulations, restrictions, even client reorganizations) that was changing daily.

The client and contractor came to realize that the two separate organizational systems created an interface, or boundary, between them that was almost impenetrable. They thus decided to try to integrate the two systems into one unified system (see Exhibit 1). This was done methodically, with a plan being drawn up, environmental impacts recognized, restructuring of the overall organization, designing the integration, and then implementing the design.

As perhaps expected, neither side's personnel were able to give up their perspective to see the larger picture. The project managers kept working on this issue, however, watched for problems, did a lot of management-by-walking-around, and gradually, the integration began to occur, gathering speed as it went. At project termination, when all costs and engineering changes were hammered out for final payment by tough external bargaining agents (rather than by principled negotiation, typically), no agreement could be reached. Instead, the project managers were brought back and allowed to terminate the project in their own fashion. They simply continued the integration process they had used earlier and quietly phased out the successful project.

EXHIBIT 1 Examples of Integrative Actions.

The Project Style Characteristics		Actions
Physical Appearance:	Counterparts working together (teamwork) Project-related pictures, charts, and schedules on office walls	Tour the site with counterpart project manager daily Make your office look like a "war room"
Myths and Stories:	We are one team with two sides Both cultures are interesting Both sides' interests should be satisfied We trust young managers Get the job done Separate yourself from the position and stick to the problem Both project managers are good, and committed to the project	Whenever possible, let the counterparts have a joint office Organize group visits to local historical sites
Ceremonies:	Gather ideas and information from all over the project organization Frequent meetings at all levels Frequent social gatherings and festivities	From time to time, attend lower-level joint project meetings Celebrate each key event completion
Management Style:	Plan, organize, and control with your counterparts Make decisions No finger pointing for wrong decisions, learn the lesson Quickly execute the decision If you need help, don't hesitate to refer to your boss	Ask counterparts for joint report on an issue Recognize high-performance managers monthly

Source: D. Z. Milosevic, "Case Study: Integrating the Owner's and the Contractor's Project Organization," *Project Management Journal*, Vol. 21.

Popular movies and television to the contrary, the intentions of foreign governments and their officials are rarely evil. Foreign governments are usually devoted to ensuring that local citizens are well-treated by invading companies, that national treasures are not disturbed, that employment for their nationals is maximized, that some profits are reinvested in the host country, that safety regulations are not violated, and that other unintended exploitations are prevented. At times, rules and regulations may result from ancient traditions—no consumption of alcoholic beverages in Islamic nations, no consumption of pork products in Israel.

The job description of any PM should include responsibility for acquiring a working knowledge of the culture of any country in which he or she is to conduct a project. As far as possible, the project should be conducted in such a way that host-country norms are honored. To do so, however, will often raise problems for management of the parent firm. An unwelcome truth is that the cultures of many countries will not offer a female PM the same level of respect shown a male PM. Thus, senior management is faced with the awkward choice of violating its own policy against sex discrimination or markedly increasing the risk of project failure. The same problem may also exist with the use of a Jewish PM in an Arab country, or an Armenian PM in Turkey.

In Chapter 5 we will discuss "virtual" projects, which are transfunctional and/or geographically dispersed. Multicultural projects are "virtual" by definition. In recent years, communication problems have been greatly eased for virtual projects through e-mail, the Internet, conference calls, and videoconferencing (Dodson, 1998). While overused e-mail may be a curse for project managers, it is also a blessing when frequent communication with other organizations is required. Of course, these technologies do not relieve the PM from the demands of cultural sensitivity. Though it is not electronic, the technology of negotiation is critical for the PM with a multicultural project. Dodson writes:

> Project management is ultimately expectation management. Effective management of expectations requires negotiation skills that eclipse more quantitative, "metrical" skills. Projects are only as successful as the degree to which the project manager is an effective negotiator....

We have already noted the difference in the bottom-up flow of information in American projects and the top-down flow in countries where the management style is authoritarian. Grinbergs et al. (1993) compare the managerial characteristics of Swiss and American managers/engineers of the same general age, education, and salary levels, all of whom were working on software projects. The study revealed that Swiss managers were "much more formal" with each other than Americans. This demonstrates the interaction of interpersonal style and language. Because we have emphasized planning so strongly in this book, we find the differences in the Swiss and American approaches to planning of special interest. "The U.S. respondents did not consider thorough planning and a long-term strategy as absolute prerequisites for beginning a project.... Though promptness is highly valued in both countries, long-term strategy is considered much more important in the Swiss company" (Grinbergs et al., 1993, p. 24).

In addition to these areas, the Swiss and Americans differed in a number of other ways of import to the PM. The Swiss showed a stronger work ethic, were more resistant to change, were more risk averse, more accepting of bureaucracy, and more focused on quality. The Americans were more collegial, more willing to experiment and innovate, had a shorter time horizon, and communicated more openly.

Dinsmore et al. (1993) list factors that they contend require special consideration by the PM heading a multicultural project. We have already noted some of these factors, and others are obvious: the importance of language and culture, the need to deal with the politics and politicians in the host nation, the fact that the PM may have to use indigenous staff members, the possibility of input supply and technology problems, and the need to obey local laws and customs. In addition, they note two other matters that may cause serious problems for the PM. First, there are additional risk factors such as kidnapping, disease, and faulty medical care. Of course, in many countries, project workers may face less risk from crime than in their home country as well as easier access to medical care. Second, the PM may have to provide for the physical and psychological needs of people who are transferred to the host nation and must live in a "strange land with different customs and way of life." They refer to this as the "expatriate way of life."

SUMMARY

This chapter addressed the subject of the PM. The PM's role in the organization and responsibilities to both the organization and the project team were discussed first. Common PM career paths were also described. Next, the unique demands typically placed on project managers were detailed and the task of selecting the PM was addressed. Last, the issue of culture and its effect on project communication and success was discussed.

The following specific points were made in the chapter.

Two factors crucial to the success of the project are its support by top management and the existence of a problem orientation, rather than discipline orientation, within the team members.

Compared to a functional manager, a PM is a generalist rather than a specialist, a synthesizer rather than an analyst, and a facilitator rather than a supervisor.

The PM has responsibilities to the parent organization, the project itself, and the project team. The unique demands on a PM concern seven areas:

- Acquiring adequate physical resources
- Acquiring and motivating personnel
- Dealing with obstacles
- Making goal trade-offs
- Maintaining a balanced outlook in the team
- Communicating with all parties
- Negotiating

The most common characteristics of effective project team members are:

- High-quality technical skills
- Political sensitivity
- Strong problem orientation
- High self-esteem

To handle the variety of project demands effectively, the PM must understand the basic goals of the project, have the support of top management, build and maintain a solid information network, and remain flexible about as many project aspects as possible.

The best person to select as PM is the one who will get the job done.

Valuable skills for the PM are technical and administrative credibility, political sensitivity, and an ability to get others to commit to the project, a skill otherwise known as leadership.

Some important points concerning the impact of culture on project management are:

- Cultural elements refer to the way of life for any group of people and include technology, institutions, language, and art.
- The project environment includes economic, political, legal, and sociotechnical aspects.
- Examples of problematic cultural issues include the group's perception of time and the manner of staffing projects.
- Language is a particularly critical aspect of culture for the project.

In the next chapter we consider the task of negotiating for the resources to implement the project plan and WBS, which will then complete our treatment of Part I: Project Initiation.

GLOSSARY

Analytic Approach   Breaking problems into their constituent parts to understand the parts better and thereby solve the problem.

Benefit-Cost   A ratio to evaluate a proposed course of action.

Champion   A person who spearheads an idea or action and "sells" it throughout the organization.

Contingency Plan   An alternative for action if the expected result fails to materialize.

Culture   The way of life of any group of people.

Discipline   An area of expertise.

Environment   Everything outside the system that delivers inputs or receives outputs from the system.

Facilitator   A person who helps people overcome problems, either with technical issues or with other people.

Functional   One of the standard organization disciplines such as finance, marketing, accounting, or operations.

Microculture   The "corporate culture" within the organization, or even project.

Systems Approach   A wide-ranging, synthesizing method for addressing problems that considers multiple and interacting relationships. Commonly contrasted with the analytic approach.

Technological   Having to do with the methods and techniques for doing something.

Trade-Off   Allowing one aspect to get worse in return for another aspect getting better.

QUESTIONS

Material Review Questions

1. How does the project act as a stepping-stone for the project manager's career?

2. Name the categories of skills that should be considered in the selection of a project manager.

3. Discuss the PM's responsibilities toward the project team members.

4. What are the major differences between functional managers and project managers?

5. What are some of the essential characteristics of effective project team members?

6. What is the most important selection characteristic of a project manager?

7. What project goals are most important during the project life cycle stages?

8. Why must project management team members have good technical skills?

9. Describe each of the four elements of culture.

10. Identify some important types of project environments.

11. Contrast culture, microculture, and multiculture.

12. In what ways is language crucial in project management?

13. Identify the five multicultural factors requiring special consideration.

Class Discussion Questions

14. Can you think of several ways to assure "breadth of communication" in a project? Do you think "socialization" off the job helps or hinders?

15. Contrast the prime law for projects, "Never surprise the boss," with the corporate adage "Bad news never travels up."

16. How does a project manager, in some cases, work like a politician?

17. What are some of the conflicts that are bound to occur between parties that have legitimate interests in the project?

18. Project managers must be generalists rather than specialists. Yet, team members need to have more specialized, technical skills. Can a generalist manage a team of specialists effectively?

19. Why do you think cost drops in importance as an objective right after the formation stage?

20. Why is it more difficult to keep the project on its time and cost schedules the later the project gets in its life cycle?

21. Suppose you have a talented scientist temporarily working for you on a client contract who is due to be transferred back to her regular job. Although you could do without her efforts at this point of the contract, you happen to know that she will be laid off for lack of work at her regular job and her personal financial situation is dire. You feel it is important that her talent be kept on the company payroll, although keeping her on the contract will increase expenses unnecessarily. Is the transfer decision a business decision or an ethical one? Why? If the decision were yours to make, what would you decide?

22. How is communication through art different than through language?

23. What should a firm do when an accepted practice in a foreign country is illegal in its own country?

24. Do you agree that the trend now is to become less of a generic project manager and more of a specialist? If so,

then how do you gain a wide range of experience for that next job opportunity?

Churchill as a Project Manager

25. How did Churchill's background qualify him as a Project Manager?

26. What are the desired traits and skills for a Project Manager?

27. How important is previous experience for a Project Manager?

A Surprise "Director of Storm Logistics" for Katrina

28. Why do you think Wilson was appointed Director?

29. What would have been the first set of tasks Wilson would have considered after requesting help?

Channel Tunnel

30. What was the role of the project manager in implementing the Channel Tunnel project?

31. What complexity was involved in planning and implementing the project?

32. Could the overruns in cost and schedule have been avoided. If so, how?

33. Identify the sub-projects within this project, if any.

Why Project Managers need to have Local Knowledge

34. Why is it important for Project Managers to consider local knowledge and cultural nuances?

35. How does local culture infl uence the outcome of a project?

36. How can a foreign project manager become aware of local practices and culture which can affect project delivery?

Success at Energo by Integrating Two Diverse Cultures

37. What was the key to solving this dilemma?

38. How did the two PMs implement their strategy?

39. What actions in Exhibit 1 might have been key to making this project a success?

INCIDENTS FOR DISCUSSION

Smithson Company

Keith Smithson is the CEO of the Smithson Company, a privately owned, medium-size computer services company. The company is 20 years old and, until recently, had experienced rapid growth. Mr. Smithson believes that the company's recent problems are closely related to the depressed Asian economy.

Brianna Smatters was hired as the director of corporate planning at Smithson six months ago. After reviewing the performance and financial statements of Smithson for the last few years, Ms. Smatters has come to the conclusion that the economic conditions are not the real problem, but rather, exacerbate the real problems. She believes that in this Internet era, Smithson Company's services are becoming obsolete but the department heads have not been able to cooperate effectively in reacting to information technology threats and opportunities. She believes that the strong functional organization impedes the kinds of action required to remedy the situation. Accordingly, she has recommended that Mr. Smithson create a new position, manager of special operations, to promote and use project management techniques. The new manager would handle several critical projects in the role of project manager.

Mr. Smithson is cool to the idea. He believes that his functional departments are managed by capable professional people. Why can't these high-level managers work together more efficiently? Perhaps a good approach would be for him to give the group some direction (what to do, when to do it, who should do it) and then put the functional manager most closely related to the problems in charge of the group. He assumes that the little push from him (Smithson) as just described would be enough to "get the project rolling."

Questions: After this explanation Ms. Smatters is more convinced than ever that a separate, nonfunctional project manager is required. Is she right? If you were Smatters, how would you sell Mr. Smithson on the idea? If a new position is created, what other changes should be made?

Newcastle Nursing and Rehabilitation Residence

The Newcastle Nursing and Rehabilitation Residence (NNRR) is a 135-bed skilled nursing home. NNRR is considering converting a 36-bed wing of their main building for use by patients who require ventilator-assisted breathing.

The rooms will be slightly smaller than optimum for ventilator patients, but just exceed the recommended minimum square footage. Enlarging the rooms is not an economic option. In the main, the conversion will require the addition of electrical wiring to power oxygen-concentrators that extract 95 percent pure oxygen from room air, portable ventilators that supply the oxygen under pressure to assist breathing, and small, motor-driven suction devices to remove excess mucus from a patient's airway. These rooms must also be connected to an emergency generator that automatically starts and supplies electrical current if the main electrical supply fails. Finally, pressure sensors must be connected from each ventilator unit to a sound device located in the hallway of the ventilator wing. These units sound a strident signal and cause a hallway light to flash if there is a sharp drop in the airway pressure of a ventilator patient. In addition to these power needs associated with ventilator patients, power outlets are also needed for several machines that dispense tube feedings of medicines and nutrition, and for IVs, radios, and similar entertainment devices. Each bed itself needs a power outlet, as does the air mattress pump. Because all rooms are double occupancy, each room needs two full sets of the outlets.

The equipment noted above is normally plugged in at all times when the patient is in his or her room. Otherwise-well patients, however, are moved daily into a "day room" equipped with a large screen TV and chairs and tables. Most patients must be moved with their portable ventilators and concentrators or bottled oxygen. Patients who are well enough, eat their meals in the day room and socialize with each other and with visitors. (The socialization is a quiet process because a large majority of the patients breathe through a tube inserted in their trachea and are unable to speak aloud.)

The Senior Administrator, Steve Murphy, has decided to set up the conversion process as a project. Mr. Murphy is considering the choice of a project manager. He is trained in business, not hospital design. He feels a Registered Nurse or Licensed Practical Nurse might be an appropriate PM. He also feels that a Respiratory Therapist (RT) might be a good choice because RTs are responsible for using the major electrical equipment. Finally, he thinks that the installation and placing of all the outlets might be better handled by a representative of the electrical contractor who must carry out the major part of the room conversion.

Questions: Who should Mr. Murphy choose? Defend your choice.

International Microcircuits, Inc.

Megan Bedding, vice-president of sales for International Microcircuits, Inc. (IM), was delighted when IM was one of the few firms invited to enter a bid to supply a large industrial customer with their major product in a small foreign country. However, her top salesperson for that region had just called and informed her of certain "expectations" of doing business in the country:

1. Local materials representing at least 50 percent of the product's value must be purchased in reciprocity.

2. The local politicians will expect continual significant donations to their party.

3. Industrial customers normally receive a 40 percent "rebate" (kickback) when they purchase goods from suppliers such as IM. (IM's profit margin is only 20 percent.)

With this new information, Megan was unsure about changing or proceeding with the bid. If it was withdrawn, a lot of effort would be wasted as well as a chance to get a foothold in the international market. But if she proceeded, how could these expectations be met in a legal and ethical way?

Question: Devise a solution that addresses Megan's concerns.

CONTINUING INTEGRATIVE CLASS PROJECT

The task for the class now is to select a project manager. But heed the advice given in the chapter that the best PM is the one "who can get the job done," not the one who is just "available." This is a particularly dangerous pitfall for a class project where everyone is busy and no one had expected to be called upon to lead a major project. And resist the temptation of naming two people as co-PMs—that rarely works unless these people have a history of working well together in previous projects. With two PMs, no one knows who is responsible for what and tasks may fall through the cracks. In theory, the work of the PM should be no more, and possibly less, than the other members of the class, especially if the project is well organized and

well run. The main responsibilities of the PM (and perhaps in concert with subteam heads) are to organize the project, schedule the tasks, and stay on top of progress. However, if problems, or maybe personality feuds, crop up, the PM may find these are taking a lot more time than was expected. When a PM is finally selected, it is important for the class, and especially any subteam heads, if such exist, to give full allegiance to the PM in getting the work done and upholding the workload they agreed to handle. Bear in mind also that there will probably be one or more people in the class who will need to do more than their fair share of the work because of unexpected problems that crop up during the term.

BIBLIOGRAPHY

Barry, V. *Moral Issues in Business*. Belmont, CA: Wadsworth, 1979.

Blanchard, K., and N. V. Peale. *The Power of Ethical Management*. New York: Morrow, 1988.

Dinsmore, P. C., and M. M. B. Codas. "Challenges in Managing International Projects." In P. C. Dinsmore, ed., *The AMA Handbook of Project Management*. New York: AMACOM, 1993.

Dodson, W. R. "Virtually International." *PM Network*, April 1998.

Dulewicz, V., and M. J. Higgs. "Design of a new instrument to assess leadership dimensions & styles." In *Henley Working Paper HWP 0311*, Henley Management College, Henley-on-Thames, UK. 2003.

Fedor, K. J., and W. B. Werther, Jr. "The Fourth Dimension: Creating Culturally Responsive International Alliances." *IEEE Engineering Management Review*, Fall 1997, as reprinted from *Organizational Dynamics*, Autumn 1996.

Ford, R. C., and F. S. McLaughlin. "Successful Project Teams: A Study of MIS Managers." *IEEE Transactions on Engineering Management*, November 1992.

Foti, R. "Today's Project Manager." *PM Network*, April 2003.

Gagnon, R. J. *An Exploratory Analysis of the Relevant Cost Structure of Internal and External Engineering Consulting*, Ph.D. dissertation. Cincinnati: University of Cincinnati, 1982.

Gagnon, R. J., and S. J. Mantel, Jr. "Strategies and Performance Improvement for Computer-Assisted Design." *IEEE Transactions on Engineering Management*, November 1987.

Gogal, H. C., and L. R. Ireland. "Project Management: Meeting China's Challenge." *Project Management Journal*, February 1988.

Grinbergs, A., and A. H. Rubenstein. "Software Engineering Management: A Comparison of Methods in Switzerland and the United States." *IEEE Transactions on Engineering Management*, February 1993.

Green, S. G. "Top Management Support of R&D Projects: A Strategic Leadership Perspective." *IEEE Transactions on Engineering Management*, August 1995.

Hauptman, O., and K. K. Hirji. "The Influence of Process Concurrency on Project Outcomes in Product Development: An Empirical Study of Cross-Functional Teams." *IEEE Transactions on Engineering Management*, May 1996.

Herzberg, F. H. "One More Time: How Do You Motivate Employees?" *Harvard Business Review*, January–February 1968.

Hughes, T. P. *Rescuing Prometheus*. New York, Pantheon, 1998.

Hunsberger, K. "Juggling Act." *PM Network*, September 2008.

Ireland, L. R., W. J. Pike, and J. L. Schrock. "Ethics for Project Managers." *Proceedings of the 1982 PMI Seminar/Symposium on Project Management*, Toronto, Ontario, Canada.

Jiang, J. J., G. Klein, and S. Margulis. "Important Behavioral Skills for IS Project Managers: The Judgments of Experienced IS Professionals." *Project Management Journal*, March 1998.

Kalu, T. C. U. "A Framework for the Management of Projects in Complex Organizations." *IEEE Transactions on Engineering Management*, May 1993.

Kent, S. "Stretched Thin." *PM Network,* April 2008.

Kloppenborg, T J., and S. J. Mantel, Jr. "Trade-offs on Projects: They May Not Be What You Think." *Project Management Journal*, March 1990.

Kotter, J. P. "What Effective General Managers Really Do." *Harvard Business Review*, November–December 1982.

Levinson, N. S., and M. Asahi. "Cross-National Alliances and Interorganizational Learning." *IEEE Engineering Management Review*, Fall 1997, as reprinted from *Organizational Dynamics*, Autumn 1995.

Lynn, L. H., and T. J. McKeown. *Organizing Business: Trade Associations in America and Japan*. Washington, D.C.: American Enterprise Institute for Public Policy Research, 1988.

The AMA Handbook of Project Management. New York: AMACOM, 1993.

Matson, E. "Congratulations, You're Promoted" and "Project: You." *Fast Company*, as reprinted in *Engineering Management Review*, Winter 1998.

Medcof, J. W., J. Hauschildt, and G. Keim. "Realistic Criteria for Project Manager Selection and Development." *Project Management Journal*, September 2000.

Mintzberg, H. *The Nature of Managerial Work*. New York: Harper & Row, 1973.

Müller, R., and R. Turner. "Leadership Competency Profiles of Successful Project Managers." *International Journal of Project Management*, Vol 28, 2010.

Nixon, M. A. "Legal Lights: Business Ethics." *Project Management Journal*, September 1987.

Norrie, J. and D. H. T. Walker. "A Balanced Scorecard Approach to Project Management Leadership." *Project Management Journal*, December 2004.

Pastin, M. *The Hard Problems of Management*. San Francisco: Jossey-Bass, 1986.

Patterson, N. "Selecting Project Managers: An Integrated List of Predictors." *Project Management Journal*, June 1991.

Pill, J. *Technical Management and Control of Large Scale Urban Studies: A Comparative Analysis of Two Cases*, Ph.D. dissertation. Cleveland: Case Western Reserve University, 1971.

Pinto, J. K., and D. P. Slevin. "The Project Champion: Key to Implementation Success." *Project Management Journal*, December 1989.

Project Management Institute. "Slow Motion," *PM Network*, April 2005, p. 1.

Robb, D. J. "Ethics in Project Management: Issues, Practice, and Motive." *PM Network*, December 1996.

Rosegger, G., and S. J. Mantel, Jr. "Competitors as Consultants: Collaboration and Technological Advance." In J. Allesch, ed., *Consulting in Innovation: Practice, Methods, Perspectives*. Amsterdam: Elsevier, 1990.

Sahlin, J. P. "How Much Technical Training Does a Project Manager Need?" *PM Network*, May 1998.

Schaefer, A. G., and A. J. Zaller. "The Ethics Audit for Nonprofit Organizations." *PM Network*, March 1998.

Scott, S. G., and R. A. Bruce. "Following the Leader in R&D: The Joint Effect of Subordinate Problem-Solving Style and Leader-Member Relations on Innovative Behavior." *IEEE Transactions on Engineering Management*, February 1998.

Shenhar, A. J. "From Theory to Practice: Toward a Typology of Project-Management Styles." *IEEE Transactions on Engineering Management*, February 1998.

Slevin, D. P. *The Whole Manager*. New York: AMACOM, 1989.

Smith, L. A., and J. Haar. "Managing International Projects." In P. C. Dinsmore, ed., *The AMA Handbook of Project Management*. New York: AMACOM, 1993.

Tannenbaum, R., and F. Massarick. "Leadership: A Frame of Reference." *Management Science*, October 1957.

The World Book. Chicago: Field Enterprises, 1997.

Whitten, N. "Attributes of the Successful Project Leader." *PM Network*, June 1996.

Zimmerer, T. W., and M. M. Yasin. "A Leadership Profile of American Project Managers." *Project Management Journal*, March 1998.

Zupek, R. "Sun Sets on Silicon Valley?" *PM Network*, May, 2010.

The following case involves a project manager who stumbles into a public project somewhat by accident. The project starts out as one thing and evolves into something else. Acquiring sufficient resources for the project is a major difficulty, and competition may be troublesome also. A consultant is hired who conducts two surveys to gather more information and makes recommendations based on the survey evidence and experience. The case illustrates the varied skills necessary to be a successful project manager and the myriad opportunities/difficulties some projects entail.

C   A   S   E

THE NATIONAL JAZZ HALL OF FAME*
Cornelis A. de Kluyver, J. Giuliano, J. Milford, and B. Cauthen

Mr. Robert Rutland, founder of the National Jazz Hall of Fame, poured himself another drink as he listened to some old jazz recordings and thought about the decisions facing him. Established about one year ago, the National Jazz Hall of Fame (NJHF) had achieved moderate success locally but had not yet attracted national recognition. Mr. Rutland wondered how much support existed nationally, what services the NJHF should provide and for whom, and what the NJHF should charge for those services. He also thought about other jazz halls of fame and their implications for the NHJF. Although he had engaged an independent consultant to find some answers, the questions still lingered.

Jazz

The word "jazz," according to Dr. David Pharies, a linguistics scholar at the University of Florida, originally meant copulation, but later identified a certain type of music. Amid the march of funeral bands, jazz music began in New Orleans in the early 1900s by combining Black spirituals, African rhythms, and Cajun music; Dixieland jazz became the sound of New Orleans. Jazz traveled from New Orleans, a major trade center, on river boats and ships and reached St. Louis, Kansas City, Memphis, Chicago, and New York. Musicians in these cities developed local styles of jazz, all of which remained highly improvisational, personal, and rhythmically complex. Over the years, different sounds emerged—swing, big band, be bop, fusion, and others—indicating the fluidity and diversity of jazz. Jazz artists developed their own styles and competed with one another for recognition of their musical ability and compositions. Such diversity denied jazz a simple definition, and

opinions still differed sharply on what exactly jazz was. It was difficult, however, to dispute Louis Armstrong's statement that "if you have to ask what jazz is, you'll never know."

Origins of the National Jazz Hall of Fame

Mr. Rutland, a history professor at the University of Virginia, which is in Charlottesville, discovered that renovation plans for the city's historic district excluded the Paramount Theatre, a local landmark. The Paramount was constructed in the 1930s and used as a performance center and later as a movie theater. It was closed in the 1970s and now was in danger of becoming dilapidated. Alarmed by the apparent lack of interest in saving the Paramount, Mr. Rutland began to look for opportunities to restore and eventually use the theater. The most attractive option to him was to establish a jazz hall of fame that would use the theater as a museum and performance center; this would capitalize on the theater's name, because the Paramount Theater in New York City was a prominent jazz hall during the 1930s and 1940s. Mr. Rutland mentioned his idea—saving the theater by establishing a jazz hall of fame—to several friends in Charlottesville. They shared his enthusiasm, and together they incorporated the National Jazz Hall of Fame and formed the board of directors in early 1983. A few prominent jazz musicians, such as Benny Goodman and Chick Corea, joined the NJHF National Advisory Board. The purpose of the NJHF was to establish and maintain a museum, archives, and concert center in Charlottesville to sponsor jazz festivals, workshops, and scholarships, and to promote other activities remembering great jazz artists, serving jazz enthusiasts, and educating the public on the importance of jazz in American culture and history.

---

*Reprinted with permission. Copyright the Darden Graduate Business School Foundation, Charlottesville, VA.

The First Year's Efforts

Immediately after incorporation, the directors began their search for funds to save the Paramount and to establish the NJHF, and soon encountered two difficulties. Philanthropic organizations refused to make grants because no one on the board of directors had experience in a project like the NJHF. In addition, government agencies such as the National Endowment for the Arts and the National Endowment for the Humanities considered only organizations in operation for at least two years. However, some small contributions came from jazz enthusiasts who had read stories about the NJHF in *Billboard*, a music industry magazine, and in the Charlottesville and Richmond newspapers.

By mid-1983, the board of directors discovered that to save the Paramount, at least $600,000 would be needed, a sum too large for them to consider. They decided, however, that out of their love for jazz they would continue to work to establish the NJHF in Charlottesville.

Despite these setbacks, Mr. Rutland and the other directors believed that the first year's activities showed promise. The NJHF sponsored three concerts at local high schools. The concerts featured such jazz greats as Maxine Sullivan, Buddy Rich, and Jon Hendricks and Company, and each concert attracted more than 500 people. Although the NJHF lost some money on each concert, the directors thought that the concerts succeeded in publicizing and promoting the NJHF. In addition, a fundraiser at a Charlottesville country club brought $2,000 to the NJHF, and Mr. Rutland started the NJHF newsletter. The collection of objects for the museum was enlarged, and Louis Armstrong and Duke Ellington were posthumously inducted into the NJHF. At the end of the first year, enthusiasm among board members was still high, and they believed that the NJHF could survive indefinitely, albeit on a small scale.

But a Hall of Fame in Charlottesville...

Mr. Rutland believed that a hall of fame could succeed in Charlottesville, though other cities might at first seem more appropriate. More than 500,000 tourists annually were attracted to Charlottesville (1980 population: 40,000) to visit Thomas Jefferson's home at Monticello, James Monroe's home at Ash Lawn, and the Rotunda and the Lawn of the University of Virginia, where total enrollment was 16,000. Mr. Jefferson designed the Rotunda and the buildings on the Lawn and supervised their construction. The Virginia Office of Tourism promoted these national landmarks as well as the city's two convention centers. In addition, 13 million people lived within a three-hour drive of Charlottesville. If Charlottesville seemed illogical for a hall of fame, Mr. Rutland reasoned, so did Cooperstown, New York, home of the Baseball Hall of Fame and Canton, Ohio, location of the Professional Football Hall of Fame. He thought that successful jazz festivals in such different places as Newport, Rhode Island, and French Lick, Indiana, showed that location was relatively unimportant for jazz. Moreover, a Charlottesville radio station recently switched to a music format called "Memory Lane," which featured classics by Frank Sinatra, Patti Page, the Mills Brothers, the Glenn Miller Orchestra, and numerous others. The station played much jazz, and won the loyalty of many jazz enthusiasts in the Charlottesville area. The success of "Memory Lane" indicated to Mr. Rutland that the Charlottesville community could provide the NJHF with a base of interest and loyalty. Most important, Mr. Rutland believed that he and his friends possessed the commitment necessary to make a jazz hall of fame succeed.

...And Halls of Fame in Other Cities?

Although no national organization operated successfully, several local groups claimed to be *the* Jazz Hall of Fame, as Billboard magazine reported.

***

Billboard 4/28/84

HALL OF FAME IN HARLEM
by Sam Sutherland and Peter Keepnews

CBS Records and the Harlem YMCA have joined forces to establish a Jazz Hall of Fame. The first induction ceremony will take place on May 14 at Avery Fisher Hall, combined with a concert featuring such artists as Ramsey Lewis, Hubert Laws, Ron Carter, and an all-star Latin Jazz ensemble. Proceeds from the concert will benefit the Harlem YMCA.

Who will the initial inductees be, and how will they be chosen? What's being described in the official literature as "a prestigious group of jazz editorialists, critics, producers, and respected connoisseurs" (and, also, incidentally, musicians—among those on the panel are Miles Davis, Dizzy Gillespie, Cab Calloway, Max Roach and the ubiquitous Dr. Billy Taylor) will do the actual selecting, but nominations are being solicited from the general public. Jazz lovers are invited to submit the names of six artists, three living and three dead, to: The Harlem YMCA Jazz Hall of Fame, New York, NY 10030. Deadline for nominations is May 1.

Billboard, 5/19/84

ONE, TWO, MANY HALLS OF FAME?
by Sam Sutherland and Peter Keepnews

Monday night marks the official launch of the Harlem YMCA Jazz Hall of Fame (Billboard, April 28), a project in which CBS Records is closely involved. The Hall's first inductees are being unveiled at an Avery Fisher Hall concert that also includes performances by, among others, Sarah Vaughan and Branford Marsalis.

The project is being touted as the first jazz hall of fame, a statement that discounts a number of similar projects in the past that never quite reached fruition. But first or not, the good people of CBS and the Harlem YMCA are apparently in for some competition.

According to a new publication known as JAMA, the Jazz Listeners/Musicians Newsletter, Dizzy Gillespie—who also is a member of the Harlem YMCA Jazz Hall of Fame committee—"promised in Kansas City, Mo. to ask musicians for help in establishing an International Jazz Hall of Fame" in that city. The newsletter quotes Gillespie, whom it describes as "honorary chairman of the proposed hall," as vowing to ask "those musicians who were inspired by jazz"—among them Stevie Wonder, Quincy Jones and Paul McCartney (?)—to contribute financially to the Kansas City project, which, as envisioned by the great trumpeter, would also include a jazz museum, classrooms and performance areas.

Is there room for two Jazz Halls of Fame? Do the people involved in the New York city project know about the Kansas City project, and vice versa? (Obviously Gillespie does, but does anyone else?) Remember the New York Jazz Museum? Remember the plaques in the sidewalk on 52nd Street (another CBS Records brainchild)?

The notion of commemorating the contributions of the great jazz musicians is a noble one. It would be a shame to see the energies of the jazz community get diverted into too many different endeavors for accomplishing the same admirable goal—which, unfortunately, is what has tended to happen in the past.

Billboard, 5/26/84

Also noted: the first inductees in the Harlem YMCA Jazz Hall of Fame (Billboard, May 19) have been announced. The posthumous inductees are, to nobody's great surprise, Louis Armstrong, Duke Ellington, Count Basie, Charlie Parker, and—a slight surprise, perhaps—Mary Lou Williams. The living honorees are Roy Eldridge, Dizzy Gillespie, Miles Davis, Ella Fitzgerald and Art Blakey.

***

The New York Jazz museum (which the 5/19/84 article referred to) was established in the early 1970s but quickly ran out of money and was closed a few years later. In the early 1960s, a jazz museum was established in New Orleans and because of insufficient funds, all that remained was the Louis Armstrong Memorial Park, the site of an outdoor jazz festival each summer. Tulane and Rutgers universities each possessed extensive archives containing thousands of phonograph records, tape recordings, posters, books, magazines, journals, and other historic pieces and memorabilia. Neither university, however, considered its archives a hall of fame.

Other Halls of Fame

The more prominent halls of fame in the U.S. were the Baseball, the Professional Football, the College Football, and the Country Music Hall of Fame. These and many other halls of fame were primarily concerned with preserving history by collecting and displaying memorabilia, compiling records, and inducting new members annually.

Mr. Rutland visited most of the other halls of fame and learned that they were usually established by a significant contribution from an enthusiast. In the case of the Country Music Hall of Fame, some country music stars agreed to make a special recording of country hits and to donate the royalties to the organization.

Mr. Rutland was especially interested in The Country Music Hall of Fame because of similarities between country music and jazz. Country music, like jazz, had a rich cultural history in America, and neither type of music was the most popular in the U.S.

The Country Music Hall of Fame (CMHF) was established in 1967 in Nashville after a cooperative fundraising effort involving the city, artists, and sponsors. By 1976, the CMHF included a museum, an archives, a library, and a gift shop. More than one-half million people visited the CMHF in 1983, partly because of the nearby Grand Ole Opry, the premier concert hall for country music where the Grand Ole Opry cable radio broadcasts originated. Of the CMHF's $2.1 million annual budget, 85 percent came from admissions, 10 percent from sales at the gift shop and by mail, and 5 percent from donations. In the past two years, the CMHF had formed the Friends of Country Music, now more than 2,000 people who donated $25 each per year and who received a country music newsletter every three months and discounts on CMHF merchandise.

The National Association of Jazz Educators

Mr. Rutland was uncertain how much and what type of support he could get from the National Association of Jazz Educators. This organization, with 5,000 members, primarily coordinated and promoted jazz education programs.

Performance programs were normally offered through music departments. Most high schools and colleges had bands that played a variety of jazz arrangements as part of their repertoire. Band conductors usually had a music degree from a major university and belonged to the National Association of Jazz Educators.

Most of the jazz appreciation courses offered in schools throughout the U.S. treated jazz as a popular art form, as a barometer of society, rather than as a subject of interest in itself. Some educators believed that jazz greats such as Louis Armstrong and Duke Ellington should be honored not as jazz musicians, but as composers like George Gershwin and Richard Rogers. Indeed, a prominent jazz historian told Mr. Rutland that jazz might benefit more from breaking down this distinction between jazz artists and composers than from reinforcing it.

The National Survey

To get some of the answers to his many questions, Mr. Rutland engaged an independent consultant who conducted two surveys; the first was a national survey and the second a tourist survey. For the national survey, the consultant designed a questionnaire to gauge the respondent's level of interest in both jazz and the concept of a National Jazz Hall of Fame, and to determine the respondent's demographics. A sample size of 1,300 was used and the mailing covered the entire continental United States. The mailing list, obtained from the Smithsonian Institution in Washington, DC, contained names and addresses of people who had purchased the "Classic Jazz Record Collection," as advertised in *Smithsonian* magazine. Of the 1,300 questionnaires, 440 were sent to Virginia residents and 860 to residents of other states in order to provide both statewide and national data. Of the questionnaires that went to other states, the majority was targeted toward major cities and apportioned according to the interest level for jazz in each city as indicated by the circulation statistics of *Downbeat*, a jazz magazine. Of the 860 questionnaires sent to the other states, 88 were sent to residents of Chicago, 88 to Detroit, 83 to New York City, 60 to San Francisco, 56 to Philadelphia, 56 to Washington, DC, 52 to Los Angeles, 46 to Charlotte, 46 to Miami, 45 to Dallas, 42 to Atlanta, 42 to Houston, 30 to Denver, 28 to Kansas City, 28 to New Orleans, 28 to St. Louis, 27 to Boston, and 15 to Seattle. Of the 1,300 questionnaires, 165, or 12.7 percent, were returned.

As shown in Exhibit 1, 79 percent of the respondents were 35 years of age or older, 73 percent were male, and

Exhibit 1. Survey Results: Demographics of Respondents

Demographics	Percentage of Respondents	Percentage of All Record Buyers*	Census Data**
Age—35+	79	37	43
Sex—Male	73	82	49
Education—Grad.+	54	24***	31
Job—Professional	57	26	22
Income—$50,000+	50	23	7
Non-profit Contr. $200/year+	75		

Source: Consumer Purchasing of Records and Pre-recorded Tapes in the U.S., 1970–1983, Recording Industry Association of America.

**Source*: U.S. Department of Commerce, Bureau of the Census, 1982.

***Source*: Simmons Market Research Bureau, 1982.

the majority were well-educated, professionals, and had an annual income of more than $50,000. Of interest also was that 75 percent of the respondents contributed $200 or more per year to different non-profit organizations. Since the sample included a large number of record buyers of age 50 or older, the consultant weighted the survey results with age data obtained from the Recording Industry Association of America to make the survey results representative of all jazz-record buyers.

The survey also showed in Exhibit 2 that swing was the most popular form of jazz, followed by Dixieland, and then more traditional forms of jazz, from which the consultant concluded that a nostalgic emphasis should gather support from jazz enthusiasts of all ages, and that later, the National Jazz Hall of Fame could promote more contemporary forms of jazz.

As for services, the survey suggested in Exhibit 3 that respondents most wanted a performance center or concert hall. A museum and seminars were also popular choices. The consultant was surprised by the strong interest in information about jazz recordings because the average respondent did not buy many records. A newsletter was rated relatively unimportant by most respondents. Most gratifying for Mr. Rutland was that respondents on average were willing to contribute between $20.00 and $30.00 per year to the National Jazz Hall of Fame, with a weighted average contribution of $23.40.

The Tourist Survey

In addition to conducting the National Survey, the consultant developed a questionnaire and interviewed approximately 100 tourists to the Charlottesville area at the Western Virginia Visitors Center near Monticello. About 140,000 tourists stopped at the center annually to collect information on attractions nearby and throughout the state. The respondents came from all areas of the country, and most were traveling for more than one day. Almost 70 percent said they like jazz, mostly Dixieland and big band, and more than 60 percent indicated they would visit a Jazz Hall of Fame. The average admission they suggested was $3.50 per person.

The Consultant's Recommendations

The consultant limited his recommendations to the results of the two surveys. As a result, the question of whether the efforts in other cities to establish a National Jazz Hall of Fame would make the Charlottesville project infeasible was still unresolved. In a private discussion, however, the consultant intimated that "if the other efforts are as clumsily undertaken as many of the previous attempts, you will have nothing to worry about." He thought it was time that a professional approach was taken toward this project. Specifically, he made three recommendations:

1. Launch a direct mail campaign to the 100,000 people on the Smithsonian jazz mailing list. The focus of the mailing should be an appeal by a jazz great such as Benny Goodman to become a Founding Sponsor of the National Jazz Hall of Fame. He estimated that the cost of the campaign would range between $25,000 and $30,000; however, with an average contribution of $25.00 per respondent, a response rate of only 2 percent would allow the National Jazz Hall of Fame to break even.

2. Appoint a full-time executive director with any funds exceeding the cost of the mailing. The principal responsibilities of the executive director would be to

Exhibit 2. Survey Results: Preferences for Different Styles of Jazz

Type of Interest	Percentage of Respondents Answering with a 4 or 5 Rating	Weighted Percentage of Respondents Answering with a 4 or 5 Rating
General Interest in Music	62	71
Dixieland	62	70
Swing	87	81
Traditional	63	66
Improvisational	41	48
Jazz Rock	25	47
Fusion	15	9
Pop Jazz	27	53
Classical	68	73

Exhibit 3. Survey Results: Preferences for Services Offered

Service	Percentage of Respondents Answering with a 4 or 5 Rating	Weighted Percentage of Respondents Answering with a 4 or 5 Rating
Performance Center	70	83
Concert Hall	66	79
Artist Seminars	50	62
Nightclub	52	57
Museum	57	57
Tourist Center	42	48
Audio-Visual Exhibitions	57	55
Shrine	55	52
Educational Programs	48	51
Record Information	71	69
History Seminars	38	54
Member Workshops	25	34
Lounge	37	45
Financial Support:		
at $10.00/year	17	13
at $20.00/year	30	26
at $30.00/year		
Number of Contributors	62	64

organize and coordinate fundraising activities, to establish a performance center and museum, and to coordinate the collection of memorabilia and other artifacts.

3. Promote the National Jazz Hall of Fame at strategic locations around Charlottesville to attract tourists and other visitors. The Western Virginia Visitors Center was a prime prospect in his view for this activity. He calculated that 50,000 tourists annually at $3.00 each would provide sufficient funds to operate and maintain the National Jazz Hall of Fame.

The consultant also identified what he considered the critical elements for his plan's success. First, the National Jazz Hall of Fame should be professional in all of its services and communications to jazz enthusiasts. Second, the executive director should have prior experience in both fundraising and direct mail; he should have a commitment to and love for jazz, as well as administrative skill and creativity. Third,

the National Jazz Hall of Fame should communicate frequently with Founding Sponsors to keep their interest and excitement alive. Finally, to ensure the enthusiastic cooperation of city officials, local merchants, and the Charlottesville community, he thought that more local prominence for the National Jazz Hall of Fame would prove indispensable.

The National Jazz Hall of Fame—Dream or Reality

As he paged through the consultant's report, Mr. Rutland wondered what to make of the recommendations. While he was encouraged by a national base of support for his idea, he was unsure how the Board of Directors would react to the consultant's proposals. With less than $2,500 in the bank, how would they get the necessary funds to implement the plan? Yet he knew he had to make some tough decisions, and quickly, if he wanted to make his dream a reality.

QUESTIONS

1. What is the project Mr. Rutland is trying to manage? Has it stayed the same?

2. Identify the various stakeholders in the project, including the competition.

3. Of the skills mentioned in the chapter that a project manager needs, which are most important here? Why?

4. What credibility does Mr. Rutland have? Is he a leader?

5. What cultures are relevant to this project? Describe the project environment.

6. What should Mr. Rutland do? Include the following issues:
   - Budget: acquiring adequate resources
     – philanthropic organizations
     – governmental agencies
     – donations
     – memberships
     – visitors
   - Budget: expenditures (consider Paramount theatre)
   - Performance: services/activities to offer
   - Competition
   - Schedule: deadlines, windows, milestones

The following reading integrates two views about the requirements for good project managers. One view concerns the personal and managerial characteristics of PMs and their ability to lead a team, regardless of the project. The other view considers the critical problems in the project in question and the PM's talents relative to these problems. A survey is first described and then the critical problems that projects face are identified from the survey responses. Next, the skills required of project managers, as indicated by the survey respondents, are detailed. Last, the skills are related back to the critical project problems for an integrated view of the requirements for a successful project manager.

DIRECTED READING

WHAT IT TAKES TO BE
A GOOD PROJECT MANAGER*
B. Z. Posner

Selecting a good project manager is not a simple task. Being an effective project manager is an ongoing challenge. The complex nature and multifaceted range of activities involved in managing projects precludes easily identifying managerial talent and continually stretches the capabilities of talented project managers. Two seemingly contradictory viewpoints have been advanced about what is required to be a good project manager.

One perspective prescribes a set of *personal characteristics* necessary to manage a project [1]. Such personal attributes include aggressiveness, confidence, poise, decisiveness, resolution, entrepreneurship, toughness, integrity, versatility, multidisciplinarity, and quick thinking.

However, Daniel Roman [2] maintains that it would take an extraordinary individual to have all of these critical personal characteristics. A more practical solution, he suggests, would be to determine the *critical problems* faced by project managers and to select a person who can handle such difficulties. The shortcoming with this second perspective, argue those like Michael Badaway [3], is that the primary problems of project managers are really not technical ones. The reason managers fail at managing projects, he contends, is because they lack critical organization and management skills.

Scholars like Roman and Badaway—as well as practitioners—may actually be raising different issues. On the one hand, good project managers understand the critical problems which face them and are prepared to deal with them. On the other hand, managing projects well requires a set of particular attributes and skills. But, are these two viewpoints really at odds with one another? In this study they were discovered to be two sides of the *same* coin!

*Reproduced from *Project Management Journal* with permission. Copyright Project Management Institute.

Study of Project Manager Problems and Skills

Questionnaires were completed by project managers during a nationwide series of project management seminars. Project managers attending these seminars came from a variety of technology-oriented organizations. Responses to the survey instrument were both voluntary and confidential.

Information about the respondents and the nature of their projects was collected. The typical project manager was a 37-year-old male, had nine people reporting to him, and was responsible for a small to moderate size project within a matrix organization structure. More specifically, there were 189 men and 98 women in the sample (N = 287) and their ages ranged from 22 to 60 years of age (X = 37.4, S.D. = 8.3). Fifty-six percent indicated that they were the formal manager of the project. The size of their immediate project group ranged from 2 to over 100 people (median = 8.9). Fifty-nine percent reported that they worked primarily on small projects (involving few people or functions, with a short time horizon) as compared to large projects (involving many people or functions, with a long time horizon). More than 63 percent indicated they were working within a matrix organization structure. No information was collected about the specific nature (e.g., new product development, R & D, MIS) of their projects.

Two open-ended questions were asked (their order was randomized). The first asked about the skills necessary to be a successful project manager. The second question investigated the most likely problems encountered in managing projects. Responses to these questions were content analyzed. Content analysis is a systematic approach to data analysis, resulting in both qualitative assessments and quantitative information. Each respondent comment was first coded and then recoded several times as patterns of responses became apparent. The two questions were:

1. What factors or variables are *most* likely to cause you problems in managing a project?

2. What *personal* characteristics, traits, or skills make for "above average" project managers? What specific behaviors, techniques, or strategies do "above average" project managers use (or use better than their peers)?

Problems in Managing Projects. There were nearly 900 statements about what factors or variables created "problems" in managing a project. Most of these statements could be clustered into eight categories as shown in Table 1. Inadequate resources was the issue most frequently mentioned as causing problems in managing a project. "No matter what the type or scope of your project," wrote one engineering manager, "if insufficient resources are allocated to the project, you have to be a magician to be successful." Not having the necessary budget or personnel for the project was a frequent complaint. However, the specific resource of time—and generally the lack thereof—was mentioned just about as often as the general inadequate resource lament. Typically, the problem of time was expressed as "having to meet unrealistic deadlines."

That resources are inadequate is caused by many factors, not the least of which being that resources are generally limited and costly. Before this hue is dismissed by veteran project managers as just so much bellyaching—"after all, there are never enough resources to go around"—it is important to examine the cause(s) of this problem. Respondents pointed out that resource allocation problems were usually created by senior management's failure to be clear about project objectives, which in turn resulted in poor planning efforts. These two problems—lack of clear goals and effective planning—were specifically mentioned by more than 60 percent of the respondents. It is painfully obvious that vague goals and insufficient planning lead to mistakes in allocating the resources needed by project managers.

Table 1 Project Management Problems

1. Resources inadequate (69)
2. Meeting ("unrealistic") deadlines (67)
3. Unclear goals/direction (63)
4. Team members uncommitted (59)
5. Insufficient planning (56)
6. Breakdown of communications (54)
7. Changes in goals and resources (42)
8. Conflicts between departments or functions (35)

Note: Numbers in parentheses represent percentage of project managers whose response was included in this cluster.

The three most significant problems reported by first-line research, development, and engineering supervisors in Lauren Hitchcock's [4] study parallels those identified by project managers. He found "insufficient definition of policy from top downward, how to define the goal of a problem, and budgeting and manpower assignments" to be the major problems confronting supervisors. It remains true that senior management needs to articulate clearly where the project should be going, why, and what it expects from project personnel.

When project goals are not clear, it is difficult (if not impossible) to plan the project efficiently. The lack of planning contributes directly to unrealistic resource allocations and schedules. People assigned to the project are unlikely, therefore, to commit energetically to the endeavor. The lack of commitment (and poor motivation) among project personnel was reported as emerging more from the problems already mentioned than from issues associated with the project's technology or organizational structure (e.g., matrix form).

The communication breakdowns (problems which occur during the life of a project) were often referred to as "inevitable." These breakdowns occur as a result of the ambiguity surrounding the project, but also result from difficulties in coordinating and integrating diverse perspectives and personalities. The project manager's challenge is to handle communication breakdowns as they arise rather than being able to predict (and control) communication problems before they happen.

How the problems confronting project managers were interrelated is exemplified by how frequently problems of communication and dealing with conflicts were linked by respondents. The linkage between these two issues was demonstrated in statements like: "My problem is being able to effectively communicate with people when we disagree over priorities." "Conflicts between departments end up as major communication hassles." Conflicts between departments were also linked to earlier problems of poor goal-setting and planning.

Managing changes (e.g., in goals, specifications, resources) contributed substantially to project management headaches. This was often mentioned as "Murphy's Law," highlighting the context or environment in which project management occurs. Planning cannot accurately account for future possibilities (or better yet, unknowns). Interestingly, less than one in 10 project managers mentioned directly a "technological" factor or variable as significantly causing them problems in managing a project.

Project Manager Skills

The second issue investigated was what project manager skills—traits, characteristics, attributes, behaviors, techniques—make a difference in successfully managing projects. Most respondents easily generated four to five items which they believed made the difference between average and superior project performance. The result was nearly 1,400 statements. These statements were summarized into six skill areas as shown in Table 2. Several factors within each are highlighted.

Table 2   Project Management Skills

1. Communication Skills (84)	4. Leadership Skills (68)
• Listening	• Sets an example
• Persuading	• Energetic
2. Organizational Skills (75)	• Vision (big picture)
• Planning	• Delegates
• Goal-setting	• Positive
• Analyzing	5. Coping Skills (59)
3. Team Building Skills (72)	• Flexibility
• Empathy	• Creativity
• Motivation	• Patience
• Esprit de corps	• Persistence
	6. Technological Skills (46)
	• Experience
	• Project knowledge

Note: Numbers in parentheses represent percentage of project managers whose response was included in this cluster.

Eighty-four percent of the respondents mentioned "being a good communicator" as an essential project manager skill. Being persuasive or being able to sell one's ideas was frequently mentioned as a characteristic of a good communicator within the project management context. Many people also cited the importance of receiving information, or good listening skills. As one systems engineer exclaimed: "The good project managers manage not by the seat of their pants but by the soles of their feet!"

Organizational skills represented a second major set of competencies. Characteristics included in this category were planning and goal-setting abilities, along with the ability to be analytical. The ability to prioritize, captured in the phrases "stays on track" and "keeps the project goals in perspective," was also identified as significant.

While successful project managers were viewed as good problem solvers, what really, differentiated them from their so-so counterparts was their *problem finding* ability. Because of their exceptional communication skills, goal clarity, and planning, effective project managers were aware of issues *before* they became problems. Problem finding gave them greater degrees of freedom, enabling them to avoid being seriously sidetracked by problems caused by unforeseen events.

The important team building skills involved developing empathetic relationships with other members of the project team. Being sensitive to the needs of others, motivating people, and building a strong sense of team spirit were identified as essential for effectively managing a project. "The best project managers use a lot of 'we' statements in describing the project," wrote one computer programmer. Being clear about the project's objectives and subsequently breaking down the project into its component parts (e.g., schedules) helped project participants to understand their interdependencies and the need for teamwork.

Several different attributes and behaviors were catalogued under leadership skills. These included setting a good example, seeing the big picture, being enthusiastic, having a positive outlook, taking initiative, and trusting people. Having a vision is closely related to goal clarity (which was included as an organizational skill). The leadership component of this competency was best expressed by one financial analyst as "the ability to see the forest through the trees." Since, as is often lamented, the only constant in managing a project is change, successful project managers require coping or stress-management skills. Respondents indicated that both flexibility and creativity were involved in effectively dealing (or coping) with change, as were patience and persistence. What project managers experience are generally high levels of stress. How well they handle stress ("grace under pressure") significantly affects their eventual success or failure.

The final cluster of skills was labeled technological. Successful project managers were seen as having relevant experience or knowledge about the technology required by the project. Seldom, however, were effective project managers seen as technological "experts." Indeed, expertise was often felt to be detrimental because it decreased flexibility and the willingness to consider alternative perspectives. Project managers do need to be sufficiently well versed in the technology to be able to ask the right questions because, as one senior military officer pointed out, "you've got to be able to know when people are blowing smoke at you."

Skills and Problems: Fundamentally Interconnected

It has been argued in the literature that project managers require certain skills in order to be effective. It has also been argued that project managers need to be able to handle certain problems in order to be effective. The results of this study suggest that these two perspectives are not contradictory but are fundamentally compatible. When the set of required skills is considered side-by-side with the set of critical problems project managers face, the complementary nature of these two perspectives is evident. This is illustrated in Table 3.

Without arguing which comes first, it is clear that either (a) project managers require certain skills in order to deal effectively with the factors most likely to create problems for them in managing the project, or (b) because certain problems are most likely to confront project managers, they require particular skills in order to handle them.

While this one-on-one matching in Table 3 obviously oversimplifies the dynamic nature of project management, it does have an inherent logical appeal. Since communication breakdowns are likely to create project management problems, effective project managers need to cultivate their communications (persuading and listening) skills. Project managers with good organizational skills are likely to be more effective at planning and subsequently allocating resources. Unless project managers are able to build strong project teams, they are likely to be plagued by problems caused by poorly committed team members and interdepartmental conflict. Project goals are likely to be more easily understood when the project manager's leadership is consistent. Interpersonal conflicts will likely diminish when project managers set clear standards of performance and

demonstrate their trust in, and respect for, others. The inevitable changes which accompany any project will be less problematic when not only coped with calmly, but also when handled with flexibility and creativity. Finally, problems created when deadlines and schedules are unrealistic may be minimized through a project manager's problem finding ability and experience in getting things back on track.

What was found underscores the claim that the primary problems of project managers are not technical, but human. Improving project managers' technological capabilities will be helpful only to the extent that this improves their ability to communicate, be organized, build teams, provide leadership, and deal comfortably with change. The challenge for technical managers, or for those moving from technical into managerial positions, is to recognize the need for, and to develop where necessary, their interpersonal skills.

References

1. Archibald, R. D. *Managing High-Technology Programs and Projects*. New York: John Wiley & Sons, 1976; Kerzner, H. *Project Management for Executives*. New York: Van Nostrand Reinhold, 1982; Stuckenbruck, L., "Ten Attributes of the Proficient Project Manager." *Proceedings of the Project Management Institute*, Montreal, 1976, 40–47; and Thamhain, H., and Wilemon, D., "Skill Requirements of Engineering Project Managers." *Twenty-Sixth IEEE Joint Engineering Management Conference*, 1978.

2. Roman, D. D. *Managing Projects: A Systems Perspective*. New York: Elsevier Science Publishing, 1985.

3. Badaway, M. *Developing Managerial Skills in Scientists and Engineers*. New York: Van Nostrand Reinhold, 1982.

4. Hitchcock, L. "Problems of First-Line Supervisors." *Research Management* Vol. 10, No. 6, 1967, 385–397.

Questions

1. What primary characteristic distinguishes the very successful project managers from the more mediocre project managers?

2. In Table 3, match the rankings between skills and problems. Why aren't the top skills matched to the main problems?

3. In Table 1, which of the problems are related to project setup (perhaps occurring before a project manager was selected) and which are related to the project manager's skills?

4. How does Table 1 compare to the discussion in the chapter?

5. How does Table 2 compare to the discussion in the chapter?

Table 3 Skills—Problems: Interconnected in Project Management

Communication	Breakdowns in communications
Organizational	Insufficient planning
	Resources inadequate
Team Building	Team members uncommitted
	Weak inter-unit integration
Leadership	Unclear goals/direction
	Interpersonal conflicts
Coping	Handling changes
Technological	Meeting ("unrealistic") deadlines

4

Managing Conflict and the Art of Negotiation

Conflict has been mentioned many times thus far in this book. This chapter is about conflict. It is also about negotiation—the skill required to resolve most conflicts. The question arises, why should there be so much conflict on projects? One of several causes is that conflict arises when people working on the same project have somewhat different ideas about how to achieve project objectives. But why should such a disagreement occur? Is there not "one best way?" There may be one best way, but exactly which way is the "one best" is a matter surrounded by uncertainty. For example, the client of the project's outputs often has a substantially different point of view than those at the input end of the project, such as suppliers, or functional managers. And other stakeholders may have even different points of view, such as the project's top management, or the local community, or the project firm's lawyers. Most conflicts have their roots in uncertainty, and negotiation is a way of managing the resultant risk. Therefore, this chapter is also about risk management, about dealing with conflicts that often arise from uncertainty.

As we will see in Chapter 6, the process of planning a project usually requires inputs from many people. Even when the project is relatively small and simple, planning may involve the interaction of almost every functional and staff operation in the organization. It is virtually impossible for these interactions to take place without conflict, and when a conflict arises, it is helpful if there are acceptable methods to reduce or resolve it. And, of course, we should mention that some people are more receptive to negotiation and compromise than others, who may be more insistent on having their own way, or see the world as trying to frustrate their every desire. Personalities vary tremendously and always need to be considered in evaluating ways to reduce conflicts in projects.

Conflict has sometimes been defined as "the process which begins when one party perceives that the other has frustrated, or is about to frustrate, some concern of his" (Thomas, 1976, p. 891). While conflict can arise over issues of belief or feelings or behavior, our concern in this chapter is focused for the most part on goal conflicts that occur when an individual or group pursues goals different from those of other individuals or groups (Raiffa, 1982, Chapter 12). A party to the conflict will be satisfied when the level of frustration has been lowered to the point where no action, present or future, against the other party is contemplated. When all parties to the conflict are satisfied to this point, the conflict is said to be resolved.

There are, of course, many ways to resolve conflict, as described in detail in the reading "Methods of Resolving Interpersonal Conflict" at the end of this chapter, such as withdrawal, smoothing, compromise, forcing, confrontation/problem-solving, and others. As noted there, confrontation/problem-solving (i.e., facing the issue directly, such as by negotiation) is the most effective method while forcing, or brute force, is the most ineffective. Brute force is, of course, a time-honored method, as is the absolute rule of the monarch, but the rule of law is the method of choice for modern societies if negotiation or arbitration has not already succeeded—in spite of occasional lapses. Conflict resolution is the ultimate purpose of law.

Organizations establish elaborate and complex sets of rules and regulations to settle disputes between the organization itself and the individuals and groups with whom it interacts. Contracts between a firm and its suppliers, its trade unions, and its customers are written to govern the settlement of potential conflicts. But the various parties-at-interest (stakeholders) do not always agree about the meaning of a law or a provision in a contract. No agreement, however detailed, can cover all the circumstances that might arise in the extensive relationships between the buyer and the seller of complicated industrial equipment, between the user and the supplier of engineering consulting services, between the producer and user of computer programs—the list of potential conflicts is endless. Our overcrowded courts are witness to the extent and variety of conflict. According to the web page of the New York State Bar Association, there are approximately 850,000 lawyers in the United States. The great majority of this group that numbers between 25 and 35 percent of the world's supply of lawyers are employed in helping conflicting parties to adjudicate or settle their differences.

In this chapter, we examine the nature of negotiation as a means of reducing or resolving the kinds of conflict that typically occur within projects. But before we begin the discussion, it must be made quite clear that *this chapter is not a primer on how to negotiate*; a course in negotiation is beyond the scope of this book (for such information, see the bibliography). Rather, this chapter focuses on the roles and applications of negotiation in the management of projects. Note also that we have given minimal attention to negotiations between the organization and outside vendors. In our experience, this type of negotiation is conducted sometimes by the project manager, sometimes by the project engineer, but most often by members of the organization's purchasing department. In any case, negotiations between buyer and seller are admirably covered by Raiffa (1982).

Debate over the proper technical approach to a problem often generates a collaborative solution that is superior to any solution originally proposed. Conflict often educates individuals and groups about the goals/objectives of other individuals and groups in the organization, thereby satisfying a precondition for valuable win-win negotiations (see Section 4.3). Indeed, the act of engaging in win-win negotiations serves as an example of the positive outcomes that can result from such an approach to conflict resolution.

In Chapter 3 we noted that negotiation was a critical skill required of the project manager. No project manager should attempt to practice his or her trade without explicit training in negotiation. In this chapter, we describe typical areas of project management where this skill is mandatory. In addition, we will cover some of the appropriate and inappropriate approaches to negotiation, as well as a few of the characteristics of successful negotiation suggested by experts in the field or indicated by our experience. We will also note some ethical issues regarding negotiation. There are probably more opportunities for ethical missteps in handling conflicts and negotiations than in any other aspect of project management. Unlike other chapters, we will use comparatively few illustrative examples. Successful negotiation tends to be idiosyncratic to the actual situation, and most brief examples do little to help transform theory into practice. We have, however, included a vignette at the end of the chapter. This vignette was adapted from "real life"; the names were changed to protect innocent and guilty alike.

Project Management in Practice
Quickly Building a School through Negotiation

The idea to build a school for orphans and poor children in an African slum in 30 days was suggested as fodder for a Norwegian television "reality" show. Only one of the 10 Scandinavian team members recruited had any construction experience and only one, Ms. Lange, a PMP, had any project management experience. As might be expected, the challenges of climate, food, language, and especially culture shock were nearly overwhelming to the small team. The heat was sweltering to the northern Europeans and the food was tasteless—Lange had to negotiate with the hotel's kitchen staff in order to add more spices in the food. But the cultural change was the

most challenging, particularly regarding time since African time was much more casual than Scandinavian time and the team was on a limited-time schedule. For example, to help secure local buy-in, Lange engaged a local carpenter to build the desks and tables for the school. When she checked back a few days before the furniture was due, she was shocked to find that he hadn't even started the work: "Time is unpredictable; I will call you," he said.

Lange found that negotiation seemed to be required for everything. "Negotiation skills definitely were the most valuable of all the project management training that I have taken." She found that she constantly needed to count to 10 in her interactions, reflect on where these people were coming from, and figure out how to create a win-win situation that would satisfy both parties. The townsfolk began to refer to her as "The Diplomat." Impressed with the foreigners who were trying to help them, the local villagers pitched in to help on the project. Lange found that, rather than going through official channels, she made better progress personally talking with many of the women who were doing the work, which solved a lot of the problems the team encountered.

However, as the end of their time there approached, success appeared unlikely. As the team considered how disappointed the children and villagers would be to not have the school completed, they decided to work in shifts throughout the night. The increased commitment paid off, and the school was completed by the time the "reality show" was over.

Source: B. G. Yovovich, " Worlds Apart," *PM Network,* Vol. 24.

4.1 CONFLICT AND THE PROJECT LIFE CYCLE

In this section, following a brief discussion of the project life cycle, we will categorize the types of conflicts that frequently occur in the project environment, and then amplify the nature of these conflicts. Finally, we will link the project life cycle with the fundamental conflict categories and discover that certain patterns of conflict are associated with the different periods in the life of a project. With this knowledge, the PM can do a faster and more accurate job of diagnosing the nature of the conflicts he or she is facing, thereby reducing the likelihood of escalating the conflict by dealing with it ineffectually.

More on the Project Life Cycle

Various authors define the stages of the project life cycle (see Figures 1-3, 1-4, and 1-5) in different ways. Two of the most commonly cited definitions are those of Thamhain et al. (1975a) and Adams et al. (1983). The former use a four-stage model with project formation, buildup, main program, and phase-out identified as the stages of the life cycle. Adams et al. also break the project life cycle into four, but slightly different, stages: conceptualization, planning, execution, and termination.

For our purposes, these two views of the cycle are not significantly different. During the first stage, senior management tentatively, sometimes unofficially, approves preliminary planning for a project. Often, this management recognition is preceded by some strictly unofficial "bootleg" work to test the feasibility of an idea. Initial planning is undertaken, basic objectives are often adopted, and the project may be "scoped out." The second stage is typified by detailed planning, budgeting, scheduling, and the aggregation of resources. In the third stage, the lion's share of the actual work on the project is accomplished. During the final stage of the life cycle, work is completed and products are turned over to the client or user. This stage also includes disposition of the project's assets and personnel. It may even include preparation for the initial stage of another related project to follow.

Categories of Conflict

All stages of the project life cycle appear to be typified by conflict. Thamhain et al. (1975a, 1975b) have done extensive research on conflict in the project. These conflicts center on such matters as schedules, priorities, staff and labor requirements, technical factors, administrative procedures, cost estimates, and, of course, personality conflicts (Afzalur, 1992). Thamhain et al. collected data on the frequency and magnitude of conflicts of each type during each stage of the project life cycle. Multiplying conflict frequency by a measure of conflict magnitude and adjusting for the proportion of PMs who reported each specific type of conflict, they derived an estimate of the "intensity" of the conflicts.

On examination of the data, it appears that the conflicts fall into three fundamentally different categories:

1. Groups working on the project may have different goals and expectations.
2. There is significant uncertainty about who has the authority to make decisions.
3. There are interpersonal conflicts between people who are parties-at-interest in the project.

Some conflicts reflect the fact that the day-to-day work on projects is usually carried out by many different units of the organization, units that often differ in their objectives and technical judgments. The result is that these units have different expectations about the project, its costs and rewards, its relative importance, and its timing. Conflicts about schedules, intra- and interproject priorities, cost estimates, and staff time tend to fall into this category. At base, they arise because the project manager and the functional managers have very different goals. The PM's concern is the project. The primary interest of the functional manager is the daily operation of the functional department.

Other conflicts reflect the fact that both technical and administrative procedures are important aspects of project management. Uncertainty about who has the authority to make decisions on resource allocation, on administrative procedures, on communication, on technological choices, and on all the other matters affecting the project produces conflict between the PM and the other parties. It is simple enough (and correct) to state that the functional manager controls who works on the project and makes technical decisions, while the project manager controls the schedule and flow of work. In practice, in the commonly hectic environment of the project, amid the day's countless little crises faced by project and functional manager alike, the distinction is rarely clear.

Finally, some conflicts reflect the fact that human beings are an integral part of all projects. In an environment that depends on the cooperation of many persons, it seems inevitable that some personalities will clash. Also, in conflicts between the project and the client, or between senior management and the project, it is the project manager who personifies the project and thus is generally a party to the conflict.

We can categorize these conflicts as conflict over differing goals, over uncertainty about the locus of authority, and between personalities. For the entire array of conflict types and parties-at-interest, see Table 4-1.

Table 4-1   Project Conflicts by Category and Parties-at-Interest

| *Parties-at-Interest* | *Categories of Conflict* | | |
	Goals	*Authority*	*Interpersonal*
Project team	Schedules Priorities	Technical	Personality
Client	Schedules Priorities	Technical	
Functional and senior management	Schedules Priorities Labor Cost	Technical Administrative	Personality

The three types of conflict seem to involve the parties-at-interest to the project in identifiable ways. The different goals and objectives of the project manager, senior management, and functional managers are a major and constant source of conflict. For example, senior management (at times, arbitrarily) is apt to fix all three parameters of the project—time, cost, and scope—and then to assume that the PM will be able to achieve all the preset targets. Underestimation of cost and time is a natural consequence of this practice, and it leads directly to conflict between the PM, as a representative of the project team, and senior management. A second consequence is that the PM tries to pass the stringent cost and time estimates along to functional managers whose units are expected to perform certain work on the project. More conflict arises when the functional managers complain that they cannot meet the time and cost restrictions. All this tends to build failure into the job of managing a project, another source of conflict between the PM and senior management.

Functional managers also may not see eye-to-eye with the PM on such issues as the project's priority or the desirability of assigning a specifically named individual to work on the project, or even the applicability of a given technical approach to the project. In addition, the client's priorities and schedule, whether an inside or outside client, may differ radically from those of senior management and the project team. Finally, the project team has its own ideas about the appropriateness of the schedule or level of project staffing. The Thamhain et al. (1975a) data show that these goal-type conflicts occur in all stages of the project's life cycle, though they are particularly serious in the early stages. Regardless of the timing, in many cases it is not certain just whose priorities are ruling.

There are, of course, a number of methods for settling conflicts about priorities between projects, as well as intraproject conflicts. Often, the project selection model used to approve projects for funding will generate a set of projects ranked by some measure of value. It is also common for senior management to determine interproject priorities. The relative importance of the various tasks in an individual project is set by the project manager, who allocates scarce resources depending on the requirements of schedule, task difficulty, resource availability, and similar considerations. The existence of these methods for resolving priority conflicts is all too often irrelevant, because there is a powerful tendency for both project and functional managers to optimize their individual interests, with little regard for the total organization.

Locus-of-authority conflicts are endemic to projects. The project team and the client tend to focus on the technical procedures, debating the proper approach to the project, or perhaps how to solve individual problems that can occur at any stage. Senior management has other fish to fry. Not only do they insist that the project manager adopt and maintain a set of administrative procedures that conform to organizational and legal standards, but they also are quite concerned with who reports to whom and whose permission is required to take what action. The astute reader will note that such concerns are not entirely appropriate for projects. Our discussions with senior managers lead us to the obvious conclusion that it is common for senior management to want the efficiency and other advantages of projects but simultaneously to attempt to maintain the managerial comforts of traditional hierarchical structures—a sure source of conflict.

The conflict-resolution potential of partnering and project charters should be quite clear. Neither technique will stop conflicts from arising, but they will sharply lower the intensity of the conflicts as well as provide a framework for resolving conflict. They will even allow an environment in which the PM and functional managers can take positions that support the total organization rather than suboptimizing the project or the function.

Project managers will often find themselves arguing for scheduling or resource priorities from functional managers who outrank them by several levels. Neither the functional nor the project managers are quite sure about who has what authority. A constant complaint of project managers is "I have to take the responsibility, but I have no authority at all."

People problems arise, for the most part, within the project team, though functional managers may clash with PMs—the former accusing the latter of being "pushy," and the latter accusing the former of "foot dragging." In our experience, most personality clashes on the project team result from differences in technical approach or philosophy of problem solving, and in the methods used to implement the project results. Of course, it is quite possible that a personality conflict causes a technical conflict. It is also possible that any type of conflict will appear, at first blush, to be a personality clash.

Next, we put these conflicts into the chronological perspective of the project life cycle.

Project Formation

In the initial stage of the project life cycle, most of the conflict centers around the inherent confusion of setting up a project in the environment of matrix management. Almost nothing about the project or its governance has been decided. Even the project's technical objectives, not clearly defined or established, are apt to be understood only in the most general sense. Moving from this state of semichaos to the relatively ordered world of the buildup stage is difficult. To make this transition, four fundamental issues must be handled, although not necessarily in the order presented here.

First, the technical objectives of the project must be specified to a degree that will allow the detailed planning of the buildup stage to be accomplished. Second, commitment of resources to the project must be forthcoming from senior management and from functional managers. Third, the priority of the project, relative to the priorities of the parent organization's other projects, must be set and communicated. We feel the project's priority must be set as early as possible in the life of the project. (While it will probably not save the project from delay in the event of a mandate, it stands as an important political signal to functional managers about which projects take precedence in case of resource conflicts.)

These conditions are not sufficient, but they are most certainly necessary if the conflicts typical of the formation stage are to be resolved—at least at a reasonable level—and not simply carried forward to the buildup stage in an exacerbated state.

The project manager who practices conflict avoidance in this stage is inviting disaster in the next. The four fundamental issues above underlie such critical but down-to-earth matters as these: *Which* of the functional areas will be needed to accomplish project tasks? *What* will be the required level of involvement of each of the functional areas? How will conflicts over resources/facility usage between this and other projects be settled? What about those resource/facility conflicts between the project and the routine work of the functions? *Who* has the authority to decide the technical, scheduling, personnel, and cost questions that will arise? Most important, *how* will changes in the parent organization's priorities be communicated to everyone involved?

Note that three of the four fundamental issues—delimiting the technical objectives, getting management commitment, and setting the project's relative priority—must be resolved irrespective of what organizational form is selected for the project. It should also be noted that the organizational structure selected will have a major impact on the ways in which the conflicts are handled. The more independent and standalone the project, the more authoritative the role played by the PM. The weaker the project and the more functional ties, the more authority is embedded in the functional managers. Lack of clarity about the relative power/influence/authority of the PM and the functional managers is a major component of all conflicts involving technical decisions, resource allocation, and scheduling.

Project Buildup

Thamhain et al. (1975a, p. 39) note that conflict occurring in the buildup stage "over project priorities, schedules, and administrative procedures...appears as an extension from the previous program phase." This is the period during which the project moves (or should move) from a general concept to a highly detailed set of plans. If the project is independent and standalone, the PM seeks a commitment of *people* from the functional departments. If the project is functionally tied down, the PM seeks a commitment of *work* from the functional departments. In either case, the PM seeks commitment from functional managers who are under pressure to deliver support to other projects, in addition to the routine, everyday demands made on their departments.

As the project's plans become detailed, conflicts over technical issues build—again, conflicts between the PM and the functional areas tend to predominate. Usually, the functional departments can claim more technical expertise than the PM, who is a "generalist." On occasion, however, the PM is also a specialist. In such situations, discussions between the functional manager and the project manager about the best technical approach often result in conflict. The total level of conflict is at its highest in this transition period.

Main Program

Schedules are still a major source of conflict in the main program phase of the project life cycle, though the proximate cause of schedule-related conflict is usually different than in the earlier stages. Project plans have been developed and approved by everyone involved (although, perhaps, grudgingly), and the actual work is under way. Let us make an assumption that is certain to be correct; let us assume that some activity runs into difficulty and is late in being completed. Every task that is dependent on this late activity will also be delayed. Some of these subsequent activities will, if sufficiently late and if the late work is not made up, delay the entire project.

In order to prevent this consequence, the PM must try to get the schedule back on track. But catching up is considerably more difficult than falling behind. Catching up requires extra resources that the functional groups who are doing the "catching up" will demand, but which the PM may not have.

The more complex the project, the more difficult it is to trace and estimate the impact of all the delays, and the more resources that must be consumed to get things back on schedule. Throughout this book we have referred to the PM's job of managing time/cost/scope trade-offs. Maintaining the project schedule is precisely an exercise in managing trade-offs, but adding to the project's cost or scaling down the project's technical capabilities in order to save time are trade-offs the PM will not take if there is any viable alternative. The PM's ability to make trade-offs is often constrained by contract, company policy, and ethical considerations. In reality, trade-off decisions are quite difficult.

Like schedule conflicts, technical conflicts are frequent and serious during the main program stage. Also like schedule conflicts, the source of technical conflict is somewhat different than in earlier stages. Just as a computer and a printer must be correctly linked together in order to perform properly, so must the many parts of a project. These linkages are known as *interfaces*. The number of interfaces increases rapidly as the project gets larger, which is to say that the system gets more complex. As the number of interfaces increases, so does the probability that problems will arise at the interfaces. The need to manage these interfaces and to correct incompatibilities is the key to the technical conflicts in the main program phase.

Project Phase-out

As in the main program stage, schedule is the major source of conflict during project phase-out. If schedule slippage has occurred in the main program stage (and it probably has), the consequences will surely be felt in this final stage. During phase-out, projects with firm deadlines develop an environment best described as hectic. The PM, project team, and functional groups often band together to do what is necessary to complete the project on time and to specification. Cost overruns, if not outrageously high, are tolerated—though they may not be forgiven and they will certainly be remembered.

Technical problems are comparatively rare during phase-out because most have been solved or bypassed earlier. Similarly, working interfaces have been developed and put in place. If the project involves implementing a technology in an outside client's system, technical conflicts will probably arise, but they are usually less intense.

Thamhain et al. (1975b, p. 41) note that personality conflicts are the second-ranked source of conflict during phase-out. They ascribe these conflicts to interpersonal stress caused by the pressure to complete the project, and to individuals' natural anxiety about leaving the project either to be assigned to another, or be returned to a functional unit. In addition, we have observed conflict, sometimes quite bitter, focused on the distribution of the project's capital equipment and supplies when the project is completed. Conflict also arises between projects phasing out and those just starting, particularly if the latter need resources or personnel with scarce talents being used by the former.

The way in which Thamhain et al. have defined conflict as having its source in differences about goals/expectations, uncertainty about authority, and interpersonal problems, precludes identifying conflict as occurring between discipline-oriented and problem-oriented team members. Recall our discussions of Hughes (1998) and de Laat (1994). We do not argue that Thamhain et al. are in error, but merely that their classification does not specifically include a type of conflict we feel is both frequent and important. Much of the conflict identified during our discussion of planning in Chapter 6, it seems to us, is due to discipline/problem-orientation differences. A clear example comes from an interview recorded during Pelled et al.'s (1994, p. 23) research on conflict in multifunctional design teams. One team member speaking of another said, "He will do whatever he thinks is right to get his [own] job done, whether or not it's good for [the company] or anyone else." In context, it is clear that this conflict was between a problem-oriented individual and one who was discipline oriented.

The upshot is simple. As we noted in the first section of Chapter 1, conflict is an inherent characteristic of projects, and the project manager is constantly beset by conflict. The ability to reduce and resolve conflict in ways that support achievement of the project's goals is a prime requisite for success as a PM. The primary tool to accomplish conflict resolution and reduction is negotiation, and the method of handling conflict established in the project formation stage will set the pattern for the entire project. Therefore, the style of negotiation adopted by the PM is critical.

Much has been written on conflict resolution. Burke's classic paper on the confrontation-problem solving method of resolving conflicts is offered as a "Reading" at the end of this chapter. The similarities between the confrontation-problem solving technique for conflict resolution and win-win negotiation covered in the following section are quite striking.

Project Management in Practice
Consideration of Waste During Project Implementation

Heathrow is the world's busiest international airport. The growth in air travel means that Heathrow is currently pushed to capacity and needs to expand. Terminal 5 has been one of Europe's largest construction projects, with 16 major projects and 147 subprojects and caters for 30 million passengers annually.

A key achievement of the project was that while working in consensus with contractors and suppliers, the project sponsor, British Airports Authority (BAA), was able to recycle or recover over 97% of waste material during the implementation phase of the project. This was enabled by taking into consideration the use of waste material during design and construction, and into operation of Terminal 5.

Design teams adopted the principles of standardisation in design, prefabrication and modularisation, dramatically reducing waste generated during construction and maximising efficiencies in material use and delivery. The innovative 'just in time' logistics strategy adopted at T5, and on-site housekeeping practices such as designated storage areas and segregated vehicle and pedestrian routes, ensured that materials were delivered to the work place as they were needed, and not stored on-site. This reduced the amount of material damaged on-site, and so reduced waste. The proactive logistics strategy also reduced the over-ordering of materials.

BAA worked with suppliers to reduce the amount of packaging delivered to the T5 site. To ensure buy in, sustainability workshops were run for suppliers focusing particularly on reducing packaging waste. Other steps were taken to reduce waste from the outset:

- All suppliers were encouraged to reduce packaging as far as possible and choose reusable materials to package their products.

- Where packaging was unavoidable, suppliers were encouraged to take back the packaging they supplied for reuse.

- Agreements with the cable suppliers enabled cable drums to be returned to the supplier for reuse.

- Standard specifications for products such as paint enabled them to be ordered in large quantities, thus reducing waste and enabling large packaging to be returned, e.g., ICI Dulux paint cans were returned to the supplier.

On-site consolidation of waste using compactors and roll packers, whilst not reducing the weight of waste, significantly reduced the volume of waste sent off-site, reducing the number of vehicle movements. Consolidation of hazardous materials during construction significantly reduced the transport of these materials.

Designated skips were provided for general, wood, metal and cardboard waste to encourage segregation for recycling. Waste cable and plasterboard were also segregated for recycling and in the offices, paper was collected through a desktop recycling box scheme. General waste was further processed and sorted by the waste contractor, who typically recycled 87% of the waste they processed.

Segregation of the hazardous waste stream was undertaken at the workface by the project teams who separated out aerosols, paints, solvents and other hazardous waste into designated hazardous waste drums. These were collected by the hazardous waste contractor, sorted and consolidated on-site prior to removal.

Lessons Learned

Working in consensus with contractors and suppliers enables the project sponsor to achieve effective waste minimisation as the promotion of recycling requires the commitment of everyone on-site. Numerous initiatives across T5, from the bottom-up, local initiatives suggested and implemented by the workforce, to the top-down strategic approach to logistics, have all contributed to the achievements in waste management at T5. With a designated team to coordinate waste management, working closely with the waste contractor promoted teamwork and a solution-led approach to waste management, generating improvements in performance.

Source: Case Study, Constructing Excellence, www.constructing-excellence.org.uk

4.2   THE NATURE OF NEGOTIATION

The favored technique for resolving conflict is *negotiation*. What is negotiation? Wall (1985, preface) defines negotiation as "the process through which two or more parties seek an acceptable rate of exchange for items they own or control." Dissatisfied with this definition, he spends part of a chapter extending and discussing the concept (Chapter 1), without a great deal of improvement. Cohen (1980, p. 15) says that "Negotiation is a field of knowledge and endeavor that focuses on gaining the favor of people from whom we want things." Other authors define negotiation differently, but do not appreciably extend Cohen's definition. Even if no single definition neatly fits all the activities we label "negotiation," we do recognize that such terms as "mediate," "conciliate," "make peace," "bring to agreement," "settle differences," "moderate," "arbitrate," "adjust differences," "compromise," "bargain," "dicker," and "haggle" (*Roget's International Thesaurus*, 1993) are synonyms for " negotiate" in some instances.

Most of the conflicts that involve the organization and outsiders have to do with property rights and contractual obligations. In these cases, the parties to negotiation see themselves as opponents. Conflicts arising inside the organization may also appear to involve property rights and obligations, but they typically differ from conflicts with outsiders in one important way: As far as the firm is concerned, they are conflicts between allies, not opponents. Wall (1985, pp. 149–150) makes this point neatly:

> Organizations, like groups, consist of interdependent parts that have their own values, interests, perceptions, and goals. Each unit seeks to fulfill its particular goal...and the effectiveness of the organization depends on the success of each unit's fulfillment of its specialized task. Just as important as the fulfillment of the separate tasks is the integration of the unit activities such that each unit's activities aid or at least do not conflict with those of the others.

One of the ways in which organizations facilitate this integration is to establish "*lateral relations* [which] allow decisions to be made horizontally across lines of authority" (Wall, 1985, p. 150). Because each unit will have its own goals, integrating the activities of two or more units is certain to produce the conflicts that Wall says should not take place. The conflicts may, however, be resolved by negotiating a solution, if one exists, that produces gains (or minimizes losses) for all parties. Raiffa (1982, p. 139) defines a Pareto-optimal solution to the two-party conflict and discusses the nature of the bargaining process required to reach optimality, a difficult and time-consuming process. While it is not likely that the conflicting parties will know and understand the complex trade-offs in a real-world, project management, many-persons/many-issues conflict (see Raiffa, 1982, Chapters 17–23), the general objective is to find a solution such that no party can be made better off without making another party worse off by the same amount or more—i.e., a Pareto-optimal solution.

The concept of a Pareto-optimal solution is important. Approaching intraproject conflicts with a desire to win a victory over other parties is inappropriate. The PM must remember that she will be negotiating with project stakeholders many times in the future. If she conducts a win-lose negotiation and the other party loses, from then on she will face a determined adversary who seeks to defeat her. This is not helpful. The proper outcome of this type of negotiation should be to optimize the outcome in terms of overall organizational goals. Although it is not always obvious how to do this, negotiation is clearly the correct approach.

During the negotiation process, an ethical situation often arises that is worth noting. Consider the situation where a firm requests an outside contractor to develop a software package to achieve some function. When the firm asks for a specific objective to be accomplished, it frequently does not know if that is a major job or a trivial task because it lacks technical competence in that area. Thus, the contractor has the opportunity to misrepresent the task to its customer, either inflating the cost for a trivial task, or minimizing the impact of a significant task in order to acquire the contract and then boosting the cost later. The ethics of the situation require that each party in the negotiation be honest with the other, even in situations where it is clear there will not be further work between the two.

4.3   PARTNERING, CHARTERING, AND SCOPE CHANGE

Projects provide ample opportunity for the project manager (PM) to utilize her or his skills at negotiation. There are, however, three situations commonly arising during projects that call for the highest level of negotiating skill the PM can muster: the use of subcontractors, the use of input from two or more functional units to design and develop the project's mission, and the management of changes ordered in the project's deliverables and/or priorities after the project is underway (de Laat, 1994; Hughes, 1998). The former probably accounts for more litigation than all other aspects of the project combined. The latter two are, in the authors' experience, by far the most common and most troublesome issues project managers report facing.

Partnering

In recent years there has been a steady growth in the frequency of outsourcing parts of projects (Smith, 1998). External suppliers, increasingly, are delivering parts of projects, including tangible products and services as well as intangible knowledge and skills. There are many reasons beyond avoidance of litigation that firms enter partnering arrangements with each other, for example, diversification of technical risk, avoidance of capital investment, reducing political risk on multinational projects, shortening the duration of the project, and pooling of complementary knowledge, among others (Beecham et al., 1998, p. 192).

Generally, relations between the organization carrying out a project and a subcontractor working on the project are best characterized as adversarial. The parent organization's objective is to get the deliverable at the lowest possible cost, as soon as possible. The subcontractor's objective is to produce the deliverable at the highest possible profit with the least effort. These conflicting interests tend to lead both parties to work in an atmosphere of mutual suspicion and antagonism. Indeed, it is almost axiomatic that the two parties will have significantly different ideas about the exact nature of the deliverable itself. The concept of "partnering" has been developed to replace this atmosphere with one of cooperation and mutual helpfulness, but the basically adversarial relationship makes cooperation difficult in the best of cases (Larson et al., 1997).

Cowen et al. (1992, p. 5) define partnering as follows:

> Project partnering is a method of transforming contractual relationships into a cohesive, cooperative project team with a single set of goals and established procedures for resolving disputes in a timely and effective manner.

They present a multistep process for building partnered projects. First, the parent firm must make a commitment to partnering, select subcontractors who will also make such a commitment, engage in joint team-building exercises, and develop a "charter" for the project. (See the next subsection for a description of such a charter.) Second, both parties must implement the partnering process with a four-part agreement on: (1) "joint evaluation" of the project's progress; (2) a method for resolving any problems or disagreements; (3) acceptance of a goal for continuous improvement (also known as "total quality management," or TQM) for the joint project; and (4) continuous support for the process of partnering from senior management of both parties. Finally, the parties commit to a joint review of "project execution" when the project is completed. Beecham et al. (1998, p. 194ff) note several things that can "doom" partnering agreements and they develop several "propositions" that lead to success. Partnering is an attempt to mitigate the risks associated with subcontracting. Consider the nature of the steps listed above. Clearly, there are specific risks that must be managed in each of them.

Each step in this process must be accompanied by negotiation, and the negotiations must be nonadversarial. The entire concept is firmly rooted in the assumption of mutual trust between the partners, and this assumption, too, requires nonadversarial negotiation. Finally, these articles focus on partnering when the partners are members of different organizations. We think the issue is no less relevant when the partners are from different divisions or departments of the same parent organization. Identical assumptions hold, identical steps must be taken, and interparty agreements must be reached for partnering to succeed.

The concept of partnering, however, goes far beyond two-party agreements between buyer and seller or interdepartmental cooperation on a project. The use of multiparty consortia to pursue technological research objectives is common. As noted in Chapter 3, SEMATECH is a consortium of semiconductor manufacturers for the purpose of conducting joint research projects in the field. The consortium was exempted from prosecution under the U.S. anti-trust laws when the National Cooperative Research Act of 1984 was passed expressly to allow such cooperation among competitors (Rosegger et al., 1990).

There are a great many such groups of competitors engaged in cooperative research and other cooperative activities (not, one hopes, in price-setting or other illegal activities). They exist worldwide and are often multinational in their membership; for example, Airbus Industry (originally British, French, Spanish, and German) and International Aero Engines (originally USA, Japan, Germany, Italy, and UK), as mentioned in Chapter 3.

Airbus Industry is not only a consortium of private firms from four different nations, but each of the four governments subsidized their respective private firms. This venture, apparently undertaken in order to foster a European competitor to USA's Boeing Aircraft, resulted in a successful competitor in the market for commercial aircraft.

Partnering, however, is not without its problems. There can be no doubt that those who have not had much experience with partnering underrate its difficulty. Partnering requires strong support from senior management of all participants, and it requires continuous support of project objectives and partnering agreements (Moore et al., 1995). Above all, and most difficult of all, it requires open and honest communication between the partners. With all of its problems, however, partnering yields benefits great enough to be worth the efforts required to make it work correctly (Baker, 1996; Larson et al., 1997).

Project Management in Practice
Habitat for Humanity Wins a Big One

Loudoun Habitat for Humanity (LHH) of Sterling, VA, had everything going its way in its proposal to the Loudoun County Housing Trust Committee for $876,000 to help purchase, build, and redevelop 21 local properties for low-income families:

- The county had a $3 million housing fund available specifically to develop housing for low- and moderate-income families.

- The $876,000 would enable LHH to apply for federal stimulus funding earmarked for projects such as this, which, together with private donations, would bring in another $2,630,000 for a total of $3.5 million.

- There was no other competing group in the area building homes for low-income families.

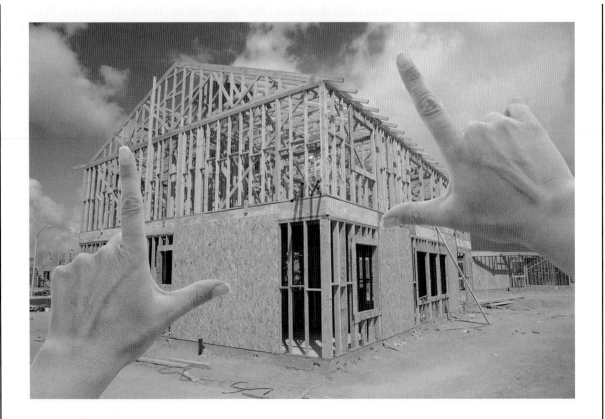

- LHH had good construction, project management, and financial expertise to successfully execute this project within the schedule and budget.

Still, LHH had to first make a successful 2-hour presentation to the Committee, convincing them of their qualifications and the attractive business case the proposal offered. But, despite prodding and frequent calls, LHH didn't hear back from the Committee, and the deadline for federal stimulus funds was approaching quickly. So LHH developed a strategy of writing letters, calling, and using any contacts available to explain the urgency of the timeline. Finally, they heard from the committee, which denied their application; apparently there had been at least one committee member who would rather use the funds to invest in high-density rentals. But this made no sense to LHH, since the county stimulus money for affordable housing would be denied—the county's political inclination didn't support high-density subsidized rentals so the zoning application would probably be rejected, and the recent U.S. fiscal crisis had reduced the value of the low-income tax credits needed to make such a project viable.

However, the Committee's recommendation had to be approved by the County Board of Supervisors, and LHH was able to make a presentation there, outlining the advantages of their proposal and the disadvantages of the high-density rentals proposal. But again, they didn't hear anything back. With time running out, they made an effort to contact each of the nine supervisors, catching three in person and delivering letters to the others. The odds were stacked against them because accepting LHH's proposal meant overturning the Committee's recommendation. The Board decided in LHH's favor, but only approved $500,000 for a major portion of their proposal. But it came just in time for LHH to win federal stimulus funds to leverage that money and allow them to proceed with the major portion of their plan.

Source: S. F. Gale, "A Closer Look," *PM Network*, Vol. 24.

Chartering

The agreements between groups partnering on large endeavors are often referred to as charters. A project (program, etc.) charter is simply a written agreement between the PM, senior management, and the functional managers who are committing resources and/or people to a specific project (program, etc.). Bear in mind, the charter may take many different forms. Typically, it details the expected deliverables, often including schedules, budgets, and resource commitments. It attests to the fact that senior management of all relevant organizations, functional managers, and the PM are "on the same page," agreeing about what is to be done, when, and at what cost. Note that if there is such an agreement, there is also an implication that none of the parties will change the agreement unilaterally, or, at least, without prior consultation with the other parties. Many projects do not have charters, which is one reason for observing that many projects are not completed on specification, on time, and on budget.

In Chapter 6, we will describe an iterative process for developing a project plan. We note that it is not uncommon for the individuals or groups who make commitments during the process of developing the project plan to sign-off on their commitments. The signed-off project plan can constitute a project charter, particularly if senior management has signed-off on the overall mission statement, *and if it is recognized as a charter by all parties to the plan.*

A somewhat less specific project charter appears in Cowen et al. (1992, Figure 2, p. 8), in which the various members of the partnering team sign a commitment to:

- Meet design intent
- Complete contract without need for litigation
- Finish project on schedule:
  —Timely resolution of issues
  —Manage joint schedule
- Keep cost growth to less than 2 percent...etc.

Of course, to meet the underlying purpose of a charter, even these less-specific terms assume an agreement on the "design intent," the schedule, and costs.

Scope Change

PMBOK Guide

Chapter 5

The problem of changing the scope expected of a project is a major issue in project management and constitutes part of the second PMBOK knowledge area. No matter how carefully a project is planned, it is almost certain to be changed before completion. No matter how carefully defined at the start, the scope of most projects is subject to considerable uncertainty. There are three basic causes for change in projects. Some changes result because planners erred in their initial assessment about how to achieve a given end or erred in their choice of the proper goal for the project. Technological uncertainty is the fundamental causal factor for either error. The foundation for a building must be changed because a preliminary geological study did not reveal a weakness in the structure of the ground on which the building will stand. An R & D project must be altered because metallurgical test results indicate another approach should be adopted. The project team becomes aware of a recent innovation that allows a faster, cheaper solution to the conformation of a new computer.

Other changes result because the client/user or project team learns more about the nature of the project deliverable or about the setting in which it is to be used. An increase in user or team knowledge or sophistication is the primary factor leading to change. A computer program must be extended or rewritten because the user thinks of new uses for the software. Physicians request that intensive care units in a hospital be equipped with laminar air-flow control in order to accommodate patients highly subject to infection who might otherwise not be admissible in an ICU. The fledgling audio-addict upgrades the specifications for a system to include very high frequencies so that his dog can enjoy the music, too.

A third source of change is the mandate. This is a change in the environment in which the project is being conducted. As such, it cannot be controlled by the PM. A new law is passed. A government regulatory unit articulates a new policy. A trade association sets a new standard. The parent organization of the user applies a new criterion for its purchases. In other words, the rules of conduct for the project are altered. A state-approved pollution control system must be adopted for each chemical refinery project. The state government requires all new insurance policies to conform to a revised law specifying that certain information must be given to potential purchasers. At times, mandates affect only priorities. The mandate in question might move a very important customer to the "head of the line" for some scarce resource or service.

To some extent, risk management techniques can be applied to scope change. Technological uncertainty can be mitigated by careful analysis of the technologies involved, including the use of technological forecasting. Risk of scope change caused by increased user knowledge can only be managed by improving the up-front communication with the client and then establishing a formal process to handle change. See Chapter 11 for more about this. Finally, mandates are, for the most part, unpredictable. These can be "managed" only by having some flexibility built into the budget and schedule of the project. Ways of doing this sensibly will be discussed in the following two chapters.

As Greek philosopher Heraclitus said, "Nothing endures but change." It is thus with projects, but whatever the nature of the change, specifications of the deliverables must be altered, and the schedule and budget recalculated. Obviously, negotiation will be required to develop new agreements between the parties-at-interest to the project. These negotiations are difficult because most of the stakeholders will have a strong interest in maintaining the status quo. If the proposed change benefits the client and increases the cost of the project, the producer will try to sequester some of the user's potential benefit in the form of added charges to offset the added cost. The client will, of course, resist. All parties must, once again, seek a Pareto-optimal solution—always a difficult task.

Change by mandate raises an additional problem. Not only are the project's deliverables, budget, and schedule usually changed, the *priorities* of other projects are typically changed too, if only temporarily while the mandate receives the system's full attention. Suddenly, a PM loses access to key resources, because they are urgently required elsewhere. Key contributors to a project miss meetings or are unable to keep promised task-delivery dates. All too often, the PM's response to this state of affairs is anger and/or discouragement. Neither is appropriate.

> This project is so important, we can't let things that are more important interfere with it.
>
> Anonymous

After discussing priorities with both PMs and senior managers, it has become clear to us that most firms actually have only three levels of priority (no matter how ornate the procedure for setting project priorities might seem to be). First, there are the high-priority projects, that is, the "set" of projects currently being supported. When resource conflicts arise within this high-priority set, precedence is typically given to those projects with the earliest due date. (More about this is in Chapter 9.) Second, there are the lower-priority projects, the projects "we would like to do when we have the time and money." Third, occasionally, there are urgent projects—mandates—that must be done immediately. "Customer A's project must be finished by the end of the month." "The state's mandate must be met by June 30." Everything else is delayed to ensure that mandates are met. As noted earlier, we will have more to say on this subject in Chapter 11.

While project charters and partnerships would certainly help the PM deal with conflicts that naturally arise during a project, the use of charters and partnering is growing slowly—though outsourcing is growing rapidly. It is understandably difficult to convince senior managers to make the firm commitments implied in a project charter in the face of a highly uncertain future. Functional managers are loath to make firm commitments for precisely the same reason. So, too, the client, aware of her or his own ignorance about the degree to which the project output will meet his or her needs, is cautious about commitment—even when a procedure for negotiating change exists.

Partnering is a recently developed concept, and in our litigious society any system for conflict resolution that asks parties to forgo lawsuits is viewed with considerable suspicion. Indeed, we find that a great many organizations preach "team building," "TQM," and "employee involvement," but many fail to practice what they preach. For each participative manager you find, we can show you a dozen micromanagers. For each team player ready to share responsibility, we can show you a dozen "blame placers." The era of project charters and partnering is approaching, but it is not yet here.

4.4 SOME REQUIREMENTS AND PRINCIPLES OF NEGOTIATION

The word "negotiation" evokes many images: the United States President and Congress on the annual federal budget, the "Uruguay Round" of the GATT talks, a player's agent and the owner of an NFL team, the buyer and seller of an apartment complex, attorneys for husband and wife in a divorce settlement, union and management working out a collective bargaining agreement, tourist and peddler haggling over a rug in an Ankara market. But as we noted in the introduction to this chapter, none of these images is strictly appropriate for the project manager who must resolve the sorts of conflicts we have considered in the previous section.

The key to understanding the nature of negotiation as it applies to project management is the realization that few of the conflicts arising in projects have to do with *whether* or not a task will be undertaken or a deliverable produced. Instead, they have to do with the precise *design* of the deliverable and/or *how* the design will be achieved, by *whom*, *when*, and at *what cost*. The implication is clear: *The work of the project will be done.* If conflicts between any of the parties to the project escalate to the point where negotiations break down and work comes to a halt, everyone loses. *One requirement* for the conflict reduction/resolution methods used by the PM is that *they must allow the conflict to be settled without irreparable harm to the project's objectives.*

A closer consideration of the attorneys negotiating the divorce settlement makes clear a second requirement for the PM negotiating conflicts between parties-at-interest to the project. While the husband and wife (or the rug peddler and tourist) may employ unethical tactics during the negotiation process and, if not found out, profit from them at the expense of the other party, it is much less likely for the attorneys representing the husband and wife to do so—particularly if they practice law in the same community. The lawyers know they will have to negotiate on other matters in the future. Any behavior that breeds mistrust will make future negotiations extremely difficult, perhaps impossible. The rug peddler assumes no further contact with the tourist, so conscience is the sole governor of his or her ethics. A *second requirement* for the conflict resolution/reduction methods used by the PM is that *they allow (and foster) honesty between the negotiators.*

The conflicting parties-at-interest to a project are not enemies or competitors, but rather allies—members of an alliance with strong common interests. It is a *requirement of all conflicting parties to seek solutions to the conflict that not only satisfy their own individual needs, but also satisfy the needs of other parties to the conflict, as well as the needs of the parent organization*. In the language of negotiation, this is called a "win-win" solution. Negotiating to a win-win solution is the key to conflict resolution in project management.

Fisher et al. (1983, p. 11) have developed a negotiation technique that tends to maintain these three requirements. They call it "principled negotiation," that is, win-win. The method is straightforward; it is defined by four points.

1. *Separate the people from the problem.* The conflicting parties are often highly emotional. They perceive things differently and feel strongly about the differences. Emotions and objective fact get confused to the point where it is not clear which is which. Conflicting parties tend to attack one another rather than the problem. To minimize the likelihood that the conflict will become strictly interpersonal, the substantive problem should be carefully defined. Then everyone can work on it rather than each other.

2. *Focus on interests, not positions.* Positional bargaining occurs when the PM says to a functional manager: "I need this subassembly by November 15." The functional manager responds: "My group can't possibly start on it this year. We might be able to deliver it by February 1." These are the opening lines in a dialogue that sounds suspiciously like the haggling of the tourist and the rug peddler. A simple "Let's talk about the schedule for this subassembly" would be sufficient to open the discussion. Otherwise each party develops a high level of ego involvement in his or her position and the negotiation never focuses on the real interests and concerns of the conflicting parties—the central issues of the conflict. The exchange deteriorates into a series of positional compromises that do not satisfy either party and leave both feeling that they have lost something important.

   In positional negotiation, the "positions" are statements of immediate wants and assume that the environment is static. Consider these positional statements: "I won't pay more than $250,000 for that property." Or, as above, "We might be able to deliver it by February 1." The first position assumes that the bidder's estimates of future property values are accurate, and the second assumes that the group's current workload (or a shortage of required materials) will not change. When negotiation focuses on interests, the negotiator must determine the underlying concern of the other party. The real concerns or interests of the individuals stating the positions quoted above might be to earn a certain return on the investment in a property, or to not commit to delivery of work if delivery on the due date cannot be guaranteed. Knowledge of the other party's interests allows a negotiator to suggest solutions that satisfy the other party's interests without agreeing with the other's position.

3. *Before trying to reach agreement, invent options for mutual gain.* The parties-in-conflict usually enter negotiations knowing the outcome they would like. As a result, they are blind to other outcomes and are not particularly creative. Nonetheless, as soon as the substantive problems are spelled out, some effort should be devoted to finding a wide variety of possible solutions—or elements thereof—that advance the mutual interests of the conflicting parties. Success at finding options that produce mutual gain positively reinforces win-win negotiations. Cohen (1980) reports on a conflict between a couple in which "he" wanted to go to the mountains and "she" wanted to go to the shore. A creative win-win solution sent them both to Lake Tahoe.

4. *Insist on using objective criteria.* Rather than bargaining on positions, attention should be given to finding standards (e.g., market value, expert opinion, law, company policy) that can be used to determine the quality of an outcome. Doing this tends to make the negotiation less a contest of wills or exercise in stubbornness. If a functional manager wants to use an expensive process to test a part, it is acceptable for the PM to ask if such a process is required to ensure that the parts meet specified quality standards.

Fisher et al. (1983) have had some success with their approach in the Harvard (Graduate School of Business) Negotiation Project. Use of their methods increases the chance of finding win-win solutions.

There are many books on negotiation, some of which are listed in the bibliography of this chapter. Most of these works are oriented toward negotiation between opponents, not an appropriate mindset for the project manager, but all of them contain useful, tactical advice for the project manager. Wall's book (1985) is an excellent academic treatment of the subject. Fisher et al. (1983) is a clear presentation of principled negotiation, and contains much that is relevant to the PM. In addition, Herb Cohen's *You Can Negotiate Anything* (1980) is an outstanding guide to win-win negotiation. The importance of negotiation is beginning to be recognized by the project management profession (Dodson, 1998; Grossman, 1995; Long, 1997; and Robinson, 1997), but the subject has not yet found its way into the Project Management Body of Knowledge in discussions about conflict.

PMBOK Guide
9.3, 9.4

Among the tactical issues covered by most books on negotiation are things the project manager, as a beginning negotiator, needs to know. For example, what should a negotiator who wishes to develop a win-win solution do if the other party to the conflict adopts a win-lose approach? What do you do if the other party tries to put you under psychological pressure by seating you so that a bright light shines in your eyes? What do you do if the other party refuses to negotiate in order to put you under extreme time pressure to accept whatever solution he or she offers? How do you settle what you perceive to be purely technical disputes? How should you handle threats? What should be your course of action if a functional manager, with whom you are trying to reach agreement about the timing and technology of a task, goes over your head and attempts to enlist the aid of your boss to get you to accept a solution you feel is less than satisfactory? How can you deal with a person you suspect dislikes you?

Almost every writer on negotiation emphasizes the importance of understanding the interests of the person with whom you are negotiating. As we noted above, the positions taken by negotiators are not truly understandable without first understanding the interests and concerns that prompt those positions. The statement that a test requested for May 15 cannot be run until June 2 may simply mean that the necessary test supplies will not be delivered until the latter date. If the PM can get the supplies from another source in time for the May 15 deadline, the test can be run on schedule. But the ability to do this depends on knowing *why* the test was to be delayed. If the negotiation remains a debate on positions, the PM will never find out that the test could have been run on time. *The key to finding a negotiator's interests and concerns is to ask "Why?" when he or she states a position.*

The following vignette demonstrates the maintenance of a nonpositional negotiating style. This vignette is based on an actual event and was described to the authors by an "actor" in the case.

Project Management in Practice
Project Assessment and Recovery

As the client looked at the project report he knew something was amiss. With the critical launch date looming, there was the risk that this project to build a new customer service facility in India would be late. The impact of any overrun could run to hundreds of thousands of euros for each week that the new facility was behind schedule. As with every ailing project, some work had been done and some successes achieved but critical work packages were slipping behind schedule and over budget.

To get an informed view of the current position, the client contracted a consultancy to undertake a project audit. They provided an independent assessment of the current state of the program against the plan. Their findings were startling—the project was 20% over budget and would miss the critical launch date by over 30 days. Something had to change if this project was to be rescued.

The following key changes were implemented.

- The first key change was to replace the 'big bang' approach (where all the integrated services would go *live* on the same day) with a phased approach.
- The appointment of an on-site project manager who set about creating accurate schedules and work estimates.
- As investigations into the cost overruns showed that the majority of this was due to schedule slippages, this became the key focus of the ongoing management of the plan. The schedule was updated on a daily basis.
- Earned Value was implemented as the management reporting and control system to drive *value for money* throughout the project.

- In addition to key milestones being identified, a risk and responsibility (RACI) matrix and a communication plan were established to keep the recovery plan on track.
- An alternative project resourcing strategy was used to bring in local suppliers at a fraction of the original budget.

The outcome of these changes was that the project was delivered ahead of the initial schedule. The first phase went *live* 3 days early, with the following phases delivered on the revised schedule. In addition, these changes were not only able to prevent a potential loss on the overall project of close to €400,000, but it clawed back some of the initial overspend so that the overall expenditure was less than €5,000 over the original budget.

By taking the drastic action of bringing in fresh ideas and implementing a rigorous project management approach to the remaining work, this company was able to prevent a potential business disaster. This demonstrates clearly the power of effective project management to turn around ailing projects as well the dangers of the 'big bang' approach.

 SUMMARY

This chapter addressed the need for negotiation as a tool to resolve project conflicts. We discussed the nature of negotiation and its purpose in the organization. We also described various categories of conflict and related them to the project life cycle. We followed this by identifying a number of requirements and principles of negotiation. Finally, we presented a short vignette illustrating an actual negotiation situation.

Specific points made in the chapter were these:

- Negotiation within the firm should be directed at obtaining the best outcome for the organization, not winning.
- There are three traditional categories of conflict: goal-oriented, authority-based, and interpersonal.
- There are also three traditional sources of conflict. They are the project team itself, the client, and functional and senior management. We added the problem/discipline orientation of people working on the project.

- Critical issues to handle in the project formation stages are delimiting technical objectives, getting management commitment, setting the project's relative priority, and selecting the project organizational structure.
- The total level of conflict is highest during the project buildup stage.
- Scheduling and technical conflicts are most frequent and serious in the project buildup and main program stages, and scheduling conflicts in particular during the phase-out stage.
- Project negotiation requirements are that conflicts must be settled without permanent damage, the methodology must foster honesty, and the solution must satisfy both individuals' and the organization's needs.
- One promising approach to meeting the requirements of project negotiation is called "principled negotiation."

In the next chapter we move to the first task of the PM, organizing the project. We deal there not only with various organizational forms, such as functional, project, and matrix, but also with the organization of the project office. This task includes setting up the project team and managing the human element of the project.

GLOSSARY

Interfaces The boundaries between departments or functions.

Lateral Relations Communications across lines of equivalent authority.

Pareto-Optimal Solution A solution such that no party can be made better off without making another party worse off by the same amount or more.

Positional Negotiation Stating immediate wants on the assumption that the environment is static.

Principled Negotiation A process of negotiation that aims to achieve a win-win result.

Parties-at-interest Those who have a vested interest in the outcome of the negotiations.

Win-win When both parties are better off in the outcome.

QUESTIONS

Material Review Questions

1. Review and justify the placement of the seven types of conflicts into the nine cells of Table 4-1.

2. Discuss each of the four fundamental issues for potential conflict during the project formation stage.

3. Identify the types of likely conflicts during the project buildup, main program, and phaseout stages.

4. What are the three main requirements of project negotiation?

5. Describe the four points of principled negotiation.

6. What is the objective of negotiation?

7. What are the four categories of conflict?

8. What is "principled negotiation"?

Class Discussion Questions

9. Summarize the vignette in the chapter in terms of the negotiation skill used. Comment on the appropriateness and ethical aspects related to "burying" the cost.

10. What will be the likely result of a win-win style manager negotiating with a win-lose style manager? What if they are both win-lose styled?

11. Reallocate the placement of the seven types of conflicts into the nine cells of Table 4-1 according to your own logic.

12. How does the type of project organization affect each of the types of conflicts that occur over the project life cycle?

13. Project managers are primarily concerned with project interfaces. At what rate do these interfaces increase with increasing project size?

14. The critical term in the concept of principled negotiation is "position." Elaborate on the multiple meanings of this term relative to negotiation. Can you think of a better term?

15. Give an example of a Pareto-optimal solution in a conflict.

16. Given that many conflicts are the result of different parties having different interests, is it possible to achieve a win-win situation?

17. The chairman of Cadbury Schweppes PLC, G.A.H. Cadbury suggests (1987) the following test for an ethical action: Would you be embarrassed to have it described in the newspaper? Is this a sufficient test for ethics? Can you think of any others?

Quickly Building a School through Negotiation

18. Is time unpredictable? What did the carpenter mean?

19. Did Ms. Lange use any of the principles of negotiation in this project?

20. At some point do you think the team had to think about the goals of the reality show compared to the needs of the African slum children?

Consideration of Waste During Project Implementation

21. Based upon this case study, does the consensus approach lead to what is best for the overall community? Why (not)?

22. What alternative approaches were possible for BAA to manage the waste material during project implementation?

23. Could the successful implementation of waste hierarchy have been possible with either a bottom-up or top-down approach?

Habitat for Humanity Wins a Big One

24. Did LHH use any of the principles of negotiation described in the chapter?

25. How did LHH use the concept of "lateral relations"?

26. How do the concepts of partnering and scope change apply, or not apply, in this example?

Project Assessment and Recovery

27. What were the key steps in bringing the project back on track?

28. Whilst some success had been achieved in the project, it was still perceived to be 'destined' to fail. What do you think the classic warning signs are of a doomed project?

 ## INCIDENTS FOR DISCUSSION

Pritchard Soap Co.

Samantha ("Sam") Calderon is manager of a project that will completely alter the method of adding perfume to Pritchard Soap's "Queen Elizabeth" gift soap line. The new process will greatly extend the number of available scents and should result in a significant increase in sales. The project had been proceeding reasonably well, but fell several weeks behind when the perfume supplier, the Stephen Marcus Parfumissary, was unable to meet its delivery deadline because of a wildcat strike.

Under normal circumstances this would not have caused problems, but the project had been subject to a particularly long evaluation study and now was in danger of not being ready for the Christmas season. The major scheduling problem concerned Pritchard's toxicity lab. Kyle Lee, lab manager, had been most cooperative in scheduling the Queen Elizabeth perfumes for toxicity testing. He had gone out of his way to rearrange his own schedule to accommodate Sam's project. Because of the strike at Marcus, however, Sam cannot have the perfumes ready for test as scheduled, and the new test date Lee has given Sam will not allow her to make the new line available by Christmas. Sam suspects that the project might not have been approved if senior management had known that they would miss this year's Christmas season.

Questions: What was the source of change in this project and how will it affect the project's priority? What are Sam's alternatives? What should she do?

Sutton Electronics

Eric Frank was still basking in the glory of his promotion to marketing project manager for Sutton Electronics Corporation, a manufacturer of electronic fire alarm systems for motels, offices, and other commercial installations.

Eric's first project involved the development of a marketing plan for Sutton's revolutionary new alarm system, which was based on a sophisticated circuitry that detected and identified a large number of dangerous gases, as well as smoke and very high temperatures. The device was the brainchild of Ira Magee, vice-president of research and the technical wizard responsible for many of Sutton's most successful products.

It was unusual for so young and relatively inexperienced an employee as Eric to be given control of such a potentially important project, but he had shown skill in handling several complex, though routine, marketing assignments. In addition, he had the necessary scientific background to allow him to understand the benefits of Magee's proposed gas-detection system.

Four weeks into the project, Eric was getting quite worried. He had tried to set up an organizational and planning meeting several times. No matter when he scheduled the meeting, the manager of the manufacturing department, Jaki Benken, was unable to attend. Finally, Eric agreed that manufacturing could be represented by young Bill Powell, a Benken protégé who had just graduated from college and joined Sutton Electronics. However, Eric was doubtful that Powell could contribute much to the project.

Eric's worry increased when Powell missed the first planning meeting completely and did not appear at the second meeting until it was almost over. Powell seemed apologetic and indicated that plant floor crises had kept him away from both meetings. The project was now five weeks old, and Eric was almost three weeks late with the marketing master plan. He was thinking about asking Ira Magee for help.

Questions: Do you think that Eric should involve Magee at this point? If so, what outcome would you expect? If not, what should he do?

CONTINUING INTEGRATIVE CLASS PROJECT

The topic of negotiation will come up in two guises during the class project: When the PM is trying to assign tasks to the class members and they are resisting, and also possibly when the PM or class is negotiating for resources with the Instructor, the Dean, or others. The topic of conflict can arise at any time and over any issue, obviously.

In all these circumstances, the individuals would be well advised to recall the principles of negotiation (or quickly refer back to this chapter). The class historian should also be noting when conflicts and bargaining occurred during the project, as well as its nature, and resolution.

BIBLIOGRAPHY

Adams, J. R., and S. E. Barndt. "Behavioral Implications of the Project Life Cycle." In D. I. Cleland and W. R. King, eds., *Project Management Handbook.* New York: Van Nostrand Reinhold, 1983.

Afzalur, R. M. *Managing Conflict in Organizations.* Westport, CT: Praeger, 1992.

Baker, K. R. "Measuring the Benefits of Partnering." *PM Network,* June 1996.

Beecham, M. A., and M. Cordey-Hayes. "Partnering and Knowledge Transfer in the U.K. Motor Industry." *Technovation,* March 1998.

Cadbury, G. A. H. "Ethical Managers Make Their Own Rules." *Harvard Business Review,* September–October 1987.

Cohen, H. *You Can Negotiate Anything.* Secaucus, NJ: Lyle Stuart Inc., 1980.

Cowen, C., C. Gray, and E. W. Larson. "Project Partnering." *Project Management Journal,* December 1992.

de Laat, P. B. "Matrix Management of Projects and Power Struggles: A Case Study of an R&D Laboratory." *IEEE Engineering Management Review,* Winter 1995, reprinted from *Human Relations,* Vol. 47, No. 9, 1994.

Fisher, R., and W. Ury. *Getting to Yes.* Harmondsworth, Middlesex, G.B.: Penguin Books, 1983.

Grossman, J. "Resolve Conflicts So Everybody Wins." *PM Network,* September 1995.

Hughes, T. P. *Rescuing Prometheus,* New York: Pantheon, 1998.

Larson, E. W., and J. A. Drexler, Jr. "Barriers to Project Partnering: Reports from the Firing Line." *Project Management Journal,* March 1997.

Long, A. "Negotiating the Right Decision." *PM Network,* December 1997.

Moore, C. C., J. D. Maes, and R. A. Shearer. "Recognizing and Responding to the Vulnerabilities of Partnering." *PM Network,* September 1995.

Pelled, L. H., and P. S. Adler. "Antecedents of Intergroup Conflict in Multifunctional Product Development Teams: A Conceptual Model." *IEEE Transactions on Engineering Management,* February 1994.

Raiffa, H. *The Art and Science of Negotiation.* Cambridge: Belknap/Harvard Press, 1982.

Robinson, T. "When Talking Makes Things Worse!" *PM Network,* March 1997.

Roget's International Thesaurus. New York: Thomas Y. Crowell, 1993.

Rosegger, G., and S. J. Mantel, Jr. "Competitors as Consultants: Collaboration and Technological Advance." J. Allesch (Ed.), *Consulting in Innovation: Practice-Methods-Perspectives,* Amsterdam: Elsevier, 1990.

Smith, M. B. "Financial Constraints on Service and Outsourcing Projects." *PM Network,* October 1998.

Thamhain, H. J., and D. L. Wilemon. "Conflict Management in Project Life Cycles." *Sloan Management Review,* Summer 1975a.

Thamhain, H. J., and D. L. Wilemon. "Diagnosing Conflict Determinants in Project Management." *IEEE Transactions on Engineering Management,* February 1975b.

Thomas, K. "Conflict and Conflict Management." In M. D. Dunnette (Ed.), *Handbook of Industrial and Organizational Psychology,* Chicago: Rand McNally, 1976.

Wall, J. A., Jr. *Negotiation: Theory and Practice.* Glenview, IL: Scott, Foresman, 1985.

The following classic article describes a number of methods for negotiating and handling conflicts. The author identifies effective and ineffective methods ranging from withdrawal to forcing. Each method is then illustrated with a number of examples. Finally, the most effective method, *Confrontation Problem Solving,* is described in terms of its many characteristics.

DIRECTED READING

METHODS OF RESOLVING
INTERPERSONAL CONFLICT*
R. J. Burke

The management of conflict in creative and useful ways, rather than its containment or abolition, has been proposed by many writers. Various strategies for dealing with conflict at different levels and for managing disagreements have also been proposed. Most of these methods have not been experimentally evaluated. Given the central and inevitable role of conflict in human affairs, a high priority of importance is to be placed on learning the most effective way to resolve it.

Purpose of This Study

In an early investigation, Burke collected questionnaire data from 74 managers, in which they described the way they and their superiors dealt with conflict between them. It was possible to relate five different methods of conflict resolution originally proposed by Blake and Mouton (1964)—Withdrawing, Smoothing, Compromising, Forcing, and Confrontation or Problem Solving—to two major areas of the superior-subordinate relationship. These were (1) constructive use of differences and disagreements, and (2) several aspects of the superior-subordinate relationship in planning job targets and evaluating accomplishments.

In general, the results showed that Withdrawing and Forcing behaviors were consistently negatively related to these two areas. Compromising was not related to these two areas. Use of Smoothing was inconsistently related, sometimes positive and sometimes negative. Only Confrontation-Problem Solving was always related positively to both. That is, use of Confrontation was associated with constructive use of differences and high scores on various measures of the superior-subordinate relationship.

This study has the dual purpose of attempting to specify more precisely the characteristics of the Confrontation-Problem Solving method of conflict resolution, and replicating Burke's earlier study using different methodology.

Method

Subjects: The respondents were managers from various organizations who were enrolled in a university course emphasizing behavioral science concepts relevant to the functions of management. Their organizational experience ranged from one year to over 30 years.

Procedure: Each respondent was asked to describe a time when he felt particularly GOOD (or BAD) about the way in which an interpersonal conflict was resolved. The specific instructions stated:

"Think of a time when you felt especially GOOD (or BAD) about the way an interpersonal conflict or disagreement (e.g., boss-subordinate, peer-peer, etc.) in which you were involved was resolved. It may have been on your present job, or any other job, or away from the work situation.

"Now describe it in enough detail so a reader would understand the way the conflict or differences were handled."

This statement appeared at the top of a blank sheet of paper.

Approximately half the respondents were first to describe the instance when they felt particularly good, followed by the instance when they felt particularly bad. The remaining respondents described the instances in the reverse order. No apparent effects were observed from the change in order, so the data from both groups will be considered together in this report.

Results

Fifty-three descriptions of effective resolution of conflict (felt especially GOOD) and 53 descriptions of ineffective resolutions of conflict (felt especially BAD) were obtained. These were provided by 57 different individuals. Some individuals provided only one example. The response rate was about 70 percent of the total available population.

The written descriptions were then coded into one of the five methods of conflict resolution proposed by Blake and Mouton.

1. *Withdrawing*—easier to refrain than to retreat from an argument; silence is golden. "See no evil, hear no evil, speak no evil."

2. *Smoothing*—play down the differences and emphasize common interests; issues that might cause divisions or hurt feelings are not discussed.

3. *Compromising*—splitting the difference, bargaining, search for an intermediate position. Better half a loaf than none at all; no one loses but no one wins.

4. *Forcing*—a win-lose situation; participants are antagonists, competitors, not collaborators. Fixed positions, polarization. Creates a victor and a vanquished.

5. *Confrontation-Problem Solving*—open exchange of information about the conflict or problem as each sees it, and a working through of their differences to reach a solution that is optimal to both. Both can win.

Table 1 presents the method of conflict resolution associated with effective resolution (left half of Table 1) and ineffective resolution (right half of Table 1). Considering the left half of the table, Confrontation-Problem Solving was the most common method for effective resolution (58.5%), followed by Forcing (24.5%), and Compromise (11.3%). The prominence of Confrontation as an effective method is consistent with Burke's earlier study but the value for Forcing was higher than expected. When these 13 cases are considered as a group, 11 of them are similar in that the party providing the written description benefited as a result of the Forcing. That is, Forcing was perceived as an effective method of resolving conflict by the victor, but not by the vanquished.

Moving to the right half of Table 1, Forcing was the most commonly used method for ineffective resolution, followed in second place by Withdrawal with only 9.4 percent. The vast majority of individuals providing written descriptions of Forcing methods were victims or "losers" as a result of Forcing behavior.

Table 1   Methods Associated with Effective and Ineffective Conflict Resolution

	Effective Resolution (N = 53)		Ineffective Resolution (N = 53)	
	N	**%**	**N**	**%**
Withdrawal	0	0.0*	5	9.4*
Smoothing	0	0.0	1	1.9
Compromise	6	11.3	3	5.7
Forcing	13	24.5*	42	79.2*
Confrontation-problem solving	31	58.5*	0	0.0*
Other (still unresolved; unable to determine how resolved; irrelevant to assignment; etc.)	3	5.7	2	3.8

*Percentage difference between groups is significant at the .05 level of confidence.

In summary, the major differences in methods of conflict resolution used to distinguish effective versus ineffective examples were: (1) significantly greater use of Confrontation in the effective examples (58.5% vs. 0.0%); (2) significantly less use of Forcing in the effective examples (24.5% vs. 79.2%); and (3) significantly less use of Withdrawal in the effective examples (0.0% vs. 9.4%).

When Forcing was seen to be effective, the authors of the examples were "winners" of a win-lose conflict; when Forcing was seen to be ineffective, the authors of the examples were "losers" of a win-lose conflict. Whether the resolution of conflict via Forcing would actually be perceived to be effective by members of the organization outside the conflict (i.e., objectively seen as effective), as it was perceived to be effective by the "winners," remains to be determined by future research.

Effective Conflict Resolution

A few of the examples of effective conflict resolution are provided to highlight specific features of Confrontation. These were taken verbatim from the written descriptions.

1. *This example highlights the presentation of a problem of mutual interest—meeting deadlines more often at the earliest opportunity (when the problem is observed). Superior is open-minded and asking for help.*

"I once was given the responsibility for managing a small group of technicians engaged in turning out critical path schedules. I spent some time trying to get organized and involved with the group, but I sensed a hostile atmosphere, accompanied by offhand sarcastic remarks. At the end of the day very little work had been accomplished.

"The next day when I came in, I called the group together and told them that we were falling behind, and asked them to help me find a solution. After the initial distrust had been dissipated, the group produced some good ideas on work reallocation, office arrangement, priorities and techniques. I told the group that all of their agreed-upon suggestions would be implemented at once, and their reply was that the backlog would be cleared in three days and would not build up again.

"Within three days the backlog was gone, the group worked together better, and for the six months I was in charge, schedules were always ready before they were required."

2. *This example highlights emphasis on facts in determining the best resolution of conflict. Both had strong convictions but one willingly moved to the other's position when facts indicated that this position was best.*

"The project engineer and I disagreed about the method of estimating the cost of alternative schemes in a highway interchange. Neither of us could agree on the other's method. Eventually I was able to satisfy him using algebra. We were both happy with the result."

3. *Like Example 2, this one highlights an emphasis on facts and the conviction that by digging and digging, the truth will be discovered. Although the superior had a vested interest in the "old" system (a product of his thinking), the discussion was never personalized. That is, it did not involve "me" versus "you," but rather a comparison of two systems, two concepts or two ideas.*

"About a year ago I developed a new system for processing the accounting of the inventory of obsolete material on hand in our plant. It was my estimation that it would prove to be an easier system to operate and control and would also involve a considerable monetary saving for the company.

"When I approached my boss with the system, he immediately turned it down as he had developed the present system and was sure it was the best possible system. As I was sure my new system was superior to the present one, I then convinced him to join me in analyzing a comparison of the two systems, pointing out the strengths and weaknesses of the two. After a period of evaluation involving many differences of opinion, we were able to resolve that my system had definite merit and should be brought into operation."

4. *This example highlights the fact that through problem solving both parties can benefit. Instead of compromising, the issues are discussed until a solution completely satisfactory to both is found. Often this is superior to the ones initially favored by the separate parties.*

"In the XXX Board of Education, there were eight inspectors of Public Schools and four superintendents. Last February the inspectors were given the assignment of developing an in-service plan for the training of teachers for the next school year. The inspectors gave the assignment to a group of three of their number who were to bring a report to the next inspectors' meeting. I was not a member of the in-service committee but in conversations with the committee members I discovered that they contemplated having an in-service program for two teachers from each school (there are about 85 schools) once a month for the entire year in mathematics. I felt that this would be a very thin coverage of our 2000 or so teachers.

"Consequently I worked on a plan whereby utilizing two Thursday mornings a month and the specialized teaching help available in XXX, every teacher would have the opportunity to become involved in an in-service training session in a subject of his or her choice once during the year. At the inspectors' meeting the subcommittee presented its report and after some procedural wrangling I was permitted to present my plan. The two were diametrically opposed and it looked as if my plan would be voted down except the chairman suggested that both plans be presented to the superintendents.

"At the meeting of the superintendents, the subcommittee made its report and I presented my plan. As the meeting progressed there was some give and take and instead of one or the other being discarded, both plans were adopted. For this school year mathematics is stressed for the first eight Thursday mornings (their plan in a rather concentrated form); then for the next eight months on the second and fourth Thursday my plan is used. We came out of this meeting with a combination of the two plans which was better than either one individually."

Ineffective Conflict Resolution

Examples 5, 6, and 7 illustrate Forcing methods of conflict resolution. A win-lose situation is set up, and usually the superior wins. The individual with the greater power triumphs (a personalized disagreement) rather than the one whose position is supported by the most factual evidence.

5. "In a previous job, I worked for a major management consulting group as a consultant. One assignment, lasting four months, was to use a simulation technique to evaluate the most preferable investment decision using defined quantitative criteria. At the end of the job two alternatives were shown to be marginally better than the other. However, later sensitivity tests also showed that the analytical technique could not rate one to be substantially better than the other.

"Therefore, I wrote a 'technically honest' report stating that our analysis could not provide the one best alternative. My manager, feeling that we were hired to recommend a 'one best' alternative, wanted to cover up the limitations of our methodology.

"We disagreed and I was overruled. The manager wrote a 'technically dishonest' version of the report and the revised report was sent to the client indicating the 'one best' alternative."

6. "Recently in my firm, management had sprung a secrecy agreement contract upon all of the technical people. No word of introduction or explanation was given. It was simply handed out and we were asked to sign it. Most of us found objection in several clauses in the agreement. However, management officials stated that the agreement would probably not stand up in a court of law. They further stated that it was something that was sent from corporate in the United States and was not their idea. The employees continued to show reluctance.

"The vice-president called on everyone individually and stated that there would be no room for advancement for anyone who did not sign the contract. As a result, everyone signed."

7. "I was assigned a project by my boss to determine the optimum way, using predetermined times, to lay out an assembly line. It would have to provide optimum efficiency with the following variables: (a) different hourly production rates (e.g., 100/hr. Mon., 200/hr. Tues.) which would mean different numbers of operators on the line; (b) different models of the product (electric motors). The group was on group incentive.

"After much research and discussion, the system was installed utilizing the floating system of assembly (operators could move from station to station in order to keep out of the bottleneck operation). This system was working out well. However, at this time I was informed by my boss that he and the foreman of the area decided that they wished to use the 'paced' system of assembly. This would mean the conveyor belt would be run at set speeds and that the stripes would be printed on the belt indicating that one device would have to be placed on each mark and operators would not float.

"I was dead against this since I had considered it and rejected it in favor of the implemented method. I was, however, given the order to use their proposed system or else. There was no opportunity for discussion or justification of the method."

8. *This example is a classic description of Withdrawal as a mode of conflict resolution. Clearly the problem is not resolved.*

"On the successful completion of a project which involved considerable time and effort, I was praised and thanked for a job well done by my immediate supervisor and his supervisor, the vice-president in charge of manufacturing. They promised me that on my next salary review I would receive a substantial increase.

"The next salary review came up and my immediate supervisor submitted an amount that he and I felt was a good increase. The amount I received was one-third of this figure. I felt insulted, cheated, and hurt that the company considered I was worth this 'token' amount.

"I had a personal interview with the vice-president where I argued that I felt I should receive more. He agreed in sort of an offhanded way—he felt the whole salary schedule should be reviewed and that my area of responsibility should be increased. He said the company wants people to 'prove themselves' before they give them increases; and he suggested a salary review. I felt I had just done this in my last project—I felt I was being put off, but agreed to the salary review.

"One month passed and nothing happened. I became frustrated—I purposely slowed down the amount of work I turned out.

"Another month passed and still no action. I became disillusioned with the company and resolved at this point to look for another position. Several months later with still no action, I resigned and accepted another position."

Inability to Resolve Conflict

These descriptions of ineffective resolution of conflict indicate that an impressive number of respondents included termination or change of employment of one member in the situation (19 of 53, 26%). These cases tended to be of two types.

The first is represented by Example 8. Here an employee decides to quit because he felt the problem was not resolved in a satisfactory manner. Forcing is likely to be associated with instances of voluntary termination.

The second centered around an inability to resolve the conflict. Then the "problem employee" (a visible symptom of the conflict) was dismissed.

9. *The following example illustrates this:*

"This concerned a young girl about 18 years old who was a typist in our office. This girl lacked a little maturity, but was not really all that bad. She was tuned to all the latest fashions in both dress and manners.

"I felt and still feel that this girl was a potentially good employee. But it was decided that she should be let go. The argument used was that she was not a good worker and lacked the proper attitude for office work. Rather than spend a little time and effort to understand the girl and perhaps develop her into a good employee, the easy way was taken and the girl was fired."

There were two other clear cases of "effective" conflict resolution resulting in voluntary employee terminations. In both instances a Forcing mode was employed and the "loser" resigned from the organization soon after. Our finding is that these were given as examples of effective conflict resolution by the "winner." In another effective example of Forcing, the "loser" was dismissed.

Conclusions

The results of this investigation are consistent with earlier studies showing the value of Confrontation-Problem Solving as a method of conflict resolution. About 60 percent of the examples of effective conflict resolution involved use of the method, while no examples of ineffective conflict resolution did. The poorest method of conflict resolution was Forcing. This method accounted for 80 percent of the examples of ineffective conflict resolution and only 24 percent of the examples of effective conflict resolution.

The latter conclusion is somewhat at odds with Lawrence and Lorsch's findings that Forcing was an effective backup method to Confrontation, from an organizational effectiveness standpoint. In fact, Burke's earlier study found that the use of these methods tended to be negatively correlated. Managers high in use of one of them tended to be low in use of the other.

Characteristics of Problem Solving

Let us now consider more specific features of Confrontation, the most effective method of resolving interpersonal conflict. Insights from the present investigation and the writings of others becomes relevant. The following then are characteristics of Confrontation as a method of managing conflict:

1. Both people have a vested interest in the outcome (Examples 1, 2, 3, and 4).

2. There is a belief on the part of the people involved that they have the potential to resolve the conflict and to achieve a better solution through collaboration.

3. There is a recognition that the conflict or the problem is mainly in the relationship between the individuals and not in each person separately. If the conflict is in the relationship, it must be defined by those who have the relationship. In addition, if solutions are to be developed, the solutions have to be generated by those who share the responsibility for assuring that the solution will work and for making the relationship last.

4. The goal is to solve the problem, not to accommodate different points of view. This process identifies the causes of reservation, doubt, and misunderstanding between the people confronted with conflict and disagreement. Alternative ways of approaching conflict resolution are explored and tested (Examples 2 and 3).

5. The people involved are problem-minded instead of solution-minded; "fluid" instead of "fixed" positions. Both parties jointly search out the issues that separate them. Through joint effort, the problems that demand solutions are identified, and later solved.

6. There is a realization that both aspects of a controversy have potential strengths and potential weaknesses. Rarely is one position completely right and the other completely wrong (Example 4).

7. There is an effort to understand the conflict or problem from the other person's point of view, and from the standpoint of the "real" or legitimate needs that must be recognized and met before problem solving can occur. Full acceptance of the other is essential.

8. The importance of looking at the conflict objectively rather than in a personalized sort of way is recognized (Example 3).

9. An examination of one's own attitudes (hostilities, antagonisms) is needed before interpersonal contact on a less effective basis has a chance to occur.

10. An understanding of the less effective methods of conflict resolution (e.g., win-lose, bargaining) is essential.

11. One needs to present "face-saving" situations. Allow people to "give" so that a change in one's viewpoint does not suggest weakness or capitulation.

12. There is need to minimize effects of status differences, defensiveness, and other barriers which prevent people from working together effectively.

13. It is important to be aware of the limitations of arguing or presenting evidence in favor of your own position while downgrading the opponent's position. This behavior often stimulates the opponent to find even greater support for his position (increased polarization). In addition, it leads to selective listening for weaknesses in the opponent's position rather than listening to understand his or her position.

Attitude, Skill, and Creativity

Two related themes run through these characteristics, one dealing with attitudes, and the other with skills (interpersonal, problem solving) of the individuals involved. As the research of Maier and his associates has shown, differences and disagreements need not lead to dissatisfaction and unpleasant experiences but rather can lead to innovation and creativity. One of the critical variables was found to be the leader's attitudes toward disagreement. The person with different ideas, especially if he or she is a subordinate, can be seen as a problem employee and troublemaker or as an innovator, depending on the leader's attitude.

There are some people that go through life attempting to sell their ideas, to get others to do things they do not want to do. They set up a series of win-lose situations, and attempt to emerge victorious. Many of these people are able to accomplish their ends. There are others who are more concerned with the quality and effectiveness of their operations, and who, with creative solutions to problems, are genuinely openminded and able and willing to learn from others (and to teach others), in a collaborative relationship.

The interpersonal skills are related to the development of a "helping relationship" and include, among other things, mutual trust and respect, candid communication, and awareness of the needs of others. The problem-solving skills center around locating and stating the problem, seeking alternatives, exploring and testing alternatives, and selecting the best alternative. Knowledge and insight gained through experience with the benefits of problem solving and the dysfunctional effects of other strategies would be valuable in developing interpersonal skills.

Further Research Needed

Two additional areas need immediate research consideration. The first needs to explore the notions of conflict resolution from the organizational as well as the individual viewpoint. Lawrence and Lorsch report that Forcing was an effective back-up mode to Confrontation from the organization's standpoint, because at least things were being done. Our data in two separate investigations indicate that this mode of conflict resolution is very unsatisfactory from the standpoint of the one forced, the "loser," and may also have dysfunctional consequences.

The second research area concerns the application of these principles of effective conflict resolution (Confrontation-Problem Solving, with their more specific attitudinal and skill components) in an attempt to arrive at more constructive use of disagreement. Preliminary results from an experiment simulating conflict situations using role playing suggest that knowledge of these principles and some limited practice in their use increases one's ability to use differences constructively in obtaining a quality solution, and decreases the tendency to engage in "limited war," as Burke called it.

References

Blake, R. R., and J. S. Mouton. *The Managerial Grid*, Houston: Gulf Publishing Company, 1964.

Blake, R. R., H. A. Shepard, and J. S. Mouton. *Managing Intergroup Conflict in Industry*, Houston: Gulf Publishing Company, 1964.

Boulding, K. "A pure theory of conflict applied to organization." In R. I. Kahn and E. Boulding (eds.), *Power and Conflict in Organizations*. New York: Basic Books, Inc., 1964, pp. 136–145.

Burke, R. J. "Methods of managing superior-subordinate conflict: Their effectiveness and consequences." Unpublished manuscript, 1969a.

Burke, R. J. "Effects of limited training on conflict resolution effectiveness." Unpublished manuscript, 1969b.

Kata, D. "Approaches to managing conflict." In R. L. Kahn and E. Boulding (eds.), *Power and Conflict in Organizations*. New York: Basic Books, Inc., 1964, pp. 105–114.

Lawrence, P. R., and J. W. Lorsch. "Differentiation and integration in complex organizations." *Administrative Science Quarterly*, 1967a, 12, 1–47.

Lawrence, P. R., and J. W. Lorsch. *Organization and Environment*, Boston: Division of Research, Harvard Business School, Harvard University, 1967b.

Maier, N. R. F. *Problem-Solving Discussions and Conferences*. New York: McGraw-Hill, 1963.

Maier, N. R. F., and L. R. Hoffman. "Acceptance and quality of solutions as related to leaders' attitudes toward disagreement in group problem-solving." *Journal of Applied Behavioral Science*, 1965, 1, pp. 373–386.

McGregor, D. *The Professional Manager*. New York: McGraw-Hill, 1967.

Shepard, H. A. "Responses to situations of competition and conflict." In R. L. Kahn and E. Boulding (eds.), *Power and Conflict in Organizations*. New York: Basic Books, Inc., 1964, pp. 127–135.

Questions

1. In Table 1, what was the second best resolution technique? What was the worst resolution technique? What do you conclude from this?

2. Which of the four examples of conflict resolution is the best example, in your opinion, of effective resolution? Why?

3. Of the ineffective resolution examples, which was the worst, in your opinion? Why?

4. Summarize or condense the 13 characteristics of Confrontation as a conflict-resolving method.

5. The article concludes on the note that conflict need not be a bad thing. Compare this view with that in the chapter concerning the win-win approach to negotiation.

5

The Project in the Organizational Structure

A firm, if successful, tends to grow, adding resources and people, developing an organizational structure. Commonly, the focus of the structure is specialization of the human elements of the group. As long as its organizational structure is sufficient to the tasks imposed on it, the structure tends to persist. When the structure begins to inhibit the work of the firm, pressures arise to reorganize along some other line. The underlying principle will still be specialization, but the specific nature of the specialization will be changed.

Any elementary management textbook covers the common bases of specialization. In addition to the ever-popular functional division, firms organize by product line, by geographic location, by production process, by type of customer, by subsidiary organization, by time, and by the elements of vertical or horizontal integration. Indeed, large firms frequently organize by several of these methods at different levels. For example, a firm may organize by major subsidiaries at the top level; the subsidiaries organize by product groups; and the product groups organize into customer divisions. These, in turn, may be split into functional departments that are further broken down into production process sections, which are set up as three-shift operating units.

In the past decade or so, a new kind of organization structure has appeared in growing numbers—the project organization, a.k.a. "enterprise project management" (Dinsmore, 1998; Levine, 1998; Williams, 1997), also known as "managing organizations by projects," the "project-oriented firm," and other names. Such organizations have been described as applying "project management practices and tools across an enterprise" (Levine, 1998). The source of these organizations is probably in the software industry that has long made a practice of developing major software application programs by decomposing them into a series of comparatively small software projects. Once the projects are completed, they are integrated into the whole application system. A great many firms, both software and nonsoftware firms alike, have now adopted a system whereby their traditional business is carried out in the traditional way, but anything that represents a change is carried out as a project. One hospital, for example, operates the usual departments in what, for them, are the usual ways. At the same time, the hospital supports several dozen projects oriented toward developing new health care products, or changing various aspects of standard medical and administrative methods.

There are many reasons for the rapid growth of project-oriented organizations, but most of them can be subsumed in four general areas. First, speed and market responsiveness have become absolute requirements for successful competition. It is no longer competitively acceptable to develop a new product or service using traditional methods in which the potential new product is passed from functional area to functional area until it is deemed suitable for production and distribution. *First-to-market* is a powerful competitive advantage. Further, in many industries it is common (and necessary) to tailor products specifically for individual clients. Suppliers of hair care products or cosmetics, for example, may supply individual stores in a drug chain with different mixes of products depending on the purchase patterns, ethnic mix of customers, and local style preferences for each store.

Second, the development of new products, processes, or services regularly requires inputs from diverse areas of specialized knowledge. Unfortunately, the exact mix of specialties appropriate for the design and development of one product or service is rarely suitable for another product or service. Teams of specialists that are created to accomplish their ad hoc purpose and disband typify the entire process. (See the PMIP sidebar on floating teams in Section 5.6 for an example of this approach.)

Third, the rapid expansion of technological possibilities in almost every area of enterprise tends to destabilize the structure of organizations. Consider communications, entertainment, banks, consumer product manufacturing and sales, the automotive industry, aircraft manufacture, heavy electrical equipment, machine tools, and so forth without end. Mergers, downsizing, reorganizations, spin-offs, new marketing channels, and other similar major disturbances all require system-wide responsiveness from the total organization. Again, no traditional mechanism exists to handle change on such a large scale satisfactorily—but project organization can.

Finally, TV, movies, novels, and other mythology to the contrary, a large majority of senior managers we know rarely feel much confidence in their understanding of and control over a great many of the activities going on in their organizations. The hospital mentioned above became a project-oriented organization because its new CEO strongly felt that she had no way of understanding, measuring, or controlling anything going on in the hospital except for the most routine, traditional activities. Transforming nonroutine activities into projects allowed her to ensure that accountability was established, projects were properly planned, integrated with other related activities, and reported routinely on their progress.

Moving from a nonproject environment to one in which projects are organized and used to accomplish special tasks, and subsequently to a full-fledged project-oriented organization presents senior management of a firm with an extraordinarily difficult transition. A full treatment of this subject is beyond the scope of this book, but several observations are in order. First, the process is time consuming. Even when the required resources are available and senior management is fully committed to the transition, it is still an arduous process. Our experience indicates that when all goes well, the transition rarely requires less than three years. In an excellent article on the process of leading fundamental change in a complex organization, Kotter (1997) lists eight steps that must be successfully completed if the change is to be accomplished. Most of these are dependent on active leadership from top management.

Whether the organization is conducting a few occasional projects or is fully project oriented and carrying on scores of projects, any time a project is initiated, three organizational issues immediately arise. First, a decision must be made about how to tie the project to the parent firm. Second, a decision must be made about how to organize the project itself. Third, a decision must be made about how to organize activities that are common to other projects.

In Chapter 3 we discussed the selection of the project manager (PM) and described the difficulties and responsibilities inherent in the PM's role. This chapter focuses on the interface between the project and its parent organization (i.e., how the project is organized as a part of its host). In the latter part of this chapter, we begin a discussion of how the project itself is organized, a discussion that will be continued in the next chapter.

PMBOK Guide
2.4.2

First we look at the three major organizational forms commonly used to house projects and see just how each of them fits into the parent organization. (These three forms are also emphasized in PMBOK.) We examine the advantages and disadvantages of each form, and discuss some of the critical factors that might lead us to choose one form over the others. We then consider some combinations of the fundamental forms and briefly examine the implications of using combination structures. Finally, we discuss some of the details of organizing the project team, describing the various roles of the project staff. We then turn to the formation and operation of a *project management office* (PMO) that can provide critically important services for all projects. The skill with which the PMO organizes, administers, and carries out its responsibilities will have a major impact on the ability of projects to meet their objectives. We also describe some of the behavioral problems that face any project team. Finally, we discuss the impact that various ways of structuring projects may have on intraproject conflict in project-oriented firms.

To our knowledge, it is rare for a PM to have much influence over the interface between the organization and the project, the choice of such interface usually being made by senior management. The PM's work, however, is strongly affected by the project's position in the organizational structure, and the PM should understand its workings. Experienced PMs do seem to mold the project's organization to fit their notions of what is best. One project team member of our acquaintance remarked at length about how different life was on two projects run by different PMs. Study of the subtle impacts of the PM on the project structure deserves more attention from researchers in the behavioral sciences.

5.1 PROJECTS IN A FUNCTIONAL ORGANIZATION

As one alternative for giving the project a "home" in a functionally structured organization, we can make it a part of one of the functional divisions of the firm, usually the function that has the most interest in ensuring its success or can be most helpful in implementing it. We commonly think of the functions of an organization as being those of Finance, Marketing, Operations (or Manufacturing), Human Resources, and so on. However, to consider a slightly different type of organization, Figure 5-1 is the organizational chart for the University of Cincinnati, a functionally organized institution. If U.C. undertook the development of a Master of Science program in Project Management (or perhaps an MPM), the project would probably be placed under the *general supervision* of the senior vice president and provost, under the *specific supervision* of the dean of the College of Business (and/or College of Engineering), and might be managed by a senior faculty member with a specialty in operations management. It might also be placed under the general supervision of the V.P. and dean for Graduate Studies and Research. Note that more than one choice of parent may exist, and if the project needs resources from some of the other functional areas, they are expected to help support the project.

Another way a project may be organized in a functional organization is to assign the work to all the relevant functional divisions with either top management overseeing the effort or else someone assigned to coordinate their efforts, perhaps as a project manager or possibly as just a facilitator. A project to increase the percentage of women in senior management might thus involve all the U.C. functions and might be coordinated through the President's office, the Affirmative Action office, or possibly using someone from Personnel in the Administration function.

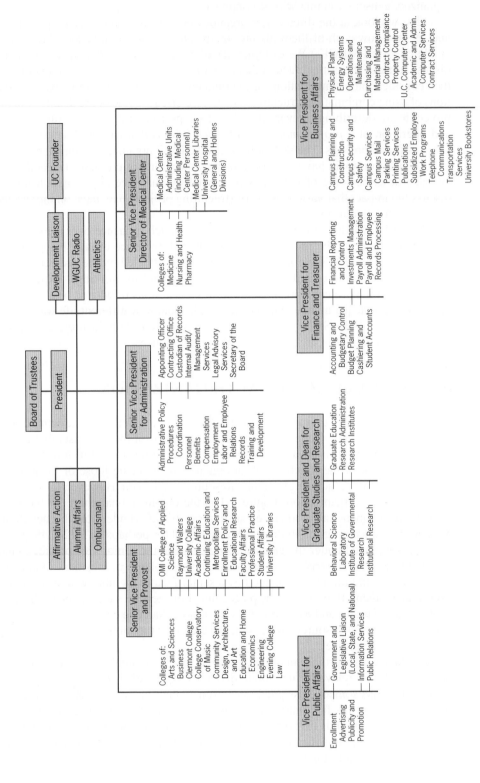

Figure 5-1 University of Cincinnati organization chart.

There are advantages and disadvantages of using a functional placement for a project, assuming that the organization is functionally organized. The major advantages are:

1. There is maximum flexibility in the use of staff. If the proper functional division has been chosen as the project's home, the division will be the primary administrative base for individuals with technical expertise in the fields relevant to the project. Experts can be temporarily assigned to the project, make the required contributions, and immediately be reassigned to their normal work.

2. Individual experts can be utilized by many different projects. With the broad base of technical personnel available in the functional divisions, people can be switched back and forth between the different projects with relative ease.

3. Specialists in the division can be grouped to share knowledge and experience. Therefore, the project team has access to whatever technical knowledge resides in the functional group. This depth of knowledge is a potential source of creative, synergistic solutions to technical problems.

4. The functional division also serves as a base of technological continuity when individuals choose to leave the project, and even the parent firm. Perhaps just as important as technological continuity is the procedural, administrative, and overall policy continuity that results when the project is maintained in a specific functional division of the parent firm.

5. Finally, and not the least important, the functional division contains the normal path of advancement for individuals whose expertise is in the functional area. The project may be a source of glory for those who participate in its successful completion, but the functional field is their professional home and the focus of their professional growth and advancement.

Just as there are advantages to using a functional placement, there are also disadvantages:

1. A primary disadvantage of this arrangement is that the client is not the focus of activity and concern. The functional unit has its own work to do, which usually takes precedence over the work of the project, and hence over the interests of the client.

2. The functional division tends to be oriented toward the activities particular to its function. It is not usually problem oriented in the sense that a project should be to be successful.

3. Occasionally in functionally organized projects, no individual is given full responsibility for the project. This failure to pinpoint responsibility usually means that the PM is made accountable for some parts of the project, but another person is made accountable for one or more other parts. Little imagination is required to forecast the lack of coordination and chaos that results.

4. The same reasons that lead to lack of coordinated effort tend to make response to client needs slow and arduous. There are often several layers of management between the project and the client.

5. There is a tendency to suboptimize the project. Project issues that are directly within the interest area of the functional home may be dealt with carefully, but those outside normal interest areas may be given short shrift, if not totally ignored.

6. The motivation of people assigned to the project tends to be weak. The project is not in the mainstream of activity and interest, and some project team members may view service on the project as a professional detour.

7. Such an organizational arrangement does not facilitate a holistic approach to the project. Complex technical projects such as the development of a jet transport aircraft or an emergency room in a hospital simply cannot be well designed unless they are designed as a totality. No matter how good the intentions, no functional division can avoid focusing on its unique areas of interest. Cross-divisional communication and sharing of knowledge is slow and difficult at best.

Project Management in Practice
Managing Risk in a Competitive Market

Tenovis is one of Germany's largest companies in the telecommunication market. Tenovis works in a wide range of telecommunication areas such as private branch exchanges (PBX), call centres, and IP-based telephony. The organisation undertook a project aimed at providing a unified, integrated tool to support service personnel in their task of administrating all of Tenovis' existing PBX platforms. Thus, this project was called Tool Harmonisation Project. Started at the end of 1999, the project's duration was planned to be approximately one year.

In this project, new and challenging technologies were to be applied. Web technology was to be used in a client-server application context. Additionally, object-oriented technology was selected for design and implementation. On the one hand, the new technologies added complexity to the project; on the other hand, they were expected to increase the project's productivity. Besides the new technologies, a new development process and a new project organisation were introduced, which involved teams from three different locations and time zones (India, France, and Germany).

In the early stages of the project, risk management was performed in an informal way. However, this intuitive risk management was considered to be no longer appropriate for a company in the telecommunication market. This market is characterised by high competition, strong demand for innovative technologies, and a very short innovation cycle. These factors usually impose risks to telecommunication projects. The introduction of new technologies and processes imposed additional risks. Hence this project was seen as particularly risky compared to other projects at Tenovis. This situation made the case for the introduction of explicit, systematic, and experience-based risk management into the project.

The following lessons were learned by the organisation with regard to managing risk:

- Risk management should be closely integrated with project management and daily project work to foster the synergy between these activities.
- Risk identification should be scheduled automatically at predefined milestones and, additionally, whenever it is seen as necessary
- Risk monitoring should be performed regularly with short intervals between two meetings.
- Risk monitoring has to sufficiently question the implementation of controlling actions and their impact on risks.
- Training of the employed risk management process is important to train the participants and raise awareness for risk management and risks.
- Process Ownership for risk management has to rest with the project manager.
- Commitment of the project manager is of utmost importance and has to be ensured from the beginning.

Source: Bernd Freimut, Susanne Hartkopf, Jyrki Kontio, Werner Kobitzsch, *"An Industrial Case Study of Implementing Software Risk Management."* Proceedings of the 8th European software engineering conference held jointly with 9th ACM SIGSOFT international symposium on Foundations of software engineering, Vienna, Austria, Session: Experiences and case studies, pages: 277–287, 2001.

5.2 PROJECTS IN A PROJECTIZED ORGANIZATION

At the other end of the organizational spectrum (in terms of project structure) is the projectized organization. Here the firm's administrative support groups (HR, Legal, Finance, Controller, etc.) report to the President or CEO as staff units. The line units are the various standalone projects being undertaken in the organization. Each project has a full complement of the functions needed for its operation, though some members may serve on two or more projects. Each standalone project is a self-contained unit with its own technical team, its own staff, and so on. Some parent organizations prescribe administrative, financial, personnel, and control procedures in detail. Others allow the project almost total freedom within the limits of final accountability. There are examples of almost every possible intermediate position. Figure 5-2 illustrates the projectized organization and its standalone projects.

As with the functional organization, standalone projects have unique advantages and disadvantages. The former are:

1. The project manager has full line authority over the project. Though the PM must report to a senior executive in the parent organization, there is a complete work force devoted to the project. The PM is like the CEO of a firm that is dedicated to carrying out the project.

2. All members of the project work force are directly responsible to the PM. There are no functional division heads whose permission must be sought or whose advice must be heeded before making technological decisions. The PM is truly the project director.

3. When the project is removed from the functional division, the lines of communication are shortened. The entire functional structure is bypassed, and the PM communicates directly with senior corporate management. The shortened communication lines result in faster communications with fewer communication failures.

4. When there are several successive projects of a similar kind, the projectized organization can maintain a more or less permanent cadre of experts who develop considerable skill in specific technologies. Indeed, the existence of such skill pools can attract customers to the parent firm. Lockheed's famous "Skunk Works" was such a team of experts who took great pride in their ability to solve difficult engineering problems. The group's name, taken from the Li'l Abner comic strip, reflects the group's pride, irreverent attitude, and strong sense of identity.

5. The project team that has a strong and separate identity of its own tends to develop a high level of commitment from its members. Motivation is high and acts to foster the task orientation discussed in Chapter 3.

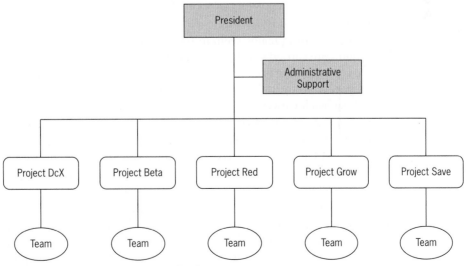

Figure 5-2 The projectized organization.

6. Because authority is centralized, the ability to make swift decisions is greatly enhanced. The entire project organization can react more rapidly to the requirements of the client and the needs of senior management.

7. Unity of command exists. While it is easy to overestimate the value of this particular organizational principle, there is little doubt that the quality of life for subordinates is enhanced when each subordinate has one, and only one, boss.

8. Projectized organizations are structurally simple and flexible, which makes them relatively easy to understand and to implement.

9. The organizational structure tends to support a holistic approach to the project. A brief explanation of the systems approach was given in Chapter 3, and an example of the problems arising when the systems approach is not used appears in Section 5.3 of this chapter. The dangers of focusing on and optimizing the project's subsystems rather than the total project are often a major cause of technical failure in projects.

While the advantages of the projectized organization make a powerful argument favoring this structure, its disadvantages are also serious:

1. When the parent organization takes on several projects, it is common for each one to be fully staffed. This can lead to considerable duplication of effort in every area from clerical staff to the most sophisticated (and expensive) technological support units. If a project does not require a full-time personnel manager, for example, it must have one nonetheless because personnel managers come in integers, not fractions, and staff is usually not shared across projects.

2. In fact, the need to ensure access to technological knowledge and skills results in an attempt by the PM to stockpile equipment and technical assistance in order to be certain that it will be available when needed. Thus, people with critical technical skills may be hired by the project when they are available rather than when they are needed. Similarly, they tend to be maintained on the project longer than needed, "just in case." Disadvantages 1 and 2 combine to make this way of organizing projects very expensive.

3. Removing the project from technical control by a functional department has its advantages, but it also has a serious disadvantage if the project is characterized as "high technology." Though individuals engaged with projects develop considerable depth in the technology of the project, they tend to fall behind in other areas of their technical expertise. The functional division is a repository of technical lore, but it is not readily accessible to members of the standalone project team.

4. Projectized project teams seem to foster inconsistency in the way in which policies and procedures are carried out. In the relatively sheltered environment of the project, administrative corner-cutting is common and easily justified as a response to the client or to technical exigency. "They don't understand our problems" becomes an easy excuse for ignoring dicta from headquarters.

5. In projectized organizations, the project takes on a life of its own. Team members form strong attachments to the project and to each other. A disease known as *projectitis* develops. A strong "we–they" divisiveness grows, distorting the relationships between project team members and their counterparts in the parent organization. Friendly rivalry may become bitter competition, and political infighting between projects is common.

6. Another symptom of projectitis is the worry about "life after the project ends." Typically, there is considerable uncertainty about what will happen when the project is completed. Will team members be laid off? Will they be assigned to low-prestige work? Will their technical skills be too rusty to be successfully integrated into other projects? Will our team ("that old gang of mine") be broken up?

5.3   PROJECTS IN A MATRIXED ORGANIZATION

In an attempt to couple some of the advantages of the standalone project in the projectized organization with some of the desirable features of the functional project, and to avoid some of the disadvantages of each, the matrixed project organization was developed. In effect, the functional and the projectized organizations represent extremes. The matrixed project organization is a combination of the two. It is a standalone project organization overlaid on the functional divisions of the parent firm.

Being a combination of standalone projectized and functional organization structures, a matrix organization can take on a wide variety of specific forms, depending on which of the two extremes (functional or standalone) it most resembles. The "projectized" or "strong" matrix most resembles the projectized organization. The "functional" or "weak" matrix most resembles the functional form of organization. Finally, the "balanced" matrix lies in between the other two. In practice, there is an almost infinite variety of organizational forms between the extremes, and the primary difference between these forms has to do with the relative power/decision authority of the project manager and the functional manager.

Because it is simpler to explain, let us first consider a strong matrix, one that is similar to a standalone project. Rather than being a standalone organization, like the standalone project, the matrix project is not separated from the parent organization. Consider Figure 5-3. Although not always the case, here the project manager of Project 1, PM_1, reports to a program manager who also exercises supervision over two other projects having to do with the same program. Project 1 has assigned to it three people from the manufacturing division, one and one-half people from marketing, one-half of a person each from finance and personnel, four individuals from R & D, and perhaps others not shown. These individuals come from their respective functional divisions and are assigned to the project full-time or part-time, depending on the project's needs. It should be emphasized that *the PM controls when and what these people will do, while the functional managers control who will be assigned to the project and how the work will be done, including the technology used.*

With heavy representation from manufacturing and R&D, Project 1 might involve the design and installation of a new type of manufacturing process for a new product Alpha. Project 2 could involve marketing for the new product. Project 3 might concern the installation of a new financial control system for the new product. All the while, the functional divisions continue on with their routine activities.

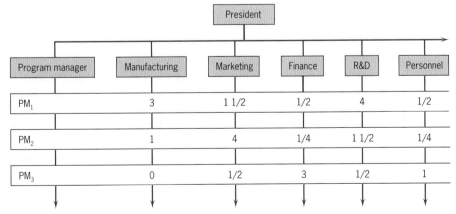

Figure 5-3   The matrix organization.

There is no single executive to whom PMs generally report. If a project is merely one of several in a specific program, the PM typically reports to a program manager, if there is one. It is not uncommon, however, for the PM to report to the manager of the functional area that has a particular interest in the project. If several projects on mathematics are being conducted for the Office of Naval Research (ONR), for instance, it would be normal for the PMs to report to the ONR section head for Mathematical Sciences. In smaller firms with only a few projects, it is common for the PM to report directly to a senior executive.

At the other end of the spectrum of matrix organizations is the functional or weak matrix. A project might, for example, have only one full-time person, the PM. Rather than having an individual functional worker actually assigned to the project, the functional departments devote *capacity* to the project, and the primary task of the PM is to coordinate the project activities carried out by the functional departments. For example, the PM of a project set up to create a new database for personnel might request that the basic design be done by the information technology (IT) group in the administrative division. The personnel job would then be added to the normal workload of the IT group. The priority given to the design might be assigned by senior management or might be the result of negotiations between the PM and the head of the IT group. In some cases, the IT group's charges for the job might also be subject to negotiation. The task could even be subcontracted to an outside vendor.

Between these extremes is the balanced matrix, which is typically anything but balanced. There are many different mixtures of project and functional responsibilities. When a functional group's work is frequently required by projects, it is common to operate the group as a functional unit rather than to transfer its people to the project. For instance, a toxicology unit in a cosmetic business, a quality assurance group in a multiproduct manufacturing firm, or a computer graphics group in a publishing firm might all be functionally organized and take on project work much like outside contractors. While the PM's control over the work is diminished by this arrangement, the project does have immediate access to any expertise in the group, and the group can maintain its technological integrity.

We have previously discussed the difference between discipline-oriented individuals and those who are problem-oriented, indicating that the latter are highly desirable as members of project teams. Both de Laat (1994) and Kalu (1993) stand as adequate testimony to the fact that discipline-oriented team members tend to become ardent supporters of their functional areas, sometimes to the detriment of the project as a whole. The resultant power struggles may stress the project manager's skills in conflict reduction.

The matrixed project approach has its own unique advantages and disadvantages. Its strong points are:

1. The project is the point of emphasis. One individual, the PM, takes responsibility for managing the project, for bringing it in on time, within cost, and to specification. The matrix organization shares this virtue with the standalone project organization.

2. Because the project organization is overlaid on the functional divisions, temporarily drawing labor and talent from them, the project has reasonable access to the entire reservoir of technology in all functional divisions. When there are several projects, the talents of the functional divisions are available to all projects, thus sharply reducing the duplication required by the standalone project structure.

3. There is less anxiety about what happens when the project is completed than is typical of the standalone project organization. Even though team members tend to develop a strong attachment for the project, they also feel close to their functional "home."

4. Response to client needs is as rapid as in the standalone project case, and the matrix organization is just as flexible. Similarly, the matrix organization responds flexibly and rapidly

to the demands made by those inside the parent organization. A project nested within an operating firm must adapt to the needs of the parent firm or the project will not survive.

5. With matrix management, the project will have—or have access to—representatives from the administrative units of the parent firm. As a result, consistency with the policies, practices, and procedures of the parent firm tends to be preserved. If nothing else, this consistency with parent firm procedures tends to foster project credibility in the administration of the parent organization, a condition that is commonly undervalued.

6. Where there are several projects simultaneously under way, matrix organization allows a better companywide balance of resources to achieve the several different time/cost/scope targets of the individual projects. This holistic approach to the total organization's needs allows projects to be staffed and scheduled in order to optimize total system performance rather than to achieve the goals of one project at the expense of others.

7. While standalone projects and functionally organized projects represent extremes of the organizational spectrum, matrix organizations cover a wide range in between. We have differentiated between strong and weak matrices in terms of whether the functional units supplied individuals or capacity to projects. Obviously, some functional units might furnish people and others only supply capacity. There is, therefore, a great deal of flexibility in precisely how the project is organized—all within the basic matrix structure—so that it can be adapted to a wide variety of projects and is always subject to the needs, abilities, and desires of the parent organization.

The advantages accruing to the matrix structure are potent, but the disadvantages are also serious. All of the following disadvantages involve conflict—between the functional and project managers, for the most part.

1. In the case of functionally organized projects, there is no doubt that the functional division is the focus of decision-making power. In the standalone project case, it is clear that the PM is the power center of the project. With matrix organizations, the power is more balanced. Often, the balance is fairly delicate. When doubt exists about who is in charge, the work of the project suffers. If the project is successful and highly visible, doubt about who is in charge can foster political infighting for the credit and glory. If the project is a failure, political infighting will be even more brutal to avoid blame.

2. While the ability to balance time, cost, and scope between several projects is an advantage of matrix organizations, that ability has its dark side. The set of projects must be carefully monitored as a set, a tough job. Further, the movement of resources from project to project in order to satisfy the several schedules may foster political infighting among the several PMs, all of whom tend to be more interested in ensuring success for their individual projects than in helping the total system optimize organization-wide goals.

3. For strong matrices, problems associated with shutting down a project are almost as severe as those in standalone project organizations. The projects, having individual identities, resist death. Even in matrix organizations, projectitis is still a serious disease.

4. In matrix-organized projects, the PM controls administrative decisions and the functional heads control technological decisions. The distinction is simple enough when writing about project management, but for the operating PM the division of authority and responsibility inherent in matrix management is complex. The ability of the PM to negotiate anything from resources to technical assistance to delivery dates is a key contributor to project success. Success is doubtful for a PM without strong negotiating skills.

5. Matrix management violates the management principle of unity of command. Project workers have at least two bosses, their functional heads and the PM. There is no way

around the split loyalties and confusion that result. Anyone who has worked under such an arrangement understands the difficulties. Those who have not done so cannot appreciate the discomforts it causes. To paraphrase Plato's comment on democracy, matrix management "is a charming form of management, full of variety and disorder."

Modern matrix management today strives to achieve many more goals than when it was adopted decades ago. For example, IBM is organized as a multi-dimensional matrix (Grant, 2008). There is a "business" organization (structured around hardware, software, and services), a "geographical" orientation (regions/countries), a "functional" home, "customer" groupings, "distribution channel" specialties, and "new business development" thrusts. If the old form of matrix management was confusing, the new form can be overwhelming. But modern organizations find that they have many more goals to achieve and must be multi-dexterous, achieving a more complex organizational integration but without hampering their flexibility, responsiveness, and performance. The solution many organizations have come up with has been to be more formal and controlling for the operational activities such as business and distribution channel goals (more centralized) while more informal (dotted-line relationships) for the functional, geographic, and customer activities, and even less formal, even voluntary or self-organizing, for knowledge management activities such as new business development.

Virtual Projects

Virtual projects are those in which work on the project team crosses time, space, organizational, or cultural boundaries. Thus, a virtual team may work in different time zones, be geographically dispersed, work in different organizations, or work in different cultures. In all cases, the rise of virtual projects has been facilitated by the use of the Internet and other communication technologies. In many of these cases, the project team is often organized in some matrix-type of structure rather than a functional or standalone project form. Kalu (1993, p. 175) further defines *virtual positions* as "task processes, the performance of which requires composite membership" in both project and functional organizations. When complex organizations conduct projects, virtual positions are typical because projects usually require input from several functional departments. This creates overlapping and shared responsibility for the work, with functional and project managers sharing responsibility for execution of the project. The reading "The Virtual Project: Managing Tomorrow's Team Today" at the end of this chapter more narrowly specifies that virtual projects exist when project team members are geographically dispersed and gives some suggestions for successfully running such projects.

Gratton (2007) also offers some rules for success when organizations find they must use geographically dispersed virtual teams for some of their projects.

- Only use virtual teams for projects that are challenging and interesting. But also be sure the project is meaningful to the company as well as the team.

- Solicit volunteers as much as possible—they'll be more enthusiastic and dedicated to the success of the project.

- Include a few members in the team who already know each other, and make sure one in every six or seven are "boundary spanners" with lots of outside contacts.

- Create an online resource for team members to learn about each other (especially how they prefer to work), collaborate, brainstorm, and draw inspiration.

- Encourage frequent communication, but not social gatherings (which will occur at more natural times anyway).

- Divide the project work into geographically independent modules as much as possible so progress in one location isn't hampered by delays in other locations.

Project Management in Practice
Software Firm Yunio Avoids Complex Technologies

Chris Mathews, co-founder and CEO of China-based startup software maker Yunio, avoids cumbersome gadgetry and complex interfaces to manage his global project teams. He prefers techniques and technologies that seem natural and comfortable for the virtual teams. His focus is clear communication, regardless of the technology used. And when a message can be sent by example, he prefers that to other, less-effective forms of communication. For instance, when working with his Chinese teams he found that it wasn't the norm for team members to let their colleagues know when they would be absent, or how to reach them. To set an example, he started e-mailing team members whenever he would be unable to attend a meeting. For individual teams or groups, he creates separate, distinct mailing lists. As his example was adopted by the teams, it became part of Yunio's culture whereby new employees automatically adopted it too.

Although Mathews uses e-mail for important matters where a written record is desirable, he finds other technologies can be more appropriate for other uses. To keep communication as simple and seamless as possible, he only uses wiki for teams larger than 15 people because it's a large investment requiring input from an online community of users to create content. Wikis become increasingly efficient, particularly for knowledge management, as the team grows. For less than 15 people, he prefers group chats but supplemented by chat logs. Instant messages don't require instant responses so they allow team members to drop a quick note to someone without requiring a response. Since his workers use instant messaging anyway, it's a natural communication tool for chats. Mathews believes that the use of tech products don't define how to manage virtual teams but rather are just part of the toolkit; smart management is about picking the most appropriate tool to communicate clearly.

Source: M. S. Zoninsein, " Less is More," *PM Network*, Vol. 24.

5.4 PROJECTS IN COMPOSITE ORGANIZATIONAL STRUCTURES

The complexities of the real world rarely lead firms to organize their projects in any of the previous "pure" forms, so what we tend to see in practice is some combination of two or three or more different forms. In a functional organization, there may be project divisions along with marketing and finance, or in a matrix division there may be a staff project reporting to the CEO (or treasurer, or . . .), and so on. We call these "composite" structures.

As an example, organization by territory is especially attractive to national organizations whose activities are physically or geographically spread, and where the products have some geographical uniqueness, such as ladies' garments. So we may have projects such as spring fashion designs being run within each territory. But suppose each territory also sells to different kinds of customers, like retailers, wholesalers, and consumers; or perhaps civilians and military. Project organization within customer divisions is typically found when the projects reflect a paramount interest in the needs of different types of customers. Then we might also have matrixed projects that cross the various territories and focus on customer preferences, or projectized if it is a single project, such as installing a customer relationship management (CRM) software database for all the territories.

If both functional and projectized divisions coexist in a firm, this would result in the composite form shown in Figure 5-4. This form is rarely observed for a long duration. What is done, instead, is to spin off the large, successful long-run projects as subsidiaries or independent operations. Many firms nurture young, unstable, smaller projects under the wing of an existing division, then wean them to standalone projects with their own identity, as in Figure 5-4, and finally allow the formation of a *venture team*—or, for a larger project, *venture firm*—within the parent company. For example, Texas Instruments did this with the Speak and Spell® toy that was developed by one of its employees, and 3M did this with their Post-It® Notes.

The composite form leads to flexibility. It enables the firm to meet special problems by appropriate adaptation of its organizational structure. There are, however, distinct dangers involved in using the composite structure. Dissimilar groupings within the same accountability center tend to encourage overlap, duplication, and friction because of incompatibility of interests. Again, we have the conditions that tend to result in conflict between functional and project managers.

Figure 5-5 illustrates another common solution to the problem of how to organize a project. The firm sets up what appears to be a standard form of functional organization, but it adds a staff office to administer all the projects. This frees the functional groups of administrative problems while it uses their technical talents. In a large specialty chemical firm, this organizational form worked so well that the staff office became the nucleus of a full-scale division of the firm whose sole purpose was to administer projects. Much has been written about the use of a "project management office" (PMO) which, as noted in earlier chapters

Figure 5-4   A functional/projectized composite organization.

Figure 5-5   A functional/staff organization.

and shown in Figure 5-5, is an equivalent structure; more will be said about the PMO in Section 5.6.

For single projects, this is basically the functional organization described earlier, but if used for multiple projects, and particularly if a PMO is used, this organization is similar to the matrix form. The main difference is that this form would typically be used for small, short-term projects where the formation of a full-fledged matrix system is not justified. This mixed form shares several advantages and disadvantages of the matrix structure, but the project life is usually so short that the disease of projectitis is rarely contracted. If the number or size of the projects being staffed in this way grows, a shift to a formal matrix organization naturally evolves.

Though the ways of interfacing project and parent organization are many and varied, most firms eventually adopt the matrix form as the basic method of housing their growing number of projects. To this base, occasional standalone, functional, and composite projects may be added if these possess special advantages; otherwise, they will be added to the matrix due to the relatively low cost of managing them and their enhanced ability to get access to broad technical support.

5.5   SELECTING A PROJECT FORM

The choice of how to organize a project is not addressed to PMs or aspiring PMs. It is addressed to senior management. Very rarely does the PM have a choice about the way the project interfaces with the parent organization. Indeed, the PM is rarely asked for input to the interface choice. Even experienced practitioners find it difficult to explain how one should proceed when trying to choose. The choice is determined by the situation, but even so, is partly intuitive. There are few accepted principles of design, and no step-by-step procedures that give detailed instructions for determining what kind of structure is needed and how it can be built. All we can do is consider the nature of the potential project, the characteristics of the various organizational options, the advantages and disadvantages of each, the cultural preferences of the parent organization, and make the best compromise we can.

In general, the functional form is apt to be the organizational form of choice for projects where the major focus must be on the in-depth application of a technology rather than, for example, on minimizing cost, meeting a specific schedule, or achieving speedy response to change. Also, the functional form is preferred for projects that will require large capital investments in equipment or buildings of a type normally used by the function.

If the firm engages in a large number of similar projects (e.g., construction projects), the projectized form of organization is preferred. The same form would generally be used for one-time, highly specific, unique tasks that require careful control and are not appropriate for a single functional area—the development of a new product line, for instance.

When the project requires the integration of inputs from several functional areas and involves reasonably sophisticated technology, but does not require all the technical specialists to work for the project on a full-time basis, the matrix organization is the only satisfactory solution. This is particularly true when several such projects must share technical experts. Another special case is when projects are created to change the way the parent organization is organized or communicates internally. Such projects typically require representation of all major parts of the parent to be successful. Matrix organizations are complex and present a difficult challenge for the PM, but are sometimes necessary.

If choice of project structure exists, the first problem is to determine the kind of work that must be accomplished. To do this requires an initial, tentative project plan (a topic covered in detail in Section 6.1). First, identify the primary deliverable(s) of the project. Next, list the major tasks associated with each deliverable. For each task, determine the functional unit that will probably be responsible for carrying out the task. These are the elements that must be involved in order to carry out the project. The problem is how best to bring them together—or, how best to integrate their work. Additional matters to be considered are the individuals (or small groups) who will do the work, their personalities, the technology to be employed, the client(s) to be served, the political relationships of the functional units involved, and the culture of the parent organization. Environmental factors inside and outside the parent organization must also be taken into account. By understanding the various structures, their advantages and disadvantages, a firm can select the organizational structure that seems to offer the most effective and efficient choice.

We illustrate the process with an example using the following procedure.

1. Define the project with a statement of the objective(s) that identifies the major outcomes desired.

2. Determine the key tasks associated with each objective and locate the units in the parent organization that serve as functional "homes" for these types of tasks.

3. Arrange the key tasks by sequence and decompose them into work packages.

4. Determine which organizational units are required to carry out the work packages and which units will work particularly closely with which others.

5. List any special characteristics or assumptions associated with the project—for example, level of technology needed, probable length and size of the project, any potential problems with the individuals who may be assigned to the work, possible political problems between different functions involved, and anything else that seems relevant, including the parent firm's previous experiences with different ways of organizing projects.

6. In light of the above, and with full cognizance of the pros and cons associated with each structural form, choose a structure.

Project Management in Practice
Trinatronic, Inc.

Project objective: To design, build, and market a laptop computer that uses open standards where possible, and is capable of running all current engineering design and office productivity software packages. To satisfy security and confidentiality considerations, the computer should be able to maintain multiple versions of its operating information without needing to use offline storage.

In addition, the computer must be able to support video and audio conferencing capabilities, and must be compatible with European Common Market and U. S. "Green" standards for energy usage. The desired price point for this computer should be 10% below what we suspect competitors could offer.

Key Tasks	Organizational Units
A. Write specifications.	Mktg. Div. and R & D
B. Design hardware, do initial tests.	R & D
C. Engineer hardware for production.	Eng. Dept., Mfg. Div.
D. Set up production line.	Eng. Dept., Mfg. Div.
E. Manufacture small run, conduct quality and reliability tests.	Mfg. Div. and Q.A. Dept., Exec. V.P. staff
F. Write (or adopt) operating systems.	Software Prod. Div.
G. Test operating systems.	Q.A. Dept., Exec. V.P. staff
H. Write (or adopt) applications software.	Software Prod. Div.
I. Test applications software.	Q.A. Dept., Exec. V.P. staff
J. Prepare full documentation, repair and user manuals.	Tech. Writing Section (Eng. Div.) and Tech. Writing Section (Software Prod. Div.)
K. Set up service system with manuals and spare parts	Tech. Writing Section (Eng. Div.) and Tech.
L. Prepare marketing program.	Mktg. Div.
M. Prepare marketing demonstrations.	Mktg. Div.

Without attempting to generate a specific sequence for these tasks, we note that they seem to belong to seven categories of work.

1. Develop and prioritize requirements.
2. Design, build, and test hardware.
3. Design, write, and test software.
4. Set up production and service/repair systems with spares and manuals.
5. Prepare and implement a make-or-buy analysis.
6. Develop release plan.
7. Design marketing effort, with demonstrations, brochures, and manuals.

Based on this analysis, it would appear that the project will need the following elements:

- Groups to design the hardware and software.
- Groups to test the hardware and write and test the software.
- A group to engineer the production system for the hardware.
- A group to design the marketing program.
- A group to prepare all appropriate documents and manuals.
- And, lest we forget, a group to administer all the above groups.

These subsystems represent at least three major divisions and perhaps a half-dozen departments in the parent organization. The groups designing the hardware and the multiple operating systems will have to work closely together. The test groups may work quite independently of the hardware and software designers, but results improve when they cooperate.

Trinatronics has people capable of carrying out the project. The design of the hardware and operating systems is possible in the current state of the art, but to design such systems at a cost of 10% below potential competitors will require an advance in the state of the art. The project is estimated to take between 18 and 24 months, and to be the most expensive project yet undertaken by Trinatronics.

Based on the sketchy information above, it seems clear that a functional project organization would not be appropriate. Too much interaction between major divisions is required to make a single function into a comfortable organizational home for everyone. Either a standalone project or matrix structure is feasible, and given the choice, it seems sensible to choose the simpler standalone project organization if the cost of additional personnel is not too high. Note that if the project had required only part-time participation by the highly qualified scientific professionals, the matrix organization might have been preferable. Also, a matrix structure would probably have been chosen if this project were only one of several such projects drawing on a common staff base.

Source: S. J. Mantel, III. Consulting project.

5.6   THE PROJECT MANAGEMENT OFFICE (PMO)

Thus far in this chapter it has been tacitly assumed that however the project has been organized, it has, or has access to, sufficient skill, knowledge, and resources to accomplish any activities that may be required. As we shall see, this assumption is not always true. A primary task of the PM is to acquire the resources, technical skills, knowledge, and whatever is needed by the project. While this may be difficult, acquisition of the project's technical resources is mainly dependent on the PM's skill in negotiation, as described in Chapter 4.

Even if the PM has all the resources needed, two problems remain. First, in the entire history of projects from the beginning of time until the day after tomorrow, no project has ever been completed precisely as it was planned. Uncertainty is a way of life for PMs and their projects. Second, the successful execution of a project is a complex managerial task and requires the use of planning, budgeting, scheduling, and control tools with which the neophyte PM may not be completely familiar. In addition, there are contractual, administrative, and reporting duties that must be performed in accord with the law, the wishes of the client, and the rules of the organizational home of the project.

Dealing with uncertainties has come to be known as *risk management*. We introduced the subject in Chapter 2 when the uncertainties of project selection were discussed. To deal with uncertainty, the parent organization must create some mechanism to manage it, a topic treated in detail in Chapter 6. In order to deal with the managerial and administrative issues in a way that meets the parent organization's rules for management and administration, many firms have created a *project management office*, or PMO. In a recent PMI (2011) survey, it was found that three out of five respondents' organizations have PMOs. This section is devoted to the investigation of how project management and administration can be organized in order to perform with efficiency, effectiveness, and consistency. The PMO and its responsibilities are detailed in the introductory chapter of PMBOK®.

PMBOK Guide
1.4.4

With the increasing role of projects in today's organizations and the move toward "management by projects," the need has arisen for an organizational entity to help manage these fast-multiplying forms of getting work done. This is the role of the Project Management

Office (PMO), a.k.a. the Project Office, the Program Management Office, the Project Support Office, and so on. There are a variety of forms of PMOs to serve a variety of needs. Some of these are at a low level in the organization and others report to the highest levels. The best PMOs (Baker, 2007) have some common characteristics, however, including the traits of being run like the best businesses (a business plan, focused, emphasis on results), enjoying strong executive support, being future-oriented learning organizations, and offering the best project leadership in the organization.

Purposes of the Project Management Office

Before discussing the purpose and services offered by PMOs, consider the following statistics reported by Block et al. (2001). When asked the reasons for initiating a PMO, almost two-thirds of the respondents indicated a need for establishing consistent project management standards and methods, and that the PMO was initiated by senior management direction. About half the respondents also indicated a need to eliminate project delays and correct poor project planning. A bit less than 40 percent wanted to improve project performance and eliminate cost overruns. Last, about a quarter of the respondents indicated they wished to reduce customer dissatisfaction. The 2011 PMI survey mentioned earlier found that having a PMO was a key practice in improving project performance, and their roles now commonly include portfolio management, program management, monitoring project success metrics, and managing project resource allocation.

A major contribution of PMOs is to establish project administration procedures for selecting, initializing and planning, budgeting, and scheduling projects as well as to serve as a repository for reports on the performance of the planning, budgeting, scheduling, and resource allocation processes. PMO files also often contain reports on risk management, project audits, evaluations, and histories. As reflected by the reasons for initiating the PMOs in the first place, 78 percent of the respondents to Block et al. (2001) indicated that their PMO established and maintained standard project processes (practices and procedures), 64 percent offered consulting help on projects, and 58 percent offered training and mentoring services. About half performed project tracking and slightly fewer conducted portfolio management. Only 28 percent maintained a stable of project managers for future project needs.

Project Management in Practice
A Project Management Office Success for the Transportation Security Administration

The Transportation Security Administration (TSA) had only 3 months and $20 million to build a 13,500 square foot coordination center, involving the coordination of up to 300 tradespeople working simultaneously on various aspects of the center. A strong Project Management Office (PMO) was crucial to making the effort a success. The PMO accelerated the procurement and approval process, cutting times in half in some cases. They engaged a team leader, a master scheduler, a master financial manager, a procurement specialist, a civil engineer, and other specialists to manage the multiple facets of the construction project, finishing the entire project in 97 days and on budget, receiving an award from the National Assn. of Industrial and Office Properties for the quality of its project management and overall facility.

Source: Project Management Institute. "PMO Speeds Success for Transportation Facility," *PM Network*, Vol 18.

Although specific goals may be articulated for the PMO, the overarching purpose is often inherent in the process itself and is unarticulated, for example, ensuring that the firm's portfolio of projects supports the organization's overall goals and strategy, as described in Chapter 2. In this case, the PMO is the critical tie between strategic management and the project managers. Another overarching purpose may be the gradual assimilation of good project management practice into the entire organization, moving it from a functionally organized to a matrixed form, not only in structure but in culture as well. In such cases, the PMO is often renamed the Enterprise Project Management Office (EPMO), or given a similar name.

In a recent study of PMOs following the financial crisis and Great Recession of 2008–9 (Gale 2010), it was found that more than half the PMOs now report to the highest levels of management and work on high-value strategic tasks such as managing the governance process (72% of those reporting), advising executives (64%), and participating in strategic planning (62%). In terms of payoffs, they reduced the number of failed projects by 31 percent, delivered 30 percent of projects under budget, and saved U.S. companies an average of $567,000 per project. PMOs show the greatest value when their project portfolio performance matches the strategic objectives of the organization. If they have no vision or mission and no measures of success, they risk getting labeled as administrative overhead and cut in tough times.

In one case, a PMO was initiated when management wanted more insight into what was happening in their projects. The PMO reorganized projects to ensure they were all in sync with the firm's goals, and had a clear business case that aligned with the organizational strategy. The PMO then not only tracked the projects but also issued monthly management reports with at-a-glance information about every project. The reports also show how each completed project helps the firm meet its objectives. To provide management with forward looking information about potential issues that might jeopardize each project's ability to deliver on its strategic goals, all projects maintain risk registers that are consolidated into a risk report at the end of each month.

It is important to understand that the role of the PMO is that of an *enabler/facilitator* of projects, not the *doer* of projects. Top management cannot allow the EPMO or the PMO to usurp the technical aspects—scheduling, budgeting, etc.—of running the project. Those are the project manager's responsibility. Although the PMO may, on occasion, become involved in some project management tasks, it should be for the purpose of facilitating liaison with top management, not to do the work of the project team.

Forms of Project Management Office

Akin to the time phasing of PMO responsibilities just noted, there are various levels of competence, sophistication, and responsibility of PMOs. That is, some organizations may only want a limited PMO that represents an information center, reporting on project progress and assessing the organization's project maturity. At the next level, the PMO may establish project management procedures and practices, promulgate lessons learned from prior projects, create a database for risk analysis, help project managers with administrative and managerial matters, and possibly even offer basic training in project management. At the upper level, the PMO may establish a resource database and monitor interproject dependencies, manage the project portfolio to ensure attainment of the organization's goals, audit and prioritize individual projects, and generally establish an enterprise project management system.

Another way of organizing the PMO has to do with the reporting level of the office. If top management wants to test the efficacy of a PMO at a lower level before approving it for the organization as a whole, they may place it in a functional department such as Information Technology or Engineering. In this role, the main responsibility of the PMO will be to help the department's project managers with their individual projects. If the PMO is established at the business level, it may take on more responsibility for good project management practices and possibly offer basic training. At higher organizational levels, the PMO's responsibilities will broaden and become less tactical and more strategic. If the eventual goal is to improve the organization's ability to execute projects, however, this is a risky way to implement a PMO! Simply because a PMO is not able to rescue a failing engineering project, for example, does not mean that it could not be extremely valuable to the organization by performing many of the preceding tasks.

In recent years, several large organizations conducting scores or more (sometimes hundreds) of projects have created multiple PMOs, each overseeing and aiding projects in their individual unit of the organization. An EPMO is occasionally also created to oversee the multiple PMOs and ensure that they follow organizational standards for managing projects. While a PMO is typically only division-wide in a large organization, the EPMO is system-wide and responsible for policy making and organizational change. The 2011 PMI survey also found that EPMOs tend to focus on the strategic aspects of project management. In such cases, PMO contact with senior management is conducted through the EPMO, typically used to manage the project selection process as well as to communicate relevant organizational policy to the PMOs, direct risk management activities, establish processes for audits and reviews, and act as the organizational repository for project records.

Tasks of the Project Management Office

To achieve its goals, PMOs and EPMOs commonly perform many of the following tasks (Block, 1999):

- Establish and enforce good project management processes such as procedures for bidding, risk analysis, project selection, progress reports, executing contracts, and selecting software
- Assess and improve the organization's project management maturity
- Develop and improve an enterprise project management system
- Offer training in project management and help project managers become certified
- Identify, develop, and mentor project managers and maintain a stable of competent candidates
- Offer consulting services to the organization's project managers
- Help project managers with administrative details such as status reports
- Establish a process for estimation and evaluation of risk
- Determine if a new project is a good "fit" for the changing organization
- Identify downstream changes (market, organization) and their impacts on current projects: Are the projects still relevant? Is there a need to change any project's scope? Are there any cost effects on the projects?
- Review and manage the organization's project risk portfolio, including limiting the number of active projects at any given time and identifying and reining in runaway projects as well as managing potential disasters
- Conduct project reviews and audits, particularly early in each project's life cycle, and report project progress relative to the organization's goals
- Maintain and store project archives
- Establish a project resource database and manage the resource pool
- Serve as a champion to pursue project management excellence in the organization and encourage discussion on the value of individual projects in the firm
- Serve as a "home" for project managers to communicate with each other and with PMO staff

- Collect and disseminate information, techniques, and lessons learned as reported in project evaluations that can improve project management practices
- Assist in project termination

Not all of these goals can be achieved at once. In the short term, or the first few months, the PMO will only be able to assess the organization's current project management practices and perhaps evaluate the progress of each of the organization's many projects. In the midterm, the PMO can start standardizing project management processes and procedures, begin helping individual projects with, for example, risk analysis and administrative details, and perhaps initiate a strategic portfolio analysis of the current projects. In the long term, or after about a year, the more comprehensive tasks may be undertaken, such as assembling a resource database, training project managers, conducting project audits, and consulting on individual projects.

In our opinion, it would be rare for a PMO or EPMO to handle, or try to handle, all of the above matters. Rather, a great many control the Project Selection Process and manage a few other project related matters, e.g., maintaining project records and archives, handling risk management, and/or training new project managers. An experienced consultant told us:

> Lately, in my travels, in most companies I come across it is the PMO's major role to create and facilitate the methodology of the project selection process in order to support upper-management's decision making. The PMO evaluates all proposed initiatives against the company's goals, estimates costs, and proves the business's proposed ROI if the initiative is funded. Once a project is selected, the PMO shifts its effort to determining if the project is meeting all of its objectives. Many PMOs do little or no direct project management support of projects as they are being carried out, but PMOs do conduct several major evaluations of all projects in a portfolio, both during the projects' life cycles and after the fact, to see if they achieve what they said they would during the selection process.

Implementing the Project Management Office

As was noted previously, the best way to implement a PMO is to treat it as a project and apply good project management procedures. In addition, given the role of this special type of project, it is also suggested that the effort not be initiated until it has the full commitment of the top managers of the organization. It should also have a senior management sponsor/champion who is determined to see this project through to success. One way to initiate the project is through a pilot program in one of the areas that falls under the responsibility of the PMO project champion. Following its completion, the pilot project can be assessed, any mistakes corrected, and the benefits publicized to the rest of the organization. As the PMO expands and interacts with more and more projects, its benefits to the organization will increase progressively with its reach. Liu et al. (2007) have shown that PMOs have a significantly positive impact on projects operating with high task uncertainty. (The positive impact of PMOs decreases as task uncertainty diminishes.)

Unfortunately, not all PMOs are successful. According to Tennant (2001), one of the primary problems of PMOs is that the executives who establish PMOs often do not understand project management practices themselves. Thus, they have unrealistic expectations of the PMO, such as providing temporary help for a project in trouble, or to obtain cost reductions from ongoing projects. The PMO is not a quick fix for saving projects that are failing; its primary objective is to improve project management processes over the long run.

PMOs cannot be expected to correct upper management failures such as inappropriate project goals, insufficient project support, and inadequate resource availability. Interestingly, a recent trend in project organizations is the outsourcing of the PMO functions themselves. One has to wonder if this is a sign of impending trouble or a wise recognition of the limitations of upper management knowledge.

5.7 THE PROJECT TEAM

> "Teamwork is a lot of people doing what I say."
>
> Anonymous Boss

PMBOK Guide
9.2–9.4

In this section we consider the makeup of the project team, bearing in mind that different projects have vastly different staffing needs. The role of the project team takes up most of Chapter 9 in PMBOK®. Then we take up some problems associated with staffing the team. Last, we deal with a few of the behavioral issues in managing this team.

To be concrete during our discussion of project teams, let us use the example of a software engineering project to determine how to form a project team. Assume that the size of our hypothetical project is fairly large. In addition to the PM, the following key team members might be needed, plus an appropriate number of systems architects, engineers, testers, clerks, and the like. This example can be applied to a construction project, a medical research project, or any of a wide variety of other types of projects. The titles of the individuals would change, but the roles played would be similar.

- *Systems Architect*   The systems architect is in charge of the basic product design and development and is responsible for functional analysis, specifications, drawings, cost estimates, and documentation.

- *Development Engineer*   This engineer's task is the efficient production of the product or process the project engineer has designed, including responsibility for manufacturing engineering, design and production of code, unit testing, production scheduling, and other production tasks.

- *Test Engineer*   This person is responsible for the installation, testing, and support of the product (process) once its engineering is complete.

- *Contract Administrator*   The administrator is in charge of all official paperwork, keeping track of standards compliance (including quality/reliability), customer (engineering) changes, billings, questions, complaints, legal aspects, costs, and negotiation of other matters related to the contract authorizing the project. Not uncommonly, the contract administrator also serves as project historian and archivist.

- *Project Controller*   The controller keeps daily account of budgets, cost variances, labor charges, project supplies, capital equipment status, etc. The controller also makes regular reports and keeps in close touch with both the PM and the company controller. If the administrator does not serve as historian, the controller can do so.

- *Support Services Manager*   This person is in charge of product support, subcontractors, data processing, purchasing, contract negotiation, and general management support functions.

Of these top project people, it is most important that the systems architect and the project controller report directly to the PM (see Figure 5-6). This facilitates control over two of the main goals of the project: technical performance and budget. (The project manager is usually

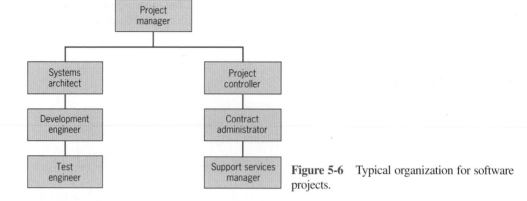

Figure 5-6 Typical organization for software projects.

in personal control of the schedule.) For a large project, all six project officials could work out of the project office and report directly to the PM.

To staff the project, the PM works from a forecast of personnel needs over the life cycle of the project. This is done with the aid of some special charts. First, a *work breakdown structure* (WBS) is prepared to determine the exact nature of the tasks required to complete the project. (The WBS is described in detail and illustrated in Chapter 6.) The skill requirements for these tasks are assessed and like skills are aggregated to determine work force needs. Be warned that development of the WBS may involve consultations with external experts. The PM needs to understand, plan for, and closely monitor the effects on current projects of these consultations. It is common for these experts to be pulled away from their own work in order to deal with planning needs arising elsewhere in a WBS. From this base, the functional departments are contacted to locate individuals who can meet these needs.

On occasion, certain tasks may be subcontracted. This option may be adopted because the appropriately skilled personnel are unavailable or cannot be located, or subcontractors can deliver for lower cost, or even because some special equipment required for the project is not available in-house. The need to subcontract is growing as firms "downsize." If the proper people (and equipment) are found within the organization, however, the PM usually must obtain their services from their home departments. Many firms insist on using "local" resources when they are available, in order to maintain better control over resource usage and quality. Typically, the PM will have to negotiate with both the functional department head and the employee, trying to "sell" the employee on the challenge and excitement of working on the project and trying to convince the department head that lending the employee to the project is in the department head's best interest.

There are some other people, not necessarily technical, who are also critical to the project's success and should report directly to the PM or to the PM's deputy (often the systems architect):

- Senior project team members who will be having a long-term relationship with the project
- Those with whom the PM will require continuous or close communication
- Those with rare skills necessary to project success.

Remember that the PM must depend on reason when trying to convince a department head to lend their valuable people to the project. The functional department head, who sees the project as a more or less glamorous source of prestige in which the department cannot share, has little natural motivation to be cooperative. Once again, project success depends on the political and negotiating skills of the PM as much as on the technical skills of the team.

Thus far, we have tacitly assumed a fairly strong matrix or projectized organization for the project in our example. In recent years, the use of weaker matrices has become more and more frequent. In many firms, when project managers are asked for the number of people who report directly to them, the answer "None!" is not uncommon. Most common of all, it seems to us, is the matrix organization with a project manager, one or two key skilled contributors who may be full-time members of the project, and a wide variety of services or capacity supplied to the project by functional groups in the parent organization. Such structures are often found in R&D projects that are part of larger programs being carried out by a parent firm. In a pharmaceutical project, for example, one or two senior scientists and laboratory technicians may be assigned to the project, but the work involved in toxicity testing, efficacy testing, and writing the product insert is supplied to the project in the form of deliverables from functional units rather than people assigned directly to the project to carry out the work.

Although the project manager has to bargain for fewer individuals in these weaker matrix structures than in the case of stronger matrices, the PM's negotiating skills are just as critical. It is typical for the success of weak-matrix projects to be dependent on the skills of the few technical specialists who are assigned directly to the project. The ability of the PM to negotiate for skilled technicians as well as for the *timely* delivery of services from functional departments is a key determinant of success.

Project Management in Practice
The Empire Uses Floating Multidisciplinary Teams

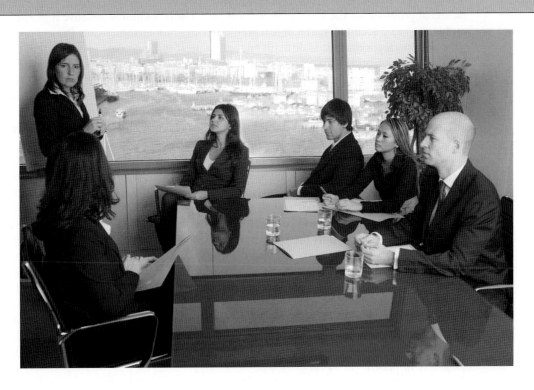

Lucasfilm Ltd., the creators of *Star Wars*, needs quick-moving, flexible, multidisciplinary teams of insiders and freelance outsiders to execute short-lived, rapidly forming and dissolving projects. Standard project management approaches are too slow for this kind of environment. They need the ability to quickly assemble teams to execute specific functions and then reassemble to fit the next set of tasks. To do this, Lucasfilm moved all their disparate units into a $350 million single-roofed complex so they can all interact as the tasks of the moment require. Managers are rootless, sweeping through office suites scattered throughout the building, depending on the talents needed for the next project. As the relentless pressure of meeting higher performance levels with tighter schedules and budgets increases for projects, this model may be the future for project management organization and leadership.

Source: B. Hindo, "The Empire Strikes at Silos," *Business Week* 2007.

5.8 HUMAN FACTORS AND THE PROJECT TEAM

PMBOK Guide

Chapter 9

With a reminder of the need for the PM to possess a high level of political sensitivity, we can discuss some other factors in managing project teams, all the while remembering that the principles and practices of good, general management also apply to the management of projects. We discuss them from the viewpoint of the PM as an individual who must cope with the personal as well as the technical victories and frustrations of life on a project. The issues of managing the project team are mainly included in the Human Resource Management knowledge area of PMBOK®.

Meeting schedule and cost goals without compromising performance appears to be a technical problem for the PM. Actually, it is only partly technical because it is also a human problem—more accurately, a technical problem with a human dimension. Project professionals tend to be perfectionists. It is difficult enough to meet project goals under normal conditions, but when, out of pride of workmanship, the professionals want to keep improving (and thus changing) the product, the task becomes almost impossible. Changes cause delays. Throughout the project, the manager must continue to stress the importance of meeting due dates. It also helps if the PM establishes, at the beginning of the project, a technical change procedure to ensure control over the incidence and frequency of change. (It would not, however, be wise for the PM to assume that everyone will automatically follow such a procedure.)

Another problem is motivating project team members to accomplish the work of the project. Unfortunately, the PM often has little control over the economic rewards and promotions of the people working on the project. This is especially true when the matrix is weak. This does not, however, mean that the PM cannot motivate members of the project team. Frederick Herzberg, who studied what motivates technical employees such as engineers, scientists, and professionals on a project team, contends that recognition, achievement, the work itself, responsibility, advancement, and the chance to learn new skills are strong motivators (see Herzberg, 1968). It is the PM's responsibility to make sure that project work is structured in such a way as to emphasize these motivational factors. We have also found that the judicious use of "thank you" notes from the PM to those functional managers who have supplied the project with capable and committed individuals and/or effective and efficient capacity is a potent motivator—copies to the relevant individuals and to the functional manager's boss, of course. (It is also important not to write such notes if the performance was mediocre or poor.)

The use of participative management is also a way of motivating people. This is not a new theory. The concept suggests that the individual worker (or team) should play a significant role in deciding what means should be employed in meeting desired ends, and in finding better ways of accomplishing things. Recent participative programs such as Six Sigma, Total Quality Management (TQM), continuous improvement teams (CIT), self-directed work teams (SDWT), and more recently, agile project management teams may have slightly different structures and vary somewhat in the amount of decision-making authority and autonomy exercised by the team, but they are all aimed at improving worker performance as well as improving production methods and product quality. We will discuss agile project management further in Chapter 6.

The adoption of such methods *empowers* the team (as well as its individual members) to take responsibility and to be accountable for delivering project objectives. Some advantages of empowerment for project teams are:

1. It harnesses the ability of the team members to manipulate tasks so that project objectives are met. The team is encouraged to find better ways to do things.

2. Professionals do not like being micromanaged. Participative management does not tell them how to work but, given a goal, allows them to design their own methods (usually within some constraints on their authority).

3. The team members know they are responsible and accountable for achieving the project deliverables.

4. There is a good chance that synergistic solutions will result from team interaction.

5. Team members get timely feedback on their performance.

6. The PM is provided a tool for evaluating the team's performance.

All of these items serve to increase motivation among members of the project team. Informal discussions with many project team leaders lead us to the same conclusions, but the success of SDWTs (and all other teams) is ultimately dependent on a clear statement of what the team is expected to accomplish. Senior management must "make the effort to clearly delineate project goals, responsibilities, and authority" in order to reap the advantages of project teams (Ford et al., 1992, p. 316; Nelson, 1998, p. 43). Finally, it is important to remember that giving a project to a team does not supersede the need for competent project management skills.

In Chapter 6, we cover the process of planning projects in detail, and we emphasize the use of the work breakdown structure (WBS) to organize the activities of the project. It is a detailed planning and scheduling technique directed toward achievement of the objectives of the project. The PM (and sometimes the client) works with members of the project team and a comprehensive set of written plans is generated by this process. The resulting document is not only a plan, but also a control mechanism. Because the system of developing the plan is participative and makes team members accountable for their specific parts of the overall plan, it motivates them, and also clearly denotes the degree to which team members are mutually dependent. The importance of this latter outcome of the planning process is not well recognized in the literature on team building.

However, bringing people together, even when they belong to the same organization and contribute their efforts to the same objectives, does not necessarily mean that they will behave like a team. Organizing the team's work in such a way that team members are mutually dependent, and recognize it, will produce a strong impetus for the group to form a real team. Project success will be associated with teamwork, and project failure will surely result if the group does not work as a team.[*] If many or most of the team members are also "problem oriented," the likelihood of the group forming an effective team is further increased. In an extensive research study on the matter, Tippet et al. (1995) conclude that overall results show that companies are generally doing a poor job of team building. Lack of effective rewards, inadequate individual and team performance feedback mechanisms, and inadequate individual and team goal-setting are all weak areas (Tippet, 1995, p. 35). Finally, Lencioni (2002) has written a wonderful little book on team building that he describes as "a leadership fable." If one can read only one work on teams, this would be our first choice.

The use of matrix project organizations raises an additional problem. Team members come and go. The constant turnover of team members makes it difficult to build and maintain a team (Bushe, 2010). When a new member of the team arrives, he or she must be brought up to date on the project. Almost always, this job is left to experienced team members, who are often beset with the pressure of their own work and resent the interruption. Some things can be done to help, if not totally solve the problem. The PM should identify some team members who are personally outgoing and knowledgeable. These individuals can be asked to meet with new members and help them engage the technical aspects of the project. The PM must, of course, make sure that this additional work can be accommodated in the schedules of the old hands. Interpersonal contact is often made easier for all parties through the use of software (Underwood, 2008). Also, increased specialization can reduce the amount of information that must be passed along, and can result in an emphasis on the fact that all team members are dependent on other team members for success. A sense of mutual dependency will also tend to raise the level of cohesiveness and commitment to all members of the project.

Another behavioral problem for the PM is interpersonal conflict. The problem is so pervasive that conflict between project team members, and between team members and outsiders (including the client) seems to be the natural state of existence for projects. It is our strong feeling that the PM who cannot manage conflict is doomed to failure. Negotiation, as we have indicated before, is the PM's primary tool for resolving conflict, but we caution the reader once again that conflict can also be a highly creative force in a project team, particularly when it is controlled by an astute PM.

In 1975, Thamhain et al. (1975) published the definitive work on the focus and nature of conflict in projects. We have found their insights just as relevant today as they were in 1975. Table 5-1, based on Thamhain et al., relates the most likely focus of conflict to specific stages of the project life cycle. The table also suggests some solutions. When the project is first organized, priorities, procedures, and schedules all have roughly equal potential as a focus of conflict. During the buildup phase, priorities become significantly more important than any other conflict factor; procedures are almost entirely established by this time. In the main program phase, priorities are finally established and schedules are the most important cause of trouble within the project, followed by technical disagreements. Getting adequate support for the project is also a point of concern. At project finish, meeting the schedule is the critical issue, but interpersonal tensions that were easily

---

*Though team formation is not even mentioned, a reading of A. S. Carlisle's (1976) article, "MacGregor," is instructive. The article is a classic on the power of delegation and was clearly the inspiration for Blanchard and Johnson's *The One Minute Manager*. The Carlisle paper reports on a plant manager who delegates most operating decisions to his subordinates and insists that they help in solving one another's problems. As a result, they form a team that would be the envy of any project manager.

ignored early in the project can suddenly erupt into conflict during the last hectic weeks of the life cycle. Worry about reassignment exacerbates the situation. Both Tables 5-1 and 5-2 show conflict as a function of stage in the project life cycle as well as by source of the conflict, but Table 5-2 also shows the *frequency* of conflict by source and stage of the life cycle.

It seems clear to us that most of the conflict on project teams is the result of individuals focusing on the project through the eyes of their individual discipline or department (de Laat, 1994; Hughes, 1998). Such people are not problem oriented and thus are rarely effective members of project teams. Dewhurst (1998, p. 34) defines a group of individuals working independently as a "Name-Only-Team" or a "NOT." If teamwork

Table 5-1   Major Sources of Conflict during Various Stages of the Project Life Cycle

Life Cycle Phase	Conflict Source	*Major Conflict Source and Recommendations for Minimizing Dysfunctional Consequences* Recommendations
Project formation	Priorities	Clearly defined plans. Joint decision making and/or consultation with affected parties. Stress importance of project to organization goals.
	Procedures	Develop detailed administrative operating procedures to be followed in conduct of project.
		Secure approval from key administrators.
		Develop statement of understanding or charter.
	Schedules	Develop schedule commitments in advance of actual project commencement.
		Forecast other departmental priorities and possible impact on project.
Buildup phase	Priorities	Provide effective feedback to support areas on forecasted project plans and needs via status review sessions.
	Schedules	Schedule work breakdown packages (project subunits) in cooperation with functional groups.
	Procedures	Contingency planning on key administrative issues.
Main program	Schedules	Continually monitor work in progress.
		Communicate results to affected parties.
		Forecast problems and consider alternatives.
		Identify potential trouble spots needing closer surveillance.
	Technical	Early resolution of technical problems.
		Communication of schedule and budget restraints to technical personnel.
		Emphasize adequate, early technical testing.
		Facilitate early agreement on final designs.
	Labor	Forecast and communicate staffing requirements early.
		Establish staffing requirements and priorities with functional and staff groups.
Phaseout	Schedules	Close schedule monitoring in project life cycle.
		Consider reallocation of available staff to critical project areas prone to schedule slippages.
		Attain prompt resolution of technical issues that may affect schedules.
	Personality and labor	Develop plans for reallocation of people upon project completion.
		Maintain harmonious working relationships with project team and support groups. Try to loosen up high-stress environment.

Source: Thamhain et al., 1975.

Table 5-2   Number of Conflicts during a Sample Project

Start	*Early*	*Main*	*Late*	*Sources of Conflict*
27	35	24	16	Project priorities
26	27	15	09	Admin. procedures
18	26	31	11	Technical trade-offs
21	25	25	17	Staffing
20	13	15	11	Support cost estimates
25	29	36	30	Schedules
16	19	15	17	Personalities

Source: Thamhain et al., 1975.

is vital to success, then for a NOT, the "work group math (is) 2 + 2 = 3 or less." The infighting that results when discipline-oriented individuals introduce conflict to a project team is perceived by most team members to be "political." If the PM allows project decisions to be dictated by the infighting, the project is apt to fail (de Laat, 1994; Pinto, 1997, p. 31).

Conflict can be handled in several ways, but one thing is certain: Conflict avoiders do not make successful project managers. On occasion, compromise appears to be helpful, but most often, gently confronting the conflict is the method of choice. Much has been written about conflict resolution and there is no need to summarize that literature here beyond noting that the key to conflict resolution rests on the manager's ability to transform a win-lose situation into win-win.

Project Management in Practice
South African Repair Success through Teamwork

When a fire broke out in the carbonate regeneration column in a major facility of Sasol, a leading South African coal, chemical, and crude-oil company, it was crucial to get it fixed immediately. It was determined that the damaged portion of the 19-foot-wide, 231-foot-long column would have to be cut out and replaced before the facility could operate again. Time was of the essence, and only 40 days were allowed for the repair project.

To achieve this unheard-of schedule, a number of special ground rules were established:

- The project is to be schedule-driven, not cost-driven
- There is no float anywhere on the project
- Always plan to reduce scheduled times, not meet them

- Resources are not to be considered as a limitation
- Communication will be continuous across all levels
- Safety will not be compromised
- Quality will not be compromised

In addition, special effort was directed toward making the project team strive to reduce time on the project. First, it was made clear that a higher premium would be placed on team performance than on individual performance. The "soft" aspects of management were always taken into consideration: making sure transport was available, accommodations were acceptable, food was available, excessive overtime was avoided, communication forms matched each member's preferences (verbal, phone, written, etc.), and so on. A communication board was installed and updated twice daily to communicate project progress, and especially time saved on the schedule with the person's name who achieved it. There were both twice-daily shift change meetings, where each shift communicated with the previous shift about progress and problems, and twice-daily planning meetings where the work activities of the next two days were planned in minute detail.

The response to this level of project team attention was overwhelming. People raised ideas for saving even five minutes on the schedule. Enthusiasm for the project, and saving project time, became the dominant culture. As a result, the project was completed in only 25 days, 15 days early, with a corresponding cost savings of over $21 million out of an $85 million budget.

Source: I. Boggon, "The Benfield Column Repair Project," *PM Network*, Vol. 10.

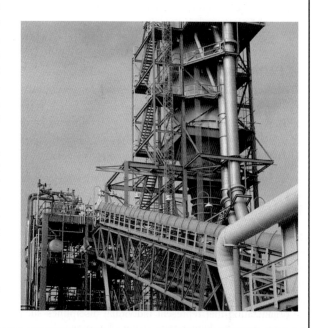

SUMMARY

This chapter described the various organizational structures that can be used for projects, and detailed their advantages. An appropriate procedure for choosing the best form was described and two examples were given. The chapter then moved into a discussion of the role of the Project Management Office. Following this, discussion turned to the project team itself, describing the organization of the project office staff and the human issues, such as motivation and conflict, the project manager will face. Specific points made in the chapter were these:

If the projectized is to be included in a functional organization, it should be placed in that unit with the greatest interest in its success or the unit that can provide the most help. Though there are advantages in this mode of organizing, the disadvantages are greater.

The projectized form of organizing has its advantages and disadvantages. Though the disadvantages are not as severe as with the functional form, they are nevertheless significant.

The matrix organization combines the functional and projectized forms in an attempt to reap the advantages of each. While this approach has been fairly successful, it also has its own unique disadvantages. There are many variants of the pure forms of organization, and various staff and "mixed" structures are commonly used to handle special projects. The best form for a particular case requires consideration of the characteristics of the project compared with the various advantages and disadvantages of each form.

A useful procedure for selecting an organizational form for a project is:

1. Identify the specific outcomes desired.
2. Determine the key tasks to attain these outcomes and identify the units within the parent organization where these tasks would normally be assigned.
3. Sequence the key tasks and group them into logical work steps.
4. Determine which project subsystems will be assigned which steps, and which subsystems must closely cooperate.
5. Identify any special firm or project characteristics, constraints, or problems that may affect how the project should be organized.
6. Consider all the above relative to the pros and cons of each organizational form as a final decision is made.

Every project should have a project office, even if it must be shared with another project.

Larger, more complex projects may include, in addition to the PM, a project engineer, manufacturing engineer, field manager, contract administrator, project controller, and support service manager. If an organization engages in multiple projects, a Project Management Office (or EPMO) may also be warranted.

Those on the project team who should report directly to the PM are the project engineer and project controller as well as:

1. Senior team members who will have a long-term relationship with the project.
2. Those with whom the PM will be continuously or closely communicating.
3. Those with rare skills needed for project success.

Perfectionism, motivation, and conflict are often the major behavioral problems facing the PM. Participative management programs can be a useful tool for addressing the first two, while gentle confrontation usually works best for the latter.

Sources of project conflict are often priorities and policies at first, schedule and technical problems during the main phase, and schedule and personal issues near termination.

In the next chapter, we move from organizational issues to project planning tasks. We address the topics of coordination, interface management, and risk management. We also present some major project management concepts and tools such as the work breakdown structure and RACI chart.

 GLOSSARY

Concurrent/Simultaneous Engineering   Originally, the use of a design team that included both design and manufacturing engineers, now expanded to include staff from quality control, purchasing, and other relevant areas.

Functional Management   The standard departments of the organization that represent individual disciplines such as engineering, marketing, purchasing, and so on.

Holistic   The whole viewed at one time rather than each piece individually.

Matrix Organization   A method of organizing that maintains both functional supervisors as well as project supervisors. A strong matrix operates closer to a projectized organization while a weak matrix operates more like a functional organization.

Mixed Organization   This approach includes both functions (disciplines) and projects in its hierarchy.

Parent Organization   The firm or organization within which the project is being conducted.

Program Manager   This person is typically responsible for a number of related projects, each with its own project manager.

Projectized Organization   This form of organizing is characterized by projects being the main subdivisions of the organization, and general administrative functions common to all projects being a staff office reporting to the President or CEO.

Project Management Office   An office to deal with multiple projects and charged with improving the project management maturity and expertise of the organization, as well as increasing the success rate of projects.

Projectitis   A social phenomenon, inappropriately intense attachment to the project.

Subcontract   Subletting tasks out to smaller contractors.

Suboptimization   The optimization of a subelement of a system, perhaps to the detriment of the overall system.

War Room   A project office where the latest detail on project progress is available. It may also be a source of technical assistance in managing the project.

Work Breakdown Structure   A basic project document that describes all the work that must be done to complete the project and forms the basis for costing, scheduling, and work responsibility (see Chapter 6).

QUESTIONS

Material Review Questions

1. What is a program manager? How does this job differ from that of a project manager?
2. Identify the advantages and disadvantages of the matrix form of organization.
3. Name the four basic types of project organization and list at least one characteristic, advantage, and disadvantage of each.
4. Give some major guidelines for choosing an organizational form for a project.
5. Why is the project management office so important?
6. Identify three ways of dealing with a conflict associated with projects.
7. What are some advantages and disadvantages of housing a project in a functional form?

8. What are the systems architect's duties?

9. What are the major sources of conflict throughout the life cycle?

10. What are the major tasks of a Project Management Office?

Class Discussion Questions

11. Discuss some of the differences between managing professionals and managing other workers or team members.

12. Human and political factors loom large in the success of projects. Given the general lack of coverage of this subject in engineering and science education, how might a PM gain the ability to deal with these issues?

13. A disadvantage of the projectized organization has to do with the tendency of project professionals to fall behind in areas of technical expertise not used on the project. Name several ways that a project manager might avoid this problem.

14. Discuss the effects of the various organizational forms on coordination and interaction, both within the project team and between the team and the rest of the firm.

15. Describe, from Table 5-2, the probable reasons for the changing number of conflicts over the course of the project in the following areas:
    (a) Priorities
    (b) Administrative procedures
    (c) Technical trade-offs
    (d) Schedules

16. How would you organize a project to develop a complex new product such as a new color fax–copy–scanner–printer machine? How would you organize if the product was simpler, such as a new disk drive?

17. What do you think may be the purpose of a work breakdown structure? How might it aid the PM in organizing the project?

18. Why do you think the average total conflict increases during the "early program phase" (Figure 5-7)?

19. What should be the role of the project manager in conflict management?

20. Is it ethical to employ participative management solely as a way to motivate employees?

21. What are the pros and cons of the head of a Project Management Office reporting to senior management? To departmental management?

22. Merck & Co., manufacturers of Vioxx, took a major financial hit when they decided to discontinue manufacture and sale of the drug. What do you think were the major items in their likely cost/benefit analysis?

Managing Risk in a Competitive Environment

23. What is the project manager's role in assessing risk within the project?

24. What special consideration does managing risk in competitive markets require?

Software Firm Yunio Avoids Complex Technologies

25. Does managing virtual teams require more attention to communication technology?

26. Would communicating by example work for non-virtual project managers?

27. What are the trade-offs project managers should consider when trying to select the most effective communication medium?

Trinatronic, Inc.

28. Consider the applicability of a "lightweight" team structure for this project.

29. Consider the applicability of a "heavyweight" or "balanced" structure.

A Project Management Office Success for the Transportation Security Administration

30. What is surprising about the success of this non-profit agency?

31. Is the role of the PMO in this case unusual?

The Empire Uses Floating Multidisciplinary Teams

32. Do you think this might be the future of project management?

33. Would this approach work for most of today's projects?

South African Repair Success through Teamwork

34. Of the special ground rules, which ones do you think really gave impetus to the speed of the project?

35. What do you think was the primary factor that changed the culture for this project?

36. Given that this project cut about 40 percent off the schedule and 25 percent off the cost, what is the message about the importance of teamwork?

INCIDENTS FOR DISCUSSION

Shaw's Strategy

Colin Shaw has been tapped to be an accounting project manager for the second time this year. Although he enjoys the challenges and opportunity for personal development afforded to him as a project manager, he dreads the interpersonal problems associated with the position. Sometimes he feels like a glorified baby-sitter handing out assignments, checking on progress, and making sure everyone is doing his or her fair share. Recently Colin read an article that recommended a very different approach for the project manager in supervising and controlling team members. Colin thought this was a useful idea and decided to try it on his next project.

The project in question involved making a decision on whether to implement an activity-based costing (ABC) system throughout the organization. Colin had once been the manager in charge of implementing a process costing system in this same division, so he felt very comfortable about his ability to lead the team and resolve this question. He defined the objective of the project and detailed all the major tasks involved, as well as most of the subtasks. By the time the first meeting of the project team took place, Colin felt more secure about the control and direction of the project than he had at the beginning of any of his previous projects. He had specifically defined objectives and tasks for each team member and had assigned completion dates for each task. He had even made up individual "contracts" for each team member to sign as an indication of their commitment to completion of the assigned tasks per schedule dates. The meeting went very smoothly, with almost no comments from team members. Everyone picked up a copy of his or her "contract" and went off to work on the project. Colin was ecstatic about the success of this new approach.

Question: Do you think he will feel the same way six weeks from now? Compare this approach with his previous approach.

Hydrobuck

Hydrobuck is a medium-sized producer of gasoline-powered outboard motors. In the past it has successfully manufactured and marketed motors in the 3- to 40-horsepower range. Executives at Hydrobuck are now interested in larger motors and would eventually like to produce motors in the 50- to 150-horsepower range.

The internal workings of the large motors are quite similar to those of the smaller motors. However, large, high-performance outboard motors require power trim. Power trim is simply a hydraulic system that serves to tilt the outboard motor up or down on the boat transom. Hydrobuck cannot successfully market the larger outboard motors without designing a power trim system to complement the motor.

The company is financially secure and is the leading producer of small outboard motors. Management has decided that the following objectives need to be met within the next two years:

1. Design a quality power trim system.
2. Design and build the equipment to produce such a system efficiently.
3. Develop the operations needed to install the system on the outboard motor.

The technology, facilities, and marketing skills necessary to produce and sell the large motors already exist within the company.

Questions: What alternative types of project organization would suit the development of the power trim system? Which would be best? Discuss your reasons for selecting this type of organization.

 ## CONTINUING INTEGRATIVE CLASS PROJECT

The job of organizing the project for speedy, competent execution on budget is a major factor in the success of every project. We are not concerned here with where the project resides in the college and who it reports to—it reports to the Instructor—but rather the internal organization of the project. It can be handled as a set of tasks where everyone in the class has some given responsibilities and a specified time to deliver the results, or through a set of teams responsible for different sets of project tasks.

If the class is small, the former may be adequate, but for a larger class, it may be more efficient and practical to set up subteams (though probably NOT a third layer of subsubteams). For a class of say 35, five or six subteams may be optimal. This gives a uniform set of about five to seven direct reports for each manager, including the PM. Of course, some subteams may need fewer workers and others more, but they should be close to the right size. Again, recall that one constraint on the organization is that the subteams cannot all be completely independent. There are two reasons for this. One is that doing some of the work across all the chapters will be more valuable to an individual student (e.g., answering all the Review Questions) than doing all the work for just one chapter and then being ignorant of all the other topics. The second is that in real projects there is typically considerable interaction, even conflict. If the project could be divided into a set of tasks that can all be done by different departments without interacting with each other, there is no need to set up a project to do the work!

◼ BIBLIOGRAPHY

Adams, J. R., and L. L. Adams. "The Virtual Project: Managing Tomorrow's Team Today." *PM Network*, January 1997.

Baker, B. "In Common." *Project Management Journal*, September 2007.

Block, T. R. "The Seven Secrets of a Successful Project Office." *PM Network*, April 1999.

Block, T. R., and J. D. Frame. "Today's Project Office: Gauging Attitudes," *PM Network*, August 2001.

Bushe, G. R., "When People Come and Go." *The Wall Street Journal*. New York: August 23, 2010.

Carlisle, A. S. "MacGregor." *Organizational Dynamics*. New York: AMACOM, Summer 1976.

Cleland, D. I. *Strategic Management of Teams*. New York: Wiley, 1996.

de Laat, P. B. "Matrix Management of Projects and Power Struggles: A Case Study of an R&D Laboratory." *IEEE Engineering Management Review*, Winter 1995, reprinted from *Human Relations*, Vol. 47, No. 9, 1994.

Dewhurst, H. D. "Project Teams: What Have We Learned?" *PM Network*, April 1998.

Dinsmore, P. C. "Converging on Enterprise Project Management." *PM Network*, October 1998.

Ford, R. C., and F. S. McLaughlin. "Successful Project Teams: A Study of MIS Managers." *IEEE Transactions on Engineering Management*, November 1992.

Gale, S. F. "The PMO Survival Guide." *PM Network*, November 2010.

Grant, R. M. "The Future of Management: Where Is Gary Hamel Leading Us?" *Long Range Planning*, 2008, pp. 469–482.

Gratton, L. "Working Together… When Apart." *Wall Street Journal*, June 16–17, 2007.

Herzberg, F. H. "One More Time: How Do You Motivate Employees?" *Harvard Business Review*, January–February 1968.

Hughes, T. P. *Rescuing Prometheus*. New York: Pantheon, 1998.

IEEE Engineering Management Review, 1st Qtr. (33:1) 2005.

Kalu, T. Ch. U. "A Framework for the Management of Projects in Complex Organizations." *IEEE Transactions on Engineering Management*, May 1993.

Kotter, J. P. "Leading Change: Why Transformation Efforts Fail." *Harvard Business Review*, March/April 1995. Reprinted in *IEEE Engineering Management Review*, Spring 1997.

Lencioni, P. *The Five Dysfunctions of a Team*. San Francisco: Jossey-Bass, 2002.

Levine, H. A. "Enterprise Project Management: What Do Users Need? What Can They Have?" *PM Network*, July 1998.

Liu, L. and P. Yetton. "The Contingent Effects of Project Performance of Conducting Project Reviews and Deploying Project Management Offices." *IEEE Transactions on Engineering Management*, November, 2007.

Likert, R J., and G. Likert. *New Ways of Managing Conflict*. New York: McGraw-Hill, 1976.

Nelson, B. "Energized Teams: Real World Examples." *PM Network*, July 1998.

Pinto, J. K. "Twelve Ways to Get the Least From Yourself and Your Project." *PM Network*, May 1997.

Project Management Institute. "Survey Reveals How Organizations Succeed." *PMI Today*, February 2011.

Tennant, D. "PMO Failure: An Observation," *PM Network*, October 2001.

Thamhain, H. J., and D. L. Wilemon. "Conflict Management in Project Life Cycles." *Sloan Management Review*, Summer 1975.

Tippet, D. D., and J. F. Peters. "Team Building and Project Management: How Are We Doing?" *Project Management Journal*, December 1995.

Underwood, R., "OK, Everybody, Let's Do This! Managing Projects and Collaborating with Co-Workers." *Inc. Magazine*, July 2008.

Williams, G. "Implementing an Enterprise Project Management Solution." *PM Network*, October 1997.

The following case describes an unusual organizational arrangement for an actual manufacturing firm. The company is largely run by the employees through teams. When projects are instituted, it is common to pass the idea through the relevant teams first, before any changes are made. However, not everything can be passed through all the teams that may be involved in the change, and this can be a source of trouble.

C A S E

DIZPLAZE
Eric Woodcock

As he drove into the employee car park, Sven Sorensen was once again thinking about how to handle the decision to install a new jig to improve the alignment of the Mark Ten line of display boxes made by the Dizplaze company, where he was the operations manager. The issue had arisen because of a series of complaints by a metro system in Germany. The passenger displays fitted at roof level inside the cars of their new fleet of trains were rattling and working loose from their mountings. These displays were the first Mark Tens to go into service anywhere, and the hope was that this customer would be an important reference. Investigations by the Dizplaze R&D department had identified the cause as poor assembly owing to the complex alignment of the display box components. Now the firm was committed to replacing all the defective display boxes.

His mind returned to the meeting he had had the previous day with Lars Anderssen, the general manager. They had discussed whether this was an issue where senior management should take the decision to install the jig, or whether it was a matter that needed to be referred to the display assembly team in the factory.

As he locked his car in the car park Sven reflected on how slow and difficult it could be to make changes at Dizplaze with its team management philosophy.

Dizplaze was founded in Malmo, Sweden, in 1972 by two electrical engineers who saw the opportunity to develop a mobile version of the mechanical dot matrix displays being installed in airports and train stations to provide passenger information. These mobile versions would have to be more robust to cope with the shocks from the movement of buses, trams and trains and they had patented a way to do this. Over the next 10 years the company grew steadily as the benefits of the new technology became accepted, and the reliability of the units improved. They replaced roller blind displays which carried route information at the front of road and rail vehicles, but which were bulky and unreliable.

Several years later, light array systems were introduced. These contained small lights which turned on and off to create either static or scrolling messages. Their main application was in passenger information displays fitted inside a vehicle.

Despite the market success labour relations within the firm became strained. The founders were outstanding technically, but lacked strong people management skills. Their investors persuaded them to employ a general manager, Anders Ekberg.

Anders quickly determined that many of the problems Dizplaze faced were because most of the employees did not feel committed to the firm—it was simply a job to them. However, the nature of the display units required a great deal of careful hand assembly to create a high quality product. Following a period of consultation with everyone in the company, Anders introduced a much more participative style of management. The company was split into a number of teams, each entirely responsible for its share of the work. There were 11 teams. Five were focussed on production: enclosure manufacture, control assembly, display assembly, final assembly and test, and packing and dispatch. The other six were: research and development (R&D), sales and marketing, purchasing, management and administration (including human resources), field service, and maintenance.

The teams set their own work schedules, allocated members to tasks, and handled the less serious disciplinary matters (poor timekeeping, not maintaining a tidy work space, etc.). They met regularly to discuss working issues and ways to be more productive. Only the more complex problems were referred to senior management to be dealt with. Teams were also given a training and development budget.

The change was a great success. In fact, the production teams were allowed to insert a small panel inside each completed display unit, signed by the people who had produced it. There were steady productivity improvements and teams came up with innovations in areas as different as the design of packaging (to reduce damage in transit) and signing in instead of clocking on. Meanwhile the R&D team were keeping pace with market developments and making sure the products remained competitive. In 2005 the first LED units were introduced, and they soon became the mainstream product line.

Overall the firm was going from strength to strength. In 2001 Anders left the business for a job in the United States, and Lars Anderssen, the operations manager, was promoted to lead the business. Sven Sorensen was recruited to fill the role of operations manager. Exhibit 1 shows the company organisation chart in 2009.

Lars enthusiastically embraced the team management culture. Between 2002 and 2006 Sven recalled a period of rapidly increasing productivity and an expanding labour force. Exhibit 2 shows the productivity trend from 2000 to 2006. Unfortunately, trouble was only just round the corner.

Although their units were sometimes found in ferries and cruise ships, Dizplaze's main customers were large bus and train operators, and most units were fitted into brand new vehicles. Public transport is an industry subject to lots of external pressures. Publicly owned operators depend on politicians for capital, and funding for new equipment may dry up in the face of other priorities. Private operators may delay new orders because interest rates are too high or revenue growth has slowed. Orders also tend to be quite large, so missing out on an order can have painful consequences. In 2007 Dizplaze suffered a series of setbacks. New bus orders were down in key markets, and only one major train contract was out for tender that they could bid on. They did not win the train contract, which meant that revenues would be at least 20% down on the previous year.

Lars' commitment to the staff of Dizplaze was that long term employment was a basic goal in return for their com-

mitment, and that he would do everything possible to avoid redundancies. A hiring freeze was put in place, and despite the reduced workload no one was laid off. Lars expected that new orders would fill the gap left by the lost train business. Several small orders came in, but not enough to cover the costs of the workforce. In February 2008, Lars announced that redundancies would be necessary. The teams were not expected to decide who would have to leave, but they were consulted on the factors that would be used to make the tough decisions. They agreed that factors such as length of service, level of relevant skills and disciplinary record should be taken into account. Even though the process was painful, almost everyone (even among those who lost their jobs) thought it was fair.

The consequence of the lay-offs was increased productivity and reduced costs. This made Dizplaze more competitive and the order book started to fill up again. From then on, temporary staff tended to be brought in to help with peaks in demand, along with more overtime for the full-time employees.

The team concept had been in place for about 20 years and had naturally evolved over that time. The format of team meetings had a common pattern and the team leaders were rotated every six months. Teams met in work time once a week for about an hour and a half. Discussions could drag on sometimes, but the advantage was that once a decision was taken it could be implemented immediately. Temporary workers could attend meetings but were not allowed to vote. There was no doubt that most of the teams were well aware of the reality of the external market when making their decisions. They knew

Exhibit 1 Organisation chart for Dizplaze

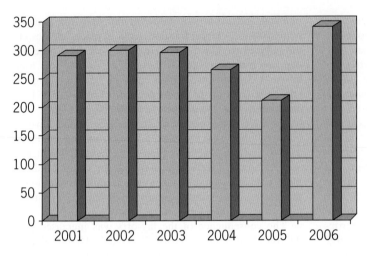

Exhibit 2   Dizplaze productivity index
(100 = Productivity in 1985)

they could not just wait for senior management to tell them what to do and complain if they did not like it. That said, they recognised there were some matters that senior management could not consult them about.

The largest team had 18 people and the smallest had six. In general, employees were very positive about team management. They felt the whole process was built on trust on both sides, and it worked well. One person remarked that it gave people a real sense of responsibility and they responded by always doing their best. Lars saw the main benefit as allowing great production flexibility. Employees did not automatically see change as a threat and staff turnover was very low.

On the other hand, many employees felt the team management process required a lot of time and energy from people, and some wondered whether working in a well-managed, conventionally organised business would actually be less demanding.

The redundancies episode strained the team approach. Members had felt that it was their duty to help devise the redundancy process, but were uncomfortable in being directly involved in an activity that would lead to people

they knew losing their jobs. It became clear that they would be less willing to take part in controversial matters, especially ones that might raise tensions within the teams. Quality was a particularly tricky area. On one occasion, a good deal of friction occurred between the R&D and control assembly teams over whether a recurrent fault was the result of bad design or poor assembly. Leaving it to the teams took almost six months to resolve, while customers were left unhappy with faulty displays, and the company had to make substantial warranty payments.

Sven Sorensen faced a dilemma over the issue of the alignment jig for the display boxes. He remained committed to the team approach and was very reluctant to do anything to undermine it. However, the market was getting tougher, and customers were becoming more demanding. Could he afford to let the display assembly team debate and deal with the quality issue on display boxes? That would reinforce the team management concept but risked delay and harm to the firm's reputation. Or must he intervene and insist on the new jig as the solution and risk damaging the team spirit and commitment everyone had worked so hard to nurture?

QUESTIONS

1. If Sven decides to go ahead and install the alignment jig without discussing it with the display assembly team, what are the potential conflicts that might arise? What are the advantages of doing this anyway?

2. If Sven decides to allow the display assembly team to make the decision, what are the potential problems? What would be the advantages?

3. If the display assembly team approves and implements the installation jig project, what form of project organization would be most appropriate?

4. Given the size of this organization and the number of projects they deal with, would it make sense to institute a Project Management Office? Is there another arrangement that might be a better alternative?

5. The team management approach has been in place for about 20 years at Dizplaze. What are the challenges in maintaining the effectiveness of this approach in a company?

6. How do you think the problem with the display boxes could have been avoided?

7. What do you recommend Sven to do?

The following reading discusses a new phenomenon in the increasingly global competitive environment—geographically dispersed project teams. The competitiveness of global firms is often facilitated by new electronic technologies, and these technologies are also useful to the success of globally dispersed project teams, as described in the article. However, other aspects of such dispersed teams are more problematic, and the article illustrates these, as well as approaches used by project managers for circumventing them. Finally, some of the advice given in the article should be useful as well for project teams that aren't geographically dispersed.

DIRECTED READING

THE VIRTUAL PROJECT: MANAGING TOMORROW'S TEAM TODAY*
J. R. Adams and L. L. Adams

Extraordinary demands are placed on project personnel—demands that require extraordinary commitments in order to accomplish the task at hand. Generating this commitment through the process of team building is a primary responsibility of any project manager. The processes of team building have been studied extensively by both academics and practitioners for decades, but until recently, nearly all of these studies were conducted within the bureaucratic setting: that is, the team members shared a common workplace, saw each other frequently, knew each other well, and expected to continue working together for an extended period of time. The team building concepts developed within such an environment naturally reflect these working conditions as either stated or implied assumptions, and the concepts derived from these studies can be assumed to hold only as long as these assumptions hold.

These concepts still hold for projects intended to support and improve bureaucratic organizations. In the vast majority of cases, however, the working conditions experienced by modern projects differ greatly from those surrounding traditional bureaucratic work. Nevertheless, the basic definitions of team building continue to emphasize the assumption of typical bureaucratic working conditions. For example, one leading textbook in the field (Kast and Rosenzweig's *Organization and Management: A Systems and Contingency Approach*, McGraw-Hill, 1985) states that "actual teamwork involves small groups of three to fifteen people that meet face-to-face to carry out their assignments." Even in PMI's current *PMBOK-Guide* (pp. 99–100), one of the five basic "tools and techniques" of team development is called "collocation," which involves "...placing all, or almost all, of the most active project team members in the same physical location to enhance their ability to perform as a team." In both of these publications, the concept of the virtual project is clearly ignored.

In the new, "virtual project" environment, team members seldom share a common workplace, may rarely see each other, may never have worked together before, and may never work together again after the project is complete. For an ever-increasing number of organizations, the world is represented by an environment of rapid technological advancement, particularly in the area of communications; complex organizational structures needed to deal with tough global competition; and dynamic markets that demand short production runs of unique products. Downsizing, outsourcing, and employee empowerment have

*Reprinted from *PM Network* with permission. Copyright Project Management Institute Inc.

become facts of life in the climate of many organizations, while job security is rapidly becoming a thing of the past. The survival of many organizations depends on the ability of the organization to rapidly change its structure, culture, and products to match the changing demands of the environment.

Let's explore the conditions faced by the modern project manager in developing an effective and productive project team within a "virtual project."

The Virtual Project The virtual project, also known as a "distributed team," is one in which the participants are geographically distributed to an extent that they may seldom, if ever, meet face-to-face as a team. The geographical distances involved do not have to be great; individuals who work in the same industrial complex may be functioning in a virtual project if their schedules do not allow them to meet face-to-face. As distances increase, however, the difficulties of communicating and building teams increase significantly. When team members are spread across several time zones, opportunity for direct communication is severely limited, and the associated costs of both face-to-face and electronic communications increase dramatically. Electronic communication takes on much more importance in virtual projects because electronic systems must assume the burden of making the development of effective project teams possible.

It is beyond the scope of this article to discuss at length the issues that are generating the need for virtual projects. Suffice it to say that the environmental conditions described above are precisely those that require project teams to be dispersed.

Jaclyn Kostner has written extensively on the virtual project. In *Knights of the TeleRound Table* (Warner Books, 1994), she documents the unique issues faced by project managers who must manage such a virtual or distributed project. The issues she defines are shown in the left-hand column of the accompanying sidebar.

Developing trust is the greatest challenge to the remote project manager. It's difficult for distant team members to get to know each other well; consequently, they tend to communicate poorly because they often are less than comfortable with each other. Both of these situations destroy the trust that is so essential to creating good teamwork. Developing a group identity across distances is also difficult because people normally associate with events that occur at their local level. Teams tend to have a problem sharing information effectively across distances. One reason for this may be the lack of informal opportunities for discussion at lunches or during coffee breaks. Developing clear structures is an issue for the virtual project manager because distant work groups need more than the traditional vision, mission, and goals

that are important for all project groups. Members of virtual teams tend to develop relationships with those who are located with them rather than with those who are at distant sites. The formation of such "cliques" can create competition or antagonism between the project manager and/or team members located elsewhere. Lastly, each distributed team member tends to have information that is somewhat different from that held by others. More important, each team member views information from a different perspective. Such inequities of information frequently increase the opportunity for miscommunication among team members.

If issues such as these are not dealt with, the virtual project experiences management difficulties far in excess of the more "typical" project with higher levels of collocation. Fortunately, the technology that has made virtual projects both possible and necessary also provides opportunities for dealing progressively with these problems.

Implementing Virtual Project Teams The sidebar includes suggestions created by virtual project managers for using the advantages of project management team building to overcome virtual team difficulties. Generally, these suggestions encourage project managers to make creative use of modern communication technologies to bring the team together and encourage the participation and sense of ownership that generates commitment to the project and team objectives.

Since it's seldom possible in the virtual project to meet face-to-face, experienced project managers recommend using a variety of electronic communications. Trust seems to develop as the individual team member learns more about the project manager, other team members, and the project. It's therefore essential that team members be encouraged to communicate with each other frequently, as well as with the project manager and the team as a whole. Virtual project managers use all forms of electronic communication—cellular phones, pagers, faxes, e-mail, Web pages, and computer-to-computer transmissions across local area and wide area networks—to distribute everything from key reports to jokes, logos, and mottoes. These communications are specifically intended to increase the common experiences shared by the team members and thus increase the bonds among them. Regularly scheduled video and telephone conference calls increase team members' exposure to project information, as well as to each other.

When cliques form as subgroups of the project team, these subgroups are managed, not ignored. Subcommittees are created to resolve project problems, specifically drawing members from different cliques together so that they learn more about each other. Team members are frequently asked to explain their viewpoints and to discuss their plans

Virtual Project Management Suggestions

Issues	Problems	Suggestions
Developing Trust	Irregular, inconsistent communication; lower level of comfort and familiarity among team members; "us vs. them" attitude.	Provide and use a variety of communication alternatives. Communicate electronically except when signatures are required. Make project management software available to all team members.
Developing Group Identity	Fewer shared experiences; lack of cohesion; little understanding of other members' roles and responsibilities.	Conduct regular teleconference meetings when the need warrants. Manage the agenda to include a variety of participants and ensure everyone is involved in the discussion. Use logos, mottoes, and creative humor. Stay in contact when meetings are not required. Note: Do not exclude anyone from group discussions.
Sharing Information	Difficulty sharing adequate levels of information across distances; lack of formal opportunities to discuss work-related issues; lack of a common system to transmit information across distances.	Use technology to develop additional information-sharing opportunities: cellular phones, pagers, faxes, telephones, e-mail, Internet, and computer-to-computer. Distribute all key reports to all team members. Put information at one central access point, e.g., a project Web page, a LAN account.
Developing Clear Structures	Uncertain roles and responsibilities of team members; clashing cultures create different expectations, few clearly defined processes for decision making.	Use standard formats for meetings. Define goals, objectives, problems, and concerns at the kickoff meeting, and reiterate them frequently. Have participants describe and define potential problems and concerns, and evaluate risks as a group.
Formation of "Cliques" or Informal Subgroups	Cliques tend to create antagonism and competition between the team and the project manager, between team members, or among the cliques themselves.	The project manager can't prevent them from forming, but can manage these subgroups. Identify and keep track of them. Create subcommittees for dealing with problems, drawing members from the different cliques. Look for opportunities to mix participants from the different cliques, and initiate or create these opportunities when necessary.
Understanding Information	Each team member has different information (inconsistent); each member has varying levels of information (incomplete); each member has a different perspective of the information. All = inequities of information.	Ask members to explain their viewpoints. Ask members to describe the actions they plan to take, and solicit possible impacts to other involved parties. Use different levels of information for different participants, as appropriate.

with the team at large to improve the common understanding of information about the project, its progress, and its prospects.

Four specific types of electronic communication, which didn't even exist just a few years ago, are being used extensively by managers of virtual projects to help overcome the lack of formal and informal personal contact among the team members.

The Internet. As technology creates conditions that demand faster reactions, team building over extensive distances, and ever-more-extensive communications, that same technology provides new approaches with which to deal with these issues. The Internet provides a means for communicating quickly and inexpensively throughout the world. It is essential for all participants in virtual project teams to have access to the Internet and e-mail. The virtual project manager relies on e-mail to exchange project data with the dispersed team, especially when team members or clients are internationally located. E-mail is a particularly good tool for exchanging the detailed information necessary to update the status of project activities. This task is difficult to accomplish verbally via telephone or videoconference because of the detail involved and the difference in time zones. Transmitting such data by facsimile can be expensive due to the volume of data involved, the frequency of needed updates, and the requirement for consistent information flows.

With e-mail as the primary mode of communication, information flows easier and faster, and the difference in time zones is less likely to be a critical failure factor. The ease of communication encourages the team to communicate more often and in more detail. Team members get to know each other more personally, and therefore develop more cohesive working relationships. One word of caution, however; many companies, in a misguided attempt to economize, are limiting the use of e-mail to "official" business, and eliminating personal comments, jokes, and other "non-essential" communications. It is precisely these "informal" transmissions that can at least partially make up for the lack of personal contact. Informal e-mail communications can replace some face-to-face contact and help generate the close working relationships, commitments, and friendships that are traditionally considered to be characteristic of successful project teams.

The Pager. A byproduct of today's business environment is that technical specialists (team members) frequently are working on multiple projects, and are considered highly valuable resources. The time of these "highly valuable resources" may be quite limited. Though regularly scheduled project meetings are critical throughout the project life cycle, these valuable resources may often be required elsewhere, and the project manager may need to help conserve their time.

One way to make the best use of a team member's time is to use a paging system. Each team member carries a pager, and the pager numbers are published with the team roster. When agenda topics don't directly relate to a particular team member or function, that person can be released from attendance, freeing up time that can then be used more productively. If an issue surfaces that requires that person's attention, he or she can be "paged" into the teleconference call. This allows for quick responses to problems and issues, and limits the number of "open action items" on meeting minutes. This procedure must be established at the project's kickoff meeting, when the project manager discusses team roles, responsibilities, and expectations. A culture must be developed within the project where each team member is expected to respond quickly to paging, especially when a 911 code, meaning an emergency needing immediate response, is attached to the pager number.

Teleconferencing.   Teleconferencing is not as new as some of the techniques noted above, but its use has expanded dramatically in recent years along with the increase of virtual projects. Everyone thinks they understand teleconferencing, but few are able to use it effectively. The lack of visual communication means that only the spoken word is available for the transfer of information, so individual speakers must identify themselves when contributing to the discussion. The medium was originally designed to provide communications between two people. When more people are added to the conference, managing the conversation flow rapidly becomes a complex issue. The goal is to assure that everyone has an opportunity to contribute and that all issues are dealt with in a reasonable period of time.

Using telephony technology for communicating among several people requires careful management and control of the communication process. The project manager cannot manage the results of the communications, but must manage the process of getting to those results. The conference needs to be well-organized and structured. A detailed agenda is essential to a productive conference call. The project manager should schedule the call in advance so that an agenda can be published and distributed at least two to three days prior to the meeting. The agenda should always include specific items of information: purpose of the teleconference, day-date-time of the call, call-in number, expected duration of the call, chair of the meeting (the project manager), a detailed listing of items to be discussed, and *the key participants for each item noted.* The project manager can then facilitate discussion among these key players, solicit input from other team members, and maintain a solution-oriented attitude. This structure allows all essential persons to share in the conversation and present their viewpoints, while keeping the team focused on the critical issues at hand. The structure also prevents side conversations and keeps the team from straying from the intended topic until a solution has been achieved.

The checklist in the accompanying sidebar is useful for developing a successful teleconference.

Videoconferencing. With a geographically dispersed team, the cost of travel, including the cost of team mem-

---

Teleconferencing Tips

- Include an overall time limit for scheduling purposes (for yourself and for your team). Anything over 1.5 hours tends to become unproductive because of the high level of concentration required to communicate in an audio-only format.

- Organize the meeting in two sequential categories. In Category 1 are those activities that on the project plan should be completed by the time the meeting occurs. In Category 2 are those activities that need to be completed prior to the next meeting.

- Have one major agenda topic called "deliverables," where the deliverables that are due or past-due are listed, along with who is responsible for completing those items. The items can be statused and assistance can be solicited from the team to expedite completion.

- Always have an "open discussion" section at the end of the agenda. Do a round-table roll call of each person to see if anyone has comments or concerns that need to be discussed or documented in the minutes. Putting the open discussion section last also keeps the focus on issues that are critical to the project, rather than on issues that may be critical to an individual. If time runs out, at least the necessities have been covered.

- Invite team members to call in or e-mail additional agenda topics, and then add these topics to the agenda for discussion. If people can't submit topics prior to agenda distribution, introduce new items only during the open discussion section so that the flow of the meeting is not disrupted.

- Talk about any major changes to the schedule, such as slippages or early completions that affect the schedule or multiple departments, at the beginning of the conference. These changes could drastically affect the items on the agenda, the flow of the conference call, or even the flow of work for your whole project.

---

bers' time during travel, is too high to justify having the team involved in periodic face-to-face status meetings. However, current issues may be too critical to rely on e-mail, teleconferencing, and one-on-one voice contact. This is a time when videoconferencing is the most appropriate form of communication.

A capability not present in other forms of electronic communication, videoconferencing allows participants to feel more involved with each other because they can communicate on many different levels. Body language and facial expressions can be observed and interpreted, in many cases transferring more meaning than the actual words. Full team participation in developing the initial work breakdown structure and the project plan, both of which occur in the kickoff meeting, is crucial to developing the commitment to the virtual project team. It is particularly appropriate to have the kickoff meeting in a site that is videoconference-accessible, if possible, so that if some people can't attend then they can still be involved.

Despite all its good points, there is a downside to videoconferencing. Some of the common problems and barriers are logistical. For example, all participants must be located at pre-arranged receiving/transmitting sites; and, although the cost has been decreasing slowly, videoconferencing is still quite expensive, especially when numerous sites and satellite-based communications are involved, so these sites may not be readily accessible.

Also, even though technology is gradually moving forward and the signal transmission speed is increasing, videoconferencing uses a wide bandwidth, which translates into a significant delay in viewing the movements and expressions of participants. This delay, as well as an individual's tendency to be uncomfortable in front of a camera, frequently combine to make the whole process somewhat stiff and stilted. This seems to be a particular problem in systems where the participants can see themselves and worry about how they look to the others.

Since the purpose of this extraordinary use of electronic communications is to increase the stability of the virtual project, it is particularly important that all team members be able to work with the detailed project plan. All team members should have access to whatever software is being used to plan and control project activities. They should also have easy access to the project files. The liberal distribution of project documentation provides enhanced communication as well as an exposure to the project cultural structure.

A basic knowledge of team building is essential to the effective management of any project. With the advent of the virtual project, however, the methods and techniques necessary for implementing the project team building process have changed. Face-to-face communications are obviously desirable, but they may no longer be possible because of time or cost constraints. Fortunately, the same technologies that have made the virtual project a possibility also provide the methods for developing effective teams of dispersed project participants.

Virtual project managers must be both knowledgeable and creative in using the modern communication technologies available to them for the purpose of enhancing the common experiences of their project team members, and hence the commitment that can be generated for the project's objectives and goals. Perhaps more important, however, is to recognize that the ability to effectively use all of the current electronic communication techniques available to the project manager is rapidly becoming a mandatory skill for anyone likely to be involved in virtual projects.

This topic deserves some extensive research in order to help the virtual project manager develop more effective methods and techniques for dealing with the task of building effective project teams from dispersed project participants.

Questions

1. Which virtual project problems are unique to the phenomenon of being dispersed and which are common project problems in any project?

2. What new electronic technologies have contributed to the problems, and solutions, of virtual project teams?

3. Of the solutions to virtual team problems, which would apply to regular project teams also?

4. Which problems described in the article are the most serious for virtual projects? Which might be fatal?

5. How might the difficulties of matrix organization change when implementing virtual projects?

P A R T

II

PROJECT PLANNING

In Part II we discuss *project planning* in terms of planning the activities, budget, and schedule for the project, as shown in the accompanying figure. Chapter 6 deals with project activity and risk planning and presents tools useful in organizing and staffing the various project tasks. It also contains a short discussion of phase-gate management systems and other ways of dealing with the problems that arise with complex projects. Budgeting, the planning and control of costs, is addressed next in Chapter 7. We also include a section on the treatment of risks in budgeting through simulation.

Scheduling, a crucial aspect of project planning, is then described in Chapter 8, along with the most common scheduling models such as the Program

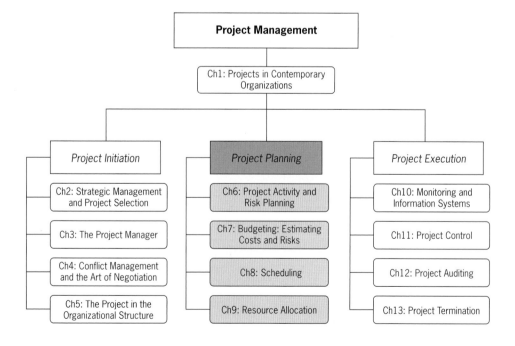

Evaluation and Review Technique (PERT) and precedence diagramming. Concluding Part II, the effect of resource allocation on the project schedule is covered in Chapter 9. For single projects, we discuss how the resource allocation problem concerns resource *leveling* to minimize the cost of the resources while still remaining on schedule. But for multiple projects, we learn that the issue is how to allocate limited resources among several projects in order to achieve the objectives of each. This chapter also describes project crashing (by the Critical Path Method) and scheduling insights from the concept of the Critical Chain.

Project Activity and Risk Planning

PMBOK Guide
Chapters 6, 11, 8

This chapter initiates our discussions of *Time, Quality, and Risk Management,* PMBOK knowledge areas 3, 5, and 8, respectively. Time management is an extensive topic which is further discussed in Chapters 8, 10, and 11. Similarly, risk will be discussed further in Chapters 7 and 8, and quality will be discussed again in Chapter 12.

In the *Reader's Digest* (March 1998, p. 49) Peter Drucker is quoted on planning: "Plans are only good intentions unless they immediately degenerate into hard work." To make such a transformation possible is no easy task. Inadequate planning is a cliché in project management. Occasionally, articles appear in project management periodicals attesting to the value of good planning. Project managers pay little attention. PMs say, or are told, that planning "takes too much time," "customers don't know what they want," "if we commit we will be held account-able," and a number of similar weak excuses (Bigelow, 1998, p. 15). Tom Peters, well-known seeker of business excellence, was quoted in the *Cincinnati Post*: "Businesses [believe] a lot of dumb things. . . . The more time you spend planning, the less time you'll need to spend on imple-mentation. Almost never the case! Ready. Fire. Aim. That's the approach taken by businesses I most respect." We strongly disagree and, as we will report below (and in Chapter 13), there is a great deal of research supporting the view that careful planning is solidly associated with project success—and none, to our knowledge, supporting the opposite position. On the other hand, sensible planners do not kill the plan with overanalysis. This leads to the well-known "paralysis by analysis." In an excellent article, Langley (1995) finds a path in-between the two extremes.

Thus far, we have dealt with initiating a project. Now we are ready to begin the process of planning the work of the project in such a way that it may be translated into the "hard work" that actually leads to the successful completion of the project. There are several reasons why we must use considerable care when planning projects. The primary purpose of planning, of course, is to establish a set of directions in sufficient detail to tell the project team exactly what must be done, when it must be done, what resources will be required to produce the delivera-bles of the project successfully, and when each resource will be needed.

As we noted in Chapter 1, the deliverables (or scope, or specifications, or objectives) of a project are more than mere descriptions of the goods and/or services we promise to deliver to the client at a quality level that will meet client expectations. The scope of a project also includes the time and cost required to complete the project to the client's satisfaction. The plan must be designed in such a way that the project outcome also meets the objectives, both direct and ancillary, of the parent organization, as reflected by the project portfolio or other strategic selection process used to approve the project. Because the plan is only an estimate of what and when things must be done to achieve the scope or objectives of the project, it is always carried out in an environment of uncertainty. Therefore, the plan must include allowances for risk and features that allow it to be *adaptive*, i.e., to be responsive to things that might disrupt it while it is being carried out. One frequent such disruption—"scope creep," or the tendency of project objectives to be changed by the client, senior management, or individual project workers with little or no discussion with the other parties actively engaged in the work of the project—is particularly common in software projects. In addition, the plan must also contain methods to ensure its integrity, which is to say it must include means of controlling the work it prescribes.

Finally, and quite apart from the deliverables required by the project itself, the plan must include any constraints on activities and input materials proscribed by law and society. Among the many sources of outside constraints are the Food and Drug Administration, the Occupational Health and Safety Administration, other federal and state laws and regulations, various engineering societies, labor unions, and the "Standard Practices" of many different industries. Such constraints are meant to protect us all from unsafe or harmful structures, machines, rugs, equipment, services, and practices.

Project Management in Practice
Beagle 2 Mars Probe a Planning Failure

As the Beagle 2 Mars probe, designed jointly by the European Space Agency and British National Space Center, headed to Mars in December of 2003, contact was lost and it was never heard from again. In retrospect, it appears that inadequate project planning (and replanning) was to blame. Excessive pressure on time, cost, and weight compromised the mission right from the start. With insufficient public funding, the design team had to spend much of their time raising private funds instead of addressing difficult technical issues. In addition, late changes forced the team to reduce the Beagle's weight from 238 pounds to 132 pounds! And when the three airbags failed to work properly in testing, a parachute design was substituted but inadequately tested due to lack of time.

A review commission recommended that in the future:

- Requisite financing be available at the outset of a project

- Formal project reviews be conducted on a regular basis
- Milestones should be established where all stakeholders reconsider the project
- Expectations of potential failure should be included in the funding consideration
- Robust safety margins should be included and funded for uncertainties

Source: Project Management Institute. "Mars or Bust," *PM Network*, Vol. 18.

There is an extensive literature on project planning. Some of it is concerned with the strategic aspects of planning, being focused on the choice of projects that are consistent with the organization's goals. Another group of works is aimed at the process of planning individual projects, given that they have been chosen as strategically acceptable. Most fields have their own accepted set of project planning processes. Except for the names given to the individual processes, however, they are all similar, as we shall soon see.

The purpose of planning is to facilitate later accomplishment. The world is full of plans that never become deeds. The planning techniques covered here are intended to smooth the path from idea to accomplishment. It is a complicated process to manage a project, and plans act as a map of this process. The map must have sufficient detail to determine what must be done next but be simple enough that workers are not lost in a welter of minutiae.

In the pages that follow we discuss a somewhat formal method for the development of a project charter (similar to a proposal, or preliminary plan) and final project plan. Almost all project planning techniques differ only in the ways they approach the process of planning. Most organizations, irrespective of the industry, use essentially the same processes for planning and managing projects, but they often call these processes by different names. What some call "setting objectives," others call "defining the scope" of the project, or "identifying requirements." What some call "evaluation," others call "test and validation." No matter whether the project is carried out for an inside or outside client, the project's "deliverables" must be "integrated" into the client's processes.

We have adopted an approach that we think makes the planning process straightforward and fairly systematic, but it is never as systematic and straightforward as planning theorists would like. At its best, planning is tortuous. It is an iterative process yielding better plans from not-so-good plans, and the iterative process of improvement seems to take place in fits and starts. The process may be described formally, but it does not occur formally. Bits and pieces of plans are developed by individuals, by informal group meetings, or by formalized planning teams (Paley, 1993), and then improved by other individuals, groups, or teams, and improved again, and again. Both the plans themselves and the process of planning should start simple and then become more complex. If the appropriate end product is kept firmly in mind, this untidy process yields a *project plan*. In this chapter we focus on designing the physical aspects of the project, defining what the project is supposed to accomplish, and who will have to do what for the project's desired output to be achieved. Here we describe the actual process of project planning. Organizing the work of the project, acquiring a project manager, and forming a project team are parts of project initiation. The project's budget and schedule are major parts of the project plan, but we delay discussion of them until Chapters 7 and 8. Indeed, what must be done to test and approve project outputs at both interim and final stages, and what records must be kept are both parts of the project plan and these are covered in later chapters, as is the part of the plan that covers terminating the project. There is nothing sacrosanct about this sequence. It is simply in the order that these parts of the project plan tend to develop naturally.

6.1   INITIAL PROJECT COORDINATION AND THE PROJECT CHARTER

It is crucial that the project's objectives be clearly tied to the overall mission, goals, and strategy of the organization, such as might be reflected in the project portfolio process. In the project charter, senior management should delineate the firm's intent in undertaking the project, outline the scope of the project, and describe how the project's desired results reinforce the organization's goals. Without a clear beginning, project planning (and later progress) can easily go astray. It is also vital that a senior manager call and be present at the *project launch meeting*, an initial coordinating meeting, as a visible symbol of top management's commitment to the project.

The individual leading the launch meeting is first to define the scope of the project as detailed in the charter. The success of the project launch meeting is absolutely dependent on the existence of a well-defined set of objectives. Unless all parties to the planning process have a clear understanding of precisely what it is the project is expected to deliver, planning is sure to be inadequate or misguided. At the launch meeting, the project is discussed in sufficient detail that potential contributors develop a general understanding of what is needed. If the project is one of many similar projects, the meeting will be short and routine, a sort of "touching base" with other interested units. If the project is unique in most of its aspects, extensive discussion may be required.

It is useful to also review the major risks facing the project during the launch meeting. The known risks will be those identified during the project selection process. These are apt to focus largely on the market reaction to a new process/product, the technical feasibility of an innovation, and like matters. The risk management plan for the project must be started at the launch meeting so that further risk identification can be extended to include the technology of the process/product, the project's schedule, resource base, and a myriad other risks facing the project but not really identifiable until the project plan has begun to take form. In addition to the matters discussed below, one of the outcomes of the project planning process will be the formulation of the project's risk management group and the initial risk management plan that the group develops during the process of planning the project.

While various authors have somewhat different expectations for the project launch meeting (e.g., see Knutson, 1995; Martin et al., 1998), we feel it is important not to allow plans, schedules, and budgets to go beyond the most aggregated level, especially if the project deliverables are fairly simple and do not require much interdepartmental coordination. To fix plans in more detail at this initial meeting tends to prevent team members from integrating the new project into their ongoing activities and from developing creative ways of coordinating activities that involve two or more organizational units. Worse still, departmental representatives will be asked to make "a ballpark estimate of the budget and time required" to carry out this first-blush plan. Everyone who has ever worked on a project is aware of the extraordinary propensity of preliminary estimates to metamorphose instantaneously into firm budgets and schedules. Remember that this is only one of a series of meetings that will be required to plan projects of more than minimal complexity. It is critical to the future success of the project to take the time required to do a technically and politically careful job of planning. "If this means many meetings and extensive use of participatory decision making, then it is well worth the effort" (Ford et al., 1992, p. 316).

Whatever the process, the outcome must be that: (1) technical scope is established (though perhaps not "cast in concrete"); (2) basic areas of performance responsibility are accepted by the participants; (3) any tentative delivery dates or budgets set by the parent organization are clearly noted; and (4) a risk management group is created. Each individual/unit accepting responsibility for a portion of the project should agree to deliver, by the next project meeting, a preliminary but detailed plan about how that responsibility will be accomplished. Such plans should contain descriptions of the required tasks, and estimates of the budgets (labor and resources) and schedules.

Project Management in Practice
Child Support Software a Victim of Scope Creep

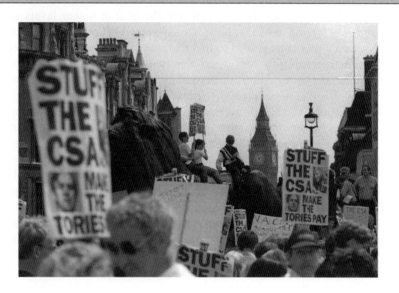

In March 2003, the United Kingdom's Child Support Agency (CSA) started using their new £456 million ($860 million) software system for receiving and disbursing child support payments. However, by the end of 2004 only about 12 percent of all applications had received payments, and even those took about three times longer than normal to process. CSA thus threatened to scrap the entire system and withhold £1 million ($2 million) per month in service payments to the software vendor. The problem was thought to be due to both scope creep and the lack of a risk management strategy. The vendor claimed that the project was disrupted constantly by CSA's 2,500 change requests, while CSA maintained there were only 50, but the contract did not include a scope management plan to help define what constituted a scope change request. And the lack of a risk management strategy resulted in no contingency or fallback plans in case of trouble, so when project delays surfaced and inadequate training became apparent, there was no way to recover.

Source: Project Management Institute. "Lack of Support," *PM Network*, Vol. 19.

PMBOK Guide

Chapter 11

Simultaneous with these planning activities, the risk management group develops a risk management plan that includes proposed methodologies for managing risk, the group's budget, schedule, criteria for dealing with risk, and required reports. Further, necessary inputs to the risk data base are described and various roles and responsibilities for group members are spelled out, as noted in PMBOK (Project Management Institute, 2008). It must be emphasized that the process of managing risk is not a static process. Rather, it is ongoing, with constant updating as more risks are identified, as some risks vanish, as others are mitigated—in other words, as reality replaces conjecture—and new conjecture replaces old conjecture.

The various parts of the project plan, including the risk management plan, are then scrutinized by the group and combined into a composite project plan. The composite plan, still not completely firm, is approved by each participating group, by the project manager, and then by senior organizational management. Each subsequent approval hardens the plan somewhat, and when senior management has endorsed it, any further changes in the project's scope must be made by processing a formal *change order*. If the project is not large or complex, informal written memoranda can substitute for the change order. The main point is that no *significant* changes in the project are made, without written notice, following top management's approval. The definition of "significant" depends on the specific situation and the people involved.

The PM generally takes responsibility for gathering the necessary approvals and assuring that any changes incorporated into the plan at higher levels are communicated to, and approved by, the units that have already signed off on the plan. Nothing is as sure to enrage functional unit managers as to find that they have been committed by someone else to alterations in their carefully considered plans without being informed. Violation of this procedure is considered a betrayal of trust. Several incidents of this kind occurred in a firm during a project to design a line of children's clothing. The anger at this *change without communication* was so great that two chief designers resigned and took jobs with a competitor.

Because senior managers are almost certain to exercise their prerogative to change the plan, the PM should always return to the contributing units for consideration and reapproval of the plan as modified. The final, approved result of this procedure is the project plan, also sometimes known as the *baseline plan*. When the planning phase of the project is completed, it is valuable to hold one additional meeting, a postplanning review (Martinez, 1994). This meeting should be chaired by an experienced project manager who is not connected with the project (Antonioni, 1997). The major purpose of the postplanning review is to make sure that all necessary elements of the project plan have been properly developed and communicated.

Outside Clients

When the project is to deliver a product/service to an outside client, the fundamental planning process described above is unchanged except for the fact that the project's scope cannot be altered without the *client's* permission. A common "planning" problem in these cases is that marketing has promised deliverables that engineering may not know how to produce on a schedule that manufacturing may be unable to meet. This sort of problem usually results when the various functional areas are not involved in the planning process at the time the original proposal is made to the potential client. We cannot overstate the importance of a carefully determined set of *deliverables*, accepted by both project team and client (Martin et al., 1998).

Two objections to such early participation by engineering and manufacturing are likely to be raised by marketing. First, the sales arm of the organization is trained to sell and is expected to be fully conversant with all technical aspects of the firm's products/services. Further, salespeople are expected to be knowledgeable about design and manufacturing lead times and schedules. On the other hand, it is widely assumed by marketing (with some justice on occasion) that manufacturing and design engineers do not understand sales techniques, will be argumentative and/or pessimistic about client needs in the presence of the client, and are generally not "housebroken" when customers are nearby. Second, it is expensive to involve so much technical talent so early in the sales process—typically, prior to issuing a bid or proposal. It can easily cost a firm more than $10,000 to send five technical specialists on a short trip to consider a potential client's needs, not including a charge for the time lost by the specialists. The willingness to accept higher sales costs puts even more emphasis on the selection process.

Project Management in Practice
Timetable Scheduling and Operational Plan Generation for London Underground

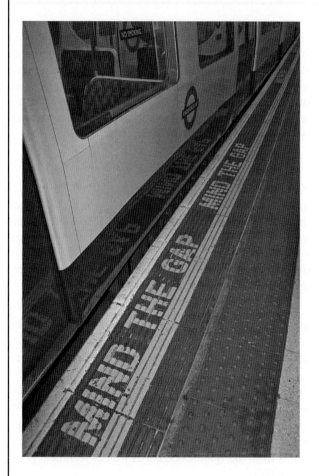

The project was for developing a system for timetable scheduling and operation plan generation, after reengineering the original software system for London Underground System (LUL).

Over 460 trains during peak hours crisscross each other over an area of 2,000 km^2, carrying over 800 million passengers a year. The London Underground is the world's oldest and most complex subway rail network. Naturally, the job of designing its train scheduling system was entrusted to one of the leaders in information technology.

CMC Ltd (CMC) was awarded a contract by London Underground in 1989, to migrate the system and to design and develop a database for its timetable scheduling and operation plan generation software. CMC successfully delivered the Computer Aided Railway Timetabling (CART) system then, and have been giving on-site support to LUL, making necessary changes to the system as and when required.

In 1998, CART was made available to the scheduling department on their Windows PC using Hummingbird's Exceed emulator. The CART software, too, was migrated to a more powerful SUN machine. The migration to the new hardware platform was done offshore in Hyderabad. The installation and setting of the Exceed software was done by the on-site team in London. This arrangement made available the usual windows application like MS Word, Excel and PowerPoint to CART users. Previously, users had to go to a different PC to do any other work.

In 2002, LUL took a decision to re-engineer CART and use Oracle as the database. LUL asked CMC to provide various solutions for implementing the new system. CMC recommended using Developer 6i with Oracle and also provided training on Oracle to LUL key staff. As proof of the concept project, CMC developed a highly customised Workflow Management

Application (WMA) using Developer 6i and Oracle 8i for the scheduling department. WMA provides automated Task Management, Resource Management and Allocation Function for the Scheduling Department. This software was part of the migration of CART from Ingres to Oracle. WMA was deployed in May 2003 and since then has been used by the scheduling department for generating timetables. CMC was responsible for the user interface, the physical database design and the coding.

After the success of WMA, CMC embarked on the mammoth task of reverse engineering each module of CART, identifying and removing obsolete pieces of code and rewriting the technical documentation. CMC is also responsible for designing a Data Bridge software which migrates user selected timetables from the CART system to the new COS (CART Oracle System) application. CMC used LUL's standard software, System Architect 2000, to create the dataflow and entity relationship diagrams. In the meantime, CMC is also responsible for maintaining and enhancing the CART application.

Source: CMC Ltd, a subsidiary of Tata Consultancy Services Limited, available at http://www.cmcltd.com/index.htm accessed, 2008-09-15.

The rejoinder to such objections is simple. It is almost always cheaper, faster, and easier to do things right the first time than to redo them. When the product/service is a complex system that must be installed in a larger, more complex system, it is appropriate to treat the sale like a project, which deserves the same kind of planning. A great many firms that consistently operate in an atmosphere typified by design and manufacturing crises have created their own panics. (Software producers and computer system salespeople, take note!) In fairness, it is appropriate to urge that anyone meeting customers face to face should receive some training in the tactics of selling.

Project Charter Elements

PMBOK Guide
4.1

Given a project charter, approvals really amount to a series of authorizations. The PM is authorized to direct activities, spend monies (usually within preset limits), request resources and personnel, and start the project on its way. Senior management's approval not only signals its willingness to fund and support the project, but also notifies subunits in the organization that they may commit resources to the project.

The process of developing the project charter varies from organization to organization, but should contain the following elements as described in PMBOK®:

- *Purpose* This is a short summary directed to top management and those unfamiliar with the project. It contains a statement of the general goals of the project and a brief explanation of their relationship to the firm's objectives (i.e., the Business Case). The Business Case includes not only market opportunities and profit potentials but also the needs of the organization, any customer requests for proposals, technological advancement opportunities, and regulatory, environmental, and social considerations.

- *Objectives* This contains a more detailed statement of the general goals of the project, what constitutes success, and how the project will be terminated. The statement should include profit and competitive aims from the Business Case as well as technical goals based on the Statement of Work (SOW).

- *Overview* This section describes both the managerial and the technical approaches to the work. The technical discussion describes the relationship of the project to available technologies. For example, it might note that this project is an extension of work done by the company for an earlier project. The subsection on the managerial approach takes note of any deviation from routine procedure—for instance, the use of subcontractors for some parts of the work.

- **Schedules** This section outlines the various schedules and lists all *milestone* events and/or phase-gates. Each summary (major) task is listed, with the estimated time obtained from those who will do the work. The projected baseline schedule is constructed from these inputs. The responsible person or department head should sign off on the final, agreed-on schedule.

PMBOK Guide
Chapter 12

- **Resources** There are three primary aspects to this section. The first is the budget. Both capital and expense requirements are detailed by task, which makes this a *project budget,* with one-time costs separated from recurring project costs. Second, is a complete list and description of all contractual items such as customer-supplied resources, liaison arrangements, project review and cancellation procedures, proprietary requirements, purchasing/procurement contracts (knowledge area 9 in PMBOK), any specific management agreements (e.g., use of subcontractors), as well as the technical deliverables and their specifications, delivery schedules, and a specific procedure for changing any of the above. Third, are the cost monitoring and control procedures. In addition to the usual routine elements, the monitoring and control procedures must also include any special resource requirements for the project such as special machines, test equipment, laboratory usage or construction, logistics, field facilities, and special materials.

- **Personnel** This section lists the expected personnel requirements of the project, especially the project manager and the sponsor/approver of the project. In addition, any special skill requirements, training needed, possible recruiting problems, legal or policy restrictions on work force composition, and security clearances, should be noted here. It is helpful to time-phase personnel needs to the project schedule, if possible. This makes clear when the various types of contributors are needed and in what numbers. These projections are an important element of the budget, so the personnel, schedule, and resources sections can be cross-checked with one another to ensure consistency.

- **Risk Management Plans** This covers potential problems as well as potential lucky breaks that could affect the project. One or more issues such as subcontractor default, unexpected technical breakthroughs, strikes, hurricanes, new markets for the technology, and sudden moves by a competitor are certain to occur—the only uncertainties are which, when, and their impact. In fact, the timing of these disasters and benefits is not random since there are definite times in every project when progress depends on subcontractors, the weather, or timely technical successes. Plans to deal with favorable or unfavorable contingencies should be developed early in the project's life. No amount of planning can definitively solve a potential crisis, but preplanning may avert or mitigate some. As Zwikael et al. (2007) report, in high-risk projects better project planning improved success on four measures: schedule overrun, cost overrun, technical performance, and customer satisfaction. They conclude that improving the project plan is a more effective risk management approach than using the usual risk management tools.

- **Evaluation Methods** Every project should be evaluated against standards and by methods established at the project's inception, allowing for both the direct and ancillary goals of the project, as described in Chapter 1. This section contains a brief description of the procedures to be followed in monitoring, collecting, storing, auditing, and evaluating the project, as well as in the post-project ("lessons learned") evaluation following project termination.

These are the elements that constitute the project charter and are the basis for more detailed planning of the budgets, schedules, work plan, and general management of the project. Once this project charter is fully developed and approved, it is disseminated to all interested parties.

Project Management in Practice
Facebook Risks Interruption to Move a Terabyte

Working on the bleeding edge of innovation is standard procedure for Facebook. To do so, however, speed is critical to their operation, and the combination of speed and innovation brings with it high risk. But Facebook is used to handling risk. For example, a recent project involved a multimillion dollar effort to move a *terabyte* of data from a near-capacity data center to a new, higher-capacity data warehouse by the end of the year, only a hundred days away, at the time. A terabyte (that is, a trillion bytes, or a million megabytes) is equivalent to 250 billion "Likes" on Facebook—a lot of data!

The project involved two phases: building and outfitting the new warehouse, and then transferring the data. The new data warehouse was designed so the servers could handle four times as much data as the current ones, and the processors and software were upgraded as well, with the result that the new data warehouse could hold eight times more data and move and manage it more efficiently, all of which represented a savings of millions of dollars in energy costs. Given the short timeline and the importance of the hardware and software working together without a hitch, the project team took many steps to reduce the risks. First, they set clear expectations with both the vendors and internal stakeholders up front so everyone could fit their objectives into those of Facebook's. Also, they conducted round-the-clock testing of the hardware, the software, and the ability of both to work together to deliver the speed, volume, and accuracy Facebook was depending on.

To transfer the data to the new warehouse, they had a choice between loading the data onto the equipment before physically moving it to the warehouse (but risking lost or damaged equipment in the move), versus moving and checking the equipment first, and then flowing the data directly to the new site (but risking a network outage or a site crash disrupting their entire website). They took the risk of the latter, but planned multiple risk avoidance steps. First they had to calculate how long it would take to flow the terabyte of data, assuming no network failures or power outages—three weeks! But there was still a risk that the data flow would use too much network capacity and affect the website. To avoid this, the team built a customer application to throttle the data by limiting and monitoring the bandwidth throughout the entire 3-week data flow. They also performed constant error-checking and data-level corrections to keep the flow synchronized, and alert the team if problems arose. Their up-front detailed planning, constant monitoring, and risk avoidance measures paid off in a successful data move to the new warehouse, on time with no delays or downtime.

Source: S. F. Gale, "A Closer Look," *PM Network*, Vol. 24.

Before proceeding, we should reiterate that this formal planning process just described is required for relatively large projects that cannot be classified as "routine" for the organization. The time, effort, and cost of the planning process is not justified for routine projects such as most plant maintenance projects. Admittedly, no two routine maintenance projects are identical, but they do tend to be quite similar. It is useful to have a generic plan for such projects, but it is meant to serve as a template that can easily be modified to fit the specific routine project at hand.

Project Planning in Action

Project plans are usually constructed by listing the sequence of activities required to carry the project from start to completion. Not only is this a natural way to think about a project; it also helps the planner decide the necessary sequence of things—a necessary consideration for determining the project schedule and duration. In a fascinating paper, Aaron and his colleagues (1993) describe the planning process used at a telecommunications firm.

Using a planning process oriented around the life-cycle events common for software and hardware product developers, they divide the project into nine segments:

- Concept evaluation
- Requirements identification
- Design
- Implementation
- Test
- Integration
- Validation
- Customer test and evaluation
- Operations and maintenance

Each segment is made up of activities and milestones (significant events). As the project passes through each of the segments, it is subjected to a series of "quality gates" (also known as "phase gates," "toll gates," etc.) that must be successfully passed before proceeding to the next segment. Note that the planning process must pass through the quality gates as well as the physical output of the project itself. For example, the requirements identification segment must meet the appropriate quality standards before the design segment can be started, just as design must be approved before implementation can begin.

Beginning in Chapter 1, we have argued that quality should be an inherent part of the project's specification/deliverables. The approach taken by Aaron et al. (1993) is a direct embodiment of our position. Indeed, it "goes us one better," by applying quality standards to the process of managing the project as well as to the project's deliverables.

6.2 STARTING THE PROJECT PLAN: THE WBS

PMBOK Guide
4.2

In this and the following sections of this chapter, and in Chapters 7 and 8 on budgeting and scheduling, we move into the details of (and some tools for) developing the project plan, essentially an elaboration of the elements of the project charter. As PMBOK® points out, the project charter is one of the major inputs to the project plan. We need to know exactly what is to be done, by whom, and when. All activities required to complete the project must be precisely delineated and coordinated. The necessary resources must be available when and where they are needed, and in the correct amounts. Some activities must be done sequentially, but some may be done simultaneously. If a large project is to come in on time and within cost, a great many things must happen when and how they are supposed to happen. Yet each of these details is uncertain and thus each must be subjected to risk management. In this section, we propose a conceptually simple method to assist in sorting out and planning all this detail. It is a *hierarchical planning system*—a method of constructing a work breakdown structure (WBS).

To accomplish any specific project, a number of major activities must be undertaken and completed. Make a list of these activities in the general order in which they would occur. This is Level 1. A reasonable number of activities at this level might be anywhere between 2 and 20. (There is nothing sacred about these limits. Two is the minimum possible breakdown, and 20 is about the largest number of interrelated items that can be comfortably sorted and scheduled at a given level of aggregation.) Now break each of these Level 1 items into 2 to 20 tasks. This is Level 2. In the same way, break each Level 2 task into 2 to 20 subtasks. This is Level 3. Proceed in this way until the detailed tasks at a level are so well understood that there is no reason to continue with the work breakdown; this will usually be at the individual worker level.

It is important to be sure that all items in the list are at roughly the same level of task generality. In writing a book, for example, the various chapters tend to be at the same level of generality, but individual chapters are divided into finer detail. Indeed, subdivisions of a chapter may be divided into finer detail still. It is difficult to overstate the significance of this simple dictum. It is central to the preparation of most of the planning documents that will be described in this chapter and those that follow.

The logic behind this simple rule is persuasive. We have observed both students and professionals in the process of planning. We noted that people who lack experience in planning tend to write down what they perceive to be the first activity in a sequence of activities, begin to break it down into components, take the first of these, break it further, until they have reached a level of detail they feel is sufficient. They then take the second step and proceed similarly. If they have a good understanding of a basic activity, the breakdown into detail is handled well. If they are not expert, the breakdown lacks detail and tends to be inadequate. Further, we noted that integration of the various basic activities was poor. An artist of our acquaintance explained: When creating a drawing, the artist sketches in the main lines of a scene, and then builds up the detail little by little over the entire drawing. In this way, the drawing has a "unity." One cannot achieve this unity by drawing one part of the scene in high detail, then moving to another part of the scene and detailing it. He asked a young student to make a pen-and-ink sketch of a fellow student. Her progress at three successive stages of her drawing is shown in Figure 6-1.

Figure 6-1 Hierarchical planning.

This illustrates the "hierarchical planning process." The PM will probably generate the most basic level (Level 1) and possibly the next level as well. Unless the project is quite small, the generation of additional levels will be delegated to the individuals or groups who have responsibility for doing the work. Maintaining the "hierarchical planning" discipline will help keep the plan focused on the project's deliverables rather than on the work at a subsystem level.

Some project deliverables may be time sensitive in that they may be subject to alteration at a later date when certain information becomes available. A political campaign is an example of such a project. A speech may be rewritten in whole or in part to deal with recently released data about the national economy, for instance. This describes a planning process that must be reactive to information or demands that change over time. This type of process is sometimes called "rolling wave planning." Nevertheless, the overall structure of the reactive planning process still should be hierarchical.

Sometimes a problem arises because some managers tend to think of outcomes when planning and others think of specific tasks (activities). Many mix the two. The problem is to develop a list of both activities and outcomes that represents an exhaustive, nonredundant set of results to be accomplished (outcomes) and the work to be done (activities) in order to complete the project.

In this hierarchical planning system, the objectives are taken from the project charter. This aids the planner in identifying the set of required activities for the objectives to be met, a critical part of the project plan. Each activity has an outcome (event) associated with it, and these activities and events are decomposed into subactivities and subevents, which, in turn, are subdivided again.

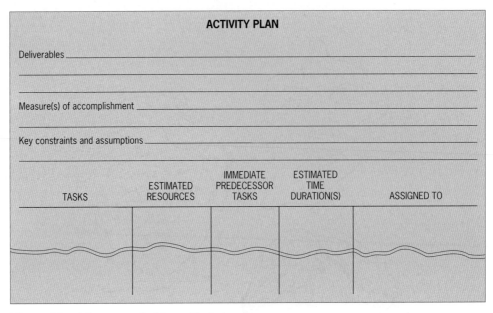

Figure 6-2   A form to assist hierarchical planning.

Assume, for example, that we have a project whose purpose is to acquire and install a large copy machine in a hospital records department. In the hierarchy of work to be accomplished for the installation part of the project, we might find such tasks as "Develop a plan for preparation of the floor site" and "Develop a plan to maintain records during the installation and test period." These tasks are two of a larger set of jobs to be done. The task ". . . preparation of the floor site" is subdivided into its elemental parts, including such items as "Get specifics on copy machine mounting points," "Check construction specifications on plant floor," and "Present final plan for floor preparation for approval." A form that may help to organize this information is shown in Figure 6-2. (Additional information about each element of the project will be added to the form later when budgeting and scheduling are discussed.)

The Work Breakdown Structure (WBS)

PMBOK Guide

5.3

Using this hierarchical planning process results in a work breakdown structure known as a WBS. The WBS is the main tool for managing the project scope as described in PMBOK®. The WBS is not one thing. It can take a wide variety of forms that, in turn, serve a wide variety of purposes. In many ways, the WBS is a simplified form of the project plan focused on the actual tasks of the project. It often shows the organizational elements associated with a project subdivided into hierarchical units of tasks, subtasks, work packages, etc. Figure 6-3 is such a WBS for a conference. The Food group in the Facilities staff has responsibility for meals and drinks, including coffee breaks and water pitchers in the conference rooms. Five different food functions are shown, each presumably broken down into more detailed tasks. In this case, the account numbers for each task are shown so that proper charges can be assigned for each piece of work done on the project.

Professor Andrew Vazsonyi has called this type of diagram a *Gozinto chart*, after the famous Italian mathematician Prof. Zepartzat Gozinto (of Vazsonyi's invention). Readers will recognize the parallel to the basic organizational chart depicting the formal structure of an organization, or the Bill of Materials in a Materials Requirements Planning (MRP) system.

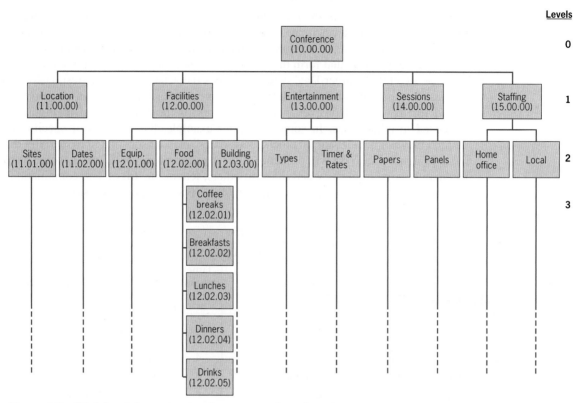

Figure 6-3 Work breakdown structure (account numbers shown).

Another form of the WBS is an outline with the top organizational (Level 1) tasks on the left and successive levels appropriately indented. Most current project management software will generate a WBS on command. Microsoft's Project®, for example, links the indented activity levels with a Gantt chart that visually shows the activity durations at any level.

In general, the WBS is an important document and can be tailored for use in a number of different ways. It may illustrate how each piece of the project contributes to the whole in terms of performance, responsibility, budget, and schedule. It may, if the PM wishes, list the vendors or subcontractors associated with specific tasks. It may be used to document that all parties have signed off on their various commitments to the project. It may note detailed specifications for any work package, establish account numbers, specify hardware/software to be used, and identify resource needs. It may serve as the basis for making cost estimates or estimates of task duration. Largely, the WBS is a planning tool but it may also be used as an aid in monitoring and controlling projects. Again, it is important to remember that no single WBS contains all of the elements described and any given WBS should be designed with specific uses in mind. Its uses are limited only by the needs of the project and the imagination of the PM. No one version of the WBS will suit all needs, so the WBS is not *a* document, but any given WBS is simply one of many possible documents.

However, in constructing the WBS, all work package information should be reviewed with the individuals or organizations who have responsibility for doing or supporting the work in order to verify the WBS's accuracy. Resource requirements, schedules, and subtask relationships can now be aggregated to form the next higher level of the WBS, continuing on to each succeeding level of the hierarchy. At the uppermost level, we have a summary of the project, its budget, and an estimate of the duration of each work element. For the moment, we are ignoring uncertainty in estimating the budget and duration of work elements.

As we noted, the actual form the WBS takes is not sacrosanct. Figure 6-4 shows a partial WBS for a college "Career Day" which includes the activities, who is responsible, the time each task is expected to take, which tasks must precede each task, and any external resources needed for that task. However, not all elements of the WBS shown in Figure 6-4 may be needed in other cases. In some cases, for example, the amounts of specific resources required may not be relevant. In others, "due dates" may be substituted for activity durations. The appearance of a WBS will probably differ in different organizations. In some plans, numbers may be used to identify activities; in others, letters. In still others, combinations of letters and numbers may be used. An example of a WBS to acquire a subsidiary is illustrated in

WBS

Steps	Responsibility	Time (weeks)	Prec.	Resources
Career Day				
1. Contact Organizations				
a. Print forms	Secretary	6	–	Print shop
b. Contact organizations	Program manager	15	1.a	Word processing
c. Collect display information	Office manager	4	1.b	
d. Gather college particulars	Secretary	4	1.b	
e. Print programs	Secretary	6	1.d	Print shop
f. Print participants' certificates	Graduate assistant	8	–	Print Shop
2. Banquet and Refreshments				
a. Select guest speaker	Program manager	14	–	
b. Organize food	Program manager	3	1.b	Caterer
c. Organize liquor	Director	10	1.b	Dept. of Liquor Control
d. Organize refreshments	Graduate assistant	7	1.b	Purchasing
3. Publicity and Promotion				
a. Send invitations	Graduate assistant	2	–	Word processing
b. Organize gift certificates	Graduate assistant	5.5	–	
c. Arrange banner	Graduate assistant	5	1.d	Print shop
d. Contact faculty	Program manager	1.5	1.d	Word processing
e. Advertise in college paper	Secretary	5	1.d	Newspaper
f. Class announcements	Graduate assistant	1	3.d	Registrar's office
g. Organize posters	Secretary	4.5	1.d	Print shop
4. Facilities				
a. Arrange facility for event	Program manager	2.5	1.c	
b. Transport materials	Office manager	.5	4.a	Movers

Figure 6-4   Partial WBS for college "Career Day."

Figures 6-5a and 6-5b. A verbal "WBS" was written in the form of a memorandum (Figure 6-5a), and was followed by the more common, tabular plan shown in Figure 6-5b. Only one page of a five-page plan is shown. The individuals and groups mentioned developed similar plans at a greater level of detail. (Names have been changed at the request of the firm.)

Occasionally, planners attempt to plan by using "Gantt charts," a network device commonly used to display project schedules (see Figure 6-6). The Gantt chart was invented as a scheduling aid. In essence, the project's activities are shown on a horizontal bar chart with the horizontal bar lengths proportional to the activity durations. The activity bars are connected to predecessor and successor activities with arrows. The project schedule integrates the many different schedules relevant to the various parts of the project. It is comprehensive and may include contractual commitments, key interfaces and sequencing, milestone events, and progress reports. In addition, a time contingency reserve for unforeseeable delays might be

---

MEMO

To allow Ajax to operate like a department of Instat, we must do the following by the dates indicated.

September 24

Ajax Management to be advised of coming under Instat operation. The Instat sales department will begin selling Ajax Consumer Division production effective Jan. 1, 1996. There will be two sales groups: (1) Instat, (2) Ajax Builder Group.

October 15

Instat Regional Managers advised—Instat sales department to assume sales responsibility for Ajax products to distribution channels, Jan. 1, 1996.

October 15

Ajax regional managers advised of sales changes effective Jan. 1, 1996.

October 15

Instat Management, Bob Carl, Van Baker, and Val Walters visit Ajax management and plant. Discuss how operations will merge into Instat.

October 22

Ajax regional managers advise Ajax sales personnel and agents of change effective Jan. 1, 1996.

October 24

Brent Sharp and Ken Roadway visit Instat to coordinate changeover.

October 29

Instat regional managers begin interviewing Ajax sales personnel for possible positions in Instat's sales organization.

November 5

Instat regional managers at Ajax for sales training session.

November 26

Walters visits Ajax to obtain more information.

November 30

Data Processing (Morrie Reddish) and Mfg. Engineering (Sam Newfield): Request DP tapes from Bob Cawley, Ajax, for conversion of Ajax to Instat eng. records: master inventory file, structure file, bill of materials file, where-used file, cross-reference Instat to Ajax part numbers, etc. Allow maximum two weeks until December 14, 1995, for tapes to be at Instat.

December 3

ADMINISTRATIVE (Val Walters): Offer Norwood warehouse for sublease.

December 3

SALES (Abbott and Crutchfield): Week of sales meeting . . . Instruction of salespeople in Ajax line . . . including procedure in writing Ajax orders on separate forms from Instat orders . . . temporarily, adding weight and shipping information, and procedure below: Crutchfield to write procedure regarding transmission of orders to Instat, credit check, and transmission of order information to shipping point, whether Norwood, San Francisco, or, later, Instat Cincinnati.

Figure 6-5a Partial WBS for merger of Ajax Hardware into Instat Corp (page 1 of 5).

WBS

Objective: Merger of Ajax Hardware into Instat Corp.			
Steps	**Due Date**	**Responsibility**	**Precedent**
1. Ajax management advised of changes	September 24	Bob Carl, Van Baker	—
2. Begin preparing Instat sales dept. to sell Ajax Consumer Division products effective 1/1/96	September 24	Bob Carl	1
3. Prepare to create two sales groups: (1) Instat, (2) Ajax Builder Group effective 1/1/96	September 24	Bob Carl	1
4. Advise Instat regional managers of sales division changes	October 15	Bob Carl	2,3
5. Advise Ajax regional managers of sales division changes	October 15	Van Baker	2,3
6. Visit Ajax management and plan to discuss merger of operations	October 15	Bob Carl, Van Baker, Val Walters	4,5
7. Advise Ajax sales personnel and agents	October 22	Van Baker	6
8. Visit Instat to coordinate changeover	October 24	Brent Sharp, Ken Roadway	6
9. Interview Ajax sales personnel for possible position	October 29	Instat regional managers	7
10. Sales training sessions for Ajax products	November 5	Instat regional managers	9
11. Visit Ajax again	November 26	Val Walters	8,10
12. Request DP tapes from Bob Cawley for conversion	November 30	Morrie Reddish, Sam Newman	6
13. Offer Norwood warehouse for sublease	December 3	Val Walters	11
14. Write order procedures	December 3	Doug Crutchfield	10
15. Sales meeting (instruction— product line and procedures)	December 3	Fred Abbott, Doug Crutchfield	14
16. DP tapes due for master inventory file, bill of materials, structure file	December 14	Bob Cawley	12
. . .			
. . .			
. . .			

Figure 6-5b   Tabular partial WBS for Ajax-Instat merger based on Figure 6-5a.

included. While it is a useful device for displaying project progress, it is somewhat awkward for project planning.

At this point, it might be helpful to sum up this section with a description of how the planning process actually works in many organizations. Assume that you, the PM, have been given responsibility for developing the computer software required to transmit medical X-rays from one location to another over the Internet. There are several problems that must be solved

Subproject		Task	Responsible Dept.	Dependent Dept.	J	F	M	A	M	J	J	A	S	O	N	D	J	F	M	A	M	J	J	A	S	O	N	D
					2011 (J–D)												2012 (J–D)											
Determine need	A1	Find operations that benefit most	Industrial							△ ▲																		
	A2	Approx. size and type needed	Project Eng.	I.E.					---	---	△	▲																
Solicit quotations	B1	Contact vendors & review quotes	P.E.	Fin., I.E., Purch.							○ ---	●	△ ○	▲	▢												
Write appropriation request	C1	Determine tooling costs	Tool Design	I.E.									○ ---		●	△												
	C2	Determine labor savings	I.E.	I.E.									---	▲	△														
	C3	Actual writing	P.E.	Tool Dsgn., Fin., I.E.													---	△ ○										
Purchase machine tooling, and gauges	D1	Order robot	Purchasing	P.E.															--- △									
	D2	Design and order or manufacture tooling	Tool Design	Purch., Tooling																			---	△				
	D3	Specify needed gauges and order or mfg.	Q.C.	Tool Dsgn., Purch.																			---	△ ○				
Installation and startup	E1	Install robot	Plant Layout	Mill-wrights																			---	△				
	E2	Train employees	Personnel	P.E. Mfg.																			---	△				
	E3	Runoff	Mfg.	Q.C.																							---	△ ▢

Legend:
* * Project completion
* ▢ Contractual commitment
* △ Planned completion
* ▲ Actual completion
* ∧ Status date
* ○ Milestone planned
* ● Milestone achieved
* --- Planned progress
* — Actual progress

Note: As of Jan. 31, 2012, the project is one month behind schedule. This is due mainly to the delay in task C1, which was caused by the late completion of A2.

Figure 6-6 Project schedule displayed as a Gantt chart.

to accomplish this task. First, the X-ray image must be translated into computer language. Second, the computerized image must be transmitted and received. Third, the image must be displayed (or printed) in a way that makes it intelligible to the person who must interpret it. You have a team of four programmers and a couple of assistant programmers assigned to you. You also have a specialist in radiology assigned part-time as a medical advisor.

Your first action is to meet with the programmers and medical advisor in order to arrive at the technical requirements for the project. From these requirements, the project mission statement and detailed specifications will be derived. (Note that the original statement of your "responsibility" is too vague to act as an acceptable mission statement.) The basic actions needed to achieve the technical requirements for the project are then developed by the team. For example, one technical requirement would be to develop a method of measuring the density of the image at every point on the X-ray and to represent this measurement as a numerical input for the computer. This is the first level of the project's WBS.

Responsibility for accomplishing the first level tasks is delegated to the project team members who are asked to develop their own WBS for each of the first level tasks. These are the second level WBS. The individual tasks listed in the second level plans are then divided further into third level WBS detailing how each second level task will be accomplished. The process continues until the lowest level tasks are perceived as "units" or "packages" of work appropriate to a single individual.

Early in this section, we advised the planner to keep all items in a WBS at the same level of "generality" or detail. One reason for this is now evident. The tasks at any level of the WBS are usually monitored and controlled by the level just above. If senior managers attempt to monitor and control the highly detailed work packages several levels down, we have a classic case of micromanagement. Another reason for keeping all items in a given level of the WBS at the same level of detail is that planners have an unfortunate tendency to plan in great detail all activities they understand well, and to be dreadfully vague in planning activities they do not understand well. The result is that the detailed parts of the plan are apt to be carried out and the vague parts of the plan are apt to be given short shrift.

In practice, this process is iterative. Members of the project team who are assigned responsibility for working out a second, third, or lower-level WBS generate a tentative list of tasks, resource requirements, task durations, predecessors, etc., and bring it to the delegator for discussion, amendment, and approval. This may require several amendments and take several meetings before agreement is reached. The result is that delegator and delegatee both have the same idea about what is to be done, when, and at what cost. Not uncommonly, the individuals and groups that make commitments during the process of developing the WBS actually *sign-off* on their commitments. The whole process involves negotiation and, of course, like any managers, delegators can micromanage their delegatees, but micromanagement will not be mistaken for negotiation—especially by the delegatees.

6.3 HUMAN RESOURCES: THE RACI MATRIX AND AGILE PROJECTS

To identify the personnel needed for the project, it may be useful to create a table that shows the staff, workers, and others needed to execute each of the WBS tasks. One such approach, called an *Organizational Breakdown Structure* (OBS), displays the organizational units responsible for each of the various work elements in the WBS, or who must approve or be notified of progress or changes in its scope, since the WBS and OBS may well not be identical. That is, some major section of the WBS may be the responsibility of two or more departments, while for other sections of the WBS, two or more, say, may all be the responsibility of one department. Such a document can be useful for department managers to see their total responsibilities for a particular project.

The Responsibility (RACI) Matrix

PMBOK Guide
9.1.2

Another approach to identifying the human resources needed for the project is to use the *RACI* (Responsible, Accountable, Consult, Inform) *matrix*. This approach is recommended by PMBOK® in its Human Resources Management chapter. This type of chart is also known as a *responsibility matrix*, a *linear responsibility chart*, an *assignment matrix*, a *responsibility assignment matrix*, and similar such names. The matrix shows critical interfaces between units that may require special managerial coordination. With it, the PM can keep track of who must approve what, who must be notified, and other such relationships. Such a chart is illustrated in Figure 6-7. If the project is not too complex, the responsibility chart can be elaborated with additional roles (see Figure 6-8). As a final example of this tool, Figure 6-9 shows one page of

WBS		Responsibility				
		Project Office				Field Oper.
Subproject	Task	Project Manager	Contract Admin.	Project Eng.	Industrial Eng.	Field Manager
Determine	A1	A		C	R	
need	A2	I	A	R	C	
Solicit quotations	B1	A	I	R		C
Write approp.	C1	I	R	A	C	
request.	C2		C	A	R	
	C3	C	I	R		I
"	"					
"	"					
"	"					

Legend:
R   Responsible
C   Consult
I   Inform
A   Accountable

Figure 6-7   RACI matrix.

	Vice-president	General manager	Project manager	Manager engineering	Manager software	Manager manufacturing	Manager marketing	Subprogram manager manufacturing	Subprogram manager software	Subprogram manager hardware	Subprogram manager services
Establish project plan	6	2	1	3	3	3	3	4	4	4	4
Define WBS		5	1	3	3	3	3	3	3	3	3
Establish hardware specs		2	3	1	4	4	4				
Establish software specs		2	3	4	1		4				
Establish interface specs		2	3	1	4	4	4				
Establish manufacturing specs		2	3	4	4	1	4				
Define documentation		2	1	4	4	4	4				
Establish market plan	5	3	5	4	4	4	1				
Prepare labor estimate			3	1	1	1		4	4	4	4
Prepare equipment cost estimate		3	1	1	1			4	4	4	4
Prepare material costs			3	1	1	1		4	4	4	4
Make program assignments			3	1	1	1		4	4	4	4
Establish time schedules		5	3	1	1	1	3	4	4	4	4

1 Actual responsibility   4 May be consulted
2 General supervision   5 Must be notified
3 Must be consulted   6 Final approval

Figure 6-8   Simplified responsibility chart.

Activities	Responsible Individuals		
	Initiate Action	*Work with*	*Clear Action with*
Distribution System and Its Administration			
1. Recommend distribution system to be used.	Mktg Officers	ILI & IHI LOB MCs M-A Cttee VP&Agcy Dir	Sr VP Mktg
	Mktg Officers	Group LOB MC M-A Cttee VP & Agcy Dir	Sr VP Mktg
	Mktg Officers	IA LOB MC M-A Cttee VP&Agcy Dir	Sr VP Mktg
Compensation			
2. Determine provisions of sales-compensation programs (e.g., commissions, subsidies, fringes).	Compensation Task Force	Mktg, S&S & Eqty Prod Offrs	President
	Compensation Task Force	Mktg, S&S & Eqty Prod Offrs	
	Compensation Task Force	Mktg, S&S & Eqty Prod Offrs	President
3. Ensure cost-effectiveness testing of sales compensation programs.	Compensation Task Force	Mktg, S&S & Eqty Prod Offrs	President
Territory			
4. Establish territorial strategy for our primary distribution system.	VP&Agcy Dir	Dir MP&R M-A Cttee	Sr VP Mktg
5. Determine territories for agency locations and establish priorities for starting new agencies.	VP&Agcy Dir	Dir MP&R M-A Cttee	Sr VP Mktg
6. Determine agencies in which advanced sales personnel are to operate.	Dir Ret Plnng Sls Dir Adv Sls	VP S & S	Sr VP Mktg

Legend: IA, ILI,IHI: Product lines
  LOB: Line of business
  MC: Management committee
  M-A Cttee: Marketing administration committee
  S&S: Sales and service
  MP&R: Marketing planning and research

Figure 6-9   Verbal responsibility chart.

a *verbal* responsibility chart developed by a firm to reorganize its distribution system. In this case, the chart takes the form of a 30-page document covering 116 major activities.

Agile project planning and management

Thus far we have been discussing the traditional method for planning projects. This method has been proven to work well for most projects. There are, however, projects for which the traditional methods do not suffice, mainly because they assume that the scope of the project can be well determined and the technology of developing the scope is well understood. This is not always the case.

From time to time we have mentioned the fact that software and IT projects have had a very high failure rate—over budget, over schedule, and delivering less than the desired output. When compared to construction projects, for example, software projects are characterized by a much higher degree of uncertainty about the exact nature of the desired output, and often by a client (user) who does not understand the complexity of the projects and lacks the knowledge to communicate fully with the project team. The result, understandably, has a high probability of client dissatisfaction with the completed project. (Much of the following description is based on Hass, 2007.)

The major source of the problem appears to be the complexity of modern business organizations. They are involved in complex relationships with each other, with multiple governments and external stakeholders, with customers, with suppliers, and operate in an environment of rapid technological change and intense global competition. Their need for complex information systems is a result of the complexity in which they operate.

Agile Project Management (APM) was developed to deal more effectively with this problem. It is distinguished by close and continuing contact between clients (users) and software developers, and an iterative and adaptive planning process. Project requirements are a result of client/developer interaction, and the requirements change as the interaction leads to a better understanding on both sides of the project requirements, priorities, and limitations.

Agile IT project teams are typically small, located at a single site, composed of a PM, the client/end user, an IT architect, two code writers, and a business analyst in the client's industry. Project team membership will, of course, vary with the nature of the project's deliverables. As noted above, the group develops the project requirements and priorities. One requirement is selected, usually the highest value or priority or most complex item, and the team tackles that item. The resulting output is tested by a test case developed as the requirement is developed. The entire team collaborates in dealing with the requirements. The PM's role is to "facilitate" rather than to "control" the process.

Project Management in Practice
Disaster Project Planning in Iceland

Natural hazards abound in the remote island nation of Iceland. Not only is it one of the most volcanically active countries in the world, but its remote and exposed location in the North Atlantic Ocean leaves it vulnerable to gales, landslides, snow avalanches, and other such natural disasters.

There are three phases of a natural disaster: the disaster itself, the response in terms of planning for the future, and the actual rebuilding project phase. Based on previous disasters, such as the 1995 avalanche in Suodavik which claimed 15 lives, it has

been proposed that the response phase be moved up in terms of contingency planning so the rebuilding phase can begin immediately after the disaster.

The normal stakeholders in an Icelandic disaster typically include the population experiencing the disaster, the local government, the insurance bodies, Iceland Catastrophe Insurance, the Landslide and Avalanche Fund, and the consulting and contracting repair organizations. In the past, the activities of these bodies have not been coordinated so every natural disaster had a delayed response to the event until all the political issues could be resolved, which often took months.

The proposal for reorganizing the response phase includes such items as:

- Documenting the response plans in a compulsory project handbook

- Charging the financing bodies with directing the actual rebuilding process

- Identifying an appropriate coordinating body for each disaster type and location

- Identifying a process for the appointment of a project manager independent, both financially and emotionally, of all the main stakeholders.

Source: G. Torfason, "Lessons from a Harsh Land: Project Management and Disaster Preparedness in Iceland," *PM Network*, February 1998, pp. 39–42.

Buried homes in Heimaey, Iceland, from the 1973 volcanic eruption.

Given several requirements, the team deals with them one at a time, each iteration being called a "sprint" during which the client agrees to "freeze" the scope. Not uncommonly, the solution to a second or third requirement may depend on altering the solution to the first requirement. One IT consultant notes (Hunsberger, 2011) that if the client changes the requirements, "we just deliver the new requirements" and ignore the previous ones. If the client wants more, they simply expand the engagement. Although agile projects provide flexibility, the trade-off is a loss of efficiency. This iterative process is not only collaborative, it must also be adaptive.

It is also obvious that problem-oriented team members who have the interpersonal skills needed for collaboration are a necessity. The willingness of team members to share knowledge is an essential condition for agile projects. Not incidentally, the willingness to share knowledge is also a key to success in traditionally organized projects (Chi-Cheng, 2009). A PM who attempts to control an agile project as he might control a traditional project is most certainly the wrong person for the job (Fewell, 2010).

The details of conducting an agile project are available through any chapter of the PMI, and the applicability of APM is much broader than just the software/IT area; this might even be the template for the future of project management for most industries. Any project that has a high-risk technology or a rapidly changing business environment is a candidate for APM, but success requires personnel who are qualified by personality, knowledge, and a desire for the APM experience (Hildebrand, 2010).

6.4 INTERFACE COORDINATION THROUGH INTEGRATION MANAGEMENT

PMBOK Guide
Chapters 4, 11

This section covers the PMBOK® knowledge area 1 concerning *Project Integration Management*. The most difficult aspect of implementing the plan for a complex project is the coordination and integration of the various elements of the project so that they meet their joint goals of scope, schedule, and budget in such a way that the total project meets its goals.

As projects become more complex, drawing on knowledge and skills from more areas of expertise—and, thus, more subunits of the parent organization as well as more outsiders—the problem of coordinating multidisciplinary teams (MTs) becomes more troublesome. At the same time, and as a result, uncertainty is increased. As the project proceeds from its initiation through the planning and into the actual process of trying to generate the project's deliverables, still more problems arise. One hears, "We tried to tell you that this would happen, but you didn't pay any attention." This, as well as less printable remarks, are what one hears when the members of an MT do not work and play well together—in other words, when the various individuals and groups working on the project are not well integrated. Rather than operating as a team, they work as separate and distinct parts, each of which has its own tasks and is not much interested in the other parts.

The intricate process of coordinating the work and timing of the different groups is called *integration management*. The term *interface coordination* is used to denote the process of managing this work across multiple groups. The RACI matrix discussed earlier is a useful aid to the PM in carrying out this task. It displays the many ways the members of the project team (which, as usual, includes all of the actors involved, not forgetting the client and outside vendors) must interact and what the rights, duties, and responsibilities of each will be.

Recent work on managing the interfaces focuses on the use of MTs to plan the project as well as design the products/services the project is intended to produce. There is general agreement that MT has a favorable impact on product/service design and delivery. Work by Hauptman et al. (1996, p. 161) shows that MTs have had a "favorable impact . . . on attainment of project budget goals, but achieves this without any adverse impact on quality, cost or schedule." The process also was associated with higher levels of team job satisfaction.

The use of MTs in product development and planning is not without its difficulties. Successfully involving cross-functional teams in project planning requires that some structure be imposed on the planning process. The most common structure is simply to define the task of

Project Management in Practice
Trying to Install a Wind Farm in the Middle of the North Sea

Denmark's objective of supplying half its national power needs through wind energy by 2025 counted heavily on DONG (Dansk Olie og Naturgas) Energy's "Horns Rev 2" 209-megawatt offshore wind farm, the largest in the world, to be located 30 km (19 mi) off the western Jutland, Denmark coast in the North Sea. Over 600 people and seven suppliers, all led by 7 project managers plus a quality control manager and a commissioning manager, constituted the multidisciplinary project team for this effort. The project consisted of installing 91 turbines over a 35 km^2 (14 mi^2) area. The 50+ meter-long blades that catch the wind and turn the turbines are mounted on shafts 115 meters (377 feet) above the surface of the water. The electricity generated by the wind farm at capacity could supply 200,000 homes.

Even though the point was to locate the farm where there was a strong, constant wind, this created

the major problem facing the team—the difficulty of working in these 36 km/h winds and icy, 3 m high (10 ft) waves out in the rough sea. Traveling to the site could take up to three hours, and labor and supplies had to be unloaded and unpacked in the harsh weather. The difficult conditions limited the time the teams could work, and increased the risk and complexity of every decision. In addition, safety issues became top priority because the work was carried out under such extreme conditions, and far from medical care. As a result, it was critical to eliminate errors and risks because once offshore, the team was coping with weather, logistics, and time, which increased the scale of any problems tenfold!

Hence, massive attention was paid to quality planning on-shore, before heading out to sea. There was a quality plan for every key event to ensure equipment and tasks would meet requirements. Every part that was delivered was rigorously inspected and anything that was missing or wrong had to be corrected before being sent out to sea. And when any troubles were encountered, they were addressed immediately. In one case, a problem arose that was going to take the supplier two months to repair; through creative troubleshooting, the team came up with a plan that would combine two tasks and in the process reduce the time to two weeks. The focus on creative problem solving among the multidisciplinary teams, rather than placing blame, allowed the project to be completed successfully. Ancillary benefits included bringing new knowledge and working practices to the company, plus enabling many members of the team to move into higher-ranking positions, including two engineers who are becoming project managers themselves.

Source: S. F. Gale, "A Closer Look," *PM Network*, Vol. 24.

the group as having the responsibility to generate a plan to accomplish whatever is defined as the project scope. There is considerable evidence that this is not sufficient for complex projects. Using MT creates what Kalu (1993) has defined as a virtual project. In Chapter 4, we noted the high level of conflict in many virtual projects (cf. de Laat, 1994). It follows that MT tends to involve conflict. Conflict raises uncertainty and thus requires risk management. Obviously, many of the risks associated with MT involve intergroup political issues. The PM's negotiating skills will be tested in dealing with intergroup problems, but the outcomes of MT seem to be worth the risks. At times, the risks arise when dealing with an outside group. For an interesting discussion of such issues and their impact on project scope, see Seigle (2001).

Bailetti et al. (1994) attacks the problem of interface management by defining and mapping all interdependencies between various members of the project team. Because the nature of these interfaces may differ during different phases of the product/service design/production process, they map each major phase separately. The logic of this approach to structuring MT is strong. The WBS and RACI matrix are a good initial source of information on interfaces, but they do not reflect the uncertainty associated with tasks on large, complex projects. Further, they implicitly assume that interfaces are stable within and across project phases—an assumption often contrary to fact. This does not ignore the value of the WBS, PERT/CPM networks, and similar tools of longstanding use and proven value in project management. It simply uses interface maps as a source of the coordination requirement to manage the interdependencies. The fundamental structure of this approach to interface management is shown in Figure 6-10.

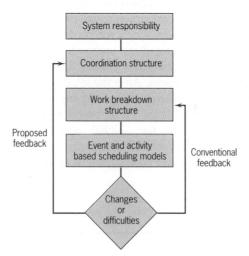

Figure 6-10 Coordination structure model of project management. *Source*: Bailetti et al., 1994.

Managing Projects by Phases and Phase-Gates

In addition to mapping the interfaces (a necessary but not sufficient condition for MT peace), the process of using MTs on complex projects must be subject to some more specific kinds of control. One of the ways to control any process is to break the overall objectives of the process into shorter term phases (or milestones) and to focus the MT on achieving the milestones, as is done in agile project management. If this is done, and if multidisciplinary cooperation and coordination can be established, the level of conflict will likely fall. At least there is evidence that if team members work cooperatively and accomplish their short-term goals, the project will manage to meet its long-term objectives; moreover, the outcome of any conflict that does arise will be creative work on the project.

The project life cycle serves as a readily available way of breaking a project up into component phases, each of which has a unique, identifiable output. Cooper et al. (1993) developed such a system with careful reviews conducted at the end of each "phase" of the life cycle. A feature of this system was feedback given to the entire project each time a project review was conducted.

Project Management in Practice
An Acquisition Failure Questions Recommended Practice

When the Belgian bank Fortis joined with the Royal Bank of Scotland and the Spanish Banco Santander to acquire the Dutch bank ABN Amro, the integration project involved over 6,000 people and was expected to take 3–4 years to complete. The objective was to evaluate what each side brought to the table and select the best technologies through extensive communication and brainstorming. The first nine months were spent evaluating every system and project that would be affected by the merger, resulting in a portfolio of 1,000 projects that needed to be accomplished. A third of the projects were IT system choices which were to be based on multiple criteria such as functionality, cost, maintainability, etc. The plan was to make the choices based on facts instead of emotions, relying on ABN Amro's data and including them in the decision making.

The biggest set of system projects involved mapping and integrating the IT systems. But ABN Amro had thousands of applications and resisted sharing their information, which led to constant conflicts, delays, and artificial obstacles. The result was that Fortis spent thousands of hours to complete even the simplest projects. The years-long project duration also hindered progress since the longer a project takes, the more conflicts, especially cultural (that can't be solved simply with additional resources), will arise. Eventually, the problems and delays depleted Fortis' capital, and, exacerbated by the global credit crisis, they went bankrupt.

Fortis was then sold to the French bank BNP Paribas. In contrast to Fortis' approach, BNP set up an 18-month project to phase out all of Fortis' systems and move Fortis' accounts and data into their own system. They integrated the Fortis team into their own organizational structure and put their own people into the key roles—there was no discussion, just work to do. It was a top-down approach that was easier, faster, and more efficient, though it didn't sit well with the Fortis employees. After the integration was complete, BNP refocused on rebuilding any lost morale. For example, most of the Fortis people kept their jobs, and BNP opened four global centers in Brussels (called BNP Paribas Fortis) to show their interest in strengthening the bank's national and global presence.

Source: S. F. Gale, "A Closer Look," *PM Network*, Vol. 24.

Another attack on the same problem was tied to project quality, again, via the life cycle (Aaron et al., 1993). They created 10 phase-gates associated with milestones for a software project. To move between phases, the project had to pass a review. (They even note that in the early stages of the project when there is no "inspectable product," that " . . . *managing quality on a project means managing the quality of the subprocesses* that produce the delivered product." Emphasis in the original.) While feedback is not emphasized in this system, reports on the finding of project reviews are circulated. The quality-gate process here did not allow one phase to begin until the previous phase had been successfully completed, but many of the phase-gate systems allow sequential phases to overlap in an attempt to make sure that the output of one phase is satisfactory as an input to the next. Another approach that also overlaps phases is called "fast tracking," and here the phases are run in parallel as much as possible to reduce the completion time of the project; of course, this also increases the project risk as well. (The use of the phase-gate process for project control is demonstrated in Chapter 11, Section 11.2.)

There are many such interface control systems, but the ones that appear to work have two elements in common. First, they focus on relatively specific, short-term, interim outputs of a project with the reviews including the different disciplines involved with the project. Second, feedback (and feedforward) between these disciplines is emphasized. No matter what they are called, it must be made clear to all involved that cooperation between the multiple disciplines is required for success, and that all parties to the project are mutually dependent on one another.

Finally, it should be stressed that phase-gate management systems were not meant as substitutes for the standard time, cost, and scope controls usually used for project management. Instead, phase-gate and similar systems are intended to create a process by which to measure project progress, to keep projects on track and aligned with the current strategy, and to keep senior management informed about the current state of projects being carried out.

6.5 PROJECT RISK MANAGEMENT

PMBOK Guide
Chapter 11

This section covers the PMBOK® knowledge area 8, concerning *Project Risk Management*. The Project Management Institute's (PMI) publication *A Guide to the Project Management Body of Knowledge (PMBOK® Guide) 3rd Edition, 2004*, states that risk management is "the systematic process of identifying, analyzing, and responding to project risk"* and consists of six subprocesses, and as we shall see below, a seventh subprocess needs to be added.

1. *Risk Management Planning*—deciding how to approach and plan the risk management activities for a project.

2. *Risk Identification*—determining which risks might affect the project and documenting their characteristics.

3. *Qualitative Risk Analysis*—performing a qualitative analysis of risks and conditions to prioritize their impacts on project objectives.

4. *Quantitative Risk Analysis*—estimating the probability and consequences of risks and hence the implications for project objectives.

---

*It is important for the reader to recall that the word "risk" has two meanings. One relates to the probability that an event will occur. The other is associated with danger or threat. The proper meaning of the word is determined by the context in which it is used.

5. *Risk Response Planning*—developing procedures and techniques to *enhance opportunities* and *reduce threats* to the project's objectives.

6. *Risk Monitoring and Control*—monitoring residual risks, identifying new risks, executing risk reduction plans, and evaluating their effectiveness throughout the project life cycle.

PMBOK Guide   We add here a seventh subprocess, based on the discussion concerning the identification of
11.2.3   risks in PMBOK®.

Project Management in Practice
Risk Analysis vs. Budget/Schedule Requirements in Australia

Sydney, Australia's M5 East Tunnel was constructed under strict budgetary and schedule requirements, but given the massive traffic delays now hampering commuters, the requirements may have been excessive. Due to an inexpensive computer system with a high failure rate, the tunnel's security cameras frequently fail, requiring the operators to close the tunnel due to inability to react to an accident, fire, or excessive pollution inside the tunnel. The tunnel was built to handle 70,000 vehicles a day, but it now carries 100,000, so any glitch can cause immediate traffic snarls. A managerial risk analysis, including the risk of overuse, might have anticipated these problems and mandated a more reliable set of computers once the costs of failure had been included.

Source: Project Management Institute. "Polluted Progress," *PM Network*, Vol. 19.

7. *The Risk Management Register*—creating a permanent register of identified risks, methods used to mitigate or resolve them, and the results of all risk management activities.

We treat each subprocess in turn, including useful tools and techniques where appropriate.

1. Risk Management Planning

It is never too early in the life of a project to begin managing risk. A sensible project selection decision cannot be made without knowledge of the risks associated with the project. Therefore, the risk management plan and initial risk identification must be carried out before the project can be formally selected for support. The risk management group must, therefore, be formed as soon as a potential project is identified.

At first, project risks are loosely defined—focusing for the most part on externalities such as the state of technology in the fields that are important to the project, business conditions in the relevant industries, and so forth. The response to external risks is usually to track the pertinent environments and estimate the chance that the project can survive various conditions. Not until the project is in the planning stage will such risks as those associated with project technology, schedule, budget, and resource allocation begin to take shape.

Because risk management often involves analytic techniques not well understood by PMs not trained in the area, some organizations put risk specialists in a project office, and these specialists staff the project's risk management activities. For a spectacularly successful use of risk management on a major project, see Christensen et al. (2001), a story of risk management in a Danish bridge construction project.

Ward (1999) describes a straightforward method for conducting PMBOK®'s six subprocesses that includes a written report on risk management, if not the creation of a risk register. Two major problems in the way that risk management is carried out by the typical organization are that (1) risk identification activities routinely fail to consider risks associated with the project's external environment; and (2) they focus on misfortune, overlooking the risk of positive things happening.

2. Risk Identification

The risks faced by a project are dependent on the technological nature of the project, as well as on the many environments (economic, cultural, etc.) in which the project exists. Indeed, the manner in which the process of risk management is conducted depends on how one or more environments impact the project. The corporate culture is one such environment. So consider, for instance, the impact of a strong corporate "cost-cutting" emphasis on how risk managers identify project risks—they will probably focus on the project's cost elements, such as personnel and resource allocation. (Note that this culture will carry over to the *process* of risk management as well—carrying out the six or seven subprocesses—not merely to the identification of risks.)

The need to consider the many environments of almost any project is clear when one examines the recent articles on risk management (e.g., Champion, 2009; Taleb, 2009). It is typical to consider only the internal environment of the project, e.g., the technical and interpersonal risks, and occasionally, negative market risks for the project. Articles on risks in IT and software projects rarely go beyond such matters—Jiang et al. (2001) is an example. This is a thoughtful development of a model for generating numerical measures for IT project risks. The specific user of the IT and the institutional setting of the project are considered, but competitors, the IT market, user industries, the legal environment, and several other relevant environments are ignored.

In Chapter 2 we described the use of the Delphi method (Dalkey, 1969) for finding numeric weights and criteria scores for the important factors in selecting projects for funding. The Delphi method is also useful when identifying project risks and opportunities for risk analysis models. Indeed, one of the first applications was forecasting the time period in which some specific technological capability would become available. The Delphi method is commonly used when a group must develop a consensus concerning such items as the importance of a technological risk, an estimate of cash flows, a forecast of some economic variable, and similar uncertain future conditions or events. Other such methods are "brainstorming," "nominal group" techniques, checklists, attribute listing, and other such creativity and idea generation methods (see the website of this book for descriptions).

Cause–effect ("fishbone") diagrams (see Figure 6-11), flow charts, influence diagrams, SWOT analysis, and other operations management techniques (Meredith et al., 2010) may also be useful in identifying risk factors. The flexibility of cause–effect diagrams makes them a useful tool in many situations. For example, the outcome of "failure" of the project can be the outcome on the right side of the fishbone and then the major factors that could cause that—bad economy, performance weakness, high pricing, competing products, etc.—can be the stems that feed into this failure, and the reasons for these various factor failures can be added to the stems. Similarly, we could put the failure factor "performance weakness" as the outcome on the right and list the factors that might cause that: weak engineering, poor materials, etc. Alternatively, we might look at the "risk" that the project might be a great success, much better than we had expected, and the factors that might cause that to occur: beat competing products to the market, booming economy, exceptionally low price, and other such positive reasons.

3. Qualitative Risk Analysis

The purpose of qualitative risk analysis is to prioritize the risks identified in the previous step so attention can be directed to the most important ones. The qualitative nature of this process makes it quite flexible, useful, and quick to apply; also, it can be used for both threats and opportunities. A subjective (or if available, objective) estimate of the probability of the

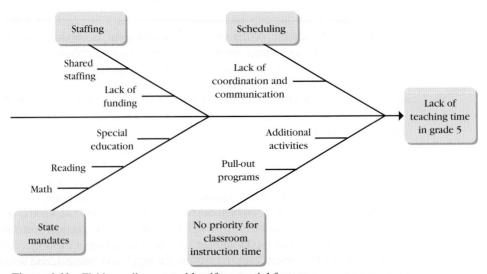

Figure 6-11   Fishbone diagram to identify potential factors

risk occurring is needed, perhaps from a Delphi approach used with a group of experts in the risk area. The probability values need not be precise, and for that matter, could just be a rank on a 1–5 scale, or even simply "low," "medium," or "high."

A sense of the impact of the threat or opportunity is also needed, and should consider all important objectives of the project, including cost, timing, scope, and ancillary objectives. To attain an overall measure of the impact, each objective should be scaled and weighted in importance. Then the impact of the threat on each objective can be found in a fashion similar to the "Getting Wheels" scoring model described in Chapter 2 with the result being a percentage of 100, a number from 1 to 5, or again just "low, medium, or high."

Once the probability and impact levels are found, a Risk Matrix can be constructed as in Figure 6-12. Here we just show the simplest version with nine cells corresponding to "low, medium, and high" categories, but a 1 to 5 range would have 25 cells to consider and a percentage of 100 range could be divided into as many cells as would be useful. As we see in Figure 6-12, for example, we have identified as "critical" those threats with a high value on one measure and a medium or high value on the other measure: in this case, high probability–medium impact, high on each, and medium probability–high impact. The other cells can be categorized in a similar fashion, and here we used just three categories in a symmetrical manner: "critical," "monitor," and "ignore." However, for some threats it may be appropriate to use four, or perhaps just two, categories, and the cells may be categorized differently for each threat. Conversely, if the Risk Matrix cell categories seem appropriate for all threats, then one matrix can be used to illustrate the distribution of all threats, as we have done in Figure 6-12 by listing the five threats (for example) in their corresponding cells.

Finally, the same approach can be used for opportunities, considering the possibility of positive impacts. In this case, the matrix shows which risk opportunities are most important to focus attention on and try to bring about, and which to ignore. The responses to both critical threats and critical opportunities will be discussed in Step 5.

Figure 6-12 Risk Matrix

4. Quantitative Risk Analysis

A quantitative risk analysis is sometimes conducted after the qualitative risk analysis has identified the critical (and perhaps some of the "monitor") risks facing a project. It is more precise (using more precise quantitative data) and typically more accurate, if the data are available. We include here three techniques: Failure Mode and Effect Analysis (FMEA) is a more rigorous approach to the Risk Matrix and includes an additional factor in the process, decision tree analysis using expected monetary values, and simulation.

Failure Mode and Effect Analysis (FMEA)   FMEA (Stamatis, 2003) is the application of a scoring model such as those used for project selection in Chapter 2. It is straightforward and extensively used, particularly in engineering, and is easily applied to risk by using six steps.

1. List the possible ways a project might fail.
2. Evaluate the severity (**S**) of the impact of each type of failure on a 10-point scale where "1" is "no effect" and "10" is "very severe."
3. For each cause of failure, estimate the likelihood (**L**) of its occurrence on a 10-point scale where "1" is "remote" and 10 is "almost certain."
4. Estimate the inability to detect (**D**) a failure associated with each cause. Using a 10-point scale, "1" means detectability is almost certain using normal monitoring/control systems and "10" means it is practically certain that failure will not be detected in time to avoid or mitigate it.
5. Find the *Risk Priority Number* (**RPN**) where $\textbf{RPN} = \textbf{S} \times \textbf{L} \times \textbf{D}$.
6. Consider ways to reduce the **S**, **L**, and **D** for each cause of failure with a significantly high **RPN**. (We discuss this in Step 5: Risk Response Planning.)

Table 6-1 illustrates the use of FMEA for the same five threats we considered in Step 4 previously, but here we use more precise data. As we see from the RPN numbers, the biggest threats are: 2. Can't acquire tech knowledge, and 3. Client changes scope. Threat 2 has a great severity, should it occur, and threat 3 is quite likely, though the severity is much less damaging. The cost threat (4) and the recession threat (5) can probably be ignored for now since their likelihoods are so low. The tight schedule (1) will have some repercussions and is also quite likely, but we will see it coming early and can probably take steps to avoid or mitigate it.

Decision Tree Analysis   This tool (Meredith et al., 2002) is simple in concept and especially useful for situations where sequential events happen over time. For example, it would be appropriate for calculating the probability of getting one head and one tail in two tosses of

Table 6-1   A FMEA example

Threat	*Severity, S*	*Likelihood, L*	*Ability to Detect, D*	*RPN*
1. Tight schedule	6	7.5	2	90
2. Can't acquire tech knowledge	8.5	5	4	170
3. Client changes scope	4	8	5	160
4. Costs escalate	3	2	6	36
5. Recession	4	2.5	7	70

Project Management in Practice
Ignoring Risk Contrasted with Recognizing Risk in Two Industries

Everyone is familiar with the U.S. oil well disaster when BP's Deepwater Horizon oil platform blew up and sank, releasing a massive oil spill into the Gulf of Mexico. BP immediately faced public and governmental questioning about whether the accident could have been prevented, whether corners had been cut, how much oil was leaking into the Gulf, what risk management procedures were followed, and many others. Unfortunately, BP didn't respond well and the oil disaster became a public relations disaster as well as an environmental one.

Oil and disaster experts point out that since the *Exxon Valdez* oil spill, which had occurred in Alaska 21 years earlier, there has been no improvement in pollution cleanup technology—the same booms and skimmers are being used now as were used then. It was clear that sooner or later, there would be another big spill; yet, the oil industry is completely unprepared for this certainty. Amazingly, these firms do not seem to consider even the most basic risk management techniques, like Murphy's Law: "What *can* go wrong, *will* go wrong." Surely it would have been

wise to use some common sense, such as employing redundant valves, and testing the casings and well equipment (e.g., blowout preventers), as they went.

Huffington Post tech blogger Philip Neches makes some interesting contrasts by describing how NASA handles such risks when they design their extremely complex spacecraft and missions. How might it fail? How likely is it to fail in this way? How serious is the failure if it does fail; is there little impact, or is it "mission critical"? A billion dollar effort, plus the lives of any astronauts, are at risk here. In contrast, BP's mission of drilling a well 1,524 m (5,000 ft) below the surface of the sea, clearly a challenge, is still much simpler. But any oil company should know that if they choose to engage in such risky projects, they will also need a plan to recover if a spill occurs, and then handle the massive negative public relations and media attention. In the long run, it's much easier to evaluate the risks up front, make the right decisions, and monitor and test as you go.

Source: S. F. Gale, "Crude Awakening," *PM Network*, Vol. 24.

a fair coin, or perhaps the probability of getting a head on the first toss and a tail on the second toss (which would have a different probability), or just the probability of getting a tail on the second toss. If we are only interested in probabilities, we call the tree a probability tree. But if there are some actions we are considering anywhere along the tree—before the first probability event, say, or between events—and we want to evaluate which action(s) would be best, then it is called a decision tree. Figure 6-13 illustrates such a tree (a solved one, here), but a very simple one with only one set of actions to choose from and one set of events; however, it could be extended to multiple actions and/or events, if desired, quite easily.

A decision tree is created from the left, with either a decision node (a square) or a probability node (a circle) occurring first. In the example shown, we are interested in deciding whether to invest in bonds, stocks, or time deposits (at a bank, for example) for some period of time (say, a year), so there are three alternatives emanating from the decision node, each one posing some risk and opportunity depending on what the economy does in the coming year. Then there is some event that affects the returns we get; in this case we have simplified the results of the economy into three simple categories of "solid growth," "stagnation," or "inflation." (Note that the probabilities of each economic outcome are identical for each decision choice because the decision we make does not affect the economy.) Under each possible outcome of the event (whose probabilities we need to be able to estimate), our decision choice will result in a different payoff, shown on the far right. Note, for example, that if we choose to invest in stocks and there is economic inflation, we will effectively lose two units of yield. To evaluate each of these outcomes and make a decision, we need a decision rule. If our rule was to "never invest in any alternative where we might lose money," then this -2 outcome would rule out the stocks decision alternative. Another rule, if we were optimists, might be to invest in whichever alternative allows us the greatest opportunity for maximizing our payoff, in which case we would choose stocks with a maximum payoff of 15 from "solid growth."

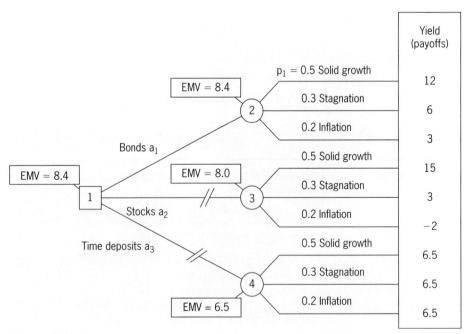

Figure 6-13 Decision tree based on expected monetary value (EMV).

However, we normally use a different rule, called Expected Monetary Value (abbreviated EMV) because this maximizes our return over the indefinite future, that is, the long run average. The process of "solving" the decision tree is to work from the right, with the outcomes (yields, in this case), and multiply each outcome times the probability of the event resulting in that outcome, called the expected value of that outcome, and then adding up all the expected values for that event node-decision choice combination. For example, the EMV for event node 2 would be $(0.5 \times 12) + (0.3 \times 6) + (0.2 \times 3) = 8.4$, which we write on the tree next to its event node. When we have done this with all of the event nodes for that decision, we compare them, double strike the lesser valued decision choices, and can then choose the best alternative choice for that decision node, in this case, "Bonds."

The use of decision trees for risk analysis easily handles both threats and opportunities, as seen in the example. The tool is attractive because it visually lays out everything that may happen in the future (that is, all risks and all decision choices). The tree can be used for individual risks, if they are independent, or joint risks on the same tree. For example, in our earlier use of FMEA, we might have interdependencies between risk 2 (can't acquire tech knowledge) and risk 3 (client changes scope). Perhaps we have a middle route to acquiring knowledge that is sufficient for the initial scope of the project, but if the client later increases the scope, this route will be inadequate. We can portray this as a decision node (alternatives to acquiring the knowledge) followed by the event node (risk) probabilities that this action will or won't be sufficient (note that in this case, as opposed to our example above, these probabilities may differ for each decision alternative), followed by the probability the client increases the scope.

Monte Carlo Simulation Like decision trees, simulation (see Meredith et al., 2002) can also handle both threats and opportunities, and sequential events as well. We start with a model; for example, "Estimated Revenues minus Estimated Costs equals Expected Profits." The advantage of simulation is that we don't need to divide probabilistic events into a limited number of categories. Instead, we estimate optimistic, typical, and pessimistic values for each probabilistic input, and use standard distributions for these events. We then randomly select inputs from these distributions a thousand or more times to generate a frequency distribution of outcomes. The frequency distributions thereby give us the probabilities of losing more than a certain amount of money, or making at least a certain amount, or taking longer, or shorter, than a certain amount of time to complete the project, and other such important information. We include two examples of this approach. In Chapter 7 we simulate project cash flows and inflation rates that are uncertain and thus subject the project to monetary risk. Then in Chapter 8 we simulate the task times of project activities to determine the effect on the overall project completion time and the risk probability of being late.

Dealing with Project Disasters Thus far, we have focused mainly on risks that might be considered normal for any firm undertaking projects. We have dealt with these risks by using an "expected value" approach, as in the PsychoCeramic Sciences example; that is, the estimated loss (or gain) associated with a risky output times the probability that the loss (or gain) will occur. We might also compare the expected loss associated with a risk to the associated expected cost of *mitigating or preventing the loss associated with the risk*. If the reduction in expected loss due to risk mitigation or prevention is greater than its cost, we would invest in the risk mitigation/prevention.

But what about the case when the loss is catastrophic, even potentially ruinous, though it may have a very low probability of occurring; e.g., a run on a bank; a strike at a critical supplier's plant; a flood that shuts down a construction project; an attack by a terrorist group on a building; or the discovery that a substance in a complex drug might cause toxic side effects? In many such cases, the cost of the risk may be massive, but the likelihood that it will occur is so small that the expected cost of the disaster is much less than many smaller, more common risks with far higher probabilities of occurring. This is typical of situations for which we purchase insurance, but what if such insurance is unavailable (usually because the pool of purchasers interested in such insurance is too small)? In the Reading: Planning for Crises in Project Management at the end of this chapter, the authors suggest four approaches for project disaster planning: risk analysis, contingency planning, developing logic charts, and tabletop exercises.

An excellent book, *The Resilient Enterprise* (Sheffi, 2005), deals with risk management concerning many different types of disasters. The book details the methods that creative businesses have used to cope with catastrophes that struck their facilities, supply chains, customer bases, and threatened their survival. The subject is more complex than we can deal with here, but we strongly recommend the book.

5. Risk Response Planning

There are four standard approaches for dealing with risk threats, and somewhat equivalently, for enhancing risk opportunities. For threats, the four are: avoid, transfer, mitigate, and accept. For opportunities they are: exploit, share, enhance, and accept. We describe the threat responses first.

- *Avoid* The idea here is to eliminate the threat entirely. This might be accomplished by using alternative resources, or adding contingent resources, at some cost of course. If the threat is client scope creep, up-front avoidance by adding scope change procedures to the contract might avoid the threat. If the threat is cost overrun, up-front de-scoping of project objectives in agreement with the client might avoid the threat. If the threat is schedule delay, contingency planning for schedule extensions might be written into the project contract. The extreme solution, of course, is to cancel the project if the threat is too great, such as bankruptcy.

- *Transfer* Although this approach does not eliminate the threat, it does remove the project contractor from the danger of the threat. The classic approach here for monetary risk is insurance, but other approaches are also available: warranties, bonding, cost-plus contracting, etc. For nonmonetary threats such as performance, or schedule, one alternative is for the client to contract (*not* subcontract) with another vendor for the portions of the project that are threatened, responsibility to the client resting with the other contractor, of course. In fact, the safest approach is to let the client perform some of these portions of the project themselves.

- *Mitigate* This is a "softening" of the danger of the threat, either through reducing the likelihood it will occur, or through reducing its impact if it does occur. Ways to reduce the likelihood are to do research or testing to improve our understanding of the probability elements of the threat and then spend some effort (and money) on reducing the more probable threats. Such efforts might involve using better materials, employing more reliable sources, simplifying the processes, shifting task times to more reliable periods, and so on, all of which usually require some investment and increase costs. For reducing the impact, similar approaches can be employed such as providing backup resources, authorizing parallel efforts, including redundancy in a system, and other such approaches, which can also be expensive.

- *Accept* The risk is accepted, either because no other response is available or because the responses are deemed too costly relative to the risk threat. This might be appropriate for non-critical threats, such as those in the "ignore" category of the risk matrix. For the critical threats, the project contractor should create a "contingency plan" so that if the threat does arise, everyone knows what actions will be taken to handle the threat. This might take the form of additional monetary or human resources, but the conditions for invoking the plan should be decided in advance so there is no confusion about whether the plan should be invoked.

We now consider the approaches for opportunities. Our discussion follows that for threat risks and many of the same ideas and examples discussed there can be applied here also.

- *Exploit* The goal here is to try to increase the probability the opportunity will occur. This might be done with higher quality resources, such as equipment, materials, or human skills, again at a cost.

- *Share* This involves partnering with another party or parties who can better capture the value of the opportunity, or at least reduce the cost of exploiting the opportunity. Joint ventures and risk-sharing partnerships are good examples of this approach.

- *Enhance* Like "mitigate" above, this involves either increasing the probability the opportunity risk will occur, or increasing its impact if it does. Again, additional resources are typically required, such as increasing the quality of the resources or the number of resources to either increase the probability or the impact of the opportunity, or both.

- *Accept* Here the project firm is prepared to capitalize on the opportunity should it occur (a contingency plan), but is not willing to invest the resources to improve the probability or impact of the opportunity occurring.

6. Risk Monitoring and Control

The topic of monitoring will be covered in detail in Chapter 11 and control in Chapter 12, so we defer our discussion of risk monitoring and control until we reach those chapters.

7. The Risk Management Register

If the risk management system has no memory, the task of risk identification will be horrendous. But the system can have a memory—at least the individuals in the system can remember. Relying on the recollections of individuals, however, is itself "risky." To ensure against this particular risk, the risk management system should maintain an up-to-date data register that includes, but is not restricted to, the following:

- identification of all environments that may impact on the project
- identification of all assumptions made in the preliminary project plan that may be a source of risk for the project
- a list of all risks identified by the risk management group, complete with their estimated impacts on the project and estimates of their probability of occurring
- a complete list of all "categories" and "key words" used to categorize risks, assumptions, and environments so that all risk management groups can access past work done on risk management
- the details of all qualitative and quantitative estimates made on risks, on states of the project's environment, or on project assumptions, complete with a brief description of the methods used to make such estimates
- minutes of all group meetings including all actions the group developed to deal with or mitigate each specific risk, including the decision to ignore a risk
- the actual outcomes of identified risks and, if a risk came to occur, the results of actions taken to mitigate or transfer the risk or invoke the contingency plan

If all this work on data collection is going to be of value to the parent organization beyond its use on the project at hand, the risk register must be available to anyone proposing to perform risk management on a project for the organization. Almost everything a risk management group does for any project should be retained in the risk register. Second, all risks must be categorized, the environments in which projects are conducted must be identified, and the methods used to deal with or mitigate them must be described.

The use of multiple key words and categories is critical because risk information must be available to managers of widely varied disciplines and backgrounds. Organizations may be conducting a great many projects at any given time. If each risk management team has to start from scratch, without reference to what has been learned by previous groups, the management of risk will be extremely expensive, take a great deal of time, and will not be particularly effective. Rest assured that even with all the experience of the past readily available, mistakes will occur. If past experience is not available, the mistakes of the past will be added to those of the future. Unfortunately, the literature on project risk management rarely mentions the value of system memory. (An exception to this generalization is Royer (2000) and the latest versions of PMBOK®.)

PMBOK Guide
11.2, 11.6

A final question remains. How well does risk management contribute to project success? In the IT industry, risk management is not associated with success, probably because it is rarely used (de Bakker et al., 2010). In those cases where it is used, with senior management support, it is influential in identifying risk. In the IT industry, however, identification rarely leads to the *management* of risk. In general, more attention is paid to risk identification than to responding to it or controlling it.

One final warning is appropriate to users of quantitative risk analysis methods. To quantify risk via simulation or any other scientific method is a reasonable picture of reality only to the extent that the assumptions made about the input data are accurate. Even if they are, such a picture of the future is not the same as managing it. As we have said elsewhere, models do not make decisions, people do. Risks should be understood, and once understood, people must decide what to do about them. Without this last step, risk identification and analysis are useless.

 ## SUMMARY

In this chapter we initiated planning for the project in terms of identifying and addressing the tasks required for project completion. We emphasized the importance of initial coordination of all parties involved and the smooth integration of the various systems required to achieve the project objectives. Then we described some tools such as the Work Breakdown Structure (WBS), the RACI matrix, and the Gozinto chart to aid in the planning process. We also briefly investigated several methods for controlling and reducing conflict in complex projects that use multidisciplinary teams. Last, we covered the process of risk management, for both threats and opportunities.

Specific points made in the chapter are these:

- The preliminary work plans are important because they serve as the basis for personnel selection, budgeting, scheduling, and control.

- Top management should be represented in the initial coordinating meeting where technical objectives are

established, participant responsibility is accepted, and preliminary budgets and schedules are defined.

- The approval and change processes are complex and should be handled by the project manager.

- Common elements of the project charter are the overview, statement of objectives/scope, general approach, contractual requirements, schedules, resources, personnel, risk management plans, and evaluation procedures.

- The hierarchical approach to project planning is most appropriate and can be aided by a tree diagram of project subsets, called a Gozinto chart, and a Work Breakdown Structure (WBS). The WBS relates the details of each subtask to its task and provides the final basis for the project budget, schedule, personnel, and control.

- A RACI matrix is often helpful to illustrate the relationship of personnel to project tasks and to identify where coordination is necessary.

- When multifunctional terms are used to plan complex projects, their task interfaces must be integrated and coordinated. The use of milestones and phase-gates throughout the project's schedule can help with this integration process.

- Risk management for both threats and opportunities has become increasingly important as projects become more complex and ill-defined. The seven subprocesses involved in managing the risks include helpful tools such as cause–effect diagrams, the risk matrix, FMEA, decision trees, simulation, a risk register, and a set of standard risk responses.

This topic completes our discussion of project activity planning. Next, we address the subject of budgeting and look at various budgeting methods. The chapter also addresses the issues of cost estimation and its difficulty, and simulation to handle budgetary risk of both costs and revenues.

GLOSSARY

Agile Project Planning An approach developed for software projects that interfaces with the customer on a short-cycle, iterative basis for constant replanning.

Bill of Materials The set of physical elements required to build a product.

Cause–Effect (Fishbone) Diagram A chart showing all the factors and subfactors that can lead to a particular threat or opportunity.

Control Chart A graph showing how a statistic is changing over time compared to its average and selected control limits.

Decision (or Probability) Tree A visual diagram showing the decision choices, event possibilities, and outcomes from the combination of both. The tree is solved by working backwards to identify the best choice.

Deliverables The physical items to be delivered from a project. This typically includes reports and plans as well as physical objects.

Earned Value A measure of project progress, frequently related to the planned cost of tasks accomplished.

Effectiveness Achieving the objectives set beforehand; to be distinguished from efficiency, which is measured by the output realized for the input used.

Engineering Change Orders Product improvements that engineering has designed after the initial product design was released.

Failure Mode and Effect Analysis (FMEA) A risk assessment process that multiplies the levels of probability, impact, and inability to detect the risk to arrive at an overall risk priority number.

Gozinto Chart A pictorial representation of a product that shows how the elements required to build a product fit together.

Hierarchical Planning A planning approach that breaks the planning task down into the activities that must be done at each managerial level. Typically, the upper level sets the objectives for the next lower level.

Integration Management Managing the problems that tend to occur between departments and disciplines, rather than within individual departments.

Materials Requirements Planning (MRP) A planning and material ordering approach based on the known or forecast final demand requirements, lead times for each fabricated or purchased item, and existing inventories of all items.

Milestones Natural subproject ending points where payments may occur, evaluations may be made, or progress may be reassessed.

Phase-Gates Preplanned points during the project where progress is assessed and the project cannot resume until re-authorization has been approved.

Project Charter A proposal for a project that summarizes the main aspects of the project for approval.

Project Plan The nominal plan for the entire project to which deviations will be compared.

RACI Matrix A table showing, for each project task, who is responsible, accountable, who can be consulted, and who needs to be informed. (Also known as a responsibility or assignment chart.)

Risk Matrix A chart showing probability on one side and impact on the other where threats and opportunities can be segmented into "critical," "monitor," and "ignore" cells.

Risk Register A database of risk information created by and available to project managers for their projects.

Simulation A process where the structure of a situation is programmed and the probability distributions of the events are selected to give a probability distribution for the variable of interest, such as time or cost.

Work Breakdown Structure (WBS) A description of all the tasks to complete a project, organized by some consistent perspective and containing a variety of information needed for that perspective.

Work Statement A description of a task that defines all the work required to accomplish it, including inputs and desired outputs.

QUESTIONS

Material Review Questions

1. Describe the approach of agile project management and how it differs from the normal approach.

2. Any successful project charter must contain nine key elements. List these items and briefly describe the composition of each.

3. What are the general steps for managing each work package within a specific project?

4. Describe the "hierarchical planning process" and explain why it is helpful.

5. What is shown on a RACI matrix? How is it useful to a PM?

6. What should be accomplished at the initial coordination meeting?

7. Why is it important for the functional areas to be involved in the project from the time of the original proposal?

8. What are the basic steps to design and use the Work Breakdown Structure?

9. What is the objective of interface management?

10. Contrast the Project Plan, the Project Charter, and the WBS.

11. Contrast milestones with phase-gates.

12. Describe how a risk matrix is constructed.

13. How would a decision tree be useful for a project manager?

14. Is the FMEA table more valuable than the risk matrix? Why (not)?

15. How far should the cause–effect diagram be broken down into subfactors?

16. Contrast the risk responses for threats and for opportunities.

Class Discussion Questions

17. What percentage of the total project effort do you think should be devoted to planning? Why?

18. Why do you suppose that the coordination of the various elements of the project is considered the most difficult aspect of project implementation?

19. What kinds of risk categories might be included in the project charter?

20. In what ways may the WBS be used as a key document to monitor and control a project?

21. Describe the process of subdivision of activities and events that composes the tree diagram known as the Work Breakdown Structure or Gozinto chart. Why is the input of responsible managers and workers so important an aspect of this process?

22. Why is project planning so important?

23. What are the pros and cons concerning the early participation of the various functional areas in the project plan?

24. Task 5-C is the critical, pacing task of a rush project. Fred always nitpicks anything that comes his way, slowing it down, driving up its costs, and irritating everyone concerned. Normally, Fred would be listed as "Notify" for task 5-C on the responsibility matrix, but the PM is considering "forgetting" to make that notation on the chart. Is this unethical, political, or just smart management?

25. How might we plan for risks that we cannot identify in the risk management section of the project charter?

26. Might milestones and phase-gates both occur at the same point of a project? Will the same activities be happening?

27. Why was agile project management developed? Do you think this might be the way of the future for project management?

28. Compare the advantages of risk matrices vs. FEMA tables for project management use.

29. Contrast decision trees and probability trees. How might each be used by project managers? Which would be the more valuable?

30. Could a cause–effect chart be used for two different risks at the same time? Would the end "problem" be the result of one risk or both concurrently?

31. Are the risk responses for threats or opportunities more important for project managers? Why?

Beagle 2 Mars Probe a Planning Failure

32. What should the project manager have done about the challenges facing this project?

33. Are the recommendations complete? Would you add anything else?

Child Support Software a Victim of Scope Creep

34. What was the source of the problem here?

35. What would you suggest to recover the project?

Timetable Scheduling and Operational Plan Generation for London Underground

36. What were the complexities involved in developing and maintaining the timetable and operational plan for London Underground?

37. Why was the timetable system upgraded and what benefits were delivered?

Facebook Risks Interruption to Move a Terabyte

38. Would you consider the completion of the first hardware phase a milestone or a phase-gate review?

39. What type of risk responses did Facebook use?

40. What other approaches might Facebook have used to handle the risks? (Hint: consider the seven risk subprocesses.)

Disaster Project Planning in Iceland

41. Given a nation so prone to disasters, why do you think it took so long to formulate a contingency disaster plan?

42. The directed reading at the end of this chapter describes four tools for crises in projects. Might any of these be useful to Iceland in the future?

Trying to Install a Wind Farm in the Middle of the North Sea

43. Contrast the difficulties and risks of this project with those of NASA in the "Ignoring Risk . . ." PMIP sidebar.

44. How important was it to have just the right competencies and dependabilities on the multidisciplinary teams?

45. Relate the detail of their "quality planning for each key event" to what you might expect their WBS to look like.

An Acquisition Failure Questions Recommended Practice

46. Do long project durations in other industries also lead to conflicts and project problems?

47. Was the difficulty in this situation due to the upset ABN Amro employees, or were there more serious project planning problems?

48. Do you agree with the "solution" exemplified by BNP? Might there be some compromise plan?

Risk Analysis vs. Budget/Schedule Requirements in Australia

49. If striving to meet schedule or budget isn't top priority, what is?

50. What type of risk analysis approach would have been most appropriate in this situation?

Ignoring Risk Contrasted with Recognizing Risk in Two Industries

51. What do you think are the reasons BP took such a relaxed attitude toward the Gulf well compared to NASA?

52. Why hasn't the oil industry funded research and technology for oil spill cleanup efforts, do you think?

53. Why didn't a billion dollar firm have a public relations department prepared for the contingency of a massive oil spill?

54. Compare NASA's approach with risk analysis as described in the chapter. Then with FMEA. What's the same? What's different?

PROBLEMS

1. Top administrators in a university hospital have approved a project to improve the efficiency of the pharmaceutical services department by the end of the fiscal year to satisfy new state regulations for the coming year. However, they are concerned about four potential threats: (1) The cost to implement the changes may be excessive, (2) The pharmacists may resist the changes, (3) The project may run much longer than expected and not be ready for the coming fiscal year, (4) The changes might reduce the quality of drug care in the hospital. The likelihood and negative impact of each threat have been solicited from the managers by a three-round Delphi process and are as follows, based on a seven-point scale where seven is the most likely and most negative impact:

Threat	Probability	Impact
1	5	3
2	6	5
3	3	4
4	4	7

Construct a risk matrix and identify what you would consider to be the "critical," "monitor," and "ignore" threats. Explain your reasoning. Recommend and justify a risk response for each threat.

2. The project manager for the project in Problem 1 has estimated the probabilities of not detecting the risks in time to react to them as follows, again on a seven-point

scale: Threat 1: 4, Threat 2: 1, Threat 3: 3, Threat 4: 6. Construct a FMEA table to determine which risks are now the "critical," "monitor," and "ignore" threats. How have they changed from Problem 1? Why? Does this new ranking seem more realistic?

3. Assume you are in a degree program in college and are concerned about getting your degree. Create a fishbone (cause–effect) diagram, with "failure to get degree" as the problem outcome. Identify at least four possible threat risks for this problem to occur. Then for each threat list at least three reasons/factors for how that threat could conceivably come to pass. Finally, review your diagram to estimate probabilities and impacts of each threat to getting your degree. Based on this analysis, what threats and factors should you direct your attention to, as the project manager of your project to get your degree.

4. The yearly demand for a seasonal, profitable item follows the distribution below:

Demand (units)	Probability
1,000	.20
2,000	.30
3,000	.40
4,000	.10

A manufacturer is considering launching a project to produce this item and could produce it by one of three methods:

a. Use existing tools at a cost of $6 per unit.

b. Buy cheap, special equipment for $1,000. The value of the equipment at the end of the year (salvage value) is zero. The cost would be reduced to $3 per unit.

c. Buy high-quality, special equipment for $10,000 that can be depreciated over four years (one fourth of the cost each year). The cost with this equipment would be only $2 per unit.

Set up this project as a decision tree to find whether the manufacturer should approve this project, and if so, which method of production to use to maximize profit. *Hint:* Compare total annual costs. Assume production must meet all demand; each unit demanded and sold means more profit.

5. Given the decision tree below for a two-stage (decision) project to enter a joint venture, find the best alternatives (among a_1-a_6 in the figure) and their expected values. The outcomes shown are *revenues* and the investment expenses are in parentheses. Node 4 represents the situation where alternative a_1 was chosen, and then the top outcome with a 70% probability occurred; note that there is no choice of alternative if the 30% probability outcome occurred. Similarly with Node 5.

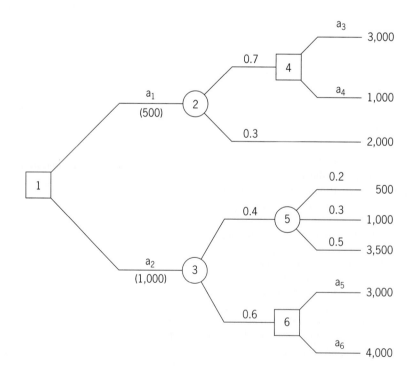

6. Medidata Inc. has identified three risk opportunities for their new medical database project. One is an opportunity to extend the database to include doctors as well as hospitals. This has a probability of a 3 and an impact on their profitability of a 3 on a 1–5 scale, where higher numbers are greater values of probability and profitability. Another is the opportunity to extend the database to other countries, particularly in Europe. For this, the probability is ranked only a 2 but the profitability impact is considered to be 4 to the higher social interest by European governments. Lastly, they might be able to interest nonusers such as pharmaceutical firms in using, or perhaps buying, their data. Here the probability is more certain, a 4, but the profitability would be only a 2. Construct an opportunity risk matrix, identify the "critical," "monitor," and "ignore" opportunities, and recommend risk responses for each opportunity.

INCIDENTS FOR DISCUSSION

Ringold's Pool and Patio Supply

John Ringold, Jr., just graduated from a local university with a degree in industrial management and joined his father's company as executive vice-president of operations. Dad wants to break John in slowly and has decided to see how he can do on a project that John Sr. has never had time to investigate. Twenty percent of the company's sales are derived from the sale of above-ground swimming pool kits. Ringold's does not install the pools. John Sr. has asked John Jr. to determine whether or not they should get into that business. John Jr. has decided that the easiest way to impress Dad and get the project done is personally to estimate the cost to the company of setting up a pool and then call some competitors and see how much they charge. That will show whether or not it is profitable.

John Jr. remembered a method called the work breakdown structure (WBS) that he thought might serve as a useful tool to estimate costs. Also, the use of such a tool could be passed along to the site supervisor to help evaluate the performance of work crews. John Jr.'s WBS is shown in Table A. The total cost John Jr. calculated was $185.00, based on 12.33 labor-hours at $15.00/labor-hour. John Jr. found that, on average, Ringold's competitors charged $229.00 to install a similar pool. John Jr. thought he had a winner. He called his father and made an appointment to present his findings the next morning. Since he had never assembled a pool himself, he decided to increase the budget by 10 percent, "just in case."

Questions: Is John Jr.'s WBS projection reasonable? What aspects of the decision will John Sr. consider?

Stacee Laboratories

Stacee Labs, the research subsidiary of Stacee Pharmaceuticals, Inc., has a long history of successful research and development of medical drugs. The work is conducted by standalone project teams of scientists that operate with little

Table A Pool Installation WBS

Works Tasks		Labor-Hours (estimated)
Prepare ground surface		2.67
Clear	1	
Rake	$\frac{1}{3}$	
Level	1	
Sand bottom	$\frac{1}{3}$	
Lay out pool frame		2.50
Bottom ring	1	
Side panels	$\frac{1}{2}$	
Top ring	1	
Add plastic liner		0.50
Assemble pool		1.66
Build wooden support		3.00
Layout	1	
Assemble	2	
Fill and test		2.00
Total		12.33

in the way of schedules, budgets, and precisely predefined objectives. The parent company's management felt that scientific research teams should not be encumbered with bureaucratic record-keeping chores, and their work should go where their inspiration takes them.

A Special Committee of Stacee Pharm's Board of Directors has completed a study of Stacee Labs and has found that its projects required a significantly longer time to complete than the industry average and, as a result, were significantly more expensive. These projects often lasted 10–15 years before the drug could be released to the market. At the same time, Stacee Labs projects had a very high success rate.

The board called in a management consultant, Ms. Millie Tasha, and asked her to investigate the research organization briefly and report to the board on ways in which the projects could be completed sooner and at lower expense. The board emphasized that it was not seeking nit-picking, cost-cutting, or time-saving recommendations that might lower the quality of Stacee Labs's results.

Ms. Tasha returned after several weeks of interviews with the lab's researchers as well as with senior representatives of the parent firm's Marketing, Finance, Government Relations, and Drug Efficacy Test Divisions, as well as the Toxicity Test Department. Her report to the Board began with the observation that lab scientists avoided contact with Marketing and Governmental Relations until they had accomplished most of their work on a specific drug family. When asked why they waited so long to involve marketing, they responded that they did not know what specific products they would recommend for sale until they had completed and tested the results of their work. They added that marketing was always trying to interfere with drug design and wanted them to make exaggerated claims or to design drugs based on sales potential rather than on good science.

Ms. Tasha also noted that lab scientists did not contact the toxicity or efficacy testing groups until scientific work was completed and they had a drug to test. This resulted in long delays because the testing groups were usually occupied with other matters and could not handle the tests promptly. It usually took many months to organize and begin both toxicity and efficacy testing.

In Ms. Tasha's opinion, the only way to make significant cuts in the time and cost required for drug research projects was to form an integrated team composed of representatives of all the groups who had a major role to play in each drug project and to have them involved from the beginning of the project. All parties could then follow progress with drug development and be prepared to make timely contributions to the projects. If this were done, long delays and their associated costs would be significantly reduced.

Questions: Do you think Millie Tasha is right? If so, how should new drug projects be planned and organized? If Stacee Pharmaceutical goes ahead with a reorganization of lab projects, what are the potential problems? How would you deal with them? Could scope creep become more of a problem with the new integrated teams? If so, how should it be controlled?

CONTINUING INTEGRATIVE CLASS PROJECT

It is now time to plan the project tasks and make assignments. First, create a work breakdown structure and a RACI matrix for the project. Identify any milestones and phase-gates. Evaluate the risks using the seven subprocesses and any appropriate tools. Make sure everyone is aware of their role in the project, their specific deadlines, and the available resources.

BIBLIOGRAPHY

Aaron, J. M., C. P. Bratta, and D. P. Smith. "Achieving Total Project Control Using the Quality Gate Method." *Proceedings of the Annual Symposium of the Project Management Institute,* San Diego, October 4, 1993.

Antonioni, D. "Post-Planning Review Prevents Poor Project Performance." *PM Network,* October 1997.

Bailetti, A. J., J. R. Callahan, and P. Di-Pietro. "A Coordination Structure Approach to the Management of Projects." *IEEE Transactions on Engineering Management,* November 1994.

Bigelow, D. "Planning Is Important—Why Don't We Do More of It?" *PM Network,* July 1998.

Champion, D. "Managing Risk in the New World." *Harvard Business Review,* October 2009.

Chi-Cheng, H. "Knowledge Sharing and Group Cohesiveness on Performance: An Empirical Study of Technology R&D Teams in Taiwan." *Technovation,* November 2009.

Christensen, P. J., and Rydberg, J. "Overcoming Obstacles." *PM Network,* November 2001.

Cooper, R.G., and E. J. Kleinschmidt, "Stage-Gate Systems for New Product Success," *Marketing Management,* Vol. 1, No. 4, 1993.

Dalkey, N. C. The Delphi Method: An Experimental Study of Group Opinion (RM-5888-PR). Santa Monica, CA: The Rand Corporation, June 1969.

de Bakker, K., A. Boonstra, and H. Wortmann, "Does Risk Management Contribute to IT Project Success? A Meta-Analysis of Empirical Evidence." *International Journal of Project Management.* Vol. 28, No. 5, 2010.

de Laat, P. B. "Matrix Management of Projects and Power Struggles: A Case Study of an R & D Laboratory." *IEEE Engineering Management Review,* Winter 1995, reprinted from *Human Relations,* Vol. 47, No. 9, 1994.

Fewell, J., "Led Astray." *PM Network,* October 2010.

Ford, R. C., and F. S. McLaughlin. "Successful Project Teams: A Study of MIS Managers." *IEEE Transactions on Engineering Management,* November 1992.

Hass, K. B. "The Blending of Traditional and Agile Project Management." *PM World Today,* May 2007.

Hauptman, O., and K. K. Hirji. "The Influence of Process Concurrency on Project Outcomes in Product Development: An Empirical Study of Cross-Functional Teams." *IEEE Transactions on Engineering Management,* May 1996.

Hildebrand, C. "Agile." *PM Network.* August 2010.

Hubbard, D. G. "Work Structuring," in P. C. Dinsmore, ed., *The AMA Handbook of Project Management.* New York: AMACOM, 1993.

Hunsberger, K. "Change Is Good." *PM Network.* February 2011.

Jiang, J. J., and G. Klein. "Software Project Risks and Development Focus." *Project Management Journal,* March 2001.

Kalu, T. Ch. U. "A Framework for the Management of Projects in Complex Organizations." *IEEE Transactions on Engineering Management,* May 1993.

Knutson, J. "How to Manage a Project Launch Meeting." *PM Network,* July 1995.

Langley, A. "Between 'Paralysis by Analysis' and 'Extinction by Instinct.'" *IEEE Engineering Management Review,* Fall 1995, reprinted from *Sloan Management Review,* Spring 1995.

Martin, P. K., and K. Tate. "Kick Off the Smart Way." *PM Network.* October 1998.

Martinez, E. V. "Executives to Project Manager: Get a Plan." *PM Network,* October 1994.

Meredith, J. R., S. M. Shafer, and E. Turban. *Quantitative Business Modeling.* Cincinnati, OH: Southwestern, 2002.

Meredith, J. R. and S. M. Shafer. *Operations Management for MBAs.* Hoboken, NJ: Wiley, 2010.

Morris, W. T. *Implementation Strategies for Industrial Engineers.* Columbus, OH: Grid, 1979.

Paley, A. I. "Value Engineering and Project Management: Achieving Cost Optimization," in P. C. Dinsmore, ed., *The AMA Handbook of Project Management.* New York: AMACOM, 1993.

Project Management Institute. *A Guide to the Project Management Body of Knowledge (PMBOK® Guide),* 3rd ed., Newtown Square, PA: Project Management Institute, 2004.

Royer, P. S. "Risk Management: The Undiscovered Dimension of Project Management." *PM Network,* September 2000. An extended version of this article appears in *Project Management Journal,* March 2000.

Seigle, G. "Government Projects: Expect the Unexpected." *PM Network,* November 2001.

Sheffi, Y. *The Resilient Enterprise.* Cambridge, MA: MIT Press, 2005.

Stamatis, D. H. *Failure Mode and Effect Analysis: FMEA from Theory to Execution,* 2nd ed. ASQ Quality Press, 2003.

Taleb, N. N., D. G. Goldstein, and M. W. Spitznagel. "The Six Mistakes Executives Make in Risk Management." *Harvard Business Review,* October 2009.

Ward, S. "Requirements for an Effective Project Risk Management Process." *Project Management Journal,* September 1999.

Whitten, N. "Do Not Make Long-Term Project Commitments." *PM Network,* February 2002.

Zwikael, O., and A. Sadeh. "Planning Effort as an Effective Risk Management Tool," *Journal of Operations Management,* Vol. 25, pp. 755–767, 2007.

 The following case illustrates the development of a project planning, management, and control system for large capital engineering projects. Senior management's goal in developing the system was primarily financial, in terms of keeping projects from exceeding budget and optimally allocate increasingly scarce investment funds. It is interesting to compare this system to that of Hewlett-Packard in the reading in Chapter 2.

C A S E

CAPRICO
Eric Woodcock

Caprico is a large maker of domestic electrical appliances based in Brazil. The firm started out in the 1970s making refrigerators, and expanded both organically and through acquisition. It now has subsidiaries (Groups) in Brazil which make washing machines, dishwashers, air conditioners, fridges and freezers, as well as smaller items like kettles and food mixers.

The Brazilian economy has grown strongly, and Caprico has also become a supplier to other markets—notably in South America, Southern Africa and Australasia. This growth has required projects to build and equip the factories to make the first products, and subsequently re-equip those factories as new products came out. The engineering department of each subsidiary has always had responsibility for planning and monitoring such projects. Project teams are ultimately answerable to the Vice President of Production in each subsidiary.

Partly because of its history of taking over established businesses, Caprico did not have a standard approach to engineering investment appraisal, or monitoring engineering projects at the management level once they are under way. Certainly there had been occasions when engineering projects went far over budget or a crucial product had been late to market. This was more of a concern as Brazil became a target market for the world's largest domestic appliance makers. Also, legislation affecting how capital spending is treated in company accounts meant that depreciation allowances were not keeping pace with inflation.

Traditionally the way most engineering projects had been appraised had been on the basis of a cost–benefit analysis, in other words, whether the investment was expected to pay off in purely financial terms. Appraisals did not usually consider the non-financial aims of projects (such as increasing customer satisfaction, for example). There had also been little effort to understand how well projects actually achieved their aims after they were finished. This also led to one project that made the most sense in purely financial terms getting approved over one that made much more sense in marketing terms. This traditional approach is illustrated in Figure 1.

Figure 1 Capital project progress prior to AGP

In response to these issues, Caprico's top management team decided to develop a corporate approach to project approval and management. Not only should this improve project outcomes, but it should also help to bind the company subsidiaries together. The task of developing the system (called "Evaluation and Management of Projects," which can be abbreviated as "AGP" in Portugese) was given to the Group Vice President for Production.

The Production VP decided to engage an external consultant to act as the architect of the AGP. After a short selection process, a consultant was appointed who was formerly head of manufacturing in the local subsidiary of an American electrical goods company and so had a clear insight into the issues faced by Caprico. He was also able to show an empathy with the style and goals of Caprico and the ability to communicate and work with staff at all levels. Alongside the external consultant would be an internal representative. The post was advertised on the internal vacancies board and 10 people came forward to apply, many seeing it as a good career development move. In the end an engineering project manager from the kitchen appliances subsidiary was chosen. The team of two would report to the Production VP and a small steering committee he had selected.

The AGP duo devised a phased approach to the development and roll out of the new system, in discussion with the Production VP. In particular, four principles were agreed:

- There would not be a "one size fits all" standard AGP across the business. The various businesses had different scales of investment, time scales of projects, and internal systems. A standard process might save some initial cost (and be easier for corporate staff to use across the business), but it would be too inflexible and probably add a good deal of unnecessary bureaucracy to many smaller projects.

- The directors of the engineering departments of the various business units would be fully involved in the development, to make sure that issues were recognised and dealt with, and—very importantly—to make sure they became committed champions and users of the new system.

- The emphasis of the AGP would be on effective planning, not on ways to recover from mistakes due to a lack of planning.

- Engineering managers would be given the time and budget to work as a group at Caprico headquarters to play their part in the development of the AGP.

Four phases were identified for the programme. At all stages the steering committee would receive regular reports of progress, and meetings would be held at the end of each phase to endorse what had been achieved. Based on their initial work, the team produced a short justification for their projects, which is shown in Figure 2.

With the principles and governance structure in place, it was possible for the two person project team to plan how the AGP development would be carried out. Indeed, the plan for the AGP would, in many ways, be a prototype for how project planning and monitoring would be done in future at Caprico.

External and internal factors make it urgent to ensure most efficient use of capital funds. Implementation of a project evaluation and management (AGP) system has been chosen as one way to improve the use of capital funds. In March the Corporate Management Committee defined this need.

Subsequently, Corporate Facilities and Manufacturing Planning performed a feasibility study on this subject. A major conclusion of the study was to develop the system internally rather than use an "off the shelf" system. An internally developed system can be tailored to the individual Groups, giving flexibility which is felt to be essential to success. Another conclusion of the study was to involve Group engineering managers in the design and implementation of the system for better understanding and acceptance.

This is the detailed plan for the design and implementation of a corporate-wide AGP system. The short-term target of the system is major capital projects; the long-term target is other types of projects, such as new product development and R&D projects. The schedule and cost are:

Completion date: 1 year from approval
Cost (in Brazilian Reais): R$200,000, of which R$60,000 is out of pocket.

Figure 2 Introduction to the AGP project plan

Here is how the AGP development was carried out.

Phase 1. Seminar for engineering department managers. A three-day seminar was held for all the engineering managers across the divisions, together with relevant staff from finance, IT and other areas who would have a major role in engineering project evaluation and management. The event began by giving all the engineering managers a short foundation course in project management. This ensured everyone understood the basic principles that are common to all well-run projects. Then everyone was taken through the corporate objectives for AGP and the approach to developing it, including their role in helping the process. The general reaction was a mixture of understanding why something had to be done, but also scepticism about how successful it would be.

Phase 2. AGP system design. Three weeks was allowed after the seminar so that the engineering managers could consider what they had heard, and for the programme team to gather views and opinions. Then a formal two-day gathering of the engineering managers was convened at Caprico headquarters to define the system. The work defined how projects would be planned and managed to a fair level of detail, including how matters like work scheduled, resource allocation, and cost allocation would be dealt with. A key role of the external consultant was to address concerns and criticisms as an outsider, thereby avoiding any internal conflict within Caprico. The aim was full consensus. On those aspects where everyone could not agree, the matter was taken away for resolution.

Phase 3. Project system development. Armed with agreed principles for the specification of the AGP and how it should work, the programme team could develop the system itself. Areas where there had not been consensus were addressed by a series of meetings to resolve differences. Only once did the Production VP have to decide on a point where agreement could not be reached.

The design of the AGP took almost four months. The contents of the AGP, and how it is intended to be used, are described later on.

Phase 4. Implementation. The AGP would be rolled out across the Caprico divisions in accordance with the plan defined in Phase 3. An important part of the roll out would be a process to monitor the effectiveness of the AGP and enable the Caprico main board to evaluate its early results.

The project plan defined in Phase 3 defined how any project should be described, in a manner that would justify its approval and allow it to be managed. The team identified a menu of 10 sections that can be included in the plan for a new project.

The sections are:

- Introduction
- Objectives
- Project structure
- Project costs
- Task network
- Project schedule
- Resource allocation
- Organisation and accountability
- Project control system
- Milestones and project sub-divisions

The team gave advice on which elements from the menu might be required, depending on the size and perceived risk of a project. Corporate staff would require comprehensive analysis on major or critical projects, whereas local project managers would be able to decide how much detail to include for smaller routine projects.

Introduction

The introduction provides an overview of the overall project. It provides an executive summary of the whole plan in language that can be understood by the corporate financial, legal, IT and other staff, as well as the engineers. It can be used by the project manager to explain the project to the project team, so that by understanding why the project is being done the team become much more committed to its success. It addresses the key questions about the project, in particular: What type of project is proposed? What is the cost-benefit relationship? What are the contingency plans in case risks materialise? Why is the project being done this way (and what alternatives have been examined)?

Objectives

The objectives of a project must be described in terms of what is to be delivered. This forces a clear and measurable definition of the scope of the project. This can be described as a Statement of Work. The description of the deliverables is part of this, but the detailed specification of those deliverables is provided as an appendix. Deliverables include not only physical items, like a production line, but also documentation, training, maintenance arrangements, etc. This focus on deliverables reduces the chance that something important will be forgotten.

Figure 3 uses the objectives of the AGP project itself as an example of project objectives.

Project Structure

The project manager must design the structure of the project to:

- Relate the specific objectives of the project to the general objectives of the business unit.
- Define the elements which, when added together, will create the deliverables.
- Define the tasks which must be done in order to create each of the elements.
- Show the hierarchical relationships between objectives, elements and tasks.

The Work Breakdown Structure is the method used to do this. The WBS is often shown as a diagram with a hierarchy of boxes, each of which represents a task. It shows how the tasks relate to each other through the connections between the lines. There is a convention for how this diagram is drawn, including how tasks are numbered.

Using a pictorial rather than a text-based WBS makes it easier to add extra bits of information into the boxes, such as time, budget or resourcing details. Figure 4 gives a text-based WBS which can be converted into a box-style format.

Project Costs

The creation of the WBS allows all the tasks to be identified and the exact scope of the project work to be established. From this information it is possible to carry out a preliminary estimate of the costs of doing the project. The estimate is a "first pass." Later work on the schedule and resources may reveal that extra time or money is needed because, for example, the same person cannot be doing two different tasks at the same time. Estimates are

---

General objectives

1. Enable better communication between Group and Corporate management with regard to the progress of major projects.

   - Enable Group management to more closely monitor the progress of major projects.
   - Provide the capability for Group personnel to better manage and control major projects.

*Specific Objectives**

1. Reporting and Control System
   - For communication of project activity within the Group and between Group and Corporate.
   - Initially for high-cost capital projects, then for "critical," then all others.

2. Procedures Manual
   - Document procedures and policies.
   - Preliminary manual available by 30 October 2012 for use in general educational seminars.

3. Computer Support Systems
   - Survey with recommendations to establish the need for and value of computer support.

4. General Educational Package
   - Provide basic project planning and control skills to personnel directly involved in project management, to be conducted by an academic authority in field.
   - Technical seminars in construction, engineering, contract administration and financial aspects of project management.

* Defined at the AGP Workshop, attended by representatives of Operating Groups.

Figure 3 Objectives of the AGP project

made at the lowest level of individual tasks in the WBS, known as work packages. A work package is a discrete piece of work which has a clear input and output and can be managed as a self-contained unit. Figure 5 shows the estimated cost of the AGP project.

Work Breakdown Structure
Caprico AGP project
1000 Project plan
2000 AGP system
2100 Design phase reports
2101 Analyse project scope
2102 Define performance reports
2103 Define project planning
2104 Define revision procedure
2105 Define approval and sign-off procedure
-
-
2121 Define record retention policy
2122 Define computer support systems requirements
2200 Procedures manual
2201 Procedures manual
2202 Final manual
2300 Reporting and control system
2301 Computer support survey
2302 PERT/CPM
2303 Scheduling
2304 Accounting
3000 General training
3100 Project planning and control seminar
3101 Objective setting
3102 WBS
-

Figure 4   Project structure

Task network

Laying out the tasks from the WBS in a task network structure allows the sequence of the project to be understood, especially how tasks interrelate to each other and where tasks can run in parallel (thereby reducing the project's overall duration). The team noted that on a number of Caprico projects no attempt was made to see whether any tasks could be done simultaneously, losing a potential opportunity to save time and cost.

The AGP does not require a task network for very small projects, but on large ones it is considered vital. It shows the critical path, and helps with detailed

Labour costs	
Development and design	R\$40,000
Attendees' time in sessions	R\$60,000
Start up time of GAP in Group	R\$40,000
Basic educational package	
Consultants' fees	R\$20,000
Attendees' travel and expenses	R\$30,000
Miscellaneous	R\$10,000
Total project cost	**R\$200,000**
Out of pocket costs:R\$60,000	

Figure 5   Project costs

planning, implementation and control. On the other hand, the version of the task network used for the project plan document and also for routine project monitoring should not contain more than 50 nodes. More than that would make the overall picture of the project hard to interpret. In a very large project, stages of the project can be represented with a few nodes on the summary network. At the stage level this part can be expanded into another network, again with up to 50 nodes.

Schedule and resource allocations

The project manager can take the information from the task network and create a project schedule. The Gantt chart format is a familiar and practical way to do this. This schedule must reflect standard work patterns, weekends, public holidays, plant and supplier shutdowns, etc., and also make realistic allowances for staff absence, training time, etc.

By adding the resource information (who does which tasks) it is possible to see on the Gantt chart instances where the same person might be assigned to do two tasks at the same time. Carrying out 'resource levelling' ensures this does not happen but may have the effect of making the project take slightly longer and cost a bit more.

Organisation and accountability

The project plan must make it clear who is responsible for managing each task and producing the agreed deliverable. This responsibility cannot be shared, and the name of the person in charge must be shown on the WBS.

For each task a responsibility matrix should be produced. This will show who is responsible for the task, but also those individuals whose authority to proceed must be obtained, who will actually do the work, who must be consulted, who may provide advice, and who will sign off the deliverable as complete. It may be that a department or individual doesn't need to be directly involved to complete the task or the project, but they may be consulted to enlist their support.

Figure 6 shows the accountability matrix for the AGP project.

Project control system

The project manager may have in place a means to monitor how well the project is doing against its time, cost and performance targets at any point. Using information gathered from timesheets, cost reports, test reports, etc., the project manager can detect whether any part of the project is drifting outside the allowable variance limits.

There is a change control process by which the project manager will assess the variance, discover its cause, plan, and then take corrective action. That may involve making adjustments to the overall project plan. Figure 7 shows how the feedback loop of control works.

Figure 8 shows the nature of the periodic reviews used for project control and their timing.

Milestones and project sub-divisions

Significant points in the project are marked with milestones. These may be points at which an important

			Engineering managers					
Activity	*AGP manager*	*Consultant*	*Small appliances Group*	*Washing and drying Group*	*Household appliances Group*	*Heating, ventilation and air conditioning Group*	*Production Vice President (Corporate)*
Project plan	I	P					A
Design-phase reports	I	P	P	P	P	P	
Procedures manual	I						A
Reporting and control system	I	P	P	P	P	P	
Computer support survey	I	P					P
Project planning and control seminar	A	I					P
Technical seminars	I		P	P	P	P	A

Legend: I = Initiate/responsibility
A = Approve
P = Provide input

Figure 6 Accountability matrix for the AGP project

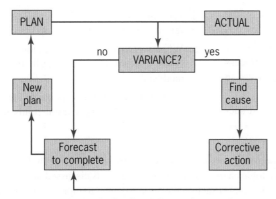

Figure 7 The basic feedback loop of control

1. Periodic status checking will be performed monthly.
2. Labour costs will be collected manually and estimated where necessary from discussion with Group engineering department.
3. Out-of-pocket costs will be collected through commitments and/or invoice payment records.
4. Monthly status reports will be issued by the AGP project manager including:
   a. Cost to date summaries
   b. Cost variances
   c. Schedule performance relative to schedule in Gantt format
   d. Changes in scope or other modifications to plan
5. Informal control will be exercised through milestone anticipation by the AGP project manager.

Figure 8   Control system

Date	*Milestone*
5th September	Project plan approved by both Corporate and Groups
26th September	Reporting and control system approved by Corporate and Groups
5th October	Organisational impact analysis report issued
7th October	Basic project planning and control seminars completed
24th March	Final procedures manual approved
	Technical seminars completed
30th June	Final impact assessment report issued

Figure 9   Milestones

deliverable has to be signed off, an important decision has to be taken, or significant funds have to be committed. Milestones are often at the end of stages.

The project should be broken up into logical subdivisions, each one typically being a series of connected tasks within the WBS. Figure 9 shows the milestones for the AGP project.

Summary

The programme team completed the design of the Project Evaluation and Management of Projects (AGP) system 12 months ago. The implementation went relatively smoothly, thanks to the ongoing consultation with the engineering managers at every step, and the regular reviews by the corporate steering committee. The roll out of AGP began with three smaller subsidiaries, and six months later the four large subsidiaries adopted it with minor changes.

Overall reaction to the system has been positive. A number of small projects have gone through the whole sequence, and although one had a serious time overrun, in general, performance was better than on projects managed using the old systems. It is too early to be sure that the system is delivering against the non-financial objectives (such as improved corporate reputation and higher customer satisfaction), but early indications are that projects are much more in tune with the needs of the external market.

 QUESTIONS

1. Which of the project planning aids described in the chapter was used in the case study? How were they different from the versions described in this chapter?
2. Compare this project with the Project Portfolio Process and Hewlett-Packard's project management process in the reading for Chapter 2.
3. What was the purpose of the AGP project? Was it successful?
4. Why are the WBS and Linear Responsibility Chart different in design to the ones in the chapter?
5. What was wrong with the previous focus on cost-benefit? Does the AGP system still include a cost-benefit analysis?
6. Why did changing depreciation legislation increase the importance of using capital funds in the most efficient way?

 The following reading applies the planning tools from emergency management to projects with their inevitable crises. The application of risk analysis, contingency plans, logic charts, and tabletop exercises is discussed in terms of both planning for and managing crises when they actually occur. Examples such as the 1996 Atlanta Olympic Games are used to illustrate the effectiveness of crisis planning tools.

DIRECTED READING

PLANNING FOR CRISES IN PROJECT MANAGEMENT*
L. M. Mallak, H. A. Kurstedt, Jr., G. A. Patzak

Project managers can't always foresee every contingency when planning and managing their projects. Many spurious events affecting project milestones and resource allocations can surface once the project is under way. Experienced project managers find crises, miscommunications, mistakes, oversights, and disasters must be managed as part of successful project management.

Project managers need effective tools to plan for and anticipate these crises. These are tools project managers may not use every day, yet they need these tools to serve them in time of emergency. The ideas and information in this paper will help project managers identify the appropriate crisis planning tools and how to use them. The project manager's experience, training, and skills should allow the understanding and use of these emergency management tools to support quicker and better decision making. In a crisis the worst decision is no decision and the second worst decision is a late one (Sawle, 1991). Managing crises better means mitigating and preparing for crises so we can reduce their occurrence and manage the consequences better if crises do occur. Based on the authors' experience in emergency management for the public and private sectors and several experiences shared in the literature, we recommend ways of planning for crises in projects.

We offer a brief list of emergency management planning tools and skills for project managers: risk analyses, contingency plans, logic charts, and tabletop exercises. These tools have different uses in different types of crises, whether they are natural, chemical/technological, or security types of crises. They also require different kinds of support—police, fire, medical, rescue, etc.

Crises are analyzed from the project management perspective, identifying the similarities and differences between crises in project management and crises in general. We discuss crisis planning strategies and tools by looking at the tools used for emergency management and investigating how we can modify them or design new tools for crisis management in projects.

Framing the Crisis

Many crises become projects once the deleterious effects are gone. A commercial airline crash, such as TWA 800 in summer 1996, where all passengers and crew died, is managed as a project once the threat of explosion and other immediate dangers diminish. However, we're concerned with crises occurring within an existing project, rather than a crisis or emergency that becomes a project.

In many of emergency management's phases and types, the primary skills required are project management skills we're already familiar with. When we're in an emergency situation and we're in the mitigation, preparedness, or recovery phase in a chronic, long-term emergency, we can readily apply our project management skills. The focus of this paper is the use of emergency management tools to aid in anticipating and planning for crises in projects. Project managers need additional tools to respond to acute emergencies—here is where emergency management tools become paramount.

The scope of application for emergency management tools will vary based on the size of the project. The tools can be quite elaborate, such as many volumes of a risk analysis or reserved space for an emergency operations center (EOC) with many dedicated phone lines. The tools can also be quite simple, such as a one to two-page list of risks in priority order or a designated office or conference room (to function as a mini-EOC) with the ability to bring in portable phones. All the tools should be used, even if just in simple form. In a small project, using one hour of a staff meeting to assign roles in the event of a crisis may suffice for more elaborate means in a larger project. The elaborateness of tools should be balanced with the cost and time required for preparation.

Typical project management requires attention to issues of cost, schedule, and quality. As the customer demands for quality increase, either the cost or the schedule must yield to balance these new demands. But at what point do increased demands reach a crisis point? Increased demands may lead to a perplexity. A perplexity is "an event with an unknown start and an unknown end." An example of a perplexity is an earthquake centered around the New Madrid (Mo.) fault line—we don't know when the earthquake will occur, for how long, nor what the extent of damage will be. In fact, the earthquake may not occur in our lifetime. The opposite of a perplexity is a process, an event with a known start and a known end and the cycle is constantly repeated (as in a manufacturing process). The concept of perplexity helps in understanding the amount and level of uncertainty faced in emergency planning for projects.

In this paper, a crisis could be externally generated, as in an earthquake, deregulation, loss of key executives through accidental death (airplane or automobile crash), or internally generated, as in a plant explosion or a strike. We use Lagadec's (1993) definition of a crisis as being an incident that upsets normal conditions, creating a disturbance that cannot be brought back to normal using existing or specialized emergency functions. A crisis, according to Lagadec, can occur when the incident passes a certain level or when the system is unstable or close to the breaking point before the incident took place. Consequently, crises considered in this paper disrupt project activities to the point where new (and typically unanticipated) decisions must be made to continue the project.

Projects have characteristics that make the design and preparation of elaborate tools difficult. First, many projects lack the permanence of a large plant, mine, or government installation. Second, emergencies in smaller projects tend to be more constrained to the site, while larger projects must deal with emergencies of greater scope and impact, such as chemical and radiological releases. Third, in a plant, a large number of people are affected by an emergency—especially the public as opposed to the workers. When the public or a large number of workers are involved, the organization's confidence in safe operations has a heavy influence, and this begets elaborateness. A simple tool can afford us most of the protection we need (e.g., 70% of maximum), while a more elaborate tool will buy us more confidence and protection (perhaps up to 99% of maximum). The more elaborate tool is worth the investment when confidence is at stake.

Tools to Help Project Managers Plan for Crises

We've chosen four types of tools used primarily in emergency management to help project managers plan for crises better. We'll describe and show how to apply risk analyses, contingency plans, logic charts, and tabletop exercises.

Risk Analysis. An essential crisis planning tool is risk analysis. Risk analysis helps us find out what can go wrong, what's most probable, and what has the greatest impact. The combination of an event's probability of occurrence and severity of consequences (e.g., catastrophic failure) determines priorities. Incident analysis can also help us understand the lessons learned in an actual crisis and develop plans to mitigate the effects of similar incidents in the future.

The 1996 Olympic Games in Atlanta presented many potential disruptions to area businesses (Bradford, 1996). Comprehensive contingency plans were needed to increase the potential for business continuity. Atlanta-based BellSouth

Business Systems' Director of Business Continuity Services John Copenhaver stated, "If you plan for a medium-case scenario and a worst-case scenario happens, it's like having no plans at all." BellSouth's plan attempted to minimize disruptions during the Olympics through special arrangements for deliveries, telecommuting, and increased modem pools so employees could work from home. BellSouth conducted a vulnerability assessment and then put systems into place to avoid interruptions to service or minimize the impact of interruptions.

Another Bell company, BellSouth Advertising and Publishing Co. (BAPCO), saw the need to develop a plan to deal with the human side of crises (traumatic stress), because those could disable a firm just as well as interruption of normal business operations (e.g., phone, equipment, facilities) (Kruse, 1993). BAPCO brought in a consultant team to deliver a one-day crisis management training session. The training was given to members of a human resources crisis team and other members of management who wanted to participate. Through counseling, housing, "BellMart," rental cars, and other support mechanisms, BAPCO weathered Hurricane Andrew much better than most South Florida organizations. BellMart was a stocked warehouse of essentials that BAPCO employees (and even their non-BAPCO neighbors) were invited to visit to take whatever they needed. Eighty-five percent of BAPCO employees were affected by the hurricane, although none were killed by the hurricane. The company pointed to several initiatives that were taken to reduce traumatic stress so that people could return to work sooner and with fewer worries. These initiatives included a rapid deployment system to immediately attend to their employees' needs, determining those needs in advance, heading off traumatic stress with constant information (daily bulletin, people sought out on phone, foot, car, etc.), bringing in BAPCO volunteers from other areas, making cash available immediately, and giving employees time off from work to get their personal lives together.

Sometimes nature surprises us and sometimes nature just tests us. The Virginia Department of Transportation (VDOT) had an opportunity to test its emergency preparedness in a potential disaster that never materialized (Slack, 1996). Hurricane Bertha threatened to slam into Virginia as a full-force hurricane, but then weakened into a tropical gale with heavy winds and rain—not the widespread destruction of a hurricane. Bertha served as a drill for VDOT's Emergency Operations Center (EOC), which used a new computer system designed to keep various safety agencies up to date with the latest information during a crisis. One of the problems VDOT faced during many natural disasters was conflicting information among VDOT, state police, local police, and other state agencies involved in emergency response. All parties now have the same information via a real-time connection, rather than each agency gathering its own information.

The availability of accurate, real-time information is not enough to mitigate crises in project management. Good implementation of risk analysis helps to plan and properly prepare for crises in projects and take steps to reduce the occurrences of crises. Engineering analyses support this process of risk analysis and make up the quantitative portion of mitigation. Cause-and-effect analyses make up the qualitative portion of mitigation and help us assess the systematic effects both forward and backward.

In emergency management, we use risk analysis to find out the risks beforehand. The use of risk analysis in this paper should be differentiated from a probabilistic risk analysis. Establishing consequences of accidents or incidents by deterministic or risk analysis provides effective tools in emergency management. In project management, we concentrate on planning and sequencing activities to maximize our efficiencies and effectively schedule resources.

Illinois Power (IP) has a risk analysis process, called the Risk Register, that was developed and implemented in 1988 and serves as a comprehensive risk assessment system. "The Risk Register is a formal process that identifies, quantifies, and categorizes the risks facing Illinois Power, develops cost-effective methods to control them, and positions the company to achieve its stated goals" (Leonard, 1995). The system continually assesses new risks, generates information for decision-making, and supports employees at all levels.

IP's Risk Register process has five phases: risk analysis, mitigation development, mitigation selection, implementation, and monitoring. In conjunction with the Risk Register, IP has a Corporate Disaster Recovery Plan. This plan is designed to "obtain information on levels of damage, resource availability, and the status of restoration activities; provide timely and accurate information to the media, government officials, regulatory authorities, employees, and the general public; give guidance on restoration activities; coordinate acquisition and allocation of resources and coordinate operations with city, county, state and federal emergency-service operations" (Leonard, 1995).

For each identified risk, IP decides on a post-loss goal—in other words, the minimum acceptable capabilities following an event. The post-loss goal sets the target for what the crisis management tool should help IP achieve and helps reduce uncertainty during and after an event.

Contingency Plans. Once the risk analysis is performed, project managers must translate those risks into contingency plans. Project managers need to sit down and ask, "What can go wrong with my project?" Once identified, the project manager has a list of risks associated with a particular project—the output of a risk analysis. Then they should ask, "Which of these risks is most likely to happen?" and "Which of these will have the greatest impact?" "On what or whom?" This last question implies the vulnerability of the organization to the identified risks. Project managers

should develop plans that use the data from a risk analysis to prepare them and their organizations for the broadest range of emergencies.

Appointing a person to be in charge of crisis planning puts responsibility and resources together, thereby reducing the need to overload already busy executives with planning for a low-probability event. Nestle U.S.A., Inc.'s headquarters are in Glendale, California, a suburb of Los Angeles. To support its contingency planning efforts, Nestle has appointed a director of business interruption planning (Ceniceros, 1995). As part of its contingency plan, Nestle has a contract with the Stouffer Renaissance Esmeralda, a resort hotel in the desert near Palm Springs, stipulating that the hotel has three days to empty out its ballroom if Nestle needs the space to resume business. The hotel was selected because it is already set up to provide comfort, food, and beverages—and that relieves the demands on Nestle managers and counselors, so they can get back into serving their customers more rapidly and effectively. "Concern for personnel in planning for business resumption is just as important as facilities or data recovery" (Ceniceros, 1995). Nestle has contracts with work-area-recovery vendors that have 72 hours to deliver office materials to the hotel. The hotel is accessible from an airport in Palm Springs, which expands access from Phoenix, should supplies need to come from elsewhere.

Nestle's contingency plan was tested with good results: "With the help of two furniture installation specialists and some hotel staff, the ballroom can quickly convert into 300 workstations complete with copy machines, computers, telecommunication cables, double-circuited power distribution panels, and everything else workers usually take for granted, such as sound barriers so business can be conducted with minimal distractions. . . . At our last exercise, we pulled together 100 workstations in 20 clock hours" (Ceniceros, 1995).

Risk analyses support planning by helping project managers pick the most probable and most severe events combined with a vulnerability assessment to see who or what is vulnerable and what will be affected. Therefore, when the crisis occurs, the project manager has thought about the crisis and what can be affected. Plans incorporating this thinking help the project manager be ready when the crisis occurs and do what is necessary to fix it. If a manager is responsible for a project, he or she should require that someone conduct a risk analysis. The risk analysis improves early recognition of warning signs; the vulnerability assessment helps identify whom to notify and how to start support to them early.

Logic Charts. Logic charts employ project flow logic to show the project flow with all dependencies in an extremely flexible, time-scale-independent diagram. Logic charts are a form of expert system because they embody the decision-making knowledge of the expert in a system that can be followed procedurally. Project flow logic is the basis for any personal computer-assisted project management tool. Project managers are skilled at charting. But, in times of crisis, different types of charts are needed.

When a crisis occurs, people need procedures to follow. Logic charts form the basis for writing these procedures. In project management, the most commonly used charts are Gantt charts for looking at activities against time and networks for looking at precedence. Emergency logic charts depend heavily on logic because of branching due to chained contingencies (e.g., "if event A and event B happened, then event C is likely").

Logic charts provide an overview of principal emergency response events and recovery operations. The charts also depict decisions, notifications, support requests, and public information actions. Use of properly prepared charts take the affected site personnel through event discovery, event assessment, identification of emergency classification level, and to the activation of on-site response actions.

Logic charts force project managers to think through the critical decisions necessary in a crisis. Project managers won't have time to go through the logic chart when the actual emergency occurs—the project manager must learn from the preparation and thinking required to construct a logic chart and feed this into or reinforce it through a tabletop exercise. When the crisis occurs, the project manager isn't thinking as clearly as usual, and the more that has been done before the crisis occurs, the better action the project manager can take.

The Oak Ridge Office (ORO) of the U.S. Department of Energy (DOE) used logic charts in its emergency response and recovery operations. ORO's logic charts offered specific steps to take based on the type of event. The first step was event discovery, where provisions for an initial response were depicted. This resulted in an event assessment leading to an initial emergency classification. Four levels of emergency classification followed, each evoking a particular response: a hazardous materials Usual Event (nonradiological), a hazardous materials Alert, a Site Emergency, and a General Emergency. A logic chart corresponding to the event discovery and initial response logic is shown in Figure 1.

Tabletop Exercises.   Tabletops and other exercises use the information from the risk analysis in the mitigation phase to simulate the decision-making and action-taking occurring in an actual crisis. A tabletop exercise involves assembling the people who will be responding to a crisis and acting out possible scenarios in advance, usually in a conference room or similar space. There, without the pressure of time or the actual crisis, people have the freedom to discuss alternatives and decide on the best courses of action in a given situation. Tabletops also provide the opportunity to rehearse the steps to take in a potential crisis. These same

techniques can help project managers prepare for possible crises that may occur in their projects.

The events or crises occurring to project managers won't be the things being tracked. What we don't track is what will go wrong. The need for tracking illustrates the use of a structured management process to catch the small problems through a thorough, systematic, and frequent review of relevant indicators (Kurstedt, Mallak, & Pacifici, 1992).

Gershanov (1995) offers a five-stage process for holding tabletop exercises. Stage 1 is to identify significant policy issues surrounding disasters in the organization. This identification may be done using an assessment tool, reviewing documents on responses to previous disasters, researching competitors' experiences, and reviewing debriefings of past exercises. Stage 2 examines these issues and isolates appropriate discussion questions. These discussion questions must be appropriate to the participants' level of responsibility in the organization. Discussion questions should address policy-level rather than operations-level concerns. Stage 3 is the tabletop exercise itself. According to Gershanov, one realistic scenario that encompasses the essential issues and problems should drive the exercise. A written version of the scenario should be available for the participants to refer to during the exercise. An outside facilitator with experience in emergency preparedness planning should run the exercise. Stage 4 is the debriefing of the exercise, providing a basis for further action and bringing a sense of closure to the exercise. Stage 5, follow-up planning, concerns how the outcomes of the debriefing will be handled and getting commitment to developing plans based on the tabletop exercise.

Tabletop exercises were used in planning for security for the 1996 Democratic National Convention (DNC) in Chicago (O'Connor, 1996). The Federal Emergency Management Agency (FEMA) facilitated tabletop exercises with members of the Chicago Police Department, the FBI, and the Secret Service to examine various scenarios and work out what would be done. Chicago Police also observed training and security practices for the 1996 Atlanta Olympic Games for lessons they could bring back to the DNC in Chicago.

Tabletop exercises are generally used in the beginning of crisis planning and focus on managerial information flows—who we talk to, what we do, who needs what information, and so forth. Issues surface in tabletops. Tabletops are a training device used to elicit understanding by carefully guiding the participants through a simulated emergency requiring a response. Although tabletop exercises are typically less expensive to conduct than drills or field exercises, they cannot substitute for the simulation of actual emergency events available through drills and field exercises.

Tabletop exercises should be conducted every quarter to keep emergency plans, procedures, and necessary thinking fresh in project managers' minds. Thinking through the decisions beforehand in an evaluative session such as a tabletop pays off when a real crisis occurs.

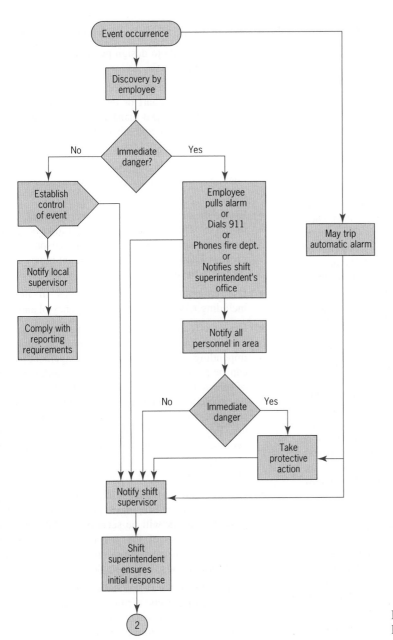

Figure 1 Event Discovery and Initial Response Logic Chart.

Tabletop exercises force managers to think through the decisions made during a crisis in advance, thereby reducing the need for decision-making during the crisis and reducing the time needed to make those decisions. "A tabletop is accomplished in controlled phases to allow discrete, individual answers, which focuses group attention on each point and thereby promotes a common understanding of roles and responsibilities and the entire response sequence by all participants" (Walker & Middleman, 1988). The tabletop exercise is a versatile tool that can be applied to all phases of project management. The overarching benefit of tabletops is they require people and systems to pay attention both during development and as the system evolves (Walker & Middleman).

One essential element to have in place for effective crisis management is a notification system. An effective notification system not only provides for contacting emergency response units, authorities, and key decision-makers, but also provides for accounting for personnel whereabouts and disposition.

Table 1   Summary of Crisis Planning Tools

Tools	Output
Risk analysis	Identification of risks
Contingency plan	Steps to take based on identified risks
Logic chart	Specific steps to take in a crisis
Tabletop exercise	Rehearse, discuss, and solidify a specific emergency response

After the 1996 Atlanta Olympics bombing, a plan to track the whereabouts of U.S. athletes and officials was deployed within 15 minutes of the blast (Lloyd, 1996). Dick Schultz, executive director of the U.S. Olympic Committee, stated: "In a two-hour time span, we not only determined the location of everybody, we had them secured. We had put together a crisis management plan for as many situations as we needed to" (Lloyd, 1996). Each U.S. athlete was issued a pager, the first time that this was ever done in an Olympics. The ability to account for all athletes and their whereabouts provides evidence for the effectiveness of their crisis plan.

Risk analysis, contingency planning, logic charts, and tabletop exercises represent several of the more common tools to help plan for crises in projects. Table 1 summarizes these tools by output. Project managers should think through their projects, in consultation with other project personnel, to select and use the tools judged to be most effective for the specific project. Once selected, these tools should be developed and tested to ensure people understand how to use them and what types of outcomes will result. Most certainly, any test of the tools results in refinement of the tools and learning on participants' behalf.

Recommendations for Project Managers

While we don't have a closed set of comprehensive strategies to offer other project managers to better plan for crises, we do have several recommendations to offer based on experience in emergency management. Considering the uncertainty involved in crisis management, we would be wary of any closed set of strategies. Crisis management, by definition, is perplexing, constantly changing, full of uncertainties, and challenging to any manager, especially the project manager. Crisis planning logically parallels the uncertain nature of crisis management. Although there is no simple solution to the complex problems posed by crises, here are our recommendations:

- Even for small projects, assign the job of developing at least a two-page risk analysis and contingency plan before the project begins. This is similar to a company appointing a manager of business interruption planning.

- Assign the job of producing a notification sequence.

- Use logic charts to design procedures that won't go awry during a crisis.

- Use tabletop exercises, because few people will look at a logic chart or even a procedure when a crisis occurs. Project managers will depend on what they've practiced, and this underscores the need and value of tabletops.

- Conduct these tabletop exercises quarterly to ensure readiness and to update procedures and responsibilities.

- Establish authority for crisis management before the crisis. The project manager isn't always the best emergency manager, so choose the person who has greatest knowledge of the operational issues associated with the crisis.

- Use emergency planning processes in projects, including risk analysis and contingency planning.

- Design effective, accurate, and timely feedback systems to provide early warning signs of failure and impending crises. A structured management process can help in focusing attention on regular tracking of relevant and critical indicators to surface the little problems before they become big ones. Become sensitive to indicators of impending project failure. Pay special attention to untracked indicators, because these are the most likely to cause trouble. Develop antennae and know when the project is going wrong.

- Choose a project manager indigenous to the country where the project is being conducted. An indigenous project manager will be sensitive to the social and political aspects of the project and its peripheral issues and will catch more problems while they're small or otherwise undetectable to the outsider.

- Be mindful of the social and political consequences of crises or events. Critics, or stakeholders, bear significant influence on project success regardless of what the indicators of cost, schedule, and quality show. Learn how to satisfy stakeholders (Mallak, Patzak, & Kurstedt, 1991). Identify one spokesperson as a liaison with the public and prepare a procedure for quick dissemination of information to all affected parties.

- Adopt a systems view and separate the crisis from the origin of the crisis. Consider the basic performance principles and problem analysis techniques popularized in total quality management programs. Look forward and backward to access the potential overall effects of the crisis.

These tools, recommendations, and strategies should help project managers to manage their crises better and perhaps to avoid some crises altogether. Making time and resources available to those in charge of crisis planning is essential; otherwise these critical tasks will be subordinated to the day-to-day activities, a vicious circle that can increase the likelihood for a larger crisis going undetected until it's too late. The regular and proper use and testing of risk analyses, contingency plans, logic charts, and tabletop exercises should surface the information, discussion of decisions and actions, and mitigation techniques that may reduce the occurrence and impact of crises in projects.

Acknowledgments

The preparation of this paper was partially funded by U.S. Department of Energy (DOE) Grant No. DE-FG05-86DP70033.

References

Bradford, M. (1996, February 2). Firms may be caught in a five-ring circus: With games on, planning will pay off. *Business Insurance,* p. 3.

Ceniceros, R. (1995, October 23). Nestle resorts to crisis. *Business Insurance,* p. 83.

Gershanov, K. M. (1995). Emergency preparedness in five easy steps. *Occupational Health and Safety,* 64 (3), 51–53.

Kruse, C. (1993, June). Disaster plan stands test of hurricane. *Personnel Journal,* 36–43.

Kurstedt, H. A., Jr., Mallak, L. A., and Pacifici, L. C. (1992). Expand quality management into the customer's environment to establish effective measures and standards. *Proceedings of the 1st International Symposium on Productivity and Quality Improvement,* February 1992, 478–485.

Lagadec, P. (1993). *Preventing chaos in a crisis.* London: McGraw-Hill.

Leonard, J. B. (1995). Assessing risk systematically: Illinois Power's risk assessment system. *Risk Management,* 42:1, p. 12.

Lloyd, J. (1996, July 28). U.S. official says athletes were safe—and feel safe. *USA Today,* p. 3C.

Mallak, L. A., Patzak, G. R., and Kurstedt, Jr., H. A. (1991). Satisfying stakeholders for successful project management. *Computers and Industrial Engineering,* 21, 429–433.

O'Connor, P. J. (1996, May 23). Security practice for convention called a success. *Chicago Sun-Times,* p. 23.

Sawle, W. S. (1991). Concerns of project managers: Crisis project management. *PM Network,* 5(1), 25–29.

Slack, C. (1996, July 15). Bertha gives VDOT center real-life situation to test computer system. *Richmond Times Dispatch,* p. D–13.

Walker, J. A., and Middleman, L. I. (1988). Tabletop exercise programs complement any emergency management system. *Proceedings of the ANS Topical Meeting on Emergency Response—Planning, Technologies, and Implementation.* Charleston, SC.

Questions

1. Planning for inevitable crises seems to be quite logical, yet is rarely done in projects. Why?

2. Would some of these tools have been of value to Iceland in the Project Management in Practice example?

3. Scenario analysis—the brainstorming of possible crises and anticipation of their outcomes—seems like another useful tool here. How does this approach compare to the tools described?

4. Which of the four tools would have the most value? Which would be easiest to implement?

5. In their recommendations to project managers regarding implementing these tools, which recommendations are most important?

7

Budgeting: Estimating Costs and Risks

In Chapter 6, we reviewed the planning process and gave some guidelines for designing the project plan. We now begin our discussion of PMBOK knowledge area 4: *Project Cost Management*. We treat the subject here in terms of planning (or budgeting) for the costs of project resources but we will reconsider the issue in Chapter 9 when we discuss the allocation of resources to project tasks.

First priority is, of course, obtaining resources with which to do the work. Senior management approval of the project budget does exactly that. A budget is a plan for allocating resources. Thus, the act of budgeting is the allocation of scarce resources to the various endeavors of an organization. The outcomes of the allocation process often do not satisfy managers of the organization who must live and work under budget constraints. It is, however, precisely the pattern of constraints in a budget that embodies organizational policy. The degree to which the different activities of an organization are fully supported by an allocation of resources is one measure of the importance placed on the outcome of the activity. Most of the senior managers we know try hard to be evenhanded in the budgetary process, funding each planned activity at the "right" level—neither overfunding, which produces waste and encourages slack management, nor underfunding, which inhibits accomplishment and frustrates the committed. (This is not to suggest that subordinate managers necessarily agree with our assessment.)

The budget is not simply one facet of a plan, nor is it merely an expression of organizational policy; it is also a monitoring and control mechanism. The budget serves as a standard for comparison, a baseline from which to measure the difference between the actual and planned uses of resources. As the manager directs the deployment of resources to accomplish some desired objective, resource usage should be monitored carefully. This allows deviations from planned usage to be checked against the progress of the project, and exception reports can be generated if resource expenditures are not consistent with accomplishments. Indeed, the pattern of deviations (variances) can be examined to see if it is possible, or reasonable, to forecast significant departures from budget. We illustrate this process in Chapter 9 when we discuss the use of "earned value" (costs derived from the project budget) to monitor and control the project and forecast the project completion time and costs. With sufficient warning, it is sometimes possible to implement corrective actions. In any event, such forecasting helps to decrease the number of undesirable surprises for senior management.

But be warned! The budget expended (resource usage) does not measure the actual level of work completed on the project. The budget alone, therefore, is not a sufficient measure of a project's progress. Budgets play an important role in the entire process of management. It is clear that budgeting procedures must associate resource use with the achievement of organizational goals or the planning/control process becomes useless. If budgets are not tied to achievement, management may ignore situations where funds are being spent far in advance of accomplishment but are within budget when viewed by time period. Similarly, management may misinterpret the true state of affairs when the budget is overspent for a given time period but outlays are appropriate for the level of task completion. Data must be collected and reported in a timely manner, or the value of the budget in identifying and reporting current problems or anticipating upcoming problems will be lost. The reporting process must be carefully designed and controlled. It is of no value if the data are sent to the wrong person or the reports take an inordinately long time to be processed through the system. For example, one manager of a now defunct, large, computer company complained that, based on third-quarter reports, he was instructed to act so as to alter the fourth-quarter results. However, he did not receive the instructions until the first quarter of the following year.

In Chapter 6, we described a planning process that integrated the planning done at different levels of the project in the work breakdown structure (WBS). If we cost the WBS, step by step, we develop a project budget. Viewed in this way, *the budget is a reflection of the WBS in another form.*

Let us now consider some of the various budgeting methods used in organizations. These are described in general first, then with respect to projects. We also address some problems of cost estimation, with attention to the details and pitfalls. We consider some of the special demands and concerns with budgeting for projects. Next, we present some techniques for improving one's skills at budget and cost estimation, or estimating and forecasting of any kind. Printouts of project budgets from PM software packages will be shown in Chapter 10 where we cover project management information systems. Last, we address the issue of risk in budgeting through the use of simulation.

7.1   ESTIMATING PROJECT BUDGETS

In order to develop a budget, we must forecast what resources the project will require, the required quantity of each, when they will be needed, and how much they will cost, including the effects of potential price inflation. Uncertainty is involved in any forecast, though some forecasts have less uncertainty than others. An experienced cost estimator can forecast the number of bricks that will be used to construct a brick wall of known dimensions within 1 to 2 percent. The errors, however, are apt to be much larger for an estimate of the number of programmer hours or lines of code that will be required to produce a specific piece of software. While the field of software science makes such estimates possible, the level of uncertainty is considerably higher and the typical error size is much larger.

In many fields, cost-estimating methods are well codified. For example, in fields such as construction, costs can often be estimated by *scaling* the various cost elements appropriately. For example, building one mile of a four-lane road can be estimated from the individual cost elements of previously constructed two-lane roads—e.g., the asphalt cost may be double while the cost of the road's shoulders may be the same. Similarly, *parametric estimating* relies on well-known statistical correlations between various factors such as the total cost of a house relative to the square feet of living area. The databases of purchasing departments include multitudes of information devoted to the techniques of estimating the quantities of materials and labor required to accomplish specific jobs. Also on the Internet are links detailing what materials, services, and machines are available, and from whom. Every business has its own rules of thumb for cost estimating. These usually distill the collective experience gained by many estimators over many years. An experienced producer of books, for example, can leaf through a manuscript and, after asking a few questions about the number and type of illustrations and the quality of paper to be used, can make a fairly accurate estimate of what it will cost to produce a book.

Project Management in Practice
Pathfinder Mission to Mars—on a Shoestring

In 1976, NASA's two Viking Mars-lander missions took six years and $3 billion (in 1992 dollars) to develop. Twenty-one years later, Mars Pathfinder and Sojourner Rover landed on Mars once again, but at a development cost of only $175 million, representing a whopping 94 percent cost reduction over the earlier mission. This amazing cost reduction was achieved through a variety of means but the most important was perhaps the philosophical one that this was a design-to-cost project rather than a design-to-performance project. Given this philosophy, the scope of the mission was intentionally limited and "scope-creep" was never an issue:

The Pathfinder Rover explores Martian terrain.

- to achieve a successful landing
- return of engineering telemetry
- acquisition and transmission of a *single*, partial panoramic image
- successful rover deployment and 7 sol (Martian day) operation on the surface
- completion of a 30 sol lander mission meeting all engineering, science, and technology objectives
- *one* successful alpha proton X-ray spectrometer measurement of a Martian rock and soil sample.

The means of limiting the cost of the mission were multiple and creative:

- development was cost-capped, with no opportunity for more funds
- identifying a set of "de-scope" options which could be implemented in case the cost grew beyond the fixed budget

- mission, flight, and ground systems designs were driven by existing hardware and system capability
- a project cash reserve of 27 percent of the total budget was held back and carefully planned for time-phased release throughout the duration of the project
- mission designers/builders transitioned into the testers/operators to save documentation, time, labor cost, and chance of error
- existing NASA mission infrastructure was used rather than designing new systems
- instituting time-phased "what if" and lien lists for real or potential current and anticipated items of cost growth during the project
- choosing to use a "single-string" but higher risk design and offsetting the risk by using more reliable parts

- 70 percent of major procurements contracts were fixed-price rather than cost-plus
- creative procurement, such as existing equipment spares, and accounting, such as lower burden rate personnel

On July 5, the Mars Sojourner Rover rolled down its deployment ramp and the resulting pictures made the headlines on newspapers around the world. The mission continued for almost three months and returned 2.6 gigabytes of scientific and engineering data, 16,000 lander camera images, 550 rover camera images, 8.5 million environmental measurements, and the results of 16 chemical rock/soil experiments and 10 technology rover experiments.

Source: C. Sholes and N. Chalfin, "Mars Pathfinder Mission," *PM Network*, Vol. 13.

We will have more to say about gathering budget data shortly. Before doing so, however, it is helpful to understand that developing project budgets is much more difficult than developing budgets for more permanent organizational activities. The influence of history is strong in the budget of an ongoing activity. Many entries are simply "last year's figure plus X percent," where X is any number the budgeter feels "can be lived with" and is probably acceptable to the person or group who approves the budgets. While the project budgeter cannot always depend on tradition as a basis for estimating the current project budget, it is not uncommon for the budgeter to have budgets and audit reports for similar past projects to serve as guides. Although we maintain that all projects are unique, many are not very different from their predecessors and can serve as reasonable guides when forecasting current project budgets. Tradition also aids the estimation process in another way. In the special case of R & D projects, it has been found (Dean et al., 1969) that project budgets are stable over time when measured as a percent of the total allocation to R & D from the parent firm, though within the project the budget may be reallocated among activities. There is no reason to believe that the situation is different for other kinds of projects, and we have some evidence that shows stability similar to R & D projects.

This notion has been formalized in the practice of "life cycle costing." The life cycles of past projects are studied as models for the way costs accrue over the life cycles of similar projects. Given information about costs during the early life of a project, the model can be used to forecast the total cost over the project's life cycle.*

A more interesting estimation technique that also depends on actual costs early in the life of a project is based on earned value analysis (Zwikael et al., 2000). (For a description of earned value analysis, see Chapter 10.) Early actual costs on a project are compared to their estimates, and the remaining costs are adjusted by assuming a constant actual-to-estimate cost ratio. The assumption of a constant ratio gives the lowest average estimation error (11 percent) of the five different predictors tested.

---

*We do not demonstrate it here, but Crystal Ball® can fit distributions to historical data. This is done by selecting the *Fit* button in CB's Distribution Gallery window. Then specify the location of the data. CB considers a wide variety of probability distributions and offers the user optional goodness-of-fit tests—see the Crystal Ball® *User Manual*.

For multiyear projects, another problem is raised. The plans and schedules for such projects are set at the beginning of project life, but over the years, the forecast resource usage may be altered by the availability of alternate or new materials, machinery, or personnel—available at different costs than were estimated, giving rise to both the risk of inflation and technological risk. The longer the project life, the less the PM can trust that traditional methods and costs will be relevant.

Tradition has still another impact on project budgeting. Every organization has its idiosyncrasies. One firm charges the project's R & D budget with the cost of training sales representatives on the technical aspects of a new product. Another adopts special property accounting practices for contracts with the government. Unless the PM understands the organizational accounting system, there is no way to exercise budgetary control over the project. The methods for project budgeting described below are intended to avoid these problems as much as possible, but complete avoidance is out of the question. The PM simply must be familiar with the organization's accounting system!

One aspect of cost estimation and budgeting that is not often discussed has to do with the *actual* use of resources as opposed to the accounting department's assumptions about how and when the resources will be used. For instance, suppose you have estimated that $5,000 of a given resource will be used in accomplishing a task that is expected to require five weeks. The actual use of the resource may be none in the first week, $3,000 worth in the second week, none in the third week, $1,500 in the fourth week, and the remaining $500 in the last week. Unless this pattern of expenditure is detailed in the plan, the accounting department, which takes a linear view of the world, will spread the expenditure equally over the five-week period. This may not affect the project's budget, but it most certainly affects the project's cash flow, a matter of major interest to the firm's comptroller. In the reading "Three Perceptions of Project Cost" at the end of this chapter, these three different views of costs and the problems they often cause are described in detail. The PM must be aware of not only the resource requirements and the specific time pattern of resource usage, but also how the expenses will affect their firm's cash flows. This subject will be revisited in Chapter 9.

Another aspect of preparing budgets is especially important for project budgeting. Every expenditure (or receipt) must be identified with a specific project task (and with its associated milestone, as we will see in the next chapter). Each element in the WBS has a unique account number to which charges are accrued as work is done. These identifiers are needed for the PM to exercise budgetary control.

With these things in mind, the issue of how to gather input data for the budget becomes a matter of some concern. There are two fundamentally different strategies for data gathering, top-down and bottom-up.

Top-Down Budgeting

This strategy is based on collecting the judgments and experiences of top and middle managers, and available past data concerning similar activities. These managers estimate overall project cost as well as the costs of the major subprojects that comprise it. These cost estimates are then given to lower-level managers, who are expected to continue the breakdown into budget estimates for the specific tasks and work packages that comprise the subprojects. This process continues to the lowest level.

The process parallels the hierarchical planning process described in the last chapter. The budget, like the project, is broken down into successively finer detail, starting from the top, or most aggregated level following the WBS. It is presumed that lower-level managers will argue for more funds if the budget allocation they have been granted is, in their judgment, insufficient for the tasks assigned. This presumption is, however, often incorrect. Instead of reasoned debate, argument sometimes ensues, or simply sullen silence. When senior managers insist on maintaining their budgetary positions—based on "considerable past experience"—junior managers feel forced to accept what they perceive to be insufficient allocations to achieve the objectives to which they must commit.

Discussions between the authors and a large number of managers support the contention that lower-level managers often treat the entire budgeting process as if it were a "zero-sum game," a game in which any individual's gain is another individual's loss. Competition among junior managers is often quite intense.

The advantage of this top-down process is that aggregate budgets can often be developed quite accurately, though a few individual elements may be significantly in error. Not only are budget categories stable as a percent of the total budget, the statistical distribution of each category (e.g., 5% for R & D) is also stable, making for high predictability (Dean et al., 1969). Another advantage of the top-down process is that small yet costly tasks need not be individually identified, nor need it be feared that some small but important aspect has been overlooked. The experience and judgment of the executive is presumed automatically to factor all such elements into the overall estimate. Questions put to subordinates, however, indicate that senior management has a strong bias toward underestimating costs.

Project Management in Practice
Øresund Bridge: Seeing Projects Through Different Lenses

The Øresund Bridge is 16.4 km long and connects the countries of Sweden and Denmark. It's innovative design, which carries a dual two-lane motorway and a double-track high-speed railway across a 7.7 km bridge, along a 4 km artificial island, and then through a 3.5 km underwater tunnel, was a project management success story. As well as being delivered 6 months ahead of schedule, it has been praised for the quality of the design.

In considering projects it is important to step away from the hard facts and to consider them from a more holistic perspective. The Øresund Bridge provides us with an opportunity to consider some of the other aspects that make this a remarkable project management success story. These aspects can be categorised as being associated with the sustainable development of the region, the social aspects of the project, the economic aspects, and the environmental aspects.

Sustainable development:

Sustainable development: The Øresund Bridge has promoted the economic and social integration of the Øresund region, as well as contributed to the regional economic development through enhanced transport infrastructure between Sweden and Denmark. By connecting the regional housing markets, businesses and labour markets, the region is now able to better compete for investment with other regions in Northern Europe.

Durability: The Øresund Bridge design promoted water run-off and included the maximum possible coat thickness on the exposed steel to provide an operational lifespan of 100 years.

Social Aspects:

Stakeholder communication: The Øresund Bridge was constructed on a sensitive marine environment, connects two countries and had an impact on a diverse population of local stakeholders (including recreational sailors, bathers and commercial fishermen). It was therefore essential that the requirements of these audiences were accommodated during the design stages of the project and that they were informed of progress during the project.

Health and Safety: The Øresund Bridge was one of the first projects in Sweden to record time lost through accidents. Through a programme of detailed planning, safety training and inspections the project achieved a rate of around 11 accidents per one million hours of work (compared to an average of 20 in Sweden). There was also one fatality on-site during the construction.

Road safety: The Øresund Bridge must be a safe operational environment. Therefore, as well as a permanently manned traffic station, well-marked emergency telephones, fire extinguishers, emergency lighting, fire alarms, and evacuation corridors (in the tunnel), the design also incorporates leading edge technologies.

This includes sensors in the tunnel to monitor carbon monoxide, nitrogen dioxide and overall visibility.

Economic Aspects:

Local employment: The Øresund Bridge was seen as a local project with up to 95% of an onsite labour force of up to 2,000 workers coming from the Øresund region. As well as the on-site labour force, there were regional subcontractors from Sweden, Norway and Denmark, as well as other suppliers from as far away as Spain (where the steel girders and concrete deck of the bridge were prefabricated).

Training: The regional government, technical colleges and universities were all involved in a programme to train local people in order to meet the skilled labour programme requirements.

Environmental Aspects:

High environmental standards: The Øresund Bridge was designed to have a zero net impact on a sensitive marine environment. As well as taking design decisions (such as prefabricating material off-site) that minimized the amount of time on, and risk of damaging, the environment, the project also spent over US$300 million on environmental protection measures. In addition, the project has benefitted the environment by creating new habitats and reducing air pollution by 50%.

Habitat creation: The Øresund Bridge required the creation of an artificial island over 4 km long. This has been allowed to develop naturally undisturbed by human interference. In 2007 a survey identified over 450 plant species and 10 bird species on the island including many rare species.

Minimal impact on water flow: The Baltic Sea is the world's largest body of brackish water which provides a unique marine ecosystem. The design of the bridge was such that the water flow, salt and oxygen would not be altered by more than 0.5%.

Flora and fauna monitoring: The flora and fauna are vital to sustaining the unique marine environment. Therefore, during the project these were continuously monitored. The information was analysed by computer models to track the overall impacts and showed that by 2000 the construction had not adversely affected the biodiversity of the strait.

Minimising light disturbance: Design decisions were made to avoid direct illumination of the water surface so as not to deter fish. In addition, the bridge illumination is minimised during the bird migration seasons to reduce the risk of distracting the birds.

By taking a broader view of the project we can see how success means more than time, cost and quality. It involves the balance between "project management success" and "project success". In addition, it becomes clearer that success often depends upon the viewpoint that you take and, therefore, that exploring your project through different lenses (in this case, technical, economic, social, environmental, sustainable) is essential if you are going to create an outstanding achievement.

Source: "http://skanska-sustainability-case-studies.com/pdfs/49/49_Oresund_v001.pdf"

Bottom-Up Budgeting

In this method, elemental tasks, their schedules, and their individual budgets are constructed, again following the WBS. The people doing the work are consulted regarding times and budgets for the tasks to ensure the best level of accuracy. Initially, estimates are made in terms of resources, such as labor hours and materials. These are later converted to dollar equivalents. Standard analytic tools such as learning curve analysis and work sampling are employed where appropriate to improve the estimates. Differences of opinion are resolved by the usual discussions between senior and junior managers. If necessary, the project manager and the functional manager(s) may enter the discussion in order to ensure the accuracy of the estimates. The resulting task budgets are aggregated to give the total direct costs of the project. The PM adds such indirect costs as general and administrative (G&A), possibly a project reserve for contingencies, and then a profit figure to arrive at the final project budget.

Bottom-up budgets should be, and usually are, more accurate in the detailed tasks, but it is critical that all elements be included. It is far more difficult to develop a complete list of tasks when constructing that list from the bottom up than from the top down. Just as the top-down method may lead to budgetary game playing, the bottom-up process has its unique managerial budget games. For example, individuals overstate their resource needs because they suspect that higher management will probably cut all budgets. Their suspicion is, of course, quite justified, as Gagnon (1982, 1987) and others have shown. Managers who are particularly persuasive sometimes win, but those who are consistently honest and have high credibility win more often.

The advantages of the bottom-up process are those generally associated with participative management. Individuals closer to the work are apt to have a more accurate idea of resource requirements than their superiors or others not personally involved. In addition, the direct involvement of low-level managers in budget preparation increases the likelihood that they will accept the result with a minimum of grumbling. Involvement also is a good managerial training technique, giving junior managers valuable experience in budget preparation as well as the knowledge of the operations required to generate a budget.

While top-down budgeting is common, true bottom-up budgets are rare. Senior managers see the bottom-up process as risky. They tend not to be particularly trusting of ambitious subordinates who may overstate resource requirements in an attempt to ensure success and build empires. Besides, as senior managers note with some justification, the budget is the most important tool for control of the organization. They are understandably reluctant to hand over that control to subordinates whose experience and motives are questionable. This attitude is carried to an extreme in one large corporation that conducts several dozen projects simultaneously, each of which may last five to eight years and cost millions of dollars. Project managers do not participate in the budgeting process in this company, nor did they, until recently, have access to project budgets during their tenure as PMs. Reconciling top-down with bottom-up budgets is obviously an area where the earlier principles of negotiation and conflict management, as described in Chapter 4, would be useful.

Work Element Costing

The actual process of building a project budget—either top-down or bottom-up or, as we will suggest, a combination of both—tends to be a straightforward but tedious process. While the budget may include revenues (e.g., milestone payments by the client), the major task in creating the budget is estimating the costs for each of the project's work elements. Basically, each work element in the work breakdown structure (WBS) is evaluated for its resource requirements, and the cost of each resource is estimated. We discuss this in more detail below and then give some suggestions for ways to improve the cost estimating process in Section 7.2.

Suppose a work element is estimated to require 25 hours of labor by a technician. The specific technician assigned to this job is paid $17.50/hr. Overhead charges to the project are 84 percent of direct labor charges. The appropriate cost appears to be

$$25 \text{ hr} \times \$17.50 \times 1.84 = \$805.00$$

but the accuracy of this calculation depends on the precise assumptions behind the 25-hr estimate. Industrial engineers have noted that during a normal 8-hr day, no one actually works for all eight hours. Even on an assembly line, workers need breaks called "personal time." This covers such activities as visiting the water cooler or toilet, having a cigarette, blowing one's nose, and all the other time-consuming activities engaged in by normal people in a normal workplace.

Project Management in Practice
Managing Costs at Massachusetts' Neighborhood Health Plan

In just a two-year period, Medicaid reduced its rate of reimbursement by 20 percent while the State of Massachusetts imposed higher eligibility requirements for health subscribers, thereby significantly reducing Neighborhood Health Plan's (NHP) revenues and threatening its viability. In the past, NHP had controlled costs by controlling hospital bed utilization and increasing preventive medicine. However, no matter how low hospital utilization is, if hospital contract rates are expensive, the cost to NHP will be high. Thus, NHP chartered a project team to help it manage costs through better selection and management of hospital contracts. More specifically, the team's charter was to develop a method to examine hospital contracts to assure that proposed rates were financially viable to NHP but high-quality care would be available when needed.

The team first selected the top 10 to 20 hospitals based on total annual payments from NHP for analysis.

From these they determined that to control costs effectively, NHP's contracting philosophy would have to change from the current 95 percent of all line items per episode to a fixed cost per episode or per day per type of stay. The team then constructed a spreadsheet that allowed cost comparisons to be made across hospitals which allowed management to bargain for lower rates or, if hospitals were inflexible, suggest to health centers what alternative hospitals to refer patients to. This and later developments by the team significantly enhanced management's ability to contain their costs while guaranteeing that quality care would be available when needed. It also allowed management to examine and respond to contracts and proposed contract changes in a timely and informed manner.

Source: J. H. Hertenstein and K. A. Vallancourt, "Contract Management = Cost Management," *PM Network*, Vol. 11.

A typical allowance for personal time is 12 percent of total work time. If personal time was not included in the 25-hr estimate made above, then the cost calculation becomes

$$1.12 \times 25 \text{ hr} \times \$17.50 \times 1.84 = \$901.60*$$

The uncertainty in labor cost estimating lies in the estimate of hours to be expended. Not including personal time ensures an underestimate.

Direct costs for resources and machinery are charged directly to the project, and are not usually subject to overhead charges. If a specific machine is needed by the project and is the property of a functional department, the project may "pay" for it by transferring funds from the project budget to the functional department's budget. The charge for such machines will be an operating cost (\$/hr or \$/operating cycle), plus a depreciation charge based on either time or number of operating cycles. Use of general office equipment, e.g., copy machines, drafting equipment, and coffeemakers, is often included in the general overhead charge.

In addition to these charges, there is also the *General and Administrative (G&A)* charge. This is composed of the cost of senior management, the various staff functions, and any other expenses not included in overhead. G&A charges are a fixed percent of either the direct costs or the total of all direct and indirect costs.

Thus, a fully costed work element would include direct costs (labor, resources, and special machinery) plus overhead and G&A charges. We advise the PM to prepare two budgets, one with overheads and G&A charges, and one without. The full cost budget is used by the accounting group to estimate the profit earned by the project. The budget that contains only direct costs gives the PM the information required to manage the project without being confounded with costs over which the PM has no control. Let us now consider a combination of top-down and bottom-up budgeting.

An Iterative Budgeting Process—Negotiation-in-Action

In Chapter 6, we recommended an iterative planning process with subordinates[†] developing WBS plans for the tasks for which they were responsible. Superiors review these plans, perhaps suggesting amendments. The strength of this planning technique is that primary responsibility for the design of a task is delegated to the individual accountable for its completion, and thus it utilizes participative management (or "employee involvement"). If done correctly, estimated resource usage and schedules are a normal part of the planning process at all planning levels. Therefore, the superior constructing a WBS at the highest level would estimate resource requirements and durations for each of the steps in the WBS. Let us refer to the superior's estimate of resource requirements for a particular task as R. Similarly, the subordinate responsible for that task estimates the resource requirements as r.

In a perfect world, R would equal r. We do not, however, live in a perfect world. As a matter of fact, the probable relationship between the original estimates made at the different levels is $R << r$. This is true for several reasons, three of which are practically universal. First, the farther one moves up the organizational chart away from immediate responsibility for doing the work, the easier, faster, and cheaper the job looks to the superior than to the one who has to do

---

*In a weak matrix project, the Technical Assistance Group representing the technician would submit a lump-sum charge to the project, calculated in much the same way. The charge would, of course, include the costs noted in the rest of this section.

[†]We use the terms "superior" and "subordinate" here for the sole purpose of identifying individuals working on different relative levels of a project's WBS. We recognize that in a matrix organization it is not uncommon for PMs ("superiors") to delegate work to individuals ("subordinates") who do not report to the PM and who may even be senior to the PM on the parent firm's organizational chart.

it. This is because the superior either does not know the details of the task, or has conveniently forgotten the details, as well as how long the job takes and how many problems can arise. Second, wishful thinking leads the superior to underestimate cost (and time), because the superior has a stake in representing the project to senior management as a profitable venture. Third, the subordinate is led to build-in some level of protection against failure by adding an allowance for "Murphy's Law" onto a budget that already may have a healthy contingency allowance.

Assuming that the superior and subordinate are reasonably honest with one another (any other assumption leads to a failure in win-win negotiations), the two parties meet and review the subordinate's WBS. Usually, the initial step toward reducing the difference in cost estimates is made by the superior who is "educated" by the subordinate in the realities of the job. The result is that the superior's estimate rises. The next step is typically made by the subordinate. Encouraged by the boss's positive response to reason, the subordinate surrenders some of the protection provided for by the budgetary "slop," and the subordinate's estimate falls. The subordinate's cost estimate is still greater than the superior's, but the difference is considerably decreased.

The pair now turn their attention to the technology of the task at hand. They carefully inspect the subordinate's work plan, trying to find a more efficient way to accomplish the desired end. It may be that a major change can be made that allows a lower resource commitment than either originally imagined. It may be that little or no further improvement is possible. Let us assume that moderate improvement is made, but that the subordinate's estimate is still somewhat greater than the superior's, although both have been altered by the negotiations thus far. What should the superior do, accept the subordinate's estimate or insist that the subordinate make do with the superior's estimate?

In order to answer this question, we must digress and reconsider the concept of the project life cycle. In Chapter 1, we presented the usual view of the project life cycle in Figure 1-3, shown here as Figure 7-1 for convenience. This view of the life cycle shows decreasing returns to inputs as the project nears completion. Figure 1-5 is also shown here as Figure 7-2 for convenience. In this case, the project shows increasing returns to inputs as the project nears completion. In order to decide whether to adopt the subordinate's resource estimate or the superior's, we need to know which picture of the life cycle represents the task under consideration. Note that we are treating

Figure 7-1 The standard stretched–S project life cycle. (Figure 1-3 reproduced.)

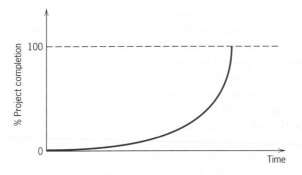

Figure 7-2 Another possible project life cycle—the stretched–J. (Figure 1-5 reproduced.)

the subordinate's task as if it were a project, which is perfectly all right because it has the characteristics of a project that were described in Chapter 1. Also note that we do not need to know the shape of the life cycle with any precision, merely if it is a stretched-S or stretched-J shape.

Remember that the superior's and subordinate's resource estimates are not very far apart as a result of the negotiations preceding this decision. If the life cycle curve is a stretched-S (as in Figure 7-1), showing diminishing marginal returns, we opt for the superior's estimate because of the small impact on completion that results from withholding a small amount of resources. The superior might say to the subordinate, "Jeremy, what can you get me for R? We will have to live with that." If, on the other hand, the life cycle curve is a stretched-J, showing increasing marginal returns as in Figure 7-2, the subordinate's estimate should be chosen because of the potentially drastic effect a resource shortage would have on project completion. In this event, the superior might say, "OK, Brandon, we have got to be sure of this job. We'll go with your numbers." If the disagreement had concerned schedule (duration) instead of resources, the negotiation process and underlying logic would be unaltered.

This is a time-consuming process. At the same time the PM is negotiating with the several subordinates responsible for the pieces of the PM's WBS, each of the subordinates is negotiating with their subordinates, and so on. This multilevel process is messy and not particularly efficient, but it allows a free-flow of ideas up and down the system at all levels. This iterative process tends to reduce the uncertainty in budget estimations. The debate over processes and their associated costs means that the uncertainty in budget estimates is very likely to be reduced.

It is worth emphasizing that ethics is just as important in negotiations within an organization as in negotiations between an organization and an outside party. In this case, the superior and subordinate have the responsibility to be honest with each other. For one thing, they must continue to work together in the future under the conditions of mutual trust. Second, it is ethically necessary to be honest in such negotiations.

Comments on the Budget Request Process

The budget process often begins with an invitation from top management for each division to submit a *budget request* for the coming year. Division heads pass the invitation along to departments, sections, and subsections, each of which presumably collects requests from below, aggregates them, and passes the results back up the organizational ladder.

This sounds like bottom-up budgeting, but there is an important difference between this procedure and a true bottom-up system. Along with the formal invitation for submission of a budget request, in the iterative system another message is passed down—a much less formal message that carries the following kinds of information: the percent by which the wage bill of the organization may be increased or must be decreased, organizational policy on adding to or cutting the work force, the general attitude toward capital expenditures, knowledge about which projects and activities are considered to be high priority and which are not, and a number of other matters that, in effect, prescribe a set of limits on lower-level managers. As the budget requests are passed back up the organization, they are carefully inspected for conformity to guidelines. If they do not conform, they are "adjusted," often with little or no consultation with the originating units. Senior management tends to adopt an autocratic stance on budget making for many reasons, but two are very common: the need to feel in control of the budget, and the feeling that a tight budget will somehow motivate subordinates to perform more efficiently. We know of no particular evidence to support such views, but they are quite common. Moreover, they lead to budgetary game playing and increase the uncertainty surrounding the budgetary process.

The less autocratic the organization (and the less pressured it is by current financial exigencies), the greater the probability that this process will allow dialogue and some compromise between managerial levels. Even the most *participative* firms, however, will not long tolerate lower-level managers who are not sensitive to messages relating to budget limitations. It makes little difference whether budget policy is passed down the system by means of formal, written policy statements or as a haphazard set of oral comments informally transmitted by some senior managers and practically neglected by others; the PM's budget request is expected to conform to policy. Ignorance of the policy is no excuse. Repeated failure to conform will be rewarded with a ticket to "corporate Siberia." It is the budget originator's responsibility to find out about budget policy. Again we see the importance of political sensitivity. The PM's channels of communication must be sensitive enough to receive policy signals even in the event that a noncommunicative superior blocks those signals.

One final comment about budgets concerns the impact of changes on the budget. Projects are known for having innumerable changes, sometimes due to scope changes by the customer, sometimes due to problems concerning the project itself such as delays, cost overruns, resource price increases, and other such matters. Obviously, for such changes the budget will always need to be reconsidered and perhaps re-estimated (and reapproved). For cases where some project tasks might exceed the budget, PMs often keep a "reserve" (e.g., 5%) from the project budget (taken from each of the task budgets proportionally) to handle unexpected task overages. Another alternative particularly useful for projects with many highly uncertain tasks is to design the project with an upfront "de-scope" strategy so that if the costs are running too high, some of the less important scope requirements can be scaled back or eliminated during the project, thereby saving cost. Regardless of the alternative used, it is always wise to consider the probability that costs will exceed the budget and what might be done ahead of time to avoid that problem.

Cost Category Budgeting vs. Project/Activity Budgeting

Another facet of budgeting has to do with the degree to which a budget is category-oriented or project/activity-oriented, a distinction we have mentioned before. The traditional organizational budget is category-oriented, often based upon historical data accumulated through a traditional, category-based, cost accounting system (Coburn, 1997; Vandament et al., 1993). Individual expenses are classified and assigned to basic budget *lines* such as phone, materials, personnel-clerical, utilities, direct labor, etc., or to production centers or processes (Brimson, 1993). These expense lines are gathered into more inclusive categories, and are reported by organizational unit—for example, by section, department, and division. In other words, the budget can be overlaid on the organizational chart. Table 7-1 shows one page of a typical, category-oriented monthly budget report for a real estate project.

With the advent of project organization, it became necessary to organize the budget in ways that conformed more closely to the actual pattern of fiscal responsibility. Under

Table 7-1   Typical Monthly Category Budget for a Real Estate Project (page 1 of 6)

	Current			
	Actual	*Budget*	*Variance*	*Pct.*
Corporate—Income Statement				
Revenue				
8430 Management fees				
8491 Prtnsp reimb—property mgmt	7,410.00	6,222.00	1,188.00	119.0
8492 Prtnsp reimb—owner acquisition	.00	3,750.00	3,750.00–	.0
8493 Prtnsp reimb—rehab	.00	.00	.00	.0
8494 Other income	.00	.00	.00	.0
8495 Reimbursements—others	.00	.00	.00	.0
Total revenue	7,410.00	9,972.00	2,562.00–	74.3
Operating expenses				
Payroll & P/R benefits				
8511 Salaries	29,425.75	34,583.00	5,157.25	85.0
8512 Payroll taxes	1,789.88	3,458.00	1,668.12	51.7
8513 Group ins & med reimb	1,407.45	1,040.00	387.45–	135.3
8515 Workmen's compensation	43.04	43.00	.04–	100.0
8516 Staff apartments	.00	.00	.00	.0
8517 Bonus	.00	.00	.00	.0
Total payroll & P/R benefits	32,668.12	39,124.00	6,457.88	83.5
Travel & entertainment expenses				
8512 Travel	456.65	300.00	156.65–	152.2
8522 Promotion, entertainment & gift	69.52	500.00	430.48	13.9
8523 Auto	1,295.90	1,729.00	433.10	75.0
Total travel & entertainment exp	1,822.07	2,529.00	706.93	72.1
Professional fees				
8531 Legal fees	419.00	50.00	369.00–	838.0
8532 Accounting fees	289.00	.00	289.00–	.0
8534 Temporary help	234.58	200.00	34.58–	117.2

traditional budgeting methods, the budget for a project could be split up among many different organizational units, which diffused control so widely that it was frequently nonexistent. It was often almost impossible to determine the actual size of major expenditure activities in a project's budget. In light of this problem, ways were sought to alter the budgeting process so that budgets could be associated directly with the projects that used them. This need gave rise to project budgeting. Table 7-2 shows a project-oriented budget divided by task/activity and expected time of expenditure. In an interesting paper, Brimson (1993) critiques both systems separately, and then combines them.

If a program consists of a set of separate projects, the use of project budgeting for each project allows those project budgets to be aggregated for the program as a whole by time periods. Moreover, the program can also have its own monthly category budget (as shown in Table 7-1, with the categories down the left side), but this may require dividing up the revenues (if any) and expenses for each of the projects' activities (tasks) into the appropriate categories. As well, each organizational unit can also present its projects' revenues and expenses by adding additional columns to Table 7-1, with one column for "regular operations" and the other columns

Table 7-2   Project Budget by Task and Month

Task	Estimate	Monthly Budget (£)							
		1	2	3	4	5	6	7	8
A	7000	5600	1400						
B	9000		3857	5143					
C	10000		3750	5000	1250				
D	6000		3600	2400					
E	12000				4800	4800	2400		
F	3000				3000				
G	9000			2571	5143	1286			
H	5000					3750	1250		
I	8000						2667	5333	
J	6000								6000
	75000	5600	12607	15114	14193	9836	6317	5333	6000

Source: Harrison, 1983.

for each project (or program). Again, however, this may take extra effort to break out the tasks by organizational unit as well as activity if the tasks involve more than one organizational unit.

The estimation of capital costs raises special problems. Accounting systems in different industries handle capital costs differently. Further, estimation requires highly specialized knowledge because the prices of some durable goods, e.g., machine tools, rise and fall in response to much different forces than affect the prices of other equipment, e.g., computer systems or aircraft. In an interesting two-part article, Sigurdsen (1996a, 1996b) notes that capital costs are variant with quantity of output and compares two methods of making capital cost estimates.

7.2   IMPROVING THE PROCESS OF COST ESTIMATING

The cooperation of several people is required to prepare cost estimates for a project. If the firm is in a business that routinely requires bids to be submitted to its customers, it will have "professional" (experienced) cost estimators on its staff. The major responsibility of the professional estimators is to reduce the level of uncertainty in cost estimates so that the firm's bids can be made in the light of expert information about its potential costs. In these cases, it is the job of the PM to generate a description of the work to be done on the project in sufficient detail that the estimator can know what cost data must be collected. Frequently, the project will be too complex for the PM to generate such a description without considerable help from experts in the functional areas.

Even with the finest of experts working to estimate resource usage, the one thing that is certain is that things will not go precisely as planned. There are two fundamentally different ways to manage the risks associated with the chance events that occur on every project. The simpler and far more common way is to make an allowance for contingencies—usually 5 or 10 percent of the estimated cost. Just why these numbers are chosen, in preference to 6 or 9, for instance, we do not know. We strongly prefer another method in which the forecaster selects "most likely, optimistic, and pessimistic" estimates. We illustrate this method in the next section when we apply simulation to the discounted cash flow problem in the PsychoCeramic Sciences example from Chapter 2.

Project Management in Practice
Completing the Limerick Nuclear Facility Under Budget

When the Limerick nuclear-power-generating facility in Pennsylvania began commercial operation, it set a construction record for nuclear facilities. In an era when it is common to hear of nuclear plants that massively overrun their budgets and completion schedules, Limerick was completed eight months ahead of its 49-month schedule and came in $400 million under its $3.2 billion budget. Limerick has truly set a standard for the industry.

It was no accident that Limerick was completed ahead of schedule and under budget. When construction started, a project goal was to complete the project eight months ahead of the planned completion, which would help keep the costs under the budget limit as well. To achieve this early target, a series of innovative approaches were taken. Two of the major ones were to accelerate ramp-up staffing and to use an extensive, fully supported second shift. The momentum of the speedy start-up set the fast pace for the remainder of the project. The second shift earned a very favorable premium, as well as having a full complement of managers and engineers to work with

the manual workers. In this fashion, the second shift productivity was equal to, if not higher than, the first shift's.

Other decisions and actions further helped either the cost or the schedule. For example, it was decided that overtime would not be worked since a second shift was being used. And as a condition of the project approval, a project labor agreement with the local unions (rather than the national) had to be developed that would eliminate strikes, lockouts, and delays and provide for peaceful resolution of disputes. Also, an incentive fee contract with the building contractor was signed whereby the contractor would share equally in cost/schedule overruns or underruns, with limits set. With such attention to the goal of an early and under-budget completion, the team, numbering almost 3,000 workers at the start, worked diligently and with high morale, beating its 4-year deadline by almost a year!

Source: T. P. Gotzis, "Limerick Generating Station No. 2," *PM Network*, Vol. 5.

Turning now to the problem of estimating direct costs,* project managers often find it helpful to collect direct cost estimates on a form that not only lists the estimated level of resource needs, but also indicates when each resource will be needed, and notes if it is available (or will be available at the appropriate time). Figure 7-3 shows such a form. It also has a column for identifying the person to contact in order to get specific resources. This table can be used for collating the resource requirements for each task element in a project, or for aggregating the information from a series of tasks onto a single form.

Note that Figure 7-3 contains no information on overhead costs. The matter of what overhead costs are to be added and in what amounts is unique to the firm, beyond the PM's control, and generally a source of annoyance and frustration to one and all. The allocation of overhead is arbitrary by its nature, and when the addition of overhead cost causes an otherwise attractive project to fail to meet the organization's economic objectives, the project's supporters are apt to complain bitterly about the "unfairness" of overhead cost allocation.

---

*Our emphasis on estimating direct costs and on focusing on resources that are "direct costed" in the WBS is based on our belief that the PM should be concerned with only those items over which he or she has some control—which certainly excludes overheads. The PM, however, may wish to add some nonchargeable items (e.g., photocopying) to the resource column of the WBS simply to "reserve" that item for use at a specific time.

Project Name_____

Date_____

Task Number _____

RESOURCES NEEDED

Resources	Person to Contact	How Many/ Much Needed	When Needed	Check (✔) if Available
People: Managers, Supervisors				
Professional & Technical				
Nontechnical				
Money				
Materials: Facilities				
Equipment				
Tools				
Power				
Space				
Special Services: Research & Test				
Typing/clerical				
Reproduction				
Others				

Figure 7-3   Form for gathering data on project resource needs.

At times, firms support projects that show a significant incremental profit over direct costs but are not profitable when fully costed. Such decisions can be justified for a number of reasons, such as:

- To develop knowledge of a technology
- To get the organization's "foot in the door"
- To obtain the parts or service portion of the work
- To be in a good position for a follow-on contract
- To improve a competitive position
- To broaden a product line or a line of business

All of these are adequate reasons to fund projects that, in the short term, may lose money but provide the organization with the real option for future growth and profitability. It is up to senior management to decide if such reasons are worth it.

Learning Curves*

If the project being costed is one of many similar projects, the estimate of each cost element is fairly routine. If the project involves work in which the firm has little experience, cost estimating is more difficult, particularly for direct labor costs. For example, consider a project that requires 25 units of a complex electronic device to be assembled. The firm is experienced in building electronic equipment but has never before made this specific device, which differs significantly from the items routinely assembled.

Experience might indicate that if the firm were to build many such devices, it would use about 70 hours of direct labor per unit. If labor is paid a wage of $12 per hour, and if benefits equal 28 percent of the wage rate, the estimated labor cost for the 25 units is

$$(1.28)(\$12/hr)(25 \text{ units})(70 \text{ hr/unit}) = \$26,880$$

In fact, this would be an underestimate of the actual labor cost because more time per unit output is used early in the production process. Studies have shown that human performance usually improves when a task is repeated. In general, performance improves by a fixed percent each time production doubles. More specifically, *each time the output doubles, the worker hours per unit decrease to a fixed percentage of their previous value.* That percentage is called the *learning rate*. If an individual requires 10 minutes to accomplish a certain task the first time it is attempted and only 8 minutes the second time, that person is said to have an 80 percent learning rate. If output is doubled again from two to four, we would expect the fourth item to be produced in

$$8(0.8) = 6.4 \text{ min}$$

Similarly, the eighth unit of output should require

$$6.4(0.8) = 5.12 \text{ min}$$

and so on. The time required to produce a unit of output follows a well-known formula:

$$T_n = T_1 n^r$$

where

T_n = the time required for the nth unit of output,

T_1 = the time required for the initial unit of output,

n = the number of units to be produced, and

r = log decimal learning rate/log 2.

The total time required for all units of a production run of size N is N

$$\text{total time} = T_1 \sum_{n=1}^{N} n^r$$

Tables are widely available with both unit and total values for the learning curves, and have been calculated for many different improvement ratios (learning rates—e.g., see Meredith et al., 2010).

---

*Occasionally, particular sections will be shaded, meaning that they can be skipped without loss of continuity.

In the example of the electronic device just given, assume that after producing the twentieth unit, there is no significant further improvement (i.e., assembly time has reached a steady state at 70 hours). Further assume that previous study established that the usual learning rate for assemblers in this plant is about 85 percent. We can estimate the time required for the first unit by letting $T_n = 70$ hours by the unit $n = 20$. Then

$$r = \log 0.85 / \log 2$$
$$= -0.1626/0.693$$
$$= -0.235$$

and

$$70 = T_1 (20)r$$
$$T_1 = 141.3 \text{ hr}$$

Now we know the time for the initial unit. Using a table that shows the total time multiplier (see Meredith et al., 2010, pp. 337–341, for example), we can find the appropriate total time multiplier for this example—the multiplier for 20 units given a learning rate of 85 percent. With this multiplier, 12.40, we can calculate the total time required to build all 20 units. It is

$$(12.40) \, (141.3 \text{ hr}) = 1752.12 \text{ hr}$$

The last five units are produced in the steady-state time of 70 hours each. Thus the total assembly time is

$$1752.12 + 5(70 \text{ hr}) = 2102.12 \text{ hr}$$

We can now refigure the direct labor cost.

$$2102.12(\$12)(1.28) = \$32,288.56$$

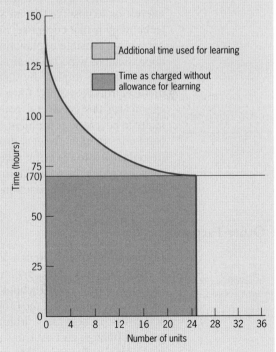

Figure 7-4   Effects of ignoring learning curve.

Our first estimate, which ignored learning effects, understated the cost by

$$\$32,288.56 - \$26,880 = \$5,408.56$$

or about 17 percent. Figure 7-4 illustrates this source of the error.

In recent years, learning curves have received increasing interest from project managers, particularly in the construction industry. Methods have been developed for approximating composite learning curves for entire projects (Amor et al., 1998), and for approximating total cost from the unit learning curve (Camm et al., 1987). Badiru (1995) has included learning curve effects in his concept of "critical resource diagramming" (discussed further in Chapter 8).

Remember that we are attempting to reduce the risk inherent in estimating costs. Therefore, for any task where labor is a significant cost factor and the production run is reasonably short, the PM should take the learning curve into account when estimating costs.

The implications of this conclusion should not be overlooked. We do not often think of projects as "production," but they are. While the construction, electronics, and aircraft assembly industries have used learning curves for many years, other industrial areas have been slow to follow. For example, research (Gagnon et al., 1987) has shown that the learning curve effect is important to decisions about the role of engineering consultants on computer-assisted design (CAD) projects. The same is assuredly true for the design of advertising campaigns or charity drives. The failure to consider performance improvement is a significant cause of errors in project cost estimation.

A Special Case of Learning—Technological Shock

If the parent organization is not experienced in the type of project being considered for selection, performance measures such as time to installation, time to achieve 80 percent efficiency, cost to install, and the like, are quite uncertain and often will be seriously underestimated. It is interesting to observe that an almost certain, immediate result of installing a new, cost-saving technology is that costs rise. Sometimes we blame the cost increases on resistance to change, but a more sensible explanation is that when we alter a system, we disturb it and it reacts in unpredictable ways. A steelmaker recalling the installation of the then new technology for manufacturing tinplate by electrolysis remarked, "We discovered and installed the world's first electrolytic method for making scrap. It took a year before we had that line running the way it was designed." Of course, if the organization is experienced, underestimation is not likely to be a serious problem. The Reliance Electric Company undertook several "18-month" plant construction projects that they predicted, accurately, would require 36 months to build from decision to the point when the plant was capable of operating at or above three-fourths capacity. (Note the potential for ethical problems here.) To the extent possible, past knowledge of system actions and reactions should be built into estimates of future project performance.

Other Factors

Depending on the reference, anywhere from about three-fifths to five-sixths of projects fail to meet their time, cost, and/or specification objectives (see, for example, Frame, 1998). The record of Information Technology (IT) projects is particularly poor, according to article after article in the journals of the Project Management Institute. Possibly the problem is that Dilbert's pointy-haired boss sets arbitrary and impossible goals. Possibly scope-creep impacts all projects [though cost overruns are not necessarily associated with changing scope (Christensen et al., 1998)]. Possibly PMs use wildly optimistic estimates in order to influence the project selection process. Or maybe they are simply unaware of good cost (or time) estimating practices. For example, there are at least 45 estimating models available for IT projects, but few IT project managers use any of them (Lawrence, 1994; Martin, 1994). Some IT workers flatly refuse to estimate time and cost for IT projects on the grounds that there is too much uncertainty—and, we suspect, in an attempt to avoid responsibility. Possibly all of these things, and even others, act together. Possibly adoption of agile project management will help reduce the failure rate.

While the number of things that can increase risk by producing errors in cost estimates is almost without limit, some problems occur with particularly high frequency. Changes in resource prices are one of these. The most commonly used solution to this problem is to increase all cost estimates by some fixed percentage. A more useful approach is to identify each input that accounts for a significant portion of project cost and estimate the direction and rate of price change for each.

The determination of which inputs account for a "significant" portion of project cost is not difficult, although it may be somewhat arbitrary. Suppose, for example, that our initial, rough cost estimate (with no provision for future price changes) for a project with an objective of setting up a small storefront accounting office is $1 million and is to be spent over a three-year period in approximately equal amounts per year. If we think personnel costs will comprise about 60 percent of that total, also spread equally over time, the wage/salary bill will be about $600,000. Split into three equal amounts, we have expenditures of $200,000 per year. If we estimate that wage/salary rates will increase by 6 percent per year, our expenses for the second year rise to $212,000 (an increase of $12,000), and to $224,720 in the third year (a further increase of $12,720). Failure to account for wage/salary inflation would result in an underestimate of project cost of $36,720. This is an error of slightly more than 4 percent of the estimated personnel cost and almost 2.5 percent of the total project budget.

Further improvements can be made by taking into account the fact that the prices of different inputs often change at very different rates and sometimes in different directions. A quick examination of the Bureau of Labor Statistics (BLS) wage and price indices, which cover a very large number of specific commodities and wage rates, will reveal that even in periods of stable prices, the prices of some things rise while others fall and still others do not change appreciably. Thus, the PM may wish to use different *inflators/deflators* for each of several different classes of labor or types of commodities. While most PMs are concerned only with price increases, any industry submitting competitive bids on projects must remember that failure to be aware of falling prices will lead to cost overestimates and uncompetitive bids.

Other elements that need to be factored into the estimated project cost include an allowance for waste and spoilage. No sane builder would order "just enough" lumber to build a house. Also, personnel costs can be significantly increased by the loss and subsequent replacement of project professionals. For example, new people go through a learning period which, as we have seen, will have a negative effect on production. Thus, it may well cost more to replace a person who leaves the project with a newcomer who has approximately the same level of experience.

We have already mentioned the inclination PMs and project sponsors have toward understating the costs of a project in order to make it appear more profitable to senior managers, as well as the proclivity of lower-level project workers to overestimate costs in order to protect themselves. If the project is in its initial planning stage as a response to a Request for Proposal (RFP) from an outside organization, over- and underestimates of cost can have a serious impact on the probability of winning the contract—or on the level of profit, if a win occurs.

Serious ethical problems may arise during the process of estimating costs and submission of bids in response to an RFP. If the job is to be paid on a cost-plus basis, or even if it is a fixed-fee project, with fee increases allowed for special circumstances, some bidders may "low ball" a contract (submit underestimated costs). By doing this, they hope to win the bid, counting on the opportunity to increase costs or to plead special circumstances once the job is underway. At times, clients have been known to give favored bidders a "last look" at supposedly sealed bids so that the favored bidder can submit a winning bid, often with an unwritten agreement to allow some cost escalation at a later date. There is considerable opportunity for unethical behavior during cost estimating and bidding. Further, estimating and bidding practices vary widely from industry to industry.

Finally, there is plain bad luck. Delays occur for reasons that cannot be predicted. Machinery with the reliability of a railroad spike suddenly breaks down. That which has never failed fails. Every project needs an "allowance for contingencies."

Project Management in Practice
The Emanon Aircraft Corporation

Emanon Aircraft is a major manufacturer of aircraft parts, specializing in landing gear parts and assemblies. They are located in a highly industrialized midwestern state. The local area suffers from somewhat higher than average unemployment, partly because Emanon has experienced a downturn in business. In the past three years, they have lost out on a number of landing gear contracts, being underbid by competitors from other areas of the country. Senior management studied the problem, but has come to no conclusion about what can be done. They have hired a consulting team from a nearby university to study the situation and make a recommendation.

Business in the aircraft industry is not significantly different than in many other industries specializing in the building of complex machines. Aircraft builders are primarily assembly operations. They build planes from subassemblies and parts manufactured by themselves or by subcontractors. When an order is received to build some number of a given type of plane, the builder (prime contractor) requests bids for the proper number of a certain part or subassembly from appropriate subcontractors.

The university consulting team studied three aspects of Emanon's landing gear operation: the manufacturing process, the cost structure, and the bidding behavior and profit structure on landing gear bids.

They determined that the manufacturing process was reasonably efficient and not significantly different from Emanon's competitors. Second, they found that all competitors were using approximately the same level of mark-up when determining their cost-plus price. When examining the cost structure, however, they noted that in the past three years, the firm consistently ran negative cost variances in material accounts. That is, the amount of material actually used in the construction of landing gears was approximately 10 percent less than the plan indicated. The team was unsure of this finding because there were only a few winning contracts for landing gears during the past three years.

An investigation was conducted on the estimating and purchase of materials for this department. It exposed the following facts. Three-and-a-half years ago, Emanon was late making a delivery of landing gear parts. The firm paid a large penalty and was threatened with loss of further business with the prime contractor. The late delivery resulted when Emanon ordered an insufficient quantity of a special steel alloy used in landing gear struts, and was unable to purchase any on the open market. The steel company required a manufacturing lead time of more than 90 days, so Emanon's delivery was late.

As a result, the purchasing official who had responsibility for this contract was demoted. The new purchasing official handled the problem in a straightforward fashion by regularly inflating the material estimates by 10 percent. The cost of material is about half of the total cost of landing gear production, which resulted in bids that were approximately 5 percent above the competition.

Source: S. J. Mantel, Jr. Consulting project.

Some writers and instructors differentiate four bases for estimating costs: experience, quantitative (statistical) methods, constraints, and worksheets. They discuss the advantages and disadvantages of each and then, typically, decide that one or another gives the best results. We feel strongly that all four are useful and that no single approach to cost-estimating should be accepted as the best or rejected out of hand. The best estimators seem to employ an eclectic approach that uses, as one said, "anything that works." The wise PM takes into account as many known influences on the project budget as can be predicted. What cannot be predicted must then, by experience, simply be "allowed for." There are two other factors, particularly common to projects involving intangible outputs such as software programming, that need to be mentioned relating to cost-estimation and the schedule. These two factors have been identified in a classic and highly readable work—*The Mythical Man-Month*—by Brooks (1975).

First, most projects involve a tangible medium that tends not to be under our control—the wood splits, the paint smears—and thus we blame implementation problems of our "good" ideas on these physical elements. So, when we are working with a purely intellectual medium that has no physical elements, such as computer code, we are highly optimistic and foolishly assume that all will go well. However, when any project consisting of a series of components can only be successful if all of the components are successful, and each component has a small probability of failing, the chances of the overall project being successful may be very poor. Consider, for example, a software program consisting of 1,000 lines of code, each of which is 0.999 reliable. The chance of the program itself working is only about 36 percent!

The second factor is what Brooks calls "the mythical man-month" and relates to our tendency to assume that workers and time are interchangeable. Thus, when a schedule slips, the traditional response is to add labor, which is like trying to douse a fire with gasoline. Our assumption that workers and time are interchangeable is correct only when a task can be partitioned such that there is no communication needed between the workers. Most projects, however, especially computer programming, are not set up that way and the more workers that are added require even more workers to train, as well as lines of communication to coordinate their efforts. Thus, three workers require three times as much pairwise intercommunication as two, and four require six times as much, etc. This result is captured in Brooks' law: *Adding manpower to a late software project makes it later*.

On Making Better Estimates*

Let us begin with the assumption that budget estimating errors are not the result of deliberate dishonesty, but derive from honest errors on the part of the PM, project cost estimators, or anyone else involved. But why do experienced managers err on their budget and schedule estimates? It is axiomatic that we should learn through experience. It is a truism that we do not. Nowhere is this more evident than in project management, and yet it is not difficult to improve one's estimating/forecasting skills.

There are two types of estimation error. First, there is *random error*, in which overestimates and underestimates are equally likely. These are errors that tend to cancel each other. If we sum these errors over many estimates, their sum will approach zero. Second, there is *bias*, which is systematic error. For biased estimates, the chance of over- and underestimates are *not* equally likely, and their sum, either positive or negative, will increase as the number of estimates increases. A measure for bias, the "tracking signal" (TS), is given in Row 4 of Figure 7-5. Using the ubiquitous Excel® we can construct a spreadsheet that captures the essence of a person's performance as an estimator. Two simple statistical measures are used:

---

*Occasionally, particular sections will be shaded, meaning that they can be skipped without loss of continuity.

	A	B	C	D	E	F	G
1	This is a template for improving one's estimating skills						
2							
3	MAR = SUM {|(A(t) / F (t)) – 1|} /n						
4	Tracking Signal = SUM{(A(t) / F (t)) – 1}/MAR						
5							Tracking
6	Period	Forecast	Actual	(A(t)/F(t)) – 1	|(A(t)/F(t)) – 1|	MAR	Signal
7	=====	======	======	========	==========	=====	======
8							
9	1	155	163	0.052	0.052		
10	2	242	240	– 0.008	0.008	0.030	1.448
11	3	46	67	0.457	0.457	0.172	2.904
12	4	69	78	0.130	0.130	0.162	3.898
13	5	75	71	– 0.053	0.053	0.140	4.120
14	6	344	423	0.230	0.230	0.155	5.205
15	7	56	49	– 0.125	0.125	0.151	4.523
16	8	128	157	0.227	0.227	0.160	5.670
17							
18	Key Formulae		Total =	0.908	1.281		
19	Cell D9	= (C9–B9)–1 copy to D10:D16					
20	Cell E9	= ABS(D9) copy to E10:E16					
21	Cell F10	= (Sum($E$9:E10))/A10 copy to F11:F16					
22	Cell G10	= (Sum($D$9:D10))/F10 copy to G11:G16					

Figure 7-5 Estimation template using ratios.

the mean absolute ratio (MAR), and the tracking signal (TS). The printout[*] of such a spreadsheet is shown in Figure 7-5. Appendix A of this book (on the book's website) includes information on probability, statistics, and forecasting.

Figure 7-5 assumes that for each period (Column A) someone has made an estimate or forecast of a variable (Column B), and that the actual value of that variable is, sooner or later, known (Column C). (It should be noted that Column A need not be time periods. This column simply counts the number of forecasts made and links them with their respective actuals.)

We will define the forecast error in terms of the *ratio* of actual to forecast. Therefore, the ratio for the first forecast (Period 1) in Figure 7-5 is

$$A(t)/F(t) = 163/155 = 1.052$$

This means that the actual was 5.2 percent higher than the forecast, which was low. In column D, we list these errors for each of the periods and then cumulate them at the bottom of the spreadsheet. Note that in columns D and E we subtract 1 from the ratio. This centers the data around zero rather than 1.0, which makes some ratios positive, indicating an actual greater than the forecast, and other ratios negative, indicating an actual less than the forecast.

---

[*]Any of the common spreadsheet programs can easily handle all of the calculations shown in this chapter and will accept formulas and calculations from any of the others.

If the cumulative percent error at the bottom of the spreadsheet is positive, which it is in this case, it means that the actuals are usually greater than the forecasts or that the size of the positive errors are, in general, larger than the size of the negative errors. The forecaster underestimates if the ratio is positive and overestimates if it is negative. The larger the percent error, the greater the forecaster's bias, systematic under- or overestimation.

Column E simply shows the absolute value of column D. Column F is the "mean absolute ratio," abbreviated MAR, which is the running average of the values in column E up to that period. (Check the formulas in the spreadsheet.) The tracking signal listed in column G is the ratio of the running sum of the values in column D divided by the MAR for that period. If the estimates are unbiased, the running sum of ratios in column D will be about zero, and dividing this by the MAR will give a very small tracking signal, possibly zero. On the other hand, if there is considerable bias in the estimates, either positive or negative, the running sum of the ratios in column D will grow quite large. Then, when divided by the mean absolute ratio this will show whether the tracking signal is >1 or <1, and therefore greater than the variability in the estimates or not. If the bias is large, resulting in large positive or negative ratios, the resulting tracking signal will be correspondingly positive or negative.

It should be noted that it is not simply the bias that is of interest to the PM, although bias is very important. The MAR is also important because this indicates the variability of the estimates compared with the resulting actual values. With experience, the MAR should decrease over time though it will never reach zero. We strive to find a forecasting technique that minimizes both the bias *and* the MAR.

7.3 RISK ESTIMATION

The duration of project activities, the amounts of various resources that will be required to complete a project, the estimates made of the value of accomplishing a project, all these and many other aspects of a project are uncertain. While a project manager may be able to reduce uncertainty, it cannot be eliminated. Decisions must be made in the face of the ambiguity that results from uncertain information. Risk estimation and analysis does not remove the ambiguity; it simply describes the uncertainties in a way that provides the decision maker with a useful insight into their nature.

To apply risk analysis, one must make assumptions about the probability distributions that characterize key parameters and variables associated with a decision and then use these to estimate the *risk profiles* or probability distributions of the outcomes of the decision. This can be done analytically or by *Monte Carlo simulation* (Meredith et al., 2002), an easy-to-use technique that is well adapted to evaluating the risk in certain situations. When the decisions involve several input variables or parameters, simulation is highly preferable to the tedious calculations required by analytic methods such as decision or probability trees. The simulation software (in our case, Crystal Ball®, an Excel® Add-In) allows the decision to be represented by a mathematical model and then selects samples from the assumed distributions for each input. The software then plugs these inputs into the model and finds the outcome(s) of the decision. This process is repeated many times and the statistical distribution of the outcomes is then displayed. The object of this process is to show the decision maker the distribution of the outcomes. This risk profile is used to assess the value of the decision along with other factors that might be relevant such as strategic concerns, socio/political factors, and impact on market share.

David Matheson, CEO of SmartOrg Inc. in California (Gale, 2007), says that "Vague terms lead to bad decisions. You need to define success in quantifiable terms so that everyone is on the same page . . . you need robust ways to discuss uncertainties quantified in the language of probability." By estimating the range and distribution for costs and revenues and using these to calculate the projected profitabilities, project managers have a way to make project selection decisions. Simulation is the perfect tool to do this!

Following a few comments about the nature of the input data and assumptions, we illustrate the use of Crystal Ball® (CB) to aid in the risk analysis of a potential investment. We show another application of CB simulation again in Chapter 8 to determine the likelihood of project completion by various times.

General Simulation Analysis

Simulation combined with sensitivity analysis is also useful for evaluating projects while they are still in the conceptual stage. Using the net present value approach, for example, we would support a project if the net present value of the cash flows (including the initial cash investment) is positive and represents the best available alternative use of the funds. When these flows are estimated for purposes of analysis, it is well to avoid the *full-cost* philosophy that is usually adopted. The full-cost approach to estimating cash flows necessitates the inclusion of arbitrarily determined overheads in the calculation—some of which are not affected by changes in product or process and thus are not relevant to the decision. The only relevant costs are those that will be changed by the implementation of the new process or product.

The determination of such costs is not simple. If the concept being considered involves a new process, it is necessary to go to the detailed *route sheet*, or *operations sequence sheet*, describing the operation in which the new process would be used. Proceeding systematically through the operating sequence step-by-step, one asks whether the present time and cost required for this step are likely to be altered if the new process concept is installed. If, and only if, the answer is yes, three estimates (optimistic, most likely, and pessimistic) are made of the size of the expected change. These individual estimated changes in production cost and time, together with upstream or downstream time and cost changes that might also result (e.g., a production method change on a part might also alter the cost of inspecting the final product), are used to generate the required cash flow information—presuming that the time savings have been properly costed. This estimation process will be explained in detail in Chapter 8.

The preceding analysis gives a picture of the proposed change in terms of the costs and times that will be affected. The uncertainty associated with each individual element of the process is included. Simulation runs will then indicate the likelihood of achieving various levels of costs and benefits. Note also that investigation of the simulation model will expose the major sources of uncertainty in the final cost and benefit distributions.

Those without considerable experience in simulation should use this tool with caution. Simulation software is indifferent to assumptions-contrary-to-fact, and cares not a wit that the experimenter specifies a statistical distribution that implies a universe that never was nor ever will be. In such cases, the results of the simulation—often taken by the unwary as an estimate of reality—are apt to mislead.

PsychoCeramic Sciences Revisited*

There is great value in performing risk analysis in order to confront the uncertainties in project selection. Reconsider the PsychoCeramic Sciences example we solved in Chapter 2, Section 2.3, devoted to finding the discounted cash flows associated with a project. Setting this problem up on Excel® is straightforward and the earlier solution is shown here in Table 7-3 for convenience. Another advantage of using Excel® is that we can simply use the NPV function

---

*Occasionally, particular sections will be shaded, meaning that they can be skipped without loss of continuity.

Table 7-3   Single-Point Estimate of the Cash Flows for PsychoCeramic Sciences, Inc.

	A	B	C	D	E	F	G
1					*Discount*	*Net Present*	*Inflation*
2	*Year*	*Inflow*	*Outflow*	*Net Flow*	*Factor*	*Value*	*Rate, p*
3	*A*	*B*	*C*	*D = B − C*	$E=1/(1 + k + p)^t$	*D*E*	
4	2010*	0.00	125,000.00	−125,000.00	1	−125,000.00	0.0300
5	2010	0.00	100,000.00	−100,000.00	0.8696	−86,956.52	0.0300
6	2011	0.00	90,000.00	−90,000.00	0.7561	−68,052.93	0.0300
7	2012	50,000.00	0.00	50,000.00	0.6575	32,875.81	0.0300
8	2013	120,000.00	15,000.00	105,000.00	0.5718	60,034.09	0.0300
9	2014	115,000.00	0.00	115,000.00	0.4972	57,175.32	0.0300
10	2015	105,000.00	15,000.00	90,000.00	0.4323	38,909.48	0.0300
11	2016	97,000.00	0.00	97,000.00	0.3759	36,465.89	0.0300
12	2017	90,000.00	15,000.00	75,000.00	0.3269	24,517.63	0.0300
13	2018	82,000.00		82,000.00	0.2843	23,309.52	0.0300
14	2019	65,000.00		65,000.00	0.2472	16,067.01	0.0300
15	2019	35,000.00		35,000.00	0.2472	8,651.46	0.0300
16							
17	**Total**	759,000.00	360,000.00	399,000.00		17,996.77	
18							
19	* t=0 at beginning of 2010						
20							
21	**Formulae**						
22	**Cell B17**		=SUM(B4:B15)	copy to C17, D17, F17			
23	**Cell D4**		=(B4−C4)	copy to D5:D15			
24	**Cell E4**		=1/(1 + .12 + G4)^0				
25	**Cell E5**		=1/(1 + .12 + G5)^1				
26	**Cell E6**		=1/(1 + .12 + G6)^(A6 − 2009)	copy to E7:E14			
27	**Cell E15**		=E14				
25	**Cell F4**		=D4*E4	copy to F5:F15			

to find the net present values; however, for pedagogic purposes and consistency we will continue with the previous method of solution. We found that the project cleared the barrier of a 12 percent hurdle rate for acceptance. The net cash flow over the project's life is just under $400,000, and discounted at the hurdle rate plus 3 percent annual inflation, the net present value of the cash flow is about $18,000. The rate of inflation is shown in a separate column because it is another uncertain variable that should be included in the risk analysis.

Now let us assume that the expenditures in this example are fixed by contract with an outside vendor. Thus, there is no uncertainty about the outflows, but there is, of course, uncertainty about the inflows. Assume that the estimated inflows are as shown in Table 7-4 and include a most likely estimate, a minimum (pessimistic) estimate, and a maximum (optimistic) estimate. (In Chapter 8, "Scheduling," we will deal in more detail with the methods and meaning of making such estimates.) Both the beta and the triangular statistical distributions are well suited for modeling variables with these three parameters. In earlier versions of CB the beta distribution was complicated and not particularly intuitive to use, so the triangular distribution was adopted as a reasonably good approximation of the beta. Use of a new beta distribution, labeled "BetaPERT" by CB in its Distribution Gallery, has been simplified in CB 11.1.1.3. We will use it in this example and in the simulations used elsewhere in this book.*

The hurdle rate of return is fixed by the firm, so the only remaining variable is the rate of inflation that is included in finding the discount factor. We have assumed a 3 percent rate with a normal distribution, plus or minus 1 percent (i.e., 1 percent represents three standard deviations).

It is important to remember that other approaches in which only the most likely estimate of each variable is used are equivalent to an assumption of certainty. The major benefit of simulation is that it allows all possible values for each variable to be considered. Just as the distribution of possible values for a variable is a better reflection of reality (as the estimator sees reality) than a single "most likely" value, the distribution of outcomes developed by simulation is a better forecast of uncertain future reality than a forecast of any single outcome can be. As any security analyst knows, a forecast of corporate quarterly earnings of $0.50–0.58 per share is far more likely to be accurate than a forecast of $0.54 per share. In general, precise forecasts will be precisely wrong.

Using CB to run a Monte Carlo simulation requires us to define two types of cells in the Excel® spreadsheet. The cells that contain variables or parameters are defined as *assumption cells*. For the PsychoCeramic Sciences case, these are the cells in Table 7-3, columns B and G, the inflows and the rate of inflation, respectively. The cells that contain outcomes of the model are called *forecast cells*, cell F17 in Table 7-3. Each forecast cell typically contains a formula that is dependent on one or more of the assumption cells. Simulations may have many assumption and forecast cells, but they must have at least one of each. Before proceeding, open Crystal Ball and make a spreadsheet copy of Table 7-3.

To illustrate the process of defining an assumption cell, consider cell B7, the cash inflow estimate for 2012. We can see from Table 7-4 that the minimum expected cash inflow is $35,000, the most likely cash flow is $50,000, and the maximum is $60,000. Also remember that we decided to model all these flows with the BetaPERT (or triangular, if you wish) distribution.

Once one has entered the original information in Table 7-3, the process of defining the assumption cells and entering the pessimistic and optimistic data is straightforward and involves six steps:**

1. Click on cell **B7** to identify it as the relevant assumption cell.
2. Select the menu option "**Define Assumptions**" at the top-left of the screen. CB's **Distribution Gallery** is now displayed as shown in Figure 7-6.
3. CB allows you to choose from a wide variety of probability distributions. Click on the **BetaPERT** (or Triangular) box and then click **OK** to select it.
4. CB's BetaPERT distribution dialog box is displayed as in Figure 7-7. It may have numbers in the boxes but ignore them. If it does not otherwise appear exactly like Figure 7-7, click "**Parameters**" in the menu at the top of the BetaPERT distribution box, and then select "**Minimum, Most Likely, Maximum**" at the top of the drop-down menu.
5. In the "**Assumption Name**" textbox at the top of the distribution box, enter a descriptive Label, for example, *Cash Inflow 2012*. Then enter the pessimistic, most likely, and optimistic estimates from Table 7-4 in the appropriate cells below the distribution.
6. Click on "**Enter**" and then on "**OK**."

---

*The instructions for its use are the same for either the beta or the triangular distribution, so the reader (or the instructor) may select either.

It is generally helpful for the reader to work the problem as we explain it. If Crystal Ball® has been installed on your computer but is not running, select **Tools, and then **Add-Ins** from Excel®'s menu. Next, click on the **CB** checkbox and select **OK**. If the CB Add-In has not been installed on your computer, download a CB trial copy using the password that accompanies this book to install it.

Table 7-4 Pessimistic, Most Likely, and Optimistic Estimates of the Cash Flows for PsychoCeramic Sciences, Inc.

Year	Minimum Inflow	Most Likely Inflow	Maximum Inflow
2012	$35,000	$50,000	$60,000
2013	95,000	120,000	136,000
2014	100,000	115,000	125,000
2015	88,000	105,000	116,000
2016	80,000	97,000	108,000
2017	75,000	90,000	100,000
2018	67,000	82,000	91,000
2019	51,000	65,000	73,000
2019 (salvage)	30,000	35,000	38,000
Total	**$621,000**	**$759,000**	**$847,000**

Figure 7-6 Crystal Ball®'s Distribution Gallery.

Figure 7-7   Crystal Ball® dialog box for model inputs assuming the BetaPERT distribution.

Now repeat steps 1–6 for the remaining cash flow assumption cells (cells B8:B15). Remember that the proper information to be entered is found in Table 7-4.

When finished with the cash flow cells, repeat the six-step procedure for assumption cells G4:G15. For this assumption select the **Normal** distribution and the entry for each cell in the series will be identical. We decided earlier to use a 3 percent inflation rate, plus or minus 1 percent. Recall that the normal distribution is "bell-shaped" and that the mean of the distribution is its center point.

Also recall that the mean, plus or minus three standard deviations, includes 99+ percent of the data. The normal distribution dialog box, Figure 7-8, calls for the distribution's mean and its standard deviation. The mean will be 0.03 (3 percent) for all cells. The standard deviation will be .0033 (one-third of 1 percent) for all cells. (Older versions of CB displayed only the first two decimal places of the standard deviation although the actual standard deviation of .0033 was used by the program.) As you enter this data you will note that the distribution will show a mean of 3 percent and a range from about 2 percent to about 4 percent.

Note that there are two cash outflows for the year 2010, but one of those occurs at the beginning of the year and the other at the end of the year. The entry at the beginning of the year is not discounted so there is no logical reason for an entry in cell G4. CB seems to like one, however, so go ahead and enter it. In the **Assumption Name:** textbox for the G4 entry, type *Inflation rate—2009.* Each of the following entries should be labeled with its appropriate year. The year 2019 raises a similar problem with two cash flows, but these both occur at the end of the year. When you constructed the spreadsheet, you probably copied cell E6 to the range E7:E15. If the inflation rate is fixed at 3 percent, that raises no problem, but when we make the inflation rate a random variable, that would allow G14 and G15, inflation for 2019, to be different. The fix is simple. First, click on **E15**. Then press the key **F2**. This shows the formula for E15 in its cell and it should appear as follows: $= 1/(1 + 0.12 + G15)^\wedge(A15\text{-}2009)$. Move

Figure 7-8 Crystal Ball® dialogue box for model inputs assuming the normal distribution.

your cursor next to the "5" in "G15." Delete the "5" and change it to "4." You may now delete the entry in cell G15; the same inflation rate will now be used for both 2015 calculations.*

Now we consider the forecast or outcome cell. In this example we wish to find the net present value of the cash flows we have estimated. The process of defining a forecast cell involves five steps.

1. Click on the cell **F17** to identify it as containing an outcome that interests us.

2. Select the menu option **Define Forecast** near the left end of the tool bar.

3. CB's **Define Forecast** dialog box is now displayed as shown in Figure 7-9. In the **Forecast Name:** textbox, enter a descriptive name such as *Net Present Value of Project*. Then enter a descriptive label such as *Dollars* in the **Units:** textbox.

4. Click **OK**. There is only one Forecast cell in this example, but there may be several. Use the same five steps for each.

5. Before leaving the **Define Forecast,** there is some additional work that will be helpful. There are several views of the output of the simulation. Click on the **View** (double arrow at right) button to choose. You may also control the precision of the output data, you can filter it if you wish, and you can decide what information about the results you would like to examine. The latter choice is made by clicking **Auto Extract.** Put a check in the "**Extract forecast . . .** " box and then check as many statistical outputs as you wish. Be sure to make an entry in the "**Starting cell**" box and choose any entry outside of the bounds of

---

*You may wonder why we spend time with this kind of detail. The reason is simple. Once you have dealt with this kind of problem, and it is common in such analyses, you won't make this mistake in the real world where having such errors called to your attention may be quite painful.

Figure 7-9 Crystal Ball® dialog box for the model forecast or outcome.

Table 7-5. (If the starting cell is within the boundary of the simulation data, the statistics will overprint your spreadsheet.) When you have completed all entries, what was Table 7-3 now appears as Table 7-5.

Table 7-5 Three-Point Estimates of Cash Flows and Inflation Rate for PsychoCeramic Sciences, Inc. All Assumptions and Forecast Cells Defined.

	A	B	C	D	E	F	G
1					*Discount*	*Net Present*	*Inflation*
2	*Year*	*Inflow*	*Outflow*	*Net Flow*	*Factor*	*Value*	*Rate, p*
3	*A*	*B*	*C*	*D = B − C*	$E = 1/(1 + k + p)^t$	*D*E*	
4	2010*	0.00	125,000.00	−125,000.00	1	−125,000.00	0.0300
5	2010	0.00	100,000.00	−100,000.00	0.8696	−86,956.52	0.0300
6	2011	0.00	90,000.00	−90,000.00	0.7561	−68,052.93	0.0300
7	2012	50,000.00	0.00	50,000.00	0.6575	32,875.81	0.0300
8	2013	120,000.00	15,000.00	105,000.00	0.5718	60,034.09	0.0300
9	2014	115,000.00	0.00	115,000.00	0.4972	57,175.32	0.0300
10	2015	105,000.00	15,000.00	90,000.00	0.4323	38,909.48	0.0300
11	2016	97,000.00	0.00	97,000.00	0.3759	36,465.89	0.0300
12	2017	90,000.00	15,000.00	75,000.00	0.3269	24,517.63	0.0300
13	2018	82,000.00		82,000.00	0.2843	23,309.52	0.0300
14	2019	65,000.00		65,000.00	0.2472	16,067.01	0.0300
15	2019	35,000.00		35,000.00	0.2472	8,651.46	0.0300
16							
17	**Total**	759,000.00	360,000.00	399,000.00		17,996.77	
18							
19	* t=0 at beginning of 2010						

We are now ready to simulate. CB randomly selects a value for each assumption cell based on the probability distributions we specified and then calculates the net present value of the cell values selected. By repeating this process many times we can get a sense of the distribution of possible outcomes.

The commands for running the simulation are roughly in the center of the toolbar. If the number of trials is not already set at 1,000, click on **Run Preferences**, and reset it. Click on the green arrow labeled "**Start**" and the simulation will run. CB summarizes the results of the simulation in the form of a frequency chart that changes as the simulations are executed. See the results of one such run in Figure 7-10.

As noted in instruction number 5 above, CB can generate considerable information about the simulation. Figure 7-11 contains some interesting information. Both the mean and median outcomes from the simulation are nicely positive and thus well above the hurdle rate of 12 percent.

There are, however, several negative outcomes and those are below the hurdle rate. What is the likelihood that this project will achieve an outcome at or above the hurdle rate? With CB, the answer is easy. Using the display shown in Figure 7-10, erase –*Infinity* from the box in the lower left corner. Type *$0* (or *$1*) in that box and press **Enter**. The boxes at the bottom of Figure 7-10 show that given our estimates and assumptions of the cash flows and the rate of inflation, there is a .90+ probability that the project will yield an outcome at or above the 12 percent hurdle rate. Other dollar amounts can be entered and the associated probabilities will be displayed.

Even in this simple example, the power of including uncertainty in project selection should be obvious. Because a manager is always uncertain about the amount of uncertainty, it is also possible to examine various levels of uncertainty quite easily using CB. We could, for instance, alter the degree to which the inflow estimates are uncertain by expanding or contracting the degree to which optimistic and pessimistic estimates vary around the most

Figure 7-10 Frequency chart of the simulation output for net present value of Psycho-Ceramic Sciences project.

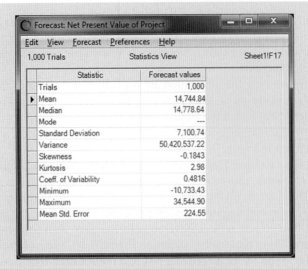

Figure 7-11 Summary statistics of the simulation output for net present value of PsychoCeramic Sciences project.

likely estimate. We could increase or decrease the level of inflation. Simulation runs made with these changes provide us with the ability to examine just how sensitive the outcomes (forecasts) are to possible errors in the input data. This allows us to focus on the important risks and to ignore those that have little effect on our decisions.

 SUMMARY

This chapter initiated the subject of project implementation by focusing on the project budget, which authorizes the project manager to obtain the resources needed to begin work. Different methods of budgeting were described along with their impacts on project management. Then, a number of issues concerning cost estimation were discussed, particularly the effect of learning on the cost of repetitive tasks and how to use the concept of the learning curve. Finally, methods for improving cost estimation skills were described.

Specific points made in the chapter were these:

- The intent of a budget is to communicate organizational policy concerning the organization's goals and priorities.

- There are a number of common budgeting methods: top-down, bottom-up, the project budget.

- A form identifying the level of resource need, when it will be needed, who the contact is, and its availability is especially helpful in estimating costs.

- It is common for organizations to fund projects whose returns cover direct but not full costs in order to achieve long-run strategic goals of the organization.

- If projects include repetitive tasks with significant human input, the learning phenomenon should be taken into consideration when preparing cost estimates.

- The learning curve is based on the observation that the amount of time required to produce one unit decreases a constant percentage every time the cumulative output doubles.

- Other major factors, in addition to learning, that should be considered when making project cost estimates are inflation, differential changes in the cost factors, waste and spoilage, personnel replacement costs, and contingencies for unexpected difficulties.

- A method for determining whether or not cost estimates are biased is described. The method can be used to improve any estimation/forecasting process.

- For handling uncertainty, risk analysis and simulation with sensitivity analysis are helpful.

In the next chapter, we address the subject of task scheduling, a topic of major importance in project management. More research and investigation have probably been conducted on the subject of scheduling than any other element of project management.

GLOSSARY

Bottom-Up Budgeting A budgeting method that begins with those who will be doing the tasks estimating the resources needed. The advantage is more accurate estimates.

Cost Categories

Direct (or Variable) Cost These costs vary with output; e.g., labor costs, material costs, and sometimes the cost of capital equipment such as machinery that performs a specific function on each unit of output.

General & Administrative Cost (G&A) The cost of administration; e.g., Accounting, Human Resources, and Legal not charged as an Indirect Cost and not included in Overhead Cost. Sometimes the G&A is not reported as a separate item but is included in overhead cost. G&A is usually charged as a fixed percent of a direct cost such as labor.

Indirect (or Fixed) Cost These costs are associated with output, but do not vary with each unit of output; e.g., the cost of capital equipment not charged per piece of output, advertising, distribution, or sales. Costs are charged as a lump sum or as a fixed percent of some direct cost such as labor.

Overhead Cost Costs incurred by the firm, but not associated with any specific product or class of products; e.g., cost of building and ground maintenance, utilities, cost of plant security, cost of health insurance and pension plans. Typically charged as a fixed percent of some direct cost such as labor.

Learning Rate The percentage of the previous worker hours per unit required for doubling the output.

Monte Carlo Simulation A procedure that imitates real-life by running thousands of values of distribution parameters to obtain an overall distribution of the outcomes of interest.

Project Budgeting Budgeting by project task/activity and then aggregating income and expenditures by project or program, often in addition to aggregation by organizational unit or category.

Risk Analysis A procedure that uses a distribution of input factors and probabilities and returns a range of outcomes and their probabilities.

Sensitivity analysis Investigation of the effect on the outcome of changing some parameters or data in the procedure or model.

Top-Down Budgeting A budgeting method that begins with top managers' estimates of the resources needed for a project. Its primary advantage is that the aggregate budget is typically quite accurate because no element has been left out. Individual elements, however, may be quite inaccurate.

Variances The pattern of deviations in costs and usage used for exception reporting to management.

QUESTIONS

Material Review Questions

1. What are the advantages of top-down budgeting? Of bottom-up budgeting? What is the most important task for top management to do in bottom-up budgeting?

2. In preparing a budget, what indirect costs should be considered?

3. Describe the purpose and use of a tracking signal.

4. Describe the top-down budgeting process.

5. What is a variance?

6. Describe the learning curve phenomenon.

7. How might you determine if cost estimates are biased?

8. What is "program budgeting"?

9. What is the difference between project and category-oriented budgets?

10. How does a risk analysis operate? How does a manager interpret the results?

Class Discussion Questions

11. Discuss ways in which to keep budget planning from becoming a game.

12. List some of the pitfalls in cost estimating. What steps can a manager take to correct cost overruns?

13. Why do consulting firms frequently subsidize some projects? Is this ethical?

14. What steps can be taken to make controlling costs easier? Can these steps also be used to control other project parameters, such as scope?

15. Which budgeting method is likely to be used with which type of organizational structure?

16. What are some potential problems with the top-down and bottom-up budgeting processes? What are some ways of dealing with these potential problems?

17. How is the budget planning process like a game?

18. Would any of the conflict resolution methods described in the previous chapter be useful in the budget planning process? Which?

19. How does the fact that capital costs vary with different factors complicate the budgeting process?

20. Why is learning curve analysis important to project management?

21. Why is it "ethically necessary to be honest" in negotiations between a superior and subordinate?

22. The chapter describes the problems of budgeting for S-shaped and J-shaped life-cycle projects. What might be the budgeting characteristics of a project with a straight line life cycle?

23. Interpret the columns of data in Figure 7-11. Does the $14,744 value mean that the project is expected to return only this amount of discounted money?

24. How would you find the probability in Figure 7-10 of an NPV of over $25,000?

25. Does the spread of the data in Table 7-4 appear realistic? Reconsider Table 7-4 to explain why the simulated outcome in Figure 7-11 is so much less than the value originally obtained in Table 7-3.

Pathfinder Mission to Mars—On a Shoestring

26. How did a change in philosophy make such a drastic difference in project cost?

27. Why was the mission scope so limited? Why even spend the money to go to Mars with such limited objectives?

28. Describe their "de-scope," "lien list," and "cash reserve" approaches.

29. Recent design-to-cost interplanetary projects have also had some spectacular failures. Is this the natural result of this new philosophy?

Øresund Bridge: Seeing projects through different lenses

30. What "lenses" are useful in exploring this project "in the round"?

31. The Øresund Bridge case shows the difference between "project management success" and "project success". How would you define these two terms?

Managing Costs at Massachusetts' Neighborhood Health Plan

32. Wouldn't higher eligibility requirements for subscribers cut NHP's health care costs? Why did this exacerbate NHP's situation?

33. Explain the trade-off between hospital utilization and contract rates.

34. How did changing from a line item pay plan to an episode plan allow comparisons and save costs?

Completing the Limerick Nuclear Facility Under Budget

35. What "trick" did the construction firm use to come in ahead of schedule and under budget?

36. What extra expenses did the contractor incur in order to finish ahead of schedule? How can one tell whether they are spending too much to finish early, thereby saving not only time but also overhead costs?

The Emanon Aircraft Corporation

37. How did inflating the material costs solve purchasing's "lateness" problem?

38. What alternatives were available to Emanon besides demoting the purchasing manager?

39. What should Emanon do now?

▮ PROBLEMS

1. Using the cost estimation template and Actuals in Figure 7-5, compare the model in the figure with the following estimates derived from a multiplicative model. Base your comparison on the mean bias, the MAR, and the tracking signal. Comment.

Period:	1	2	3	4	5	6	7	8
Estimated:	179	217	91	51	76	438	64	170

2. Conduct a discounted cash flow calculation to determine the NPV of the following project, assuming a required rate of return of 0.2. The project will cost $75,000 but will result in cash inflows of $20,000, $25,000, $30,000, and $50,000 in each of the next four years.

3. In Problem 2, assume that the inflows are uncertain but normally distributed with standard deviations of $1,000, $1,500, $2,000, and $3,500, respectively. Find the mean forecast NPV using Crystal Ball®. What is the probability the actual NPV will be positive?

4. A production lot of 25 units required 103.6 hours of effort. Accounting records show that the first unit took 7 hours. What was the learning rate?

5. If unit 1 requires 200 hours to produce and the labor records for an Air Force contract of 50 units indicates an average labor content of 63.1 hours per unit, what was the learning rate? What total additional number of labor-hours would be required for a follow-on Air Force contract of 50 units? What would be the average labor content of this second contract? Of both

contracts combined? If labor costs the vendor $10/hour on this second contract and the price to the Air Force is fixed at $550 each, what can you say about the profitability of the first and second contracts, and hence the bidding process in general?

6. Your firm designs PowerPoint slides for computer training classes, and you have just received a request to bid on a contract to produce the slides for an 8-session class. From previous experience, you know that your firm follows an 85 percent learning rate. For this contract it appears the effort will be substantial, running 50 hours for the first session. Your firm bills at the rate of $100/hour and the overhead is expected to run a fixed $600 per session. The customer will pay you a flat fixed rate per session. If your nominal profit margin is 20 percent, what will be the total bid price, the per session price, and at what session will you break even?

7. A light manufacturing firm has set up a project for developing a new machine for one of its production lines. The most likely estimated cost of the project itself is $1,000,000, but the most optimistic estimate is $900,000 while the pessimists predict a project cost of $1,200,000. The real problem is that even if the project costs are within those limits, if the project itself plus its implementation costs exceed $1,425,000, the project will not meet the firm's NPV hurdle. There are four cost categories involved in adding the prospective new machine to the production line: (1) engineering labor cost, (2) nonengineering labor cost, (3) assorted material cost, and (4) production line downtime cost.

The engineering labor requirement has been estimated to be 600 hours, plus or minus 15 percent at a cost of $80 per hour. The nonengineering labor requirement is estimated to be 1,500 hours, but could be as low as 1,200 hours or as high as 2,200 hours at a cost of $35 per hour. Assorted material may run as high as $155,000 or as low as $100,000, but is most likely to be about $135,000. The best guess of time lost on the production line is 110 hours, possibly as low as 105 hours and as high as 120 hours. The line contributes about $500 per hour to the firm's profit and overhead. What is the probability that the new machine project will meet the firm's NPV hurdle?

8. A four-year financial project has estimates of net cash flows shown in the following table. It will cost $65,000

to implement the project, all of which must be invested at the beginning of the project. After the fourth year, the project will have no residual value. Assume that the cash flow estimates for each year are best represented by a triangular distribution and that the hurdle rate is 20 percent.

(a) Use Crystal Ball® to find the expected NPV of the project.

(b) What is the probability that the project will yield a return greater than the 20 percent hurdle rate?

Year	Pessimistic	Most Likely	Optimistic
1	$14,000	$20,000	$22,000
2	19,000	25,000	30,000
3	27,000	30,000	36,000
4	32,000	35,000	39,000

9. If an inflation rate of 2 percent, normally distributed with a standard deviation of .333 percent, is assumed, what is the expected NPV of the project in Problem 8, and what is the probability that it will qualify?

10. A dot-com startup has decided to upgrade its server computers. It is also contemplating a shift from its Unix-based platform to a Windows-based platform. Three major cost items will be affected whichever platform they choose: hardware costs, software conversion costs, and employee training costs. The firm's technical group has studied the matter and has made the following estimates for the cost changes in $000s.

Using Crystal Ball® and assuming that the costs may all be represented by BetaPERT distributions, simulate the problem 1,000 times. Given the information resulting from the simulation, discuss the decision problem.

	Windows			Unix		
	Low	Likeliest	High	Low	Likeliest	High
Hardware	100	125	200	80	110	210
Software	275	300	500	250	300	525
Training	9	10	15	8	10	17.5

INCIDENTS FOR DISCUSSION

Preferred Sensor Company

Sean Cole has been appointed project manager of the Preferred Sensor Company's new sensor manufacturing process project. Sensors are extremely price-sensitive, and Preferred has done a great deal of quantitative work so it

can accurately forecast changes in sales volume relative to changes in pricing.

The company president, "Dude" Sensor, has considerable faith in the firm's sensitivity model and insists that all projects that affect the manufacturing cost of sensors be run against the sensitivity model in order to generate data to calculate the return on investment. The net result is that project managers, like Sean, are under a great deal of pressure to submit realistic budgets so go/no-go project decisions can be made quickly. Dude has canceled several projects that appeared marginal during their feasibility stages and recently fired a project manager for overestimating project costs on a new model sensor. The project was killed very early in the design stage and six months later a competitor introduced a similar sensor that proved to be highly successful.

Sean's dilemma is how to go about constructing a budget that accurately reflects the cost of the proposed new manufacturing process. Sean is an experienced executive and feels comfortable with his ability to come close to estimating the cost of the project. However, the recent firing of his colleague has made him a bit gun-shy. Only one stage out of the traditional four-stage sensor manufacturing process is being changed, so he has detailed cost information about a good percentage of the process. Unfortunately, the tasks involved in the process stage being modified are unclear at this point. Sean also believes that the new modification will cause some minor changes in the other three

stages, but these changes have not been clearly identified. The stage being addressed by the project represents almost 50 percent of the manufacturing cost.

Questions: Under these circumstances, would Sean be wise to pursue a top-down or a bottom-up budgeting approach? Why? What factors are most relevant here?

General Ship Company

General Ship Company has been building nuclear destroyers for the Navy for the last 20 years. It has recently completed the design of a new class of nuclear destroyer and will be preparing a detailed budget to be followed during construction of the first destroyer.

The total budget for this first destroyer is $90 million. The controller feels the initial project cost estimate prepared by the planning department was too low because the waste and spoilage allowance was underestimated. Thus, she is concerned that there may be a large cost overrun on the project and wants to work closely with the project manager to control the costs.

Question: How would you monitor the costs of this project?

CONTINUING INTEGRATIVE CLASS PROJECT

Although probably a minor task for this project, create a program budget using both top-down and bottom-up budgeting.

Reconcile any differences by discussion between the PM, subgroup leaders, and the student(s) responsible for the task.

BIBLIOGRAPHY

Amor, J. P., and C. J. Teplitz. "An Efficient Approximation for Project Composite Learning Curves." *Project Management Journal*, September 1998.

Badiru, A. B. "Incorporating Learning Curve Effects into Critical Resource Diagramming." *Project Management Journal*, June 1995.

Brimson, J. A. "Activity Product Cost." *IEEE Engineering Management Review*, Spring 1993.

Brooks, F. P. *The Mythical Man-Month*. Reading, MA: Addison-Wesley, 1975.

Camm, J. D., J. R. Evans, and N. K. Womer. "The Unit Learning Curve Approximation of Total Cost." *Computers in Industrial Engineering*. Vol. 12, No. 3, 1987.

Chase, R. B., and N. J. Aquilano. *Production and Operations Management*, *5th ed*. Homewood, IL: Irwin, 1989.

Christensen, D. S., and J. A. Gordon. "Does a Rubber Baseline Guarantee Cost Overruns on Defense Acquisition Contracts?" *Project Management Journal*, September 1998.

Coburn, S. "How Activity Based Costing Was Used in Capital Budgeting." *Management Accounting*, May 1997.

Dean, B. V., S. J. Mantel, Jr., and L. A. Roepcke. "Research Project Cost Distributions and Budget Forecasting." *IEEE Transactions on Engineering Management*, November 1969.

Frame, J. D. "Risk Assessment Groups: Key Component of Project Offices." *PM Network*, March 1998.

Gagnon, R. J. *An Exploratory Analysis of the Relevant Cost Structure of Internal and External Engineering Consulting*, Ph.D. dissertation. Cincinnati: University of Cincinnati, 1982.

Gagnon, R. J., and S. J. Mantel, Jr. "Strategies and Performance Improvement for Computer-Assisted Design." *IEEE Transactions on Engineering Management*, November 1987.

Gale, S. F. "The Bottom Line," *PM Network*, August 2007.

Harrison, F. L. *Advanced Project Management*. Hants, England: Gower, 1983.

Lawrence, A. O. "Using Automated Estimating Tools to Improve Project Estimating." *PM Network*, December 1994.

Martin, J. E. "Selecting an Automated Estimating Tool for IS Development Projects." *PM Network*, December 1994.

Meredith, J. R., S. M. Shafer, and E. Turban. *Quantitative Business Modeling.* Cincinnati, OH: Southwestern, 2002.

Meredith, J. R., and S. M. Shafer. *Operations Management for MBAs, 4th ed.* Hoboken, NJ: Wiley, 2010.

Sigurdsen, A. "Principal Errors in Capital Cost Estimating Work, Part 1: Appreciate the Relevance of the Quantity-Dependent Estimating Norms." *Project Management Journal*, September 1996a.

Sigurdsen, A. "Principal Errors in Capital Cost Estimating, Part 2: Appreciate the Relevance of the Objective Cost Risk Analysis Method." *Project Management Journal*, December 1996b.

Vandament, W. F., and D. P. Jones. *Financial Management: Progress and Challenges.* San Francisco: Jossey-Bass, 1993.

Zwikael, O., S. Globerson, and T. Raz. "Evaluation of Models for Forecasting the Final Cost of a Project." *Project Management Journal*, March 2000.

 The following case and the answers to the questions at the end describe the stringent criteria this disguised but well-known firm uses to select among projects that offer major profit opportunities for the firm. In addition, the firm intentionally ties the criteria to their strategic goals so that each adopted project moves the organization farther in the competitive direction they have chosen by adding to their core competencies. The case also illustrates how the firm integrates their marketing, operations, engineering, and finance functions to forge a competitive advantage for the firm in the marketplace.

C A S E

GUJARAT AUTO
Eric Woodcock

Pradip Mistry, Finance Director of Gujarat Auto, walked through the Arrivals Hall at Ahmedabad airport in India and turned his mobile phone back on after his flight from Bangalore. Among the 10 messages was one from his assistant to say that the TPK proposal was ready for him to review. He had set aside the whole day to do this, for he had to make a recommendation to Dilip Patel, the company's Executive Vice-President, about what course to take. The proposal had been put together by Saini Nehwal, a very promising young project manager, for whom this assignment was a very important chance to impress the executive team at Gujarat Auto.

The TPK project was just the kind of opportunity that fitted Gujarat Auto's strategic ambitions, but it also carried a lot of risk. Before making his recommendation to Dilip Patel, Pradip Mistry wanted to understand every aspect of the proposal.

History of Gujarat Auto

Gujarat Auto started out as a joint venture between an Indian engineering company and a German diesel engine manufacturer in the 1960s. After the joint venture agreement came to an end, the Indian parent set up Gujarat Auto as an autonomous subsidiary. The company's fortunes blossomed as India's economy began to grow dramatically, thanks to burgeoning demand for tractors, trucks and stationary electricity generators.

Gujarat Auto's major customers had always been Indian manufacturers, many of whom had sourced engines on a product line by product line basis, with relatively short production runs. Under pressure to reduce costs and improve product quality, those firms had been examining the concept of single sourcing components—going for more standardised designs and entering contracts for larger quantities from a single supplier. Another advantage of this approach would be that they would have a close relationship with one company and so be able to set purchase schedules at shorter notice and keep down stocks of built engines.

The TPK opportunity

One of the largest Indian tractor makers, TPK, had decided that rather than make its own engines (which it has done for 40 years) it would buy them in. In part, that decision was because the TPK design was out of date and the costs of developing a new engine would be much more than TPK was prepared to spend. Instead it had issued just such a request—not only to domestic Indian suppliers, but also to several of the major global diesel engine manufacturers—for the exclusive supply of all its engines for five years, potentially encouraging foreign firms to set up new operations or joint ventures in India.

This opportunity had presented Gujarat Auto with a dilemma. If they did not bid for this contract, they would be opening the door to competitors to take 100% of the engines bought by one of India's biggest customers—as well as forgoing the sizable and profitable aftermarket business. On the other hand, while a successful bid would involve the kind of high capital investment that would deter rivals and new entrants, the risks involved in bidding were very high.

None of Gujarat Auto's current factories was big enough to handle the envisaged volume required by TPK. Furthermore, TPK had made it clear that a single source supplier would have to be able to meet peak demand from TPK's own factories, without holding stock or lengthening order lead times.

As he sipped his tea, Pradip Mistry reflected on the questions Dilip Patel had asked him at their last discussion about the proposal.

- Gujarat Auto already achieved a high return on investment (ROI) from its current operations. Would the new investment dilute that?

- Would the investment in new plant and equipment be offset by a reduction in labour and other costs?

- How certain is the mid- to long-term revenue from TPK? This proposal required an investment in new facilities before knowing whether at least one long-term contract would be in place to recoup the investment.

- Did this proposal maximise ROI, Gujarat Auto's sales potential, or total profit?

Pradip Mistry looked again at the expected profit after tax and average rate of return—based on sales of 70,000 engines per year.

The Gujarat Auto business strategy

Gujarat Auto also had a series of strategic principles which had been applied consistently to investment decisions. Pradip Mistry made a note (in priority order) of the ones he felt were most relevant to this proposal.

1. Bid only to sell products that will maintain high sales margins over the long term.

2. Develop only products in which the product technology or the production process offers a significant edge against the competition, to enable Gujarat Auto to maintain a technical lead.

3. Employ the most advanced technology in new projects that is either known by us, or is the next logical step in our technological advancement.

4. Encourage projects which allow project managers to develop their skills as "intrapreneurs" (entrepreneurs inside the business) and project champions.

5. Operate small factories with fewer than 500 employees to ensure high efficiency and good working relations.

Demand Forecasts

Three scenarios were included in the proposal to test the robustness of the investment case:

Scenario 1 assumed that the new engine would be successful, with TPK increasing its output in line with economic growth in India, and maintaining exclusive supply beyond the first five years.

Scenario 2 assumed that after five years, TPK decided to dual source, and began to take engines from another company.

Scenario 3 assumed that the TPK product line did not do well, perhaps because TPK suffered from new competition in the tractor market, or worse, the engine was a technical and market failure. The three scenarios are set out in Table 1.

Manufacturing strategy

In truth, however, there could be little real confidence in these forecasts. The Indian tractor market was becoming highly dynamic. New competitors from places like China were already making inroads, and farmers were seeing fluctuating prices for their produce which affected their confidence about investing in expensive equipment like a tractor. The proposal noted that "every effort should be made to minimise our exposure on this investment and maximise our flexibility."

Gujarat Auto had been monitoring developments in the market for some time and it was not a surprise when TPK announced their plan to single source. In anticipation of this, Pradip Mistry had authorised a study to be carried out on how Gujarat Auto could scale up to produce tens of thousands of engines from a single factory.

Table 1   Demand Forecasts

Year	Scenario 1	Scenario 2	Scenario 3
Year 1	69,000	69,000	69,000
Year 2	73,000	72,000	72,000
Year 3	90,000	81,000	77,000
Year 4	113,000	95,000	68,000
Year 5	125,000	87,000	62,000
Year 6	145,000	74,000	47,000

The main parts of the factory would be a machine shop (where the crankcase, cylinder head, crankshaft and piston rods would be machined in different areas) and an assembly shop (where these parts, and components bought in from other suppliers, would be put together to create the finished engine).

Three manufacturing methods were considered for the machine shop: batch machining of parts using computer numerically controlled (CNC) equipment, a flexible manufacturing system (FMS), and high volume, low-unit-cost transfer machines. The transfer machines would be ideal for very high volumes of standardised parts, but changeovers would be slow and expensive.

The conclusion was that the FMS was the best route, as it would allow Gujarat Auto to produce different versions of the TPK engine at a realistic cost, and also supply engines to other customers if required. Not only would the FMS be able to produce different versions of the engine, it would also be able to machine different materials, such as aluminium and cast iron.

The option of using robots for a significant part of the engine assembly was examined in detail. This had attractions, but it was felt that without a firm commitment from TPK, the high initial investment could not be justified. Instead the factory would be designed to allow robotic assembly to be introduced later.

In line with the flexibility of the plant, the new factory would have innovative working practices.

- Machine operators would be trained to do most of the maintenance of their own machines.
- All operators and assembly workers would be responsible for inspecting their own work.
- There would be only four skill groups on the factory and everyone would be trained to do whatever work was required within that skill group. Thus a worker in skill group 3 might be asked to spend a month working in assembly at that skill level and then a month in the machine shop at skill group 3.
- There would be no time clocks in the factory.

Two specialist firms made proposals for the entire design, construction and fitting out of the new factory. Gujarat Auto was also in discussion with four vendors of machining and assembly equipment. This involvement was crucial, since design for manufacture would be a key factor in ensuring that the new engines were reliable and performed well.

An organisation structure was defined, and a schedule for ramping up employment to the full level. The forecasts of factory output assumed a learning rate of 80% over the first 1,000 engines from the new factory.

Financial considerations

The financial consequences of investing in the new factory were considered from various angles. The consequences of doing nothing were examined, recognising that Gujarat Auto had a successful track record in producing engines for a wide range of customers in moderate volumes. Also examined were the likely effects

Table 2   New factory site capital costs in Indian rupees (₹)

Land and site preparation	
Land	₹14,760,000
Access roads and car park	₹7,440,000
Landscaping	₹1,320,000
Building costs	
Building	₹93,600,000
Ventilation and air conditioning	₹13,560,000
Power supply	₹12,300,000
Employee services	₹10,620,000
Legal fees and permits	₹1,560,000
Auxiliary equipment	
Company signage	₹1,500,000
Containers, racks, etc.	₹1,980,000
Factory data centre	₹8,880,000
Coolant disposal	₹5,820,000
Furnishings	₹3,060,000
Forklift trucks	₹4,320,000
Total	₹180,720,000

on other parts of the business. Gujarat Auto operated three factories in western India. The new plant would probably be located closer to the TPK main factory in the state of Uttar Pradesh, in north eastern India. One possibility was closing one of the existing factories and transferring its work to the new one, since this would be closer to more of Gujarat Auto's customers.

For the TPK proposal the investment in the new factory could be summarised as:

The cost of the production equipment for the new factory would be ₹115,660,000 and it would need ₹20,000,000 of working capital at start up. All equipment would be depreciated over eight years; the building would be depreciated over 25 years. The business case assumed that the manufacturing cost of each engine (including overheads and transport to TPK) would be ₹16,220, and the selling price to TPK would be ₹19,400.

Pradip Mistry had been discussing the whole proposal with his colleagues. One manager asked what difference it would make if TPK took only 70% of the forecast volume in Year 3, or alternatively, if they took 50% more than the forecast. At what point would additional plant and machinery be considered?

Another manager doubted that a substantial share of the volume would be lost to the competition after the end of the five-year exclusive contract. That would only occur if Gujarat Auto fell behind technically or produced poor quality products—neither of which seemed likely. He also questioned the high margins assumed in the proposal. Surely the bidding process would mean that whoever got the TPK contract would have to manage quite low margins as a reward for getting an exclusive deal.

Pradip Mistry had his own concerns about the project. He wondered about the volatility in the market for agricultural equipment. He worried about how aggressively foreign competitors would bid in order to gain a foothold in the Indian market. He worried whether Gujarat Auto could afford not to get this business.

QUESTIONS

1. How did Gujarat Auto handle the risk that their assumptions about the sales of engines to TPK might be too optimistic?
2. Were Gujarat Auto's costs for the new factory in Table 2 derived from a top-down or bottom-up process?
3. What were the answers to Dilip Patel's questions?
4. What other factors are relevant to this issue?
5. How do the changes in assumptions mentioned by the other managers affect the proposal?
6. What recommendation should Pradip Mistry make to Dilip Patel? Why?

This article clearly describes the importance and impact of cost-related issues on a project. These issues can significantly alter the profitability and even success of a project. Costs are discussed from three viewpoints: that of the project manager, the accountant, and the controller. Not only are the amounts of expenditures and encumbrances important, but their timing is critical also. Perhaps most important is having a project cost system that accurately reports costs and variances in a way that can be useful for managerial decisions.

DIRECTED READING

THREE PERCEPTIONS OF PROJECT COST*
D. H. Hamburger

Project cost seems to be a relatively simple expression, but "cost" is more than a four letter word. Different elements of the organization perceive cost differently, as the timing of project cost identification affects their particular

*Reprinted from *Project Management Journal* with permission. Copyright by the Project Management Institute.

organizational function. The project manager charged with on-time, on-cost, on-spec execution of a project views the "on cost" component of his responsibility as a requirement to stay within the allocated budget, while satisfying a given set of specified conditions (scope of work), within a required time frame (schedule). To most project managers this simply means a commitment to project funds in accordance with a prescribed plan (time-based budget). Others in the organization are less concerned with the commitment of funds. The accounting department addresses expense recognition related to a project or an organizational profit and loss statement. The accountant's ultimate goal is reporting profitability, while positively influencing the firm's tax liability. The comptroller (finance department) is primarily concerned with the organization's cash flow. It is that person's responsibility to provide the funds for paying the bills, and putting the unused or available money to work for the company.

To be an effective project manager, one must understand each cost, and also realize that the timing of cost identification can affect both project and corporate financial performance. The project manager must be aware of the different cost perceptions and the manner in which they are reported. With this knowledge, the project manager can control more than the project's cost of goods sold (a function often viewed as the project manager's sole financial responsibility). The project manager can also influence the timing of cost to improve cash flow and the cost of financing the work, in addition to affecting revenue and expense reporting in the P&L statement.

Three Perceptions of Cost

To understand the three perceptions of cost—commitments, expenses, and cash flow—consider the purchase of a major project component. Assume that a $120,000 compressor with delivery quoted at six months was purchased. Figure 1 depicts the order execution cycle. At time 0 an order is placed. Six months later the vendor makes two shipments, a large box containing the compressor and a small envelope containing an invoice. The received invoice is processed immediately, but payment is usually delayed to comply with corporate payment policy (30, 60, 90, or more days may pass before a check is actually mailed to the vendor). In this example, payment was made 60 days after receipt of the invoice or 8 months after the order for the compressor was given to the vendor.

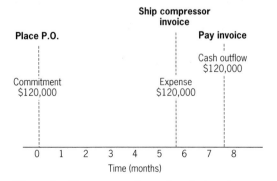

Figure 1   Three perceptions of project cost.

Commitments—The Project Manager's Concern

Placement of the purchase order represents a *commitment* to pay the vendor $120,000 following satisfactory delivery of the compressor. As far as the project manager is concerned, once this commitment is made to the vendor, the available funds in the project budget are reduced by that amount. When planning and reporting project costs the project manager deals with commitments. Unfortunately, many accounting systems are not structured to support project cost reporting needs and do not identify commitments. In fact, the value of a purchase order may not be recorded until an invoice is received. This plays havoc with the project manager's fiscal control process, as he cannot get a "handle" on the exact budget status at a particular time. In the absence of a suitable information system, a conscientious project manager will maintain personal (manual or computer) records to track his project's commitments.

Expenses—The Accountant's Concern

Preparation of the project's financial report requires identification of the project's revenues (when applicable) and all project *expenses*. In most conventional accounting systems, expenses for financial reporting purposes are recognized upon receipt of an invoice for a purchased item (not when the payment is made—a common misconception). Thus, the compressor would be treated as an expense in the sixth month.

In a conventional accounting system, revenue is recorded when the project is completed. This can create serious problems in a long-term project in which expenses are accrued during each reporting period with no attendant revenue, and the revenue is reported in the final period with little or no associated expenses shown. The project runs at an apparent loss in each of the early periods and records an inordinately large profit at the time revenue is ultimately reported—the final reporting period. This can be seriously misleading in a long-term project which runs over a multi-year period.

To avoid such confusion, most long-term project P&L statements report revenue and expenses based on a "percentage of completion" formulation. The general intent is to "take down" an equitable percentage of the total project revenue (approximately equal to the proportion of the project work completed) during each accounting period, assigning an appropriate level of expense to arrive at an acceptable period gross margin. At the end of each accounting year and at the end of the project, adjustments are made to the recorded expenses to account for the differences between actual expenses incurred and the theoretical expenses recorded in the P&L statement. This can be a complex procedure. The misinformed or uninformed project manager can place the firm in an untenable position by erroneously misrepresenting the project's P&L status; and the rare unscrupulous project manager can use an arbitrary assessment of the project's percentage of completion to manipulate the firm's P&L statement.

There are several ways by which the project's percentage of completion can be assessed to avoid these risks. A typical method, which removes subjective judgments and the potential for manipulation by relying on strict accounting procedures, is to be described. In this process a theoretical period expense is determined, which is divided by the total estimated project expense budget to compute the percentage of total budget expense for the period. This becomes the project's percentage of completion which is then used to determine the revenue to be "taken down" for the period. In this process, long delivery purchased items are not expensed on receipt of an invoice, but have the value of their purchase order prorated over the term of order execution. Figure 2 shows the $120,000 compressor in the example being expensed over the six-month delivery period at the rate of $20,000 per month.

Cash Flow—The Comptroller's Concern

The comptroller and the finance department are responsible for managing the organization's funds, and also assuring the availability of the appropriate amount of cash for payment of the project's bills. Unused funds are put to work for the organization in interest-bearing accounts or in other ventures. The finance department's primary concern is in knowing when funds will be needed for invoice payment in order to minimize the time that these funds are not being used productively. Therefore, the comptroller really views project cost as a *cash outflow*. Placement of a purchase order merely identifies a future cash outflow to the comptroller, requiring no action on his part. Receipt of the invoice generates a little more interest, as the comptroller now knows that a finite amount of cash will be required for a particular payment at the end of a fixed period. Once a payment becomes due, the comptroller provides the funds, payment is made, and the actual cash outflow is recorded.

It should be noted that the compressor example is a simplistic representation of an actual procurement cycle, as vendor progress payments for portions of the work (i.e., engineering, material, and delivery) may be included in the purchase order. In this case, commitment timing will not change, but the timing of the expenses and cash outflow will be consistent with the agreed-upon terms of payment.

The example describes the procurement aspect of project cost, but other project cost types are treated similarly. In the case of project labor, little time elapses between actual work execution (a commitment), the recording of the labor hours on a time sheet (an expense), and the payment of wages (cash outflow). Therefore, the three perceptions of cost are treated as if they each occur simultaneously. Subcontracts are treated in a manner similar to equipment purchases. A commitment is recorded when the subcontract is placed and cash outflow occurs when the monthly invoice for the work is paid. Expenses are treated in a slightly different manner. Instead of prorating the subcontract sum over the performance period, the individual invoices for the actual work performed are used to determine the expense for the period covered by each invoice.

Thus the three different perceptions of cost can result in three different time-based cost curves for a given project budget. Figure 3 shows a typical relationship between commitments, expenses, and cash outflow. The commitment curve leads and the cash outflow curve lags, with the expense curve falling in the middle. The actual shape and the degree of lag/lead between the curves are a function of several factors, including: the project's labor, material, and subcontract mix; the firm's invoice payment policy; the delivery period for major equipment items; subcontract performance period and the schedule of its work; and the effect of the project schedule on when and how labor will be expended in relation to equipment procurement.

The conscientious project manager must understand these different perceptions of cost and should be prepared to plan and report on any and all approaches required by management. The project manager should also be aware

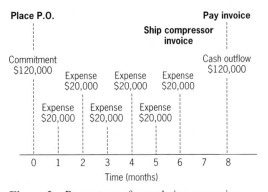

Figure 2   Percentage of completion expensing.

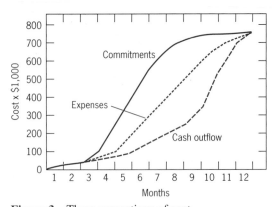

Figure 3   Three perceptions of cost.

of the manner in which the accounting department collects and reports "costs." Since the project manager's primary concern is in the commitments, he or she should insist on an accounting system which is compatible with the project's reporting needs. Why must a project manager resort to a manual control system when the appropriate data can be made available through an adjustment in the accounting department's data processing system?

Putting Your Understanding of Cost to Work

Most project managers believe that their total contribution to the firm's profitability is restricted by the ability to limit and control project cost, but they can do much more. Once the different perceptions of cost have been recognized, the project manager's effectiveness is greatly enhanced. The manner in which the project manager plans and executes the project can improve company profitability through influence on financing expenses, cash flow, and the reporting of revenue and expenses. To be a completely effective project manager one must be totally versed in the cost accounting practices which affect the firm's project cost reporting.

Examination of the typical project profit & loss statement (see Table 1) shows how a project sold for profit is subjected to costs other than the project's costs (cost of goods sold). The project manager also influences other areas of cost as well, addressing all aspects of the P&L to influence project profitability positively.

Specific areas of cost with examples of what a project manager can do to influence cost of goods sold, interest expense, tax expense, and profit are given next.

Cost of Goods Sold (Project Cost)

- Evaluation of alternate design concepts and the use of "trade-off" studies during the development phase of a project can result in a lower project cost, without sacrificing the technical quality of the project's output. The application of value engineering principles during the initial design period will also reduce cost. A directed and controlled investment in the evaluation of alternative design concepts can result in significant savings of project cost.

- Excessive safety factors employed to ensure "onspec" performance should be avoided. Too frequently the functional members of the project team will apply large safety factors in their effort to meet or exceed the technical specifications. The project team must realize that such excesses increase the project's cost. The functional staff should be prepared to justify an incremental investment which was made to gain additional performance insurance. Arbitrary and excessive conservatism must be avoided.

- Execution of the project work must be controlled. The functional groups should not be allowed to stretch out the project for the sake of improvement, refinement, or the investigation of the most remote potential risk. When a functional task has been completed to the project manager's satisfaction (meeting the task's objectives), cut off further spending to prevent accumulation of "miscellaneous" charges.

- The project manager is usually responsible for controlling the project's contingency budget. This budget represents money that one expects to expend during the term of the project for specific requirements not identified at the project onset. Therefore, these funds must be carefully monitored to prevent indiscriminate spending. A functional group's need for a portion of the contingency budget must be justified and disbursement of these funds should only be made after the functional group has exhibited an effort to avoid or limit its use. It is imperative that the contingency budget be held for its intended purpose. Unexpected problems will ultimately arise, at which time the funds will be needed. Use of this budget to finance a scope change is neither advantageous to the project manager nor to management. The contingency budget represents the project manager's authority in dealing with corrections to the project work. Management must be made aware of the true cost of a change so that financing the change will be based on its true value (cost-benefit relationship).

- In the procurement of equipment, material, and subcontract services, the specified requirements should be identified and the lowest priced, qualified supplier found. Adequate time for price "shopping" should be built into the project schedule. The Mercury project proved to be safe and successful even though John Glenn, perched in the Mercury capsule atop the Atlas rocket prior to America's first earth orbiting flight, expressed his now famous concern that "all this hardware was built by the low bidder."

Table 1 Typical Project Profit & Loss Statement

Revenue (project sell price)	$1,000,000
(less) cost of goods sold	
(project costs)	($ 750,000)
Gross margin	$ 250,000
(less) selling, general &	
administrative expenses	($ 180,000)
Profit before interest and taxes	$ 70,000
(less) financial expense	($ 30,000)
Profit before taxes	$ 40,000
(less) taxes	($ 20,000)
Net profit	$ 20,000

The project manager should ensure that the initial project budget is commensurate with the project's required level of reliability. The project manager should not be put in the position of having to buy project reliability with unavailable funds.

- Procurement of material and services based on partially completed drawings and specifications should be avoided. The time necessary for preparing a complete documentation package before soliciting bids should be considered in the preparation of the project schedule. Should an order be awarded based on incomplete data and the vendor then asked to alter the original scope of supply, the project will be controlled by the vendor. In executing a "fast track" project, the project manager should make certain that the budget contains an adequate contingency for the change orders which will follow release of a partially defined work scope.

- Changes should not be incorporated in the project scope without client and/or management approval and the allocation of the requisite funds. Making changes without approval will erode the existing budget and reduce project profitability; meeting the project manager's "on-cost" commitment will become extremely difficult, if not impossible.

- During periods of inflation, the project manager must effectively deal with the influence of the economy on the project budget. This is best accomplished during the planning or estimating stage of the work, and entails recognition of planning in an inflationary environment for its effect by estimating the potential cost of two distinct factors. First, a "price protection" contingency budget is needed to cover the cost increases that will occur between the time a vendor provides a firm quotation for a limited period and the actual date the order will be placed. (Vendor quotations used to prepare an estimate usually expire long before the material is actually purchased.) Second, components containing certain price-volatile materials (e.g., gold, silver, etc.) may not be quoted firm, but will be offered by the supplier as "price in effect at time of delivery." In this case an "escalation" contingency budget is needed to cover the added expense that will accrue between order placement and material delivery. Once the project manager has established these inflation-related contingency budgets, the PM's role becomes one of ensuring controlled use.

Financial Expense

- The project's financial cost (interest expense) can be minimized by the project manager through the timing of order placement. Schedule slack time can be used to defer the placement of a purchase order so that the material is not available too early and the related cash outflow is not premature. There are several risks associated with this concept. Delaying an order too long could backfire if the desired material is unavailable when needed. Allowing a reasonable margin for error in the delivery cycle, saving some of the available slack time for potential delivery problems, will reduce this risk. Waiting too long to place a purchase order could result in a price increase, which can more than offset the interest savings. It is possible to "lock-up" a vendor's price without committing to a required delivery date, but this has its limitations. If vendor drawings are a project requirement, an "engineering only" order can be placed to be followed by hardware release at the appropriate time. Deferred procurement, which takes advantage of available slack time, should be considered in the execution of all projects, especially during periods when the cost of money is excessively high.

- Vendors are frequently used to help "finance the project" by placing purchase orders which contain extended payment terms. Financially astute vendors will build the cost of financing the project into their sell price, but only to the extent of remaining competitive. A vendor's pricing structure should be checked to determine if progress payments would result in a reduced price and a net project benefit. A discount for prompt payment should be taken if the discount exceeds the interest savings that could result from deferring payment.

- Although frequently beyond the project manager's control, properly structured progress payment terms can serve to negate most or all project financial expenses. The intent is simple. A client's progress payment terms can be structured to provide scheduled cash inflows which offset the project's actual cash outflow. In other words, maintenance of a zero net cash position throughout the period of project execution will minimize the project's financial expense. In fact, a positive net cash position resulting from favorable payment terms can actually result in a project which creates interest income rather than one that incurs an interest expense. Invoices to the client should be processed quickly, to minimize the lost interest resulting from a delay in receiving payment.

- Similarly, the project manager can influence receipt of withheld funds (retention) and the project's final payment to improve the project's rate of cash inflow. A reduction in retention should be pursued as the project nears completion. Allowing a project's schedule to indiscriminately slip delays project acceptance, thereby delaying final payment. Incurring an additional expense to resolve a questionable problem should be considered whenever the expense will result in rapid project acceptance and a favorable interest expense reduction.

- On internally funded projects, where retention, progress payments, and other client related financial considerations are not a factor, management expects to achieve payback in the shortest reasonable time. In this case, project spending is a continuous cash outflow process which cannot be reversed until the project is completed and its anticipated financial benefits begin to accrue from the completed work. Unnecessary project delays, schedule slippages, and long-term investigations extend system startup and defer the start of payback. Early completion will result in an early start of the investment payback process. Therefore, management's payback goal should be considered when planning and controlling project work, and additional expenditures in the execution of the work should be considered if a shortened schedule will adequately hasten the start of payback.

Tax Expense and Profit

- On occasion, management will demand project completion by a given date to ensure inclusion of the project's revenue and profit within a particular accounting period. This demand usually results from a need to fulfill a prior financial performance forecast. Delayed project completion by only a few days could shift the project's entire revenue and profit from one accounting period to the next. The volatile nature of this situation, large sums of revenue and profit shifting from one period to the next, results in erratic financial performance which negatively reflects on management's ability to plan and execute their efforts.

- To avoid the stigma of erratic financial performance, management has been known to suddenly redirect a carefully planned, cost-effective project team effort to a short-term, usually costly, crash exercise, directed toward a project completion date, artificially necessitated by a corporate financial reporting need. Unfortunately, a project schedule driven by influences external to the project's fundamental objectives usually results in additional cost and reduces profitability.

- In this particular case, the solution is simple if a percentage of completion accounting process can be applied. Partial revenue and margin take-down during each of the project's accounting periods, resulting from this procedure (rather than lump sum take-down in a single period at the end of the project, as occurs using conventional accounting methods)

will mitigate the undesirable wild swings in reported revenue and profit. Two specific benefits will result. First, management's revenue/profit forecast will be more accurate and less sensitive to project schedule changes. Each project's contribution to the overall forecast will be spread over several accounting periods and any individual performance change will cause the shift of a significantly smaller sum from one accounting period to the next. Second, a project nearing completion will have had 90–95 percent of its revenue/profit taken down in earlier periods, which will lessen or completely eliminate management pressure to complete the work to satisfy a financial reporting demand. Inordinate, unnecessary spending to meet such unnatural demands can thereby be avoided.

- An Investment Tax Credit,* a net reduction in corporate taxes gained from a capital investment project (a fixed percentage of the project's installed cost), can be earned when the project actually provides its intended benefit to the owner. The project manager should consider this factor in scheduling the project work, recognizing that it is not necessary to complete the entire project to obtain this tax benefit as early as possible. Failure to substantiate beneficial use within a tax year can shift this savings into the next tax year. The project manager should consider this factor in establishing the project's objectives, diligently working toward attainment by scheduling the related tasks to meet the tax deadline. Consideration should also be given to expenditures (to the extent they do not offset the potential tax savings) to reach this milestone by the desired date.

- In managing the corporate P&L statement, the need to shift revenue, expenses, and profit from one tax period to the next often exists. By managing the project schedule (expediting or delaying major component procurements or shifting expensive activities), the project manager can support this requirement. Each individual project affords a limited benefit, but this can be maximized if the project manager is given adequate notice regarding the necessary scheduling adjustments.

- Revenue/profit accrual based on percentage of completion can create a financial problem if actual expenses greatly exceed the project budget. In this case the project's percentage of completion will accumulate more quickly than justified and the project will approach a theoretical 100 percent completion before all work is done. This will "front load"

---

*The proposed tax law revisions under consideration in Congress at the time this article was written include a provision which eliminates the Investment Tax Credit.

revenue/profit take-down and will ultimately require a profit reversal at project completion. Some managers may find this desirable, since profits are being shifted into earlier periods, but most reputable firms do not wish to overstate profits in an early period which will have to be reversed at a later time. Therefore, the project manager should be aware of cost overruns and, when necessary, reforecast the project's "cost on completion" (increasing the projected cost and reducing the expected profit) to reduce the level of profit taken down in the early periods to a realistic level.

Conclusion

Cost is not a four-letter word to be viewed with disdain by the project manager. It is a necessary element of the project management process which the project manager must comprehend despite the apparent mysteries of the accounting systems employed to report cost. The concept of cost is more than the expenses incurred in the execution of the project work: the manner in which cost is treated by the organization's functional elements can affect project performance, interest expenses, and profitability. Therefore,

the conscientious project manager must develop a complete understanding of project cost and the accounting systems used to record and report costs. The project manager should also recognize the effect of the timing of project cost, and the differences between commitments, expenses, and cash flow. The project manager should insist on the accounting system modifications needed to accommodate project cost reporting and control requirements. Once an appreciation for these concepts has been gained, the project manager can apply this knowledge towards positively influencing project and organizational profitability in all areas of cost through control of the project schedule and the execution of the project's work.

Questions

1. What is the major point of the article?
2. How does the accountant view project costs?
3. How does the controller view project costs?
4. How does the project manager view project costs?
5. What other costs does the project manager need to be cognizant of? What actions should the PM take concerning these other costs?

8

Scheduling

The previous chapter initiated our discussion of project implementation. In this and the following three chapters, we continue with the implementation of the project plans we made in Chapter 6. In this chapter, we examine some scheduling techniques that have been found to be useful in project management. We cover the Program Evaluation and Review Technique (PERT), the Critical Path Method (CPM), Gantt charts, and briefly discuss Precedence Diagramming and report-based methods. Risk analysis and management will be considered as an inherent feature of all scheduling methods, and a simulation of a project schedule will be demonstrated.

In Chapter 9, we consider the special problems of scheduling when resource limitations force conflicts between concurrent projects, or even between two or more tasks in a single project. We also look at Goldratt's "critical chain" (1997) and ways of expediting activities by adding resources. Following a discussion of the monitoring and information system function in Chapter 10, we discuss the overall topic of project control in Chapter 11.

8.1 BACKGROUND

A schedule is the conversion of a project work breakdown structure (WBS) into an operating timetable. As such, it serves as the basis for monitoring and controlling project activity and, taken together with the plan and budget, is probably the major tool for the management of projects. In a project environment, the scheduling function is more important than it would be in an ongoing operation because projects lack the continuity of day-to-day operations and often present much more complex problems of coordination. Indeed, project scheduling is so important that a detailed schedule is sometimes a customer-specified requirement. A properly designed, detailed schedule can also serve as a key input in establishing the monitoring and control systems for the project.

Not all project activities need to be scheduled at the same level of detail. In fact, there may be several schedules (e.g., the master schedule, the development and testing schedule, the assembly schedule). These schedules are typically based on the previously determined WBS, and it is good practice to create a schedule for each major task level in the WBS that will cover the work packages. It is rarely necessary, however, to list all work packages. One can focus mainly on those that need to be monitored for maintaining adequate control over the project. Such packages are usually difficult, expensive, or have a relatively short time frame for their accomplishment.

The basic approach of all scheduling techniques is to form a network of activity and event relationships that graphically portrays the sequential relations between the tasks in a project. Tasks that must precede or follow other tasks are then clearly identified, in time as well as function. Such a network is a powerful tool for planning and controlling a project, and has the following benefits:

- It is a consistent framework for planning, scheduling, monitoring, and controlling the project.
- It illustrates the interdependence of all tasks, work packages, and work elements.
- It denotes the times when specific individuals and resources must be available for work on a given task.
- It aids in ensuring that the proper communications take place between departments and functions.
- It determines an expected project completion date.
- It identifies so-called critical activities that, if delayed, will also delay the project completion time.
- It also identifies activities with slack that can be delayed for specified periods without penalty, or from which resources may be temporarily borrowed without harm.
- It determines the dates on which tasks may be started—or must be started if the project is to stay on schedule.
- It illustrates which tasks must be coordinated to avoid resource or timing conflicts.
- It also illustrates which tasks may be run, or must be run, in parallel to achieve the predetermined project completion date.
- It relieves some interpersonal conflict by clearly showing task dependencies.
- It may, depending on the information used, allow an estimate of the probability of project completion by various dates, or the date corresponding to a particular a priori probability.

Project Management in Practice
Production Scheduling

A plastics manufacturer company based in Suffolk in the UK needed to address a scheduling problem. At any one time they have over 5,000 live orders waiting to be fulfilled, each for different designs, materials, colours, decoration, packaging . . . . The list goes on. It is enough to keep even the most agile team of planners busy.

A common manufacturing conundrum is how to achieve an optimum balance between the flexibility that customers demand and the lower costs that manufacturing efficiencies can deliver. Customers require ever shorter lead times, smaller batch sizes to keep inventory costs down and customised products. In contrast, manufacturers prefer long production runs to minimise setup costs, long lead times for better scheduling and standardised products.

Navigating this tight rope is a core function handled by the company's planning department. For many years they had relied on a manual system with cards representing the production job for each order, placed on a scheduling board. These cards would be cut to length representing the job duration, and have the details of the job written on them. The length would be calculated based on factors such as batch size, machine tool used and wastage.

Considering that typically there are 3 to 4 customer amendments to each order before it reaches manufacture, the manual system was starting to creak at the seems. In search of a solution they turned to their long-term partner, the IT consultancy

D T Systems, who had already developed the other components of their manufacturing system.

Initially the planners expressed some serious concern as to the feasibility of the project, given the complexity of the tasks involved and the knowledge required to perform those tasks efficiently. However, working in close collaboration D T Systems proto-typed a computerised scheduling system.

As the software developed, the planners' attitude gradually changed from pessimism to one of optimism. 'If it can do all of that, could it do this as well?' They're now wondering how they got by before. The interface mirrors the planning boards but is in real-time.

- Jobs are viewed within a time-line against their allocated machine.
- Jobs are sized automatically, according to various production calculations.
- Jobs as placed so they are produced in time, but can be moved by the planner.
- Jobs are colour coded to indicate plain, decorated, etc.
- Jobs requiring planner action flash.
- Jobs breech any non-working days or machine maintenance periods.
- Jobs show and take into account latest production.
- Mouse over job, shows full job details.
- Zoom in and out, and change scale.
- Mismatched machine/job combinations are highlighted.
- Jobs that will be late are highlighted.
- Pop-up links from the job to all other areas of the system.
- Job highlight feature to indicate all jobs meeting specified criteria.

The schedule acts as a "command centre" for the planner, where all of their multivarious tasks can be quickly and easily coordinated to all other areas of the information system. This tight integration allows information to flow freely between the different departments. When an order is amended in the Sales department, the associated job flashes on the planners schedule.

The combination of automatic calculation, rapid searching, a simple user interface and immediate access to information has had a substantial impact on planner productivity. The overall number of labour hours required to plan production has reduced significantly, even though, due to business growth the company is actually now processing 40% more orders than it was two years ago. "This has made a very significant difference to the time it takes to manage orders through the business," said the Commercial Director. They are now intending to role the system out to the remaining production departments and continue to harness the benefits created by this new integrated planning approach.

Overview

Industry Sector: Manufacturing

Business Situation

Requirement for a computerised solution to replace an outmoded manual production scheduling system that involved many time-consuming, labour-intensive tasks.

Solution

An integrated, computerised scheduling system that provides the planner with a "command centre" to orchestrate the planning process.

Benefits

- Labour saving due to increased planner productivity.
- Increased production efficiency due to better planning and use of better information.
- Increased analysis—labour-intensive tasks automated, freeing planner to add value by performing more analysis.
- Tight integration with other areas of the business has greatly reduced the paper trail associated with new and amended orders.
- Command Centre—planners can rapidly access all aspects of a job, e.g., sales order, machine setup, materials, etc.
- Increased visibility—the schedules are viewable in read-only mode from other departments.

Source: Production Scheduling Case Study, DT Systems Ltd, available at http://www.dtsystems.co.uk/Portals/0/Production%20 Scheduling.pdf, accessed 2008-09-16. Reproduced by permission of DT Systems Ltd.

8.2 NETWORK TECHNIQUES: PERT (ADM) AND CPM (PDM)

With the exception of Gantt charts, to be discussed below, the most common approach to project scheduling is the use of network techniques such as PERT and CPM. The Program Evaluation and Review Technique (PERT) was developed by the U.S. Navy in cooperation with Booz Allen Hamilton and the Lockheed Corporation for the Polaris missile/submarine project in 1958. The Critical Path Method was developed by DuPont, Inc., during the same time period.

In application, PERT has primarily been used for R&D projects, the type of projects for which it was developed, though its use is more common on the "development" side of R&D than it is on the "research" side. CPM was designed for construction projects and has been generally embraced by the construction industry. (There are many exceptions to these generalities. The Eli Lilly Company, for example, uses CPM for its research projects.)

The use of PERT has decreased sharply in recent years because a large majority of project management software generates CPM networks. The two methods are quite similar and are often combined for educational presentation.

Originally, PERT was strictly oriented to the time element of projects and used probabilistic activity time estimates to aid in determining the probability that a project could be completed by some given date. CPM, on the other hand, used deterministic activity time estimates and was designed to control both the time and cost aspects of a project, in particular, time/cost trade-offs. In CPM, activities can be "crashed" (expedited) at extra cost to speed up the completion time. Both techniques identified a project critical path with activities that could not be delayed, and also indicated activities with slack (or float) that could be somewhat delayed without lengthening the project completion time. Some writers insist on a strict differentiation between PERT and CPM. This strikes us as unnecessary. One can estimate probabilistic CPM times, and can "crash" PERT networks.

We might note in passing that the critical activities in real-world projects typically constitute less than 10 percent of the total activities. In our examples and simplified problems in this chapter, the critical activities constitute a much greater proportion of the total because we use smaller networks to illustrate the techniques.

PMBOK Guide

Chapter 6

For almost half a century, PERT and CPM networks have been used in project management. However, in 2005, the Project Management Institute (PMI) renamed PERT as ADM (Arrow Diagram Method) and CPM as PDM (Precedence Diagram Method) in the PMBOK®. In general, we will simply refer to either as a "network," but if we wish to refer specifically to a PERT (ADM) network where the activities are shown as arrows on the network, we will call it an AOA (activity-on-arrow) network, and if we refer to a CPM (PDM) network where the activities are shown as nodes, we will call it an AON (activity-on-node) network, as explained in the following subsection.

> As of tomorrow, employees will only be able to access the building using individual security cards. Pictures will be taken next Wednesday, and employees will receive their cards in two weeks.

Terminology

Let us now define some terms used in our discussion of networks.

Activity A specific task or set of tasks that are required by the project, use up resources, and take time to complete.

Event The result of completing one or more activities. An identifiable end state that occurs at a particular time. Events use no resources.

Network The arrangement of all activities (and, in some cases, events) in a project arrayed in their logical sequence and represented by arcs and nodes. This arrangement (network) defines the project and the activity precedence relationships. Networks are usually drawn starting on the left and proceeding to the right. Arrowheads placed on the arcs are used to indicate the direction of flow—that is, to show the proper precedences. Before an event can be *realized*—that is, achieved—all activities that immediately precede it must be completed. These are called its *predecessors*. Thus, an event represents an instant in time when each and every predecessor activity has been finished.

Path The series of connected activities (or intermediate events) between any two events in a network.

Critical Activities, events, or paths which, if delayed, will delay the completion of the project. A project's *critical path* is understood to mean the sequence of critical activities (and critical events) that connects the project's start event to its finish event and which cannot be delayed without delaying the project.

To transform a project plan into a network, one must know what activities comprise the project and, for each activity, what its predecessors (or successors) are. An activity can be in any of these conditions: (1) it may have a successor(s) but no predecessor(s); (2) it may have a predecessor(s) but no successor(s); and (3) it may have both predecessor(s) and successor(s). The first of these is an activity that starts a network. The second ends a network. The third is in the middle. Figure 8-1 shows each of the three types of activities. Activities are represented here by rectangles (one form of what in a network are called "nodes") with arrows to show the precedence relationships. As noted earlier, this activity-on-node (AON) notation is used for PDM/CPM networks. When there are multiple activities with no predecessors, it is usual to show them all emanating from a single node called "START,"* as in Figure 8-2. Similarly, when multiple activities have no successors, it is usual to show them connected to a node called "END."

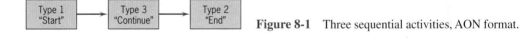

Figure 8-1 Three sequential activities, AON format.

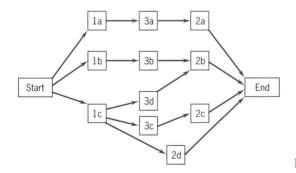

Figure 8-2 Activity network, AON format.

*It is traditional to use the word "START" to note the beginning of a network. The PMI used "START" in the first two editions of its Guide to the Project Management Body of Knowledge (PMBOK). However, in the third edition of PMBOK they started denoting the first node in a network as "BEGIN." We will stay with "START."

The interconnections depend on the technological relationships described in the WBS. For example, when one paints a room, filling small holes and cracks in the wall and masking windows and woodwork are predecessors to painting the walls. Similarly, removing curtains and blinds, as well as pictures and picture hooks from the wall are predecessors to spackling and masking. It is the nature of the work to be done that determines predecessor–successor relationships.

In the preceding examples, rectangles (nodes) represented the activities; hence it was called an activity-on-node (AON) network. Another format for drawing networks is AOA (activity-on-arrow), as shown in Figure 8-3. Here, the activities are shown on the arrows and the (circular) nodes represent events. And as noted earlier, this is the standard notation for ADM/PERT networks. If the project begins with multiple activities, they can all be drawn emanating from the initial node and multiple activities can terminate in a single node at the end of the project.

Throughout most of this chapter we adopt the AON format, but we will also demonstrate AOA network construction. This chapter is intended as an introduction to project scheduling at a level sufficient for the PM who wishes to use most commercial computerized project scheduling packages. For a deeper understanding of PERT and CPM, we refer the reader to Dean (1985) or Moder et al. (1983).

Recall the planning documents we developed in Chapter 6. In particular, the WBS contains the information we need. It is a list of all activities that must be undertaken in order to complete a specified task, the time each activity is expected to take, any nonroutine resources that will be used by the activity, and the predecessor activities for each activity. For example, we might have a WBS like that shown in Figure 8-4.

Figure 8-3   Activity network, AOA format.

WBS

Objective: To complete. . . . .
. . . .
Measures of Performance. . . . .
. . . .
Constraints . . . .

Tasks	*Precedence*	*Time*	*Cost*	*Who Does*
a	—	5 days	—	—
b	—	4 days	—	—
c	a	6 days	—	—
d	b	2 days	—	—
e	b	5 days	—	—
f	c,d	8 days	—	—

Figure 8-4   Sample WBS.

Constructing the Network, AON Version

We begin with the node called "START." Activities **a** and **b** have no predecessors, so we draw arrows out of START to each of them (Figure 8-5a). As explained above, the arrowheads show the direction of precedence. Activity **c** follows **a**, activity **d** follows **b**, and activity **e** also follows **b**. Let's add these to our network in Figure 8-6a. Now, activity **f** follows both **c** and **d**. The WBS does not indicate any further activity is required to complete the task, so we have reached the end of this particular plan. We thus draw arrows from activities **e** and **f** to the node END, as shown in Figure 8-7a. Many of the project management software packages will generate these networks on request.

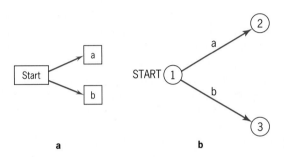

Figure 8-5 Sample of network construction.

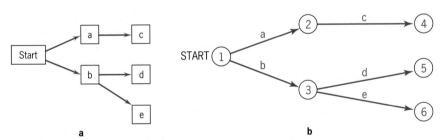

Figure 8-6 Sample of network construction.

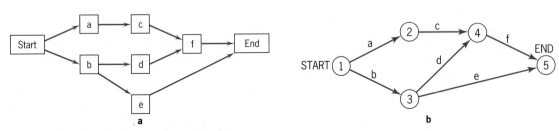

Figure 8-7 Sample of network construction.

Constructing the Network, AOA Version

Again, we begin with a node (event) called "START." Activities **a** and **b** have no predecessors, so we draw arrows labeled "**a**" and "**b**" from START and terminating in circle-shaped nodes numbered "1" and "2" for easy identification (Figure 8-5b). Activity **c** follows **a**, activity **d** follows **b**, and activity **e** also follows **b**. Let's add these arrows to our AOA network, labeling the arrows and nodes sequentially as we go (Figure 8-6b).

Note that activity **f** must follow both **c** and **d**, but any given activity must have its source in one and only one node. Therefore, **c** and **d** must terminate at the same node. Erase activity **d** and its node—it is now clear that hand-drawn networks should be drawn in pencil—and redraw **d** to end at the same node that terminates **c**. We now add activity **e** following **b**, and **f** following **c** and **d**. Because **e** and **f** have no successors, they will terminate at the END node (Figure 8-7b).

The choice between AOA and AON representation is largely a matter of personal preference. As we noted above, AON is typically used in the most popular PC-based commercially available computer software, and AON networks are easier to draw. AOA networks are slightly harder to draw because they sometimes require the use of *dummy* activities to aid in indicating a particular precedence, via a dashed arc. A dummy activity has no duration and uses no resources. Its sole purpose is to indicate a technological relationship. (AON networks do not require the use of dummy activities.) AOA networks clearly identify events in the network. These must be added as "zero-duration" activities in AON networks.

Figure 8-8 illustrates the proper way to use a dummy activity if two activities occur between the same *two* events. Figure 8-8 also shows why dummy activities may be needed for AOA networks. An activity is identified by its starting and ending nodes as well as its "name." For example, activities **a** and **b** both start from node 1 and end at node 2. Many computer programs that are widely used for finding the critical path and time for networks require the nodes to identify which activity is which. In our example, **a** and **b** would appear to be the same, both starting at node 1 and ending at node 2. Figure 8-9 illustrates how to use a dummy activity in AOA format when activities **a**, **b**, and **c** must precede activity **d**, but only **a** and **b** must precede activity **e**. Last, Figure 8-10 illustrates the use of dummy activities in a more complex setting. AON networks are widely used, but some firms favor AOA networks, so the PM should be familiar with both types.

Gantt (Bar) Charts and Microsoft Project® (MSP)

PMBOK Guide
6.5.3

One of the oldest but still one of the most useful methods of presenting project schedule information is the Gantt chart, developed around 1917 by Henry L. Gantt, a pioneer in the field of scientific management. The Gantt chart shows planned and actual progress for a number of tasks displayed as bars against a horizontal time scale. It is a particularly effective and easy-to-read method of indicating the actual current status for each of a set of tasks compared to the planned progress for each item of the set. As a result, the Gantt chart can be helpful in expediting, sequencing, and reallocating resources among tasks, as well as in the valuable but mundane job of keeping track of how things are going. In addition, the charts usually contain a number of special symbols to designate or highlight items of special concern to the situation being charted. Although the 3rd edition of PMBOK started calling these "bar charts," we will continue calling them Gantt charts here.

There are several advantages to the use of Gantt charts. First, even though they may contain a great deal of information, they are easily understood. While they do require frequent updating (as does any scheduling/control device), they are easy to maintain *as long as task*

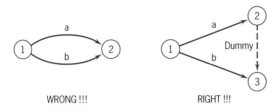

Figure 8-8   Networking concurrent activities.

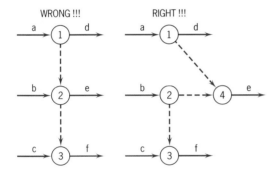

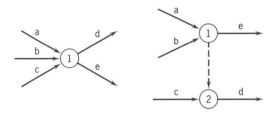

Figure 8-9   Activity **c** not required for **e**.

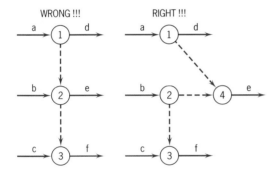

Figure 8-10   **a** precedes **d**; **a** and **b** precede **e**; **b** and **c** precede **f** (**a** does not precede **f**).

requirements are not changed or major alterations of the schedule are not made. Gantt charts provide a picture of the current state of a project. Gantt charts, however, have a serious weakness. If a project is complex with a large set of activities, it may be very difficult to follow multiple activity paths through the project. Gantt charts are powerful devices for communicating to senior management, but networks are usually more helpful in the hands-on task of managing the project.

Another significant feature of Gantt charts is that they are as easy to construct as a network. We use the example in the previous subsection to demonstrate how to construct such a chart.

As is true of many things, it is important for the student to be able to understand just what it is that networks and Gantt charts show (and what they do not show) before using MSP or other software to draw complex networks and Gantt charts that the student will have to understand and use. Drawing networks and charts by hand is a quick way to develop that understanding. Once understanding is gained, however, software is easier, faster, and given a project of a size that reflects reality, far more cost effective.

Consider the example in Figure 8-4 that was just used to illustrate how to draw a network. When we open MSP we begin by clicking on Gantt chart from either the task tab or the view tab. We will now see the form that is used to enter WBS data into the program. Entering the data is straightforward. We begin by entering an activity named "START." We assign it a duration of 0 days which makes it a "milestone" rather than a true "activity." We now enter activity **a** with a duration of five days, and then continue with the rest of the activities. At the end of the list, we add FINISH with zero days duration, the project ending milestone.

The software automatically assigns a WBS (ID) number to each activity as you enter it. You may delete or add columns if you wish. If you do not enter a specific start date, the MSP will default to the present date for its start date. As you enter data from the WBS, MSP will draw an AON network and a Gantt chart automatically. (The Gantt chart will be visible to the right of the WBS information. The Network Diagram will be visible by selecting the View tab and choosing Network Diagram in the Task Views group.) If the activity names and durations are entered without noting the appropriate predecessor information, all activities will be assumed to start on the same start date. As the predecessor information is entered, the proper relationships between the activities are shown; see Figures 8-11 and 8-12.

Our concern so far has simply been to show the technological dependencies in a network or Gantt chart. A glance at the AON network or the Gantt chart shows something interesting. If we sum up the activity times for all activities in the WBS, we see that there are 30 days of work to schedule. But, as the network and chart show, the project is scheduled to start on January 17 and will be completed on February 11. That is 25 days, not 30. Further, MSP defaults to a work calendar with a five-day week. If the calendar is adjusted to a seven-day week, the project will require only 19 days to be completed. It can be finished as early as February 5. Calculation-by-hand is not at all difficult, but MSP can do it faster and easier. It is important, however, to remember that software makes assumptions about such things as the number of days worked in a week, the number of hours per day that are worked, and several other matters that will be considered later. These assumptions

ID	Task Name	Duration	Start	Finish	Predecessors
1	Start	0 days	1/17	1/17	
2	a	5 days	1/17	1/21	1
3	b	4 days	1/17	1/20	1
4	c	6 days	1/24	1/31	2
5	d	2 days	1/21	1/24	3
6	e	5 days	1/21	1/27	3
7	f	8 days	2/1	2/10	4,5
8	Finish	0 days	2/11	2/11	6,7

Project: Sample Project   Manual Task ▧▧▧▧▧   Milestone ◆

Figure 8-11   MSP plan and Gantt chart for sample project in Figure 8-4.

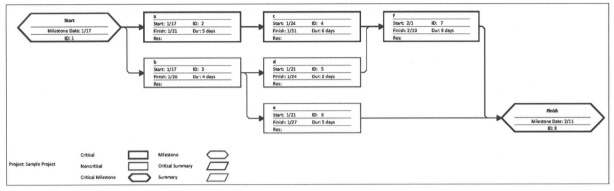

Figure 8-12   An MSP AON network for sample project in Figure 8-4.

may be changed if one wishes, but they must be considered every time the software is used to map a project.

This example illustrates both the strength and weakness of the Gantt chart. Its major strength is that it is easy to read. All popular project management software will prepare Gantt charts, and most have some options available for customization. On balance, ease of construction and ease of use have made the Gantt chart the most popular method for displaying a project schedule. Nonetheless, an AON network is still most useful for the PM to exercise control over the schedule, and the viewer may be misled if the Gantt chart is not read carefully or if it does not contain all appropriate information (Wilkens, 1997).

An Important Aside on Estimating Activity Times

Before solving the network to find the critical path and critical time of the entire network, we must note that *it is vital to good project management to be meticulously honest in estimating the time required to complete each of the various tasks included in the project*. Note that we did not say "meticulously accurate." This would not be possible in the uncertain world in which we all live. We said "honest," which means that time estimates should be unbiased, best-guesses. It is unfortunate that this commandment is often disregarded.

Estimates of the time required to complete project activities should be estimated in the same way that required resources are estimated. As described in Chapter 7, both the project manager and the people carrying out the activity should make estimates of the resource requirements. They should also make estimates of the activity duration. If duration estimates differ significantly between the two sources, the duration should be negotiated as in Ch. 7.

The tendency of too many managers is to set deadlines earlier than the project requires in order to "insure" that the task will be completed in time. In an excellent, short article in the *Wall Street Journal*, Jared Sandberg (2007) points out that the false early deadline is common. A false deadline does not insure that a task or project will be completed in time. Quite the opposite, it frequently results in tasks being completed late. The lie is easily discovered and the result is that no one takes that manager's deadlines seriously thereafter. Some managers set deadlines on all tasks given to subordinates. They treat routine work and critically important work in the same way. This violates a primary rule of good time management, and the result is that "urgent" but unimportant tasks often squeeze out truly important activities, making them late.

Other sources of bias in time estimates result when project sponsors underestimate time and resource requirements in an attempt to insure that their project will pass the barriers to project selection, and when workers overestimate time and resource usage to ensure successful task completions and project delivery.

Given that schedules are based on honest best-guesses, other major problems can cause serious errors in time estimates. In some projects, the client is directly engaged in evolving project deliverables, which means that deliverables, and thus activities, are likely to change before the project is completed. In many complex projects, not all activities are fully understood until the project has completed some earlier activities. These problems led to the development of agile project management that uses an iterative process for making time and resource estimates for these later, not-well-understood activities. The same problem arises in a multiproject environment when one project "borrows" a critical resource from another project. Then, activities on the borrowed-from project may be delayed. This actual or potential lateness may not be discovered unless the project manger conducts frequent, periodic, schedule-status reviews—a technique called "iterative scheduling," which allows appropriate rescheduling in conjunction with the client (Wheatly, 2010). Wheatly says the following five clues can indicate when iterative scheduling is needed: late or vague progress reports, overdue deliverables, static progress indicators, longer work hours for team members, and a noticeable increase in minor "issues" affecting the project. With this short sermon, we return to solving the network we have created.

Project Management in Practice
Election Returns within Three Hours

Panama's presidential election on May 3, 2009 was a tense drama, as most are, but in two-and-a-half hours after the polls closed, the country heard the outcome. Given that many of the nation's citizens are located in small, remote villages, and others in dense jungles, miles from the nearest landlines, this was an impressive achievement. But it was no accident—it was the outcome of a project to restore faith in the government of a country racked by the fraud of the 1983 Manuel Noriega dictatorship.

The essence of the project boiled down to two thrusts. The first was a decades-long continuing effort by Panama's Electoral Tribunal to establish a valid electoral database through mandatory birth and death records, plus biometric data (fingerprints, photo-recognition software, etc.) to capture key milestones in each citizen's life so only eligible citizens could vote, only once and only for the candidates and issues relevant to their location.

The second thrust was technological, involving the establishment and use of highly secure communication channels, including telephone lines, satellite phones, VHF radio links, and for this election, a new wireless application protocol (WAP) that was written from scratch, encrypted, authenticated, and extensively tested. To be sure it worked smoothly and securely, polling station attendants were trained in using the app and then the app was simulated for 12 extensive tests at polling stations. During the simulations, security experts and "ethical hackers" from the United States tested and probed the system's defenses, resulting in last-minute changes to both the software and the procedures for using it, such as password access.

In the press center for the election where voting details by province would be immediately posted, a giant 19-foot by 25-foot monitoring screen was installed to report the vote. This screen was surrounded by four smaller screens to provide more voting details such as number of valid, blank, and null votes, level of voting participation, local issues, interactive maps of the nation, and so on. Not surprisingly, the Electoral Tribunal responsible for elections is already preparing for the 2014 election

and plans to extend the system to other elections, such as legislative and city mayoral and councilor elections.

Source: M. Wheatley, "Calling the Election," *PM Network*, Vol. 24.

Solving the Network

Let us now consider a small project with 10 activities in order to illustrate the network technique. Table 8-1 lists the activities, their most likely completion times, and the activities that must precede them. The table also includes optimistic and pessimistic estimates of completion time for each activity in the list. Actual activity time is expected rarely to be less than the optimistic time or more than the pessimistic time. (More on this matter shortly.)

Beginning with a node named START, connect the three activities with no predecessors (**a**, **b**, and **c**) to the Start node as in Figure 8-13.

Activity **d** has a predecessor of **a**, and thus it follows **a**. Activities **e**, **f**, and **g** all must follow both **b** and **c** as predecessors. Activity **h** follows **c**. Activity **j** follows both **d** and **e**. Activity **i** follows **g** and **h**. Because there are no more activities, we must be at the end of the network. Add a node labeled "END" and connect any nodes without successor activities, in this case, **j**, **f**, and **i**, reading from top to bottom. As stated earlier, always show the direction of a connection with an arrowhead.

Table 8-1   Project Activity Times and Precedences

Activity	Optimistic Time	Most Likely Time	Pessimistic Time	Immediate Predecessor Activities
a	10	22	22	—
b	20	20	20	—
c	4	10	16	—
d	2	14	32	a
e	8	8	20	b, c
f	8	14	20	b, c
g	4	4	4	b, c
h	2	12	16	c
i	6	16	38	g, h
j	2	8	14	d, e

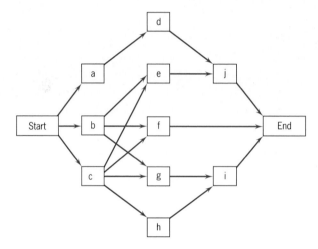

Figure 8-13   The AON network from Table 8-1.

Calculating Activity Times

The next step is to calculate expected activity completion times from the data in Table 8-1. These expected completion times are found by using the three time estimates (optimistic, pessimistic, and most likely) in the table. Remember that these estimates are an expression of the risk associated with the time required for each activity. (The optimistic, pessimistic, and most likely estimates made for activity times are equally applicable to the estimates of resource usage made in Chapter 7, as are the calculations that follow.)

Once again, a short digression is helpful. Precisely what is meant by "optimistic," "pessimistic," and "most likely"? Assume that all possible times for some specific activity might be represented by a statistical distribution (e.g., the asymmetrical distribution in Figure 8-14). The "most likely" time, m, for the activity is the mode of this distribution. In theory, the "optimistic" and "pessimistic" times are selected in the following way. The PM, or whoever is attempting to estimate a and b, is asked to select a such that the actual time required by the activity will be a or greater about 99 percent of the time. Similarly, b is estimated such that about 99 percent of the time the activity will have a duration of b or less. (Some project managers or workers may be uncomfortable making estimates at this level of precision, but we will delay dealing with this problem for the moment.)

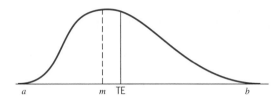

Figure 8-14 Distribution of all possible activity times for an activity.

The expected time, TE, is found by

$$TE = (a + 4m + b)/6$$

where

- a = optimistic time estimate
- b = pessimistic time estimate
- m = most likely time estimate, the mode

Note in Table 8-1 that some activity durations are known with certainty, which is to say that a, b, and m are the same (see activity **g**, for instance). Note further that the most likely time may be the same as the optimistic time ($a = m$) as in activity **e**, or that the most likely time may be identical to the pessimistic time ($m = b$) as in activity **a**. The range about m may be symmetric where

$$m - a = b - m$$

as in activity **c**, or may be quite asymmetric, as in activities **h** and **i**.

The above formula for calculating expected times is based on the beta statistical distribution.[*] This distribution is used rather than the more common normal distribution because it is highly flexible in form and can take into account such extremes as where $a = m$ or $b = m$.

TE is an estimate of the mean of the distribution. It is a weighted average of a, m, and b with weights of 1-4-1, respectively. Again, we emphasize that this *same method can be applied to finding the expected level of resource usage given the appropriate estimates of the modal resource level as well as optimistic and pessimistic estimates.*

This process of estimating activity times occasionally comes under criticism. In general, critics argue that when activity times are set, these come to be considered as targets. This argument maintains that PERT/CPM success is due to the *process* of estimating times rather than to the estimates themselves. That is, the estimates are said to become self-fulfilling prophecies. An additional argument (Williams, 1995) is that actual activity times are rarely less than the estimate of the mode, and are often greater, accounting for the right skew of the distribution. The cause is attributed to Parkinson's law—that work expands to fill the allotted time. If problems occur, the activity may require more time, but it will almost never require less. While no one, to the best of our knowledge, had proven this empirically, there is some anecdotal evidence that supports this notion. There is, however, also anecdotal evidence that supports the traditional assumption that three-time activity duration estimates are the "best guesses" of people who have experience in similar activities. In any event, our purpose here is to estimate the range of time required for each activity rather than argue with the underlying logic of the estimation process.

---

[*]We remind readers who would like a short refresher on elementary statistics and probability that one is available in Appendix A on this book's website.

> "Doing it right is no excuse for not meeting the schedule. No one will believe you solved this problem in one day! Now, go act busy for a few weeks and I'll let you know when it's time to tell them."

Table 8-2   Expected Activity Times (TE), Variances (σ^2), and Standard Deviations (σ)

Activity	Expected Time, TE	Variance, σ^2	Standard Deviation, σ
a	20	4	2
b	20	0	0
c	10	4	2
d	15	25	5
e	10	4	2
f	14	4	2
g	4	0	0
h	11	5.4	2.32
i	18	28.4	5.33
j	8	4	2

The results of the expected value calculations are shown in Table 8-2 and are included in the activity nodes of Figure 8-14 as well. Also included in the table and in the nodes are measures of the uncertainty for the duration of each activity, the *variance*, σ^2, that is,

$$\sigma^2 = ((b - a)/6)^2$$

and the *standard deviation*, σ, which is given by

$$\sigma = \sqrt{\sigma^2}$$

This calculation of σ is based on the assumption that the standard deviation of a beta distribution is approximately one-sixth of its range, $(b - a)/6$.

Later in this chapter, we will argue for an amendment to the estimation procedure for the variance of activity times if the estimates of a and b are not made at the 99 percent level. Note that the format and calculations of Tables 8-1 and 8-2 lend themselves to the use of a spreadsheet program such as Excel,® as we did in Chapter 7. The equations for TE, σ^2, and σ can be entered once and copied to the rest of the rows.

Critical Path and Time

Consider again the project shown in Figure 8-15. Assume, for convenience, that the time units involved are days, that the first figure is the expected time, and that the second figure is the variance. How long will it take to complete the project? (For the moment we will treat the expected times as if they were certain.) If we start the project on day 0, shown as ES (earliest start) at the upper left of each node in Figure 8-16, we can begin simultaneously working on activities **a**, **b**, and **c**, each of which has no predecessor activities. We will complete activity **a** in 20 days, activity **b** in 20 days, and activity **c** in 10 days, shown as EF (earliest finish) at the upper right of each of their respective nodes. These early finish times represent the earliest times that the following activities can begin.

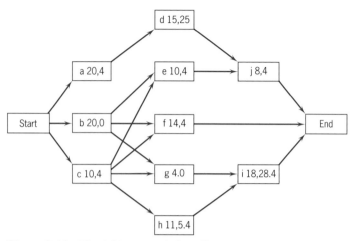

Figure 8-15   The AON network from Table 8-2, showing activity durations and variances.

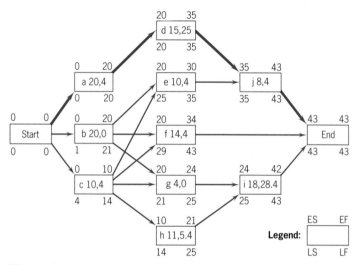

Figure 8-16   AON network showing earliest and latest start and finish times, and critical (bolded) path.

Note that activity **e** not only requires the completion of activity **b**, but also requires the completion of activity **c**, as shown by the two incoming arrows. Activity **e** cannot begin until all paths leading to it have been completed. Therefore, the ES for activity **e** is equal to the EF of the *latest* activity leading to it, 20 for activity **b**.

Proceeding similarly, we see that activity **j** has two predecessor activities, **d** and **e**. Activity **d** cannot start until day 20, (ES = 20) and it requires 15 days to complete. Thus, it will end (EF) a total of 35 days from the start of the project. Activity **e** may also start after 20 days but it requires only 10 days, a total of 30 days from the project start. Because activity **j** requires the completion of both activities **d** and **e**, its ES is 35 days, the longest of the paths to it. Activity **i** has an ES of 24 days, the longest of the two paths leading to it, and END, the completion of the network, has a time of 43 days. The remaining ESs and EFs are shown in Figure 8-16.

As can be seen, the longest of the paths through the network is **a-d-j** using 43 days, which means that 43 days is the shortest time in which the entire network can be completed. This is called the *critical time* of the network, and **a-d-j** is the *critical path*, usually shown as a heavy line as in Figure 8-16.

In a simple network such as our example, it is easy to find and evaluate every path between start and finish to find the longest path. However, many real networks are considerably more complex, and finding all the paths can be taxing. Using the method illustrated above, there is no need to worry about the problem. Every node is characterized by the fact that one or more activities lead to it. Each of these activities has an expected duration and originates in an earlier node. As we proceed to calculate the ES and EF of each node, beginning at the start, we are *actually finding the critical path and time to each of the nodes* in the network. Note that activity **i** has an ES of 24 days, and its critical path is **b-g**, rather than **c-h** which requires 21 days, or **c-g**.

Although we will assume throughout this chapter that we always employ the "as-soon-as possible" approach to scheduling tasks ("early start"), there are situations where other approaches are sometimes used. One example is the simultaneous start, where all resources are launched at the beginning. Another is the simultaneous finish, where a facility can be moved to its next location once all the tasks are finished. Of course, delay early on in a project runs the risk of delaying the overall project if some other activities inadvertently become delayed. One important reason for using an "as-late-as-possible" approach, described below, is that it delays the use of resources as much as possible, thereby optimizing the cash flow of the project, but again at some risk of delay.

Slack (aka, Float)

We will now focus on the latest possible starting times (LS) for the activities. As noted in the previous section, the ES for an activity is equal to the largest EF for its preceding activities. An important question for the PM is this: What is the latest time (LS) activity **i** could start without making the entire project late?

Refer again to Figure 8-16. The project has a critical time of 43 days. Activity **i** must therefore be finished by day 43, indicated by LF (latest finish time), placed at the bottom right of its node. Also, activity **i** requires 18 days to be accomplished. Therefore, **i** *must* be started no later than day 25 ($43 - 18 = 25$) if the project is to be completed on day 43. The LS for activity **i** is thus 25, placed at the lower left corner of the node. Because **i** cannot begin until activities **g** and **h** have finished, the latest time (LF) for each of these is also day 25. The difference between the LS and the ES for an activity is called its *float* or *slack*. In the case of activity **i**, it must be started no later than day 25, but *could* be started as early as day 24, so it has one day of slack. It should be immediately obvious that all activities on the critical path have zero slack.* Zero slack activities cannot be delayed without making the project late.

For another example, consider activity **f**. Its ES is day 20, which is equal to the EF of its predecessor activity **b**. The LS for activity **f** is $43 - 14 = 29$. If **f** is started later than day 29, it will delay the entire project. Activity **f** has slack of $LS - ES = 29 - 20 = 9$ days.

To find the slack for any activity, we make a backward pass (right to left) through the network just as we made a forward pass (left to right) to find the critical path and time, and the ESs and EFs for successor activities. There is one simple convention we must adopt: *When there are two or more noncritical activities on a path, it is conventional to calculate the slack for each activity as if it were the only activity in the path.* Thus, when finding the slack

---

* "Float" and "slack" are synonyms. The PMI writes of "float." MSP uses the term "slack." We simply use the term "slack" out of habit.

Table 8-3   Times and Slacks for Network
in Figure 8-16

Activity	LS	ES	Slack
a	0	0	0
b	1	0	1
c	4	0	4
d	20	20	0
e	25	20	5
f	29	20	9
g	21	20	1
h	14	10	4
i	25	24	1
j	35	35	0

for activity **i**, for example, we assume that none of **i**'s predecessors are delayed. Of course, if some activity, **x**, had six days of slack, and if an earlier activity was late, causing the event to be delayed say two days, then activity **x** would have only four days of slack, having lost two days to the earlier delay.

It is simple to calculate slack for activities that are immediate predecessors of the final node. As we move to earlier activities, it is just a bit more complicated. Consider activity **g**. Remembering our assumption that the other activities in the same path use none of the available slack, we see that activity **i** must follow **g**, and that **g** follows activities **b** and **c**. Starting with activity **i**'s LS of 25, we subtract four days for **g** (25 − 4 = 21). Thus **g** can begin no later than day 21 without delaying the network. The ES for **g** is day 20, so **g** has one day of slack.

As another example, consider activity **e**. Activity **e** must be completed by day 35, the LS of activity **j**. The LS for **e** is thus 35 − 10 = 25. Its ES is day 20, so activity **e** has five days of slack. Table 8-3 shows the LS, ES, and slack for all activities.

On occasion, the PM may negotiate an acceptable completion date for a project which allows for some slack in the entire network. If, in our example, an acceptable date was 50 working days after the project start, then the network would have a total of 50 − 43 = 7 days of slack.

Some writers and MSP differentiate between "total" slack or float and "free" slack or float. Total slack is LF – EF or LS – ES as described above. Free slack is defined as the time an activity can be delayed without affecting the start time of *any* successor activity. Activity **h** could be delayed three days without affecting the start time of activity **i**. Activity **h** has three days of free slack and four days of total slack.

Precedence Diagramming

One shortcoming of the AOA network method is that it does not allow for leads and lags between two activities without greatly increasing the number of subactivities to account for this. In construction projects, in particular, it is quite common for the following restrictions to occur. (Node designations are shown in Figure 8-17.)

- **Finish to Start**   Activity 2 must not start before Activity 1 has been completed. This is the typical arrangement of an activity and its predecessor. Other finish–start arrangements are also possible. If the predecessor information had been written "1FS + 2 days," Activity 2 would be scheduled to start at least two days after the completion of Activity 1, as shown in Figure 8-17. For instance, if Activity 1 was the pouring of a concrete sidewalk, Activity 2 might be any activity that used the sidewalk.

Figure 8-17   Precedence diagramming conventions.

- **Start to Start**   Activity 5 cannot begin until Activity 4 has been underway for at least two days. Setting electrical wires in place cannot begin until two days after framing has begun.

- **Finish to Finish**   Activity 7 must be complete at least one day before Activity 8 is completed. If Activity 7 is priming the walls of a house, Activity 8 might be the activities involved in selecting, purchasing, and finally delivering the wallpaper. It is important not to hang the paper until the wall primer has dried for 24 hours.

- **Start to Finish**   Activity 11 cannot be completed before 7 days since the start of Activity 10. If Activities 10 and 11 are the two major cruising activities in a prepaid weeklong ocean cruise, the total time cannot be less than the promised week. The S–F relationship is rare because there are usually simpler ways to map the required relationship.

Precedence diagramming is an AON network method that easily allows for these leads and lags within the network. MSP handles leads and lags without problems. Network node times are calculated in a manner similar to AON/AOA times. Because of the lead and lag restrictions, it is often helpful to lay out a Gantt chart to see what is actually happening. The richer set of precedence relationships allowed by AON is pertinent for a variety of projects, particularly construction projects. [For more details on this technique, see Al-Hammed et al. (1998).] Most current project management software will allow leads, lags, delays, and other constraints in the context of their standard AON network and Gantt chart programs.

Once Again, Microsoft Project®

Figures 8-18 and 8-19 depict the three-time Gantt chart and network diagram using the data in Table 8-4. The data to perform a PERT Analysis can be calculated by hand for small projects or by using Excel®. Notice in both figures that it is sometimes difficult to tell which activities precede activities **e**, **f**, **g**, and **h**. (Check Table 8-4.)

In the next section we show how to determine the probability that a project will be completed in a specified time. To do this, the standard deviation, σ, and variance, σ^2, for each activity duration are needed. MSP does not calculate these numbers. The variances and

ID	Task Name	Duration	Start	Finish
1	Start	0 days	1/18	1/18
2	a	20 days	1/18	2/6
3	b	20 days	1/18	2/6
4	c	10 days	1/18	1/27
5	d	15 days	2/7	2/21
6	e	10 days	2/7	2/16
7	f	14 days	2/7	2/20
8	g	4 days	2/7	2/10
9	h	11 days	1/28	2/7
10	i	18 days	2/11	2/28
11	j	8 days	2/22	3/1
12	Finish	0 days	3/1	3/1

Figure 8-18   Gantt Chart of Table 8-4.

Figure 8-19   AON network of Table 8-4.

Table 8-4   MSP Gantt Chart Version of Project Described in Table 8-1.

ID	Task Name	Predecessors	Optimistic Duration	Most Likely Duration	Pessimistic Duration	Expected Duration
1	Start		0 days	0 days	0 days	0 days
2	a	1	10 days	22 days	22 days	20 days
3	b	1	20 days	20 days	20 days	20 days
4	c	1	4 days	10 days	16 days	10 days
5	d	2	2 days	14 days	32 days	15 days
6	e	3, 4	8 days	8 days	20 days	10 days
7	f	3, 4	8 days	14 days	20 days	14 days
8	g	3, 4	4 days	4 days	4 days	4 days
9	h	4	2 days	12 days	16 days	11 days
10	i	8, 9	6 days	16 days	38 days	18 days
11	j	5, 6	2 days	8 days	14 days	8 days
12	Finish	10, 11, 7	0 days	0 days	0 days	0 days

standard deviations for the activities in the project demonstrated here are shown in Table 8-2. Recall that

$$\sigma = (b - a)/6$$

and

$$\sigma^2 = ((b - a)/6)^2$$

Exhibits Available from Software, a Bit More MSP

As we noted earlier and you have seen just above, project management software can illustrate the project as a Gantt chart and, in addition, show precedences, times, and other activity elements directly on the chart. Moreover, AOA and AON network diagrams, calendars, and other displays and reports can also be shown. For example, Figure 8-20 shows an MSP Gantt chart for the project of Table 8-1 with the critical path, path connections, and LS and LF times depicted on the chart. It is simple to customize the information shown; for instance, early start and finish times, slack, special resource requirements, and several other items can be added to the nodes.

As another example, Figure 8-21 shows the basic Gantt chart for a video production project, including a summary task (ID 3) and two milestones. Figure 8-22 is the AON network diagram showing the critical path, path connections, task durations, milestones, resources, start and finish dates, and ID numbers. Figure 8-23 is the project calendar showing the calendar scheduling of the tasks on a monthly calendar with the critical path tasks highlighted. The calendar view depicted in Figure 8-23 is the default MSP view showing the tasks continuing over the weekends *even though no work may actually be conducted.* MSP's calendar default

ID	Task Name	Estimated Duration	Start	Finish	Late Start	February						March	
						1/16	1/23	1/30	2/6	2/13	2/20	2/27	3/6
1	Start	0 days	1/18	1/18	1/18								
2	a	20 days	1/18	2/6	1/18								
3	b	20 days	1/18	2/6	1/19								
4	c	10 days	1/18	1/27	1/22								
5	d	15 days	2/7	2/21	2/7								
6	e	10 days	2/7	2/16	2/12						5 days		
7	f	14 days	2/7	2/20	2/16							9 days	
8	g	4 days	2/7	2/10	2/8								
9	h	11 days	1/28	2/7	2/1				3 days				
10	i	18 days	2/11	2/28	2/12							1 day	
11	j	8 days	2/22	3/1	2/22								
12	Finish	0 days	3/1	3/1	3/1								

Project: Table 8-4   Task ▬▬▬▬ Summary ▬▬▬▬ Slack ──────
                      Milestone ◆ Critical ▬▬▬▬

Figure 8-20   An MSP Gantt chart of the project in Table 8-4 showing activity durations and schedule, critical path, path connections, slack, and earliest and latest start and finish times.

work schedule is 8 hours per day, 5 days per week unless the user specifies a different work-week schedule, such as one that *does* work over the weekends.

Project progress should also be monitored and input to the software for updating the charts and reports. Such progress is indicated directly on the Gantt chart, such as that shown in Figure 8-24 for the video project. Note in the figure how the project completion milestone has been delayed to match actual completion dates of the updated project's tasks.

Uncertainty of Project Completion Time

When discussing project completion dates with senior management, the PM should try to determine the probability that a project will be completed by the suggested deadline—or find the completion time associated with a predetermined level of risk. With the information in Table 8-2, this is not difficult.

If we assume that the activities are statistically independent of each other, then the variance of a set of activities is equal to the sum of the variances of the individual activities comprising the set. From your study of statistics, recall that the variance of a population is a measure of the population's dispersion and is equal to the square of the population's standard deviation. The variances in which we are interested are the variances of the activities on the critical path and, as we will see shortly, of other paths that are close to being critical.

The critical path of our example includes activities **a**, **d**, and **j**. From Table 8-2 we find that the variances of these activities are 4, 25, and 4, respectively; and the variance for the critical path is the sum of these numbers, 33 days. Assume, as above, that the PM has promised to

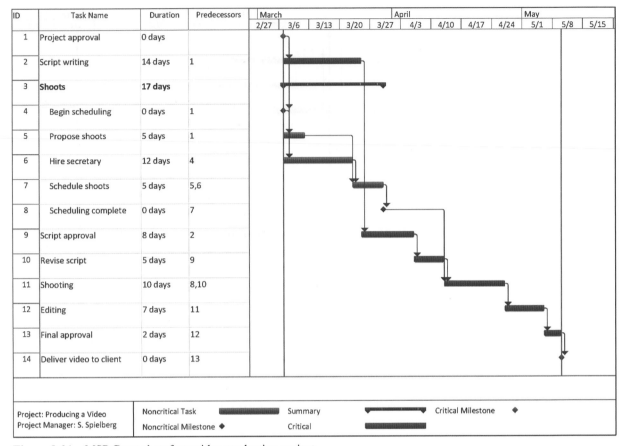

ID	Task Name	Duration	Predecessors
1	Project approval	0 days	
2	Script writing	14 days	1
3	**Shoots**	**17 days**	
4	Begin scheduling	0 days	1
5	Propose shoots	5 days	1
6	Hire secretary	12 days	4
7	Schedule shoots	5 days	5,6
8	Scheduling complete	0 days	7
9	Script approval	8 days	2
10	Revise script	5 days	9
11	Shooting	10 days	8,10
12	Editing	7 days	11
13	Final approval	2 days	12
14	Deliver video to client	0 days	13

Project: Producing a Video
Project Manager: S. Spielberg

Figure 8-21   MSP Gantt chart for a video production project.

Figure 8-22   An MSP AON network for video project with critical path, durations, dates, milestones, and ID numbers.

Figure 8-23 MSP calendar for video project; critical path is in bold print.

Figure 8-24 MSP Gantt chart for video project tracking progress to date.

complete the project in 50 days. What are the chances of meeting that deadline? We find the answer by calculating Z, where

$$Z = (D - \mu)\sqrt{\sigma_\mu^2}$$

and

D = the desired project completion time

μ = the critical time of the project, the sum of the TEs for activities on the critical path

σ_μ^2 = the variance of the critical path, the sum of the variances of activities on the critical path

Z = the number of standard deviations of a normal distribution (the *standard normal deviate*)

Z, as calculated above, can be used to find the probability of completing the project on time. Using the numbers in our example, $D = 50$, $\mu = 43$, and $\sigma_\mu^2 = 33$ (the square root of σ_μ^2 is 5.745), we have

$$Z = (50 - 43)/5.745$$
$$= 1.22 \text{ standard deviations}$$

We turn now to Table 8-5, which shows the probabilities associated with various levels of Z. (Table 8-5 also appears on the inside rear cover.) We go down the left column until we find $Z = 1.2$, and then across to column .02 to find $Z = 1.22$. The probability value of $Z = 1.22$ shown in the table is .8888, or almost 89 percent, which is the likelihood that we will complete the critical path of our sample project within 50 days of the time it is started. Figure 8-25 shows the resulting probability distribution of the project completion times.*

We can work the problem backward, too. What deadline is consistent with a .95 probability of on-time completion? First, we go to Table 8-5 and look through the table until we find .95. The Z value associated with .95 is 1.645. (The values in the table are not strictly linear, so our interpolation is only approximate.) We know that μ is 43 days, and that $\sqrt{\sigma_\mu^2}$ is 5.745. Solving the equation for D, we have

$$D = \mu + 5.745 \,(1.645)$$
$$= 43 + 9.45$$
$$= 52.45 \text{ days}$$

Thus, we conclude that there is a 95 percent chance of finishing the project by 52.45 days. However, that is not quite true. There is a 95 percent chance of finishing path **a-d-j** in 52.45 days. Remember that this is a stochastic network. ("Stochastic"—sta kas' tik—is much nicer to say than "probabilistic" and means the same thing.) If the activities of the project are

Figure 8-25   Probability distribution of project completion times.

---

*Our use of the normal distribution is allowed by the Central Limit theorem which attests to the fact that the sum of independent activity times is normally distributed if the number of activities is large.

Table 8-5   Cumulative (Single Tail) Probabilities of the Normal Probability Distribution
(Areas under the Normal Curve from $-\infty$ to Z)

Example: the area to the left of $Z = 1.34$ is found by following the left Z column
down to 1.3 and moving right to the .04 column. At the intersection read .9099.
The area to the right of $Z = 1.34$ is $1 - .9099 = .0901$. The area between the mean
(center line) and $Z = 1.34$ is $.9099 - .5 = .4099$.

z	.00	.01	.02	.03	.04	.05	.06	.07	.08	.09
.0	.5000	.5040	.5080	.5120	.5160	.5199	.5239	.5279	.5319	.5359
.1	.5398	.5438	.5478	.5517	.5557	.5596	.5636	.5675	.5714	.5753
.2	.5793	.5832	.5871	.5910	.5948	.5987	.6026	.6064	.6103	.6141
.3	.6179	.6217	.6255	.6293	.6331	.6368	.6406	.6443	.6480	.6517
.4	.6554	.6591	.6628	.6664	.6700	.6736	.6772	.6808	.6844	.6879
.5	.6915	.6950	.6985	.7019	.7054	.7088	.7123	.7157	.7190	.7224
.6	.7257	.7291	.7324	.7357	.7389	.7422	.7454	.7486	.7517	.7549
.7	.7580	.7611	.7642	.7673	.7704	.7734	.7764	.7794	.7823	.7852
.8	.7881	.7910	.7939	.7967	.7995	.8023	.8051	.8078	.8106	.8133
.9	.8159	.8186	.8212	.8238	.8264	.8289	.8315	.8340	.8365	.8389
1.0	.8413	.8438	.8461	.8485	.8508	.8531	.8554	.8577	.8599	.8621
1.1	.8643	.8665	.8686	.8708	.8729	.8749	.8770	.8790	.8810	.8880
1.2	.8849	.8869	.8888	.8907	.8925	.8944	.8962	.8980	.8997	.9015
1.3	.9032	.9049	.9066	.9082	.9099	.9115	.9131	.9147	.9162	.9177
1.4	.9192	.9207	.9222	.9236	.9251	.9265	.9279	.9292	.9306	.9319
1.5	.9332	.9345	.9357	.9370	.9382	.9394	.9406	.9418	.9429	.9441
1.6	.9452	.9463	.9474	.9484	.9495	.9505	.9515	.9525	.9535	.9545
1.7	.9554	.9564	.9573	.9582	.9591	.9599	.9608	.9616	.9625	.9633
1.8	.9641	.9649	.9656	.9664	.9671	.9678	.9686	.9693	.9699	.9706
1.9	.9713	.9719	.9726	.9732	.9738	.9744	.9750	.9756	.9761	.9767
2.0	.9772	.9778	.9783	.9788	.9793	.9798	.9803	.9808	.9812	.9817
2.1	.9821	.9826	.9830	.9834	.9838	.9842	.9846	.9850	.9854	.9857
2.2	.9861	.9864	.9868	.9871	.9875	.9878	.9881	.9884	.9887	.9890
2.3	.9893	.9896	.9898	.9901	.9904	.9906	.9909	.9911	.9913	.9916
2.4	.9918	.9920	.9932	.9925	.9927	.9929	.9931	.9932	.9934	.9936
2.5	.9938	.9940	.9941	.9943	.9945	.9946	.9948	.9949	.9951	.9952
2.6	.9953	.9955	.9956	.9957	.9959	.9960	.9961	.9962	.9963	.9964
2.7	.9965	.9966	.9967	.9968	.9969	.9970	.9971	.9972	.9973	.9974
2.8	.9974	.9975	.9976	.9977	.9977	.9978	.9979	.9979	.9980	.9981
2.9	.9981	.9982	.9982	.9983	.9984	.9984	.9985	.9985	.9986	.9986
3.0	.9987	.9987	.9987	.9988	.9988	.9989	.9989	.9989	.9990	.9990
3.1	.9990	.9991	.9991	.9991	.9992	.9992	.9992	.9992	.9993	.9993
3.2	.9993	.9993	.9994	.9994	.9994	.9994	.9994	.9995	.9995	.9995
3.3	.9995	.9995	.9995	.9996	.9996	.9996	.9996	.9996	.9996	.9997
3.4	.9997	.9997	.9997	.9997	.9997	.9997	.9997	.9997	.9997	.9998

of uncertain duration, no one knows how long it will take to complete each of them. Therefore, no one knows how long any path through the network might take—except that it will undoubtedly be equal to or less than the sum of the pessimistic estimates of all activities in the path and will be equal to or greater than the sum of the optimistic estimates of all activities in the path—*assuming that the estimates are accurate*. When the project is initially analyzed, the path that originally appeared to be the critical path may or may not actually be critical. We will return to this issue several times before this chapter is complete.

Note that as D approaches μ, Z gets smaller, approaching zero. Table 8-5 shows that for $Z = 0$, the chance of on-time completion is 50–50. The managerial implications are all too clear. If the PM wants a reasonable chance of meeting a project deadline, there must be some slack in the project schedule. When preparing a project budget, it is quite proper to include some allowance for contingencies. The same principle holds for preparing a project schedule. The allowance for contingencies in a schedule is *network slack*, and the wise PM will insist on some.

Finally, to illustrate an interesting point, let's examine an apparently noncritical path, activities **b-g-i**. The variance of this path (from Figure 8-16) is $0 + 0 + 28.4 = 28.4$, which is slightly less than the variance of the critical path. The path time is 42 days. The numerator of the fraction $(D - \mu)/\sqrt{\sigma_\mu^2}$ is larger, and in this case the denominator is smaller. Therefore, Z will be larger, and the probability of this path delaying project completion is less than for the apparently critical **a-d-j** path. But consider the noncritical path **c-h-i** with a time of $10 + 11 + 18 = 39$ days, and a total variance of 37.8. (Remember, we are trying to find the probability that this noncritical path with its higher variance but shorter completion time will make us late, given that the critical path is 43 days.)

$$Z = (50 - 39)/6.15$$
$$Z = 1.79$$

The result is that we have a 96 percent chance for this noncritical path to allow the project to be on time.

If the desired time for the network equaled the critical time, 43 days, we have seen that the critical path has a 50–50 chance of being late. What are the chances that the noncritical path **c-h-i** will make the project late? D is now 43 days, so we have

$$Z = (43 - 39)/6.15$$
$$= .65$$

$Z = .65$ is associated with a probability of .74 of being on time, or $1 - .74 = .26$ of being late.

Assuming that these two paths (**a-d-j** and **c-h-i**) are independent, the probability that *both* paths will be completed on time is the product of the individual probabilities, $(.50)(.74) = .37$, which is considerably less than the 50–50 we thought the chances were—hence, the probabilities computed using just the critical path are *always optimistic*, sometimes just a little but occasionally by a great deal! If the paths are not independent, the calculations become more complicated. We will describe an easier and more accurate way to determine project completion probabilities using *simulation* in the next section. Therefore, it is a good idea to always check noncritical paths that have activities with large variances and/or path times that are close to critical in duration (i.e., those with little slack).

This leads us to what is often referred to as *merge bias* (Hulett, 1996). Any time two or more paths of a network come together or merge we have the case noted just above: the probability of both paths being on time is the product of the probabilities for the individual paths. If one of the paths is critical and the others have a reasonable amount of slack (and/or low path variance compared to the critical path), the problem of merge bias is rarely serious. If,

Solved Problem

Consider the following project (times given in days).

Activity	a	m	b	Predecessors
a	1	4	7	—
b	2	2	2	—
c	2	5	8	a
d	3	4	5	a
e	4	6	8	c,b
f	0	0	6	c,b
g	3	6	9	d,e

Find:

1. The network.
2. All expected activity times, variances, and slacks.
3. The critical path and expected completion time.
4. The probability the project will be done in 23 days.
5. The completion time corresponding to 95% probability.

Answer

1.

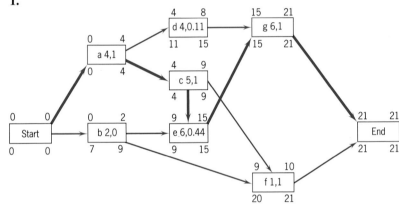

Legend:

ES	EF
LS	LF

2. Activity	TE	σ^2	Slack
a	4	1.00	0
b	2	0	7
c	5	1.00	0
d	4	0.11	7
e	6	0.44	0
f	1	1	11
g	6	1	0

3. Critical path is a-c-e-g for a time of 21 days.
4. $Z = (23 - 21)/\sqrt{3.44} = 1.078$ for a probability of 85.9%.
5. $P = 0.95$ corresponds to $Z = 1.65 = (T - 21)/1.855$, or $T = 24.06$ days.

however, a second path has low slack and significant path variance, we cannot ignore it and should use simulation.

Simulation is an obvious way to check the nature and impacts of interactions between probabilistic paths in a network. While this used to be difficult and time consuming, software has now been developed which simplifies matters greatly. There are several excellent risk management and simulation software packages that link directly to one or more of the popular spreadsheet application packages. We prefer Crystal Ball®—a copy comes with this book—but Risk+® and @Risk® are also well regarded. All the above allow easy simulation of network interactions and yield data that show the probability of completing the networks by specific times (Levine, 1996). These simulations, of course, include the results of potential path mergers. As we have stated earlier, the methods noted here can also be applied to risk analysis for resources. If resource usage is related to the time required by an activity, then the uncertainty about time means that there is also uncertainty about resource use. If the relationship between activity time and resource use is known or can be assumed to be roughly linear over short periods of time, it is not difficult to estimate the resource equivalents of the simulation.

Toward Realistic Time Estimates

The calculations of expected network times, and the uncertainty associated with those time estimates performed in the preceding sections are based, as we noted, on estimating optimistic and pessimistic times at the .99 level. That is, a is estimated such that the actual time required for an activity will be a or higher 99 percent of the time and will be b or lower 99 percent of the time. We then noted, parenthetically, that sometimes project managers are uncomfortable making estimates at that level of precision.

Fortunately, in practice it is not necessary to make estimates at the one-in-a-hundred level. Unless the underlying distribution is very asymmetric, no great error is introduced in finding TE if the pessimistic and optimistic estimates are made at the 95 percent, or even at the 90 percent levels; that is to say, only once in 20 times (or 10 times for the 90 percent level) will the actual activity time be greater than or less than the pessimistic or optimistic estimates, respectively. *The formula for calculating the variance of an activity, however, must be modified.*

Recall that the calculation of variance is based on the assumption that the standard deviation of a beta distribution is approximately one-sixth of its range. Another way of putting this assumption is that a and b are estimated at the -3σ and $+3\sigma$ limits, respectively—roughly at the $99+$ percent levels. Let the 95 percent estimates be represented by a' and b' and 90 percent estimates by a'' and b''. If we use a 95 or 90 percent estimation level, we are actually moving both a and b in from the distribution's tails so that the range will no longer represent $\pm 3\sigma$. See Figure 8-26.

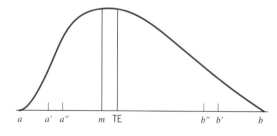

Figure 8-26 a, m, and b estimates at the 99, 95, and 90 percent levels.

It is simple to correct the calculation of variance for this error. Consider the 95 percent estimates. Referring to Table 8-5 we can find the Z associated with .95 of the area under the curve from a' to ∞. For .95, Z is approximately -1.645. (Of course, this applies to the normal distribution rather than to the beta distribution, but this heuristic appears to work quite well in practice.) Similarly, $Z = 1.645$ for the area under the curve from $-\infty$ to b'.

The range between b' and a' represents $2(1.645)\sigma = 3.29\sigma$, rather than the 6σ used in the traditional estimate of the variance. Therefore, when estimating a' and b' at the 95 percent level, we should change the variance calculation formula to read

$$\sigma^2 = ((b' - a')/3.29)^2$$

For estimates at the 90 percent level (a'' and b'' in Figure 8-26), Z is approximately 1.28 and the variance calculation becomes

$$\sigma^2 = ((b'' - a'')/2.56)^2$$

In order to verify that this modification of the traditional estimator for the variance of a beta distribution gave good estimates of the true variance, we ran a series of trials using Statistical Analysis Systems' (SAS) PROC IML for beta distributions of different shapes and estimated a and b at the 95 and 90 percent levels. We then compared these estimates of a and b with the true variance of the distribution and found the differences to be quite small, consistently under 5 percent.

It is important to repeat that some managers do not have confidence in making estimates at the 99 percent level and prefer the 90 or 95 percent levels. If estimates are made at these levels, however, use of the traditional calculation for variance ($\{[b - a]/6\}2$) will result in a serious underestimation of path variances and introduce considerable error into estimates of the probabilities of completing projects by specific dates. But again, we caution readers that nothing will help the PM manage risk if the input data are biased or carelessly developed.

Project Management in Practice
Hosting the Annual Project Management Institute Symposium

Planning and implementing a national conference for a society that will draw about 1,000 attendees is a major project. The tasks involved in hosting such an event are considerable and involve selecting a program committee, choosing a theme, contacting exhibitors, making local arrangements, planning the program, and on and on.

Pittsburgh was selected as host city/chapter for the 1992 Project Management Institute's annual September seminar/symposium. The objectives for the event were three: (1) to deliver a high-quality, value-added program that would be useful and last for years to come, (2) to offer a social and guest program that would reflect well on the host city, and (3) to meet strict financial criteria. The first task after selecting the city and hotel facilities was to put together the project team

and chairperson. This included managers in charge of each of the tracks, the social program, the local arrangements, and all the other details. The project team was organized using a functional approach. Pittsburgh PMI Chapter officers had most of the primary responsibilities, with members from nine other chapters assisting in other duties.

Next was the development of the work breakdown structure, shown in Figure A, and the Gantt chart of activity schedules, shown in Figure B. As seen in the Gantt chart, scheduling all the work for a major conference such as this is an overwhelming effort. In the WBS, the major task was the development of the technical program. For PMI '92, the technical program offered 22 workshops composed of 70 technical

---

WORK BREAKDOWN STRUCTURE AND TASKS

S/S Project Management
Recruit Project Team
Establish Organizational
  Procedures
Establish CAO Support
  Levels and Budget
Issue Reports to VP-Tech
  and Board of Directors
Develop S/S Goals and
  Objectives
Assemble and Issue Post-
  S/S Report

Technical Program
Develop S/S Theme
Strategize Tracks and SIGs
Recruit Technical Program
  Team
Develop Selection Process
  Procedures
Interface with Education
  Committee on Workshops
Plan and Issue Call for
  Papers/Panel Discussion
Recruit Invited Papers/
  Panel Discussions
Recruit Moderators
Develop and Issue Master
  Schedule for Presentations
Select Printer
Plan and Issue Abstract
  Books and Proceedings
Organize Awards for
  Speakers' Breakfasts

Identify Audio/Visual
  Requirements
Develop and Issue Post-S/S
  Technical Report

Social Guest Program
Establish Objectives
Identify Available Activities
Analyze Cost-Benefit
Identify Recommendations
Complete Contracts
Recruit Staff

Speakers
Identify Candidates and
  Related Benefits and
  Costs
Make Recommendations and
  Obtain Approval
Complete Contracts
Maintain Periodic Contact
Host Speakers

Publicity/Promotion
Theme Establishment and
  Approval
Logo Development and
  Approval
Video Production
Promotional Materials
Identification and Approval
Advertising: PMI, Public and
  Trade Media Releases
Regional Newsletter Articles

Finance
Initiate Code of Accounts
Develop Procedures of
  Financial Operation
Develop Independent
  Auditing Procedure
Initiate Separate Banking
  Account
Develop Cash Flow
  Estimates/Projections
Develop and Issue Standard
  Reports
Interact with CAO on
  Account Reconciliation
Develop and Issue Post-S/S
  Financial Report

Corporate Sponsorship
Establish Participation
  Philosophy
Target Prime Corporations
Solicit Participation
Recognition

**Facilities Vendor/CAO
Support**
Contract with Host and
  Backup Hotels
Staff Recruiting
(Details to Be Identified and
  Scheduled with PMI
  Exective Director and
  Events Manager)

Figure A   The work breakdown structure.

---

papers, special panel discussions, and case studies. The technical tracks included engineering and construction, pharmaceuticals, utilities, software, automotive, R&D, defense, education, and manufacturing. The workshops included sessions on preparing for the PMI certification examinations, learning about Taguchi concepts of statistical quality control, and future practice in project management. All of these also required careful scheduling.

The vendor program included exhibits by dozens of vendors and a large number of showcase sessions

for in-depth demonstrations of their wares. The social program included a golf tournament, numerous social activities to meet with colleagues, tours of Pittsburgh's attractions, and a wide variety of entertainment opportunities.

All in all, a conference such as PMI's is as difficult a project as many firms face in their competitive markets.

Source: PMI Staff, "Catch the Spirit ... at Pittsburgh," *PM Network*, Vol. 6.

Figure B Gantt chart.

8.3 RISK ANALYSIS USING SIMULATION WITH CRYSTAL BALL®*

As we have emphasized often in this book, life with projects is characterized by uncertainty. The time required to carry out an activity, the cost and availability of a resource, the success of a research experiment, the wishes of the client, and the actions of a competitor, as well as

---

*Occasionally, particular sections will be shaded, meaning that they can be skipped without loss of continuity.

the vagaries of the weather, ups and downs of interest rates, and the random moods of a senior manager are typical of the things that can upset the most carefully planned and managed project. While it is possible through careful preplanning to reduce somewhat the degree of uncertainty surrounding any project, uncertainty can never be eliminated. We can, however, manage the uncertainty so as to reduce the impact of the ambiguities existing in our uncertain world.

As we noted previously, one method of managing the uncertainty is to perform risk analysis on such data as we have involved in our managerial decisions. This requires us to make assumptions about the probability distributions of the variables and parameters affecting our decisions. These assumptions allow us to adopt Monte Carlo simulation models and evaluate the impact of given managerial decisions. The decision is modeled mathematically. Individual values for each variable in the model are selected at random from the probability distributions we specified, and the outcome of the model is calculated. This process is repeated many times, and the model's output for each repetition is used to construct a statistical distribution of all of the outcomes. This distribution shows the *risk profile* of the decision. The risk profile is considered along with the parent organization's strategies and policies, the wishes of the client, and many other factors when making the decision.

In Chapter 7, we used Crystal Ball® (CB) to simulate a decision process that measured whether or not a project was above an organization's hurdle rate of return. We have noted several times that the same kind of simulation might be used to manage the uncertainty involved in deciding at what level to budget a project. We can now examine its use in scheduling projects. Let us reconsider the data we have previously analyzed from Table 8-1. The analytical approach to finding the duration of the critical path of the network as well as path times for the network's other paths is based on our assumption that the probability distribution used for activity times was best described as a beta distribution. CB can thus use the beta distributions to generate random numbers for the simulation.

Figure 8-27 shows a model for simulating project completion times. It is surprisingly simple for what seems to be such a complex problem. Having entered CB, we label the columns, first one for each activity, and then one for each path through the network, and finally one for "completion time." The most difficult job one faces is identifying all of the paths to be evaluated. For small networks, this is not difficult, but for large networks, it may be. The MSP network of the problem can be a major help.

Recalling that it is easier to follow instructions if the software is running, entering the data into the spreadsheet that CB presents to you is simple.

1. After entering the appropriate column labels, click on space **A3** with the cursor and enter "20" from your earlier solution that assumes a beta distribution. Click on that number to fix the entry in place.
2. Click on **Define Assumption**.
3. The gallery of distributions will appear, click on BetaPERT, and then on **OK**.
4. In the BetaPERT **Distibution** box, enter from Table 8-4 (Section 8.2) the pessimistic, most likely, and optimistic estimates for activity **a** and click on **OK**. Note that assumption cells are colored green.

An anomaly worth mentioning concerns activity **b**. If you call up the BetaPERT distribution and attempt to enter 20-20-20, the three times given in the problem, CB will not allow it,

	A	B	C	D	E	F	G	H	I	J	K	L	M	N	O	P	Q	R	S
1	Activity	Activity	Activity	Activity	Activity	Activity	Activity	Activity	Activity	Activity	Path	Path	Path	Path	Path	Path	Path	Path	Completion
2	a	b	c	d	e	f	g	h	i	j	a-d-j	b-e-j	b-f	b-g-i	c-e-j	c-f	c-g-i	c-h-i	Time
3	18	20	10	16	12	14	4	10	20	8	42	40	34	44	30	24	34	40	44
4																			
5																			
6	**Key**																		
7	*Formulas:*																		
8	Cell K3	=A3 + D3 + J3																	
9	Cell L3	=B3 + E3 + J3																	
10	Cell M3	=B3 + F3																	
11	Cell N3	=B3 + G3 + I3																	
12	Cell O3	=C3 + E3 + J3																	
13	Cell P3	=C3 + F3																	
14	Cell Q3	=C3 + G3 + I3																	
15	Cell R3	=C3 + H3 + I3																	
16	Cell S3	=MAX(K3:R3)																	

Figure 8-27 Crystal Ball® simulation-ready spreadsheet for project described in Table 8-1.

because these numbers will not define a distribution. Do not define cell B3 as an assumption cell. Merely enter 20 in the cell and continue with the next entry. It will be treated by CB as a "constant," which, of course, it is. Activity **g** is also a cell listing a constant or deterministic time. These cells will not be colored.

5. Continue entering data until you have completed all activities.

6. If you counted carefully, you found eight paths through the network (cf. rows 8–15 in Figure 8-27). Enter the path identification for each and then enter the formula for path duration for each of the paths. Note that these formulas simply sum the activity TEs for each path.

7. Now enter the formula that calculates the project duration in cell S3, labeled "Completion time" (cf. row 16). Click on cell S3 and then on **Define Forecast**. Type in "Project Completion Time," or whatever you select for a title, and click **OK**. The formula will find the longest of the paths for each simulation. That will be the critical path for any given trial.

8. Now click on the green arrow. You can watch the results being shown on your screen in the form of a statistical distribution.

The statistical distribution you see when running a simulation will be similar to Figure 8-28, the project completion time frequency chart. (If you wish to find out the likelihood of completing the project in 52 days, for example, simply enter the number 52, or number of your choice, in the box that reads "+ Infinity." Then press **Enter**. The probability you seek will appear in the **Certainty** cell, as in Fig. 8-29.)

If you click on **Create Report** and **Extract Data**, you can see other information, Figures 8-30 and 8-31. Figure 8-30 shows several interesting statistics about the distribution in Figure 8-28. The distribution of 1,000 completion times had a mean of 47.8 days and a median of 47.6 days. Recall that the expected critical path completion time with the beta distribution was 43 days. The greater mean time found by simulation is due to the impact of path mergers. The **Percentiles** data in Figure 8-31 show the percent of the trials completed at or below the days shown.

The value of simulation is well demonstrated by this simple example. The problem of gathering a large amount of information about path mergers, the probability of completion for a number of different times, and the impact of different assumptions about activity distributions by use of analytical methods is formidable even with spreadsheets to handle the calculations. Simulation handles these issues easily.

At times, PMs avoid the whole issue by suggesting that all they "really need to know" is the expected time of completion, the fastest time the project could be completed, and the latest possible time for completion. If one examines the optimistic and pessimistic times for each activity, we can readily find those times. The fastest time is 30 days and the critical path is **b-e-j**; the slowest time is 70 days with critical path **c-h-i**. The likelihood of either path occurring, that is, that activities **b**, **e**, and **j** all take minimum values at the same time (or that **c**, **h**, and **i** take on their maximum values), is so small as to be negligible. [If the estimates are made at the 3σ level, the probability that an activity would have a duration at or less than the optimistic estimate is $(1-.9987) = .0013$. The probability that all three activities would simultaneously be at or below their estimates is $.0013^3 = .000000002$, and this ignores the more improbable

Figure 8-28 CB frequency chart for project completion time.

Figure 8-29 CB probability chart of project completion time in 52 days.

condition that all other activities would simultaneously maintain the required small values.]
The project could, of course, be delayed for far more than 70 days, but that would be caused
by some external, catastrophic event not contemplated when generating the original time
estimates. (The possibility that this type of event may occur is precisely why we will advise
PMs to continue to update risk identification, assessment, and analysis as long as the project
is underway.)

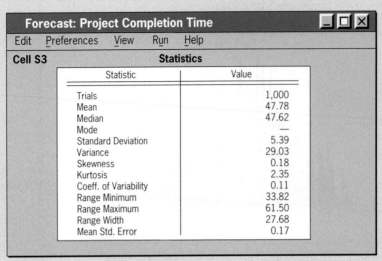

Figure 8-30   CB summary statistics for project completion time.

Forecast: Project Completion Time		
Edit Preferences View Run Help		
Cell S3	**Percentiles**	
Percentile		Days
0%		33.82
10%		40.87
20%		42.85
30%		44.49
40%		45.91
50%		47.62
60%		48.90
70%		50.83
80%		52.77
90%		55.11
100%		61.50

Figure 8-31   CB percentile probabilities of completing project in *n* days.

Traditional Statistics or Simulation?

The PM no longer has much choice about dealing with uncertainty. When the first edition of this book was written in 1985, three-time PERT/CPM was used by a few hardy souls, but uncertainty was more or less ignored by a large majority of those involved with projects.

"Allowances for contingencies" were made as a sort of insurance against time and budget over-runs, but little more attention was paid to risk. Times have changed. Formal risk management systems are now standard practice in many firms, and risk management is used by many others on specific types of projects that are considered "risky." The management of risk is not an issue. The only issue is how to do it.

The subject of project scheduling brings the problem of choosing the methods used to perform quantitative risk analysis into focus. The standard statistical methods were explained and demonstrated in the subsection on "Uncertainty of Project Completion Time," in this chapter. Following the section on traditional methods, we demonstrated and discussed simulation as a way of accomplishing essentially the same analysis, but more accurately and easily. We recommend simulation—*but only after the analyst has a good understanding of the traditional statistical approach.*

Both methods require that the three time estimates be made and that the TE be found for each activity. TE (and variance) is easily calculated on almost any commercially available spreadsheet. Using statistics, TE and variance must also be found for each path—again, easily done by computer. Most real projects, however, are larger than the hypothetical projects we used here to explain and illustrate the techniques of project management. When dealing with larger projects and their many paths, it is difficult merely to find those paths that may be critical or near critical. This must be done whether using statistics or simulation. But the statistical method requires one to analyze potential path mergers by hand. This increases the difficulty to extraordinary levels, not to mention adding a horrendous level of tedium. Of course, whichever method is chosen, it is rarely required to evaluate every path carefully. Paths that are significantly shorter than the critical path can usually be safely ignored. Unless their variance is extremely high, there is little chance they will affect the project duration.

Irrespective of the method chosen, the PM will not know much about activity durations until the project gets underway. The actual critical path cannot be known until it becomes an historical fact. Even if we make three time estimates for activities and then calculate TE for each, that does not make the TEs certain. As the project gets underway, it often seems like everything tends to disrupt the schedule: worker personalities, miscommunication, team characteristics, the PM's personality, the client, upper management, resources. And if we cannot determine which path through a project will turn out to be the critical path until after the fact, we also cannot determine how much slack any given path will have. As noted earlier, the wise PM will recalculate the network and critical path regularly, and always with updated data.

Nonetheless, careful analysis, be it by traditional statistics or by simulation, is important. It provides much better insight into the risks associated with project duration than the PM can get in any other way—including a call to Miss Cleo. The result is that the PM cannot devote his or her managerial attention solely to the critical path. There is no way of knowing which path will turn out to be critical, and thus attention must be given to all activities and paths. It is useful, every once in a while, for the PM to remember that if an activity has a great deal of slack, the people working on that activity have no sense of urgency about completing it. The activity is apt to lose its slack rapidly.

Crystal Ball® is an excellent piece of software and makes simulation a reasonably easy tool with which to simulate project durations. We prefer CB because it is user friendly, and also because it can display its results in a wide variety of formats. CB also allows the user to interact with the software by responding immediately to changes in the parameters of a simulation.

Project Management in Practice
Rapid Project Deployment at Kineo

In June 2008 Canon were exhibiting at a major media and print fair in Germany. Over 400,000 people were expected to attend this fair and Canon was expected to have 25,000 business conversations at the event. Canon's performance at this fair would have a direct impact on the profitability of their Print Division.

With over 500 staff attending the event, Canon believed it was critical that these people were supported and trained to deliver a consistent message on Canon's business approach and the value it could bring to its customers. Less than 6 weeks before the event, Canon approached Kineo, a provider of e-training, to see if it was possible to develop and deliver a module to support Canon at this fair. The product would have to be attractive and engaging for the staff, fully support Canon's brand, and allow the exhibition staff to qualify potential clients quickly. In addition, it should allow for the recording and tracking of the learner's score and be available in both English and German. And all in 6 weeks.

To deliver such a demanding project in such a short time, Kineo had to deploy a lean approach to project management, which was at the heart of their practice. A small dedicated team of Canon and Kineo engineers collaborated on the prototype using frequent conference calls to work through rapid iteration cycles. Changes were made on the same day they were identified to allow for further iterations and the team operated with a real spirit of partnership and collaboration, striving to deliver a quality product within a demanding time constraint.

The quality of the e-learning material did not suffer because of these constraints. Over 400 people went through the e-learning material prior to the conference and over 90% of these passed the assessment first time. The volume of user queries was low and the feedback was overall very positive.

In summary, the Kineo–Canon project is a demonstration of the way that a collaborative spirit in your project team can overcome seemingly impossible challenges.

www.kineo.com/documents/kineo_canon_case_study.pdf accessed on the 7th April 2011.

8.4 USING THESE TOOLS

The development of user-friendly software such as Microsoft Project®, Crystal Ball®, and Excel® that do similar jobs has made the use of tools we have described thus far available to anyone with a project to manage. We are aware that gathering the input data for the software is usually more difficult than entering and processing it, but it is doable. For example, refer to the Apartment Complex example (Figure 8-32). The information in this example was gathered and processed by people who had just been introduced to the subject.

Figure 8-32 is a portion of a 48-step WBS for the syndication of an apartment complex. Note that several of the steps are obvious composites of multistep tasks designed for a lower level (e.g., see steps 1–4). Figure 8-33 is an AON network of Figure 8-32. The firm also has a Gantt chart version of the network that is used for tracking each project. Figure 8-32 also contains three time estimates of the "calendar" time used for each step (in days) and of the

Task	a days (hours)	m days (hours)	b days (hours)
1. Product package received by Secy. in Real Estate (R.E.) Dept.	n/a	(.3)	(.4)
2. Secy. checks for duplicates, and forwards all packages in Atlanta region (but not addressed to R.E staff member) to Atl. via fast mail. Atl. office sends copy of submittal log to L.A. office on weekly basis.	n/a	(.2)	(.3)
3. Secy. dates, stamps, logs, checks for duplication, makes new file, checks for contact source, adds to card file all new packages. Sends criteria letter to new source. Sends duplication letter. Forwards package to Admin. Asst. (AA).	(.7)	(.7)	(.9)
4. AA reviews package, completes Property Summary Form, forwards to L.A. Reg. Acquisit. Director officer or to R.E. staff member to whom package is addressed (RAD).	(.5)	(.5)	(.7)
Total 1–4	1(1.7)	1(1.7)	3(2.3)
5. Person to whom package forwarded determines action. (May refer to other or retain for further review.) "Passes" sent to Secy. for files. "Possibles" retained by RAD for further review.	1(.5)	1(.5)	1(1)
•	•	•	•
•	•	•	•
•	•	•	•
48. Legal issues Post Closing Memorandum.	2(5)	5(8)	10(10)

Figure 8-32 WBS for syndication of an apartment complex.

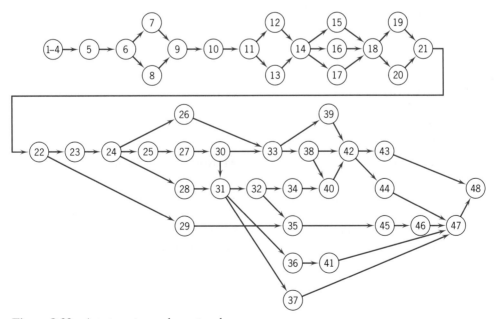

Figure 8-33 Apartment complex network.

"resource" time used for each step (in hours). The time estimate 2(10) is read "2 days, 10 labor-hours." The duplicate data are useful for scheduling workloads. The model served as a template for a complex problem and not only improved the process but shortened the time required to carry it out.

We are reluctant to give advice about which tools to use. If the PM indulges in a bit of experimentation with the major systems, their relative advantages and disadvantages in a given application will become evident.

SUMMARY

In this chapter the scheduling aspect of project implementation was addressed. Following a description of the benefits of using a network for planning and controlling a project, the AOA and AON approaches were described, as were Gantt charts.

Specific points covered in the chapter were these:

- Scheduling is particularly important to projects because of complex coordination problems.

- The network approach to scheduling offers a number of specific advantages of special value for projects.

- Critical project tasks typically constitute fewer than 10 percent of all the project tasks.

- Network techniques can adopt either an activity-on-node or activity-on-arc framework without significantly altering the analysis.

- Networks are usually constructed from left to right, indicating activity precedence and event times as the network is constructed. Through use of the network, critical activities and events are identified, early and late activity start times are found, available slacks for each activity are determined, and probabilities of project completion by various times are calculated.

- Gantt charts, a monitoring technique, are closely related to network diagrams, but are more easily understood and provide a clearer picture of the current state of the project. However, while offering some advantages, they also have some drawbacks, such as not clearly indicating task precedence and dependencies.

In the next chapter, we investigate the scheduling problem further when multiple projects require a set of common resources to be shared. Again, a number of techniques are useful for resource allocation and activity expediting under such circumstances.

GLOSSARY

Activity   A specific project task that requires resources and time to complete.

Activity-on-Arrow   (Activity-on-Node)   The two ways of illustrating a network: placing the activities on the arcs or on the nodes.

Arc   The line connecting two nodes.

Crash   In CPM, an activity can be conducted at a normal pace or at an expedited pace, known as crashing, at a greater cost.

Critical   An activity or event that, if delayed, will delay project completion.

Event   An end state for one or more activities that occurs at a specific point in time.

Gantt Chart   A bar chart illustrating multiple, time-based activities on a horizontal time scale.

Milestone   A clearly identifiable point in a project or set of activities that commonly denotes a reporting requirement or completion of a large or important set of activities.

Network   A combination of interrelated activities and events depicted with arcs and nodes.

Node   A point where one or more lines (arrows) begin or terminate, commonly used for depicting an event or activity.

Path   A sequence of lines and nodes in a network.

Project Management Information System (PMIS)
The systems, activities, and data that allow information flow in a project, frequently computerized but not always.

Trade-off The amount of one factor that must be sacrificed in order to achieve more or less of another factor.

QUESTIONS

Material Review Questions

1. Define *activity*, *event*, and *path* as used in network construction. What is a dummy activity?

2. What characteristic of the critical path times makes them critical?

3. What two factors are compared by Gantt charting? How does the Gantt chart differ in purpose from the WBS?

4. Contrast total slack and free slack.

5. When is each scheduling technique appropriate to use?

6. What is the difference between activity-on-node and activity-on-arrow diagrams?

7. How does simulation determine the probabilities of various project completion times?

8. Briefly summarize how a network is drawn.

9. Define "late start time," "early start time," and "early finish time."

10. How is the critical path determined?

11. What is "slack" and why is it important?

Class Discussion Questions

12. How do you think the 3-times network technique could be used to estimate costs for manufacturing?

13. What are some benefits of the network approach to project planning? What are some drawbacks?

14. What is your position on the statements in the Using These Tools section?

15. Why is AOA or AON of significant value to the project manager?

16. How is uncertainty in project scheduling dealt with?

17. How would you calculate free slack?

18. How are activity times estimated?

19. Should the critical path activities be managed differently from noncritical path activities? Explain.

20. Precedence diagramming extends the standard task relationship in a network to three additional situations. Can you think of any others?

Production Scheduling

21. What are the common problems encountered during planning and scheduling?

22. How does the availability of automated information improve operational costs?

23. What are the long term benefits of implementing a computerized scheduling system?

Election Returns within Three Hours

24. Which of Panama's two thrusts do you think was the more difficult? Why?

25. Do you think other countries could replicate Panama's system? Would they?

26. If another country wanted fast returns like Panama, which aspects of the system might they ignore? Why?

Hosting the Annual Project Management Institute Symposium

27. Elaborate on the uniqueness of this work breakdown structure.

28. Based on the Gantt chart, when did the symposium actually occur?

29. Why are there activities scheduled after the symposium? When is the project finally done?

Rapid Product Development at Kineo

30. In this project we saw how projects can be driven by demanding timescales. What other types of project have tight timescales?

31. Success in the Kineo project is attributed to which key processes? What else do you think is important in situations such as this?

PROBLEMS

1. Given the following information, draw the AON diagram:

Activity	Immediate Predecessor
1	—
2	—
3	1, 4
4	2
5	2
6	3, 5

2. Convert the AON diagram below to an AOA diagram.

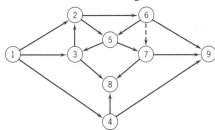

3. Find three errors in the diagram below.

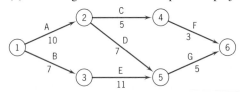

4. Given the diagram below, find:
(a) The critical path.
(b) How long it will take to complete the project.

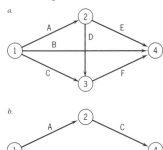

5. Convert the AOA diagram in Problem 4 to an AON diagram. How would the AON diagram change if there had been a dummy from node 2 to node 3 in Problem 4?

6. Convert each of the following AOA diagrams into AON diagrams.

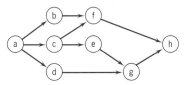

7. Given the following activities and precedences, draw an AOA or AON diagram:

Activity	Immediate Predecessor
A	—
B	—
C	A
D	A, B
E	A, B
F	C
G	D, F
H	E, G

8. Given the following network,

(a) What is the critical path?
(b) How long will it take to complete this project?
(c) Can activity **B** be delayed without delaying the completion of the project? If so, how many days?

9. Given the estimated activity times below and the network in Problem 8 above,

Activity	a	m	b
A	6.5	7.5	14.5
B	8.5	10.5	12.5
C	2.5	3.5	4.5
D	6.5	7.5	8.5
E	5.5	5.5	9.5
F	5.5	7.5	9.5
G	4.5	6.5	8.5
H	2.5	3.5	3.5

what is the critical path probability that the project will be completed within:
(a) 21 days?
(b) 22 days?
(c) 25 days?

10. Activity*	a	m	b
AB	3	6	9
AC	1	4	7
CB	0	3	6
CD	3	3	3
CE	2	2	8
BD	0	0	6
BE	2	5	8
DF	4	4	10
DE	1	1	1
EF	1	4	7

*The nomenclature AB means the activity *between* nodes A and B.

Find

(a) The AOA network and the critical path.
(b) All event slacks.
(c) Critical path to event D.
(d) Critical path probability of completion in 14 days.
(e) The effect if CD slips to 6 days; to 7 days; to 8 days.

11.

Activity†	TE
AB	1
AC	2
AD	3
DC	4
CB	3
DE	8
CF	2
BF	4
IJ	2
CE	6
EF	5
FG	10
FH	11
EH	1
GH	9
EJ	3
GI	8
HJ	6

(a) Draw the AOA diagram.
(b) Find the critical path.
(c) Find the completion time.

12. The Denver Iron & Steel Company is expanding its operations to include a new drive-in weigh station. The weigh station will be a heated/air-conditioned building with a large floor and small office. The large room will have the scales, a 15-foot counter, and several display cases for its equipment.

Before erection of the building, the project manager evaluated the project using AON analysis. The activities, with their corresponding times, were recorded in Table A.

Using AON analysis, find the critical path, the slack times, and the expected completion time.

13. Miracle Marketing has received a contract from a large pharmaceutical firm to design a nationwide advertising campaign for their recently approved cancer drug. The drug is easily taken, compared with current intravenous drugs, and can be administered from home. Miracle Marketing has assigned to the task a project manager who, in turn, has delegated minor subprojects to subordinate managers.

The project was evaluated using AOA analysis. Due to the extensive length of the project, many activities were combined: The following is the result.

Activity*	Time (months)
AB: Obtain patient lists	3
BC: Select interviewees	6
BD: Engage interviewers	2
BF: Train interviewers	5
BE: Interview patients	4
CD: Collate results	9
DG: Summarize data	20
FG: Analyze results	6
EH: Identify main advantages	11
EI: Select advantages for ads	19
GJ: Determine media mix	1
HK: Compare to ad budget	3
IL: Revise mix for budget	9
LM: Select ad style	12
KN: Choose ad type	7
JO: Design ad campaign	4
MN: Check with sponsor	15
NP: Revise ad campaign	13
OP: Present for approval	10

Find the critical path and expected completion time.

Table A

#	Activity	Optimistic	Most Likely	Pessimistic	Preceding Tasks
			Times		
1	Lay foundation	8	10	13	—
2	Dig hole for scale	5	6	8	—
3	Insert scale bases	13	15	21	2
4	Erect frame	10	12	14	1, 3
5	Complete building	11	20	30	4
6	Insert scales	4	5	8	5
7	Insert display cases	2	3	4	5
8	Put in office equipment	4	6	10	7
9	Finishing touches	2	3	4	8, 6

---

†See nomenclature note in Problem 10.

*See nomenclature note in Problem 10.

14. The following chart was prepared at the beginning of a HRM (Human Resource Management) crash hiring project. The project begins with two activities: Assemble interview team (A) and Budget resources (B).

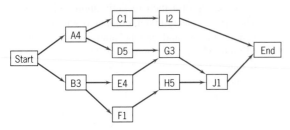

The duration, in days, follows the letter of each activity. What is the critical path? Which activities should be monitored most closely?

At the end of the first week, it was noted that activity **A** was completed in 2.5 days, but activity **B** required 4.5 days. What impact does this have on the project? Are the same activities critical?

15. Given the following financing project being considered by a venture firm, find the critical path probability of completion by 17 weeks. By 24 weeks. By what date is management 90 percent sure completion will occur?

Times (weeks)

Activity*	Optimistic	Most Likely	Pessimistic
1–2: Collect firm data	5	11	11
1–3: Analyze data	10	10	10
1–4: Determine need	2	5	8
2–6: Determine profitability	1	7	13
3–6: Evaluate risk	4	4	10
3–7: Interview owners	4	7	10
3–5: Check references	2	2	2
4–5: Evaluate industry	0	6	6
5–7: Evaluate economy	2	8	14
6–7: Decide funding	1	4	7

If the venture firm can complete the project for the customer within 18 weeks, it will receive a bonus of $10,000. But if the project delays beyond 22 weeks, it must pay a penalty of $5,000 due to lost opportunity.

*See nomenclature note in Problem 10.

If the firm can choose whether or not to bid on this project, what should its decision be if the project is only a breakeven one normally?

16. Given an auditing project with the following activities,

Activity	Standard Deviation	Critical?	Duration
a, add	2	yes	2
b, balance	1		3
c, count	0	yes	4
d, deduct	3		2
e, edit	1	yes	1
f, finance	2		6
g, group	2	yes	4
h, hold	0	yes	2

Using the critical path, find:
(a) The probability of completing this project in 12 weeks (or less), as the client desires.
(b) The probability of completing this project in 13 weeks (or less).
(c) The probability of completing this project in 16 weeks (or less), the client's drop-dead date.
(d) The number of weeks required to assure a 92.5 percent chance of completion, as guaranteed by the auditing firm.

17. The following network is a compressed representation of the prospectus of a start-up firm that plans to develop a new, bioelectronic computer chip.

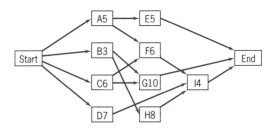

Note that four activities, the biological elements, can start immediately.

Find:
(a) The critical path.
(b) The earliest time to complete the project.
(c) The slack on activities **E**, **F**, and **H**.

18. The events of the project below are designated as 1, 2, and so on.
(a) Draw the network.
(b) Find the critical path.
(c) Find the slacks on all the activities.

Activity	Prec. Evt.	Suc. Evt.	TE (weeks)	Prec. Activ.
a	1	2	3	none
b	1	3	6	none
c	1	4	8	none
d	2	5	7	a
e	3	5	5	b
f	4	5	10	c
g	4	6	4	c
h	5	7	5	d, e, f
i	6	7	6	g

19. Given the following network (times are in weeks), determine:
    (a) The ES, LS, EF, and LF for each activity.
    (b) The slacks on all activities.
    (c) The critical activities and path.

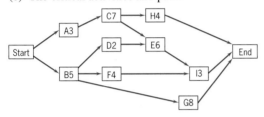

20. Given the schedule in Table B for a liability work package done as part of an accounting audit in a corporation, find:
    (a) The critical path.
    (b) The slack time on "process confirmations."
    (c) The slack time on "test pension plan."
    (d) The slack time on "verify debt restriction compliance."

Table B

Activity	Duration (days)	Preceding Activities
a. Obtain schedule of liabilities	3	none
b. Mail confirmation	15	a
c. Test pension plan	5	a
d. Vouch selected liabilities	60	a
e. Test accruals and amortization	6	d
f. Process confirmations	40	b
g. Reconcile interest expense to debt	10	c, e
h. Verify debt restriction compliance	7	f
i. Investigate debit balances	6	g
j. Review subsequent payments	12	h, i

21. In the website development project network shown in the following figure, the number alongside each activity designates the activity duration (TE) in weeks.

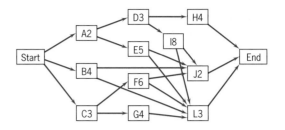

Determine:
(a) The ES and LS for each activity.
(b) The earliest time that the website can be completed.
(c) The slack on all activities.
(d) The critical activities.
(e) The critical path.

22. Given the following information regarding a project concerning an initial public offering (IPO),

Activity	TE (weeks)	Preceding Activities
a: Check feasibility	3	none
b: Determine funding	1	none
c: Find possible banks	3	a
d: Select two possibles	4	a
e: Interview two banks	4	b
f: Analyze funding costs	5	b
g: What chance of success?	2	c, e
h: Sign contract	3	f

(a) Draw the network.
(b) What is the critical path?
(c) When will the offering be available (completion of the project)?
(d) What is the effect on the project if activity **e** (approvals) takes an extra week? Two extra weeks? Three extra weeks?

23. Construct a network for the aerospace launch project below and find its critical path.

Activity	TE (weeks)	Preceding Activities
a: Check controls	3	none
b: Check propellants	5	a
c: Check personnel	3	a
d: Assemble items	1	c
e: Move to launch pad	3	b
f: Run system tests	4	b, d
g: Check astronauts	2	c
h: Ground stations go?	3	g, f
i: Countdown	1	e, h

24. Construct a network for the following training and development project.

Activity	TE (weeks)	Preceding Activities
a: Select personnel	3	none
b: Invite personnel	5	none
c: Budget ok?	14	a
d: Prepare materials	5	a
e: Engage instructor	4	b
f: Select date	7	b
g: Remind personnel	8	d, e
h: Start project	5	g, f

(a) Draw the network.
(b) Find the critical path.
(c) Assume activity **a** (hire trainers) took 5 weeks. Replan the project.
(d) From where would you suggest transferring resources, and to what activities, so that the original target training date may be maintained?

25. Resolve part (d) of Problem 10 assuming the values of *a* and *b* are given at the 95 percent level. Repeat, assuming the values are given at the 90 percent level.

26. Using the information below, draw an AOA network. Find the critical path and use it to compute the number of days you would be 95 percent sure the project would be completed. Calculate the slack, earliest start, and latest start times for each activity and show in table form. Does any path come close to causing a problem in determining the probability of project completion based on the critical path alone?

Activity	Time (days)		
	a	m	b
1–2	6	8	10
1–3	5	6	7
1–4	6	6	6
2–6	0	0	0
2–7	10	11	12
3–6	12	14	16
4–5	5	8	11
4–9	7	9	11
5–6	8	10	12
5–9	0	0	0
6–7	14	15	16
6–8	10	12	14
7–10	9	12	15
8–10	0	4	14
9–11	5	5	5
10–11	7	8	9

27. Given the following activities required for staging a community play on Independence Day,
(a) Construct an AON diagram.

(b) Determine the earliest completion time for the play and the critical path.
(c) Based on the critical path, what completion date are you 80% confident of achieving? 40% confident?
(d) Will a 1-day delay in this project be serious?

Activity	Predecessor	Time (days)		
		a	m	b
1	—	2	4	6
2	—	5	5	5
3	2	3	5	7
4	1	7	10	13
5	1	11	12	13
6	2, 4	5	6	7
7	3	9	10	11
8	3, 6	5	7	9
9	4	7	9	11
10	5	3	3	3
11	7	15	17	19
12	8	6	8	10
13	9, 10	7	8	15
14	7	12	14	16
15	12, 13	16	17	18

28. Draw an AON network using the following data and find the probability of completing the critical path of the operatic project in 44 days, the official opening date.

Activity	Predecessor	Time (days)		
		a	m	b
1	—	6	10	14
2	1	0	1	2
3	1	16	20	30
4	2	3	5	7
5	4	2	3	4
6	3	7	10	13
7	4	1	2	3
8	7	0	2	4
9	3, 7	2	2	2
10	9	2	3	4
11	8	0	1	2
12	10, 11	1	2	3

29. Simulate Problem 27 to find the probabilities of project completion. Use a triangular distribution for defining activity time distributions. After a 1,000-trial simulation, examine the statistical information generated and compare the output of the simulation with your findings in Problem 27. Briefly explain the significant similarities and differences.

30. Simulate Problem 28 to find the probabilities of project completion. Use a BetaPERT distribution for defining activity time distributions. After a 1,000-trial simulation, examine the statistical information generated and compare the output of the simulation with your findings in Problem 28. Briefly explain the significant similarities and differences.

31. In the following table are listed tasks, duration in weeks, and predecessors.

Task	Predecessors	Duration
a	—	2
b	—	2
c	a, b	4
d	c	3
e	a, b, c	1
f	d, e	2
g	f	3
h	g	1

(a) Construct a Gantt chart using MSP.
(b) Assuming the default 5-day workweek, calculate the critical path of the project.
(c) Calculate the project duration.

32. In the following table, project activities in days are listed with three time estimates for duration in days and predecessors for the activities.

Activity	Optimistic Time	Most Likely Time	Pessimistic Time	Predecessors
a	5	7	12	—
b	8	8	8	—
c	2	6	10	a
d	12	14	19	a, b
e	6	6	12	c, d
f	3	12	18	b, e
g	6	8	10	f

(a) Calculate the expected time of each activity using MSP.
(b) Construct a Gantt chart using MSP.
(c) Use MSP to draw a network diagram.
(d) Assuming a 5-day workweek, calculate the critical path of the project.
(e) Calculate the slack for the activities.

INCIDENTS FOR DISCUSSION

Yankee Chair Company

The Yankee Chair Company was anxious to get a new model rocking chair onto the market. Past efforts to introduce new models had resulted in frustrating failures. Bret Ricks, president of Yankee Chair, was determined that it would not happen again with the newest model. He had no confidence in his current management team, so he hired Jan Dymore, a local consultant, to organize and manage this project. He assigned a Yankee Chair manager, Tom Gort, to work with Dymore to start developing some talent for project management within the company. Dymore decided to set up a PERT network and guided Gort through the process of listing activities, assigning precedence, and estimating completion times. She also explained the critical path concept to Gort, who by this time had a reasonable grasp of the project direction. At the first review session with Mr. Ricks, the PERT approach was accepted enthusiastically, but toward the end of the review Dymore made some critical remarks about the product design and was subsequently released from the project.

Ricks then asked Gort if he could carry on the PERT approach by himself. Gort jumped at the chance, but later in his office he began to question whether or not he really could use the PERT network effectively. Dymore had made a guess at what the critical path would be and how long the project would take, but she had also told Gort that several other calculations had to be made in order to calculate the exact time estimates for each activity and the variances of those activity times. Gort really did not understand the mathematics involved and certainly did not want to look bad in Ricks' eyes, so he decided to take Dymore's guess at

the critical path and get the best possible estimates of those activity times. By concentrating his attention on the critical path activities and ignoring the variance issues, he figured he could bring the project in on time.

Questions: Will Gort's approach work? How much more of a gamble is Gort taking than any project manager normally takes? What should Gort watch out for?

Cincinnati Software

Cincinnati Software, which currently specializes in the installation of manufacturing resource planning (MRP II) systems in small firms, is planning a major expansion into installing the new enterprise resource planning (ERP) systems. This major expansion into the hottest software area will be organized as an in-house project of strategic importance. The company has selected a project manager and team to follow the project through to completion. The project team is very interested in selecting an appropriate scheduling technique for the project. The project manager has thus set the following guidelines for the selection process: simple; able to show durations of events, the flow of work, and the relative sequence of events; able to indicate planning and actual flow, which items may proceed at the same time, and how far they are from completion. The assistant project manager favors the Gantt chart, the finance representative likes PERT, and the information technology department head prefers CPM.

Questions: If you were the project manager, which method would you use, and why?

CONTINUING INTEGRATIVE CLASS PROJECT

It is now time to construct the project schedule. You may do this by hand or using a software package for project management as mentioned in Chapter 1. You will need a network diagram, the critical path(s) and near-critical paths, the probability of completion by the due date, and calendar or Gantt chart schedule showing milestones and phase gates. If risk analysis was included in your assignments, you should also run Crystal Ball® to show the distribution of completion times and probabilities.

BIBLIOGRAPHY

Al-Hammed, A., and S. Assaf. "A Survey of Cost Reduction Techniques Used by Construction Firms in Saudi Arabia." *American Association of Cost Engineers Transactions*, 1988.

Badiru, A. B. "Activity-Resource Assignments Using Critical Resource Diagramming." *Project Management Journal*, September 1993.

Dean, B. V. *Project Management: Methods and Studies.* New York: Elsevier, 1985.

Evans, J. R., and D. L. Olson, *Introduction to Simulation and Risk Analysis*, Upper Saddle River, NJ: Prentice-Hall, 1998.

Goldratt, E. M. *Critical Chain*, Great Barrington, MA, North River, 1997.

Hulett, D. T. "Schedule Risk Analysis Simplified." *PM Network*, July 1996.

Levine, H. A. "Risk Management for Dummies, Part 2." *PM Network*, April 1996.

Moder, J. J., C. R. Phillips, and E. W. Davis. *Project Management with CPM, PERT, and Precedence Diagramming*, *3rd ed.* New York: Van Nostrand Reinhold, 1983.

Project Management Institute. *A Guide to the Project Management Body of Knowledge*, *4th ed.* Newtown Square, PA: Project Management Institute, 2008.

Sandberg, J. "Rise of False Deadline Means Truly Urgent Often Gets Done Late." *Wall Street Journal*, January 28, 2007.

Wheatly, M. "Up for Adaptation." *PM Network,* July 2010.

Wilkens, T. T. "Are You Being Misled by Your Progress Gantt Chart?" *PM Network*, August 1997.

Williams, T. M. "What Are PERT Estimates?" *Journal of the Operational Research Society*, Vol. 44, No. 12, 1995.

The following case presents a realistic situation facing a construction firm that has just won a competitive contract. The realistic conditions complicating the project are described in detail, as are the alternatives offered by the staff for dealing with these complexities.

C A S E

TOPLINE ARENA
Eric Woodcock

The year is 2010. Lotus Construction had won the contract to build the new Topline Arena in one of China's fastest growing cities. This would be an important venue in the city, able to host sports like basketball and table tennis, stage rock concerts and put on conferences and mid-sized exhibitions. The arena had to be ready by 15 February 2011 in order to host the National Teachers' Convention, which opens on 30 March. The contract to build the arena was with a large property development company and if all went according to plan, Lotus could produce a profit before tax of ¥2,000,000 (Chinese Yuan Renminbi). However, the contract included a penalty clause that would charge Lotus ¥100,000 for each week or part of a week they were late in handing over the Topline Arena. The main tasks in the project are set out in the appendix.

The project began on 31 January and all was going smoothly through the spring and summer. The site was cleared; the foundations for the arena area were finished and the excavations were complete for the seating galleries and the roof structure. Then on 15 October Lotus received notification of something completely unexpected. The local utility company had discovered a large fracture in a primary water main running alongside the arena site. This presented two major risks to the project. The first was that leaking water would undermine the arena foundations, rendering it unsafe. The second was that the arena could not open if the fracture was not repaired because a fall in water pressure would mean the hundreds of water sprinklers in the arena would not operate in case of fire. The utility company was carrying out further investigations. There was a 50:50 chance that the work would be so urgent that it had to begin on 1 December, otherwise it could be delayed until the following spring after the arena had opened. This would be a major undertaking right next to the arena site. If work started on 1 December, arena construction would probably have to stop whilst the repairs were made because vibrations from the arena site could cause a complete collapse of the water main and endanger workers. The new utility company survey would also determine whether this was so.

The contract with the property company had not foreseen such a crisis, and Lotus's insurance would not cover it for the consequential damages of a late completion. The project team had to think urgently about how to deal with this situation and yet maintain the promised completion date.

Zhao Jiu Hui of the Lotus team had been to see the utility company, and based on their discussions, she had estimated there was a 70% chance that the fracture repair would take 8 weeks, and a 30% chance it would take 12 weeks. She believed that the chances that work could continue on the arena during the repair were very slim. One positive factor was that the workforce on the arena could be temporarily redeployed to a nearby infrastructure project, so the labor costs over any shutdown would be negligible.

The team's troubles increased when the chief site engineer joined the meeting with the latest long range weather forecast. The project plans had been done on the expectation of a mild winter as the temperature trends of the last 15 years suggested this. However, the latest forecast predicted much colder temperatures. Cold weather affects how strong concrete will be when it sets, and he suggested that a third of pouring after 1 December would require special heaters that cost ¥3,000 a week to hire and operate. The chief site engineer predicted a 33% chance that the weather after 1 December would be cold enough to require heaters.

On top of that, any delay to the finish date would add ¥3,000 per week in extra overhead costs.

The management team were asked to come up with ideas on how to cope with the water main repair and also deal with the effects of the predicted cold weather. Five proposals were put forward:

1. Accelerate the pouring of the seat gallery supports. This would add ¥130,000 to the costs but save 6 weeks on the duration of this activity.

2. As proposal 1, but also put a double shift on the foundations for the arena floor. This would cost an extra ¥65,000, but cut the duration of this activity down to 9 weeks.

3. Many activities cannot begin until the roof is on. So use three shifts plus some overtime to complete the roof 6 weeks earlier than planned. This would cost an extra ¥60,000.

4. Do nothing until 1 December. If the weather is very cold, defer concrete pouring until it warms up and heat when necessary. If the utility company insists arena work is halted, wait until the water main repair is done, then carry out all remaining activities as quickly as possible. The duration of any activity cannot be cut to less than one third of its originally planned duration. The additional costs on each week of an activity would be ¥20,000.

5. Take no action and proceed as originally planned. Hope that work can continue while the water main is repaired and that the weather stays mild over the winter.

At the next emergency planning meeting, Jiang Wei, the project director, looked round the room and said to his team, "Well, we have five clear proposals here. Which one do you recommend we take?"

Appendix: The construction sequence

The Topline Arena is an indoor structure with a seating capacity of 20,000. The project begins with clearing the site, an activity that lasts 8 weeks. Once the site is clear, the work can start simultaneously on the structure itself and on the main floor and stage. The work in the main floor area involves subsurface drainage which lasts 8 weeks, followed by main floor foundation. Only with the completion of the main floor foundation (14 weeks) can the installation of the main floor and stage take place, an activity that consumes 12 weeks. The work on the structure itself starts with excavation, followed by the pouring of concrete footings. Each of these activities takes 4 weeks. Next comes the pouring of supports for seat galleries (12 weeks), followed by erecting pre-cast galleries (13 weeks). The seats can then be poured (4 weeks) and are ready for painting. However, the painting (3 weeks) cannot begin until the dressing rooms are completed (4 weeks). The dressing rooms can be completed only after the roof is erected (8 weeks). The roof must be erected on a steel structure which takes 4 weeks to install. This activity can start only after the concrete footings are poured. Once the roof is erected, work can start simultaneously on the lights (5 weeks) and on the scoreboard and other facilities (4 weeks). Assume that there are 28 days in February and that February 15 falls on a Monday.

Questions

1. Analyse the five proposals and make recommendations based on expected costs.

2. What other basis might be used to make a decision besides expected costs? What might the decision be in that case?

3. What other factors might enter into the decision, such as behavioral, organizational and political?

4. What decision would you make if you were the project director?

C H A P T E R

9

Resource Allocation

PMBOK Guide

6.3

In the previous chapter, we looked at a special type of resource allocation problem, that of allocating time among project tasks, better known as *scheduling*. Now we consider the impact on the schedule of the allocation of physical resources as well, a topic considered along with scheduling in PMBOK. Also, we are concerned with using resources in both individual and in multiple, simultaneous projects. The subject relates directly to the topic of scheduling because altering schedules can alter the need for resources and—just as important—alter the timing of resource needs. At any given time, the firm may have a fixed level of various resources available for its projects. The fixed resources might include labor-hours of various types of special professional or technical services, machine-hours of various types of machinery or instrumentation, hours of computing time, specialized locations, and similar scarce resources needed for accomplishing project tasks. For example, if the need for some resource varies between 70 and 120 percent of resource capacity, then that resource will be underutilized (and wasted if no alternative use exists) at one point in the project and in insufficient supply at another. If the project schedule can be adjusted to smooth the use of the resource, it may be possible to avoid project delay and, at the same time, not saddle the project with the high cost of excess resources allocated "just to make sure."

This chapter addresses situations that involve resource problems. We discuss the trade-offs involved, the difference between allocation to one project and allocation between multiple projects, the relationship between resource loading and leveling, and some of the approaches employed to solve allocation problems, including the Critical Path Method (CPM), Goldratt's "critical chain," and several other approaches to the problem of scheduling under conditions of resource scarcity. We begin with resource conflicts in a single project, and extend the discussion to the multiple project case. Although CPM is not actually a resource allocation method, we include it here because we view time as a resource, and trade-offs between time and other resources are a major problem in resource management. Finally, we note the major impact that current project management software has had on the PM's ability—and willingness—to deal with resource loading and leveling.

Project Management in Practice
Expediting Los Angeles Freeway Repairs after the Earthquake

Some years ago, at 4:31 A.M., a 6.8 magnitude earthquake hit Los Angeles and collapsed large sections of four major freeways, snarling one million commuters in daily gridlock for the indefinite future. Clearly, solutions to this crisis were of the highest priority. "Caltrans," the California Department of Transportation, sprung into action with a three-pronged attack. First, they rushed into emergency response, fanning out to conduct visual inspections and close dangerous segments of the roads and freeways. Second, they initiated interim traffic management strategies for all closed segments, utilizing parallel streets and old bypass roads to expand their capacity, change their signage and striping, and redirect adjacent traffic including traffic signal timing. Last, they planned for speedy demolition and rebuilding of the damaged portions of the freeways. Time was all-important and Caltrans used every tradeoff available to expedite the repairs which would normally take years to complete.

1. California's governor signed an Emergency Declaration allowing Caltrans to streamline its contracting procedures so that RFPs, bids, and evaluations that usually took four months could be completed in five days.

2. Significant incentives/disincentives were built into the contracts, the incentive depending on the value of the construction under consideration. One firm spent heavily on overtime, extra equipment rentals, and bonuses to keep working 24 hours a day, rain or shine, and came in 74 days ahead of a contractual date of 140 days, thereby earning a $14.8 million bonus that became the talk of the town!

3. All resources of the Federal Highway Administration were made available to work with Caltrans.

4. "Force Account" contracting was employed for immediate selection of sole-source contractors. The contractor then began work immediately under the direction of a Caltrans Resident Engineer.

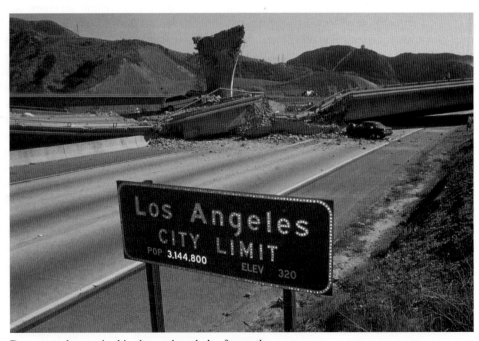

Damage to be repaired in the earthquake's aftermath.

5. Major project management processes were initiated including disaster response and an earthquake recovery task force consisting of top executives in local and national governmental agencies.

6. Millions in additional funds were made available through Caltrans' Director, a declaration of a state of emergency by President Clinton, and eventually Congress.

Source: J. B. Baxter, "Responding to the Northridge Earthquake," *PM Network*, Vol. 8.

9.1 CRITICAL PATH METHOD—CRASHING A PROJECT

When it was first developed in 1958, CPM used AON notation and included a way of relating the project schedule to the level of physical resources allocated to the project. This allowed the PM to trade time for cost, or vice versa. In CPM, two activity times and two costs were often specified for each activity. The first time/cost combination was called *normal*, and the second set was referred to as *crash*. Normal times are "normal" in the same sense as the *m* time estimate of the three times used in PERT. Crash times result from an attempt to expedite the activity by the application of additional resources—for example, overtime, special equipment, and additional staff or material.

It is standard practice with AOA and AON to estimate activity times under the assumption of resource loadings that are normal. To discuss a time requirement for any task without some assumption about the level of resources devoted to the task makes no real sense. At the same time, it does not make sense to insist on a full list of each and every resource that will be spent on each of the hundreds of activities that may comprise a network. Clearly, there must have been some prior decision about what resources would be devoted to each task, but much of the decision making is, in practice, relegated to the common methods of standard practice and rules of thumb. The allocation problem requires more careful consideration if it is decided to speed up the accomplishment of tasks and/or the total project. We need to know what additional resources it will take to shorten completion times for the various activities making up the project.

While standard practice and rules of thumb are sufficient for estimating the resource needs for normal progress, careful planning is critical when attempting to expedite (crash) a project. Crash plans that appear feasible when considered activity by activity may incorporate impossible assumptions about resource availability. For example, we may need to crash some activities on the Wild Horse Dam Project. To do so, we have all the labor and materials required, but we will need a tractor-driven crawler crane on the project site not later than the eighth of next month. Unfortunately, our crane will be in Decatur, Illinois, on that date. No local contractor has a suitable crane for hire. Can we hire one in Decatur or Springfield and bring ours here? And so it goes. When we expedite a project, we tend to create problems; and the solution to one problem often creates several more problems that require solutions.

Difficulties notwithstanding, the wise PM adopts the Scout's motto: "Be prepared." If deterministic time estimates are used, and if project deadlines are firm, there is a high likelihood that it will be necessary to crash the last few activities of most projects. The use of three probabilistic activity time estimates may reduce the chance that crashing will be needed because they include identification and estimation of risks and uncertainties that are sometimes forgotten or ignored when making deterministic time estimates. Even so, many things make crashing a way of life on some projects—things such as last-minute

Table 9-1   An Example of Two-Time CPM

Activity	Precedence	Duration, Days (normal, crash)	Cost (normal, crash)
a	—	3, 2	$ 40, 80
b	a	2, 1	20, 80
c	a	2, 2	20, 20
d*	a	4, 1	30, 120
e**	b	3, 1	10, 80

*Partial crashing allowed

**Partial crashing *not* allowed

Table 9-2   Activity Slopes–Cost per Period for Crashing

Activity	Slope ($/day)
a	40/−1 = −40
b	60/−1 = −60
c	—
d	90/−3 = −30
e	−70 (2 days)

changes in client specifications, without permission to extend the project deadline by an appropriate increment, i.e., scope creep. An example of one of the problems that commonly result from the use of deterministic time estimates can be seen in the boxed example that follows.

Consider the data in Table 9-1. First, we compute a cost/time slope for each activity that can be expedited (crashed). Slope is defined as follows:

$$\text{Slope} = \frac{\text{crash cost} - \text{normal cost}}{\text{crash time} - \text{normal time}}$$

that is, the cost per day of crashing a project. The slope is negative, indicating that as the time required for a project or task is decreased, the cost is increased. Note that activity c cannot be expedited. Table 9-2 shows the time/cost slopes for our example.

An implication of this calculation is that activities can be crashed in increments of one day (or one period). Often, this is not true. A given activity may have only two or three technically feasible durations. The "dollars per day" slope of such activities is relevant only if the whole crash increment is useful. For example, if an activity can be carried out in either eight days or four days, with no feasible intermediate times, and if an uncrashable parallel path goes critical when the first activity is reduced from eight down to six days, then the last two days (to four days) of time reduction are useless. Of course, if the PM needs to complete the project two days earlier, reducing the duration of one activity by four days may be the easiest and cheapest way to do it. (And there are times when the PM may expedite activities that have little or no impact on the network's critical time, such as when the resources used must be made available to another project.)

Project Management in Practice
Architectural Associates, Inc.

Architectural Associates, Inc. (AAI) specializes in large, industrial, retail, and public projects, including shopping malls, manufacturing complexes, convention centers, and the like. The firm is considered to be one of the region's most effective and creative design studios. The entire space devoted to design is a single, open area and workstations are laid out in such a way as to encourage communication between individuals working on a common project.

A senior executive of AAI noticed that for the past year or two, the chance of bringing design projects in on time and on budget had decreased to the point where the only uncertainty was how late and how much over budget a project would be.

An examination of the workplace disclosed a large, green felt display board mounted on the wall where it was visible to the entire design staff. The board listed the names of individual designers and technicians vertically, and design contract numbers across the horizontal axis. The times allocated for work on each project by appropriate staff members were shown at the intersections of the rows and columns. The time estimates were made by senior managers, themselves architects, based on their experience. The individuals with direct responsibility for design work generally felt that the time estimates were reasonable.

The work process was studied and the following problem was revealed. If the design of the electrical systems involved in a plan was estimated to take five days, for example, the individual(s) responsible for the work planned it in such a way that it used the five days allowed. If a problem occurred on the first day, the worker(s) simply stayed late or speeded up work the next day in order to get back on schedule. Problems on the second day, and even on the third and fourth days were handled in the same way, by crashing the work. Problems occurring on the fifth day, however, could not be handled so easily and this part of the project would be late. Because most of the different systems (the mechanicals, landscape, etc.) were designed simultaneously and staffed to require about the same number of days (rather than being sequential), and because problems were very likely to arise late in the design process of at least one of the systems, the overall design project, which required all tasks to be completed on time, was almost invariably late.

In an attempt to solve the problem, a simple checkmark to show job assignments was substituted for time allocations on the green board. Additionally, senior management made normal, optimistic, and pessimistic time estimates for each task and calculated "TE," also used to help estimate project cost. These estimates, however, were not given to the design staff who were simply told to do the work involved as efficiently and effectively as they could. The result was that the degree to which actual task times were early or late increased slightly, but the average time required for the various tasks was decreased because task schedules were now designed for efficiency rather than to meet management's expectations.

Source: S. J. Mantel, Jr. Consulting project.

One must remember that crashing a project results in a change of the technology with which something is done. In the language of economics, it is a change in the "production function." At times, crashing may involve a relatively simple decision to increase groups of resources already being used. If the project, for instance, is to dig a ditch of a certain length and depth, we might add units of labor-shovel to shorten the time required. On the other hand, we might replace labor-shovel units with a Ditch Witch. Technological discontinuities in outcomes usually result. Different amounts of labor-shovel input may result in a job that takes anywhere from one to three days. Use of the Ditch Witch may require three hours. There may be no sensible combination of resources that would complete the job in, say, six hours. It is important to remember that when we change technology, we may also be changing the level of risk in carrying out the activity. In some cases, technology cannot be changed, and task duration is fixed. A 30-day toxicity test for a new drug requires 30 days—no more, no less.

Not only do changes in technology tend to produce discontinuities in outcomes, they also tend to produce discontinuities in cost. As the technology is changed to speed a project, the relationship of input cost to activity duration is apt to jump as we move from less to more sophisticated production systems. For an extended treatment of this subject, see Nicholas (1990, Chapter 13).

When crashing a project, our first task is to develop a table or graph of the cost of a project as a function of the project's various possible completion dates. Starting with the normal schedule for all project activities, crash selected activities, one at a time, to decrease project duration at the minimum additional cost. To crash a project, follow two simple principles: First, focus on the critical path(s) when trying to shorten the duration of a project, with the exception we noted above, when a resource used by an activity not on the critical path is needed for another project. Crashing a noncritical activity will not influence project duration. Second, when shortening a project's duration, select the least expensive way to do it.

Given these guides, consider the network shown in Figure 9-1a that was constructed from the data in Table 9-1. It is easier to illustrate the impact of crashing on an activity-on-arrow (AOA) network than on an activity-on-node (AON) network, so we use that approach here. Also, we use dummy activities in this case not to illustrate precedence but to show time durations and slack on the time axis. As indicated in Tables 9-1 and 9-2, activity **d** can be partially crashed but activity **e** involves a technological discontinuity and must take either three days to complete at $10 or one day at $80. In general, the impact of having such a technological discontinuity is that the best solution for crashing n days might not be part of the best solution for crashing $n + 1$ days. Rather, it may be best to crash the activity with the technological discontinuity at $n + 1$ days and not crash another activity that could be crashed for n days. This situation is illustrated in the discussion that follows.

The network's critical path is **a-b-e**, the project duration is 8 days, and the normal total cost is $120, as illustrated in the network of Figure 9-1a. The decision about which activities to crash depends on how much we need to reduce the duration of the project. To reduce the total network duration by 1 day, we must reduce the time required by one of the activities along the critical path. Inspecting Table 9-2 to see which critical activity can be reduced at the least cost, we find it is activity **a** which adds $40 to the project's current cost of $120. Activity **b** could be crashed at a cost of $60 or we could even crash **e** 2 days for a cost of $70. Of course, crashing **e** would only shorten the project duration by one day because when **e** is shortened, the path **a-d-dummy**, seven days long, becomes the critical path and does not allow the project to be shortened to 6 days. Of the three options, crashing **a** is the lowest cost and therefore preferable; see Figure 9-1b. Notice that crashing **a** also shortens **a-d-dummy** and **a-c-dummy** by 1 day.

Suppose the project must be crashed by 2 days. What are the options? Reconsidering Table 9-2 and Figure 9-1a, we see that we could crash activity **e** for 2 days ($70), but path **a-d-dummy** (7 days' duration) must also be crashed at least 1 day. We choose **d** ($30/day) because it is cheaper than **a** ($40). The cost of crashing is $100, and the total project cost is $120 + $100 = $220. Alternatively, we could crash **a** and **b**, also for a cost of $100 ($40 + $60). Arbitrarily, we choose the latter option (Figure 9-1c).

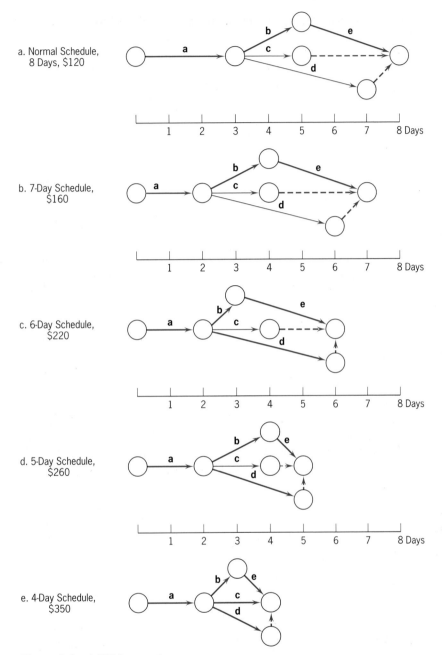

Figure 9-1   A CPM example.

Now suppose we wanted to crash the project by 3 days, from the original 8 days down to 5 days. Clearly **e** must be crashed by 2 days, costing $70, and **a** or **b** by a day. We choose **a**, the cheapest, for an additional $40. This leaves **d** to be crashed by 1 day for another $30, resulting in a total crashing cost of $140 and a project cost of $120 + $140 = $260 (Figure 9-1d). Note that we did not crash **b** this time, as we did for 6 days. This is due to the technological discontinuity in activity **e**.

Last, let us consider crashing the project by 4 days down to a project duration of 4 days. Since we crashed **e**, the technological discontinuity, to reach a 5-day duration, all the remaining activities can be incrementally crashed. Thus, we can simply inspect Figure 9-1d to see what else needs incremental crashing to reduce the project by another day. Notice in Figure 9-1d that **a-b-e** and **a-d-dummy** are both critical paths. Only **b** and **d** can still be crashed so we crash each by 1 day for an additional cost beyond the 5-day schedule of Figure 9-1d of $60 + $30 = $90 for a total project cost of $260 + $90 = $350 (Figure 9-1e). Note that **c** is now critical so *all* activities are critical. Since the critical paths **a-b-e** and **a-c** are at their full extent of crashing, the project duration cannot be further reduced, even though activity **d** could be crashed another day. Thus, Figure 9-1e is *not* the all-crash network, although it equals the all-crash time schedule of four days.

Another approach to CPM would have been starting with an all-crash schedule costing $380 and "relaxing" the activities one at a time. Of course, the activities relaxed first should be those that do not extend the completion date of the project. In our example, this is possible because **d** does not need to be at one day and so could be extended by one day at a cost saving of $30 without altering the project's completion date. This can be seen in Figure 9-1e, where activity **d** is shown taking two days with a project cost of $350. Continuing in this manner and relaxing the most expensive activities first would eventually result in the all-normal schedule of eight days and a cost of $120, as shown in Figure 9-1a.

Whether or not all this crashing is worthwhile is another matter. On the cost side, Figure 9-2 shows the time/cost relationship of crashing the project. On the benefit side, some projects have penalty clauses that make the parent organization liable for late delivery—and sometimes bonuses for early delivery. Starting at the right (all-normal) side of Figure 9-2, note that it becomes increasingly costly to squeeze additional time out of the project. Charts such as the one shown in Figure 9-2 are useful to the PM in exercising control over project duration and cost. They are particularly helpful in dealing with senior managers who may argue for early project completion dates with little understanding of the costs involved. Similarly, such data are of great benefit when clients plead for early delivery. If the client is willing to pay the cost of crashing, or if the firm is willing to subsidize the client, the PM can

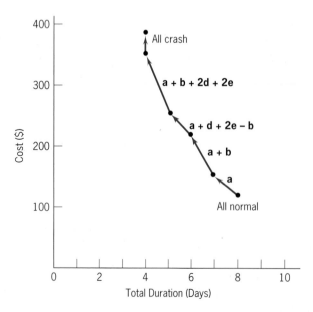

Figure 9-2 CPM cost-duration history.

Table 9-3   Official Pace of a Project

Title	Normal	Rush	Blitz
Approved Project Definition	Full	Some abbreviations from normal pace.	Only as necessary for major management decisions, purchasing and design engineering.
Study of Alternates	Reasonable	Quick study of major profitable items.	Only those not affecting schedule.
Engineering Design	Begins near end of Approved Project Definition.	Begins when Approved Project Definition 50–75% complete	Concurrently with such Approved Project Definition as is done.
Issue Engineering to Field	Allows adequate time for field to plan and purchase field items. Usually $\frac{1}{2}$–2 months lead time between issue and field erection.	Little or no lead time between issue and field erection.	No lead time between issue and field erection.
Purchasing	Begins in latter stages of Approved Project Definition.	Approved Project Definition. Rush purchase of all long delivery items. Many purchases on "advise price" basis.	Done concurrently with such Approved Project Definition as is done. Rush buy anything that will do job. Overorder and duplicate order to guarantee schedule.
Premium Payments	Negligible	Some to break specific bottlenecks.	As necessary to forestall any possible delays.
Field Crew Strength	Minimum practical or optimum cost.	Large crew with some spot overtime.	Large crew; overtime and/or extra shifts.
Probable Cost Difference Compared with Normal Pace, as a Result of:			
— Design and Development	Base	5–10% more	15% and up, more
— Engineering and Construction Costs	Base	3–5% more	10% and up, more
Probable Time	Base	Up to 10% less	Up to 50% less

afford to listen with a sympathetic ear. (While we advise the PM to ignore overhead cost over which he or she has no control, it should be noted that indirect costs are often altered when a project is crashed.)

Some organizations have more than one level of crashing. Table 9-3 illustrates such a case. In this example, the firm has two distinct levels of expediting a project: *rush* and *blitz*. The differences in the precedence relationships between tasks are noted in the table, as are differences in resource commitments. The last two rows of the table show the expected changes in cost and time if the project is expedited.

Fast-Tracking

Another way to expedite a project is known as "fast-tracking." This term has been applied mostly to construction projects, but the technique can be used in many other types of projects. It refers to overlapping the design and build phases of a project. Because design is usually completed before construction starts, overlapping the two activities will result in shortening the project duration. Beginning to build before design is completed might also, however, result in an increased number of change orders, subsequent loss of productivity, increased cost, and loss of time. Studies of construction projects revealed, however, that while there were more design changes in fast-tracked projects, the total number of project change orders was not significantly different than in similar projects that were not fast-tracked (Ibbs et al., 1998). Fast-tracking seems to be a reasonable way to expedite construction projects, as well as other types of projects when the early "build" or "carry out" steps are fairly routine and well understood. It is a partial use of the basic concept in phase-gate project management and is dependent on effective feed-back and feed-forward communication.

Solved Problem

Given the following network (time in days):

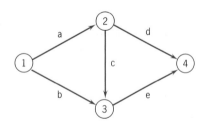

Activity	Crash Time, Cost	Normal Time, Cost	Partial Crashing?
a	3, $60	3, $60	No
b	6, 80	7, 30	Yes
c	2, 90	5, 50	No
d	5, 50	6, 30	No
e	2, 100	4, 40	Yes

Find the lowest cost to complete the project in 10 days.

Answer:
Current time and cost: 12 days and $210

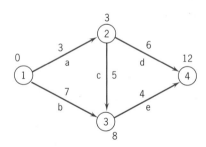

Since the critical path is **a-c-e**, we only initially need consider these three activities:

a: cannot be crashed

c: can cut three days at an extra cost of $40 but, due to **b**, only results in project completion by day 11. To reach 10 days, cut **b** by one day, total extra cost $90.

e: can cut **e** by two days for an extra cost of $60 and results in project completion by day 10.

Thus, cut **e** two days at a cost of $60.

Project Management in Practice
Thirty Days to Rescue

Global Healthcare Project (GHP) of California, USA, conducts various community projects in poor communities and regions across the globe. Previously, they had helped the residents of Pueblo Nuevo, Guatemala, set up a local pharmacy for their remote village in the northwest mountain highlands. Recently, the community again requested GHP's help in setting up an ambulance service since people couldn't reach a hospital when there was an emergency. GHP assembled a volunteer team of 22 university students to provide an ambulance, set up an emergency call system, and train some of the residents to act as EMTs (emergency medical technicians). However, the students could only be gone for 30 days, so this had to be a very fast project.

However, GHP found that the resource and infrastructure needs were overwhelming:

- There was no suitable vehicle in the community to buy and convert into an ambulance. Moreover, they wanted this project to be a "community-owned" effort with the community owning the ambulance and maintaining the system.

- The nearest hospital was three hours away down rough mountain terrain.

- There was no basic equipment available for the ambulance, not even oxygen tanks.

- Very few villagers had a driver's license or the time to spend as an ambulance driver.

- Ongoing funding was needed for the ambulance and supplies and maintenance.

- Training the driver-EMTs faced problems of limited education and medical knowledge, as well as literacy, language, and other difficulties.

The first task for the project team upon arrival was to find and register the vehicle. They did locate an acceptable vehicle four hours away near the Mexican border but it couldn't be registered in the name of the community without engaging a lawyer and going through a lot of paperwork. This was done, but it took almost the full 30 days. They equipped the vehicle with mountain terrain tires to handle the rough trails. They skipped trying to equip the ambulance with any equipment other than simple medical supplies.

They eventually located 3 residents who had driver's licenses, could handle driving on mountain terrain, were trainable, and had the time to drive patients to the hospital. To secure ongoing funding, the community agreed to add a surtax on the pharmacy for the supplies and maintenance. The trainers threw out the training manual and instead just demonstrated emergency-response procedures. For the call system, GHP arranged for a satellite phone number that could always reach one of the three driver-EMTs.

As the team was preparing to depart, a young girl required emergency transport to the hospital near midnight and got there safely with the new phone-ambulance system, a tribute to the efforts of the project team! The ambulance returned the next morning.

Source: J. Danko, "Rescue Squad," *PM Network,* Vol. 24.

9.2   THE RESOURCE ALLOCATION PROBLEM

A shortcoming of the scheduling procedures covered in the previous chapter is that they do not address the issues of resource utilization and availability. The focus is on time rather than physical resources. Also, in the discussion that follows it will not be sufficient to refer to resource usage simply as "costs." Instead, we must refer to individual types of labor, specific facilities, kinds of materials, individual pieces of equipment, and other discrete inputs that are relevant to an individual project but are limited in availability. In addition, we commonly must consider two types of resources: (1) those that are needed in a specific amount for an activity (e.g., 2 machine hours, 5 yards of cement,12 labor days), and (2) those that are needed to accompany the labor for as long as the labor is used, such as a machine. This chapter will always clarify which type of these two types of resources we are considering at the time. Last, we must not forget that time itself is always a critical resource in project management, one that is unique because it can neither be inventoried nor renewed. **One cannot save time—one can only spend more or less of it.**

The relationship between progress, time, and resource availability/usage is the major focus of this chapter. Schedules should be evaluated not merely in terms of meeting project milestones, but also in terms of the timing and use of scarce resources. A fundamental measure of the PM's success in project management is the skill with which the trade-offs among scope, time, and cost are managed. It is a continuous process of cost-benefit analysis: "I can shorten this project by a day at a cost of $400. Should I do it?" "If I buy 300 more hours of engineering time, I may be able to improve performance by 2 or 3 percent. Should I do it?" Of course, all such estimates are uncertain. What are the risks and how should we deal with them?

Occasionally it is possible that some additional (useful) resources can be added at little or no cost to a project during a crisis period. At other times, some resources in abundant supply may be traded for scarce ones. Most of the time, however, these trades entail additional costs to the organization, so a primary responsibility for the PM is to make do with what is available.

The extreme points of the relationship between time use and resource use are these:

- ***Time Limited:*** The project must be finished by a certain time, using as few resources as possible. But it is time, not resource usage, that is critical.
- ***Resource Limited:*** The project must be finished as soon as possible, but without exceeding some specific level of resource usage or some general resource constraint.

The points between these two extremes represent time/resource-use trade-offs. As in Figure 9-2, they specify the times achievable at various resource levels. Equivalently, they specify the resources associated with various completion times. Clearly, the range of time or resource variability is limited.

Occasionally, both time and resources may be limited, but in this case the specifications cannot also be fixed. If all three variables—time, cost, specifications—are fixed, the system is "overdetermined." The PM has lost all flexibility to perform the trade-offs that are so necessary to the successful completion of projects. Of course, it is possible that all three variables might be fixed at levels that allowed the PM plenty of maneuvering room, but this is most unlikely. Far more likely, our project manager acquaintances tell us, is the case in which senior management assigns budgets, schedules, and specifications without regard for the uncertainties of reality. It is the PM's responsibility, possibly with help from the project's champion, to

---

Project Management in Practice
Benefit/Cost Analysis Saves Chicago's Deep Tunnel Project

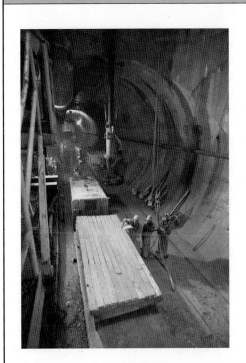

A creative approach to benefit/cost analysis comes from the Chicago Deep Tunnel Project, conceived in the 1970s and now scheduled for completion in just a few more years at a cost of $3–4 billion. The project consists of 110 miles of 300-foot underground tunnels, plus reservoirs and pollution-control systems for holding both sewage and excess rainwater. However, escalating costs over the years have reduced the benefit-cost ratio to less than 3 and the federal government was forced to reconsider their spending on it. With the threat of a loss in funding, the project was redesigned to improve the benefits while reducing the costs by $100 million, thereby boosting the benefit-cost ratio to above four, thus meeting federal standards.

Source: Project Management Institute. "Digging Deep," *PM Network,* Vol. 20.

warn senior management of the impropriety of such restrictions in spite of the chance that a senior manager might respond with "I'll get someone who can... !" If our advice seems a bit strong, we refer you to Jim McCarthy's Rule #25 (McCarthy, 1995, pp. 88–89, or see Mantel et al., 2011, pp. 123–124): "Don't accept task dates, features, and resource dictates from managers unfamiliar with the task."

On occasion, it may be that one or more tasks in a project are *system-constrained*. A system-constrained task requires a fixed amount of time and known quantities of resources. Some industrial processes—heat treating, for instance—are system-constrained. The material must "cook" for a specified time to achieve the desired effect. More or less "cooking" will not help. When dealing with a system-constrained task or project, no trade-offs are possible. The only matter of interest in these cases is to make sure that the required resources are available when needed.

In the following sections, we discuss approaches for understanding and using these relationships in various project situations.

9.3   RESOURCE LOADING

Resource loading describes the amounts of individual resources an existing schedule requires during specific time periods. Therefore, it is irrelevant whether we are considering a single work unit or several projects; the loads (requirements) of each resource type are simply listed as a function of time period. Resource loading gives a general understanding of the demands a project or set of projects will make on a firm's resources. It is an excellent guide for early, rough project planning. Obviously, it is also a first step in attempting to reduce excessive demands on certain resources, regardless of the specific technique used to reduce the demands. Again, we caution the PM to recognize that the use of resources on a project is often nonlinear. Much of the project management software does not recognize this fact (Gilyutin, 1993).

If resources of a project are increased by X percent, the output of the project usually does not increase by X percent, and the time required for the project does not decrease by X percent. The output and time may not change at all, or may change by an amount seemingly not related to X. An increase of 20 percent in the number of notes played does not necessarily improve the quality of the music. Any time the resource base of a project is altered from standard practice, the risk that the project may not be successful is changed, often increased.

Given a WBS, deriving a resource-loading document is not difficult. Figure 6-4 (Chapter 6) shows part of a WBS for a "Career Day" at a college. The part of the WBS shown lists the personnel resources needed for each activity. (The hours required are included in the WBS, but were not printed in Figure 6-4.) Utilizing data in the WBS, MSP generated Figure 9-3, the resource usage calendar. Each of the human resources used in the project is listed, followed by the name of the activities in which the resource is used. The total hours of work for each resource called for by the WBS are shown together with the amount planned for each activity. The schedule for resource loading is derived and the loading is then shown for each resource for each week (or day or month) of the project. It should be clear that if the information in this calendar were entered into a Crystal Ball®/Excel® spreadsheet along with estimates of the variability of resource times, the resource loading for any or all of these resources could be estimated by simulation.

An examination of Figure 9-3 shows that the secretary is overloaded during late May and early June. Assuming that there is only one secretary, during the week of May 30 he or she

			Career Day Project Resource Usage Calendar													
			May					June					July			
ID	Resource Name	Work	25	2	9	16	23	30	6	13	20	27	4	11	18	25
1	**Secretary**	**1,020 hrs**	24h	40h	40h	40h	88h	120h	102h	40h	40h	40h	40h	40h	40h	40h
	Print forms	240 hrs														
	Gather college particulars	160 hrs	24h	40h	40h	40h	16h									
	Print programs	240 hrs					24h	40h	40h	40h	40h	40h	16h			
	Advertise in college paper	200 hrs					24h	40h	36h	0h	0h	0h	24h	40h	36h	
	Organize posters	180 hrs					24h	40h	26h	0h	0h	0h	0h	0h	4h	40h
2	**Program Manager**	**1,440 hrs**	40h	40h	40h	16h	24h	40h	40h	40h	16h					
	Contact organizations	600 hrs	16h													
	Select guest speaker	560 hrs														
	Organize food	120 hrs	24h	40h	40h	16h										
	Contact faculty	60 hrs					24h	36h								
	Arrange facility for event	100 hrs						4h	40h	40h	16h					
3	**Office Manager**	**180 hrs**	24h	40h	40h	40h	16h				20h					
	Collect display information	160 hrs	24h	40h	40h	40h	16h									
	Transport materials	20 hrs									20h					
4	**Graduate Assistant**	**1,140 hrs**	24h	40h	40h	40h	64h	80h	80h	56h	40h	40h	16h			
	Print participants' certificates	320 hrs														
	Organize refreshments	280 hrs	24h	40h	40h	40h	40h	40h	40h	16h						
	Send invitations	80 hrs														
	Organize gift certificates	220 hrs														
	Arrange banner	200 hrs					24h	40h	40h	40h	40h	16h				
	Class announcements	40 hrs										24h	16h			
5	**Director**	**400 hrs**	24h	40h	40h	40h	40h	40h	40h	40h	40h	40h	16h			
	Organize liquor	400 hrs	24h	40h	40h	40h	40h	40h	40h	40h	40h	40h	16h			

Figure 9-3   Resource usage calendar for Career Day Project.

must work 17+ hours per day of a 7-day week (or 24 hours per 5-day week). This is apt to try the patience of the most determined and loyal employee. Graduate assistants are certainly considered slaves by their faculty masters, but are usually indentured for only 20 hours per week of servitude. Unless there are four GAs, the project will have problems. It is the job of the PM to deal with these problems, either by adding people or by changing the schedule in such a way that the demand for resources does not exceed resource capacities.

Because the project WBS is the source of information on activity precedences, durations, and resources requirements, it is the primary input for both the project schedule and its budget. The WBS links the schedule directly to specific demands for resources. Thus, the AOA network technique can be modified to generate time-phased resource requirements. A Gantt chart could be adapted, but the AOA diagram, particularly if modified to illustrate slacks as in Figure 9-1, will be helpful in the analysis used for resource leveling. Let us illustrate with the AON network used as an example in the previous chapter, but converted to an AOA diagram. The AOA network (from Table 8-2) is illustrated in

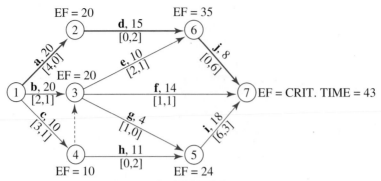

Figure 9-4 The AOA network of Table 8-2.

Figure 9-4, and resource usage is illustrated for two hypothetical resources, A and B, on the arcs. The expected activity time is shown above the arc, and resource usage is shown in brackets just below the arc, with the use of A shown first and B second—e.g., [5, 3] would mean that five units of A and three units of B would be used on the activity represented by the arc. Figure 9-5 shows the "calendarized" AOA diagram, similar to the familiar Gantt chart. Resource demands can now be summed by time period across all activities.

The loading diagram for resource A is illustrated in Figure 9-6a, and that for resource B in Figure 9-6b. The loads are erratic and vary substantially over the duration of the project. Resource A, used in tasks **a**, **b**, and **c**, has a high initial demand that drops through the middle of the project and then climbs again. Resource B, on the other hand, has low initial use but increases as the project develops. The PM must be aware of the ebbs and flows of usage for each input resource throughout the life of the project. It is the PM's responsibility to ensure that the required resources, in the required amounts, are available when and where they are needed. In the next three sections, we will discuss how to meet this responsibility.

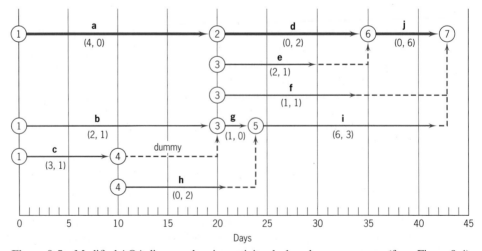

Figure 9-5 Modified AOA diagram showing activity slack and resource usage (from Figure 9-4).

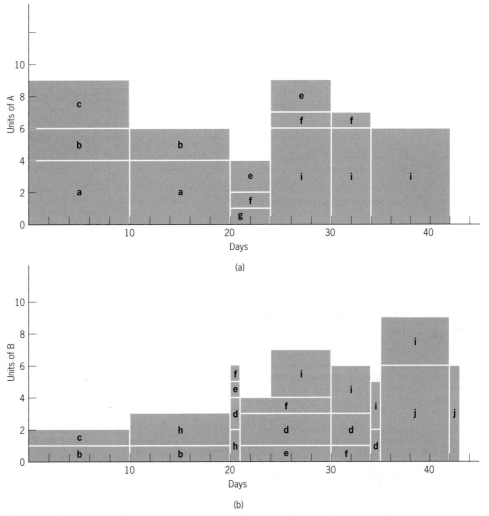

Figure 9-6 (a) Load diagram for resource A. (b) Load diagram for resource B.

9.4 RESOURCE LEVELING

In the preceding example, we noted that the project began with the heavy use of resource A, used smaller amounts during the middle of the project, and then continued with rising usage during the project's latter stages. Usage of B started low and rose throughout the project's life. Large fluctuations in the required loads for various resources are a normal occurrence—and are undesirable from the PM's point of view. Resource leveling aims to minimize the period-by-period variations in resource loading *by shifting tasks within their slack allowances.* The purpose is to create a smoother distribution of resource usage.

There are several advantages to smoother resource usage. First, much less hands-on management is required if the use of a given resource is nearly constant over its period of use. The PM can arrange to have the resource available when needed, can have the supplier furnish constant amounts, and can arrange for a backup supplier if advisable. Moreover, the PM can do this with little error. Second, if resource usage is level, the PM may be able to use a "just-in-time" inventory policy without much worry that the quantity delivered will be wrong. If the resource being leveled is people, leveling improves morale and results in fewer problems in the personnel and payroll offices because of increasing and decreasing labor levels.

Not only are there managerial implications to resource leveling, there are also important cost implications. When resources are leveled, the associated costs also tend to be leveled. If resource use increases as time goes by, and if resources are shifted closer to the present by leveling, costs will be shifted in the same way. The opposite is true, of course, if resource usage is shifted to the future. Perhaps most important from a cost perspective is leveling employment throughout a project or task. For most organizations, the costs of hiring and layoff are quite significant. It is often less expensive to level labor requirements in order to avoid hiring and layoff, even if it means some extra wages will be paid. In any case, the PM must be aware of the cash flows associated with the project and of the means of shifting them in ways that are useful to the parent firm.

The basic procedure for resource leveling is straightforward. For example, consider the simple AOA network shown in Figure 9-7a. The activity time is shown above the arc, and resource usage (one resource, workers) is in brackets below the arc. Activities **a**, **b**, and **c** follow event 1, and all must precede event 4. Activity **a** requires two workers and takes two days, **b** requires two workers and takes 3 days, and **c** needs 4 workers and 5 days. (We addressed the problem of trade-offs between labor and activity time in the first section of this chapter.) If all these tasks are begun on their early start dates, the resource loading diagram appears as shown in Figure 9-7b, steps of decreasing labor demand varying from eight workers to four workers. If, however, task **b** is delayed for 2 days, the full length of its slack in this particular case, the resource loading diagram is smoothed, as shown in Figure 9-7c. The same result would have occurred if **b** were started as early as possible and task **a** were delayed until day 3.

Resource leveling is a procedure that can be used for almost all projects, whether or not resources are constrained. If the network is not too large and there are only a few resources, the leveling process can be done manually. For larger networks and multiple resources, resource leveling becomes extremely complex, far beyond the power of manual solutions. Fortunately, a number of computer programs can handle most leveling problems efficiently.

Reconsider the load diagrams of Figures 9-6a and b. Assume it is desired to smooth the loading of resource B, which is particularly jagged. Both activities **e** and **f** can be delayed (**e** has 5 days of slack and **f** has 9). If we delay both for one day, we remove the peak on day 20 without increasing any of the other peaks (see Figure 9-8b). If we do this, however, it also alters the use of resource A and deepens the "valley" on day 20 (see Figure 9-8a). If we further delay **f** another 7 days in order to level the use of A toward the end of the project, we would deepen the valley between days 20 and 24, and the resultant use of A would be as shown by the dotted lines on Figure 9-8a. Activity **f** would begin on day 28 (and would become critical). The effect on the usage of B is easy to see (Figure 9-8b). The change would lower usage by one unit beginning on day 21 (remember that we have already delayed **f** one day), and increase usage by one unit beginning on day 35, continuing to the end of the project. This action increases peak use of B from nine to ten units.

It is important to emphasize that if the network under consideration is more complex and the number of resources to be leveled is realistically large, a manual leveling process is out of the question. Computer-aided leveling is not only mandatory, it is also helpful because it allows the PM to experiment with various patterns of resource usage through simulation. In the next section, we raise the most general problem of minimizing resource usage while still achieving various completion dates—or the inverse problem, minimizing completion times while operating with specified limits on resources.

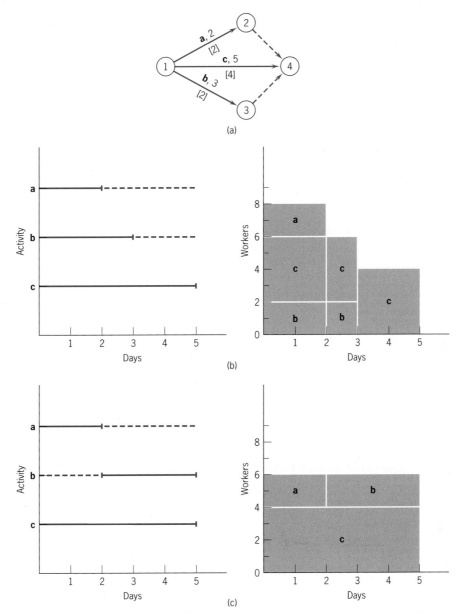

Figure 9-7　(a) The network. (b) Before resource leveling. (c) After resource leveling.

Resource Loading/Leveling and Uncertainty

Figure 9-9 is a resource loading chart for a software engineering group in a large company, constructed by importing MSP resource loading information into an Excel® spreadsheet and then displaying it graphically. There are 21 engineers in the group, nominally scheduled to work 40 hours a week, resulting in a weekly capacity of

$$21 \times 40 = 840 \text{ labor-hours each week.}$$

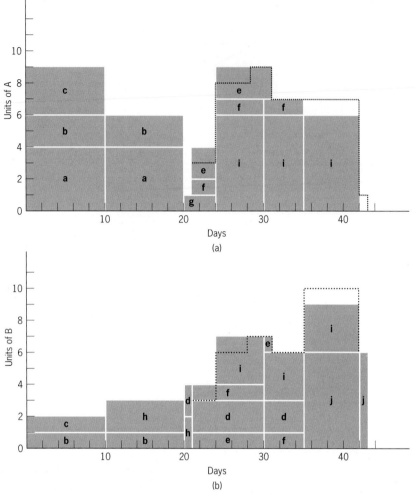

Figure 9-8 (a) Load diagram for resource A with activities **e** and **f** delayed by one day each. (b) Load diagram for resource B with activities **e** and **f** delayed by one day each.

The graph covers February through September, a period of 34 weeks. Thus, the total engineering capacity for the period shown is

$$34 \times 840 = 28,560 \text{ labor-hours.}$$

As shown, the total labor-hours required for the period is 28,282, so we see that there is excess capacity, a nice situation normally. However, there are two problems. As is clear in the loading chart, the demand for engineering labor is not evenly distributed throughout the period, hitting a major peak in the late March–early April time frame and then a few more times later in the period. This is counterbalanced by weeks throughout the time period where less-than-full capacity is required; however, this is not helpful since the engineers are employed for 40-hour weeks so the undercapacity times are wasted.

There are some alternatives used to address these kinds of situations. First, we can try to level the demand, moving some of it forward and some back, depending on our

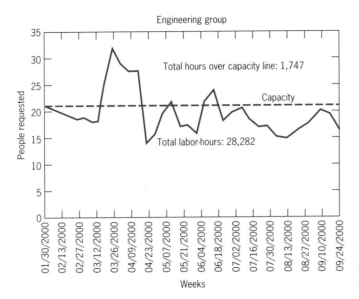

Figure 9-9 Thirty-four-week resource loading chart for a software engineering group.

flexibility in this production environment. Second, we can try to alter the supply of engineering hours, asking the engineers to trade off time between periods of overcapacity and periods of undercapacity. We might expend additional resources, bringing in contract engineers to handle the overload period, or subcontract the workload, but such suggestions would almost certainly be rejected by senior management because of security worries by our clients. Perhaps it would be cheaper to let the work be delayed a few weeks and try to catch up later. We will identify other ways of resolving this element of uneven demand a bit later.

But there is another problem with this situation, which is that we try not to schedule a scarce resource for more than 85–90 percent capacity. The reason is due to disruptions, emergencies, maintenance requirements, personnel issues, and simple inefficiency of any resource that is scheduled for full production over an extended time period. Let us consider the case of the engineers, in particular. Over this 34-week period that includes the summer, there will probably be most of the scheduled 2-week vacations (if not longer). If 15 engineers are scheduled for vacations during this period, that will remove 15×2 weeks $\times 40 =$ 1,200 labor-hours from the capacity. In addition, there are three national holidays during this period: Memorial Day, the Fourth of July, and Labor Day, resulting in a further loss of $21 \times 3 \times 8$ hours $= 504$ hours. These two scheduled sets of events have now reduced our capacity to $28,560 - 1,200 - 504 = 26,856$ labor-hours, 5 percent less than the demand over the period.

What about unscheduled events and disruptions? Illnesses will surely occur in this long time frame. Furthermore, will the facilities, equipment, materials, and the work itself be ready for the engineers when they move to the next task? Will everything show up precisely when it is needed? Will there be no delays in the work preceding what the engineers are expected to do? Will there be no scope changes in the preceding work, thus delaying the succeeding tasks scheduled for the engineers? As you can see, we expect there to be "unexpected" delays for multiple reasons, hence the admonition to never schedule a resource for more than 85–90 percent of its capacity.

But what about manufacturing situations in which machines and processes are commonly run near capacity for extended durations? These situations are not projects but rather routine production environments, assembly lines, for example. New work is scheduled to arrive precisely when the previous work has been completed. Planning is extensive, maintenance is carefully scheduled, experience in what can go wrong is abundant, resources are carefully controlled and monitored, and so on. That is not the situation of projects, which by definition are nonroutine. Depending on experience, when planning routine types of manufacturing processes, we try to have line capacity just slightly in excess of our average demand for the line's output. This policy is a sure course to disaster when applied to project management.

Now, what do we do about our software engineers? As it happens, some groups of professionals, such as engineers, are employed with the understanding that there will be periods of overtime required (for which they are generally not paid) and periods when things will be slack and they are relatively free to come and go as they please. In reality, engineers often work 50 to 60 hours per week for extended periods, and if a prolonged period of insufficient work is available at the company, management may lay off some engineers. As can be seen, a workweek of, say, 55 hours $\times$ 21 engineers $\times$ 34 weeks $\times$ 85 percent capacity = 33,379 labor-hours, more than sufficient for the 28,282 labor-hours required—but not much more than sufficient.

9.5   CONSTRAINED RESOURCE SCHEDULING

Far too often, PMs are surprised by resource constraints. The cause of this condition is usually the direct result of a failure to include resource availability in risk identification activities. The lack of a resource where and when it is needed can have many causes, but the most common causes are not difficult to identify and mitigate: failure of a supplier to produce and/or deliver, the assignment of the resource to another activity, and loss or theft of a resource. PMs often apply risk management techniques to resources known to be scarce, but neglect to consider the more common resources that usually cause the problems.

There are two fundamental approaches to constrained resource allocation problems: heuristics and optimization models. Heuristic approaches employ rules of thumb that have been found to work reasonably well in similar situations. They seek better solutions. Optimization approaches seek the best solutions but are far more limited in their ability to handle complex situations and large problems. We will discuss each separately.

Most PC software designed for project management will level resources and solve the problems of overscheduling resources. They require priority rules to establish which activities take precedence. The priority rules the programs use vary somewhat, but most packages offer a choice. For example, reconsider the video project used to demonstrate MSP output forms in Chapter 8. We can include the resource requirement for each activity directly on the Gantt chart, as in Figure 9-10, but we can also show separate diagrams that illustrate the demand or "load" for each of the resources as in Figure 9-11. Figures 9-11 and 9-12 show a resource conflict for the producer and the resource leveling solution. Note the changes in the scheduled finish dates for the leveled solution.

Heuristic Methods

Heuristic approaches to constrained resource scheduling problems are in wide, general use for a number of reasons. First, they are the only feasible methods of attacking the large, nonlinear,

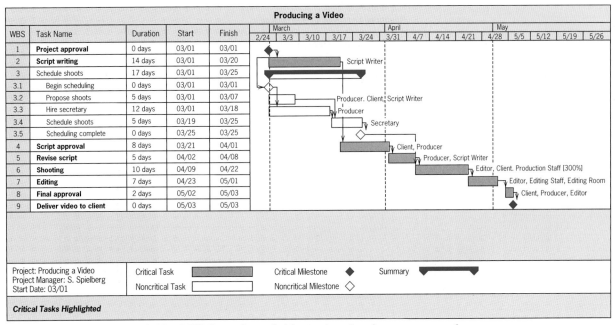

Figure 9-10 MSP Gantt chart of video project showing resource needs.

complex problems that tend to occur in the real world of project management. Second, while the schedules that heuristics generate may not be optimal, they are usually quite good—certainly good enough for most purposes. Commercially available computer programs handle large problems and have had considerable use in industry. Further, modern simulation techniques allow the PM to develop many different schedules quickly and to determine which, if any, are significantly better than current practice. If a reasonable number of simulation runs fail to produce significant improvement, the PM can feel fairly confident that the existing solution is a good one.

Most heuristic solution methods start with the PERT/CPM schedule and analyze resource usage period by period, resource by resource. In a period when the available supply of a resource is exceeded, the heuristic examines the tasks in that period and allocates the scarce resource to them sequentially, according to some priority rule. The major difference among the heuristics is in the priority rules they use. Remember that the *technological necessities always take precedence*. Some of the most common priority rules are:

As Soon as Possible   The default rule for scheduling. This provides the general solution for critical path and time.

As Late as Possible   All activities are scheduled as late as possible without delaying the project. The usual purpose of this heuristic is to defer cash outflows as long as possible.

Shortest Task First   Tasks are ordered in terms of duration, with the shortest first. In general, this rule will maximize the number of tasks that can be completed by a system during some time period.

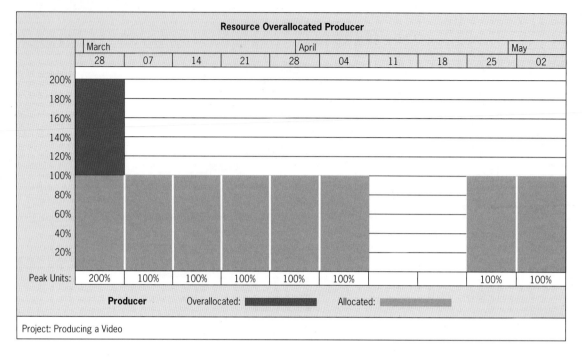

Figure 9-11   MSP load diagram showing resource conflict (producer used beyond capacity).

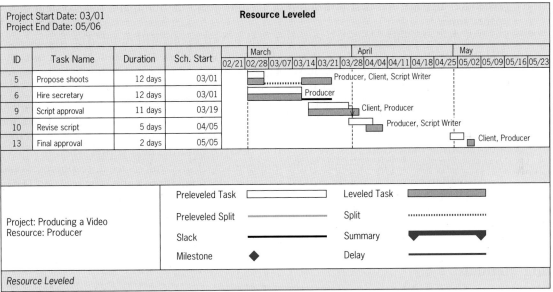

Figure 9-12 MSP rescheduling to level producer resource usage without exceeding capacity.

Most Resources First Activities are ordered by use of a specific resource, with the largest user heading the list. The assumption behind this rule is that more important tasks usually place a higher demand on scarce resources.

Minimum Slack First This heuristic orders activities by the amount of slack, least slack going first. (It is common, when using this rule, to break ties by using the shortest-task-first rule.)

Most Critical Followers Tasks are arranged by number of critical activities following them. The ones with the greatest number of critical followers go first.

Most Successors This is the same as the previous rule, except that all followers, not merely critical ones, are counted.

Arbitrary Priorities are assigned to activities according to some rule not associated with task length, slack, or resource requirements. Such rules might be that tasks on projects of higher value to the parent organization (or for the project of a favored customer) are taken before those of lower value.

There are many such priority rules employed in scheduling heuristics. From time to time researchers subject several of the more popular of the project management software programs to tests of their ability to handle such tasks as allocating constrained resources and resource leveling. Although their findings vary somewhat because of slightly different assumptions, the minimum-slack-first rule was found to be best or near-best quite often and rarely caused poor performance. It usually resulted in the minimum amount of project schedule slippage, the best utilization of facilities, and the minimum total system occupancy time.

As the scheduling heuristic operates, one of two events will result. The routine runs out of activities (for the current period) before it runs out of the resources, or it runs out of resources before all activities have been scheduled. (Rarely is the supply of resources precisely equal to the demand.) If the former occurs, the excess resources are left idle, assigned elsewhere in the organization as needed during the current period, or applied to future tasks required by the project—always within the constraints imposed by the proper precedence relationships. If one or more resources are exhausted, however, activities requiring those resources are slowed or delayed until the next period when resources can be reallocated. For example, if the minimum-slack-first rule is used, resources would be devoted to critical or nearly critical activities, delaying those with greater slack. Delay of an activity uses some of its slack, so the activity will have a better chance of receiving resources in the next period's allocation. Repeated delays move the activity higher and higher on the priority list.

Optimizing Methods

In the past several years, a wide range of attacks have been made on the problems of resource allocation and scheduling when resources are constrained. Some of these depend on sophisticated mathematical and/or graphical tools and may be quite powerful in what they can do. The methods to find an optimal solution to the constrained resource scheduling problem fall primarily into two categories: mathematical programming (linear programming, LP, for the most part) and enumeration. In the late 1960s and early 1970s, limited enumeration techniques were applied to the constrained resource problem with some success. Advances in linear programming (LP) techniques now allow LP to be used on large constrained resource scheduling problems. Other approaches have combined programming and enumeration methods.

Project Management in Practice
Benefits of Resource Constraining at Pennsylvania Electric

Pennsylvania Electric Company, headquartered in Johnstown, PA, operates generating facilities with a capacity of 6,950 megawatts to serve 547,000 customers over an area of 17,600 square miles. The Generation Division Planning Group is responsible for planning all maintenance and capital projects. In the early 1980s, the group used manual methods of planning with hand-drawn charts. Of course, planning is now computerized, which is faster, allows "what-if" analyses, and controls more than just the previously monitored critical path.

A special feature of the computerized system is its resource constraining module which establishes labor requirements across all jobs. In the pilot program to test the new software, $300,000 was saved when it was discovered that a particular job could be done with 40 percent fewer mechanics than normally used and still complete the job on time.

After worker-hours are input to the program by activity, actual progress is monitored (see figure) and schedule and cost deviations are highlighted for management attention. This allows management to make

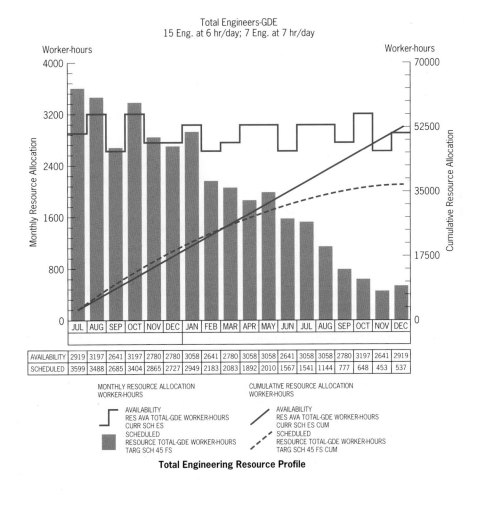

Total Engineers-GDE
15 Eng. at 6 hr/day; 7 Eng. at 7 hr/day

	JUL	AUG	SEP	OCT	NOV	DEC	JAN	FEB	MAR	APR	MAY	JUN	JUL	AUG	SEP	OCT	NOV	DEC
AVAILABILITY	2919	3197	2641	3197	2780	2780	3058	2641	2780	3058	3058	2641	3058	3058	2780	3197	2641	2919
SCHEDULED	3599	3488	2685	3404	2865	2727	2949	2183	2083	1892	2010	1567	1541	1144	777	648	453	537

MONTHLY RESOURCE ALLOCATION
WORKER-HOURS

CUMULATIVE RESOURCE ALLOCATION
WORKER-HOURS

AVAILABILITY
RES AVA TOTAL-GDE WORKER-HOURS
CURR SCH ES

SCHEDULED
RESOURCE TOTAL-GDE WORKER-HOURS
TARG SCH 45 FS

AVAILABILITY
RES AVA TOTAL-GDE WORKER-HOURS
CURR SCH ES CUM

SCHEDULED
RESOURCE TOTAL-GDE WORKER-HOURS
TARG SCH 45 FS CUM

Total Engineering Resource Profile

adjustments to recover the schedule, slow the project down, or acquire more funds to get the project back on schedule. Obviously, there are always some emergencies outside the plan that must be handled on an exception basis. But with this software, management knows what effect different actions will have on the basic plan and can thereby make the best use of available resources to handle the emergency with minimal impact on the plan.

Source: A. J. Cantanese, "At Penelec, Project Management Is a Way of Life," *Project Management Journal*, Vol. 21.

9.6 MULTIPROJECT SCHEDULING AND RESOURCE ALLOCATION*

In Chapter 2, we described a method for strategically selecting the best set of projects that would help achieve the organization's strategic goals. This method, called the Project Portfolio Process, ended with a set of high-priority projects that could be adequately funded by the organization. However, the process did not consider the scheduling and allocation of limited, individual critical resources among the projects. In some cases, a particular machine, or skilled employee may be needed on two or more projects at the same time. This involves multiproject scheduling and resource allocation.

Scheduling and allocating resources to multiple projects are much more complicated than for the single-project case. The most common approach is to treat the several projects as if they were each elements of a single large project. (A more detailed explanation is given below when we consider a specific multiproject scheduling heuristic.) Another way of attacking the problem is to consider all projects as completely independent; see the works by Kurtulus et al. (1982, 1985) for example. As they show, these two approaches lead to different scheduling and allocation outcomes. For either approach, the conceptual basis for scheduling and allocating resources is essentially the same.

There are several projects, each with its own set of activities, due dates, and resource requirements. In addition, the penalties for not meeting time, cost, and scope goals for the several projects may differ. Usually, the multiproject problem involves determining how to allocate resources to, and set a completion time for, a new project that is added to an existing set of ongoing projects. This requires the development of an efficient, dynamic multiproject scheduling system.

To describe such a system properly, standards are needed by which to measure scheduling effectiveness. Three important parameters affected by project scheduling are: (1) schedule slippage, (2) resource utilization, and (3) in-process inventory. The organization (or the PM) must select the criterion most appropriate for its situation.

Schedule slippage, the time past a project's due or delivery date, is often considered the most important of the criteria. Slippage may well result in penalty costs that reduce profits. Further, slippage of one project may have a ripple effect, causing other projects to slip. Indeed, expediting a project in order to prevent slippage may, and usually does, disturb the overall organization to the point where slippage due to resource shortages may then be caused in other projects. The loss of goodwill when a project slips and deliveries are late is important to all producers. As is the case with many firms, Northrop Grumman Corporation jealously guards its reputation for on-time delivery. During a project to install a new machine control system on a production line, Northrop Grumman insisted that the project be designed to minimize disturbance to operations in the affected plant and avoid late shipments. This increased the cost of the project, but the firm maintained its delivery schedules.

---

*Shaded sections can be skipped without loss of continuity.

While it is relatively easy to measure the costs of excess *resource utilization* due to less than optimal scheduling, the costs of uncoordinated multiproject scheduling can also be high, especially in service firms. In the real estate syndication firm example at the end of Chapter 8, the scarce resource is executive judgment time. If two deals arrive at the same time, one must wait. This is undesirable because other potential buyers are seeking properties.

The third standard of effectiveness, the amount of *in-process inventory*, concerns the amount of work waiting to be processed because there is a shortage of some resource(s). The remedy involves a trade-off between the cost of in-process inventory and the cost of the resources, usually capital equipment, needed to reduce the in-process inventory levels. It is almost axiomatic that the most time-consuming operation in any production system involving much machining of metals is an operation called "wait."

These three criteria cannot be optimized at the same time. As usual, trade-offs are involved. A firm must decide which criterion is most applicable in any given situation, and then use that criterion to evaluate its various scheduling and resource allocation options. Adler et al. (1996) found that some highly successful firms had been applying work-process schedule management to product/service development projects. Specifically, they found that project schedules are faster when the firm does fewer of them ("in-process inventory"), increasing bottleneck capacity ("resource utilization") pays large dividends, and eliminating unnecessary workload ("in-process inventory") and processes decreases the variation in service times.

As noted earlier, the minimum-slack-first rule is the best overall priority rule and generally results in minimum project slippage, minimum resource idle time, and minimum system occupancy time (i.e., minimum in-process inventory). But the most commonly used priority rule is first-come, first-served—which has little to be said for it except that it fits the client's idea of what is "fair," if the client is at the head of the line. In any case, individual firms may find a different rule more effective in their particular circumstances and should evaluate alternative rules by their own performance measures and system objectives.

Given these observations, let us examine some examples of the various types of multiproject scheduling and resource allocation techniques. We begin with a short description of several heuristics, and then discuss one heuristic in greater detail.

Heuristic Techniques

Because of the difficulties with the analytical formulation of realistic problems, major efforts in attacking the resource-constrained multiproject scheduling problem have focused on heuristics. We touched earlier on some of the common general criteria used for scheduling heuristics. Let us now return to that subject.

There are scores of different heuristic-based procedures in existence. A great many of the procedures have been published (see Davis et al., 1975, for example), and descriptions of some are generally available in commercial computer programs.

The most commonly applied rules were discussed in Section 9.5. The logical basis for these rules predate AOA and AON. They represent rather simple extensions of well-known approaches to job-shop scheduling. Some additional heuristics for resource allocation have been developed that draw directly on AOA and AON. All these are commercially available for computers, and most are available from several different software vendors in slightly different versions.

Resource Scheduling Method In calculating activity/project priority, give precedence to that activity/project that results in the minimum increase in project duration(s). The comparison is made on a pairwise basis among all activities/projects in the conflict set.

Minimum Late Finish Time This rule assigns priorities to activities/projects on the basis of finish times as determined by AOA or AON. The earliest late finishers are scheduled first.

Greatest Resource Demand   This method assigns priorities on the basis of total resource requirements, with higher priorities given for greater demands on resources. Resource requirements must be stated in common terms, usually dollars. This heuristic is based on an attempt to give priority to potential resource bottleneck activities.

Greatest Resource Utilization   This rule gives priority to that combination of activities that results in maximum resource utilization (or minimum idle resources) during each scheduling period. This rule was found to be approximately as effective as the minimum slack rule for multiple project scheduling, where the criterion used was project slippage.

Most Possible Jobs   Here, priority is given to the set of activities that results in the greatest number of activities being scheduled in any period.

Heuristic procedures for resource-constrained multiproject scheduling represent the only practical means for finding workable solutions to the large, complex multiproject problems normally found in the real world. Let us examine one multiproject heuristic in somewhat more detail.

A Multiproject Scheduling Heuristic

To attack this problem, recall the hierarchical approach to project planning we adopted in Chapter 6. A project plan is a nested set of plans, composed of a set of generalized tasks, each of which is decomposed into a more detailed set of work packages that are, in turn, decomposed further. The decomposition is continued until the work packages are simple enough to be considered "elemental." A network diagram of a project might be drawn for any level of task aggregation. A single activity (arrow) at a high level of aggregation would represent an entire network of activities at a lower level (see Figure 9-13). Another level in the planning hierarchy is shown as a Gantt chart in Figure 9-14.

If an entire network is decomposed into subnetworks, we have the equivalent of the multiproject problem where each of the projects (subnetworks) is linked to predecessor and successor projects (other subnetworks). In this case, the predecessor/successor relationships depend on the technology of the parent project. In the true multiproject case, these relationships may still depend on technological relationships; for example, a real estate development project being dependent on the outcome of a land procurement project. The relationships may, however, be determined more or less arbitrarily, as when projects are sequenced on a first-come, first-served basis, or by any other priority-setting rule, or undertaken simultaneously in the hope that some synergistic side effects might occur. Or the relationship among the projects may simply be that they share a common pool of resources.

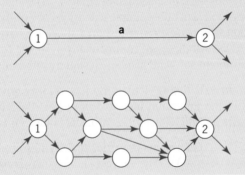

Figure 9-13   Task **a** decomposed into a network of subtasks.

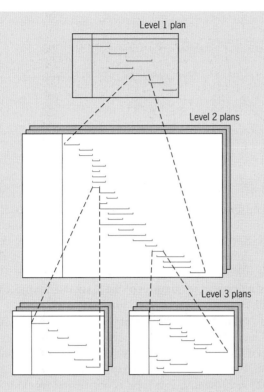

Figure 9-14 Hierarchy of Gantt charts. *Source:* F. L. Harrison (1983). *Advanced Project Management.* Hants, U.K.: Gower.

With this conceptual model, assume we have a set of projects. Each individual project is represented by a network of tasks. We can form a single network of these projects by connecting them with dummy activities (no resources, no duration) and/or pseudoactivities (no resources, some duration). Both dummy activities and pseudoactivities represent dependency relationships, but these dependencies, as noted above, may be technological or arbitrary.*

As usual, and excepting dummy and pseudoactivities, each task in each network requires time and resources. The amount of time required may or may not vary with the level of resources applied to it. The total amount of resources and/or amounts of individual resources are limited in successive scheduling periods. Our problem is to find a schedule that best satisfies the sequence and resource constraints and minimizes the overall duration of the entire network. The resulting schedule should indicate when to start any activity and at what level of resources it should be maintained while it is active.

Weist's heuristic (SPAR-1, Scheduling Program for Allocation of Resources) allocates resources to activities in order of their early start times. In the first period, we would list all available tasks and order them by their slack, from least to most. (Calculation of slack is based on the assumption that activities will be supported at *normal* resource levels.) Activities are selected for support and scheduling one by one, in order. As activities at the top of the list are supported, the relevant resource stocks are debited. Tasks are scheduled sequentially until the list of available jobs is completed, or until the stock of one or more necessary resources is depleted. If we deplete resources before completing the task list, remaining tasks are delayed until the next period. Postponed activities lose slack and rise toward the top of the priority list.

---

*This exposition is based on Weist's (1967) work, and on Corwin's (1968) application of Weist's papers to resource allocation among multiple R&D projects.

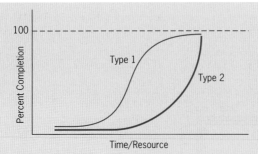

Figure 9-15 Project or task life cycles.

Thus, resources are devoted to activities until the supply of available resources or activities is exhausted. If we use up the resources before all critical activities are scheduled, we can adopt one of two subheuristics. First, we may be able to borrow resources from currently active, but noncritical, tasks. Second, we may "deschedule" a currently active, noncritical task. The former presumably slows the progress of the work, and the latter stops it. In both cases, some resources will be released for use on critical tasks. Obviously, if a critical task is slowed, descheduled, or not supported, the duration of the associated project will be extended.

The decision about which of these courses of action to take, borrowing or descheduling, can be made by adopting the same logic used in Chapter 7 when we discussed the budget negotiations between subordinate and superior. The decision to borrow or deschedule depends on our estimate of the impact either action would have on the task under consideration, given its current state of completion. Figure 9-15 shows two different versions of the project or task life cycle discussed in Chapter 7. If the task is a Type 1, borrowing would minimize the damage to the task unless it is quite near completion and we are willing to accept the outcome in its current state, in which case we can deschedule. If the task is Type 2, borrowing is apt to have a catastrophic effect on the task and we should either deschedule it (and start it again later) or reject it as a source of resources.

As we have noted, many commercially available software packages have the ability to schedule constrained resources and deal with resource conflicts. We should note in passing that the case of resource shortages applies not to resources in general but to one or two highly specific resources, typically. Many of the packages will allow the user to solve the problem either automatically, using the program's heuristics, or by hand, in which case the user can adopt any method desired. If a set of projects is linked together by dummy activities so that it can be treated like a single project, the software will report resource usage conflicts; that is, cases in which the scheduled utilization of a resource is greater than the supply of that resource.

9.7 GOLDRATT'S CRITICAL CHAIN*

In the previous section, we showed that the problem of constrained resource scheduling of multiple projects could be reduced to the problem of scheduling activities using scarce resources in the case of a single project. However, the best-known attack on the resource-constrained scheduling problem is Goldratt's *Critical Chain* (1997). The celebrated author of *The Goal* (Goldratt et al., 1992) applies his Theory of Constraints to the constrained resource scheduling problem. The original focus of the Theory of Constraints to project management was the single project case, but it, too, is just as applicable to multiple projects.

---

*This section, parts of which were contributed by our colleague Scott Shafer, may be skipped without loss of continuity.

If we consider all the comments we have heard about the problems PMs have to deal with on a daily basis, many are brought up over and over again. Further, it is interesting to note that these statements are made by PMs working in construction, manufacturing, software development, R&D, marketing, communications, maintenance, . . . and the list of industries could easily be extended. For example, the following issues are raised with high frequency, and this short list is only indicative, not nearly exhaustive.

- Senior management changes the project's scope without consultation, without warning, and without changing the budget or schedule.
- Project due dates are set with little regard given to availability of resources.
- There is no possible way of accomplishing a project without exceeding the given budget.
- Project work loads and due dates are set by the sales group, not by the nature of the projects and the level of resources needed.
- Project due dates are set unrealistically short as an "incentive" for people to work harder and faster.

It appears that these, and many other, problems are generic. They are independent of the area of application. Note that all of these issues concern trading off time, cost, and scope. To deal with the strong optimistic bias in many project schedules, let us consider just a few of the things that tend to create it.

1. ***Thoughtless optimism***   Some PMs, apparently with a strong need to deny that lateness could be their fault, deal with every problem faced by their projects as strict exceptions, acts of chance that cannot be forecast and hence need not be the subject of planning. These individuals simply ignore risk management.

2. ***Capacity should be set to equal demand***   Some senior managers refuse to recognize that projects are not assembly lines and are not subject to standard operations management line of balance methods. Refer back to Section 9-4, subsection "Resource Loading/Leveling and Uncertainty," for proof of the need for capacity to exceed demand for projects.

3. ***The "Student Syndrome"***   This phrase is Goldratt's term for his view that students always want more time to complete a project. Given more time, they delay starting the project until the last possible moment. One of the common occurrences is for activities with high slack to be delayed and ignored until the slack is gone. If *any* problems arise with such activities, they will be late.

4. ***Multitasking to reduce idle time***   Consider a situation where there are two projects, A and B, each with three sequential activities and with you as the only resource required by both projects. Each activity requires 10 days. In Figure 9-16 see two Gantt charts for sequencing the activities in the two projects. In the first, switch from project A (dark) to project B (light) for each of the three activities, that is, carry out Activity 1 for project A, then Activity 1 for project B, then Activity 2 for A, and so forth. In the second sequence, complete project A before starting project B. In both cases, the total time required will be 60 days. In the second, note that project A is completed after 30 days and B after 60 days. In the first chart, however, Project A will be finished after 50 days and B after 60 days. While the total time required is the same, project A has been delayed for 20 days by the multitasking. Further, this ignores the fact that switching back and forth between tasks is neither a particularly efficient nor effective way to complete two different jobs.

5. ***Complexity of networks makes no difference***   Consider two different projects as seen in Figure 9-17. Assume that each activity requires 10 days and is known with certainty.

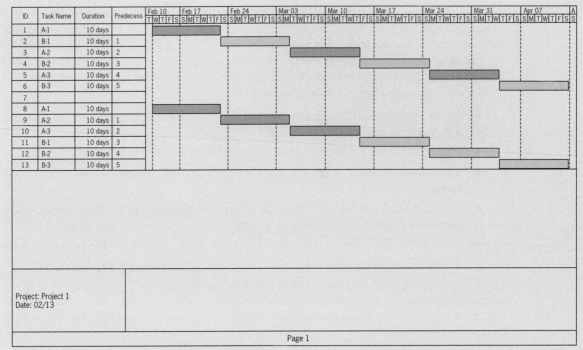

Figure 9-16   Effect of multitasking on project completion given fixed activity times.

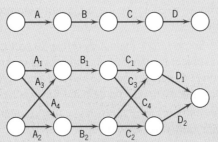

Figure 9-17   Two levels of 40-day network complexity.

Clearly, both projects are completed in 40 days though one is considerably more complex than the other. But let's get a bit more real. Assume that each activity is stochastic, with normally distributed times. The mean time is 10 days, and the standard deviation is 3 days. If we simulate the projects 500 times, we get the results shown in Tables 9-4 and 9-5. Table 9-4, covering the simulation of the simple network, shows (as we expected) a mean project completion time of about 40 days. Table 9-5 covers the simulation of the complex network, and its mean completion time is about 46 days. Complexity, uncertainty, and merging paths all join to make trouble.

6. ***People need a reason to work hard***   Senior managers of our acquaintance have been known to argue that project workers—and they include project managers in that category—"always" have enough slack time in their activity duration estimates to make sure that they can complete the activities on time and "without too much sweat." Therefore, it makes some managerial sense to cut back on the time allowances until they can serve as an incentive to the project team. It has, however, long been known that for people with a high need for achievement, the maximum level of motivation is associated with only moderate, not high, levels of risk of failure.

Table 9-4 Project Simulation Statistics for Simple Network #1

Forecast: Completion Time Network #1	
Edit Preferences View Run Help	
Cell U3	**Statistics**

Statistic	Value
Trials	500
Mean	39.97
Median	40.23
Mode	—
Standard Deviation	5.85
Variance	34.18
Skewness	0.09
Kurtosis	2.86
Coeff. of Variability	0.15
Range Minimum	24.32
Range Maximum	56.97
Range Width	32.65
Mean Std. Error	0.26

Table 9-5 Project Simulation Statistics for Complex Network #2

Forecast: Completion Time Network #2	
Edit Preferences View Run Help	
Cell V3	**Statistics**

Statistic	Value
Trials	500
Mean	46.31
Median	46.25
Mode	—
Standard Deviation	4.53
Variance	20.51
Skewness	0.05
Kurtosis	2.78
Coeff. of Variability	0.10
Range Minimum	34.83
Range Maximum	59.02
Range Width	24.18
Mean Std. Error	0.20

7. *Game playing*   This is possibly the most common cause of late projects. It is certainly a major cause of frustration for anyone involved in a project. Senior managers, firm in the belief that project workers add extra time and resources to activity time and budget estimates in order to insure a safe and peaceful life on their portion of a project, routinely cut schedules and budgets. Project workers, suspecting that senior management will cut schedules and budgets without regard to any logic or reason, increase their schedules and budgets as much as they guess will be allowed. Each assumes that the other is not to be trusted. The outcome is simple. Rather than practice careful risk management, each blames the other for any lateness or budget overage. As we noted in the "Aside" in Chapter 8, unbiased honesty in estimates on the part of both worker and manager is mandatory for any reasonable chance of on-schedule performance of projects.

Do Early Finishes and Late Finishes Cancel Out? So What?

One of the tacit assumptions of probabilistic networks is that early and late activity completions cancel out. This assumption might be sensible were it not for the matters listed in the previous subsection. Assume two activities, A and B. A is a predecessor of B. If activity A is late, then activity B will start late by whatever amount of lateness is bequeathed to it by A. Similarly, if in spite of all the forces tending to thwart such things, activity A finishes early, B will start early. The assumption, which is also a tacit assumption of both the analytical and simulation methods of finding a path's duration, is generally true for the first case, when A is late. But for the case when A is early, *the assumption is rarely true*. Unfortunately, a finish by A in less than its expected duration almost never translates to a start by B before its expected start time.

With a few exceptions, the fact that early finishes do not become early starts is ignored by most people involved with projects. Goldratt writes about the phenomenon (1997, Chapter 13 and elsewhere), and a few others have also briefly discussed the matter. There is a mild debate as to the reason for this deplorable condition. Goldratt feels that project workers will avoid admitting that an activity has been completed early.

Others point out that when the activity schedule is set, it is presumed that the activity will start immediately after the most likely finish date of its (latest) predecessor. The reason is simple—its resources will not be available until that date. There is also a logical explanation of why the start of a successor is usually delayed until its predetermined expected start time. Some say that project workers will not report finishes before the most likely duration. The logic of this position depends on an inherent distrust between project workers and senior management. If an early finish is reported, workers assume that the shorter-than-normal activity duration will be the expectation for similar activities in the future. Senior managers, the argument proceeds, do not really understand the uncertainty faced by project workers. Senior management will assume that if an activity can be finished early once, it can be finished early again, or that they were correct in their assumption that workers "pad" their time and resource estimates. The chance event of an early finish is, thus, used to substantiate a shortened duration estimate in the future.

There is also a logical explanation of why a successor activity does not receive resources until its predetermined expected start, which is, by definition, equal to the expected finish of the latest predecessor activity. A stochastic network has little in common with an assembly line; nonetheless, we find some managers attempting to delay the deployment of resources to a project as long as possible. If we agree to start a project as soon as its predecessors are completed, we must contemplate having the resources available and waiting well before the activity's expected start. Idle resources, however, are not acceptable to managers trained in a just-in-time view of the world. Assembly lines are reasonably predictable; projects are not.

The Critical Chain

In addition to the problems of multitasking, thoughtless optimism, the student syndrome, and the other things we have mentioned, Goldratt adds several more common practices (e.g., "safety time") and argues that all of these lead to a vicious cycle that makes projects substantially late. Using the logic of his Theory of Constraints, Goldratt recommends that new projects should be scheduled based on the availability of scarce resources. He then suggests that "time buffers" be added in the schedules of resources that feed bottleneck (scarce) resources, and the bottleneck resources themselves.

The proper scheduling helps the problems caused by poor multitasking, but does not lead to more realistic project duration estimates. The buffers act as safety time, but here it is added to a path or two rather than to every activity or to the project as a whole. It can be shown by elementary statistics that the safety time needed to protect a path, called *path buffers*, is considerably less than the sum of the safety times needed to protect each activity in the path. Similarly, Goldratt suggests a *project buffer*, but also suggests that activity durations be decreased to the point where the workers have no desire to act out the student syndrome. In fact, he recommends that task durations should have a high probability of being insufficient. (In this, we disagree with Goldratt, because it raises the probability of lateness and violates our plea for strict honesty unless the high probability is made public, at which point it would usually be disregarded.)

Finally, Goldratt argues that two activities scheduled to be carried out in parallel and using the same scarce resource are not independent as the traditional theory would assume.* If the supply of the scarce resource is not sufficient to allow both activities to be carried out simultaneously, then whichever of the two is given priority immediately lengthens the other activity's path but not its actual duration.

Assume that two parallel paths compose a project, A_1-B and A_2-C. A_1 and A_2 require the same scarce resource. **B** and **C** use different resources. A_1 requires 7 days, A_2 requires 5 days, **B** needs 10 days, and C needs 6 days and thus, the path A_1-**B** is 17 days and the path A_2-**C** is 11 days. If there is not enough of the scarce resource to fund both **A** activities, they must be done sequentially. If A_1 is done first, A_2 cannot start until A_1 is complete, thereby adding 7 days to the A_2-**C** path, making it 18 days long and increasing the project finish date by 1 day. If A_2 is done first, 5 days will be added to the A_1-**C** path, making it 22 days, a 5-day increase over its original 17-day duration. If this problem seems familiar, it is. This is precisely the issue we dealt with when we examined the process of resource leveling in Section 9-4.

Using Goldratt's meaning of the word "dependent," the activities of a project can be ordered into paths based on their resource dependencies as well as on their technological precedence requirements. The longest of these paths of sequentially time-dependent activities is known as the "critical chain." A project, therefore, is composed of its critical chain and of noncritical chains that feed into it—see Figure 9-18. There are two sources of delay for the project. One

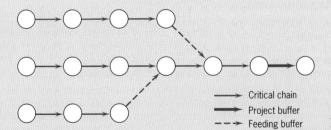

Critical chain
Project buffer
Feeding buffer

Figure 9-18 Project and feeder buffers.

---

*The word "dependent" has two different meanings in this context. Two parallel activities using the same scarce resource depend on one another in the sense that the ability to *start* one depends on the existence of priorities indicating which of the two competing activities gets first use of the scarce resource. At the same time, they may be statistically independent, which means that the *duration* of one activity does not depend on the duration of the other.

comes from a delay of one or more activities in the critical chain. The second results from a delay in one or more of the activities on a noncritical or "feeder" chain because such delays could delay activities on the critical chain. A project buffer protects the critical chain, and feeding buffers protect the feeder paths. Resources used by activities on the critical chain are given priority so that they are available when required.

SUMMARY

In this chapter, we looked at the problem of allocating physical resources, both among the multiple activities of a project and among multiple projects. The continuous problem to the PM is finding the best trade-offs among resources, particularly time. We considered resource loading, allocation, and leveling, and presented methods and concepts to aid in all these tasks.

Specific points made in the chapter were these:

- The critical path method (CPM) is a network constructed in the same manner as PERT, but it also considers the possibility of adding resources to tasks (crashing) to shorten their duration, thereby expediting the project. This can also be done with PERT.

- The resource allocation problem is concerned with determining the best trade-offs between available resources, including time, throughout the duration of a project.

- Resource loading is the process of calculating the total load from project tasks on each resource for each time period of the project's duration.

- Resource leveling is concerned with evening out the demand for various resources required in a project by shifting tasks within their slack allowances. The aid of a computer is mandatory for realistic projects.

- There are two basic approaches to addressing the constrained resources allocation problem:

  — *Heuristic methods* are realistic approaches that may identify feasible solutions to the problem.

They essentially use simple priority rules, such as shortest task first, to determine which task should receive resources and which task must wait.

  — *Optimizing methods*, such as linear programming, find the best allocation of resources to tasks but are limited in the size of problems they can efficiently solve.

- For multiproject scheduling, three important measures of effectiveness are schedule slippage, resource utilization, and level of in-process inventory.

- When a new project is added to a multiproject system, the amount of slippage is directly related to the average resource load.

- Mathematical programming models for multi-project scheduling aim either to minimize total throughput time for all projects, minimize the completion time for all projects, or minimize the total lateness (or lateness penalty) for all projects. These models are limited to small problems.

There are a number of heuristic methods, such as the resource scheduling method, available for the multiproject scheduling problem.

In the next chapter, we move to the ongoing implementation of the project and consider the project information systems used for monitoring progress, costs, scope, and so on. The chapter also describes some available computer packages for this function.

GLOSSARY

Cost/Time Slope The ratio of the increased cost for expediting to the decreased amount of time for the activity.

Followers The tasks that logically follow a particular task in time.

Heuristic A formal process for solving a problem, like a rule of thumb, that results in an acceptable solution.

Mathematical Programming A general term for certain mathematical approaches to solving constrained optimization problems, including linear programming, integer programming, and so on.

Predecessors The tasks that logically precede a particular task in time.

Priority Rules Formal methods, such as ratios, that rank items to determine which one should be next.

Resource Leveling Approaches to even out the peaks and valleys of resource requirements so that a fixed amount of resources can be employed over time.

Resource Loading The amount of resources of each kind that are to be devoted to a specific activity in a certain time period.

Successors See followers.

Tree Search The evaluation of a number of alternatives that logically branch from each other like a tree with limbs.

QUESTIONS

Material Review Questions

1. Identify several resources that may need to be considered when scheduling projects.

2. What is resource loading? How does it differ from resource leveling?

3. What is an activity slope and what does it indicate?

4. Name four priority rules. What priority rule is best overall? How would a firm decide which priority rule to use?

Class Discussion Questions

9. Why are large fluctuations in the demands for particular resources undesirable? What are the costs of resource leveling? How would a PM determine the "best" amount of leveling?

10. When might a firm choose to crash a project? What factors must be considered in making this decision?

11. Why is the impact of scheduling and resource allocation more significant in multiproject organizations?

12. How much should a manager know about a scheduling or resource allocation computer program to be able to use the output intelligently?

13. With the significantly increased power of today's computers, do you think the mathematical programming optimization approaches will become more popular?

14. What are some of the limitations of AON networks?

15. Why is leveling of resources needed?

16. What are some implications of resource allocation when an organization is involved in several projects at once?

17. What are some of the indirect costs of crashing?

18. How might AON be used for strategic planning purposes?

5. Name three efficiency criteria that might be considered when choosing a multiproject scheduling system.

6. What are two methods for addressing the constrained resources allocation problem?

7. How does the task life cycle type affect our attempts to level the resource loads?

8. Describe the concept "critical chain" in your own words.

19. List all the various ways that resources greatly increase scheduling complexity.

20. Goldratt suggests setting task durations so short there is a high probability they will not be done on time. What is his thinking here? Do you agree with him?

Expediting Los Angeles Freeway Repairs after the Earthquake

21. Of the six constraints, which were cost trade-offs and which were scope trade-offs?

22. In what way were the performance trade-offs made? That is, how did they affect performance?

23. What kinds of resource allocation approaches discussed in the chapter were used in this situation?

Architectural Associates, Inc.

24. Was the problem here one of those described in Critical Chain? Which one, if so?

25. Describe how the change effectively solved the problem.

Thirty Days to Rescue

26. What "lessons learned" could you suggest for GHP from this project for similar, future projects?

27. Does this project sound like a "mission impossible?" In what regards?

28. What would you suggest to GHP regarding overcoming the short time span for this kind of project?

Benefit/Cost Analysis Saves Chicago's Deep Tunnel Project

29. Have you any comment about the duration of this project?

30. How do you think Chicago improved the benefit-cost ratio of the project?

Benefits of Resource Constraining at Pennsylvania Electric

31. Why would the planning group use 40% more mechanics than necessary?

32. What does the availability in the chart represent? Why do the monthly values move up and down?

33. What does the scheduled amount represent? Why does it drop off toward the end? How can it exceed the availability?

PROBLEMS

1. Given the following network, determine the first activity to be crashed by the following priority rules:
   (a) Shortest task first
   (b) Minimum slack first
   (c) Most critical followers
   (d) Most successors

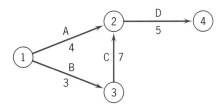

2. Using the network above and the additional information below, find:
   (a) The crash cost per day
   (b) Which activities should be crashed to meet a project deadline of 13 days at minimum cost. Assume partial crashing is allowed.

Activity	Crash Time (days)	Crashed Cost (total)	Normal Time (days)	Normal Cost
A	3	$500	4	$300
B	1	325	3	250
C	4	550	7	400
D	3	250	5	150

3. Consider the following network for conducting a two-week (10 working days) computer training class:

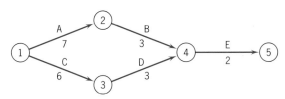

   (a) Construct a schedule showing:
       ESs for all activities
       LSs for all activities
       Slacks for all activities
       Critical path
   (b) Given the following:

Activity	Crash Time (days)	Crashed Cost (total)	Normal Time (days)	Normal Cost
A: Obtain instructor	4	$800	7	$500
B: Locate a room	2	350	3	200
C: Check costs	4	900	6	500
D: Room open?	1	500	3	200
E: Schedule class	1	550	2	300
		$3100		

   1. Find the crash cost per day.
   2. Which activities should be crashed to meet a project deadline of 10 days with a minimum cost? Assume partial crashing.
   3. Find the new cost.
   4. Is partial crashing an appropriate assumption in this kind of project?

4. Given the following highway rerouting project,

Activity	Immediate Predecessor	Activity Time (months)
A: Schedule crew	—	4
B: Schedule equipment	—	6
C: Plan new route	A	2
D: Costs meet budget?	B	6
E: Inform public	C, B	3
F: Put out signs	C, B	3
G: Begin rerouting	D, E	5

   (a) Draw the network.
   (b) Find the ESs, LSs, and slacks.
   (c) Find the critical path.
   (d) If the project has a 1 1/2-year deadline for reopening, should we consider crashing some activities? Explain.

5. Given the following network for a stock repurchase project with outside consulting resource demands, construct a modified Gantt AOA chart with resources and a resource load diagram. Suggest how to level the outside consulting load if you can split operations.

$$\text{code:} \frac{\text{activity, time}}{\text{resource units}}$$

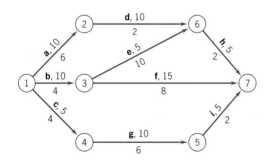

6. Consider the following activity information and the constraint that the project must be completed in 16 weeks.

Activity	Prec. Evt.	Suc. Evt.	TE (weeks)	Prec. Activ.
a	1	2	3	none
b	1	3	6	none
c	1	4	8	none
d	2	5	7	a
e	3	5	5	b
f	4	5	10	c
g	4	6	4	c
h	5	7	5	d,e,f
i	6	7	6	g

In addition, activities **c, f, h**, and **i** may be crashed as follows. Assume partial crashing.

Activity	Crash Time (weeks)	Additional Cost per Week
c	7	$40
f	6	20
h	2	10
i	3	30

Find the best schedule and its cost.

7. The following data were obtained from a study of the times required to conduct a consumer test panel study:

Activity	Crash Schedule Time	Crash Schedule Cost	Normal Schedule Time	Normal Schedule Cost
1–2: City center	3	$6	5	$4
1–3: City northeast	1	5	5	3
2–4: City south	5	7	10	4
3–4: City southeast	2	6	7	4
2–6: City west	2	5	6	3
4–6: County east	5	9	11	6
4–5: County north	4	6	6	3
6–7: County south	1	4	5	2
5–7: County west	1	5	4	2

Note: Costs are given in thousands of dollars, time in weeks.
   (a) Find the all-normal schedule and cost.
   (b) Find the all-crash schedule and cost.
   (c) Find the total cost required to expedite all activities from all-normal (case a) to all-crash (case b).
   (d) Find the *least-cost* plan for the all-crash time schedule. Start from the all-crash problem (b). Assume partial crashing.

8. Given the data in Problem 7, determine the first activities to be crashed by the following priority rules:
   (a) Shortest task first.
   (b) Most resources first (use normal cost as the basis).
   (c) Minimum slack first.
   (d) Most critical followers.
   (e) Most successors.

9. Consider the project network below. Suppose the duration of both activities **A** and **D** can be reduced to one day, at a cost of $15 per day of reduction. Also, activities **E, G,** and **H** can be reduced in duration by one day at a cost of $25 per day of reduction. What is the least-cost approach to crash the project two days? What is the shortest "crashed" duration, the new critical path, and the cost of crashing?

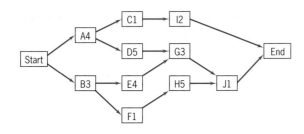

10. Given a network for an HR training project with normal times and crash times (in parentheses), find the cost-duration history. Assume indirect costs for facilities and equipment are $100 per day. The data are:

Activity	Time Reduction, Direct Cost per Day
1–2: Obtain room	$30 first, $50 second
2–3: Select trainer	$80
3–4: Invite personnel	$25 first, $60 second
2–4: Check budget	$30 first, $70 second, $90 third

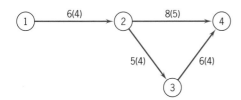

11. Reconsider Problem 2, assuming a fixed overhead cost of $30 per day but no project deadline. What is the least-cost crash program? What if the overhead cost was $40? What if it was $60?

12. The network for shooting a TV commercial as shown in the table has a fixed cost of $90 per day, but money can be saved by shortening the project duration. Find the least-cost schedule.

Activity	Normal Time	Crash Time	Cost Increase (1st, 2nd, 3rd day)
1–2: Contract personnel	7	4	$30, 50, 70
2–3: Obtain stage props	9	6	40, 45, 65
1–3: Rent equipment	12	10	60, 60
2–4: Contract studio	11	9	35, 60
3–4: Set time and date	3	3	—

13. Given the following project to landscape a new building site,

Activity	Immediate Predecessor	Activity Duration (days)	Resource Used
A: Get plants	—	2	X, Y
B: Get flowers	A	2	X
C: Obtain soil	A	3	X
D: Obtain fertilizer	B, C	4	X, Y
E: Select labor	D	3	W, X
F: Set date	D	1	W, X, Y
G: Begin	E, F	2	X, Y

(a) Draw a Gantt chart using MSP.
(b) Find the critical path and project duration in days.
(c) Given that each resource is assigned 100% to each task, identify the resource constraints.
(d) Level the resources and determine the new project duration and critical path.
(e) Identify what alternative solutions can be used to shorten the project duration and not over-allocate the resources.

14. Assume that a resource used by activities **e**, **f**, **g**, and **h** in the figure below is scarce. To which activity would you assign the resource, based on the following rules?

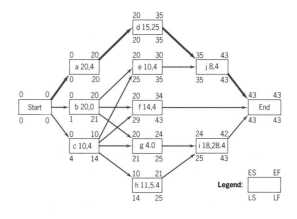

a. Minimum slack.
b. Most successors.
c. Most critical followers.
d. Shortest task first.
e. As late as possible.

15. Given the following project (all times are in days):

Activity	Pre-decessor	Normal Time	Normal Cost	Crash Time	Crash Cost
a	—	5	$50	3	$150
b	—	4	40	2	200
c	b	7	70	6	160
d	a, c	2	20	1	50
e	a, c	3	30	—	—
f	b	8	80	5	290
g	d	5	50	4	100
h	e, f	6	60	3	180

(a) Draw the network and find the critical path, time, and cost for an all-normal level of project activity.
(b) Calculate the crash cost-per-day (all activities may be partially crashed).
(c) Find the optimal way of getting an 18-day delivery time. What is the project cost?
(d) Find the optimal way of getting a 16-day delivery time. What is the project cost?
(e) Calculate the shortest delivery time for the project. What is the cost?

 ## INCIDENTS FOR DISCUSSION

Bryce Power Tool Company

Kevin Ertle is the director of information technology (IT) for the Bryce Power Tool Company. A decision was made recently to upgrade Bryce's legacy systems to a comprehensive ERP system. The president of Bryce has indicated that he expects the modernization program to result in a significant improvement in new product time to market. Ertle is concerned with the possibility that his department will not have adequate resources to support the upgrade. Kevin believes he has enough staff to handle the aggregate IT requirements, but he is not too sure he will be able to supply the proper IT personnel at the times and quantities requested by the company's project managers.

To complicate matters further, the upgrade will be under the control of four different business unit project managers. Each major market segment has been recognized as a separate business unit with the authority to select IT subsystems for their segment based on a schedule that makes sense for it. Kevin knows a little bit about resource allocation techniques. He remembers that one of the most effective allocation techniques is to work first on the activity with the minimum slack, so he has instructed his staff to approach any tasks they are assigned as members of a project team on that basis.

Questions: Is this technique a reasonable way to schedule the IT resources of Bryce? Why or why not? What complication is added by making this four separate projects?

Critical Care Hospital

Critical Care Hospital will be purchasing a CATSCAN (computerized axial tomography scanner) in the next six months. The CATSCAN equipment will be installed in the radiology department and will require a significant renovation for the area. The scanner will arrive in about five months, but the construction project cannot be started until the unit is set in place. This will result in a project length of approximately 12 months. The hospital estimates the equipment will generate an income of $25,000 per month and is therefore in a hurry to complete the project. The project manager feels she may be able to cut the time on some aspects of the project, but at an increased cost. She has decided, in an effort to make the best decision, to use a resource allocation version of CPM.

Questions: What information must the project manager gather to use this method properly? How should she use this version of CPM to reduce the project time?

 ## CONTINUING INTEGRATIVE CLASS PROJECT

Although the budget didn't allow for additional resources to speed up activities that fell behind schedule, you have some slack paths in the project where you can borrow people to help with problem activities. Based on the tasks that constitute the critical path, determine where you would borrow resources from if each task were to fall behind schedule, assuming other tasks stayed on schedule. (That is, you can't borrow people from a task that is at the beginning of the project to help with a critical path task that is at the end of the project.)

BIBLIOGRAPHY

Adler, P. S., A. Mandelbaum, V. Nguyen, and E. Schwerer. "Getting the Most Out of Your Product Development Process." *Harvard Business Review*, March–April 1996.

Corwin, B. D. "Multiple R and D Project Scheduling with Limited Resources." *Technical Memorandum No. 122*, Department of Operations Research, Cleveland: Case Western Reserve University, 1968.

Davis, E. W., and J. H. Patterson. "A Comparison of Heuristic and Optimum Solutions in Resource-Constrained Project Scheduling." *Management Science*, April 1975.

Gilyutin, I. "Using Project Management in a Nonlinear Environment." *Project Management Journal*, December 1993.

Goldratt, E. M., and J. Cox. *The Goal*. Great Barrington, MA: North River, 1992.

Goldratt, E. M. *Critical Chain*. Great Barrington, MA: North River, 1997.

Harrison, F. L. *Advanced Project Management*. Hants, Great Britain: Gower, 1983.

Ibbs, C. W., S. A. Lee, and M. I. Li. "Fast-Tracking's Impact on Project Change." *Project Management Journal*, December 1998.

Kurtulus, I., and E. W. Davis. "Multi-Project Scheduling: Categorization of Heuristic Rules Performance." *Management Science*, February 1982.

Kurtulus, I., and S. C. Narula. "Multi-Project Scheduling: Analysis of Project Performance." *IEEE Transactions on Engineering Management*, March 1985.

Mantel, S. J., Jr., J. R. Meredith, S. M. Shafer, and M. M. Sutton. *Project Management in Practice, 4th ed.* Hoboken, NJ: Wiley, 2011.

McCarthy, J. *Dynamics of Software Development*. Redmond, WA: Microsoft Press, 1995.

Nicholas, J. M. *Managing Business & Engineering Projects*. Englewood Cliffs, NJ: Prentice Hall, 1990.

Piney, C. "Critical Path or Critical Chain: Combining the Best of Both." *PM Network*, December 2000.

Raz, T., R. Barnes, and D. Dvir. "A Critical Look at Critical Chain Project Management." *Project Management Journal*, December 2003.

Trietsch, D. "Why a Critical Path by Any Other Name Would Smell as Sweet." *Project Management Journal*, March 2005.

Weist, J. D. "A Heuristic Model for Scheduling Large Projects with Limited Resources." *Management Science*, February 1967.

Wheatley, M. "Future Perfect." *PM Network*, April 2004.

The following case describes the evolution of a new product and the project devised to take it to market. As well as discussing the issues of developing a work breakdown structure, network diagram, schedule, and resource loading diagrams for each of the involved departments, the case also brings up the issues of time–cost trade-offs, cash flows, and resource leveling.

C A S E

D. U. SINGER HOSPITAL PRODUCTS CORP.
Herbert F. Spirer

D. U. Singer Hospital Products Corp. has done sufficient new product development at the research and development level to estimate a high likelihood of technical success for a product of assured commercial success: A long-term antiseptic. Management has instructed Singer's Antiseptic Division to make a market entry at

the earliest possible time; they have requested a complete plan up to the startup of production. Marketing and other plans following startup of production are to be prepared separately after this plan has been completed.

Project responsibility is assigned to the division's Research and Development Group; Mike Richards, the project scientist who developed the product, is assigned responsibility for project management. Assistance will be required from other parts of the company: Packaging Task Force, R & D Group; Corporate Engineering; Corporate Purchasing; Hospital Products Manufacturing Group; Packaged Products Manufacturing Group.

Mike was concerned about the scope of the project. He knew from his own experience that a final formula had yet to be developed, although such development was really a "routine" function. The remaining questions had to do with color, odor, and consistency additives rather than any performance-related modification. Fortunately, the major regulatory issues had been resolved and he believed that submission of regulatory documentation would be followed by rapid approval as they already had a letter of approval contingent on final documentation.

But there were also issues in packaging that had to be resolved; development of the packaging design was one of his primary concerns at this time. Ultimately, there will have to be manufacturing procedures in accordance with corporate policies and standards: capital equipment selection and procurement, installation of this equipment and startup.

Mike was concerned about defining the project unambiguously. To that end, he obtained an interview with S. L. Mander, the group vice-president.

When he asked Mander where his responsibility should end, the executive turned the question back to him. Mike had been prepared for this and said that he would like to regard his part of the project as done when the production process could be turned over to manufacturing. They agreed that according to Singer practice, this would be when the manufacturing operation could produce a 95 percent yield of product (fully packaged) at a level of 80 percent of the full production goal of 10 million liters per year.

"But I want you to remember," said Mander, "that you must meet all current FDA, EPA, and OSHA regulations and you must be in compliance with our internal specification—the one I've got is dated September and is RD78/965. And you know that manufacturing now—quite rightly, I feel—insists on full written manufacturing procedures."

After this discussion, Mike felt that he had enough information about this aspect to start to pin down what had to be done to achieve these results. His first step in this effort was to meet with P. H. Docent, the Director of Research.

*Tasks which must be accounted for in a network plan are identified by lower-case alphabetic symbols in parentheses. Refer to Exhibit 1.

"You are naive if you think that you can just start right in finalizing the formula," said Docent. "You must first develop a product rationale (**a**).* This is a formally defined process according to company policy. Marketing expects inputs at this stage, manufacturing expects their voice to be heard, and you will have to have approvals from every unit of the company that is involved; all of this is reviewed by the Executive Committee. You should have no trouble if you do your homework, but expect to spend a good eight weeks to get this done."

"That certainly stretches things out," said Mike. "I expected to take 12 weeks to develop the ingredient formula (**b**) and you know that I can't start to establish product specifications (**c**) until the formula is complete. That's another three weeks."

"Yes, but while you are working on the product specifications you can get going on the regulatory documentation (**d**). Full internal specifications are not required for that work, but you can't start those documents until the formula is complete."

"Yes, and I find it hard to believe that we can push through both preparation of documents and getting approval in three weeks, but Environmental swears it can be done."

"Oh, it can be done in this case because of the preparatory work. Of course, I won't say that this estimate of three weeks is as certain as our other time estimates. All we need is a change of staff at the Agency and we are in trouble. But once you have both the specifications and the approval, you can immediately start on developing the production processing system (**g**)."

"Yes, and how I wish we could get a lead on that, but the designers say that there is too much uncertainty and they won't move until they have both specifications and regulatory documentation and approval. They are offering pretty fast response; six weeks from start to finish for the processing system."

"They are a good crew, Mike. And of course, you know that you don't have to delay on starting the packaging segment of this project. You can start developing the packaging concept (**e**) just as soon as the product rationale has been developed. If my experience is any judge, it will take a full eight weeks; you'll have to work to keep the process from running forever."

"But as soon as that is finished we can start on the design of the package and its materials (**f**), which usually takes about six weeks. Once that is done we can start developing the packaging system (**h**), which shouldn't take longer than eight weeks," concluded Mike. At this point he realized that although Docent would have general knowledge, he needed to talk directly to the Director of Manufacturing.

"The first step, which follows the completion of the development of processing and packaging systems," said the Director of Manufacturing, "is to do a complete study of the facilities and equipment requirements (**i**). You won't be able to get that done in less than four weeks. And that must precede the preparation of the capital equipment list (**j**) which should take about three-quarters as long. Of course, as soon as the development of both the process system and packaging system are completed, you could start on preparing the written manufacturing facilities procedures (**q**)."

"But," said Mike, "Can I really finish the procedures before I have installed the manufacturing facilities (**p**)?"

"No, quite right. What you can do is get the first phase done, but the last three of the 10 weeks it will take to do that will have to wait for the installation of the manufacturing facilities."

"Then this means that I really have two phases for the writing, that which can be completed without the manufacturing facilities installation (**q**), and that which has to wait for them (**q'**)."

"True. Now you realize that the last thing you have to do after completing the procedures and installing the equipment and facilities is to run a pilot test (**r**) which will show that you have reached a satisfactory level?"

"Yes. Since that must include debugging, I've estimated a 6-week period as adequate." The Director of Manufacturing assented. Mike continued, "What I'm not sure of is whether we can run all the installation tasks in parallel."

"You can let the purchase orders run and carry out the procurement of process equipment (**k**), packaging equipment (**l**), and facilities (**m**) as soon as the capital equipment list is complete. The installation of each of these types of equipment and facilities can start as soon as the goods are on hand (**n, o, p**)."

"What do you estimate for the times to do these tasks?" asked Mike. The Director of Manufacturing estimated 18, 8, and 4 weeks for the purchasing phases for each of the subsystems in that order and 4 weeks for each of the installations. "Then I can regard my job as done with the delivery of the procedures and when I show my 95 percent yield," said Mike, and the Director of Manufacturing agreed, but reminded Mike that none of the purchasing cycles could start until the capital equipment list had been prepared and approved (**j**) which he saw as a 3-week task.

The executive committee of D. U. Singer Hospital Products Corporation set a starting date for the project of March 10 and asked Mike to project a completion date with his submission of the plan. The committee's request implied that whatever date Mike came up with was acceptable, but Mike knew that he would be expected to show how to shorten the time to complete the project. However, his task in making the schedule was clear; he had to establish the resource requirements and deal with calendar constraints as best as he could.

To this end, Mike had to get an estimate of resources, which he decided to do by making a list of the activities and asking each group involved what was their level of employee input. The results of this survey are shown in Exhibit 1. For example, activity **a** takes 8 weeks and requires 12 worker-weeks from R&D, or an average of 1.5 workers for the entire 8-week duration of activity **a**.

For the purposes of overall planning, the accounting department told Mike that he could estimate a cost of $600 per week per employee. This would enable him to provide a cash flow forecast along with his plan, which the chief accountant said would be expected, something that Mike had not realized.

Mike knew that it was customary at D. U. Singer to provide the following as parts of a plan to be submitted to the executive committee:

A. Statement of objectives.

B. Work breakdown structure.

C. An activity-on-node network.

D. A determination of the critical path(s) and the duration along the path.

E. An activity list, early-start schedule, slack list, and master schedule. Assume that every activity begins at its early start, regardless of resource constraints.

F. A period labor requirements table for each group and the project as a whole.

G. A cumulative labor requirements table for each group and the project as a whole. Include line graphs to illustrate the cumulative loads.

H. A schedule based on the best leveling of labor requirements that could be achieved without lengthening project duration by more than 14 percent in calendar days.

I. A cash-flow requirements graph for the project, assuming that charges are uniformly distributed throughout the activity.

EXHIBIT 1   Labor Requirements (Worker-weeks)

Activity	Packaging Task Force	R&D Group	Corp. Eng.	H-P Manuf.	Pack. Prod. Manuf.	Maint.	Purchasing	Material & Other Direct Charges
a—prod. rationale	1	12	1	1	2	0	0	$ 0
b—dev. formula	0	16	4	2	0	0	0	500
c—prod. spec.	1	6	3	1	1	0	1	0
d—reg. document	0	12	4	2	0	0	0	0
e—dev. pkg. concept	12	8	4	2	8	0	2	4,000
f—design pkg.	12	2	3	0	3	0	3	2,000
g—dev. proces. sys.	0	18	12	12	0	0	0	0
h—dev. pkg. sys.	24	8	8	0	8	0	2	0
i—study facil./eqpt. req.	0	4	16	2	2	0	0	0
j—capital equip. list	0	1	3	0	0	0	1	0
k—procure proces. eqpt.	0	1	1	1	0	0	7	40,000
l—procure pkg. eqpt.	1	0	1	0	1	0	9	160,000
m—procure facil.	0	0	1	1	1	1	6	30,000
n—install proces. eqpt.	0	2	4	8	0	4	1	4,000
o—install pkg. eqpt.	2	0	4	0	8	4	1	8,000
p—install mfg. facil.	0	0	5	5	5	10	1	6,000
q,q'—written procedures	5	5	5	10	15	10	0	5,000
r—pilot test	3	6	6	6	6	6	0	0

 QUESTIONS

1. Construct the nine elements of the plan identified above.

2. Analyze the plan for potential problems.

3. Analyze the plan for opportunities.

4. Should the executive committee approve the plan? Why or why not?

5. What alternatives might the executive committee suggest for analysis?

P A R T III

PROJECT EXECUTION

Part III of the text now gets into actual *project execution*, as shown in the accompanying figure. Chapter 10 examines the information requirements of a project and the need for monitoring critical activities. Included in this chapter is a description of some common project management information systems (PMIS). There are many such systems available, and several are briefly discussed, but in this book we will use Microsoft Project®, by far the most popular project management software.

Chapter 11 then describes the control process in project management—keeping the project under control and bringing it back into alignment with plans when our monitoring shows that it is deviating. This chapter

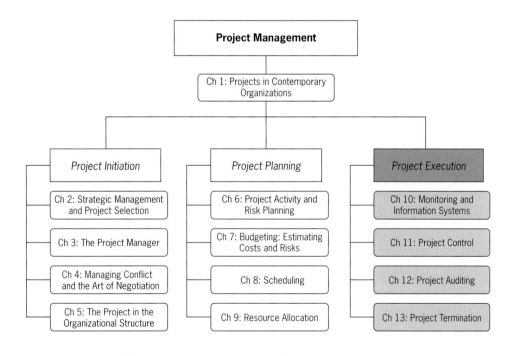

covers standards for comparison and tools to help the manager keep the project in control. Chapter 12 deals with methods for both ongoing evaluations and terminal audits of a project, as well as identifying factors associated with project success and failure. Last, Chapter 13 describes the different forms of project termination, such as outright shutdown, integration into the regular organization, or extension into a new project. Each form presents unique problems for the project manager to solve.

10

Monitoring and Information Systems

In this chapter, perhaps more than in any other, it would be helpful if we could consider everything at once. How is it possible to discuss monitoring without specifying what is to be controlled? On the other hand, how is it possible to specify a control system without understanding what aspects of a project are subject to measurement and how the measurement is to be accomplished? As a matter of fact, one could just as easily argue that evaluation, the primary subject of Chapter 12, should precede both monitoring and control. The placement of these chapters is arbitrary, and readers may feel free to read them in any order. Irrespective of the order in which one considers these subjects, however, their interdependence is clear.

Our fundamental approach to evaluation and control of projects is that these activities are, at base, the opposite sides of project selection and planning. The logic of selection, such as by the Project Portfolio Process, or any of the methods described in Chapter 2, dictates the components to be evaluated, and the details of planning expose the elements to be controlled. The ability to measure is prerequisite to either. Thus, all of the project's objectives as delineated in the project selection process must be examined and measures for each included in the monitoring system. If a weighted factor model is used, the measures can usually be integrated into a single evaluation measure. For a continuously operating project selection system, monitoring the critical project measures as the project proceeds through its life cycle, such as by the Project Management Office as described in Chapter 5, is required so projects can be terminated, if necessary, and new projects initiated. Much more will be said about this in Chapters 12 and 13.

Many more evaluative measures are needed, for example, for the maintenance of a risk management system. Not only must the project performance be monitored, but the environment within which the project exists must also be observed and recorded. *Monitoring* is collecting, recording, and reporting information concerning any and all aspects of project performance that the project manager or others in the organization wish to know. In our discussion it is important to remember that monitoring, as an activity, should be kept distinct from controlling (which uses the data supplied by monitoring to bring actual performance into approximate congruence with planned performance), as well as from evaluation (through which judgments are made about the quality and effectiveness of project performance).

First we expand on the nature of this link between planning and control, including a brief discussion of the various aspects of project performance that need to be monitored. We also examine some of the problems associated with monitoring a project. Finally, we discuss choosing computer software packages that can greatly increase the speed and effectiveness of project monitoring.

This book is addressed to practicing PMs as well as students of project management. Students resist the idea that PMs do not have immediate access to accurate information on every aspect of the project. But PMs know it is not always easy to find out what's going on when working on a project. Records are frequently out of date, incomplete, in error, or "somewhere else" when needed. Throughout the chapter, our primary concern is to ensure that all parties interested in the project have available, *on a timely basis*, the information needed to exercise effective control over the project and the uncertainties that impact on it. The other uses for monitoring (e.g., auditing, learning from past mistakes, or keeping senior management informed), important as they are, must be considered secondary to the control function when constructing the monitoring system.

One final note: In this chapter, we frequently refer to a "project monitor," a "project controller," or even to the "group" or "office" responsible for monitoring. These individuals and groups do in fact exist on most large projects. On a small project, it is likely that the person in charge of monitoring is the same person as the project controller—and the same person as the PM. That is, when we refer to the project monitor and controller, we are referring to *roles* needed in project management, not necessarily to different individuals.

10.1   THE PLANNING-MONITORING-CONTROLLING CYCLE

Throughout this book we have stressed the need to plan, check on progress, compare progress to the plan, and take corrective action if progress does not match the plan. The key things to be planned, monitored, and controlled are time (schedule), cost (budget), and scope (performance). These, after all, encompass the fundamental objectives of the project.

There is no doubt that some organizations do not spend sufficient time and effort on planning and controlling projects. It is far easier to focus on doing, especially because it appears to be more effective to "stop all the talk and get on with the work." We could cite firm after firm that incurred great expense (and major losses) because the planning process was inadequate for the tasks undertaken.

Project Management in Practice
Tracking Scope Creep: A Project Manager Responds

Dear Editor:

The two-part *Scope Creep* article in the Winter and Spring issues of *Today's Engineer* presented an interesting case study. The engineering-only solution, however, misses the bigger issue—lack of a formal project management process. It is unfortunate that the need for formal project management is omitted from the article. A formal project management process is the cornerstone of on-time and on-schedule projects. Such a process includes:

- A formal project plan development process
- A tracking system capable of providing variance analysis data
- Managing project scope, schedule, and resource changes throughout the project life cycle.

This case study depicts an all-too-familiar scenario:

1. An engineer is selected as project manager—usually with no formal project management training.

2. The project team is composed of primarily engineers—marketing and other functional organizations are viewed as project outsiders, rather than team members, and do not participate in the planning process.

3. Project objectives and deliverables are poorly defined—usually by engineering—including only engineering deliverables.

4. A comprehensive work breakdown structure, task completion criteria, and network diagram are nonexistent—progress measurement is therefore somewhat arbitrary and difficult to ascertain.

5. Task duration estimates are probably determined by someone other than the task owner—making estimates invalid.

6. The project schedule is pasted together to look good and match target dates—missing the opportunity to use critical path method (CPM) to develop a credible schedule.

7. Resource requirements, including people and budget, are guesses—usually without the benefit of using a comprehensive CPM-developed preliminary schedule.

8. A risk management plan does not exist—most project risks are treated as surprises.

9. The project plan is not validated and baselined by the project sponsor—missing the opportunity to obtain team and sponsor commitment prior to implementation.

10. A formal project tracking and change management system does not exist—impossible to track a project without a plan to measure progress against and to manage changes.

Project management, like engineering, is a discipline that must be learned. Project management is not for everyone. It requires a different skill set than, say, engineering or marketing.

Source: J. Sivak, "Scope Creep: A Project Manager Responds," ©1998 IEEE. Reprinted with permission from *Today's Engineer*, Vol. 1, No. 3 (Summer), p. 8, 1998.

- A major construction project ran over budget by 63 percent and over schedule by 48 percent because the PM decided that, since "he had managed similar projects several times before, he knew what to do without going into all that detail that no one looks at anyway."

- A large industrial equipment supplier "took a bath" on a project designed to develop a new area of business because they applied the same planning and control procedures to the new area that they had used (successfully) on previous, smaller, less complex jobs.

- A computer store won a competitive bid to supply a computer, five terminals, and associated software to the Kansas City office of a national firm. Admittedly insufficient planning made the installation significantly late. Performance of the software was not close to specified levels. This botched job prevented the firm from being invited to bid on more than 20 similar installations planned by the client.

The planning (budgeting and scheduling) methods we propose "put the hassles up front." They require a significantly greater investment of time and energy early in the life of the project, but they significantly reduce the extent and cost of poor performance and time/cost overruns. Note that this is no guarantee of a trouble-free project, merely a decline in the risk of failure.

It is useful to perceive the control process as a *closed-loop* system, with revised plans and schedules (if warranted) following corrective actions. We delay a detailed discussion on control until the next chapter, but the planning-monitoring-controlling cycle is continuously in process until the project is completed. The information flows for such a cycle are illustrated in Figure 10-1. Note the direction of the flows, information flowing from the bottom toward the top and authority flowing from the top down.

It is also useful to construct this process as an internal part of the organizational structure of the project, not something external to and imposed on it or, worse, in conflict with it. Finally, experience tells us that it is also desirable, though not mandatory, that the planning-monitoring-controlling cycle be the normal way of life in the parent organization. What is good for the project is equally good for the parent firm. In any case, unless the PM has a smoothly operating monitoring/control system, it will be difficult to manage the project effectively. In Chapters 12 and 13, we will discuss research indicating that planning and control are clearly associated with project success.

Designing the Monitoring System

The first step in setting up any monitoring system is to identify the key factors to be controlled. Clearly, the PM wants to monitor scope, cost, and time but must define precisely which specific characteristics of scope, cost, and time should be controlled and then establish exact boundaries within which control should be maintained. There may also be other factors of importance worth noting, at least at milestones or review points in the life of the project. For example, the number of labor hours used, the number or extent of process or output changes, the level of customer satisfaction, and similar items may be worthy of note on individual projects.

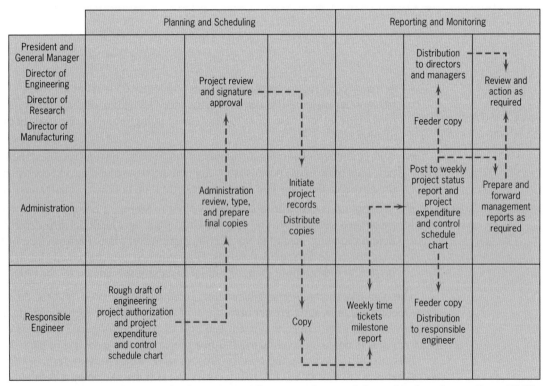

Figure 10-1   Project authorization and expenditure control system information flow. *Source:* Dean (1968).

But the best sources of items to be monitored are the project WBS, change of scope orders, and the risk management plan. The WBS describes what is being done, when, and the planned level of resource usage for each task, work package, and work element in the project. Monitoring the risks found in the risk management plan keeps the PM and project team alert to specific risks and thus lowers the probability of surprises. The monitoring system is a direct connection between planning and control. If it does not collect and report information on some significant element of the plan, control can be faulty or missing. The WBS furnishes the key items that must be measured and reported to the control system, but it is not sufficient. For example, the PM might want to know about changes in the client's attitudes toward the project. Information on the morale of the project team might be useful in preparing for organizational or personnel changes on the project. These two latter items may be quite important, but are not usually reflected in the project's WBS.

Unfortunately, it is common to focus monitoring activities on data that are easily gathered—rather than important—or to concentrate on "objective" measures that are easily defended at the expense of softer, more subjective data that may be more important to control. Above all, monitoring should concentrate primarily on measuring various facets of output rather than intensity of activity. It is crucial to remember that effective PMs are not primarily interested in how hard their project teams work. They are interested in achieving results.

The measurement of project performance usually poses the most difficult data gathering problem. There is a strong tendency to let project inputs serve as surrogate measures for output. If we have spent 50 percent of the budget (or of the scheduled time), we assume we have also completed 50 percent of the project or reached 50 percent of our performance goal. If the item being referenced is a small work unit, it does not make a significant difference if we are wrong. If, however, the reference is to a task or to the entire project, the assumption of input/output proportionality (hereafter, the "proportionality rule") is often seriously misleading.

Further, it is common to specify performance to a level of precision that is both unnecessary and unrealistic, or a level of lenience that is worthless. For example, a communications software project specified that a telephone "information" system had to locate a phone number and respond to the querier in 5 seconds or less. Is 5.1 seconds a failure? Does the specification mean 5 seconds or less every time, or merely that response times should average 5 seconds or less? Is the specification satisfied if the response time is 5 seconds or less 90 percent of the time?

The monitoring systems we describe in this chapter, however, focus mainly on time and cost as measures of performance, not scope (performance). While we are most certainly concerned with keeping the project "on spec," and do consider some of the problems of monitoring output, the subject is not fully developed here because the software designed to monitor projects is not constructed to deal with performance adequately.

Given all this, performance criteria, standards, and data collection procedures must be established for each of the factors to be measured. The criteria and data collection procedures are usually set up for the life of the project. The standards themselves, however, may not be constant over the project's life. They may change as a result of altered capabilities within the parent organization or a technological breakthrough made by the project team; but, perhaps more often than not, standards and criteria change because of factors that are not under the control of the PM. For example, they may be changed by the client. One client who had ordered a special piece of audio equipment altered performance specifications significantly when electronic parts became available that could filter out random noises. This is, of course, a change in scope, a serious matter that we discuss in detail later under the topic of "control."

Perhaps the most common error made when monitoring data is to gather information that is clearly related to project performance but has little or no probability of changing significantly from one collection period to the next. Prior to its breakup, the American Telephone and Telegraph Company used to collect monthly statistics on a very large number of indicators of operating efficiency. The extent of the collection was such that it filled a telephone-book-sized volume known as "Ma Bell's Green Book." For a great many of the indicators, the likelihood of a significant change from one month to the next was extremely small. When asked about the matter, one official remarked that the mere collection of the data kept the operating companies "on their toes." We feel that there are other, more positive and less expensive ways of motivating project personnel. Certainly, "collect everything" is inappropriate as a monitoring policy.

Therefore, the first task is to examine the WBS in order to extract scope, time, and cost goals. These goals should relate in some fashion to each of the different levels of detail; that is, some should relate to the project, some to its tasks, some to the work packages, and so on. Data must be identified that measure achievement against these goals, and mechanisms designed that gather and store such data. If at least some of the data do not relate to the work unit level, no useful action is apt to be taken. In the end, it is the detailed work of the project that must be altered if any aspect of project performance is to be changed. A reading of the fascinating book *The Soul of a New Machine* (Kidder, 1981) reveals the crucial roles that organizational factors, interpersonal relationships, and managerial style play in determining project success. Also of value is a paper by Mekhilef et al. (2005) that develops a method to find and analyze the ways in which individuals introduce dysfunction into decision processes.

How to Collect Data*

Given that we know *what type* of data we want to collect, the next question is *how* to collect this information. At this point in the construction of a monitoring system, it is necessary to define precisely what pieces of information should be gathered and when. In most cases, the PM has options. Questions arise. Should cost data be gathered before or after some specific event? Is it always mandatory to collect time and cost information at exactly the same point in the process? What do we do if a specific item is difficult to collect because the data source (human) fears reporting any information that might contribute to a negative performance evaluation? What do we do about the fact that some use of time is reported as "hours charged" to our project, and we are quite aware that our project has been charged for work done on another project (but for the same customer) that is over budget? Are special forms needed for data collection? Should we set up quality control procedures to ensure the integrity of data transference from its source to the project information system? Such questions merely indicate the broad range of knotty issues that must be handled.

A large proportion of all data collected takes one of the following forms, each of which is suitable for some types of measures.

1. **Frequency counts** A simple tally of the occurrence of an event. This type of measure is often used for "complaints," "number of times a project report is late," "days without an accident," "bugs in a computer program," and similar items. The data are usually easy to collect and are often reported as events per unit time or events as a percent of a standard number. Even with such simple counts, data may be difficult to collect. Items such as "errors" or "complaints" often go unreported by individuals or groups not particularly eager to advertise malperformance.

---

*Shaded sections may be skipped without loss of continuity.

2. ***Raw numbers*** Dates, dollars, hours, physical amounts of resources used, and specifications are usually reported in this way. These numbers are reported in a wide variety of ways, but often as direct comparisons with an expected or standard number. Also, "variances" are commonly reported either as the difference between actual and standard or as the ratio of actual to standard. Differences or ratios can also be plotted as a time series to show changes in system performance. When collecting raw project data, it is important to make sure that all data are collected from sources that operate on the same time intervals and with the same rules for data collection.

3. ***Subjective numeric ratings*** These numbers are subjective estimates, usually of a quality, made by knowledgeable individuals or groups. They can be reported in most of the same ways that objective raw numbers are, but care should be taken to make sure that the numbers are not manipulated in ways only suitable for quantitative measures. (Recall Chapter 2 for comments on measurements.) Ordinal rankings of performance are included in this category.

4. ***Indicators*** When the PM cannot measure some aspect of system performance directly, it may be possible to find an indirect measure or indicator. The speed with which change orders are processed and changes are incorporated into the project is often a good measure of team efficiency. Response to change may also be an indicator of the quality of communications on the project team. Of course this measure may vary with the complexity of the change. Therefore, when using indicators to measure performance, the PM must make sure that the link between the indicator and the desired performance measure is as direct as possible and is not affected by (or is corrected for) other variables.

5. ***Verbal measures*** Measures for such performance characteristics as "quality of team member cooperation," "morale of team members," or "quality of interaction with the client" frequently take the form of verbal characterizations. As long as the set of characterizations is limited and the meanings of the individual terms consistently understood by all, these data serve their purposes reasonably well.

After data collection has been completed, reports on project progress should be generated. These include project status reports, time/cost reports, and variance reports, among others. Causes and effects should be identified and trends noted. Plans, charts, and tables should be updated on a timely basis. Where known, "comparables" should be reported, as should statistical distributions of previous data if available. Both help the PM (and others) to interpret the data being monitored. Figures 10-2 and 10-3 illustrate the use of such data. Figure 10-2 shows the results of a count of "bugs" found during a series of tests run on a new piece of computer software. (Bugs found were fixed prior to subsequent tests.) Figure 10-3 shows the percent of the time a computer program retrieved data within a specified time limit. Each point represents a series of trials.

The PM can fit a statistical function to the data shown in Figure 10-2 and make a rough estimate of the number of tests that will have to be run to find some predetermined number

Figure 10-2   Number of bugs found during test of Datamix program.

Figure 10-3 Percent of specified performance met during repeated trials.

of additional bugs in the program. By fitting a curve (formally or "by eyeball") to the data in Figure 10-3, the PM can estimate the cost and time (the number of additional trials and adjustments) required to get system performance up to the specified level. (Curve and distribution fitting is easily done by use of Crystal Ball®.)

The nature of *timeliness* will be amplified next, but it is important that the PM make sure that the AON/AOA and Gantt charts in the project war room (office) are frequently updated. Monitoring can serve to maintain high morale on the project team as well as to alert team members to problems that will have to be solved. The purpose of the monitoring system is to gather and report data. The purpose of the control system is to act on the data. To aid the *project controller*, it is helpful for the *monitor* to carry out some data analysis. Significant differences from plan should be highlighted or "flagged" so that they cannot be overlooked by the controller. The methods of statistical quality control (see Evans et al., 2011) are very useful for determining what size variances are "significant" and sometimes even help in determining the probable cause(s) of variances. Where causation is known, it should be noted. Where it is not known, an investigation may be in order. (It is also useful to remember that some things are more easily fixed than understood, in which case investigations may not be cost-effective.)

At base, this provides a *management by exception* reporting system for the PM. But management by exception has its flaws as well as its strengths. It is essentially an "after-the-fact" approach to control. Variances occur, are investigated, and only then is action taken. The astute PM is far more interested in preventing problems than curing them. Therefore, the monitoring system should develop data streams that indicate variances yet to come. Obviously, such indicators are apt to be statistical in nature, hinting at the likelihood of a future problem rather than predicting it with certainty.

In creating the monitoring system, some care should be devoted to the issues of honesty and bias. The former is dealt with by setting in place an internal audit. The audit serves the purpose of ensuring that the information gathered is honest. No audit, however, can prevent bias. In general, data are biased by those who report them, advertently or inadvertently.

The issue of creating an atmosphere that fosters honesty on a project is widely ignored, but it is of major importance. The PM can tolerate almost any kind of behavior except dishonesty. Projects are vulnerable to dishonesty, far more vulnerable than the ongoing operations of the parent organization. Standard operations are characterized by considerable knowledge about expected system performance. When the monitoring system reports information that deviates from expectations, it is visible, noteworthy, and tends to get attention. In the case of many projects, expectations are not so well known. Deviations are not recognized for what they are. The PM is often dependent on team members to call attention to problems. To get this cooperation, the PM must make sure that the bearer of bad news is not punished; nor is the admitter-to-error executed. On the other hand, the hider-of-mistakes can be sent to Siberia.

There is some tendency for project monitoring systems to include an analysis directed at the assignment of blame. This practice has doubtful value. While the managerial dictum "rewards and punishments should be closely associated with performance" has the ring of good common sense, it is actually not good advice. Instead of motivating people to better performance, the practice is more apt to result in lower expectations. If achievement of goals is directly measured and directly rewarded, tremendous pressure will be put on people to understate goals and to generate plans that can be met or exceeded with minimal risk and effort.

Project Management in Practice
Drug Counseling Program

A social service agency applied for and received funding for a special project to counsel male drug addicts between 18 and 24 years of age, and to secure full-time employment for each client (or part-time employment for clients who were still in school). To qualify for the program, the addicts must have been arrested for a crime, but not be classed as "repeat offenders." Further, the addict must be living with at least one member of his family who is a parent or guardian. Among other conditions placed on the grant, the agency was asked to develop a measure of effectiveness for the counseling program that was acceptable to the funding agency.

The primary measure of effectiveness adopted by most drug programs was "rate of recidivism." A recidivistic incident is defined as any re-arrest for a drug-related crime, or any behavior that resulted in the individual reentering the social service system after completing the program and being discharged.

While a "re-arrest" is most surely recidivistic, there were several cases in which former clients contacted the agency and asked to be re-admitted to the program. These voluntary re-admissions resulted when a former client either began to use drugs again or was fearful that he would begin again. It seemed to the agency professionals that voluntary re-admissions were successes, not failures.

A new measure of effectiveness was developed to replace "rate of recidivism." It was composed of scores on three different measures, combined with equal weighting.

1. Number of successive weeks of "clean urines."
2. Number of successive months of satisfactory employment (or schooling) experience.
3. Number of successive months of satisfactory behavior at home.

Scores on the second and third measures were based on interviews with employers, teachers, and parent(s).

Source: S. J. Mantel, Jr. Consulting project.

10.2 INFORMATION NEEDS AND REPORTING

Everyone concerned with the project should be appropriately tied into the project reporting system (Back et al., 2001). The monitoring system ought to be constructed so that it addresses every level of management, but reports need not be of the same depth or at the same frequency for each level. Lower-level personnel have a need for detailed information about individual tasks and the factors affecting such tasks. Report frequency is usually high. For the senior management levels, overview reports describe progress in more aggregated terms with less individual task detail unless senior management has a special interest in a specific activity or task. Reports are issued less often. In both cases, the structure of the reports should reflect the WBS, with each managerial level receiving reports that allow the exercise of control at the relevant

Figure 10-4 Reporting and information flows between organizations working on a common project.

level. At times it may be necessary to move information between organizations, as illustrated in Figure 10-4, as well as between managerial levels.

The proliferation of electronic mechanisms, along with a wide array of software, have made the process of collecting and disseminating information much faster and less arduous than previously. In addition to its use for conducting the routines of project management, the Internet is a rich source of information, including databases on almost anything, patent information, and technical aid for managing projects, to mention only a small fraction of readily available information. Many current project management software packages allow easy connection to the Internet and e-mail to transmit information, charts, networks, and reports practically anywhere. The material can be altered or updated and returned to the sender with minimal effort beyond that needed to move the information to the next cubicle.

> "E-mail is not to be used to pass on information or data. It should be used only for company business."

The Reporting Process

The relationship of project reports to the project WBS is the key to the determination of both report content and frequency. Reports must contain data relevant to the control of specific tasks that are being carried out according to a specific schedule. The frequency of reporting should be great enough to allow control to be exerted during or before the period in which the task is scheduled for completion. For example, efficacy tests of drugs do not produce rapid results in most cases. Thus, there is no reason for weekly (and perhaps not even monthly) reports on such tests. When test results begin to occur, more frequent reports and updates may be required.

In addition to the criterion that reports should be available in time to be used for project control, the timing of reports should generally correspond to the timing of project milestones. This means that project reports may not be issued periodically—excepting progress reports for senior management. There seems to be no logical reason, except for tradition, to issue weekly, monthly, quarterly, etc., reports. Few projects require attention so neatly consistent with the calendar. This must not be taken as advice to issue reports "every once in a while." Reports should be scheduled in the project plan. They should be issued on time. The report schedule, however, need not call for *periodic* reports.

The distribution of project reports depends on who is interested. For senior management, there may be only a few milestones, even in large projects. For the PM there may be many critical points in the project schedule at which major decisions must be made, large changes in the resource base must be initiated, or key technical results achieved. Similar points relevant to lower levels relate to finer detail and occur with higher frequency. Individual senior managers have widely varying preferences in the frequency and content of reports they wish to see. The PM is well advised to supply them. But irrespective of the senior manager's wishes, the PM must make sure that relevant information about progress is always included—and reported in a way it cannot be overlooked. It is also counterproductive to delay reporting on a current or immediately potential crisis until the next routine report is due.

The nature of the monitoring reports should be consistent with the logic of the planning, budgeting, and scheduling systems. The primary purpose is, of course, to ensure achievement of the project plan through control. There is little reason to burden operating members of the project team with extensive reports on matters that are not subject to control—at least not by them. For example, overhead costs or the in-house rental cost of the project war room are simply not appropriate considerations for a team member who is supervising a research experiment in polymer chemistry or designing the advertising campaign for a new brand of coffee. The scheduling and resource usage columns of the project WBS will serve as the key to the design of project reports.

There are many benefits of detailed, timely reports delivered to the proper people. Among them are:

- Mutual understanding of the goals of the project
- Awareness of the progress of parallel activities and of the problems associated with coordination among activities
- Understanding the relationships of individual tasks to one another and to the overall project
- Early warning signals of potential problems and delays in the project
- Minimizing the confusion associated with change by reducing delays in communicating the change
- Higher visibility to top management, including attention directed to the immediate needs of the project
- Keeping the client and other interested outside parties up to date on project status, particularly regarding project costs, milestones, and deliverables.

Report Types

> "One day my boss asked me to submit a status report to him concerning a project I was working on. I asked him if tomorrow would be soon enough. He said, 'If I wanted it tomorrow, I would have waited until tomorrow to ask for it!' "

For the purposes of project management, we can consider three distinct types of reports: routine, exception, and special analysis. The routine reports are those issued on a regular basis; but, as we noted above, *regular* does not necessarily refer to the calendar. For senior management, the reports will usually be periodic and at major milestones, but for the PM and lower-level project personnel, critical events may be used to trigger routine reports. At times, it may be useful to issue routine reports on resource usage periodically, occasionally on a weekly or even daily basis.

Exception reports are useful in two cases. First, they are directly oriented to project management decision making and should be distributed to the team members who will have prime responsibility for decisions or who have a clear "need to know." Second, they may be issued when a decision is made on an exception basis and it is desirable to inform other managers as well as to document the decision—in other words, as part of a sensible procedure for protecting oneself. (PMs should be aware that overuse of exception reporting will be perceived by top management as sheeplike, overly cautious behavior.)

Special analysis reports are used to disseminate the results of special studies conducted as part of the project or as a response to special problems that arise during the project. Usually they cover matters that may be of interest to other PMs, or make use of analytic methods that might be helpful on other projects. Studies on the use of substitute materials, evaluation of alternative manufacturing processes, availability of external consultants, capabilities of new software, and descriptions of new governmental regulations are all typical of the kinds of subjects covered in special analysis reports. Distribution of these reports is usually made to anyone who might be interested.

Meetings

To celebrate his 50th birthday, columnist Dave Barry listed "25 things you will learn in 50 years of living." The sixteenth was "If you had to identify, in one word, the reason why the human race has not and never will achieve its full potential, that word would be 'meetings.' " For a large majority of project managers and workers, meetings are as welcome as bad checks or unmentionable diseases. There is no doubt that meetings of project teams are necessary and often helpful. The main complaints are that they are interminably long, come to no conclusions, and waste everyone's time. Indeed, a short commentary on how not to run a meeting is entitled, "Creative Time Wasting" (Nevison, 1995).

Thus far, we have implicitly assumed that "reports" were written and disseminated by hard-copy, e-mail, or by Internet. Far more often, however, all three types of reports are delivered in face-to-face meetings, or in telephone conference calls. Indeed, senior managers usually insist on face-to-face meetings for staying informed about project progress, and these meetings may touch on almost any subject relevant to the project (or not). Project review meetings can be either highly structured (see Knutson, 1996, for instance) or deceptively casual, but they are always important.

A large majority of project meetings do not concern senior management. They are project team meetings, occasionally including the client, and concern the day-to-day problems met on all projects. There is no particular reason that these meetings need to be conducted in a manner that is so dreaded by attendees. A few simple rules can remove most of the pain associated with project meetings.

- Use meetings for making group decisions or getting input for important problems. Avoid "show-and-tell" meetings, sometimes called "status and review meetings." If the latter type of meeting has been used to keep project team members informed about what others are doing on the project, insist that such information be communicated personally or electronically by the relevant individuals to the relevant individuals. Only when there is a clear need, such as informing senior management of the project's status, and it is difficult for team members to "get together" on their own, are status and review meetings appropriate.
- Have preset starting and stopping times as well as a written agenda. Stick with both, and above all, do not penalize those who show up on time by making them wait for those who are tardy.
- Make sure that you (and others) do your homework prior to the meeting. Be prepared!
- If you chair the meeting, take your own minutes. Reality (and the minutes become reality as soon as the meeting is over) is too important to be left to the most junior

person present. Distribute the minutes as soon as possible after the meeting, no later than the next work day.

- Avoid attributing remarks or viewpoints to individuals in the minutes. Attribution makes people quite wary about what they say in meetings and damps creativity as well as controversy. Also, do not report votes on controversial matters. It is, for example, inappropriate to report in the minutes that the project team voted to send a "Get Well" card to the boss; 4 yea and 3 nay.

- Avoid overly formal rules of procedure. A project meeting is not a parliament and is not the place for Robert's Rules of Order, though courtesy is always in order.

- If a serious problem or crisis arises, call a meeting for the purpose of dealing with that issue only. The stopping time for such meetings may be "When the problem has been solved." Some types of meetings should never be held at all. A large, diversified manufacturing firm holds monthly "status and review" meetings in each of its divisions at which the managers of all projects report to a Project Review Committee (PRC). The divisional PRCs are made up of senior managers. At least one, and we are told more than one, of the PRCs apparently models its meetings on "Hell Week" at a nearby university fraternity. Hazing and humiliating the project managers who must report to the committee is standard practice. The results are to be expected. Projects are managed defensively. Creativity is avoided. Project managers spend time printing and distributing résumés. The best PMs do not stay long.

In 1976, Antony Jay (1995) wrote a classic article on how to conduct a meeting. We recommend it; it is still a classic.

Common Reporting Problems

There are three common difficulties in the design of project reports. First, there is usually too much detail, both in the reports themselves and in the input being solicited from workers. Unnecessary detail (or too frequent reporting) usually results in the reports not being read. Also, it prevents project team members from finding the information they need. Furthermore, the demand for large quantities of highly detailed input information often results in careless preparation of the data, thereby casting doubt on the validity of reports based on such data. Finally, the preparation and inclusion of unnecessary detail are costly, at the very least.

A second major problem is the poor interface between the project information system and the parent firm's information system. In our experience, the PM may try to force a connection. It rarely works well. The parent organization's information system must serve as the definitional prototype for the project's information system. Obviously, different types of reports must be constructed for managing the project, but they can be built by using standard data, for the most part. The PM can feel free to add new kinds of data to the information base but cannot insist that costs, resource usage, and the like be reported in the project differently from how they are reported in the parent organization. (Clearly, this rule does not apply to information generated or requested by the PM for the purpose of project management.)

The project-oriented firm or the organization that simultaneously conducts a large number of projects can justify a customized project database and report system specifically tailored to its special needs. In such cases, the interface between the project information system and the organization's overall information system must be carefully designed to ensure that data are not lost or distorted when moving from one system to the other. It is also important to make sure that when cost/scope data are reported, the data represent appropriate time periods.

The third problem concerns a poor correspondence between the planning and the monitoring systems. If the monitoring system is not tracking information directly related to the project's plans, control is meaningless. This often happens when the firm's existing information system is used for monitoring without modifications specifically designed for project management. For example, an existing cost tracking system oriented to shop operations would be inappropriate for a project with major activities in the area of research and development. But as we just noted, the PM's problem is to fit standard information into a reporting and tracking system that is appropriate for the project.

The real message carried by project reports is in the comparison of actual activity to plan and of actual output to desired output. Variances are reported by the monitoring system, and responsibility for action rests with the controller. Because the project plan is described in terms of scope, time, and cost, variances are reported for those same variables. Project variance reports usually follow the same format used by the accounting department, but at times they may be presented differently.

10.3   EARNED VALUE ANALYSIS

Thus far, our examples have covered monitoring for parts of projects. The monitoring of performance for the entire project is also crucial because performance is the *raison d'être* of the project. *Individual* task performance must be monitored carefully because the timing and coordination between individual tasks is important. But overall project performance is the crux of the matter and must not be overlooked. One way of measuring overall performance is by using an aggregate performance measure called *earned value*.

The Earned Value Chart and Calculations

PMBOK Guide
7.3.2

There is a considerable body of literature devoted to earned value. To note only a few of the available items, see Anbari (2003), the Flemming references, Hatfield (1996), Project Management Institute (2004), and Singletary (1996). One must, however, exercise some care when reading any article on the subject. Various ratio index numbers have almost as many names (and hence, acronyms) as there are writers. Some authors take further license; see Brandon (1998) for instance, and also see the subsequent *Project Management Journal's* Correspondence column (September 1998, p. 53) for readers' reactions. We will adopt and stick to the PMBOK version of things, but will also note the names and acronyms used by Microsoft's Project®.* Any other names/acronyms will be identified with the author(s). A history of earned value from its origin in PERT/Cost together with its techniques, advantages, and disadvantages is reported in a series in *PM Network* starting with Flemming et al. (1994).

A serious difficulty with comparing actual expenditures against budgeted or *baseline* expenditures for any given time period is that the comparison fails to take into account the amount of work accomplished relative to the cost incurred. The earned value of work performed (*value completed*) for those tasks in progress is found by multiplying the estimated percent physical completion of work for each task by the planned cost for those tasks. The result is the amount that should have been spent on the task thus far. This can then be compared with the actual amount spent.

Making an overall estimate of the percent completion of a project without careful study of each of its tasks and work units is not sensible—though some people make such estimates nonetheless. Instead, it is apparent that at any date during the life of a project the following general condition exists: Some work units have been finished, and they are 100 percent complete; some work units have not yet been started, and they are 0 percent complete; other units have been started but are not yet finished, and for this latter group we may estimate a percent completion.

---

*Earlier versions of Microsoft Project® used a slightly different way to calculate earned value variances.

As we said, estimating the "percent completion" of each task (or work package) is nontrivial. If the task is to write a piece of software, percent completion can be estimated as the number of lines of code written divided by the total number of lines to be written—given that the latter has been estimated. But what if the task is to test the software? We have run a known number of tests, but how many remain to be run?

There are several conventions used to aid in estimating percent completion:

- *The 50–50 rule.* Fifty percent completion is assumed when the task is begun, and the remaining 50 percent when the work is complete. This seems to be the most popular rule, probably because it is relatively fair and doesn't require the effort of attempting to estimate task progress. Since it gives credit for half the task as soon as it has begun, it is excessively generous at the beginning of tasks, but then doesn't give credit for the other half until the task is finally complete, so is excessively conservative toward the end of tasks, thereby tending to balance out on an overall basis.

- *The 0–100 percent rule.* This rule allows no credit for work until the task is complete. With this highly conservative rule, the project always seems to be running late, until the very end of the project when it appears to suddenly catch up. Consequently, the earned value line will always lag the planned value line on the graph.

- *Critical input use rule.* This rule assigns task progress according to the amount of a critical input that has been used. Obviously, the rule is more accurate if the task uses this input in direct proportion to the true progress being made. For example, when building a house, the task of building the foundation could be measured by the cubic yards (or meters) of concrete poured, the task of framing the house could relate to the linear feet (meters) of lumber used, the roofing task could relate to the sheets of 4 X 8 foot plywood used, and the task of installing cabinets might be measured by the hours of skilled cabinet labor expended.

- *The proportionality rule.* This commonly used rule is also based on proportionalities, but uses time (or cost) as the critical input. It thus divides actual task time-to-date by the scheduled time for the task [or actual task cost-to-date by total budgeted task cost] to calculate percent complete. If desirable, this rule can be subdivided according to the subactivities within the task. For example, suppose progress on a task is dependent on purchasing (or building) a large, expensive machine to do a long and difficult task, but the machine itself does not make any substantial task progress. We could create a table or graph of the use of money (or time, if the machine had to be built) relative to task progress which would show a large amount of money (or time) being expended up front for the machine, but with little (or no) progress per se being made. This would then be followed by a continuing expenditure of a smaller stream of money (or time) to run the machine and finish the job, perhaps in direct proportion to the progress.

These rough guides to "percent completion" are not meant to be applied to the project as a whole, though sometimes they are, but rather to individual activities. For projects with few activities, rough measures can be misleading. For projects with a fairly large number of activities, however, the error caused by percent completion rules is such a small part of the total project time/cost that the errors are insignificant. More serious is the tendency to speak of an entire project as being "73 percent complete." In most cases this has no real meaning—certainly not what is implied by the overly exact number. Some authors assume that making estimates of percent completion is simple (Brandon, 1998, p. 12, col. 2, for instance). The estimation task is difficult and arbitrary at best, which is why the 50–50 and other rules have been adopted.

A graph illustrating the concept of earned value such as that shown in Figure 10-5 can be constructed using the above rules and provides a basis for evaluating cost and scope to date. If the total value of the work accomplished is in balance with the planned (baseline)

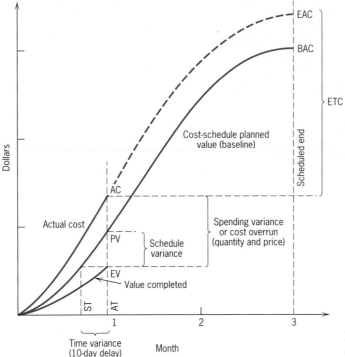

Figure 10-5   Earned value chart.

cost (i.e., minimal scheduling variance), as well as its actual cost (minimal cost variance), then top management has no particular need for a detailed analysis of individual tasks. Thus the concept of earned value combines cost reporting and aggregate scope reporting into one comprehensive chart. The baseline cost to completion is indicated on the chart and referred to as the budget at completion (BAC). The actual cost to date can also be projected to completion, as will be shown further on, and is referred to as the estimated cost at completion (EAC).

We identify several variances on the earned value chart following two primary guidelines: (1) A negative variance is "bad," and (2) the cost and schedule variances are calculated as the earned value minus some other measure. Specifically, the *cost* (or sometimes the *spending*) *variance* (CV) is the difference between the amount of money we budgeted for the work that has been performed to date, that is, the *earned value*, EV, and the actual cost of that work (AC). The *schedule variance* (SV) is the difference between the EV and the cost of the work we scheduled to be performed to date, or the planned value (PV). The *time variance* is the difference in the time scheduled for the work that has been performed (ST) and the actual time used to perform it (AT).* In compact form,

$$EV - AC \; = \; \text{cost variance (CV, overrun is negative)}$$
$$EV - PV \; = \; \text{schedule variance (SV, behind is negative)}$$
$$ST - AT \; = \; \text{time variance (TV, delay is negative)}$$

Typically, variances are defined in such a way that they will be negative when the project is behind schedule and/or over cost. As we have noted, however, this practice is not universal either in the literature or in practice.

---

*A fourth variance can be found. It is the difference between the cost that the project budget says should have been expended to date (PV) and the actual cost incurred to date by the project (AC). PV − AC is what we call the *resource flow variance*. (Note that the resource flow variance is not a "cash flow" variance.)

The variances are also often formulated as ratios rather than differences so that the cost variance becomes the Cost Performance Index (CPI) = EV/AC, the schedule variance becomes the Schedule Performance Index (SPI) = EV/PV, and the time variance becomes the Time Performance Index (TPI) = ST/AT. Use of ratios is particularly helpful when an organization wishes to compare the performance of several projects (or project managers), or the same project over different time periods. As we just noted, however, the accuracy and usefulness of all these performance measures depend on the degree in which estimates of percent completion reflect reality.

Cost and schedule variances (or CPI and SPI) are very commonly used. A short example illustrates their application. Assume that operations on a work package were expected to cost $1,500 to complete the package. They were originally scheduled to have been finished today. At this point, however, we have actually expended $1,350, and we estimate that we have completed two-thirds of the work. What are the cost and schedule variances?

$$\text{cost variance} = EV - AC$$
$$= \$1,500(2/3) - 1,350$$
$$= -\$350$$
$$\text{schedule variance} = EV - PV$$
$$= \$1,500(2/3) - 1,500$$
$$= -\$500$$
$$CPI = EV/AC$$
$$= \$(1,500(2/3))/1,350$$
$$= .74$$
$$SPI = EV/PV$$
$$= \$(1,500(2/3))/1,500$$
$$= .67$$

In other words, we are spending at a higher level than our budget plan indicates, and given what we have spent, we are not as far along as we should be (i.e., we have not completed as much work as we should have). We can also use SPI to calculate the time variance TV if we realize that the scheduled time, ST, should conceptually be in proportion to (EV/PV): $ST = (AT)(EV/PV)$. Since $TV = ST - AT$, then $TV = (AT)((EV/PV) - 1) = (AT)(SPI - 1)$. (This can be derived through simple trigonometry.)

It is, of course, quite possible for one of the indicators to be favorable while the other is unfavorable. We might be ahead of schedule and behind in cost, or vice versa. There are six possibilities in total, all illustrated in Figure 10-6. The scenario shown in Figure 10-5, where both SV and CV are negative, is captured in arrangement d of Figure 10-6. The example immediately above, which also results in negative values of SV and CV, is arrangement c of Figure 10-6. Barr (and others) combines the two indexes, CPI and SPI, to make a type of "critical ratio" (described further in Chapter 11) called the Cost–Schedule Index (Barr, 1996, p. 32).

$$CSI = (CPI)(SPI)$$
$$= (EV/AC)(EV/PV)$$
$$= EV^2/(AC)(PV)$$

In our case,

$$= \$(1,500(2/3))^2/(1,350)(1,500)$$
$$= \$1,000,000/2,025,000$$
$$= 0.49$$

As Barr writes, CSI < 1 is indicative of a problem.

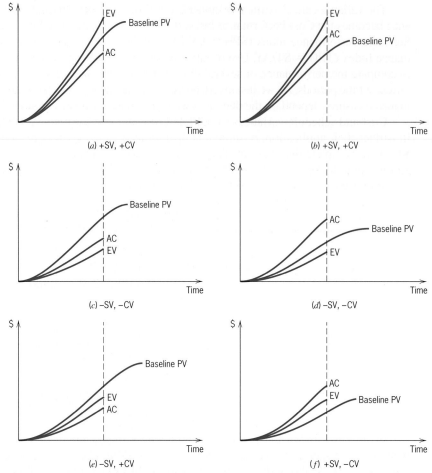

Figure 10-6 Six possible arrangements of AC, EV, and baseline PV resulting in four combinations of positive and negative schedule variance (SV) and cost variance (CV). (Figure 10-5 is arrangement *d*.)

One can continue the analysis to forecast the future of this work unit under the condition when no measures are taken to correct matters. The cost to complete the work unit can be estimated as the budgeted cost of the entire unit, less the earned value to date, adjusted by the CPI to reflect the actual level of performance. The budget at completion (BAC) in our example is $1,500. The earned value to date (EV) is $1,500 X 2/3 = $1,000. The estimated cost to complete (ETC), assuming the same cost efficiency level, can be projected as:

$$ETC = (BAC + EV)/CPI$$
$$= \$(1,500 + 1,000)/0.74$$
$$= \$676$$

The estimated cost at completion (EAC)—and we use Barr's term (1996) rather than Microsoft's FAC or any of the many other names in the literature—is the amount expended to date (AC) plus the estimated cost to complete (ETC):

$$EAC = ETC + AC$$
$$= \$676 + 1,350$$
$$= \$2,026$$

PMBOK Guide

7.3.2.2

rather than the original estimate of $1,500. For a complete description of this approach to estimating the total cost of a work unit, or a set of work units, see Barr (1996) and the Flemming and Koppelman works. We also could consider the ETC as a probabilistic number, and, given upper and lower bounds and an estimated distribution for ETC, we can easily apply simulation to find a distribution for EAC.

The PMBOK also considers two other ways to calculate ETC. If you assume that the team is now going to do all the future work at the originally budgeted rate, then ETC = BAC − EV. Another possible assumption is that the team will do all the future work at a rate that considers both the cost and schedule deviations to date, in which case ETC = (BAC − EV)/(CPI)(SPI) or just (BAC − EV)/CSI. Recognize that if the team is behind schedule, this implies a crash schedule to catch up, which will further inflate the costs.

Note: The planned values (PV) for each task would normally be known from the WBS and budget for the project tasks. However, when distributing PV over the scheduled time for a task (e.g., 3 weeks) for comparison to EV for monitoring purposes during the actual project, consideration should be given to how each task's EV is going to be determined. For example, if the PV is assumed to be generated in proportion to the time spent on the task, then the use of a 0–100 percent rule for EV will result in the project always appearing behind schedule. This is fine if the person monitoring the project understands that this difference of measurement methods is the cause of the "behind schedule" appearance. However, an alternative approach would be to distribute the PV for each task in the same manner that the EV is going to be measured for each task, and then the comparison of the EV to the PV will be more realistic.

Thus far, the focus has been on measuring performance on a work unit rather than on the project as a whole. Where dealing with a specific work unit, the estimates of costs and time can be fairly precise. Even the estimate of percent completion can be made without introducing too much error when using, as we did above, the proportionality rule. Given the relatively short time frame and relatively small cost compared to the whole project, errors are not apt to be significant. Random errors in estimating will tend to cancel out and we can aggregate the work unit data into larger elements, e.g., tasks or even the whole project. (Bias in estimating is, of course, a different matter.) Although the measurement error may be minimal, for most projects there is still no sound basis for estimating percent completion of the project as a whole.

Even if this aggregation is feasible, the use of earned value analysis for forecasting project schedules and costs does not mean that the forecasts will make it possible to correct malperformance. The case for remediation is not hopeful. In a study of more than 700 projects carried out under Department of Defense contracts, the chances of correcting a poorly performing project more than 15 percent complete were effectively nil (Flemming et al., 1996). The study concludes that if the beginning of the project was underestimated and took longer and cost more than the plan indicated, there was little or no chance that the rest of the project would be estimated more accurately. For relatively small deviations from plan, the PM may be able to do a lot of catching up.

If the earned value chart shows a cost overrun or scope underrun, the PM must figure out what to do to get the system back on target. Options include such things as borrowing resources from activities performing better than expected, or holding a meeting of project team members to see if anyone can suggest solutions to the problems, or perhaps notifying the client that the project may be late or over budget. Of course, careful risk analysis at the beginning of the project can do a great deal to avoid the embarrassment of notifying the client and senior management of the bad news.

Example: Updating a Project's Earned Value

We use a simple example to illustrate the process of determining the baseline budget and interim earned value and actual costs for a project. Table 10-1 presents the basic project information, and updated information as of day 7 in the project. The planned AON diagram is

Table 10-1   Earned Value Example (today is day 7)

Activity	Predecessor	Days Duration	Budget, $	Actual Cost, $
a	—	3	600	680
b	a	2	300	270
c	a	5	800	
d	b	4	400	
e	c	2	400	

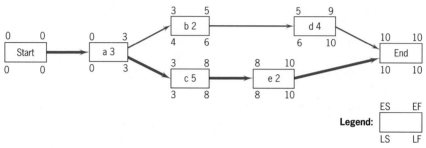

Figure 10-7   Example AON diagram.

shown in Figure 10-7, where path **a-c-e** is the critical path, with project completion expected at day 10. What has actually happened in the project is that the first activity, **a**, took 4 days instead of the planned 3 days to complete, delaying the start of both activities **b** and **c**. Activities **b** and **d** are proceeding as expected, except of course for their one-day delay in initiation, but anyway, path **a-b-d** was not the critical path for the project.

Activities **a** and **b** are both completed and their actual costs are shown in Table 10.1. (The costs to date for activities **c** and **d** are not known.) However, due to its delay, activity **a** cost $80 more than budgeted. Hence, the project manager is trying to cut the costs of the remaining activities, and we see that activity **b** came in $30 under budget, which helps but does not fully offset the previous overrun.

The baseline budget (PV) using the 50–50 rule is calculated in Figure 10-8 and graphed in Figure 10-10 (solid line) where the BAC is listed as $2,500. The project's status and earned value (EV) as of day 7 are given in Figure 10-9 and shown in Figure 10-10 as a dotted line. Included in the figure is the actual cost (AC, the dashed line in Figure 10-10) for the two completed activities. As shown in Figure 10-10, the schedule variance is currently 0 and the cost variance is $1,500 − 950 = +550.

But notice how these figures do not give a very accurate picture of project progress. The earned value up to now has been trailing the baseline and has only caught up because the 50–50 rule doesn't have any activity beginning or ending at day 6; however, with expediting activity **c**, we may in fact be back on schedule by day 8. The cost variance, however, is highly affected by the fact that actual costs are not recorded until the activity is 100 percent complete, combined with the impact of the 50–50 rule. The result is that the baseline and earned value cost figures will tend to converge when activities begin but the actual costs will lag them considerably. Even though the proportionality rule would more accurately delay the aggregation of earned value costs, there would still be a positive bias if the actual costs were not calculated until the activities were completed. It would be more accurate, but considerably more complex, to apportion actual costs according to percentage activity completion. These effects are illustrated further in some of the problems at the end of the chapter.

Day

Activity	0	1	2	3	4	5	6	7	8	9	10
a	300		300								
b				150	150						
c				400				400			
d						200			200		
e									200	200	
Total	300		300	550	150	200		400	400	200	
Cum. Total	300	300	600	1150	1300	1500	1500	1900	2300	2500	

Figure 10-8   Example baseline (PV) budget using the 50–50 rule.

Day

Activity	0	1	2	3	4	5	6	7	8	9	10
a	300			300							
b					150	150					
c					400						
d							200				
e											
EV	300			300	550	150	200				
Cum. EV	300	300	300	600	1150	1300	1500				
Actual Cost				680		270					
Cum. AC	0	0	0	680	680	950	950				

Figure 10-9   Example status at day 7.

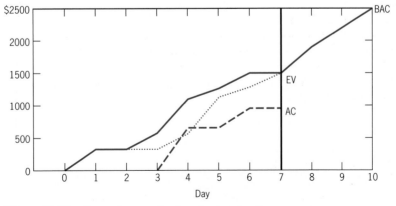

Figure 10-10   Example earned value chart at day 7.

MSP Variance and Earned Value Reports

Figure 10-11 shows an earned value budget for the Career Day project described in Chapter 6. It includes all the budget, actual, and earned value figures for each work package in the project, as well as projections at completion. The budget was generated as a standard report from MSP. (Similar reports are available through most other PC project management software packages.) Note that the project is reported on at the work package level. The first two tasks, *Contact Organizations* and *Banquet and Refreshments*, have been completed, and the third task, *Publicity and Promotion*, is currently underway. Note that in the first task, the fifth work package, "Print Programs," finished early (PV < EV). The first four work packages under *Publicity and Promotion* have been completed, but the fifth and seventh are only partially finished. The sixth work package has not been started, nor has the fourth task, *Facilities*, been started. A compressed Gantt chart is shown on the right side.

The three columns of data on the right, BAC, FAC, and Variance, are "Budget at Completion," "Forecast at Completion" (same as EAC), and the Variance or difference between BAC and FAC. For all activities that have been completed, BAC = EV and FAC = AC. Note that the final variance is not calculated for tasks that are incomplete; see "Advertise in college paper" and "Organize posters," for example. *Advertise in college paper* is 50 percent complete, and *Organize posters* is 45 percent complete. That is, for *Advertise in college paper*, the EV of $82.50 is 50 percent of the BAC. Similarly for *Organize posters*, $335.25 is 45 percent of the BAC of $745.00. When the two work packages are completed, however, and if there is still a cost variance, then BAC and FAC will no longer be equal. For a completed work package, the cost variance EV − AC = BAC − FAC.

Name	PV	EV	AC	Sch. Variance	Cost Variance	BAC	FAC	Variance	Jan	Feb	Mar	Jan	Feb	Mar
Contact Organizations	$3,797.00	$3,980.00	$3,920.00	$183.00	$60.00	$3,980.00	$3,920.00	$60.00						
Print forms	$645.00	$645.00	$645.00	$0.00	$0.00	$645.00	$645.00	$0.00						
Contact organizations	$840.00	$840.00	$728.00	$0.00	$112.00	$840.00	$728.00	$112.00						
Collect display information	$660.00	$660.00	$660.00	$0.00	$0.00	$660.00	$660.00	$0.00						
Gather college particulars	$520.00	$520.00	$520.00	$0.00	$0.00	$520.00	$520.00	$0.00						
Print programs	$687.00	$870.00	$922.00	$183.00	($52.00)	$870.00	$922.00	($52.00)						
Print participants' certificates	$445.00	$445.00	$445.00	$0.00	$0.00	$445.00	$445.00	$0.00						
Banquet and Refreshments	$1,220.00	$1,220.00	$1,200.00	$0.00	$20.00	$1,220.00	$1,200.00	$20.00						
Select guest speaker	$500.00	$500.00	$500.00	$0.00	$0.00	$500.00	$500.00	$0.00						
Organize food	$325.00	$325.00	$325.00	$0.00	$0.00	$325.00	$325.00	$0.00						
Organize liquor	$100.00	$100.00	$100.00	$0.00	$0.00	$100.00	$100.00	$0.00						
Organize refreshments	$295.00	$295.00	$275.00	$0.00	$20.00	$295.00	$275.00	$20.00						
Publicity and Promotion	$2,732.00	$2,297.75	$2,039.00	($434.25)	$258.75	$3,010.00	$2,870.00	$140.00						
Send invitations	$700.00	$700.00	$560.00	$0.00	$140.00	$700.00	$560.00	$140.00						
Organize gift certificates	$330.00	$330.00	$330.00	$0.00	$0.00	$330.00	$330.00	$0.00						
Arrange banner	$570.00	$570.00	$570.00	$0.00	$0.00	$570.00	$570.00	$0.00						
Contact faculty	$280.00	$280.00	$280.00	$0.00	$0.00	$280.00	$280.00	$0.00						
Advertise in college paper	$165.00	$82.50	$65.00	($82.50)	$17.50	$165.00	$165.00	$0.00						
Class announcements	$99.00	$0.00	$0.00	($99.00)	$0.00	$220.00	$220.00	$0.00						
Organize posters	$588.00	$335.25	$234.00	($252.75)	$101.25	$745.00	$745.00	$0.00						
Facilities	$200.00	$0.00	$0.00	($200.00)	$0.00	$200.00	$200.00	$0.00						
Arrange facility for event	$52.00	$0.00	$0.00	($52.00)	$0.00	$52.00	$52.00	$0.00						
Transport materials	$148.00	$0.00	$0.00	($148.00)	$0.00	$148.00	$148.00	$0.00						

Project: Career Day
Date: 3/24

| Critical | Progress | ◇ Milestone |
| Noncritical | Summary | ◇ Rolled up |

Figure 10-11   MSP budget sheet for Career Day project (cf. Chapter 6).

Milestone Reporting

We referred earlier to milestone reports. A typical example of such a report is shown in Figure 10-12 and Figure 10-13. In this illustration, a sample network with milestones is shown, followed by a routine milestone report form. A model top management project status report is illustrated in the next chapter. When filled out, these reports show project status at a specific time. They serve to keep all parties up to date on what has been accomplished. If accomplishments are inadequate or late, these reports serve as starting points for remedial planning.

Figure 10-12 shows the network for a new product development project for a manufacturer. A steady flow of new products is an essential feature of this firm's business, and each

---

Project Management in Practice
Earned Value at CERN

The Large Hadron Collider (LHC) has been described as the largest, the most expensive and the most complex scientific instrument ever built by mankind. Built by the European Organisation for Nuclear Research (CERN) it measures over 27 km in circumference, cost in excess of $4.4 billion and involved scientists from over 100 countries in its design. The challenges of delivering such a unique mega-project were immense, and in the early stages the project slipped behind schedule and was running at 18% over budget.

To enhance the project management of the LHC project, the Aymar review implemented an Earned Value system in 2002. The aim of this system was to provide a clear picture on the cost and schedule performance for over 12,000 defined work units. Through an earned value system it is easy to take an objective view of project performance; to identify the under- or over-budgeted items, to identify items that are ahead or behind schedule. Most importantly you can integrate these perspectives to provide a holistic view of project performance with a clear focus on achievement rather than activity.

In reviewing their implementation of Earned Value the team at CERN identified some important lessons for future projects. Firstly, design the Earned Value Work Breakdown Structure (WBS) to be less than 500 activities (rather than the 12,000 CERN used). Secondly, have the WBS defined to the same level of granularity (e.g., do not have one work package worth thousands of Swiss Francs and the others worth millions). Thirdly, make the accountability for the lowest level of the WBS clear and transparent, and fourthly, make 80% of your budget activities fall in the range of 0.2–2% of the total budget (for example, if your budget is $1 million and 50,000 hours, then 80% of the activities should have an individual planned value of between $2k and $20k, or 100 hours and 1,000 hours).

Sources: CERN (2006) "AIS group keeps CERN on track" *CERN Computer Newsletter*, Vol. 41, No. 2, April–May 2006, pp. 1–2.

De Jurgen De Jonghe, J. and Bonnal, P. "Big Bang at CERN" presentation to the 11th PMI BeNelux Day, www.pmibeneluxday.org/

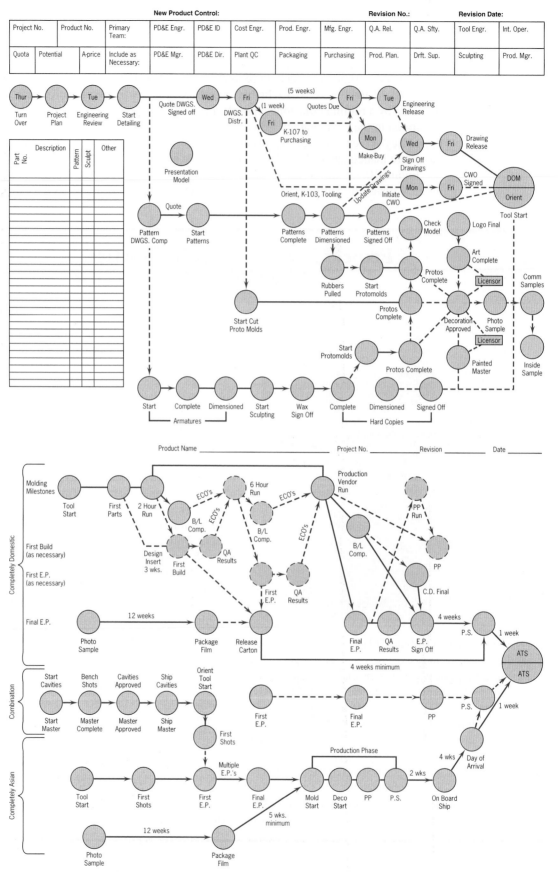

Figure 10-12 Sample project network with sign-off control.

NAME					PROJECT PLAN	ENGR. REVIEW	DESIGN REVIEW	QUOTE QUES.	PAT SCULP COMPL.	PAT SCULP COMPL	QUOTES DUE	MAKE BUY
PROJECT NO.	PRODUCT NO.	MFG SOURCE	TURNOVER	ORIGINAL								
A = PRICE	QUOTA	POTENTIAL		CURRENT								
				ACTUAL								

ENGR. RELEASE	PROJECT REVIEW	RELEASE DWGS.	TOOL START	PHOTO SAMPLES	INSIDE SAMPLES	PKG. FILM	INSTR. LAYOUT	INSTR. FILM ART	FINAL PARTS	FIRST EP	FINAL EP	EP SIGN-OFF	ORIENT PS	OBS	PROD. PILOT	PT SIGN-OFF	PROD. START	ATS

Figure 10-13 Milestone monitoring chart for Figure 10-12.

new product is organized as a project as soon as its basic concept is approved by a project selection group. If we examine Figure 10-12 closely, we see that the sign-off control boxes at the top of the page correspond with sequences of events in the network. For example, look at the bottom line of the upper network in Figure 10-12. The design of this product requires a sculpture that is formed on an armature. The armature must be constructed, and the sculpture of the product completed and signed off. Note that the sculpture is used as a form for making models that are, in turn, used to make the prototype product. The completion of the sculpture is signed off in the next-to-last box in the lower line of boxes at the top of the page.

The upper network in Figure 10-12 is primarily concerned with product design and the lower network with production. The expected times for various activities are noted on the network, along with the various operations that must be performed. Figure 10-13 is a summary milestone report. Each project has a series of steps that must be completed. Each has an original schedule that may be amended for use as a current schedule. Steps are completed in actual times. This form helps program managers coordinate several projects by trying to schedule the various steps to minimize the degree to which the projects interfere with one another by being scheduled for the same facilities at the same time.

The next section of this chapter, which considers computerized project management information systems, contains several other examples of project reports.

10.4 COMPUTERIZED PMIS (PROJECT MANAGEMENT INFORMATION SYSTEMS)*

The project examples used in Chapters 8 and 9 were small, so that the concepts could be demonstrated. But real projects are often extremely large, with hundreds of tasks and thousands of work units. Diagramming, scheduling, and tracking all these tasks is clearly a job for the computer, and computerized PMISs were one of the earlier business applications for computers. Initially, the focus was on simple scheduling packages, but this quickly extended to include costs, earned values, variances, management reports, and so on.

---

*Occasionally, particular sections will be shaded, meaning that they can be skipped without loss of continuity.

The earlier packages ran on large, expensive mainframe computers; thus, only the larger firms had access to them. Still, the use of these packages for managing projects on a day-to-day basis was not particularly successful. This was because of the inability of project managers to update plans in real time, mainframe computers typically being run in a batch rather than online mode. With the development and proliferation of desktop (and laptop) computers, and servers, and the corresponding availability of a wide variety of project management software, project managers now use at least one PMIS.

These server or desktop computer-based PMISs are considerably more sophisticated than earlier systems and use the computer's graphics, color, and other features more extensively. Many systems can handle almost any size project, being limited only by the memory available in the computer. Many will handle multiple projects and link them together to detect resource over-allocation; e.g., Microsoft Project® can consolidate more than 1,000 projects. The PMIS trend has been to integrate the project management software with spreadsheets, databases, word processors, communication, graphics, and the other capabilities of Windows-based software packages. The current trend is to facilitate the global sharing of project information, including complete status reporting, through local networks or the Internet rather than using standalone systems.

Throughout this text we have illustrated software output from one project management software package, Microsoft's Project® (MSP). Surveys of project management tools published in *Project Management Journal* and elsewhere listed MSP as being used by about half of all respondents. Primavera Project Planner®, a system designed for very large projects, is a distant second. The development of these and other powerful software systems was accompanied by the development of desktop computers with memory, power, and speed undreamed of a decade ago. With project files stored in large memory banks on anything from a mainframe to workstations, servers, and PC's, the software and project files became available on LAN and WAN systems, as well as through the Internet so everyone involved, no matter where they were globally, could interact with the system in real time.

The reader interested in current capabilities would be wise to refer to recent annual or monthly software reviews such as those in the Project Management Institute's occasional software surveys, *PCMagazine* and *Federal Computer News*. Reviews of software are also widely available on the Internet at such magazine-sponsored Web sites as "qualitymag.com" and "zdnet.com" or sites sponsored by the software producers.

Finally, it is worth noting that these systems can very easily be misused or inappropriately applied—as can any tools. The most common error of this type is managing the PMIS rather than the project itself. This and other such errors were long ago described by Thamhain (1987):

- *Computer paralysis*. Excessive computer involvement with computer activity replacing project management; loss of touch with the project and its realities.

- *PMIS verification*. PMIS reports may mask real project problems, be massaged to look good, or simply verify that real problems exist, yet are not acted upon.

- *Information overload*. Too many reports, too detailed, or the distribution of reports, charts, tables, data, and general information from the PMIS to too many people overwhelms managers and effectively hides problems.

- *Project isolation*. The PMIS reports replace useful and frequent communication between the project manager and top management, or even between the PM and the project team.

- *Computer dependence*. PM or top management wait for the computer reports/results to react to problems rather than being proactive and avoiding problems in the first place.

- **PMIS misdirection**. Due to the unequal coverage of the PMIS, certain project sub-areas are overmanaged and other areas receive inadequate attention; symptoms of problems are monitored and managed (budget overruns, schedule slippages), rather than the problems themselves.

We have also found that problems can result when someone other than the PM attempts to update projects without involving the PM in the changes.

Choosing Software

When choosing project management software, the potential user should read several software surveys conducted with project managers, for example, Libratore et al., 2003. Such surveys are now last year's news and thus, obsolete, but they clearly indicate the sorts of capabilities that are important to most users. We would, however, strongly warn against allowing the organization's software technicians from making the choice, unaided. Software that appeals to software specialists is not necessarily the optimal choice for the project manager.

The following characteristics of generally desirable attributes in project management software are based on a number of user surveys and the comments of experienced PMs.

- **Friendliness**. For the novice user, this includes clear and logical manuals, help screens, tutorials, a menu-driven structure, easy editing, and so on. For firms implementing project management, this means the existence of an organized training program on the use of the software conducted by trainers who have some understanding of project management.

- **Schedules**. Gantt charts are mandatory, as well as automatic recalculation with updates of times, costs, and resources. Plots of earliest start, scheduled start, slack/float, latest finish, planned finish, and actual finish times are desirable. The software should also be able to display AON or AOA networks. The time units for schedule display (and resource usage) should vary from minutes to months. The ability to handle three-time schedule inputs is desirable.

- **Calendars**. Either a job shop and/or calendar dates are necessary, plus the ability to indicate working days, nonworking days, and holidays for each resource used.

- **Budgets**. The ability to include a budget for planning, monitoring, and control. Especially desirable is the ability to interface this with a spreadsheet program.

- **Reports**. Individualizing report formats is most desirable. Again, having the ability to interface the reports with a word processing package is highly desirable.

- **Graphics**. The ability to see the schedule and interactions is especially important. For Gantt charts, the software should be able to show the technical dependencies between work units or tasks.

- **Charts**. Charts for responsibility and histograms for resources were deemed particularly useful.

- **Migration**. The ability to transfer data to and from spreadsheets, word processors, database programs, graphics programs, and desired add-on programs. The ability to interface with telecommunication systems and the Internet is required for most applications.

- **Consolidation**. The ability to aggregate multiple projects into a single database for determination of total resource usage and detection of resource conflicts. The software must have the ability to recalculate all schedules and resource records when updated information is added.

We would add one more:

- *Access*. The ability to access and download from the corporate database crucial information such as labor hours and accounts payable.

It is heartening to note that many of the current project management software packages have available almost all of the characteristics noted above. It is important, however, to remember that no one package will meet all needs. Numerous trade-offs exist not only between price and capability but also between functional capability, ease of use, complexity, and speed. In general, there are six areas of PMIS internal capabilities, separate from the ability to migrate data and communicate externally, that should be considered. These are project planning, resource management, risk management, tracking/monitoring, report generation, and decision aiding. The potential purchaser of a PMIS should consider the intended use of the package, the background and needs of all the potential users, and the organizational setting where the package is to be employed, including the needs and orientation of those who will be receiving the reports and graphics.

A general PMIS selection process roughly based on Levine's dated but still excellent work (1987) is as follows:

1. Establish a comprehensive set of selection criteria, considering capabilities in project planning, resource management, tracking/monitoring, report generation, earned value/variance analysis, and risk management.

2. Set priorities for the criteria, separating "must have" items from "nice to have" items and "not needed" items.

3. Conduct a preliminary evaluation of the software packages relative to the criteria using vendor-supplied data, product reviews, and software surveys.

4. Limit the candidate packages to three and obtain demos of each, evaluating the vendors at the same time in terms of interest, software maintenance, and support.

5. Evaluate each package with a standard project typical of your current and projected future needs. Make note of any weaknesses or strengths that are particularly relevant to your situation.

6. Negotiate on price, particularly if you are making a volume purchase or contemplating a site license. Include descriptions of vendor support, training, and product maintenance in the contract.

 ## SUMMARY

In this chapter, we reviewed the monitoring function, relating it to project planning and control, and described its role in the project implementation process. The requirements for monitoring were discussed, in addition to data needs and reporting considerations. Last, some techniques for monitoring progress were illustrated and some computerized PMISs were described.

Specific points made in the chapter were:

- It is important that the planning-monitoring-controlling cycle be a closed-loop cycle based on the same structure as the parent system.

- The first task in designing the monitoring system is to identify the key factors in the project WBS to be monitored and to devise standards for them. The factors should concern results, rather than activities.

- The data collected are usually either frequency counts, numbers, subjective numeric ratings, indicators, or verbal measures.

- Project reports are of three types: routine, exception, and special analysis.

- Project reports should include an amount of detail appropriate to the target level of management with a frequency appropriate to the need for control (i.e., probably not weekly or other such regular basis). More commonly, reports occur near milestone dates.

- Three common project reporting problems are too much detail, poor correspondence to the parent firm's reporting system, and a poor correspondence between the planning and monitoring systems.

- The earned value chart depicts scheduled progress, actual cost, and actual progress (earned value) to allow the determination of spending, schedule, and time variances.

- There exist a great number of computerized PMISs that are available for PMs, with software evaluations occurring regularly in various magazines.

- Project managers' preferred PMIS features were friendliness, schedules, calendars, budgets, reports, graphics, networks, charts, migration, and consolidation.

In the next chapter, we move into the final phase of project implementation, project control. We discuss the different types of control and describe some techniques useful to the PM in controlling the project.

GLOSSARY

Computer Paralysis   Excessive fascination or activity with the computer rather than the project itself such that the project suffers.

Cost (or spending) Variance   The budgeted cost of the work performed less the actual cost of the work performed.

Earned Value   An approach for monitoring project progress that relies on the budgeted cost of activities completed to ascribe value.

Friendliness   When applied to computer use, this term refers to how easy it is to learn and/or use a computer or software package.

Hard Copy   Printed information output, as opposed to screen output.

Information Overload   Having an excess of information so that the information desired is difficult to locate.

Migration   The ability to move files and data between software packages.

Monitor   To keep watch in order to take action when progress fails to match plans.

Schedule Variance   The budgeted cost of work completed less the budgeted cost of work scheduled at this time.

Software   The instructions for running a computer.

Spreadsheet   A matrix of data used with a computer. As the data in particular cells are changed, the results of other cells change also to keep in accordance.

Time Variance   The scheduled time for the work completed less the actual time.

Variance   A deviation from plan or expectation.

Windowing   A computer software feature that allows different functions to be conducted in a separate section of the screen, called a window.

QUESTIONS

Material Review Questions

1. Define *monitoring*. Are there any additional activities that should be part of the monitoring function?

2. Identify the key factors that need to be considered when setting up a monitoring system.

3. List some factors that would be difficult to monitor.

4. Describe routine reports and some problems with them.

5. What are the primary difficulties experienced in the design of project reports?

Class Discussion Questions

11. Discuss the benefits of timely, appropriate, and detailed information. How can a value be assigned to these characteristics?

6. Describe the three variances of an earned value chart and explain their significance.

7. Can you identify other symptoms of computer misuse besides those in Section 10.4?

8. What types of measures do data come in?

9. What is the purpose of "earned value"? How would the progress of the project as a whole be calculated?

10. Describe the various ways that earned value can be found.

12. What are the advantages for a PM of having a computerized system over a manual one? The disadvantages?

13. A project is usually a one-time activity with a well-defined purpose. What is the justification of setting up a PMIS for such a project?

14. A more intensive, and extensive, monitoring system is needed in project management than in a functional organization. Why?

15. The earned value chart is an attempt to put the three-dimensional concept of Figure 1-1 (see Chapter 1) into a two-dimensional format. Is it successful? What is missing?

16. How might a variance be traced back to its source?

17. How would a Project Management Information System differ from an ordinary Management Information System?

18. What type of general purpose software might project managers find useful?

19. How should a PMIS be chosen?

20. Discuss the uses of a PMIS in the different stages of the project life cycle.

21. Is it unethical, in an attempt to avoid a "shoot-the-messenger" response, to simply not mention bad news?

22. Which method of estimating earned value seems the most accurate? Which one would you recommend? Why?

Tracking Scope Creep: A Project Manager Responds

23. Is the point of the letter to the editor about scope creep, or tracking? What is it about?

24. The author criticizes the selection of engineers for projects. Is the author saying engineers don't make good project managers?

25. In terms of monitoring and tracking, which of the 10 oversights is probably most crucial?

Drug Counseling Program

26. Which of the five kinds of data forms is the first measure? The second?

27. Which measures of the three would be the most accurate? The most reliable?

Earned Value at CERN

28. What was the prime purpose behind the implementation of earned value at CERN?

29. How does Earned Value help to address and manage these issues?

PROBLEMS

1. Find the schedule and cost variances for a project that has an actual cost at month 22 of $540,000, a scheduled cost of $523,000, and an earned value of $535,000.

2. A sales project at month 5 had an actual cost of $34,000, a planned cost of $42,000, and a value completed of $39,000. Find the cost and schedule variances and the CPI and SPI.

3. A software development project at day 70 exhibits an actual cost of $78,000 and a scheduled cost of $84,000. The software manager estimates a value completed of $81,000. What are the cost and schedule variances and CSI? Estimate the time variance.

4. A project to develop a county park has an actual cost in month 17 of $350,000, a planned cost of $475,000, and a value completed of $300,000. Find the cost and schedule variances and the three indexes.

5. A consulting project has an actual cost in month 10 of $23,000, a scheduled cost of $17,000, and a value completed of $20,000. Find the schedule and cost variances and the three indexes.

6. A project to develop technology training seminars is 5 days behind schedule at day 65. It had a planned cost of $735,000 for this point in time, but the actual cost is only $550,000. Estimate the schedule and cost variances. Re-estimate the variances if the actual cost had been $750,000.

7. Given an activity in an advertising project whose planned cost was $12,000 but actual cost to date is $10,000 so far and the value completed is only 70 percent, calculate the cost and schedule variances. Will the client be pleased or angry?

8. For the following test marketing project at week 6:
   a. Ignore the far right "% Complete" column and using the 50–50 percent completion rule for PV and EV, calculate the cost, schedule, and time variances. Also calculate the CPI, SPI, CSI, and the ETC and EAC.
   b. Repeat the calculations in 8a, but now using the "% Complete" column. Assume that the PV values are based on time proportionality but the "% Complete" values for EV are from the workers actually doing the tasks.

Activity	Predecessors	Duration (weeks)	Budget, $	Actual Cost, $	% Complete
a: Build items	—	2	300	400	100
b: Supply stores	—	3	200	180	100
c: Create ad program	a	2	250	300	100
d: Schedule ads	a	5	600	400	20
e: Check sale results	b, c	4	400	200	20

9. At week 24 of a project to shoot a television commercial, what should the expenditures be? If the earned value is right on schedule but the actual expenses are $9,000, what are the cost and schedule variances? What are the three indexes, the ETC, and the EAC? Use the proportionality rule.

Activity	Pre-decessors	Duration (weeks)	Budget, $
a: Write script	—	6	900
b: Screen actors	—	6	1,200
c: Select actors	a	6	1,200
d: Contract studio	a	12	1,800
e: Obtain props	b, c	14	1,400
f: Schedule date	b, c, d	10	1,500
g: Shoot commercial	d, e	16	800

10. Resolve Problem 8b using MSP. Omit the calculations for CPI, SPI, and CSI.

11. Resolve the earned value example of Table 10-1 by recomputing Figures 10-8 and 10-9 using the 0–100% rule.

12. Repeat Problem 11 using the time proportionality rule and the following new data for % completion of each task: a: 100; b: 100; c: 80 (cost 600); d: 50 (cost 200); e: 0.

13. Draw an earned value chart for the end of the first week (5 days) assuming the time proportionality rule for the project illustrated in the following network diagram given the following costs and percentage completions:

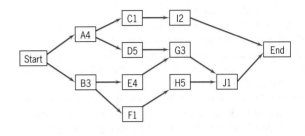

Activity	Budget, $	Actual, $	% Complete
A	600	400	100
B	300	450	100
C	150	100	100
D	750	60	10
E	400	150	30
F	100	50	100
G	200	0	0
H	400	0	0
I	100	0	0
J	100	0	0

14. The following project is at the end of its sixth week. Find the cost and schedule variances. Also find the CPI, SPI, ETC, and EAC for the project.

Activity	Pre-decessors	Duration (weeks)	Budget, $	Actual Cost, $	% Complete
a	—	2	300	400	100
b	—	3	200	180	100
c	a	2	250	300	100
d	a	5	600	400	20
e	b, c	4	400	200	20

INCIDENTS FOR DISCUSSION

Jackson Insurance and Title Company

Mark Suturana joined the Jackson Company six months ago. He is an experienced management information systems executive who has been given the task of improving the responsiveness of Jackson's data processing group to the end user. After several months of investigation, Mark felt certain he understood the current situation clearly enough to proceed. First, approximately 90 percent of all end user requests came to data processing (DP) in the form of a project, with the DP output either the final product of the project, or, more commonly, one step of a project. Accordingly, Mark felt he should initially direct his efforts toward integrating DP's approach to projects with the company's formal project management system.

It has been Mark's experience that most problems associated with DP projects revolve around poor project definition and inadequate participation by the end user during the system design phase. Typically, the end user does not become heavily involved in the project until the new system is ready to install. At that point, a great deal of work is required to adapt the system to meet end-user requirements. Mark decided to institute a procedure that put end-user cooperation and participation on the front end of the project. The idea was to define the objective and design of the system so thoroughly that implementation would become almost mechanical in nature rather than an introduction to the end user of "his or her new system."

Mark also recognized that something had to be done to control the programming quality of DP's output. A more effective front-end approach to DP projects would subject DP managers to more intense pressure to produce results within user's needs, including time constraints. Mark was concerned that the quality of the DP output would deteriorate under those conditions, especially given the lack of technical expertise on the part of end users and outside project managers. To solve this problem, Mark recommended the creation of a DP quality assurance (QA) manager who would approve the initial steps of the projects and review each additional step. The QA manager would have the authority to declare any step or portion of the output inadequate and to send it back to be reworked.

Questions: Is this a good control system for DP? Why or why not? Does it also represent a good control point for company projects using DP to accomplish one portion of the project objective? What would be your answer if you were a non-DP project manager? Might scope creep become a problem under this new system? If so, how should Mark control it?

The U.S. Army Corps of Engineers

The U.S. Army Corps of Engineers has contracted with a medium-size excavation firm to construct a small series of three earthen dams as part of a flood control project in North Carolina. For economic reasons, dams #1 and #2 have to be constructed at the same time and dam #3 can be built only after #1 and #2 are completed. There is also a very important scheduled completion date that has to be met (relating to next year's flood season). The project is being handled by Bryan Johnson, who has been with the company for about a year.

This is a new job for Bryan in that he had never before headed more than one project at a time. About three months into the building of dams #1 and #2, he began to notice an information problem. He had supervisors from dams #1 and #2 reporting to him, but he never knew how far along they were in relation to each other. Since dam #3 cannot be built until both dams are fully complete, he cannot tell if it will be started on time and therefore completed on time. Realizing the situation was becoming serious, he began to wonder about how he could coordinate the projects. How could he tell where the projects were in relation to each other? How far were they *jointly* behind? Bryan's major problem was his inability to monitor and record the dual projects effectively.

Questions: What would you recommend to Bryan?

 CONTINUING INTEGRATIVE CLASS PROJECT

Devise a plan for monitoring the project tasks. Then create an earned value table and chart to fill out as the project progresses. Unless outside resources are substantial, the main "costs" you will be tracking will be labor hours to complete the tasks. Generate the planned value (PV) history for the project, the cumulative PV, and the EAC. Decide how you will determine the earned value (EV) for the tasks as they progress. For example, worker estimates, 50–50, what?

BIBLIOGRAPHY

Anbari, F. T. "Earned Value Project Management Method and Extensions." *Project Management Journal*, December 2003.

Back, W. E., and K. A. Moreau. "Information Management Strategies for Project Management." *Project Management Journal*, March 2001.

Barr, Z. "Earned Value Analysis: A Case Study." *PM Network*, December 1996.

Brandon, D. M., Jr. "Implementing Earned Value Easily and Effectively." *Project Management Journal*, June 1998.

Dean, B. V. *Evaluating, Selecting, and Controlling R&D Projects*. New York: American Management Association Research Study 89, 1968.

Evans, J. R., and W. M. Lindsay. *Management for Quality and Performance Excellence, 8th ed.* Florence, KY, 2011.

Flemming, Q. W., and J. M. Koppelman. *Earned Value Project Management*. Upper Darby, PA: Project Management Institute, 1996.

Flemming, Q. W., and J. M. Koppelman. "The Earned Value Body of Knowledge." *PM Network*, May 1996.

Flemming, Q. W., and J. M. Koppelman. "Forecasting the Final Cost and Schedule Results." *PM Network*, January 1996.

Flemming, Q. W., and J. M. Koppelman. "Taking Step Four with Earned Value: Establish the Project Baseline. *PM Network*, May 1995.

Flemming, Q. W., and J. M. Koppelman. "Taking Step Three with Earned Value: Estimate and Budget Resources." *PM Network*, January 1995.

Flemming, Q. W., and J. M. Koppelman "The 'Earned Value' Concept: Back to the Basics." *PM Network*, January 1994.

Hatfield, M. A. "The Case for Earned Value." *PM Network*, December 1996.

Jay, A. "How to Run a Meeting." *IEEE Engineering Management Review*, Winter 1995, reprinted from the *Harvard Business Review*, March–April 1976.

Kidder, T. *The Soul of a New Machine*. Boston: Little, Brown, 1981.

Knutson, J. "How to Prepare and Conduct a Project Review." *PM Network*, October 1996.

Levine, H. A. "PM Software Forum." *Project Management Journal*, 1987 in (all issues). See "Hints for Software Selection," June and December 1987.

Libratore, M. J., and B. Pollack-Johnson. "Factors Influencing the Usage and Selection of Project Management Software." *IEEE Transactions on Engineering Management*, May 2003.

Mekhilef, M., and J. S. Le Cardinal. "A Pragmatic Methodology to Capture and Analyse Decision Dysfunctions in Development Projects." *Technovation*, April 2005.

Nevison, J. M. "Creative Time Wasting." *PM Network*, November 1995.

Project Management Institute. *A Guide to the Project Management Body of Knowledge, 4th ed.* Newtown Square, PA: Project Management Institute, 2008.

Project Management Institute. *Software Survey*. Newtown Square, PA: Project Management Institute, 2001.

Singletary, N. "What's the Value of Earned Value?" *PM Network*, December 1996.

Thamhain, H. J. "The New Product Management Software and Its Impact on Management Style." *Project Management Journal*, August 1987.

 The following case illustrates how easily a project can get into massive trouble when the customer changes policies, responsibilities, or managers on a project and the contractor fails to monitor these events. Because the terminology is rather specialized, it tends to mislead the reader into focusing on the technology instead of the crucial events happening on the project. There are also a great number of players in the project, and keeping them straight takes careful documentation. Finally, the case raises legitimate questions about how formally to manage a project when the customer is disposed to be rather informal and casual about activities.

C   A   S   E

KROON CHEMISCHE FABRIEK
Eric Woodcock

Kroon Chemische Fabriek extends over 80 hectares on the outskirts of Rotterdam in the Netherlands. Its parent company—IC Spezial—is based in Hamburg and has five plants spread across Germany, Belgium, and the Netherlands. KCF produces a wide range of speciality chemicals for industrial customers throughout Europe. The nature of the processes means that parts of the chemical plant have to be shut down periodically for cleaning, upgrading and safety checks.

New equipment often has to be installed during these shutdowns to comply with changing health, safety and environmental regulations. These planned shutdowns are known in KCF as Planned Off-Lines (or POLs), because the plant is deliberately taken out of production, or "off line." KCF has this work done by external contractors who are selected through a bidding process for each POL. Contractors not only do the physical work; they often train KCF personnel in how to use and maintain new equipment and provide certification.

Two years ago, one of these contractors, de Groote Site Service, found itself in a very awkward position. It had completed a POL 15 months ago. The project was originally agreed to be a fixed price contract for a clearly specified package of work. However, there had been delays outside de Groote's control and KCF had also asked it to install new air quality monitors. As a result, the contract was changed to time and materials, with a price significantly higher than the original fixed price deal. KCF was now insisting it was not responsible for the enormous overrun and was refusing to pay the full bill. Sitting in his office in Amsterdam, Peter Rikkers, de Groote's project manager on the job, reflected on the situation his firm was in. He was clear in his own mind that de Groote was not at fault, and had a right to insist on full payment or start legal action. However, de Groote had always had a good relationship with KCF and Peter knew that maintaining that good relationship with this very important customer took priority over recovering all their costs.

Background

De Groote had been working with KCF since 1995, and relations between the two companies were gener-

ally very cordial. In fact, de Groote maintained an on-site office at the Rotterdam site. Three years ago de Groote representatives worked with KCF to develop a fixed-contract for around $250,000 for what seemed a straightforward POL.

Even before the work Peter worried about potential problems. The contract assumed that de Groote would be able to work on three mixing vessels at the same time, but there were rumours that an extension to a big order meant this might not happen. He also felt that the time allowed for the cleaning of three large mixing vessels was optimistic but had been overruled by his boss. It had also become apparent from reading KCF reports that there was more corrosion in several of the steam pipes than de Groote's original inspection suggested.

De Groote representatives approached Anita Wolkers, the KCF site manager, after six weeks of work and explained that the project could not be completed under the original terms because of the additional work required and the consequent extra time needed. Anita asked for a revised budget and schedule and gave approval for work to be billed on a time and materials basis.

Then late in October and without warning, KCF announced that it would not accept de Groote's certification of staff. Instead, it had decided at a corporate level to start to do its own certification. Introducing this into the current POL was time consuming, because de Groote and KCF staff had to work together so that KCF could certify the de Groote training programme. This included KCF insisting on making several changes to the training courses.

On-site, the work of cleaning the mixing vessels was indeed going more slowly than expected. KCF did not release each mixing vessel according to the revised schedule. In an effort to contain KCF's costs, de Groote offered to send some of its staff home until the vessels were available. Anita refused, saying she wanted the staff available on-site so that they could start work as soon as each vessel became available.

Peter sent detailed letters to everyone who was defined on the original purchase order as KCF's

Exhibit 1 Key Events on the KCF POL

Date	Activity
31 August	Verbal authority from Anita Wolkers to work on a time and materials basis.
1 September	All three mixing vessels scheduled to be made available. None ready.
11 September	First mixing vessel handed to de Groote for POL work.
22 September	According to original contract POL scheduled to be finished on this day.
23 September	Second mixing vessel handed over. Memo received from Wolkers confirming authorisation on 31 August.
2 October	Third mixing vessel handed over.
14 October	POL complete.

representatives (including Anita Wolkers), explaining the situation and the likely time scale and cost consequences for KCF. The only response was an assurance from Anita that the contract was now on a time and materials basis.

Initially de Groote had 20 engineers, technicians and training personnel on-site. When the project was at its peak, almost 50 de Groote staff were there. The original contract was for $250,000, but the extra work and time delays meant that the eventual bill de Groote presented to KCF was over $750,000, and the job took 44 days, rather than 22 days, to complete (see Exhibit 1). Some of this arose from dealing with the steam pipe corrosion and fitting air quality monitors. However, a significant part of the bill was caused by having de Groote staff on-site waiting for parts of the KCF plant to be made available for POL work.

Changes to Purchasing Procedures

To make matters even more complicated, throughout the period that the POL was being agreed and delivered, KCF was changing its purchasing procedures from a centralised model (where everything was dealt with at the headquarters in Hamburg) to a decentralised one, where purchasing was managed at each of the five sites. Traditionally, the original contract would be agreed with the central purchasing team in Hamburg, but any extra scope of work would be agreed with the on-site technical people. Now, the Rotterdam site would be responsible for every aspect of the procurement, including contract changes. The changes became effective the middle of September.

Unfortunately, de Groote was not properly briefed on this change of process and behaved as it has always done. Because of the long-standing relationship between the companies, projects had often been devised and managed quite informally. The original order would always be processed in Hamburg but variations would be discussed and agreed with the technical people on-site. Therefore, de Groote had sent the purchase order to Erna Timmerman, the purchasing officer in Hamburg.

Under the new arrangements, Willem van der Veer was assigned to be the on-site contracts manager at KCF. De Groote was not informed of this change, although some of its staff knew who de Veer was because he was at the technical presentations the company had given when the plans for this project were being discussed.

Presenting the Invoice

Four weeks after the POL was completed, de Groote submitted its final price estimate to Anita Wolkers. It came to $800,000, but excluded additional services worth $175,000 which de Groote was prepared to supply at no cost. These services were mainly to do with the change to the certification programme which KCF had introduced. A copy was sent to Erna Timmerman.

The initial reaction from Anita was that the estimate looked fine, because all the extra costs had been explained and KCF was certainly responsible for the delays and she sent a note to that effect to de Groote, with a copy to Erna Timmerman.

One month later, at a meeting at KCF, a team from de Groote formally presented the invoice for $800,000 to Anita Wolkers and several of her colleagues. Willem van der Veer was invited but did not attend the meeting. The invoice was reviewed by Anita and sent on to the Hamburg office for payment.

Normally KCF paid its invoices within 60 days. After 90 days had passed, de Groote became concerned. Certainly, there was a great deal of supporting paperwork with the invoice that KCF would have to go through, but that had not delayed invoice payment in the past.

Relations between de Groote and KCF remained cordial, but no new major contracts were signed.

Peter Rikkers rang Anita Wolkers and he was reassured there was not a problem and that payment would be forthcoming. However, it was four months later when KCF made a payment of $600,000. Then, Jacob Reuter, de Groote's regional sales manager, received a letter from a IC Spezial's Commercial Director, Hans Rimmel, requesting a meeting. On 6 June, Reuter and

Kim Flier, de Groote's contract manager, took the train to Rotterdam for the meeting. Peter Rikkers could not attend as he was dealing with an urgent matter with another customer. Neither Reuter nor Flier knew quite what to expect.

The Negotiations

At the meeting, Hans Rimmel was joined by Willem van der Veer and his boss, Laura Houtman. Rimmel informed the de Groote team that, because the original agreement was fixed price, it would not pay any more towards the $800,000 de Groote said it was owed. In fact, KCF declared that de Groote owed KCF $150,000 plus interest for the amount they believed they had overpaid.

Jacob Reuter pointed out that Anita Wolker, the site manager, had accepted that the special factors meant the contract should become time and materials. A long discussion ensued, at the end of which KCF conceded that it could be considered to be partly time and materials. But they accused de Groote of loading the job with extra people and that the bill was still far too high.

A further meeting was set for two weeks later. At that meeting Jacob Reuter produced evidence to show that the staffing estimates agreed with KCF had been fully complied with, the productivity of the work was on target, and that there had been a series of factors outside de Groote's control that had caused the costs to rise. These included the late availability of equipment for POL work and the changes to the staff certification process. He then presented KCF with a new invoice for $125,000 to cover most of the $175,000 in additional costs they had previously been prepared to absorb.

All discussions and agreements about the content of the job as it went along had been with the site and technical people at the plant. Jacob and Laura Houtman asked that they be included in the discussions because they felt the commercial team did not understand the technical factors involved. KCF refused, and all discussions were with the commercial people only.

Two months later KCF offered a further $200,000 to bring the matter to a close. de Groote had to weigh up the case for pressing for full and fair payment versus the importance of maintaining the business of one of de Groote's most important customers.

The Consequences for de Groote

The whole episode had ongoing consequences for de Groote. The next time KCF came to it and two other firms with an invitation to bid for a major piece of POL work, the terms and conditions of the deal were very strongly in favour of KCF. Gone were any traditions of close, informal working; the new regime wanted tight contracts and arms length relationships with suppliers. de Groote offered a deal based on modified terms, but KCF insisted on its own. de Groote's proposal won top marks from the technical group and also offered the best price, but KCF awarded the work to a competitor who was willing to accept the new terms. As it happens, the competitor finished the POL 10 days early, but industry rumours suggested they found themselves in contention with KCF over getting paid for unexpected extra work.

Advice for Project Managers

Looking at the whole experience, Laura Houtman recognised three areas where things might have been done better that she wrote in an e-mail to her colleagues:

- Understand who is really authorised to spend the customer's money. Clearly, at the end, it was not the site director, even though she acted like she was.

- Do not assume traditional ways of working will endure and there will always be strong mutual trust. It is better to provide reports and invoices on a frequent basis so that the customer knows exactly where they are financially.

- The biggest lesson was to involve the commercial team far more. That means building relations with those people at the start and making sure that any agreements with the technical people are endorsed by the commercial staff.

In summary, Laura saw the project manager's job as being to:

- Know who the decision makers are
- Ask the right questions of the right people
- Control the customer
- Get money for work performed
- Persevere.

Questions

1. What did Peter Rikkers and de Groote do well in this situation? What could have been done better?

2. What factors that were outside Peter Rikkers' control interfered with his efforts to work with KCF?

3. What skills does it take to be an effective interface with the customer? Has this project been successful for de Groote?

4. In what ways was the project scope expanded? Would you consider this to be "scope creep"?

5. Is the customer always right? Do you think any of the "common reporting problems" described in the chapter may have occurred here?

6. Should de Groote try to win back KCF's business at this time? How could de Groote eventually win back NLP's business? What should he do?

CHAPTER

11

Project Control

In the previous chapter, we described the monitoring and information gathering process that would help the PM control the project. Control is the last element in the implementation cycle of planning–monitoring–controlling. Information is collected about system performance, compared with the desired (or planned) level, and action taken if actual and desired performance differ enough that the controller (manager) wishes to decrease the difference. Note that reporting performance, comparing the differences between desired and actual performance levels, and accounting for why such differences exist are all parts of the control process. In essence, control is the *act* of reducing the difference between plan and reality.

Although this chapter is primarily directed to the exercise of control by the project manager, we must note that the Project Management Office, or other project overseer reporting to upper management, also has a project control function. The aim of the project is to help achieve some strategic objective of the organization; thus, the regular deliberations of the PMO, council, or group charged with implementing the Project Portfolio Process (or any other project selection mechanism) must include an appraisal of the continuing value of the project in achieving those objectives. Using the information gained from monitoring the project, as well as information concerning changes in the organizational goals, resources, and strategy, this group may need to take some form of action (control) regarding the project, such as redirecting it, getting it back on track, or perhaps even terminating it.

A special kind of control is exercised through risk management. The group responsible for risk management, be it the PMO or a specific group devoted to the subject, may exert its actions on the project but also may act on the environment, the major source of risk for the project. As you will see, a great many of the things that can go wrong with project scope, cost, or schedule are the result of uncertainty. And the lion's share of the uncertainty has its source in systems that lie outside the project, its environment. When feasible, the group may act on these outside systems to decrease or remove threats to the project, but often they are beyond the group's influence. All that can be done is to act on the project in order to mitigate or counteract or enhance the actions of these external systems. In our opinion, far too little attention is given to risk identification and management.

As has been emphasized throughout this book, control is focused on three elements of a project—scope, cost, and time. The PM is constantly concerned with these three aspects of the project. Is the project delivering what it promised to deliver, or more? Is it making delivery at or below the promised cost? Is it making delivery at or before the promised time? It is strangely easy to lose sight of these fundamental targets, especially in large projects with a wealth of detail and a great number of subprojects. Large projects develop their own momentum and tend to get out of hand, going their own way independent of the wishes of the PM and the intent of the proposal.

Think, for a moment, of a few of the things that can cause a project to require the control of scope, costs, or time.

Scope

Unexpected technical problems arise.

Insurmountable technical difficulties are present.

Quality or reliability problems occur.

Client requires changes in system specifications.

Interfunctional complications and conflicts arise.

Technological breakthroughs affect the project.

Intrateam conflicts arise on interpretation of specifications, or solutions to technical problems.

Market changes increase or decrease the project's value.

Cost

Technical difficulties require more resources.

The scope of the work increases.

Initial bids or estimates were too low.

Reporting was poor or untimely. Budgeting was inadequate.

Corrective control was not exercised in time.

Input price changes occurred.

Time

Technical difficulties took longer than planned to solve.

Initial time estimates were optimistic.

Task sequencing was incorrect.

Required inputs of material, personnel, or equipment were unavailable when needed.

Necessary preceding tasks were incomplete.

Customer-generated change orders required rework.

Governmental regulations were altered.

These are only a few of the relatively "mechanistic" problems that can occur. Actually, there are no purely mechanistic problems on projects. All problems have a human element, too. For example, humans, by action or inaction, set in motion a chain of events that leads to a failure to budget adequately, creates a quality problem, leads the project down a technically difficult path, or fails to note a change in government regulations. If, by chance, some of these or other things happen (as a result of human action or not), humans are affected by them. Frustration, pleasure, determination, hopelessness, anger, and many other emotions arise during the course of a project. They affect the work of the individuals who feel them—for better or worse. It is over this welter of confusion, emotion, fallibility, and general cussedness that the PM tries to exert control.

All of these problems, always indeterminate combinations of the human and mechanistic subsystems, call for intervention and control by the project manager. There are infinite "slips 'twixt cup and lip," especially in projects where the technology or the deliverables are new and unfamiliar, and PMs, like most managers, find control is a difficult function to perform. There are several reasons why this is so. One of the main reasons is that PMs, again like most managers, do not discover problems. Managers discover what Russell Ackoff (1974) once described as a "mess." A "mess" is a general condition of a system that, when viewed by a manager, leads to a statement that begins, %#^@*&+#!" and goes downhill from there. It is the discovery of a mess that leads the PM to the conclusion that there is a problem(s) lurking somewhere around.

In systems as complex as projects, the task of defining the problem(s) is formidable, and thus knowing what to control is not a simple task. Another reason control is difficult is because, in spite of an almost universal need to blame some person for any trouble, it is often almost impossible to know if a problem resulted from human error or from the random application of Murphy's Law. PMs also find it tough to exercise control because the project team, even on large projects, is an "in-group." It is "we," while outsiders are "they." It is usually hard to criticize friends, or subject them to control. Further, many PMs see control as an ad hoc process. Each need to exercise control is seen as a unique event, rather than as one instance of an ongoing and recurring process. Whitten (1995) offers the observation that projects are drifting out of control if the achievement of milestones is being threatened. He also offers some guidelines on how to resolve this problem and bring the project back in control.

Because control of projects is such a mixture of feeling and fact, of human and mechanism, of causation and random chance, we must approach the subject in an extremely orderly way. In this chapter, we start by examining the general purposes of control. Then we consider the basic structure of the process of control. We do this by describing control theory in the form of a cybernetic control loop. While most projects offer little opportunity for the actual application of automatic feedback loops, this system provides us with a comprehensive but reasonably simple illustration of all the elements necessary to control any system. From this model, we then turn to the types of control that are most often applied to projects. The design of control systems is discussed, as are the impacts that various types of controls tend to have on the humans being controlled. The specific requirement of "balance" in a control system is also covered, as are two special control problems: control of creative activities, and control of change.

All in all, it is our opinion that of all the major tasks of project management, control is the least understood. Most PMs are ill-at-ease while in the role of exercising control. Many seem to associate the notion of disciplinarian with control. A few simple suggestions might help. Avoid heavily criticizing people for actions they know (now) are wrong. A simple reminder will do. Avoid criticizing people in public under any circumstances. Recall, from time to time, that the people working for you are reasonably bright and almost never act out of malice—unless you have just violated the immediately preceding rule. Above all, remember that placing blame does not fix the problem. Fix first, blame later—if you still have the energy and "simply must."

Project Management in Practice
Regaining Control of Nuclear Fusion

In 1996, the U.S. Dept. of Energy (DOE) initiated a project to build a National Ignition Facility (NIF) to help learn how to achieve a controlled, self-sustaining nuclear fusion reaction known as "ignition." The facility would require a 500,000 square-foot area to house 192 laser beams directed by mirrors mounted on a 10-story tall structure onto the center of a 33-foot diameter concrete-shielded target chamber. The deadline was September 2001.

However, unexpected risks stymied the effort. First, El Niño rains flooded the worksite the following year. After construction resumed, workers then

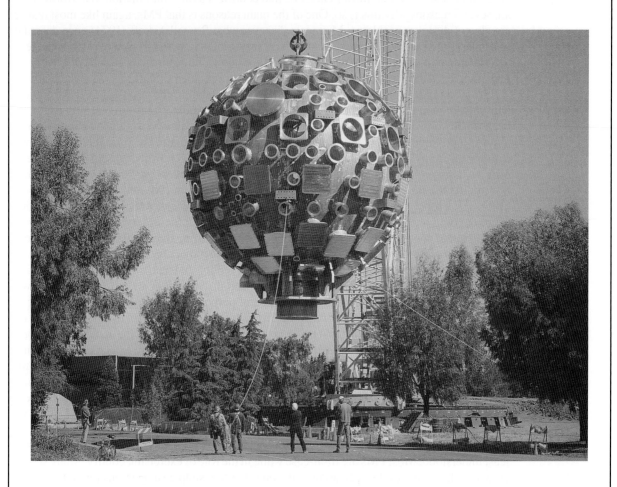

uncovered a 16,000-year-old mammoth, requiring an archaeological team to come on-site to excavate "Niffy," as they called him. But more importantly, two other factors stopped progress completely in 1999: 1) Laser installation was much more complex and demanded much higher cleanliness standards than could be provided. 2) Inadequate systems engineering greatly underestimated the engineering complexity and scope of the project.

To regain control, the DOE developed a new baseline with a bottom-up reassessment of costs, schedules, risks, and contingencies, which then had to be approved by the DOE and the U. S. congress. These estimates were then reviewed by outside scientific and technical experts to validate their accuracy. To ensure the project's performance at the level of best practice, the DOE adopted PMBOK standards and in particular, an earned value system of cost and schedule management. After approval, 12,000 contracts were awarded to over 8,000 vendors, representing an almost $2 billion effort to complete the NIF, which proceeded smoothly to completion in 2009. The month after completion NIF successfully fired a 192-beam laser shot delivering 1.1 megajoules of infrared energy to the center of the target chamber, an historic level of energy all concentrated in a few billionths of a second.

The successful turnaround and control of the NIF project is attributed to the strategic use of project management principles, and resulted in the NIF winning the PMI 2010 Project of the Year award.

Source: K. Hunsberger, "Sparking Ignition," *PM Network,* Vol. 24.

▨ 11.1   THE FUNDAMENTAL PURPOSES OF CONTROL

The two fundamental objectives of control are:

1. The regulation of results through the alteration of activities.

2. The stewardship of organizational assets.

Most discussions of the control function are focused on regulation. The PM needs to be equally attentive to both regulation and conservation. Because the main body of this chapter (and much of the next) concerns the PM as regulator, let us emphasize the conservationist role here. The PM must guard the physical assets of the organization, its human resources, and its financial resources. The processes for conserving these three different kinds of assets are different.

Physical Asset Control

Physical asset control requires control of the *use* of physical assets. It is concerned with asset maintenance, whether preventive or corrective. At issue also is the timing of maintenance or replacement as well as the quality of maintenance. Some years ago, a New England brewery purchased the abandoned and obsolete brewing plant of a newly defunct competitor. A PM was put in charge of this old facility with the instruction that the plant should be completely "worn out" over the next five-year period, but that it should be fully operational in the meantime. This presented an interesting problem: the controlled deterioration of a plant while at the same time maintaining as much of its productive capability as possible. Clearly, both objectives could not be achieved simultaneously, but the PM met the spirit of the project quite well.

Physical inventory, whether equipment or material, must also be controlled. It must be received, inspected (or certified), and possibly stored prior to use. Records of all incoming shipments must be carefully validated so that payment to suppliers can be authorized. With the exploding growth of outsourcing (even within projects) and the development of supply chains, both domestic as well as global, the difficulties of physical asset control have grown enormously. The proper design and operation of supply chains, known as supply chain management, or SCM (see Meredith et al., 2010, Chapter 7; Lee, 2003), is imperative to business as well as project success these days. The same precautions applied to goods from external suppliers must also be applied to suppliers from inside the organization. Even such details as the project library, project coffee maker, project office furniture, and all the other minor bits and pieces must be counted, maintained, and conserved.

Human Resource Control

Stewardship of human resources requires controlling and maintaining the growth and development of people. Projects provide particularly fertile ground for cultivating people. Because projects are unique, differing one from another in many ways, it is possible for people working on projects to gain a wide range of experience in a reasonably short time.

While the measurement of physical resource conservation is accomplished through standard audit procedures, the measurement of human resource conservation is far more difficult. Such devices as employee appraisals, personnel performance indices, and screening methods for appointment, promotion, and retention are not particularly satisfactory devices for ensuring that the conservation function is being properly handled. The accounting profession has worked for some years on the development of *human resource accounting*, and while the effort has produced some interesting ideas, human resource accounting is not well accepted by the accounting profession.

Financial Resource Control

Though accountants have not succeeded in developing acceptable methods for human resource accounting, their work on techniques for the conservation (and regulation) of financial resources has most certainly resulted in excellent tools for financial control.

The techniques of financial control, both conservation and regulation, are well known. They include current asset controls, and project budgets as well as capital investment controls. These controls are exercised through a series of analyses and audits conducted by the accounting/controller function for the most part. Representation of this function on the project team is mandatory. The structure of the techniques applied to projects does not differ appreciably from those applied to the general operation of the firm, but the context within which they are applied is quite different. One reason for the differences is that the project is accountable to an outsider—an external client, or another division of the parent firm, or both at the same time.

The importance of proper conformance to both organizational and client control standards in financial practice and record keeping cannot be overemphasized. The parent organization, through its agent, the project manager, is responsible for the conservation and proper *use of* resources owned by the client or owned by the parent and charged to the client. Clients will insist on, and the courts will require the practice of, *due diligence* in the exercise of such responsibility. While some clients may not be aware of this responsibility on the part of firms with whom they contract, the government is most certainly aware of it. In essence, due diligence requires that the organization proposing a project conduct a reasonable investigation, verification, and disclosure, in language that is understandable, of every material fact relevant to the firm's ability to conduct the project, and to omit nothing where such omission might ethically mislead the client. It is not possible to define, in some general way, precisely what might be required for any given project. The firm should, however, make sure that it has legal counsel competent to aid it in meeting this responsibility.

One final note on the conservationist role of the controller—the mind-set of the conservationist is often antithetical to the mind-set of the PM, whose attention is focused on the *use* of resources rather than their *conservation*. The conservationist reminds one of the fabled librarian who is happiest when all the books are ordered neatly on the library shelves. The PM, often the manager and controller at one and the same time, is subject to this conflict and has no choice but to live with it. The warring attitudes must be merged and compromised as best they can. For an excellent work on the role of the manager as steward, see Block (1993).

11.2   THREE TYPES OF CONTROL PROCESSES

The process of controlling a project (or any system) is far more complex than simply waiting for something to go wrong and then, if possible, fixing it. We must decide at what points in the project we will try to exert control, what is to be controlled, how it will be measured, how much deviation from plan will be tolerated before we act, what kinds of interventions should be used, and how to spot and correct potential deviations before they occur. In order to keep these and other such issues sorted out, it is helpful to begin a consideration of control with a brief exposition on the theory of control.

No matter what our purpose in controlling a project, there are three basic types of control mechanisms we can use: "cybernetic" control, go/no-go control, and postcontrol. In this section we will describe these three types and briefly discuss the information requirements of each. While few cybernetic control systems are used for project control, we will describe them here because they clearly delineate the elements that must be present in *any* control system, as well as the information requirements of control systems.

Project Management in Practice
Delhi Metro

The Delhi Mass Rapid Transit System (MRTS), or Delhi Metro, is a rapid transit system in the Indian National Capital Territory of Delhi. It was built and is operated by the Delhi Metro Rail Corporation Limited (DMRC).

The Delhi Metro was opened on December 24, 2002. It became the second underground rapid transit system in India, after the one in operation in Kolkata. Unlike the Kolkata Metro, the Delhi Metro has a combination of elevated, at-grade and underground lines. Trains operating within the network typically travel at speeds below 80 km/h (50 mph) and stop for about 20 seconds at each MRTS station. The MRTS rolling stock are manufactured by ROTEM, relying on 1,676 mm (5 ft 6 in) track gauge (broad gauge). As of 2008, the metro system has a total network length of 68 km, with 62 stations (13 underground, 48 elevated and 1 at-grade station) on 3 separate lines.

The concept of a metro for Delhi was first formalized in the Delhi Master Plan of 1960, and the legal framework for the metro was laid out in the *Metro Railways (Construction of Works) Act* of 1978.

Actual work towards building the metro, however, only started in March 5, 1995, when the DMRC was established. After the previous problems experienced by the Kolkata Metro, which was badly delayed and 12 times over budget due to "political meddling, technical problems and bureaucratic delays," the DMRC was given full powers to hire people, decide on tenders and control funds.

Physical construction work started on October 1, 1998. Aside from one major problem in 2000, where the Ministry of Railways forced the system to use broad gauge despite the DMRC's preference for standard gauge, construction proceeded smoothly. The first line opened on December 24, 2002 and the entire Phase I of the project was completed in December 2005, on budget and almost three years ahead of schedule, an achievement described as "nothing short of a miracle" by *BusinessWeek*.

Phase I of the network comprises 65.11 km of route length with 13.01 km underground called Metro corridor and 52.10 km surface/elevated called Rail Corridor.

Phase II of the network comprises 128 km of route length and 79 stations, and was (at the time this case was prepared) still under construction, with the first section opened in June 2008 and a target completion date of 2010.

Phase III (112 km) and IV (108.5 km) are planned to be completed by 2015 and 2020 respectively, with the network spanning 413.8 km by then, making it larger than London's Underground (408 km). As the city expands beyond its city limits, there will be further extensions of the network in suburbs, because the northern outskirts of Delhi (Narela) and the suburbs beyond it (Kundli, Sonepat), and the south-eastern suburb of Greater Noida are currently left untouched in the Delhi Metro Masterplan 2021. Northern extensions would be provided by extending Yellow line (Line 2) northwards. Also, plans have been mooted to construct a new line from Noida Sector-62 to Greater Noida which will intersect Indraprastha-Noida Sector-32 line (Blue line), which is already under construction.

Each train consists of four coaches and can carry up to 240 seated and 400 standing passengers. The trains operate at intervals of 3 to 4.5 minutes between 6:00 to 23:00. Coaches on all trains are well ventilated and air-conditioned at a temperature of 20~22°C.

All metro stations and trains are monitored constantly by more than 1,200 closed-circuit cameras, and specially trained Delhi Metro police are stationed at all stations and on trains to deal with law and order is-sues in the system. Trains are at platform level with a small platform gap to allow easy movement of passengers. The Delhi Metro is also one of the few metros in the world to have plainclothes metro-marshals on trains. Intercoms are provided in each train car for emergency communication between the passengers and the driver.

Eating, drinking, smoking, and chewing of gum are prohibited in the entire system. Automated station announcements are recorded in Hindi and English. Many stations have services such as ATMs, food outlets, cafés, and convenience stores.

The achievements of the Delhi Metro project are mainly in the area of bringing to the country the state-of-art technology in all areas of metro workings. In this effort, the project succeeded in ensuring transfer of technology to a large extent, with the scope for further extension of Delhi Metro or for taking up Metro Systems in other cities. This will make India almost self-sufficient in this regard. Another notable achievement of the project is compressing the whole implementation period for Phase-I from the originally planned 10 years to 7 years. DMRC has also been able to set up certain benchmarks in regard to quality and safety in construction. The public have appreciated the way DMRC executed this project with minimal inconvenience to the city and high standards of environmental protection.

DMRC has been able to bring to India a number of new technologies hitherto not known in the coun-try. These are: driving of tunnels with earth pressure balanced mechanical shields, ballast-less track tech-nology, high-speed turnouts, a sophisticated signalling system with automatic train protection, a sophisticated telecommunication system between the trains and the operation control centre, new design features for highly economical and lightweight metro coaches, and a foolproof ticketing system using "Contactless Smart Cards."

Precast concrete leads to better quality and aesthetics, and is the most appropriate choice for any fast track construction. This has been adopted on a large scale in the viaduct of Delhi Metro project. The main reason for not utilising the precast concrete in India before was that the initial cost of infrastructure required to implement the precast concrete technology was high (as compared to other construction techniques) and it would be economical only if the project is large and standardisation of structural components is possible. Further, both the client and the contractor need to realise the advantages and potential of precast concrete construction.

Thus, in addition to being on time and within budget, the Delhi Metro project is credited with adopting innovative technologies to achieve successful project implementation.

Source: Interview with E Sreedharan, Managing Director, Delhi Metro Rail Corporation Limited, in *The Indian Concrete Journal*, November 2002. Reproduced by permission.

Cybernetic Control

Cybernetic, or steering, control is by far the most common type of control system. (*Cyber* is the Greek word for "helmsman.") The key feature of cybernetic control is its automatic operation. Consider the diagrammatic model of a cybernetic control system shown in Figure 11-1.

As Figure 11-1 shows, a system is operating with inputs being subjected to a process that transforms them into outputs. It is this system that we wish to control. In order to do so, we must monitor the system output. This function is performed by sensors that measure one or more aspects of the output, presumably those aspects one wishes to control. Measurements taken by a sensor are transmitted to the comparator, which compares them with a set of predetermined standards. The difference between actual and standard is sent to the decision maker, which determines whether or not the difference is of sufficient size to deserve correction. If the difference is large enough to warrant action, a signal is sent to the effector, which acts on the process or on the inputs to produce outputs that conform more closely to the standard.

A cybernetic control system that acts to reduce deviations from standard is called a *negative feedback loop*. If the system output moves away from standard in one direction, the control mechanism acts to move it in the opposite direction. The speed or force with which the control operates is, in general, proportional to the size of the deviation from standard.

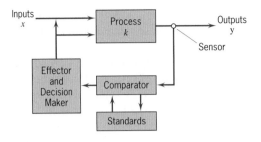

Figure 11-1 A cybernetic control system.

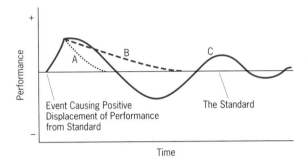

Figure 11-2 Typical paths for correction of deviation of performance from standard.

(Mathematical descriptions of the action of negative feedback loops are widely available. See, for example, van Gigch, 1978.) The precise way in which the deviation is corrected depends on the nature of the operating system and the design of the controller. Figure 11-2 illustrates three different response patterns. Response path A is direct and rapid, while path B is more gradual. Path C shows oscillations of decreasing amplitude. An aircraft slightly deflected from a stable flight path would tend to recover by following pattern C.

Information Requirements for Cybernetic Controllers In order to establish total control over a system, the controller must be able to take a counteraction for every action the system can take. For complex systems, particularly those containing a human element, this is simply not possible. Thus, we need a strategy to aid the PM in developing a control system. One such strategy is to use a cost/benefit approach to control—to control those aspects of the system for which the expected benefits of control are greater than the expected costs. However, relatively few elements of a project (as opposed to the elements of a system that operates more or less continuously) are subject to automatic control. An examination of the WBS will reveal which of the project's tasks are largely mechanistic and represent continuous types of systems. If such systems exist, and if they operate across a sufficient time period to justify the initial expense of creating an automatic control, then a cybernetic controller might be useful.

Given the decisions about what to control, the information requirements of a cybernetic controller are easy to describe, if not to meet. First, the PM must define precisely what characteristics of an output (interim output or final output) are to be controlled. Second, standards must be set for each characteristic. Third, sensors must be acquired that will measure those characteristics at the desired level of precision. Fourth, these measurements must be compared to a "standard" signal. Fifth, the difference between the two is sent to the decision maker which, if it is sufficiently large, then transmits a signal to the effector that causes the operating system to react in a way that will counteract the deviation from standard.

Perhaps the most difficult task in creating a cybernetic control system is setting the standards for each element of output we wish to control. For some things, a single standard with a range of error that can be tolerated might be appropriate. In most cases, however, the standards must be set by the PM and/or the client and/or senior management about what is acceptable output at each stage of a project. These standards are a common subject for negotiation between the interested parties.

The Critical Ratio (CR, described in the next section) and Earned Value analysis (EV, in Chapter 10) can both be used in cybernetic control systems. For example, the cost and schedule variance indices (CPI and SPI) can be entered as standards and specific deviations from the desired cost/schedule results to date can be used to trigger an investigation and resulting control of the relevant process. Deviations from a desired level of CR might be used similarly.

Knowledge of cybernetic control is important because all control systems are merely variants, extensions, or nonautomatic modifications of such controls. Because most projects have relatively few mechanistic elements that can be subjected to classic cybernetic controls, this concept of control is best applied to tracking the system and automatically notifying the PM when things threaten to get out of control.

Go/No-Go Controls

Go/no-go controls take the form of testing to see if some specific precondition has been met. Most of the control in project management, if it exists at all, falls into this category. This type of control can be used on almost every aspect of a project. For many facets of the project's scope, cost, and time, it is sufficient to know that the predetermined specifications have been met. Certain characteristics of output may be required to fall within precisely determined limits if the output is to be accepted by the client. In regard to time and cost, there may be penalties associated with nonconformance with the approved plans. Penalty clauses that make late (or too early) delivery costly for the producer are often included in the project contract. Cost overruns may be shared with the client or borne by the project. Some contracts arrange for the first $X of cost overrun to be shared by client and producer, with any further overrun being the producer's responsibility. The number and type of go/no-go controls on a project are limited only by the imagination and desire of the contracting parties.

The project plan, budget, and schedule are all control documents, so the PM has a predesigned control system complete with prespecified milestones as natural control checkpoints. Extra milestones can also be inserted, such as special reviews to make sure the project is still on course to meet its return on investment goals, or whatever else might be involved in a continue/terminate decision. Control can be exercised at any level of detail that is supported by detail in the plans, budgets, and schedules. The parts of a new jet engine, for instance, are individually checked for quality conformance. These are go/no-go controls. The part passes or it does not, and every part must pass its own go/no-go test before being used in an engine. Similarly, computer programs are tested for bugs. The program passes its tests or it does not.

Go/no-go controls operate only when and if the controller uses them. In many cases, go/no-go controls function periodically, at regular, preset intervals. The intervals are usually determined by clock, calendar, or the operating cycles of some machine system. Such periodicity makes it easy to administer a control system, but it often allows errors to be compounded before they are detected. Things begin to go awry just after a quarterly progress check, for instance, and by the time the next quarterly check is made, some items may be seriously out of control. Project milestones typically do not occur at neat, periodic intervals; thus, *controls should be linked to the actual plans and to the occurrence of real events, not simply to the calendar.* Senior management should review reports on all projects at reasonably frequent intervals.

The PM must keep abreast of all aspects of the project, directly or through deputies. Competent functional managers understand the importance of *follow-up*, and the project manager's work provides no exception. Control is best exerted while there is still time for corrective action. To this end, the PM should establish an *early warning system* so that potential problems can be exposed and dealt with before they turn into full-fledged disasters. One way to construct such an early warning system is to set up a project forecast data sheet. On this sheet, outputs or progress are forecast by period. Actual output or progress is then checked against the forecast, period by period. Sometimes projects, especially information system projects, get "stuck" in their progress, absorbing large quantities of resources but yielding no progress or value. Keil et al. (2010) call these "black hole" projects and offer a variety of suggestions to help turn them around.

As we have said before, for an early warning system to work, it must be clear that the messenger who brings bad news will not be shot, and that anyone caught sweeping problems and mistakes under the rug will be. As we have also said before, the most important rule for any subordinate is the Prime Law of Life on a project: Never let the boss be surprised! Controls have a tendency to terrorize the insecure and to induce high anxiety in everyone else. The result is avoidance, and avoidance is exactly what the PM cannot tolerate. Unless deviation from plan is discovered, it cannot be corrected. Therefore, a spirit of trust between superior and subordinate at all levels of the project is a prime requisite for the effective application of control.

Phase-Gated Processes One form of go/no-go control that has gained popularity (Cooper, 1994) is that of phase-gated processes (also known as stage gates, toll gates, quality gates, and so on). Rather than waiting until the project is completed, and then finding out that it doesn't achieve the objectives of the organization, the phase-gate process controls the project at various points throughout its life cycle to make sure it remains on course and of value to the organization. This process is most commonly used for new product/service development projects where it is important to constantly evaluate the match between the changing, dynamic market and the changing nature of the new product/service under development. At the launch of the new development project, a series of "gates" are planned, whereby the project cannot continue with funding until each gate has been successfully passed.

Although often placed at natural project milestones, there may be more or fewer gates than milestones, but the purpose is different—milestones are natural "end-of-phase" points within a project whereas gates are meant to catch problems early on. The initial gates tend to be conceptual- and performance-based while the latter are more market oriented, such as whether we should commit to producing this prototype for the mass market. Figure 11-3 shows one Power Point slide from a presentation to senior management using a "quality-gate" system for reporting progress on the firm's projects.

The criteria for passing each gate are developed in the project planning stage. There is a wide range of reasons for terminating a project midstream; for example, most of the benefits have already been achieved and further expenditures aren't justified, or the market potential of the project has changed substantially. Other possible reasons easily come to mind: critical personnel have left the organization, the project life-cycle costs have gotten out of hand, a competitor has already come out with a better product at a cheaper price, and so on.

We recommend above that senior managers should review reports on all projects at frequent intervals. In actual practice, reporting on the progress of each project in terms of the project's phase-gates appears to be a uniquely helpful approach for senior managers.

Discovery-Driven Planning and Learning Plans Another more recent type of go/no-go control has been proposed by McGrath et al. (1995) and Rice et al. (2008) which reverses the evaluation process. Instead of trying to determine whether the project is achieving the numbers it needs to at this stage of the project, it looks at how valid the initial assumptions now appear to be regarding the project: the market, the customer's needs, the progress that has been made, performance expected in the future, costs to date and expected at completion, schedule to date and expected at completion, and so on. An assumptions checklist for each stage is prepared with the most critical assumptions first and when the project reaches that stage, the assumptions are checked for validity. If a critical assumption is

Milestone Tracking
CRS-J3

Quality Gate Milestone Tracking		Q9	Q8	Q7	Q6	Q5	Q4	Q3	Q2	Q1	
		Business Review	Req'ts	HLD	Release Commit	Iteration Planning	Handoff to Test	Test Complete	Perf Results	GA	
Products/Programs											
CRS-J3	Std Interval		5/14	7/9	8/6		11/5	12/31	12/31	11/14	
	Commit		5/14	6/4	7/9						
	Revised			6/8	7/22						
	Actual		**5/14**	**6/8**							
% Over (Under) Plan			0.0%	13.3%	0.0%		0.0%	0.0%	0.0%	0.0%	
Developers: 3			Testers: 0		Architects: 2		July Dev, Test, Arch	3	8	2	

- **Quality Gate 8 approved on 05/14**
- **Successfully completed the Design Documents and Annotated MRD**
- **Quality Gate 7 approved on 06/08**
- **Quality Gate 6 is targeted for 07/22 (original 07/09 – Delay is due to the COMMCO work planning)**
- **Revised Targets:**
  - Gate 4 – 08/25
  - Gate 1 – 10/13
  - Customer Commit – 10/14

Operations Update – Engineering
6/15
Page 16

Figure 11-3   A quality-gate application.

not met, the project must be replanned or the assumptions revised as appropriate. If no plan can satisfy all the revised assumptions, the project is terminated.

Information Requirements for Go/No-Go Controls   Most of the input information needed to operate go/no-go project control has already been referenced directly or implied by the previous discussion. The project proposal, plans, specifications, schedules, and budgets (complete with approved change orders) contain all the information needed to apply go/no-go controls to the project. Milestones are often key events that serve as a focus for ongoing control activity. These milestones are the project's deliverables in the form of in-process output or final output. If the milestones occur on time, on budget, and at the planned level of quality, the PM and senior management can take comfort from the fact that things are proceeding properly.

Except for a few important projects, senior managers usually cannot keep up with the day-to-day or week-to-week progress of work; nor should they try. Senior management does, however, need a monthly or quarterly status review for all projects. The project status report contains a list of the important milestones for each project together with the status of each. If many of the projects are similar—such as construction projects or marketing projects, for example—the milestones will be of similar type, and one table can show the status of several projects in spite of the fact that each milestone may not be applicable to each and every project. The Elanco Animal

Task	Project #1	Project #2	Project #3
Priorities set	C	C	C
PM selected	C	C	C
Key members briefed on RFP	C	C	C
Proposal sent	C	C	C
Proposal accepted as negotiated	C	C	C
Preliminary design developed	C	W/10	C
Design accepted	C	W/12	C
Software developed	C	NS/NR	N/A
Product test design	C	W/30	W/15
Manufacturing scheduled	C	NS/HR	W/8
Tools, jigs, fixtures designed	W/1	NS/HR	W/2
Tools, jigs, fixtures delivered	W/2	NS/HR	W/8
Production complete	NS/HR	NS/HR	NS/HR
Product test complete	NS/HR	NS/HR	NS/HR
Marketing sign-off on product	NS/HR	NS/HR	NS/HR

Notes:

N/A—Not applicable	W—Work in progress (number refers to month required)	NS—Not started
C—Completed		NR—Need resources
		HR—Have resources

Figure 11-4   Sample project status report.

Health Company, a division of Eli Lilly and Company, uses such a report. A generalized version of Elanco's Project Status Report is shown in Figure 11-4. The Gantt chart (see Chapter 8) is also a convenient way to present senior managers with information on project status.

The PM should ensure that the status reports given to senior management contain information that is current enough to be actionable (and always as accurate as required for control). Some firms are now putting such control information on the Internet to make it instantly available to all parties on a worldwide basis. Some guidelines for this approach are given in Seesing (1996). The PM is well advised to insist that status reports make clear the implications of specific conditions where those implications might be overlooked—or not understood—by senior managers. If meetings between senior management and project managers are used to report project status and progress, it is critical to remember that the process employed in such meetings should not be punitive or intimidating. As we pointed out in Chapter 10, punitive meetings do far more damage than good.

Postcontrol

Postcontrols (also known as postperformance controls or reviews, or postproject controls or reviews) are applied after the fact. One might draw parallels between postcontrol and "locking the barn after the horse has been stolen," but postcontrol is not a vain attempt to alter what has already occurred. Instead, it is a full recognition of George Santayana's observation that "Those who cannot remember the past are condemned to repeat it." Cybernetic and go/no-go controls are directed toward accomplishing the goals of an ongoing project. Postcontrol is directed toward improving the chances for *future* projects to meet their goals. The PMBOK recognizes the value of what is called "Organizational Process Assets" (OPA) and in the Project Time Management chapter there states: "The lessons-learned knowledge base contains historical information regarding activities lists used by previous similar projects that can be considered when defining project schedule activities." (See Project Management Institute, 2008.)

Postcontrol is applied through a relatively formal document that is usually constructed with four distinct sections.

PMBOK Guide
2.4.3; 6.1.1.3

The Project Objectives   The postcontrol report will contain a description of the objectives of the project. Usually, this description is taken from the project proposal, and the entire proposal often appears as an appendix to the postcontrol report. As reported here, project objectives include the effects of all change orders issued and approved during the project.

Because actual project performance depends in part on uncontrollable events (strikes, weather, failure of trusted suppliers, sudden loss of key employees, and other acts of God), the key initial assumptions made about risks during preparation of the project budget and schedule should be noted in this section. A certain amount of care must be taken in reporting these assumptions. They should not be written with a tone that makes them appear to be excuses for poor performance. At the same time, it is useful to remember that brevity is a virtue when writing postcontrol reports on routine projects unless the uncontrollable events are apt to occur with some frequency. While it is clearly the prerogative, if not the duty, of every PM to protect him- or herself politically, he or she should do so in moderation to be effective.

Milestones, Gates, and Budgets   This section of the postcontrol document starts with a full report of project performance against the planned schedule and budget. This can be prepared by combining and editing the various project status reports made during the project's life. Significant deviations of actual schedule and budget from planned schedule and budget should be highlighted. Explanations of why these deviations occurred will be offered in the next section of the postcontrol report.

The Final Report on Project Results   When significant variations of actual from planned project performance are indicated, no distinction should be made between favorable and unfavorable variations. Like the tongue that invariably goes to the sore tooth, project managers tend to focus their attention on trouble. While this is quite natural, it leads to complete documentation on why some things went wrong and little or no documentation on why some things went particularly well. Both sides, the good and the bad, should be chronicled here.

Recommendations for Performance and Process Improvement   The culmination of the postcontrol report is a set of recommendations covering the ways that future projects can be improved. Many of the explanations appearing in the previous sections are related to one-time happenings—sickness, weather, strikes, or the appearance of a new technology—that of themselves are not apt to affect future projects, although other, different one-time events may affect them. But some of the deviations from plan were caused by happenings that are very likely to recur. Examples of recurring problems might be a chronically late supplier, a generally noncooperative functional department, a habitually optimistic cost estimator, or a highly negative project team member. Provision for such things can be factored into future project plans, thereby adding to predictability and control. This is risk identification and management in practice. We cannot overemphasize the importance of this section. It is the critical element of the OPA.

Just as important, the process of organizing and conducting projects can be improved by recommending the continuation of managerial methods and organizational systems that appear to be effective, together with the alteration of practices and procedures that do not. In this way, the conduct of projects will become smoother, just as the likelihood of achieving good results, on time and on cost, is increased. In thinking about the ways to improve the management of future projects, it is essential to remember that we need not wait for the next generation of projects to introduce more effective methods for managing projects. We can usually introduce them when they are discovered, after clearing them with the PMO or whatever body controls the organization's project management protocol. Project management is a steadily evolving science. Thoughtful PMs and project workers help it evolve.

Postcontrol can have a considerable impact on the way projects are run. A large, market-driven company in consumer household products developed new products through projects that were organized in matrix form, but had a functional tie to the marketing division. PMs were almost always chosen from the marketing area. Members of the project team who represented R & D had argued that they should be given a leadership role, particularly early in the project's life. Marketing resisted this suggestion on the grounds that R & D people were not market oriented, did not know what would sell, and were mainly interested in pursuing their own "academic" interests. After reading the perennial R & D request in a postcontrol report, the program manager of one product line decided to reorganize a project as requested by R & D. The result was not merely a successful project, but was the first in a series of related projects based on extensions of ideas generated by an R & D group not restricted to work on the specific product sought by marketing. Following this successful experiment, project organization was modified to include more input from R & D at an earlier stage of the project.

There is no need to repeat the information requirements for postcontrol here. It should be noted, however, that we have not discussed the postcontrol audit, a full review and audit of all aspects of the project. This is covered in Chapter 12. The postcontrol report is a major source of input for the postcontrol audit.

11.3 THE DESIGN OF CONTROL SYSTEMS

Irrespective of the type of control used, there are some important questions to be answered when designing any control system: Who sets the standards? Will they achieve the project's goals? What output, activities, and behaviors should be monitored? How timely must the monitoring be? How great must a difference between standard and actual be before it becomes actionable? What are the most appropriate actions for each situation? What rewards and penalties can be used? Who should take what action?

In addition to being sensible, a good control system should also possess some other characteristics.

- The system should be flexible. Where possible, it should be able to react to and report unforeseen changes in system performance.
- The system should be cost effective. The cost of control should never exceed the value of control. One study (Heywood et al., 1996) has found that the cost of control in projects ranges from as much as 5 percent of total project costs for small projects to less than 1 percent for very large projects.
- The control system must be truly useful and satisfy the real needs of the project.
- The system must operate in an ethical manner.
- The system must operate in a timely manner. Problems must be reported while there is still time to do something about them, and before they become large enough to destroy the project.
- Sensors and monitors should be sufficiently accurate and precise to control the project within limits that are truly functional for the client and the parent organization.
- The system should be as simple as possible to operate.
- The control system should be easy to maintain. Further, the control system should signal if it goes out of order.
- Control systems should be fully documented when installed, and the documentation should include a complete training program in system operation.

No matter how designed, all control systems we have described use feedback as a control process. Let us now consider some more specific aspects of control. To a large extent, the PM is trying to anticipate problems or catch them just as they begin to occur. The PM wants to keep the project out of trouble because upper management often bases their continuing funding decision on a milestone or stage-gate review of the project. If all is not going well, other technological alternatives may be recommended; or if things are going badly, the project may be terminated. Thus, the PM must monitor and control the project quite closely.

The control of scope, cost, and time usually requires different input data. To control scope, the PM may need such specific documentation as engineering change notices, test results, quality checks, rework tickets, scrap rates, and maintenance activities. Of particular importance here is carefully controlling any changes, usually increases, in scope due to "scope creep," the natural inclination of the customer to change the deliverables as they obtain better information about their needs over time. Scope creep is not always the fault of the customer, however; sometimes the team members themselves, in an effort to do their best work, unwittingly increase the scope of the project. The PM must be constantly on guard to identify such changes. We will have more to say about this shortly.

For cost control, the manager compares budgets to actual cash flows, purchase orders, labor hour charges, amount of overtime worked, absenteeism, accounting variance reports, accounting projections, income reports, cost exception reports, and the like. To control the schedule, the PM examines benchmark reports, periodic activity and status reports, exception reports, AOA or AON networks, Gantt charts, the project schedule, earned value graphs, and probably reviews the WBS.

The PM may find a particular activity perplexing or not understand why it is taking longer than it should or costing more than expected. An audit would provide the data to explain the unusual nature of the discrepancy. The PM may choose to do the audit or have the organization's accountant perform the work.

A large variety of new tools have recently become available for the control of projects such as benchmarking, quality function deployment, stage-gate processing, self-directed teams, the design-build approach, and so on. Thamhain (1996) describes these tools and offers suggestions for selecting and implementing them according to individual circumstances of the project.

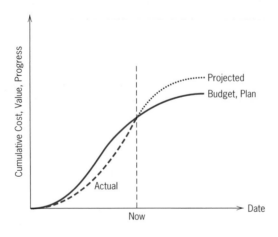

Figure 11-5   Trend projection.

Some of the most important analytic tools available for the project manager to use in controlling the project are variance analysis and trend projection, both of which were discussed in Chapter 10. The essence of these tools is shown in Figure 11-5. A budget, plan, or expected growth curve of time or cost for some task is plotted. Then actual values are plotted as a dashed line as the work is actually finished. At each point in time a new projection from the actual data is used to forecast what will occur in the future if the PM does not intervene. Based on this projection, the manager can decide if there is a problem, what action alternatives exist, what they will cost and require, and what they will achieve. Trend projection charts can even be used for combined scope/cost/time charts, as illustrated in Figure 11-6.

Project Management in Practice
Schedule and Cost Control for Australia's New Parliament House

Over seven years in the making, Australia's new Parliament House at Canberra is actually a suite of buildings costing about $982 million! Meant to be an enduring symbol of the values and expectations of Australia and a source of pride for its citizens, the complex will consist of 5,000 rooms, 40,000 items of furniture, 50,000 square meters of stonework, 7,350 doors, and 170,000 square meters of drywall. To excavate the site, over one million cubic meters of rock was moved, and 170,000 cubic meters of concrete was poured to form the foundation. At its busiest point, the complex was costing $1.2 million per working day.

Given the immensity of the project, the information systems to control its design, construction, and furnishing were equally extensive. Procedures were devised for planning, cost control, tendering, contract commencement, drawing and samples, purchasing, stores control, contracts administration, accounts, general administration, and accident prevention. In the area of contracts alone, 540 separate contracts were awarded; while 20,000 drawings were prepared, with 750,000 prints issued. Thus, computerized systems were developed for the data associated with contracts and bids, drawings, information requests, site instructions, change proposals, shop drawings, asset registers, time reporting, cost reporting, budgetary control, contracts payments, consultants' fees, and reimbursables.

Time control is based on monitoring at four levels of detail, giving progressively more programming detail on aspects of the project. Special purpose programs are included for specific problems or requirements. In addition to exception reports, progress review and coordination meetings help management focus attention on the areas of concern. The overall control system is illustrated in the previous figure.

Cost control is based on the philosophy that 80 percent of the cost is designed in and only 20 percent is due to construction variations. Thus, attention was focused on three points during the design process: early on, to identify allocations and deviations; halfway through to check costs again; and at the completion. Still, ongoing cost control is necessary and performance against budget is measured monthly. Forecasts are also revised every six months to check for any problems ahead.

With such attention to control, the citizens of Australia are looking forward to the completion of their new "house."

Source: T. R. Nixon, "Project Management at the New Parliament House, Canberra," *Project Management Journal,* September 1987.

Project Control Process

Level 1
Master
programme

Level 2
Zone summary
programmes

Level 3
Working
level
programmes

Level 4
2 to 4 week
ahead barcharts

Special
purpose
programmes

Contractors'
programmes

The old parliament house (foreground) and the complex of buildings that comprise the new parliament house (background) in Canberra, Australia.

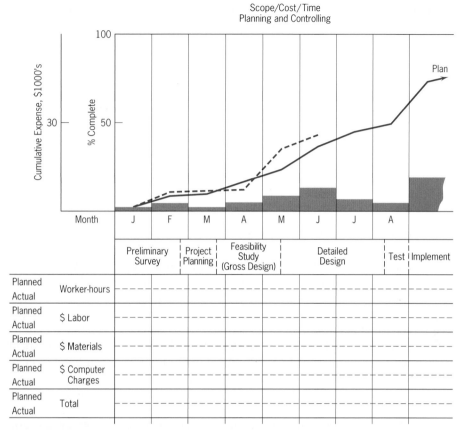

Figure 11-6   Integrated scope/cost/time chart. *Source:* Murdick (1984).

Critical Ratio Control Charts

On occasion it may be worthwhile, particularly on large projects, for the PM to calculate a set of critical ratios for all project activities. The critical ratio is

(actual progress/scheduled progress) $\times$ (budgeted cost/actual cost)

The critical ratio is made up of two parts—the ratio of actual progress to scheduled progress, and the ratio of budgeted cost to actual cost. *Caeteris paribus,** to quote any economist who ever lived, a ratio of actual to scheduled progress greater than one is "good." If the ratio is less than one, it is "bad." Similarly with the ratio of budgeted to actual cost—never forgetting *caeteris paribus*. Assuming moderately accurate measures for each element of each ratio (an assumption that rivals *caeteris paribus* for its *chutzpa*), the critical ratio is a good measure of the general health of the project. Note that the critical ratio is the product of the two separate

---

*For those who have never been blessed with a course in economics, this Latin phrase means "other things being equal." The phrase is the economist's equivalent of the physicist's frictionless plane. It does not and cannot exist in fact.

Table 11-1   (Actual Progress/Scheduled Progress) × (Budgeted Cost/Actual Cost)

Task Number	Actual Progress		Scheduled Progress		Budgeted Cost		Actual Cost		Critical Ratio
1	(2	/	3)	×	(3	/	2)	=	1.00
2	(2	/	3)	×	(6	/	6)	=	0.67
3	(3	/	3)	×	(4	/	6)	=	0.67
4	(3	/	2)	×	(6	/	6)	=	1.50
5	(3	/	3)	×	(6	/	4)	=	1.50

ratios. This way of combining the two underlying ratios weights them equally, allowing a "bad" ratio for one part to be offset by an equally "good" ratio in the other. The PM may or may not agree that this results in a valid measure of project "health."

Consider Table 11-1. We can see that the first task is behind schedule but also has a correspondingly lower cost, which is below budget. Hence, even though the project is running late, the critical ratio shows no problems. If lateness is, in fact, no problem for this activity, the PM need take no action. The second task is on budget but its physical progress is lagging. Even if there is slack in the activity, the budget will probably be overrun. The third task is on schedule, but cost is running higher than budget, creating another probable cost overrun. The fourth task is on budget but ahead of schedule. A cost saving may result. Finally, the fifth task is on schedule and is running under budget, another probable cost saving.

Tasks 4 and 5 have critical ratios greater than 1 and might not concern some PMs, but the thoughtful manager wants to know why they are doing so well (and the PM may also want to check the information system to validate the unexpectedly favorable findings). The second and third activities need attention, and the first task may need attention also. The PM may set some critical-ratio control limits intuitively. The PM may also wish to set different control limits on different activities, controlling progress in the critical path more closely than on paths with high slack.

The critical ratio can also be used with earned values, bearing in mind that "progress" in earned value nomenclature is expressed in monetary units, and we only have three measures instead of four. Clearly, actual progress is EV, scheduled progress is PV, and actual cost is AC. But what then is budgeted cost? Logically, this would be planned value, but if we use PV for budgeted cost, we wind up with the same dilemma we had for Task 1 in Table 11-1: Although the project was substantially late, the critical ratio indicated that everything was fine. It is preferable to use earned value, and then the critical ratio does show that there is a problem. As a result, the critical ratio becomes precisely the cost schedule index, CSI.

The use of EV for budgeted cost doesn't completely solve the possibility of a misleading critical ratio, unfortunately. There can still be instances where the earned value is less than the planned value (a problem!) but the actual cost is so much less than the planned value that the critical ratio is still greater than one, or where the actual cost exceeds the planned value (a problem) but the earned value sufficiently exceeds the planned value that the critical ratio is again greater than one.

Charts can be used to monitor and control the project through the use of these ratios. Figure 11-7 shows an example. Note that the PM will ignore critical ratios in some ranges, and that the ranges are not necessarily symmetric around 1.0. Different types of tasks may

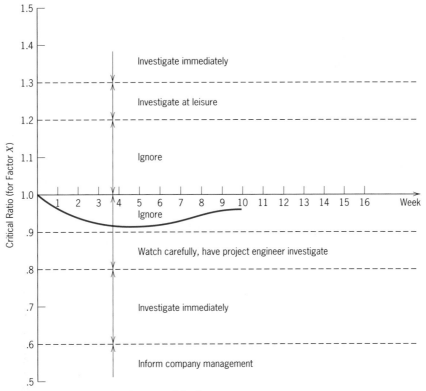

Figure 11-7 Critical ratio control limits.

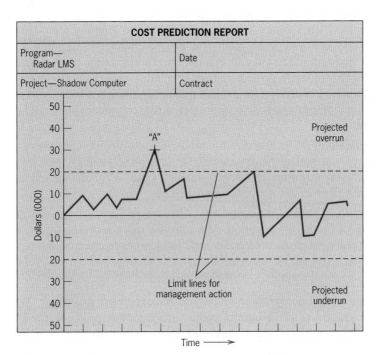

Figure 11-8 Cost control chart. *Source:* Hajek (1977).

have different control limits. Control charts can also be used to aid in controlling costs (Figure 11-8), work force levels, and other project parameters.

Benchmarking

PMBOK Guide

Table 3-1

Another recent addition to the arsenal of project control tools is *benchmarking*, or making comparisons to "best in class" practices across organizations. Benchmarking controls the project management *process* rather than the project itself. This concept is explained and demonstrated in many recent publications (see, e.g., Byrne, 1999; Thamhain, 1996). One case study (Gupta et al., 1997) points out the importance of including the customer's perceptions in the benchmarking study or else the data may be accurate but not give the firm any insight into why customers don't recognize their top-level quality. A benchmarking study (Ibbs et al., 1998) to generate input for the Project Management Maturity Model measured project processes, tools, techniques, and practices across a range of industries, the six life-cycle phases, and the nine knowledge areas of the PMBOK. Graphs were then generated to show the distribution of scores in these industries across the various factors.

Another recent study (Toney, 1997) benchmarked Fortune 500 firms in terms of best practices and key success factors for projects being conducted in functional organizations. The conclusions of the study were reported in four major areas, as described next. These areas are typically the responsibility of the Project Management Office.

- ***Promoting the benefits of project management*** Have the project manager report to a senior executive with multifunctional authority. Identify and nurture senior officers who champion project management. Conduct training in project management. Participate in project management benchmarking forums. Partner with educational and professional project management organizations. Use a variety of sources to communicate the benefits of project management to senior management.

- ***Personnel*** Pay for project management skills and high-risk projects through bonuses, stock options, and other incentives. Employ team-based pay. Create job descriptions and career paths for project managers. Develop a checklist for project manager selection and evaluation criteria. Offer project manager development programs. Design project manager retention programs. Offer advanced training and continuing education for project managers. Design a broadly based project manager evaluation process based on project skills, customer satisfaction, negotiation skills, and so on.

- ***Methodology*** Standardize the organization's project management methods. Integrate the project management processes. Develop project management into a core competence of the organization. Develop a standard process for change management. Develop a standard process for conflict management.

- ***Results of project management*** Measure project performance and the impact of the project on the organization. Measure the value received from the project. Measure the riskiness of the project. Identify the lessons learned from the project.

We are adding another "best practice" to be handled by the PMO:

- ***On-course improvement in project management practices*** When improvements are suggested to the current project management protocol, the PMO should review them immediately and, if approved, institute them as soon as possible.

11.4 CONTROL OF CHANGE AND SCOPE CREEP

In earlier chapters, we discussed the fact that the original plans for projects are almost certain to be changed before the projects are completed. Project changes, we noted earlier, result from three basic causes: (1) uncertainty about the technology on which the work of the project or its output is based; (2) an increase in the knowledge base or sophistication of the client/user leading to scope creep; and (3) a modification of the rules applying to the process of carrying out the project or to its output. All three of these causes are especially common in software projects, where scope creep is legendary. When either the process or output of a project is changed, there is almost always a concomitant change in the budget and/or schedule. For example, the lead contractor on the Dallas Cowboys's new Cowboys Stadium, the largest domed stadium in the world, experienced 1,500 scope changes during construction, all oriented toward enhancing the fans' experience (Hunsberger, 2010). Since there were over 250 subcontractors building the new stadium, all of whom had to be coordinated, retasked, and rescheduled, these changes resulted in major increases in the budget, which were even further exacerbated by the constraint that the project could *not* be delayed!

Conversations in recent years with more than 500 project managers have convinced us that coping with changes and changing priorities is perceived as the most important single problem facing the PM—or if not the most important, certainly the most irritating. When a senior financial officer of a toy manufacturing firm makes an offhand, negative comment about the color of a toy, and triggers a "total redesign" of the toy, thereby invalidating an already approved design, schedule, and budget, the project manager and the design artist may consider murder. (It is probable that a knowledgeable jury would find such action justifiable.)

Hussain et al. (2005) conducted a well-designed survey of more than 1,000 project managers searching for the PM's identification of the "greatest problem of project management." Their findings differed from our informal survey of attendees at project management seminars. They found that "organization," "resource," and "time" issues were the three most important problems, while "change" ranked seventh of 11 choices. Our casual, open-ended question was "What kind of problem arising on projects bugs you the most?" Coping with change (design, schedule, personnel, resources, scope, etc.) had the largest response in our open-ended query. Nevertheless, we recommend the work of Hussain et al. (2005) to our readers' attention.

The most common changes, however, are due to the natural tendency of the client and project team members to try to improve the product or service. New demands and scope requirements become apparent to the client which were not realized at the time of project initiation. Hunsberger (2011) agrees and attributes scope creep to just two reasons: (1) stakeholders only being consulted at the beginning of the project, and (2) requirements changing due to new information about the needs of the project. New technologies become available or better ideas occur to the team as work progresses. As noted earlier, the later these changes are made in the project, the more difficult and costly they are to complete. Without control, a continuing accumulation of little changes can have a major negative impact on the project's schedule and cost.

Leffingwell (1997) suggests that interaction between the project team and the customer should be regularized by partnering. The customer may then take some official responsibility for helping to manage project scope. When the client is a part of the parent organization, the problem is often more difficult. Jealousy, mistrust, and conflict between departments (e.g., the traditional battle between marketing and engineering) leads to uncontrolled scope creep and to inevitable delays and budget overruns (Gibson, 1998).

Project Management in Practice
Major Scope Creep in a Consultancy Project

A major utility services company headhunted a senior project manager with a very explicit brief "to do something with management information." The project manager knew the organisation and had great confidence that he could provide a workable solution for the company within six months. This solution was to be based, at a strategic level, on the Balanced Scorecard. At an IT level it would be based upon a data warehouse that would allow the dimensions of the scorecard to be drilled down (from company to business unit, then down into contract, then into region, subcontractor and eventually the labour gang). This data would then be used as the stimulus for a series of performance improvement plans using a Total Quality Management toolkit.

At a conceptual level the project worked well. It received the sign-off from the client board and the investment in the IT equipment was made and additional staff recruited to service the IT requirements (e.g., processing data, producing reports). However, as the project started to roll out, the shape, size, and dimensions of the project began to change considerably.

One of the key changes came through because of the strength of the initial concept. The board were so taken by the idea of the scorecard that they were keen to have scorecards for the ancillary departments as well as the core "front line" contracts. This resulted in valuable time being drawn away from these crucial work packages and being placed on "nice to have" work. In short, the project was consumed by its own (potential) success and made progress slower than anticipated due to the lead consultant being overcommitted.

The second key challenge was identified when the project was rolled out in a pilot zone. The translation from a concept to practice identified that there was a key shortfall across the organisation in IT capabilities as well as Total Quality Management techniques. Rather than providing a short introduction to the Total Quality Management toolkit, the consulting team had to spend significant time on-site training, coaching and supporting a large population of junior managers.

In addition, the managers who used the techniques wanted slight changes to the functionality or appearance of the system. For example, one regional manager was colour-blind and so required that the traffic light reports (a key part of the data warehouses visualisation of performance information) were awash with shades of greys rather than the intended green and red indicators of good and poor performance. Each of these changes was a slight modification which in itself did not seem onerous but combined to create a significant volume of extra work and an unstable system.

The final shift to the project came when the initial work on the project identified that there was a large turnover in the workforce. This spawned a subsidiary project to initiate a staff satisfaction survey and to implement a series of actions to enhance staff conditions and morale. This was deemed to be under the remit of the consultant and again drew him away from the prime purpose.

Upon the successful rollout of the pilot, the company won a "world class supplier" accolade from their key client. From this perspective, the project was a great success and helped to secure future work with the client. However, from a project management perspective, it was a "challenged" project that was delivered late and would have been significantly over budget if the actual man hours had been paid for (rather than the consultant using his weekends to "catch up" with the core activities of the project).

In reflecting back on the experience, the consultant identified three key mistakes he had made:

- Firstly, his assumptions about the organisation he was going to work in: Undertaking a review of all of the dimensions of the project (e.g., capability of using the technology, the process, and the techniques) would have identified that significant work would be required on the human aspect of the project.

- Secondly, running the project without a formal control board: As project management was not seen as a key requirement in the company (which had a "let's get on and do it" ethos) a formal structure to steer the project to success was not initiated. Consequently, the project could change course without the formal evaluation of the potential consequences of changes. Such a control board would have kept the focus on the core activities (the scorecards for the contracts) rather than seeing the energy dissipated across a wider range of projects.

- Thirdly, the lack of formal project management, particularly a change request process: This resulted in an unstructured process of review and approval where pressure was placed on the adherence to senior managers wishes for local modifications rather than having a clear evaluation of the positive benefit of minor changes.

There is, however, no insurance against the risks associated with project changes. Total quality management and employee involvement will help if both the deliverable and the process by which it is to be produced are carefully studied by thoughtful teams that represent the interests of the major stakeholders in any project: the client, senior management, the project team, and the community. Since prevention of change is not possible, the PM's best hope seems to lie in controlling the process by which change is introduced and accomplished. Control of change is, therefore, one of the primary concerns of risk management.

Control of scope creep is accomplished with a formal *change control system* which, in some industries, is a part of their *configuration management system* responsible for integrating and coordinating changes throughout the systems development cycle. The purpose of the formal change control system is to:

- review all requested changes to the project (both content and procedures)
- identify all task impacts
- translate these impacts into project scope, cost, and schedule
- evaluate the benefits and costs of the requested changes
- identify alternative changes that might accomplish the same ends
- accept or reject the requested changes
- communicate the changes to all concerned parties
- ensure that the changes are implemented properly
- prepare monthly reports that summarize all changes to date and their project impacts

The following simple guidelines, applied with reasonable rigor, can be used to establish an effective change control procedure. The guidelines can also be integrated into the risk management system as a way to manage the risks imposed by scope creep.

1. All project contracts or agreements must include a description of how requests for a change in the project's plan, budget, schedule, and/or deliverables will be introduced and processed.
2. Once a project is approved, any change in the project will be in the form of a *change order* that will include a description of the agreed-upon change together with any changes in the plan, budget, schedule, and/or deliverables that result from the change. For any but minor changes, a risk identification and analysis study should be performed. In order to study the potential impact of change, it is often possible to conduct a simulation study.

Project Management in Practice
Better Control of Development Projects at Johnson Controls

The Automotive Systems Group of Johnson Controls was having trouble controlling their product development programs with each project being managed differently, disagreements about who was responsible for what, projects failing because of rapid company growth, and new employees having trouble fitting into the culture. For a solution, they went to their most experienced and successful project managers and condensed their knowledge into four detailed procedures for managing projects. Because these procedures are now common to all projects, they can be used to train new employees, standardize practices, create a common language, tie together different company functions, create common experiences, act as implicit job descriptions, and create a positive overall project management culture.

The first procedure is project approval for authorizing the expenditure of funds and use of resources. The sales department must first provide a set of product/market information, including financial data, project scope, critical dates, and engineering resource requirements before management will approve the project. Thus, projects are now scrutinized much more closely before work is started and money spent—when more questions are asked and more people are involved, better decisions tend to be made.

The second procedure is the statement-of-work, identifying agreements and assumptions for the project. Here, both the customer and top management must sign off before product design work begins, thereby reducing misunderstandings regarding not only product specifications, prices, and milestones but also intangible product requirements, explicit exclusions, and generic performance targets. Maintaining this documentation over the life of the project has helped avoid problems caused by late product changes from the customer, particularly for 3–5 year projects where the personnel rotate off the project. Customers have, however, been slow to agree to this level of documentation because it limits their ability to change timing, prices, and specifications late in the program when they are more knowledgeable about their needs.

The third procedure is the work breakdown structure, consisting of nine critical life-cycle phases running from definition through production. Included in each of these nine phases are four key elements: the tasks, the timing of each task, the responsible individuals, and the meeting dates for simultaneous engineering (a formalized procedure at Johnson Controls).

The fourth procedure is a set of management reviews, crucial to successful project completion. Both the content and timing of these reviews are specified in advance and progression to the next phase of a project cannot occur until senior management has approved the prespecified requirements, objectives, and quality criteria for that phase. The procedure also specifies questions that must be answered and work that must be reviewed by senior management.

Through the use of these procedures, which are updated and improved with each new project experience, the learning that occurs in the organization is captured and made useful for future projects.

Source: W. D. Reith and D. B. Kandt, "Project Management at a Major Automotive Seating Supplier," *Project Management Journal*, Vol. 22.

3. The project manager must be consulted on all desired changes prior to the preparation and approval of the change order. The project manager's approval, however, is not required.

4. Changes must be approved, in writing, by the client's agent as well as by an appropriate representative of senior management of the firm responsible for carrying out the project.

5. Once the change order has been completed and approved, the project master plan should be amended to reflect the change, and the change order becomes a part of the master plan.

The process of controlling change is not complicated. If the project is large, Roman (1986, p. 274) suggests a change control board, a group representing all interested parties that processes all requests for change. For the typical small- or medium-sized project, however, the problem of handling change need not be complex. The main source of trouble is that too many project managers, in an attempt to avoid anything that smacks of bureaucracy, adopt an informal process of handling requests for change. Misunderstanding often arises from this informality, and the PM finds that the project becomes committed to deliver a changed output of extended scope, but will have to swallow the additional cost involved, and will have to scramble to meet the old, unchanged schedule.

The problems associated with dealing with change orders informally are particularly severe in the case of software and information system projects. The severity of the problem of dealing with change in software projects, it seems to us, is caused by two, interrelated factors. First, software and information systems experts too often fail to explain adequately to the client the real nature of the systems they develop. Second, clients too often fail to make an adequate effort to understand the systems that become the lifeblood for their organizations. The development of *agile* approaches for managing IT projects, or the use of the formal process for change suggested above, should help reduce the degree of misunderstanding and disappointment.

Difficult as it may be, control is an important part of the PM's job on every project. Perhaps the most helpful advice we can give the PM is, in the language of the 1970s, to "hang loose." One effective project manager of our acquaintance tells his project team, "I will not accept crises after 4:30 P.M. You are limited to one crisis per day. Crises are not cumulative. If you don't get yours in today, you do not get two tomorrow." All this is said, of course, with good humor. Team members understand that the PM is not serious, but his projects seem to progress with exceptional smoothness. Crises do occur from time to time, but everyone on the team works to prevent them by applying control in an effective and timely manner.

11.5   CONTROL: A PRIMARY FUNCTION OF MANAGEMENT*

With a few rare exceptions, control of projects is always exercised through people. Senior managers try to exercise governance of project managers, and project managers try to exert control over the project team and others representing functions that are involved with the project. The purpose is always the same—to avoid problems and bring the actual schedule, budget, and deliverables of the project into congruence with the plan. The reading at the end of this chapter compares the reasons these senior managers think projects run into problems with those of the project managers. Their perspectives are considerably different—the senior managers lay the blame for problems on insufficient up-front and contingency planning while the project managers stress the impact of customer and management changes and technical and staffing problems.

In this final section, we discuss the design and use of control systems with some emphasis on the ways in which people respond to various types of control. A number of the points we cover

*Shaded sections can be skipped without loss of continuity.

in these sections are discussed at greater length in William Newman's (1975) excellent classic, *Constructive Control*. Its insights are as fresh today as they were when the book was written.

Also, it should be noted that much of the literature on Six-Sigma, total quality management (TQM), ISO 9000 standards, employee involvement (EI), and the functioning of teams is devoted to techniques for developing creativity and synergistic problem solving through effective teamwork. What is almost never discussed is the implicit assumption that teams have a sense of direction, and are attempting to achieve some specified objectives. All of this implies control. Even the most chaotic brainstorming session is aimed at the solution of specific problems. Control is a necessary and inherent part of life in any organization. It is not helpful to think of control as coercive, though, at times, it may be. We prefer to think of control as the maintenance of ethical, goal-directed behavior. The PM is always subject to such eternal verities as the law of gravity, and the brute fact that the exercise of managerial control will result in distorting the behavior of subordinates. The job of the PM/controller is to set controls that will encourage those behaviors/results that are deemed desirable and discourage those that are not.

By and large, people respond to the goal-directedness of control systems in one of three general ways: (1) by active and positive participation and goal seeking; (2) by passive participation in order to avoid loss; and (3) by active but negative participation and resistance—usually not active resistance to the goal, but failure to undertake those activities that will result in goal achievement. Which of the three resemble a given individual's reaction to control depends on several variables, including such things as the specific control mechanism used, the nature of the goal being sought, and the individual's basic tolerance for being controlled. While human response to specific types of control is typified by its variety, some generalizations are possible.

Cybernetic Controls   Human response to steering controls tends to be positive. Steering controls are usually viewed as helpful rather than as a source of unwelcome pressure if the controlees perceive themselves as able to perform inside the prescribed limits. Contrary to the popular song, it is not the "impossible dream" that motivates goal-seeking behavior, but rather a moderately good chance of success. Of course, response to steering control is dependent on the individual's acceptance of the goal as appropriate. Indeed, no control system is acceptable if the objective of control is not acceptable.

Go/No-Go Controls   Response to go/no-go controls tends to be neutral or negative. The reason appears to be related to the inherent nature of this type of control system. With go/no-go control systems, "barely good enough" results are just as acceptable as "perfect" results. The control system itself makes it difficult for the worker to take pride in high-quality work because the system does not recognize gradations of quality. In addition, it is all too common to be rather casual about setting the control limits for a go/no-go control; the limits should be very carefully set. While go/no-go control is the most frequent type of control exercised on projects, the impact of such control on the project team seems, to us, to be less negative than Newman (1975, pp. 41–42) suggests. Perhaps this is because *project team performance* is the primary focus of control rather than specific items of work performed by individuals.

Postcontrols   Postcontrols are seen as much the same as a report card. Whether reaction to postcontrol is positive, neutral, or negative seems to depend on the "grade" received. In cases where a series of similar projects must be undertaken, postcontrols are regarded as helpful in planning for future work, but considerable care must be devoted to ensuring that controls are consistent with changing environmental conditions. Changes in project management methods resulting from changes suggested and tested by the PMO are seen as very helpful, particularly if they result from project worker involvement.

Balance in a Control System

> My sister passed away, and her funeral was scheduled for Monday. When I told my boss, he said she died so that I would have to miss work on the busiest day of the year. He then asked if we could change her burial to Friday. He said, "That would be better for me."

When developing a control system, it is important that the system be *well balanced*. A balanced control system is cost effective, well geared for the end results sought, and not overdone. The causes of imbalance are legion. For example, the application of across-the-board controls is usually not a good idea. Treating everyone alike appeals to a naive sense of equity, but better results are usually achieved by treating everyone individually.

Across-the-board freezes on expenditures or on hiring tend to reward those who have already overspent or overhired and to penalize the frugal and efficient. The side effects of this are often quite odd. Some years ago, Procter & Gamble put a freeze on hiring into effect for an engineering development laboratory. Project managers who were shorthanded hired temporary labor, including highly skilled technicians from Manpower and similar firms. P & G's accounting system allowed temporary labor to be charged to material accounts rather than to the salary account. The lesson to be learned is that results-oriented, creative project managers tend to see across-the-board controls as a challenge and thus a barrier to be circumvented.

Other common causes of imbalance are these:

1. Placing too much weight on easy-to-measure factors and too little weight on difficult-to-measure, soft factors (the so-called intangibles).

2. Emphasizing short-run results at the expense of longer-run objectives—possibly one of the most serious problems facing industry today.

3. Ignoring the changes in the structure of organizational goals that result from the passage of time or changes in the firm's circumstances. For example, high quality and strict adherence to delivery schedules might be extremely important to a new firm. Later, perhaps, expense control might be more important.

4. Overcontrol by an aggressive executive often causes trouble. In an attempt to create a reputation for on-time delivery, one overly zealous PM put so much pressure on the project team that on-time shipments took precedence over proper test procedures. The result was serious malfunctions of the product and its subsequent recall.

5. Monitoring and controlling items may lead some people to ignore anything that is not measured. "If it isn't counted, it doesn't count," is the attitude. This factor was responsible for the failure of many attempts at Management-by-Objectives.

Achieving balance in a control system requires that several principles must be simultaneously upheld. Perhaps most important is the need to tie controls directly to project objectives. Start by defining the desired results as precisely as possible. System actions that can cause deviation from the desired results are then examined and controls are designed for these actions, beginning with those that can be the source of serious deviation, particularly those that cause trouble with high frequency or without advance notice, such as scope creep.

The PM should also examine all controls in terms of the probable reactions of individuals to the proposed controls. One asks, "How will the various members of the project team react to this control?" If negative reaction is likely, the control should be redesigned.

The problem of developing a good balance between long-run and short-run control objectives is delicate, not because the blending is inherently difficult, but because the PM is often preoccupied with urgent short-run problems rather than longer-run problems that can always be "temporarily" set aside no matter how important the results may be at some later date. Even the timing and sequences of monitoring and controlling can affect the likelihood of time and cost overruns (Partovi et al., 1993).

A good rule for the controller is to place the control as close as possible to the work being controlled and to design the simplest possible mechanism to achieve control. Giving the worker direct control over quality has had impressive results in Japanese production processes as well as at the Lincoln Electric Company in the United States. Similar results were achieved by a major producer of housing units. Carpenters, masons, electricians, and other workers were given considerable discretion over specific production methods. Projects on which this approach was employed showed significantly improved quality when compared to projects built by standard methods.

The most important step in constructing a balanced control system must be taken far in advance of the time when control systems are usually designed. Every step of project planning must be undertaken with the understanding that *whatever work is planned will also have to be controlled.* As we have emphasized, planning and control are opposite sides of the same coin. No amount of planning can solve the current crisis, but planning combined with the design and installation of appropriate control mechanisms can go a long way toward crisis prevention.

An excellent example of integrating the planning and control functions is provided by Mead Data Central, a producer of large-scale database systems and a subsidiary of Mead Corporation. In its *Project Management Development Guide*, Mead describes six stages of the project life cycle. For each stage, the purpose is carefully explained and the deliverables for that stage are listed. For example, the list of deliverables for the feasibility stage contains these items: project description, project number, preliminary business case, project requirements document, and so forth. For each deliverable, the individual(s) and/or groups responsible are noted. This was among the earliest examples of what later came to be known as a "phase-gate" system.

A senior executive at a large industrial firm that carries out many projects each year sees control in a slightly different light. Noting that differences between plan and reality usually represent problems for project managers, he remarked: "If you are solving problems faster than they are arriving to be solved, you have the project under control. If not, you haven't."

Controlling Creative Activities

Some brief attention should be paid to the special case of controlling research and development projects, design projects, and similar processes that depend intimately on the creativity of individuals and teams. First, the more creativity involved, the greater the degree of uncertainty surrounding outcomes. Second, too much control tends to inhibit creativity. But neither of these dicta can be taken without reservation. Control is not necessarily the enemy of creativity; nor, popular myth to the contrary, does creative activity imply complete uncertainty. While the exact outcomes of creative activity may be more or less uncertain, the process of getting the outcome is usually not uncertain. If the potential payoff for the creative activity is high, the need for careful risk management is also high.

In order to control creative projects, the PM must adopt one or some combination of three general approaches to the problem: (1) process review, (2) personnel reassignment, and (3) control of input resources.

Process Review   The process review focuses on the process of reaching outcomes rather than on the outcomes per se. Because the outcomes are partially dependent on the process used to achieve them, uncertain though they may be, the *process* is subjected to control. For example, in research projects the researcher cannot be held responsible for the outcome of the research, but can most certainly be held responsible for adherence to the research proposal, the budget, and the schedule. The process is controllable even if the precise results are not.

Control should be instituted at each project milestone, an obvious opportunity for phase-gate controls. If research results are not as expected or desired, milestones provide a convenient opportunity to assess the state of progress, the value of accomplishment to date, the probability of valuable results in the future, and the desirability of changes in the research design. Again, the object of control is to ensure that the research design is sound and is being carried out as planned or amended. The review process should be participative. Unilateral judgments from the superior are not apt to be accepted or effective. Care must be taken not to overstress method as opposed to result. Method is controllable, and should be controlled, but results are still what count.

Personnel Reassignment   This type of control is straightforward—individuals who are productive are kept; those who are not are moved to other jobs or to other organizations. Problems with this technique can arise because it is easy to create an elite group. While the favored few are highly motivated to further achievement, everyone else tends to be demotivated. It is also important not to apply control with too fine an edge. While it is not particularly difficult to identify those who fall in the top and bottom quartiles of productivity, it is usually quite hard to make clear distinctions between people in the middle quartiles.

Control of Input Resources   In this case, the focus is on efficiency. The ability to manipulate input resources carries with it considerable control over output. Obviously, efficiency is not synonymous with creativity, but the converse is equally untrue—creativity is not synonymous with the extravagant use of resources.

The results flowing from creative activity tend to arrive in batches. Considerable resource expenditure may occur with no visible results, but then, seemingly all of a sudden, many outcomes may be delivered. The milestones for application of resource control must therefore be chosen with great care. The controller who decides to withhold resources just before the fruition of a research project is apt to become an ex-controller.

Sound judgment argues for some blend of these three approaches when controlling creative projects. The first and third approaches concentrate on process because process is observable and can be affected. But process is not the matter of moment; results are. The second approach requires us to measure (or at least to recognize) output when it occurs. This is often quite difficult. Thus, the wise PM will use all three approaches: checking process and method, manipulating resources, and culling those who cannot or do not produce.

SUMMARY

As the final subject in the project implementation part of the text, this chapter described the project control process in the planning-monitoring-controlling cycle. The need for control was discussed and the three types available were described. Then the design of control systems was addressed, including management's role, achieving the proper balance, and attaining control of creative activity as well as handling changes.

- Control is directed to scope, cost, and time.
- The two fundamental purposes of control are to regulate results through altering activity and to conserve the organization's physical, human, and financial assets.
- The three main types of control processes are cybernetic (either first-, second-, or third-order), go/no-go, and postcontrol.
- The postcontrol report contains four sections:
  –Project objectives
  –Milestones and budgets
  –Final project results
  –Recommendations for improvement
- The trend projection curve, critical ratios, and the control chart are useful control tools.
- Control systems have a close relationship to motivation and should be well-balanced; that is, cost-effective, appropriate to the desired end results, and not overdone.
- Three approaches to the control of creativity are process review, personnel reassignment, and control of inputs.
- The most irritating problem facing a PM is the control of change.

In the next chapter, we initiate the project termination part of the text, beginning with evaluation and auditing. This topic is closely related to the postcontrol topics in this chapter.

GLOSSARY

Champion A person with organizational clout who takes on personal responsibility (though not usually day-to-day management) for the successful completion of a project for the organization.

Control Assuring that reality meets expectations or plans. Usually involves the process of keeping actions within limits to assure that certain outcomes will in fact happen.

Control Chart A chart of a measure of performance—commonly a quality characteristic—over time, showing how it changes compared to a desired mean and upper and lower limits.

Critical Ratio A ratio of progress (actual/scheduled) times a cost ratio (budgeted/actual).

Cybernetic An automatic control system containing a negative feedback loop.

Early Warning System A monitoring system that forewarns the project manager if trouble arises.

Go/No-Go Initially, a type of gauge that quickly tells an inspector if an object's dimension is within certain limits. In the case of project management, this can be any measure that allows a manager to decide whether to continue, change, or terminate an activity or a project.

QUESTIONS

Material Review Questions

1. What is the purpose of control? To what is it directed?
2. What are the three main types of control system? What questions should a control system answer?
3. What tools are available to the project manager to use in controlling a project? Identify some characteristics of a good control system.
4. What is the mathematical expression for the critical ratio? What does it tell a manager?
5. How is creativity controlled?
6. What are go/no-go gauges?
7. What is a champion?
8. Describe a cybernetic control system.
9. What should the postcontrol report include?
10. How should change be controlled?
11. Describe the phase-gate process.

Class Discussion Questions

12. How might the project manager integrate the various control tools into a project control system?

13. How could a negative feedback control system be implemented in project management to anticipate client problems?

14. How does the earned value approach achieve the objective of the trend projection curve in Figure 11-5?

15. What other project parameters besides schedule and cost might a control chart be used for? How would their limits be set?

16. Control systems are sometimes classified into two categories, preventive and feedback. How do the three types of systems described in the chapter relate to these two categories?

17. How do internal and external controls differ?

18. What are some difficulties encountered when attempting project control?

19. How might the information required for control systems be collected?

20. How might the information collected through the control system be used on subsequent projects?

21. How does the control of creative projects differ from the control of ordinary projects?

22. Where might ethical issues arise for a PM in the stewardship of the company's resources?

23. Why is the control of change such a difficult problem for a PM? How might a change control system help?

24. Give a numeric example where using the CSI as the critical ratio would be misleading.

Regaining Control of Nuclear Fusion

25. Why do you think the complexity of the task was so greatly underestimated?

26. Why weren't standard project management principles used from the start, do you suppose?

27. What type of control did they employ here: cybernetic, go/no-go, or postcontrol? Justify your answer.

28. What tools from the chapter would have been useful to them in this project?

Delhi Metro

29. What are the factors that contribute to the successful implementation of an infrastructure project?

30. How do infrastructure projects benefit from past project experience?

31. What are the barriers to adopting innovative technologies whilst implementing projects?

Schedule and Cost Control for Australia's New Parliament House

32. How were costs controlled in this project?

33. Where in the controlling process was "scope creep" controlled?

Major Scope Creep in a Consultancy Project

34. What were the key reasons behind the project being delayed?

35. What should the consultant have done differently to avoid the issues identified in the case?

Better Control of Development Projects at Johnson Controls

36. Summarize the unique way Johnson achieved control over their projects.

37. How did "scope creep" enter the projects in the past? Which procedure is now directed at controlling this effect?

38. Which of the four procedures is probably most critical to successful projects?

39. What is the term used in the chapter for the senior management review described in the fourth procedure?

PROBLEMS

1. Given the following information, calculate the critical ratios and indicate which activities are on target and which need to be investigated. Comment on the situation for each of the activities.

Activity	Actual Progress	Scheduled Progress	Budgeted Cost	Actual Cost
A	2 days	2 days	$40	$35
B	4 days	6 days	$30	$40
C	1 day	3 days	$50	$70
D	3 days	2 days	$25	$25

2. Calculate the critical ratios for the following activities and indicate which activities are probably on target and which need to be investigated. Comment on each activity.

Activity	Actual Progress	Scheduled Progress	Budgeted Cost	Actual Cost
A	4 days	4 days	$60	$40
B	3 days	2 days	$50	$50
C	2 days	3 days	$30	$20
D	1 day	1 day	$20	$30
E	2 days	4 days	$25	$25

3. Given the following information about a showroom renovation, which activities are on time, which are early, and which are behind schedule?

Activity	Budgeted Cost	Actual Cost	Critical Ratio
A: Plan changes	$60	$40	1.0
B: Solicit bids	$25	$50	0.5
C: Select contractor	$45	$30	1.5
D: Schedule date	$20	$20	1.5
E: Start renovation	$50	$50	0.67

4. Design and plot a critical ratio for a computer installation project that had planned constant, linear progress from 0 to an earned value of 200 over a 100-day duration. In fact, progress for the first 20 days has been: 2, 3, 4, 6, 7, 9, 12, 14, 15, 17, 20, 21, 21, 22, 24, 26, 27, 29, 31, 33. What can you conclude about this project?

5. Design and plot a critical ratio for a Web site project that has planned constant, linear spending from 0 to a total of 1,000 over a 100-day duration. In fact, daily spending for the first 15 days has been: 11, 10, 9, 10, 11, 12, 11, 9, 8, 9, 10, 12, 14, 11, 7. What can you conclude about this project?

6. Industrial Building, Inc., has two project teams installing virtually identical, 4-story commercial buildings for a customer in two separate cities. Both projects have a planned daily cost of 100 and a planned daily earned value of 100. The first six days for each team have progressed as follows:

Day	Team A: Earned Value	Team B: Earned Value	A: Cost	B: Cost
1	90	90	95	95
2	92	88	98	94
3	94	95	101	102
4	98	101	106	109
5	104	89	116	99
6	112	105	126	118

Compare the two projects in terms of general progress and according to critical ratios.

7. Samson Building, Ltd., is also constructing an identical building for the same customer as in Problem 6 and has the following earned values and costs for the first six days: EV: 90, 88, 95, 101, 89, 105; Cost: 92, 88, 93, 98, 85, 100. Compare this project to the two in Problem 6.

8. The following information (in AOA format) concerns progress at day 40 of an Internet marketing project. Determine if the project is in control based on time and cost to date. If not, what is the cost overage or underage?

Activity	Days Duration	Budget	Actual Cost	% Completed
1-2: Contact sites	10	300	250	100
2-3: Solicit costs	8	400	450	100
2-4: Design ads	12	350	380	100
4-3: Evaluate budget	0	0	0	
3-5: Shoot ads	18	405	400	70
5-6: Place ads	16	450	—	0

9. Determine if the following test marketing project at week 6 is in control. If not, what is out of control? If it is in control, are both budget and schedule in control?

Activity	Predecessors	Duration (weeks)	Budget, $	Actual Cost, $	% Completed
a: Build items	—	2	300	400	100
b: Supply stores	—	3	200	180	100
c: Create ad program	a	2	250	300	100
d: Schedule ads	a	5	600	400	20
e: Check sale results	b, c	4	400	200	20

10. At week 24 of a project to shoot a television commercial, the project manager is worried about her budget since costs have risen to $7,500. Is there a cost overage? If so, how much is it? Is the schedule ahead or behind? Overall, does the project appear to be in control?

Activity	Predecessors	Duration (weeks)	Budget, $	% Completed
a: Write script	—	6	900	100
b: Screen actors	—	6	1200	100
c: Select actors	a	6	1200	100
d: Contract studio	a	12	1800	100
e: Obtain props	b, c	14	1400	100
f: Schedule date	b, c, d	10	1500	40
g: Shoot commercial	d, e	16	800	0

INCIDENTS FOR DISCUSSION

Speciality Service, Inc.

Speciality Service, Inc., is a field computer repair operation serving the small commercial industry in seven states. Speciality Service has one operation in each state, and they vary in size from 50 to 240 employees. A disturbing trend has been developing for the last couple of years that Speciality Service management wishes to stop. The incidence of tardiness and absenteeism is on the increase. Both are extremely disruptive in a custom packing operation. Speciality Service is nonunion in all seven locations, and since management wants to keep this situation, it wants a careful, low-key approach to the problem. Jason Horn, assistant personnel manager, has been appointed project manager to recommend a solution. All seven operations managers have been assigned to work with him on this problem.

Jason has had no problem interfacing with the operations managers. They have very quickly agreed that three steps must be taken to solve the problem:

1. Institute a uniform daily attendance report that is summarized weekly and forwarded to the main office. (Current practice varies from location to location, but comments on attendance are normally included in monthly operations reports.)

2. Institute a uniform disciplinary policy, enforced in a uniform manner.

3. Initiate an intensive employee education program to emphasize the importance of good attendance.

The team has further decided that the three-point program should be tested before a final recommendation is presented. They have decided to test the program at one location for two months. Jason wishes to control and evaluate the test by having the daily attendance report transmitted to him directly at headquarters, from which he will make the final decision on whether to present the program in its current format or not.

Questions: Does this monitoring and control method appear adequate? What are the potential problems?

Night Tran Construction Company

Night Tran Construction Company specializes in building small power plants, mostly for utility companies. The company was awarded a contract approximately two years ago to build such a power plant. The contract stated a project duration of three years, after which a 1 percent penalty would be invoked for each additional month of construction. Project records indicate the utility plan is only 50 percent completed and is encountering continuing problems. The owner of Night Tran Company, concerned over the potential losses, investigated the project and found the following: There was an excessive number of engineering design changes; there was a high work rejection rate; and the project was generally understaffed. As a result, she directed the project manager to develop a better system of project control and present this method to the board members in one week.

Questions: If you were the project manager, what characteristics would you be looking for in the new control system? Will a new control system be adequate for the problem? Will it control scope creep? Explain.

 CONTINUING INTEGRATIVE CLASS PROJECT

Decide what type of control system you plan to use for the project and describe it—you may wish to use subteam leaders in the control process if you have them. Then design a critical ratio control chart for the project that you will use as the project progresses. Once again, the costs will probably be the labor hours put in by members of the class. How will you determine actual progress?

 BIBLIOGRAPHY

Ackoff, R. L. "Beyond Problem Solving." *Decision Sciences*, April 1974.

Block, P. *Stewardship*. San Francisco: Berrett-Koehler, 1993.

Byrne, J. "Project Management: How Much Is Enough?" *PM Network*, February 1999.

Cooper, R. G. "The New Product Process: A Decision Guide for Management." *Journal of Marketing Management*, Vol. 3, No. 3 (Winter), 1994.

Gibson, L. "Project Scope Creep." *Today's Engineer*, Spring 1998.

Gupta, V. K., and D. J. Graham. "A Customer-Driven Quality Improvement and Management Project at Diamond Offshore Drilling." *Project Management Journal*, September 1997.

Hajek, V. G. *Management of Engineering Projects*. New York: McGraw Hill, 1977.

Heywood, G. E., and T. J. Allen. "Project Controls: How Much Is Enough?" *PM Network*, November 1996.

Hunsberger, K. "The Best of the Best." *PM Network*, September 2010.

Hunsberger, K. "Change Is Good." *PM Network*, February 2011.

Hussain, R., and S. Wearne. "Problems and Needs of Project Management in the Process and Other Industries." *Transactions of the Institution of Chemical Engineers*, Part A, April 2005.

Ibbs, C. W., and Y.-H. Kwak. "Benchmarking Project Management Organizations." *PM Network*, February 1998.

Keil, M., and M. Mähring. "Is Your Project Turning into a Black Hole?" *California Management Review,* Fall 2010.

Lee, H. L. "Aligning Supply Chain Strategies with Product Uncertainties." *IEEE Engineering Management Review*, 2nd Qtr. 2003.

Leffingwell, D. "Engage! Involve the Customer to Manage Scope." *PM Network*, August 1997.

McGrath, R. G., and I. Macmillan, "Discovery-Driven Planning." *Harvard Business Review*, July–August 1995.

Meredith, J. R., and S. M. Shafer. *Operations Management for MBAs, 4th ed.* New York: Wiley, 2010.

Murdick, R. G. *Information Systems for Modern Management, 3rd ed.* Englewood Cliffs, NJ: Prentice Hall, 1984.

Newman, W. H. *Constructive Control.* Englewood Cliffs, NJ: Prentice Hall, 1975.

Partovi, F. Y., and J. Burton. "Timing of Monitoring and Control of CPM Projects." *IEEE Transactions on Engineering Management*, February 1993.

Project Management Institute. *A Guide to the Project Management Body of Knowledge, 4th ed.* Newtown Square, PA: Project Management Institute, 2008.

Project Management Institute. "Q&A: On Track." *PM Network*, October 2002.

Rice, M. P., G. C. O'Connor, and R. Pierantozzi. "Implementing a Learning Plan to Counter Project Uncertainty." *MIT Sloan Management Review,* Winter 2008.

Roman, D. D. *Managing Projects: A Systems Approach.* New York: Elsevier, 1986.

Seesing, P. R. "Distributing Project Control Database Information on the World Wide Web." *PM Network*, October 1996.

Thamhain, H. J. "Best Practices for Controlling Technology-Based Projects." *Project Management Journal*, December 1996.

Toney, F. "What the *Fortune* 500 Know about PM Best Practices." *PM Network*, February 1997.

van Gigch, J. P. *Applied General Systems Theory, 2nd ed.* New York: Harper & Row, 1978.

Whitten, N. "Managing Priorities Effectively." *PM Network*, July 1995.

The following case illustrates the control actions a small firm's president used to implement a successful project that saved his firm and launched it into a new area of business. The project had many points of crisis, and control was required to keep it on track. Although the project involved the implementation of a new technology, many of the critical issues requiring careful control were human and behavioral. The case includes important data for economic analysis of the project, its justification, and the justification of a potential follow-on project.

C A S E

PEERLESS LASER PROCESSORS
Jack R. Meredith, Marianne M. Hill, and James M. Comer*

Owner and President Ted Montague was sitting at his desk on the second floor of the small Groveport, Ohio, plant that housed Peerless Saw Company and its new subsidiary, Peerless Laser Processors, Inc. As he scanned over the eight-page contract to purchase their third laser system, a

*Reprinted by permission. Copyright J. R. Meredith.

1,200-watt computerized carbon dioxide (CO_2) laser cutter, he couldn't help but reflect back to a similar situation he faced three years ago in this same office. Conditions were significantly different then. It was amazing, Ted reflected, how fast things had changed in the saw blade market, especially for Peerless, which had jumped from an underdog to the technology leader. Market data and financial statements describing the firm and its market environment are given in Exhibits 1 and 2.

History of Peerless Saw Company

Peerless Saw Company was formed in 1931, during the Great Depression, in Columbus, Ohio, to provide bandsaw blades to Ford Motor Company. It survived the Depression and by 1971, with its nonunionized labor force, it was known for its quality bandsaw and circular saw blades.

But conditions inside the firm warranted less optimism. The original machines and processes were now very old and breaking down frequently, extending order backlogs to 20 weeks. However, the owners were nearing retirement and didn't want to invest in new machinery, much less add capacity for the growing order backlog which had been building for years.

By 1984 the situation had reached the crisis point. At that point Ted Montague had appeared and, with the help of external funding, bought the firm from the original owners. Ted's previous business experience was in food processing, and he had some concern about taking charge of a metal products company. But Ted found the 40 employees, 13 in the offices and 27 (divided among two shifts) on the shop floor, to be very helpful, particularly since they now had an owner who was interested in building the business back up.

Within two years Ted felt comfortable with his knowledge of the business. At that point he had a feel for what he believed were the more serious problems of the business and hired both a manufacturing manager and a manufacturing engineer, Con Wittkopp, to help him solve the problems. The most shopworn machines at Peerless were the over 30-year-old grinding machines and vertical milling machines. Committed to staying in business, Ted arranged for capital financing to design and build a new facility and replace some of the aging equipment. In 1987 the firm moved into new quarters in Groveport, not far from Columbus, with an additional 7,000 square feet of floor space. He also ordered seven new grinders from Germany and five new vertical mills. In order to determine what bottlenecks and inefficiencies existed on the shop floor, Ted also devised and installed a cost tracking system.

Laser Cutting Technology

By 1988, the competition had grown quite strong. In addition to the growing number of direct domestic competitors, foreign firms were mounting a devastating attack on the more common saw blade models, offering equivalent quality off the shelf for lower prices. Furthermore, many users were now tipping their own blades, or even cutting them themselves, further reducing the salable market. Sales were down while costs continued to increase and the remaining equipment continued to age and fail. Ted and Con looked into new technologies for saw blade cutting. They felt that Computer Numerical Control (CNC) machining couldn't be adapted to their needs, and laser cutting had high setup times, was underpowered, and exhibited a poor cut texture. (Ted remarked that "It looked as though an alligator had chewed on it.")

By early 1991, advances in laser cutting technology had received a considerable amount of publicity, so Ted and Con signed up to attend a seminar on the subject sponsored by Coherent, one of the leaders in industrial laser technology. Unfortunately, at the last minute they were unable to attend the seminar and had to cancel their reservations.

Ted was under pressure from all sides to replace their worn-out punch presses. No longer able to delay, he had contracts made up to purchase three state-of-the-art, quick-change, Minster punch presses. As he sat at his desk on the second floor of the Groveport building, scanning the Minster, Inc. contracts one last time before signing, Con came in with a small piece of sheet steel that had thin, smooth cuts through it.

It seems that a salesperson had been given Ted and Con's names from the seminar registration list and decided to pay them a call. He brought a small piece of metal with him that had been cut with a laser and showed it to Con. This was what Con brought into Ted's office. Impressed with the sample, Ted put the contracts aside and talked to the salesperson. Following their talk, Ted made arrangements to fly out to Coherent's headquarters in Palo Alto, California, for a demonstration.

In July 1991, Ted and Con made the trip to Palo Alto and were impressed with the significant improvements made in laser cutting technology in just a few years. Setups were faster, the power was higher, and the cuts were much

Sales		$5,028,067
Costs:		
Materials	1,860,385	
Labor	905,052	
Variable overhead	1,106,175	
G&A	553,087	
Contribution to profit		603,368

EXHIBIT 1   Peerless Financial Data, 1993.

Year	Sales (M)	Market Share (%)
1993	$5.028	29
1992	3.081	27
1991	2.545	25
1990	2.773	25

EXHIBIT 2   Sales and Market Data, 1993

cleaner. Following this trip, they arranged to attend the Hanover Fair in Germany in September to see the latest European technology. There they were guaranteed that the newer, higher powered lasers could even cut one-quarter-inch steel sheets.

In November, Ted and Con returned to Palo Alto, making their own tests with the equipment. Satisfied, Ted signed a contract for a 700-watt laser cutter,* one of the largest then available, at a price close to $400,000, although the cutter couldn't be delivered until September 1992.

In addition to the risk of the laser technology, another serious problem now faced Ted and Con—obtaining adequate software for the laser cutter. Ted and Con wanted a package that would allow off-line programming of the machine. Furthermore, they wanted it to be menu driven, operable by their current high school educated workers (rather than by engineers, as most lasers required), and to have pattern search capability.

Coherent, Inc. was simply not in the off-line software business. Since Ted and Con did not want to learn to write their own software for the cutter, Coherent suggested a seminar for them to attend where they might find the contact they needed.

Con attended the session but was shocked at the "horror stories" the other attendees were telling. Nevertheless, someone suggested that he contact Battelle Laboratories in Columbus for help. Fearing their high class price tag but with no other alternative, Ted and Con made arrangements to talk with the Battelle people.

The meeting, in March 1992, gave Ted and Con tremendous hope. Ted laid out the specifications for the software and, surprisingly, it appeared that what they wanted could possibly be done. The price would be expensive, however—around $100,000—and would require seven months to complete. The timing was perfect. Ted arranged for a September completion, to coincide with the delivery of the laser cutter. In the next seven months Con worked closely with Battelle, constantly redesigning and respecifying the software to improve its capabilities and avoid unsolvable problems and snags.

Finally, in September 1992, a 2-inch stack printout of code, programmed into a computer, was delivered and matched via an interface with the recently delivered laser cutter. But when the system was turned on, nothing happened. As Ted remarked, "Disaster City!" The software problem was solved within a day but the laser cutter had to be completely rebuilt on-site. For almost 100 days the bugs had to be worked out of the system. "It was just awful."

The months of debugging finally resulted in a working system by December. Meanwhile, Ted and the machine

---

*The contract included extensive ancillary equipment and hardware.

operator, Steve, spent four hours every Friday morning in training at Battelle to learn how to use the system. Con and another operator did the same on Friday afternoons. Con and Ted later remarked that the "hardest" part of the training was learning to find the keys on the keyboard.

Initially, Ted and Con thought that they might have enough business to keep the laser busy during one shift per day. As it turned out, running the system was considerably more operator dependent than they had expected for a computerized system. Though anyone in the shop could learn to use the system, the operator had to learn how to work with the system, finessing and overriding it (skipping routines, "tricking" it into doing certain routines) when necessary to get a job done. Ted described this as "a painful learning curve." Thus, only an experienced operator could get the volume of work through the system that was "theoretically" possible. Nevertheless, once thoroughly familiar with the system, one operator could easily handle two cutters at the same time, and probably even three.

Within the next 17 months, Peerless put 4,000 saw patterns on the system and started running the cutter for two full shifts. Due to increased demand they added another laser cutter, using the same computer system, and by November 1993 were running both cutters throughout two full shifts.

Marketplace and Competitive Effects

As of 1994, Peerless saw a number of improvements in their operations, and some significant changes in their market as well. In 1989 they had a 14-week delivery lead time. Part of the reason for this was that 25 percent of their orders had to be renegotiated with the customer because the old tooling couldn't handle the job. This slowed down the work tremendously. With the laser cutter this has been reduced to just three weeks, heat treating being the bottleneck (two full weeks).

Though they weren't making any blades that could not be made in 1989, their product mix changed considerably. In 1989 they made primarily 8-, 10-, 12-, and 14-inch saw blades. With the new capabilities of the laser cutter they were now making a much wider variety of blades, and more complex blades as well. As a matter of fact, they were producing the more difficult blades now, and at less cost. For example, with the laser cutter, it took one-seventh the amount of time to cut a blade as it did previously, and one-eighth the number of machine operators. The resulting average cost saving was 5 to 10 percent per blade, reaching a maximum of 45 percent savings (on labor, material, and variable overhead) on some individual blades. Although cost savings allowed Peerless to cut prices on their blades, more significantly, they had an improved product, faster lead times, and more production capability.

Production capability was of particular importance. Peerless found that the ability to do things for customers that simply couldn't be done before changed the way customers ordered their blades. Because of their new capability, they were now seeing fewer repeat orders (although the batch size remained about the same) and considerably more "creativity" on the part of their customers. Orders now came to them as "The same pattern as last time except…" Customers were using Peerless's new capability to incrementally improve their saw blades, trying to increase capacity, or productivity, or quality by even 1 or 2 percent, based on their previous experimentation. Peerless had discovered, almost by accident, a significant competitive advantage.

Ted was intrigued with the way the laser cutter had revived Peerless. He stated that, based on payback or return on investment (ROI) criteria, he could not have justified the investment in the laser cutter beforehand. But more significantly, if he were to go through the figures now, after the tremendous success of the laser cutter, he still would not be able to justify the cutter on payback or ROI grounds. The point was, the new technology had changed the market Peerless was selling to, although the customers remained largely the same. The laser cutter in fact "created" its own market, one that simply could not exist prior to this technology. It filled a need that even the customers did not know existed.

Despite the increased speed of the laser cutter, it was not necessary to lay anyone off, though some employees' jobs changed significantly. The laser system was purposely packaged so that the existing employees could work with it and contribute to its success, even though they may have had only high school educations.

Ted continued to push the concept of a small, high-quality, technologically advanced business staying ahead of the same foreign competition that was wreaking havoc on the major corporations in America.

Ted summarized the benefits the new technology brought as:

- Decreased product cost
- Increased product quality
- Ability to use a sophisticated technology
- Ability to do what couldn't be done before, more responsive to the market
- An inspiration to visiting customers
- A positive image for the firm
- Adds "pizzazz" and "mystique" to the firm
- Allows entry into new fields

Peerless in 1994

In September 1994 Ted created a new division, Peerless Laser Processors, Inc. to handle general laser cutting of other types of parts besides saw blades. By then, Peerless had logged 10,000 hours on the laser cutters and had placed 6,000 patterns on the system, adding new ones at the rate of 300 a month. Due to continuing customer requests that had never originally been considered, or even dreamed of, the software has been under constant revision and improvement by Battelle. Ted noted that, even though the need for revisions is expected to continue, it would neither pay to hire a software programmer nor would the job be interesting enough to keep one for long.

Ted and Con felt that generic computer-assisted design/computer-aided manufacturing (CAD/CAM) systems available today would not help their situation. The unneeded capabilities tend to slow down the system, and in their new business the main competitive factor, given other constants such as quality, is: "How fast can you do the job?"

Peerless also hired two additional sales representatives, with one now in the field and two in the office at all times. They also hired an engineer to develop new applications on a full-time basis for Peerless Laser Processing. As Con noted, "The problem is recognizing new applications while still doing your own work." They discovered, for example, that they could now make their own shuttles for their double disk grinders instead of purchasing them.

Peerless now has five U.S. competitors in the laser cutting business. Of course, Germany and Japan, among others, are still major competitors using the older technology. For the future, Ted sees the lasers becoming more powerful and having better control. He sees applications growing exponentially, and lasers doing welding and general fabrication of parts as well. He sees other technologies becoming competitive also, such as water jet and electrodischarge machining (EDM).

For Peerless, Ted's immediate goal is to attain a two-week lead time for saw blades and even better customer service, possibly including an inventory function in their service offerings. For the long run, Ted's goal is to become a "showcase" operation, offering the best in technology and quality in the world. As Ted put it: A company is like a tree. It only succeeds if it continues to grow, and you've got to grow wherever there's an opportunity. There are a maximum number of saw blades needed in the world, but no cap on what else the technology can do. We're only limited by our own imagination and creativeness and desire to make technology do things. That's our only restriction. What it fundamentally comes down to is this: Is a railroad a railroad or a transportation company? Are we a saw blade company or are we a company that fabricates metals into what anyone wants?

QUESTIONS

1. How did the laser cutter "save" Peerless Saw Company when it could not be justified on payback or ROI grounds?

2. Compare the decision Ted faces now—the 1,200-watt laser purchase—with the decision he faced in 1991 when he was considering the three punch presses. Structure the investment decision for each of these cases, considering costs, benefits, and risks. How has the decision environment changed? Is Ted more or less comfortable with this decision? How is this decision easier? How is it harder?

3. What do you think the potential problems might be in purchasing the 1,200-watt laser? What about the potential benefits? Will this laser have the same impact on the business as the first laser? What are the strategic variables involved in these decisions?

4. Calculate the variable cost per blade of laser cutting with this new system. Assume that the variable cost of the laser is $4/hour, that the laser cuts at the rate of 40 inches per minute, that a typical blade of 14 inches diameter sells for $25, and the same computer and software will be used as currently. Material load time

for a 10-blade sheet of steel is one minute. Use a 3-inch arbor hole size and assume that a cut tooth doubles the cut distance. Compare this cost to the cost of variable overhead per blade in Exhibit 1.

5. Using the data in question 4, estimate the costs and revenues for this new system to perform a payback analysis (in months). What do you have to assume in addition to do the payback analysis?

6. What are the organizational/behavioral considerations involved in this purchase? Are they the same as the first laser? How might this system be more or less justifiable on a noneconomic basis than the first laser system?

7. Of the three major types of control systems—cybernetic, go/no-go, and postcontrol—which would have been the most useful with the first laser and why? With this new laser and why?

8. Ted is thinking about offering 25 of his largest customers the opportunity to tie into his system directly from their offices. What benefits would this offer to the customers and Peerless? What problems might it pose?

The following article reports on a study of hundreds of project managers and the challenges and barriers they perceived in successfully controlling projects. The potential problems leading to schedule slips and budget overruns are identified and compared to the directly observed reasons. Also, the general managers' reasons for the slips and overruns are compared to the project managers' reasons, and significant differences are noted. Last, the criteria that seem to be important to control are listed and discussed.

The value of this article for managers is the insight it gives concerning what needs to be controlled to bring about successful projects. The major factors are defining a detailed project plan that includes all key project personnel, reaching agreement on the plan among the project team members and the customer, obtaining the commitment of management, defining measurable milestones, and detecting problems early.

DIRECTED READING

CONTROLLING PROJECTS ACCORDING TO PLAN*
H. J. Thamhain and D. L. Wilemon

Few project managers would argue the need for controlling their projects according to established plans. The challenge is to apply the available tools and techniques effectively. That is, to manage the effort by leading the multifunctional

*Reprinted from *Project Management Journal* with permission. Copyright by the Project Management Institute.

personnel toward the agreed-on objectives within the given time and resource constraints. Even the most experienced practitioners often find it difficult to control programs in spite of apparent detail in the plan, personnel involvement, and even commitment. As summarized in Table 1, effective program management is a function of properly defining the work, budgets, and schedules and then monitoring progress. Equally important, it is related to the ability to keep personnel involved and interested in the work, to obtain and refuel commitment from the team as well as from upper management, and to resolve some of the enormous complexities on the technical, human, and organizational side.

Responding to this interest, a field study was initiated to investigate the practices of project managers regarding their project control experiences. Specifically, the study investigates:

1. Type of project control problems experienced by project managers.
2. Project management practices and performance.
3. Criteria for effective project control.

Method of Investigation

Data were collected over a period of three years from a sample of over 400 project leaders in predominantly technical undertakings, such as electronics, petrochemical, construction, and pharmaceutical projects. The data were collected mostly by questionnaires from attendees of project management workshops and seminars, as well as during in-plant consulting work conducted by the authors. Selectively, questionnaires were followed up by personal interviews. All data were checked for relevant sourcing

Table 1 Challenges of Managing Projects According to Plan

Rank	Challenge	Frequency (mentioned by % of PMs)
1	Coping with end-date driven schedules	85%
2	Coping with resource limitations	83%
3	Communicating effectively among task groups	80%
4	Gaining commitment from team members	74%
5	Establishing measurable milestones	70%
6	Coping with changes	60%
7	Working out project plan agreement with team	57%
8	Gaining commitment from management	45%
9	Dealing with conflict	42%
10	Managing vendors and subcontractors	38%
11	Other challenges	35%

to assure that the people who filled in the questionnaire had the minimum project leadership qualifications we established. These included: two years of experience in managing multidisciplinary projects, leading a minimum of three other project professionals, and being formally accountable for final results.

Sample Characteristics

The final qualifying sample included 304 project leaders from 183 technical projects. The leaders had an average of 5.2 years of project management experience. As shown by the sigma/standard deviation,* the sample data are distributed widely:

Number of Project Leaders in Sample	304
Number of Projects in Sample	183
Number of Project Leaders per Project	1.66 ($\sigma = 1$)
Project Size (Average)	\$850K ($\sigma = 310K$)
Project Duration (Average)	12 Months ($\sigma = 4$)
Multidisciplinary Nature (Average)	8 Team Members ($\sigma = 5$)
Project Management Experience/PM	5.2 Years ($\sigma = 2.5$)
Number of Previous Projects/PM	6 ($\sigma = 4.5$)

Data were collected in three specific modes: (1) Open-ended questions leading to a broad set of data, such as condensed in Table 2, and used for broad classifications and further, more detailed investigations; (2) Specific questions, requested to be answered on a tested five-point scale, such as shown in Figure 1. The scores enabled subsequent data ranking and correlation analysis; and (3) Interviews leading to a discussion of the previous findings and further qualitative investigations into the practices and experiences of project managers and their superiors.

All associations were measured by utilizing Kendall's Tau rank-order correlation. The agreement between project managers and their superiors on the reason for project control problems was tested by using the nonparametric Kruskal-Wallis one-way analysis of variance by ranks, setting the null-hypothesis for agreement at various confidence levels depending on the strength of the agreement or disagreement as specified in the write-up.

Discussion of Results

The results of this study are being presented in four parts. First, the reasons for poor project control are

---

*The distribution of the sample data is skewed. The sigma/standard deviation listed in parentheses corresponds to the positive side only.

Table 2   Potential Problems* (subtle reasons) Leading to Schedule Slips and Budget Overruns

01   Difficulty of Defining Work in Sufficient Detail
02   Little Involvement of Project Personnel During Planning
03   Problems with Organizing and Building Project Team
04   No Firm Agreement to Project Plan by Functional Management
05   No Clear Charter for Key Project Personnel
06   Insufficiently Defined Project Team Organization
07   No Clear Role/Responsibility Definition for Project Personnel
08   Rush into Project Kick-off
09   Project Perceived as Not Important or Exciting
10   No Contingency Provisions
11   Inability to Measure True Project Performance
12   Poor Communications with Upper Management
13   Poor Communications with Customer or Sponsor
14   Poor Understanding of Organizational Interfaces
15   Difficulty in Working across Functional Lines
16   No Ties between Project Performance and Reward System
17   Poor Project Leadership
18   Weak Assistance and Help from Upper Management
19   Project Leader Not Involved with Team
20   Ignorance of Early Warning Signals and Feedback
21   Poor Ability to Manage Conflict
22   Credibility Problems with Task Leaders
23   Difficulties in Assessing Risks
24   Insensitivity to Organizational Culture/Value System
25   Insufficient Formal Procedural Project Guidelines
26   Apathy or Indifference by Project Team or Management
27   No Mutual Trust among Team Members
28   Too Much Unresolved/Dysfunctional Conflict
29   Power Struggles
30   Too Much Reliance on Established Cost Accounting System

*The tabulated potential problems represent summaries of data compiled during interviews with project personnel and management.

analyzed as they relate to budget overruns and schedule slips. Second, the less tangible criteria for these control problems are discussed. This part shows that many of the reasons blamed for poor project performance, such as insufficient front-end planning and underestimating the complexities and scope, are really rooted in some less obvious organizational, managerial, and interpersonal problems. Third, the relationship between project performance and project management problems is

discussed, and fourth, the criteria for effective project controls are summarized.

The Reasons for Poor Project Control.   Figure 1 on page 514 summarizes an investigation into 15 problem areas regarding their effects on poor project performance. Specifically, project managers and their superiors (such as senior functional managers and general managers) indicate on a five-point scale their perception of how frequently certain problems are responsible for schedule slips and budget overruns. The data indicate that project leaders perceive these problem areas in a somewhat different order than their superiors.

While *project leaders* most frequently blame the following reasons as being responsible for poor project performance:

1. Customer and Management Changes
2. Technical Complexities
3. Unrealistic Project Plans
4. Staffing Problems
5. Inability to Detect Problems Early

Senior management ranks these reasons somewhat differently:

1. Insufficient Front-End Planning
2. Unrealistic Project Plans
3. Underestimated Project Scope
4. Customer and Management Changes
5. Insufficient Contingency Planning

On balance, the data support the findings of subsequent interviews that project leaders are more concerned with external influences such as changes, complexities, staffing, and priorities while senior managers focus more on what should and can be done to avoid problems. In fact, the differences between project leaders' and senior/superior management's perceptions were measured statistically by using a Kruskal–Wallis analysis of variance by ranks, based on the following test statistics:

Strong Agreement: If acceptable at <99% confidence

Agreement: If acceptable at <90% confidence

Weak Agreement: If acceptable at <80% confidence

Disagreement: If rejected at 80% confidence

Project leaders disagree with their superiors on the ranking of importance for all but six reasons. What this means is that while both groups of management actually agree on the basic reasons behind schedule slips and budget overruns, they attach different weights. The practical implication of this finding is that senior management expects proper project planning, organizing, and tracking from project leaders. They further believe that the "external" criteria, such as customer changes and project complexities, impact project performance only if the project had not been defined properly and sound management practices were ignored. On the other side, management's view that some of the subtle problems, such as sinking team spirit, priority shifts, and staffing, are of lesser importance might point to a potential problem area. Management might be less sensitive to these struggles, get less involved, and provide less assistance in solving these problems.

Less Obvious and Less Visible Reasons for Poor Performance. Managers at all levels have long lists of "real" reasons why the problems identified in Figure 1 occur. They point out, for instance, that while insufficient front-end planning eventually got the project into trouble, the real culprits are much less obvious and visible. These subtle reasons, summarized in Table 2, strike a common theme. They relate strongly to organizational, managerial, and human aspects. In fact, the most frequently mentioned reasons for poor project performance can be classified in five categories:

1. Problems with organizing project team
2. Weak project leadership
3. Communication problems
4. Conflict and confusion
5. Insufficient upper management involvement

Most of the problems in Table 2 relate to the manager's ability to foster a work environment conducive to multidisciplinary teamwork, rich in professionally stimulating and interesting activities, involvement, and mutual trust. The ability to foster such a high-performance project environment requires sophisticated skills in leadership, technical, interpersonal, and administrative areas. To be effective, project managers must consider all facets of the job. They must consider the task, the people, the tools, and the organization. The days of the manager who gets by with technical expertise or pure administrative skills alone, are gone. Today the project manager must relate socially as well as technically. He or she must understand the culture and value system of the organization. Research and experience show that effective project management is directly related to the level of proficiency at which these skills are mastered. This is also reflected in the 30 potential problems of our study (see Table 2) and the rank-order correlations summarized in Table 3. As indicated by the correlation figure of $\tau = +.45$, the stronger managers felt about the reasons in Figure 1, the stronger they also felt about the problems in Table 2 as reasons for poor project performance. This correlation is statistically significant at a confidence level of 99 percent and supports the conclusion that both sets of problem areas are related and require similar skills for effective management.

Management Practice and Project Performance. Managers appear very confident in citing actual and potential problems. These managers are sure in their own mind that these problems, summarized in Figure 1 and Table 2, are indeed related to poor project performance. However, no such conclusion could be drawn without additional data and the specific statistical test shown in Table 3. As indicated by the strongly negative correlations between project performance and (1) potential problems ($\tau = -.55$) and (2) actual problems ($\tau = -.40$), the presence of either problem will indeed result in lower performance. Specifically, the stronger and more frequently project managers experience these problems, the lower was the manager judged by superior managers regarding overall on-time and on-budget performance.

Furthermore, it is interesting to note that the more subtle potential problems correlate most strongly to poor performance ($\tau = -.55$). In fact, special insight has been gained by analyzing the association of each problem to project performance separately. Taken together, it shows that the following problems seem to be some of the most crucial *barriers* to high project performance:

- Team organization and staffing problems
- Work perceived as not important, challenging, having growth potential
- Little team and management involvement during planning

Table 3   Correlation of Project Management Practices to Performance

Potential Problems vs. Actual	Correlation of (1) Potential Problems (Table 2) and (2) Directly Observed Reasons by PMs (Figure 1)	$\tau = +.45*$
Potential Problems vs. Performance	Correlation of (1) Potential Problems (Table 2) and (2) Project Performance (top management judgment)	$\tau = -.55*$
Actual Problems vs. Performance	Correlation of (1) Directly Observed Reasons (Figure 1) and (2) Project Performance (top management)	$\tau = -.40*$

*99% Confidence Level (p = .01)
All Tau values are Kendall Tau Rank-Order Correlation.

Rank by		Reason or Problem	Rarely 1	Sometimes 2	Often 3	Most Likely 4	Always 5	Agreement between GM & PM
General Managers	Project Managers							
1	10	Insufficient Front-End Planning					GM (PM at ~2.5)	Disagree
2	3	Unrealistic Project Plan						Agree
3	8	Project Scope Underestimated						Disagree
4	1	Customer/Management Changes						Disagree
5	14	Insufficient Contingency Planning						Disagree
6	13	Inability to Track Progress						Disagree
7	5	Inability to Detect Problems Early		PM	GM			Disagree
8	9	Insufficient Number of Checkpoints						Agree
9	4	Staffing Problems						Agree
10	2	Technical Complexities						Disagree
11	6	Priority Shifts						Disagree
12	11	No Commitment by Personnel to Plan						Disagree
13	12	Uncooperative Support Groups						Agree
14	7	Sinking Team Spirit						Agree
15	15	Unqualified Project Personnel						Disagree
								Agree

Figure 1 Directly observed reasons for schedule slips and budget overruns.

- Conflict, confusion, power struggle
- Lacking commitment by team and management
- Poor project definition
- Difficulty in understanding and working across organizational interfaces
- Weak project leadership
- Measurability problems
- Changes, contingencies, and priority problems
- Poor communications, management involvement and support

To be effective, project leaders must not only recognize the potential barriers to performance, but also know where in the life cycle of the project they most likely occur. The effective project leader takes preventive actions early in the project life cycle and fosters a work environment that is conducive to active participation, interesting work, good communications, management involvement, and low conflict.

Criteria for Effective Project Control

The results presented so far focused on the reasons for poor project performance. That is, what went wrong and why were analyzed. This section concentrates on the lessons learned from the study and extensive interviews investigating the forces driving high project performance. Accordingly, this section summarizes the criteria which seem to be important for controlling projects according to plan. The write-up follows a recommendations format and flows with the project through its life cycle wherever possible.

1. **Detailed Project Planning.** Develop a detailed project plan, involving all key personnel, defining the specific work to be performed, the timing, the resources, and the responsibilities.

2. **Break the Overall Program into Phases and Subsystems.** Use Work Breakdown Structure (WBS) as a planning tool.

3. **Results and Deliverables.** Define the program objectives and requirements in terms of specifications, schedule, resources, and deliverable items for the total program and its subsystems.

4. **Measurable Milestones.** Define measurable milestones and checkpoints throughout the program. Measurability can be enhanced by defining specific results, deliverables, technical performance measures against schedule, and budget.

5. **Commitment.** Obtain commitment from all key personnel regarding the problem plan, its measures and results. This commitment can be enhanced and maintained by involving the team members early in the

project planning, including the definition of results, measurable milestones, schedules, and budgets. It is through this involvement that the team members gain a detailed understanding of the work to be performed, develop professional interests in the project and desires to succeed, and eventually make a firm commitment toward the specific task and the overall project objectives.

6. ***Intra-Program Involvement.*** Assure that the interfacing project teams, such as engineering and manufacturing, work together, not only during the task transfer, but during the total life of the project. Such interphase involvement is necessary to assure effective implementation of the developments and to simply assure "doability" and responsiveness to the realities of the various functions supporting the project. It is enhanced by clearly defining the results/deliverables for each interphase point, agreed upon by both parties. In addition, a simple sign-off procedure, which defines who has to sign off on what items, is useful in establishing clear checkpoints for completion and to enhance involvement and cooperation of the interphasing team members.

7. ***Project Tracking.*** Define and implement a proper project tracking system which captures and processes project performance data conveniently summarized for reviews and management actions.

8. ***Measurability.*** Assure accurate measurements of project performance data, especially technical progress against schedule and budget.

9. ***Regular Reviews.*** Project should be reviewed regularly, both on a work package (subsystem) level and total project level.

10. ***Signing-On.*** The process of "signing-on" project personnel during the initial phases of the project or each task seems to be very important to a proper understanding of the project objectives, the specific tasks, and personal commitment. The sign-on process is greatly facilitated by sitting down with each team member and discussing the specific assignments, overall project objectives, as well as professional interests and support needs.

11. ***Interesting Work.*** The project leader should try to accommodate the professional interests and desires of supporting personnel when negotiating their tasks. Project effectiveness depends on the manager's ability to provide professionally stimulating and interesting work. This leads to increased project involvement, better communications, lower conflict, and stronger commitment. This is an environment where people work toward established objectives in a self-enforcing mode requiring a minimum of managerial controls. Although the scope of a project may be fixed, the project manager usually has a degree of flexibility in allocating task assignments among various contributors.

12. ***Communication.*** Good communication is essential for effective project work. It is the responsibility of the task leaders and ultimately the project manager to provide the appropriate communication tools, techniques, and systems. These tools are not only the status meetings, reviews, schedules, and reporting systems, but also the objective statements, specifications, list of deliverables, the sign-off procedure, and critical path analysis. It is up to the project leaders to orchestrate the various tools and systems, and to use them effectively.

13. ***Leadership.*** Assure proper program direction and leadership throughout the project life cycle. This includes project definition, team organization, task coordination, problem identification, and a search for solutions.

14. ***Minimize Threats.*** Project managers must foster a work environment that is low on personal conflict, power struggles, surprises, and unrealistic demands. An atmosphere of mutual trust is necessary for project personnel to communicate problems and concerns candidly and at an early point in time.

15. ***Design a Personnel Appraisal and Reward System.*** This should be consistent with the responsibilities of the people.

16. ***Assure Continuous Senior Management Involvement, Endorsement, and Support of the Project.*** This will surround the project with a priority image, enhance its visibility, and refuel overall commitment to the project and its objectives.

17. ***Personal Drive.*** Project managers can influence the climate of the work environment by their own actions. Concern for project team members, ability to integrate personal goals and needs of project personnel with project goals, and ability to create personal enthusiasm for the project itself can foster a climate of high motivation, work involvement, open communication, and ultimately high project performance.

A Final Note

Managing engineering programs toward established performance, schedule, and cost targets requires more than just another plan. It requires the total commitment of the performing organization plus the involvement and help of the sponsor/customer community. Successful program managers stress the importance of carefully designing the project planning and control system as well as the structural and authority relationships. All are critical to the implementation of an effective project control system. Other organizational issues, such as management style, personnel appraisals and compensation, and intraproject communication, must be carefully considered to make the system self-forcing; that is, project personnel throughout the organization must feel that participation in the project is desirable regarding the fulfillment of their professional needs and wants. Furthermore, project personnel must be convinced that management involvement is helpful in their work. Personnel must be convinced that identifying the true project status and communicating potential problems early will provide them with more assistance to problem solving, more cross-functional support, and in the end will lead to project success and the desired recognition for their accomplishments.

In summary, effective control of engineering programs or projects involves the ability to:

- Work out a detailed project plan, involving all key personnel
- Reach agreement on the plan among the project team members and the customer/sponsor
- Obtain commitment from the project team members
- Obtain commitment from management

- Define measurable milestones
- Attract and hold quality people
- Establish a controlling authority for each work package
- Detect problems early

Questions

1. Why do project managers and senior general managers see the reasons for project difficulty differently?

2. Why do the potential problems correlate more strongly with poor performance than the actual problems?

3. Overall, what do you conclude are the reasons for poor project performance?

4. Relate the findings in this article to the PM in Practice SF Turnback project control process and the PM in Practice Johnson Controls project management procedures.

5. Of the types of control discussed in the chapter, which type(s) is this article referring to?

Project Auditing

In the previous chapter, we discussed postcontrol. Postcontrol cannot change the past, but it tries to capture the essence of project successes and failures so that future projects can benefit from past experiences. To benefit from past experiences implies that one understands them, and understanding requires evaluation. But project evaluation is not limited to after-the-fact analysis. While the project as a whole is evaluated when it has been completed (the basis for postcontrols), project evaluation should be conducted at a number of points during the life cycle.

A major vehicle for evaluation (but by no means the only one) is the *project audit*, a more or less formal inquiry into any aspect of the project. We associate the word *audit* with a detailed examination of financial matters, but a project audit is highly flexible and may focus on whatever matters senior management desires. Note that there are also other types of audits such as *ethics audits* which can be helpful when employing project management in an organization. For example, as Schaefer et al. (1998, p. 40) note, "Ethics is not a matter of right or wrong; it is a process by which an organization evaluates decisions," a process that is most certainly relevant to project management! (We should add that Webster defines "ethics" as a "system or code of morals" and "ethical" as "conforming to the standards of a profession.") And in addition to project audits, there are also other kinds of project evaluations, such as project *reviews**; see also Sangameswaran (1995) for more details.

The term *evaluate* means to set the value of or appraise. Project evaluation appraises the progress and performance of a project compared to that project's planned progress and performance, or compared to the progress and performance of other, similar projects. The comparison is made by measuring the project against several different types of standards. The evaluation also supports any management decisions required for the project. Therefore, the evaluation must be conducted and presented in a manner and format that assures management that all pertinent data have been considered. The evaluation of a project must have credibility in the eyes of the management group for whom it is performed and also in the eyes of

---

*The reading "An Assessment of Postproject Reviews" at the end of this chapter examines four such evaluations and summarizes the pros and cons of conducting such evaluations.

the project team on whom it is performed. Accordingly, the project evaluation must be just as carefully constructed and controlled as the project itself.

In this chapter, we describe the project audit/review/evaluation, its various forms and purposes, and some typical problems encountered in conducting an audit/evaluation. For an excellent general work on evaluation, see Meyers (1981).

12.1   PURPOSES OF EVALUATION—GOALS OF THE SYSTEM

Certainly the major element in the evaluation of a project is its "success." In a study of a variety of different kinds and sizes of industrial projects (Shenhar et al., 1997), 127 project managers identified 13 factors constituting four independent dimensions of project success, from their perspective as project managers. The first and most straightforward dimension is the project's *efficiency* in meeting both the budget and the schedule. This has been the primary focus of our discussion of project management and control thus far, meeting the time, cost, and scope objectives of the project. The second and most complex dimension is that of *customer impact/satisfaction*. This dimension includes meeting the project's technical and operational specifications but also includes factors relating to loyalty and repurchase: fulfilling the customer's needs, actual use by the customer, solving a major operational problem of the customer, and the perennial challenge of customer satisfaction.

The third dimension is *business/direct success*, measured here primarily in terms of level of commercial success and market share. For internal projects, however, the factors might include such measures as yields, cycle times, processing steps, quality, and so on. The last dimension, somewhat more difficult and nebulous to ascertain, is *future potential*. This includes factors relating to opening a new market, developing a new line of products or services, or if an internal project, developing a new technology, skills, or competences. Next, we will note some additional dimensions for evaluating projects that go beyond those discussed by Shenhar et al. (1997).

Beyond the straightforward considerations of project success, another primary purpose of evaluation is to help translate the achievement of the project's goals into a contribution to the parent organization's goals. To do this, all facets of the project are studied in order to identify and understand the project's strengths and weaknesses. It is the equivalent of an application of Six-Sigma or TQM to project management. The result is a set of recommendations for improvements that can help both ongoing and future projects to:

- Identify problems earlier
- Clarify scope, cost, and time relationships
- Improve project performance
- Locate opportunities for future technological advances
- Evaluate the quality of project management
- Reduce costs
- Improve the process of risk identification and management
- Speed up the achievement of results
- Identify mistakes, remedy them, and avoid them in the future
- Provide information to the client
- Reconfirm the organization's interest in and commitment to the project

For brevity, we will refer to the stated project objectives, including customer satisfaction, as the project's "direct goals." They ignore, however, many costs and benefits to the project, to its team members, and to the parent organization that are not overtly established as objectives, such as the preceding list of project improvements. Evaluation often makes recommendations that relate to these ancillary, unplanned but important contributions to the project and its parent. Some examples of recommendations concerning these "ancillary goals" include attempts to:

- Improve understanding of the ways in which projects may be of value to the organization
- Improve the processes for organizing and managing projects, better known as the firm's project management "maturity"
- Provide information and experience for entering new markets
- Provide a congenial environment in which project team members can work creatively together
- Identify organizational strengths and weaknesses in project-related personnel, general management, and decision-making techniques and systems
- Identify and improve the response to risk factors in the firm's use of projects
- Allow access to project policy decision making by external stakeholders
- Improve the way projects contribute to the professional growth of project team members
- Identify project personnel who have high potential for managerial leadership

The identification of ancillary goals is a difficult and politically delicate task. Although the adjective "ancillary" is not a sufficient descriptor, it is the best single word we could find. Synonyms are "helpful," "subsidiary," "accessory," and the like, and we have all these things in mind. In addition, the ancillary goals are usually not overtly identified. Interviews with the individuals in charge of making decisions about projects will help to expose the ancillary goals that the firm is seeking by supporting the project. But for the most part, they are "hidden" by accident, not by purpose. Finding them often requires deductive reasoning. Organizational decisions and behaviors imply goals, often very specific goals, that are simply not spelled out anywhere in the organizational manuals. For example, most executives desire to operate their organizations in such a way that people enjoy the work they do and enjoy working together, but only occasionally do firms publish such statements. Few firms would disavow this objective, they simply do not *overtly* subscribe to it. Even so, this particular objective affects the decisions made in almost every firm we know.

At times, however, ancillary goals and the parties-at-interest that support them can be readily identified. Some examples are: goals that govern the treatment of animals that may be involved in a project, goals that demand highly specific processing of information about a project output (e.g., pharmaceutical drugs), or goals that control the production processes associated with a project (e.g., antipollution). Whether clearly identified or not, and whether measured or not, ancillary goals affect decisions made on all projects.

A reasonable attempt to identify as many goals as possible is valuable. Frequently, recognition of an ancillary goal is required to understand why certain decisions on projects are made. The desire to identify individuals who have high potential for leadership may explain why a given person with relatively little experience is given a specific project responsibility. Ancillary goals add several additional dimensions to project evaluation.

There are tough problems associated with finding the ancillary goals of a project. First, and probably the most important, is the obvious fact that one cannot measure performance against an unknown goal. Therefore, if a goal is not openly acknowledged, project team members need not fear that their performance can be weighed and found wanting. The result is that goals appearing in the project proposal must be recognized and are a source of some anxiety in members of the project team. But "unwritten" goals can often be ignored. Again, ancillary goals are rarely disclaimed; they are merely not mentioned.

Whether or not anxiety about meeting ancillary goals is deserved is not relevant. Particularly in this era of corporate "restructuring," anxiety is present. It is heightened by the fear that an evaluation may not be conducted "fairly," with proper emphasis on what is being accomplished rather than stressing shortcomings. If the self-image of the project team is very strong, this barrier to finding ancillary goals of the project may be weak, but it is never absent.

A second problem arises during attempts to find the ancillary goals of a project. Individuals pursue their own ends while working for organizations. At times, however, people may be unwilling to admit to personal goals—goals they may see as not entirely consistent with organizational objectives. For example, a person may seek to join a project in order to learn a new skill, one that increases that person's employment mobility. At times, the scientific direction taken by R & D projects is as much a function of the current interest areas of the scientists working on the project as it is the scientific needs of the project. While such purposes are not illegitimate or unethical, they are rarely admitted.

A third problem arises through lack of trust. Members of a project team are never quite comfortable in the presence of an auditor/evaluator. If the auditor/evaluator is an "outsider"—anyone who cannot be identified as a project team member—there is fear that "we won't be understood." While such fears are rarely specific, they are nonetheless real. If the auditor/evaluator is an "insider," fear focuses on the possibility that the insider has some hidden agenda, is seeking some personal advantage at the expense of the "rest of us." The motives of insider and outsider alike are distrusted. As a result, project team members have little or no incentive to be forthcoming about their individual or project ancillary goals.

Finally, a fourth problem exists. Projects, like all organizations that serve human ends, are multipurposed. The diverse set of direct and ancillary, project and individual goals do not bear clear, organizationally determined on (or accepted) priorities. Various members of the project team may have quite different ideas about which purposes are most important, which come next in line, and which are least important. In the absence of direct questions about the matter, no one has to confront the issue of who is right and who is wrong. As long as the goals and priorities are not made explicit, project team members can agree on *what* things should be done without necessarily agreeing on (or even discussing) *why* those things should be done. Thus, if some of the project's objectives are not openly debated, each member can tolerate the different emphases of fellow team members. No one is forced to pick and choose, or even to discuss such matters with co-workers.

All in all, the task of finding the ancillary goals of a project is difficult. Most evaluations simply ignore them, but the PM is well advised to take a keen interest in this area, and to request that evaluations include ancillary goals, the project's and the parent organization's, if not those of individuals. Even though one must usually be satisfied with rough, qualitative measures of ancillary-goal achievement, the information can be valuable. It may provide insight into such questions as: What sorts of things motivate people to join and work on projects? What sorts of rewards are most effective in eliciting maximum effort from project personnel? What are the major concerns of specific individuals working on the project?

In Chapter 5, we alluded to the importance of the project management "war room" (office, PMO) as a meeting place for the project team, a display area for the charts that show the project's progress, a central repository for project files and reports, and an office for the PM and other project administrators. The war room is also the "clubhouse" for the project team members and serves an important ancillary goal. It is to the project what the local pub was to "that old gang of mine." The camaraderie associated with a successful, well-run project provides great satisfaction to team members. The PMO, therefore, fills an emotional need as well as meeting its more mundane, direct administrative goals. The best PMOs (Baker, 2007) also, however, offer the best project leadership in the organization and are proud of it, enjoying strong executive support and the admiration of others in the organization who would love to be a part of this future-oriented, well-run learning team.

Project Management in Practice
Lessons from Auditing 110 Client/Server and Open Systems Projects

In an 11-year audit of 110 client/server and open systems projects, one auditor boiled the differences between success and failure down to four foundational concepts.

1. *Objectivity regarding scope, budget, deadlines, and solution design.* Lack of objectivity in these areas is one of the basic causes of project failure. Decisions concerning the business case for initiating the project and establishing all of its parameters need to be scrutinized for bias and inadequate diligence.

2. *Experienced people at all levels in the project.* Having experienced people on both the client side and the contractor side helps in a number of areas: maintaining a cooperative, problem-solving attitude, enforcing milestones and deliverables, using professional project management techniques, and maintaining continuous user involvement.

3. *Authority matched with responsibility.* Since a project is usually established with a certain scope but limited budget and schedule, the project manager needs to have the authority to make tradeoffs between these objectives. This level of authority needs to be present on both the client side as well as the contractor side.

4. *Accountability sufficient to ensure that all parties perform as promised or are definitely held responsible.* Accountability needs to be thoroughly detailed in the original contracts and purchase orders. It should include details concerning the project champion, the original estimator, suppliers, the client team and users, and the contractor team. Keeping projects short, such as under six months, keeps from diluting accountability through personnel turnover.

Source: T. Ingram, "Client/Server and Imaging: On Time, On Budget, As Promised," *PM Network*, Vol. 9.

12.2   THE PROJECT AUDIT

The project audit is a thorough examination of the management of a project, its methodology and procedures, its records, its properties, its budgets and expenditures, and its degree of completion. It may deal with the project as a whole, or only with a part of the project. The formal report may be presented in various formats, but should, at a minimum, contain comments on the following points:

1. *Current status of the project.* Does the work actually completed match the planned level of completion?

2. *Future status.* Are significant schedule/cost/scope changes likely? If so, indicate the nature of the changes.

3. *Status of crucial tasks.* What progress has been made on tasks that could decide the success or failure of the project?

4. *Risk assessment.* What is the potential for project failure or monetary loss?

5. *Information pertinent to other projects.* What lessons learned from the project being audited can be applied to other projects being undertaken by the organization?

6. *Limitations of the audit.* What assumptions or limitations affect the data in the audit?

Note that the project audit is not a financial audit. The audit processes are similar in that each represents a careful investigation of the subject of the audit, but the outputs of these processes are quite different. The principal distinction between the two is that the financial audit has a limited scope. It concentrates on the use and preservation of the organization's assets. The project audit is far broader in scope and may deal with the project as a whole or any component or set of components of the project. Table 12-1 lists the primary differences between financial and project audits.

While the project audit may be concerned with any aspect of project management, it is not a traditional management audit. Management audits are primarily aimed at ensuring that the organization's management systems are in place and operative. The project audit goes beyond this. Among other things, it is meant to ensure that the project is being *appropriately* managed. Some managerial systems apply fairly well to all projects; for example, the techniques of planning, scheduling, budgeting, and so forth. On the other hand, some management practices should differ with different types of projects. See Ruskin et al. (1985) for an interesting discussion of the project management audit and Sangameswaran (1995) and Corbin et al. (2001) for some guidance on auditing do's and don'ts.

We maintain that software projects are not *significantly* different from other types of projects. We stand on that position, but we also note that they possess some unique characteristics worthy of recognition and response, thus the rise of agile management for projects with uncertain scope. For example, computer-based projects are ordinarily very labor-intensive while many manufacturing projects, for instance, are highly capital intensive. A thoughtful manager will simply not adopt the same managerial approach to each. The need for and value of a participative style (Six-Sigma, TQM, EI, etc.) is well established in the case of labor-intensive projects where problems are often ill-structured. If the project is capital intensive and characterized by well-structured problems, the need for and value of a participative style is *relatively* diminished. (The reader must not read these statements as degrading the value of participative management. It is simply more valuable and relevant in some cases than others.)

Table 12-1   Comparison of Financial Audits with Project Audits

	Financial Audits	*Project Audits*
Status	Confirms status of business in relation to accepted standard	Must create basis for, and confirm, status on each project
Predictions	Company's state of economic well-being	Future status of project
Measurement	Mostly in financial terms	Financial terms plus schedule, progress, resource usage, status of ancillary goals
Record-keeping system	Format dictated by legal regulations and professional standards	No standard system, uses any system desired by individual organization or dictated by contract
Existence of information system	Minimal records needed to start audit	No records exist, data bank must be designed and used to start audit
Recommendations	Usually few or none, often restricted to management of accounting system	Often required, and may cover any aspect of the project or its management
Qualifications to the audit report	Customary to qualify statements if conditions dictate, but strong managerial pressure not to do so	Qualifications focus on shortcomings of audit process (e.g., lack of technical expertise, lack of funds or time)

To sum up, the management audit looks at managerial systems and their use. The project audit studies the financial, managerial, and technical aspects of the project as an integrated set applied to a specific project in a specific organizational environment.

Depth of the Audit

There are several practical constraints that may limit the depth of the project auditor's investigation. Time and money are two of the most common (and obvious) limits on the depth of investigation and level of detail presented in the audit report. Of course, there are costs associated with the audit/evaluation process over and above the usual costs of the professional and clerical time used in conducting the audit. Accumulation, storage, and maintenance of auditable data are important cost elements. Remember that such storage may be critically important in meeting the test of "due diligence" noted in Chapter 11. (Remember, too, that destruction of business data may be illegal under certain circumstances.)

Also serious, but less quantifiable, are two often overlooked costs. First, no matter how skilled the evaluator, an audit/evaluation process is always distracting to those working on the project. No project is completely populated with individuals whose self-esteem [defined by Ambrose Bierce (1991) as "an erroneous appraisement"] is so high that evaluation is greeted without anxiety. Worry about the outcome of the audit tends to produce an excessive level of self-protective activity, which, in turn, lowers the level of activity devoted to the project. Second, if the evaluation report is not written with a "constructive" tone, project morale will suffer.* Depending on the severity of the drop in morale, work on the project may receive a serious setback.

It is logical to vary the depth of the investigation depending on circumstances and needs unique to each project. While an audit can be performed at any level the organization wishes, three distinct levels are easily recognized and widely used: the general audit, the detailed audit, and the technical audit. The general audit is normally most constrained by time and resources and is usually a brief review of the project, touching lightly on the six concerns noted earlier. A typical detailed audit is conducted when a follow-up to the general audit is required. This tends to occur when the general audit has disclosed an unacceptable level of risk or malperformance in some part(s) of the project.

At times, the detailed audit cannot investigate problems at a satisfactory technical level because the auditor does not possess the technical knowledge needed. In such cases, a technical audit is required. Technical audits are normally carried out by a qualified technician under the direct guidance of the project auditor. In the case of very advanced or secret technology, it may be difficult to find qualified technical auditors inside the organization. In such cases, it is not uncommon for the firm to use academic consultants who have signed the appropriate nondisclosure documents. Although not a hard and fast rule, the technical audit is usually the most detailed.

Timing of the Audit

Given that all projects of significant size or importance should be audited, the first audits are usually done early in the project's life. The sooner a problem is discovered, the easier it is to deal with. Early audits are often focused on the technical issues in order to make sure that key technical problems have been solved or are under competent attack. Ordinarily, audits done later in the life cycle of a project are of less immediate value to the project, but are of more value to the parent organization. As the project develops, technical issues are less likely to be matters of concern. Conformity to the schedule and budget becomes the primary interest.

---

*The evaluator is well advised to remember two fundamental principles: (1) Constructive criticism does not feel all that constructive to the criticizee; and (2) Fix first, then blame—if you have any energy left.

Management issues are major matters of interest for audits made late in the project's life (e.g., disposal of equipment or reallocation of project personnel).

Postproject audits are conducted with several basic objectives in mind. First, a postproject audit is often a legal necessity because the client specified such an audit in the contract. Second, the postproject audit is a major part of the Postproject Report, which is, in turn, the main source of managerial feedback to the parent firm. Third, the postproject audit is needed to account for all project property and expenditures.

Additional observations on the timing and value of audits are shown in Table 12-2.

Format and Use of the Audit Report

The type of project being audited and the uses for which the audit is intended dictate some specifics of the audit report format. Within any particular organization, however, it is useful to establish a general format to which all audit reports must conform. This makes it possible for project managers, auditors, and organizational management all to have the same understanding of, and expectations for, the audit report as a communication device. If the audit report is to serve as a communication device, there must also be a predetermined distribution list for such documents. When distribution is highly restricted, the report is almost certain to become the focus for interpersonal and intergroup conflict and tension.

While a few PMs insist on a complicated format for evaluation reports tailored to their individual projects, the simpler and more straightforward the format, the better. The information should be arranged so as to facilitate the comparison of predicted versus actual results. Significant deviations of actual from predicted results should be highlighted and explained in a set of comments. This eases the reader's work and tends to keep questions focused on important issues rather than trivia. This arrangement also reduces the likelihood that senior managers will engage in "fishing expeditions," searching for something "wrong" in every piece of data and sentence of the report. Once again, we would remind PMs of the dictum "Never let the boss be surprised."

Negative comments about individuals or groups associated with the project should be avoided. Write the report in a clear, professional, unemotional style and restrict its content to information and issues that are relevant to the project. The following items cover the *minimum* information that should be contained in the audit report.

1. *Introduction* This section contains a description of the project to provide a framework of understanding for the reader. Project objectives (direct goals) must be clearly delineated.

Table 12-2 Timing and Value of Project Audits/Evaluations

Project Stage	Value
Initiation	Significant value if audit takes place early—prior to 25 percent completion of initial planning stage
Feasibility study	Very useful, particularly the technical audit
Preliminary plan/schedule budget	Very useful, particularly for setting measurement standards to ensure conformance with standards
Baseline schedule	Less useful, plan frozen, flexibility of team limited
Evaluation of data by project team	Marginally useful, team defensive about findings
Implementation	More or less useful depending on importance of project methodology to successful implementation
Postproject	More or less useful depending on applicability of findings to future projects

If the objectives are complex, it may be useful to include explanatory parts of the project proposal as an addendum to the report.

2. *Current Status*   Status should be reported as of the time of the audit and, among other things, should include the following measures of performance:

    Cost: This section compares actual costs to budgeted costs. The time periods for which the comparisons are made should be clearly defined. As noted in Chapter 7, the report should focus on the *direct* charges made to the project. If it is also necessary to show project *total* costs, complete with all overheads, this cost data should be presented in an *additional* set of tables.

    Schedule: Performance in terms of planned events or milestones should be reported (see Figures 10-15 and 11-5 as examples). Completed portions of the project should be clearly identified, and the percent completion should be reported on all unfinished tasks for which estimates are possible. Make sure that the method used for estimating percent completion does not mislead readers (c.f. Section 10.3).

    Scope: This section compares work completed with resources expended. Earned value charts or tables (see Figures 10-7 and 10-13) may be used for this purpose if desired, but they may lack the appropriate level of detail. The requirement here is for information that will help to pinpoint problems with specific tasks or sets of tasks. Based on this information, projections regarding the timing and amounts of remaining planned expenditures are made.

    Quality: Whether or not this is a critical issue depends on the type of project being audited. Quality is a measure of the degree to which the output of a system conforms to prespecified characteristics. For some projects, the prespecified characteristics are so loosely stated that conformity is not much of an issue. At times, a project may produce outputs that far exceed original specifications. For instance, a project might require a subsystem that meets certain minimum standards. The firm may already have produced such a subsystem—one that meets standards well in excess of the current requirements. It may be efficient, with no less effectiveness, to use the previously designed system with its excess performance. If there is a detailed quality specification associated with the project, this section of the report may have to include a full review of the quality control procedures, along with full disclosure of the results of quality tests conducted to date.

3. *Future Project Status*   This section contains the auditor's conclusions regarding progress together with recommendations for any changes in technical approach, schedule, or budget that should be made in the remaining tasks. Except in unusual circumstances, for example, when results to date distinctly indicate the undesirability of some preplanned task, the auditor's report should consider only work that has already been completed or is well under way. No assumptions should be made about technical problems that are still under investigation at the time of the audit. Project audit/evaluation reports are not appropriate documents in which to rewrite the project proposal.

4. *Critical Management Issues*   All issues that the auditor feels require close monitoring by senior management should be included in this section, along with a brief explanation of the relationships between these issues and the objectives of the project. A brief discussion of time/cost/scope trade-offs will give senior management useful input information for decisions about the future of the project.

5. *Risk Management*   This section should contain a review of major risks associated with the project and their projected impact on project time/cost/scope. If alternative decisions exist that may significantly alter future risks, they can be noted at this point in the report. Once again, we note that the audit report is not the proper place to second-guess those who wrote the project proposal. The Postproject Report, on the other hand, will often contain sections on the general subject of "If only we knew then what we know now."

6. *Caveats, Limitations, and Assumptions*   This section of the report may be placed at the end or may be included as a part of the introduction. The auditor is responsible for the accuracy and timeliness of the report, but senior management still retains full responsibility for the interpretation of the report and for any action(s) based on the findings. For that reason, the auditor should specifically include a statement covering any limitations on the accuracy or validity of the report.

Responsibilities of the Project Auditor/Evaluator

First and foremost, the auditor should "tell the truth." This statement is not so simplistic as it might appear. It is a recognition of the fact that there are various levels of truth associated with any project. The auditor must approach the audit in an objective and ethical manner and assume responsibility for what is included and excluded from consideration in the report. Awareness of the biases of the several parties interested in the project—including the auditor's own biases—is essential, but extreme care is required if the auditor wishes to compensate for such biases. (A note that certain information *may* be biased is usually sufficient.) Areas of investigation outside the auditor's area of technical expertise should be acknowledged and assistance sought when necessary. The auditor/evaluator must maintain political and technical independence during the audit and treat all materials gathered as confidential until the audit is formally released.

Walker et al. (1980) develop an even stronger case for the "independence" of the auditor. They argue that independence is essential for management's ability to assemble information that is both timely and accurate. They also list the following steps for carrying out an audit:

- Assemble a small team of experienced experts
- Familiarize the team with the requirements of the project
- Audit the project on-site
- After completion, debrief the project's management
- Produce a written report according to a prespecified format
- Distribute the report to the PM and project team for their response
- Follow up to see if the recommendations have been implemented

If senior management and the project team are to take the audit/evaluation seriously, all information must be presented in a credible manner. The accuracy of data should be carefully checked, as should all calculations. The determination of what information to include and exclude is one that cannot be taken lightly. Finally, the auditor should engage in a continuing evaluation of the auditing process in a search for ways to improve the effectiveness, efficiency, and value of the process.

12.3   THE PROJECT AUDIT LIFE CYCLE

Thus far, we have considered the project audit and project evaluation as if they were one and the same. In most ways they are. The audit contains an evaluation, and an evaluator must conduct some sort of audit. Let us now consider the audit as a formal document required by contract with the client. If the client is the federal government, the nature of the project audit is more or less precisely defined, as is the audit process.

Like the project itself, the audit has a *life cycle* composed of an orderly progression of well-defined events. There are six of these events.

Project Management in Practice
Management of the Typhoon Project

The National Audit Office (NAO) is a government department that scrutinises public (government) spending on behalf of the UK Parliament. Its activities are focussed on improving financial management and reporting, making better use of information and ensuring that services are delivered cost-effectively. As well as undertaking financial audits of all government departments it also publishes about 60 "value for money" reports per year on key projects. In March 2011 the NAO published its report on the Management of the Typhoon Project. The key objective of this report was to evaluate effectively that the Ministry of Defence is managing this project in order to achieve full cost and operational value from this investment.

Background to the Project

In the 1980s the United Kingdom government collaborated with Germany, Italy and Spain on the design, development and production of the Eurofighter Typhoon. Together the four partners committed to buy 472 of the aircraft in three stages, or tranches. A further 87 aircraft were purchased by Saudi Arabia and Austria.

The collaboration agreement shared the production of the aircraft across the partner countries (for example, an Italian company builds the left wing, whilst the right wing is built by a Spanish company). In addition, all of the countries are partners in the strategic decision making and governance arrangements. The contract to be part of this collaboration was so restrictive that when Germany sought to withdraw from the project in the early 1990s due to the prohibitive costs they found that the penalties would be so huge that they were in effect locked in for the duration.

The UK's Ministry of Defence initially committed to buying 323 aircraft. However, changes to the global context resulted in this being reduced to a commitment to buy 160 Eurofighter Typhoons. The first one was delivered in 2003 and the last one is expected to be delivered in 2015.

The total cost of the initial procurement, upgrading and support of the aircraft is estimated to be £37 billion.

Current Position of the Project

70 aircraft have now been delivered to the UK Ministry of Defence. However, whilst the initial project was conceived during the Cold War and the Typhoon was designed mainly for an air-to-air combat role, the current operational requirements are for the aircraft to conduct both air-to-air and ground attack missions. Consequently, the aircraft already delivered will have to be upgraded to provide this additional capability.

The audit reported on the following key points:

- The collaborative management structures have proven to be complex and inefficient. The report highlights the lengthy process by which key decisions require consensus. Consequently, it has taken up to seven years to agree and deliver some of these upgrades. These inefficient arrangements have contributed in £2.2 billion cost increase.

- The chair of the Programme Board has accountability from bringing together a wide array of components (e.g., training, equipment, personnel, infrastructure, doctrine and concepts, organisation, information and logistics). However, they can only influence the groups responsible for the delivery of these components; they cannot compel them to deliver. In addition, they do not attend all of the strategic decision making meetings.

- The collaborative contracts for the delivery of spares and repair of equipment have caused problems. These supply issues have contributed to a shortfall in flying hours of 13% in 2009–10 which has had an impact on the training of the pilots on the more complex tasks. It has also led to the number of serviceable planes being reduced as parts are taken from one plane to service others.

- The development costs for the Typhoon have more than doubled to £6.7 billion from the original approval in 1987. As the report states, these costs are fixed irrespective of the number of planes actually made.

- The production cost of £13.5 billion is within the original approval. However, the Ministry of defence is buying 72 (30%) fewer aircraft than originally planned.

- Taking into account the development and production costs, the price per aircraft has risen by 75%.

- The capability of the aircraft has increased (e.g., with the enhanced ground attack capability) and so overall the Ministry of defence believes it can meet the required military tasks with fewer aircraft.

1. *Project Audit Initiation*   This step involves starting the audit process, defining the purpose and scope of the audit, and gathering sufficient information to determine the proper audit methodology.

2. *Project Baseline Definition*   This phase of the cycle normally consists of identifying the performance areas to be evaluated, determining standards for each area through benchmarking or some other process, ascertaining management performance expectations for each area, and developing a program to measure and assemble the requisite information.

   Occasionally, no convenient standards exist or can be determined through benchmarking. For example, a commodity pricing model was developed as part of a large marketing project. No baseline data existed that could serve to help evaluate the model. Because the commodity was sold by open bid, the firm used its standard bidding procedures. The results formed baseline data against which the pricing model could be tested on an "as if" basis. Table 12-3 shows the results of one such test. CCC is the firm and the contracts on which it bid *and won*, together with the associated revenues (mine net price × tonnage), are shown. Similar information is displayed for Model C, which was used on an "as if" basis, so the Model C Revenue column shows those bids the model *would have won*, had it actually been used.

3. *Establishing an Audit Database*   Once the baseline standards are established, execution of the audit begins. The next step is to create a database for use by the audit team. For example, consider the database required by the CCC pricing model test in Table 12-3. Depending on the purpose and scope of the audit, the database might include information needed for assessment of project organization, management and control, past and current project status, schedule performance, cost performance, and output quality, as well as plans for the future of the project. The information may vary from a highly technical description of performance to a behaviorally based description of the interaction of project team members.

   Because the purpose and scope of audits vary widely from one project to another and for different times on any given project, the audit database is frequently quite extensive. The required database for project audits should be specified in the project master plan. If this is done, the necessary information will be available when needed. Nonetheless, it is important to avoid collecting "anything that might be useful," since this can place extraordinary information collection and storage requirements on the project.

4. *Preliminary Analysis of the Project*   After standards are set and data collected, judgments are made. Some auditors eschew judgment on the grounds that such a delicate but weighty responsibility must be reserved to senior management. But judgment often requires a fairly sophisticated understanding of the technical aspects of the project, and/or of statistics and probability, subjects that may elude some managers. In such an event, the auditor must analyze the data and then present the analysis to managers in ways that communicate the real meaning of the audit's findings. It is the auditor's duty to brief the PM on all findings

Table 12-3   Performance against Baseline Data

| | | Bid Performance for Model "C" | | | | |
| | | Award | | | | |
Destination	Tonnage	CCC Bid	Model "C" Bid	Mine Net Price	CCC Revenue	Model "C" Revenue
D1-2	3800		X	$4.11		$15,618
D1-7	1600		X	3.92		6,272
D2-7	1300		X	4.11		5,343
D3-2	700		X	5.13		3,591
D3-3	500	X		5.22	$2,610	
D3-4	600		X	5.72		3,432
D3-5	1200		X	5.12		6,144
D3-6	1000		X	5.83		5,830
D4-6	700		X	4.88		3,416
D4-8	600		X	5.34		3,204
D5-1	500	X		3.54	1,770	
D6-1	1000	X	X	4.02–3.92	4,020	3,920
D6-2	900	X		4.35	3,915	
D6-5	200	X		3.75	750	
D6-6	800		X	3.17		2,536
D7-5	1600		X	5.12		8,192
D7-8	2600		X	5.29		13,754
D8-2	1600	X	X	4.83	7728	7,728
D8-3	2400		X	4.32		10,368
				Total revenue	$20,793	$99,348
				Total tonnage	4700	21,500
				Average mine net	$4.42	$4.62

and judgments *before* releasing the audit report. The purpose of the audit is to improve the project being audited as well as to improve the entire process of managing projects. It is not intended as a device to embarrass the PM.

5. *Audit Report Preparation*   This part of the audit life cycle includes the preparation of the audit report, organized by whatever format has been selected for use. A set of recommendations, together with a plan for implementing them, is also a part of the audit report. If the recommendations go beyond normal practices of the organization, they will need support from the policy-making level of management. This support should be sought and verified *before* the recommendations are published. If support is not forthcoming, the recommendations should be modified until satisfactory. Figure 12-1 is one page of an extensive and detailed set of recommendations that resulted from an evaluation project conducted by a private social service agency.

6. *Project Audit Termination*   As with the project itself, after the audit has accomplished its designated task, the audit process should be terminated. When the final report and recommendations are released, there will be a review of the audit process. This is done in order to improve the methods for conducting the audit. When the review is finished, the audit is truly complete and the audit team should be formally disbanded.

12.4   SOME ESSENTIALS OF AN AUDIT/EVALUATION

For an audit/evaluation (hereafter, simply a/e) to be conducted with skill and precision, for it to be credible and generally acceptable to senior management, to the project team, and to the

---

Final Report, Agency Evaluation, Sub-Committee II
Physical Plant, Management of Office, Personnel Practices

Summary of Recommendations

Recommendations which require Board action.

1. The Board of _____ should continue its efforts to obtain additional funds for our salary item.

2. The cost of Blue Cross and Blue Shield insurance coverage on individual employees should be borne by _____.

Recommendations which can be put into effect by *Presidential Order* to committees, staff, or others.

3. The House Committee should activate, with first priority, the replacement of the heating/air-conditioning system. Further, this committee should give assistance and support to the Secretary to the Executive Director in maintenance and repair procedures.

4. A professional library should be established even if part-time workers must share space to accomplish this.

5. Our insurance needs should be re-evaluated.

6. All activities related to food at meetings should be delegated to someone other than the Secretary to the Executive Director.

7. Majority opinion—positions of Administrative Assistant and Bookkeeper will need more time in the future. Minority opinion—positions of Administrative Assistant, Bookkeeper, and Statistical Assistant should be combined.

8. The Personnel Practices Committee should review job descriptions of Bookkeeper and Statistical Assistant and establish salary ranges for those two positions and that of the Administrative Assistant.

9. Dialogue between the Executive Director, his secretary, and the Administrative Assistant should continue in an effort to streamline office procedures and expedite handling of paperwork.

10. The written description of the Personnel Practices Committee should include membership of a representative of the nonprofessional staff.

11. The Personnel Practices Committee should study, with a view toward action, the practice of part-time vs. full-time casework staff.

Figure 12-1   Sample recommendations for a social service agency.

client, several essential conditions must be met. The a/e team must be properly selected, all records and files must be accessible, and free contact with project members must be preserved.

The A/E Team

The choice of the a/e team is critical to the success of the entire process. It may seem unnecessary to note that team members should be selected because of their ability to contribute to the a/e procedure, but sometimes members are selected merely because they are available. The size of the team will generally be a function of the size and complexity of the project. For a small project, one person can often handle all the tasks of an a/e audit, but for a large project, the team may require representatives from several different constituencies. Typical areas that might furnish a/e team members are:

- The project itself
- The accounting/controller department
- Technical specialty areas
- The customer
- The marketing department
- Senior management
- Purchasing/asset management
- The personnel department
- The legal/contract administration department

The main role of the a/e team is to conduct a thorough and complete examination of the project or some prespecified aspect of the project. The team must determine which items should be brought to management's attention. It should report information and make recommendations in such a way as to maximize the utility of its work. The team is responsible for constructive observations and advice based on the training and experience of its members. Members must be aloof from personal involvement with conflicts among project team staff and from rivalries between projects. The a/e is a highly disciplined process, and all team members must willingly and sincerely subject themselves to that discipline.

Access to Records

In order for the a/e team to be effective, it must have free access to all information relevant to the project. This may present some problems on government projects that may be classified for reasons of national security. In such cases, a subgroup of the a/e team may be formed from qualified ("cleared") individuals.

Most of the information needed for an a/e will come from the project team's records and those of the Project Office, and/or from various departments such as accounting, personnel, and purchasing. Obviously, gathering the data is the responsibility of the a/e team, and this burden should not be passed on to the project management team, though the project team is responsible for collecting the usual data on the project and keeping project records up to date during the project's life.

In addition to the formal records of the project, some of the most valuable information comes from documents that predate the project—for example, correspondence with the customer that led to the RFP, minutes of the Project Selection Committee, and minutes of senior management committees that decided to pursue a specific area of technical interest. Clearly, project status reports, relevant technical memoranda, change orders, information about project organization and management methods, and financial and resource usage information are also important. The a/e team may have to extract much of these data from other documents because the required information is often not in the form needed. Data collection is time-consuming, but careful work is absolutely necessary for an effective, credible a/e.

As information is collected, it must be organized and filed in a systematic way. Systematic methods need to be developed for separating out useful information. Most important, stopping rules are needed to prevent data collection and processing from continuing far past the point of diminishing returns. Priorities must be set to ensure that important analyses are undertaken before those of lesser import. Also, safeguards are needed against duplication of efforts. The careful development of forms and procedures will help to standardize the process as much as possible.

Access to Project Personnel and Others

Contact between a/e team members and project team members, or between the a/e team and other members of the organization who have knowledge of the project, should be free. One exception is contact between the a/e team and the customer; such contacts are *not made without clearance* from senior management. This restriction would hold even when the customer is represented on the audit team, and should also hold for in-house clients.

In any case, there are several rules that should be followed when contacting project personnel. Care must be taken to avoid misunderstandings between a/e team members and project team members. Project personnel should always be made aware of the in-progress a/e. Critical comments should be avoided. Particularly serious is the practice of delivering on-the-spot, off-the-cuff opinions and remarks that may not be appropriate or represent the consensus opinion of the a/e team.

The a/e team will undoubtedly encounter political opposition during its work. If the project is a subject of political tension, attempts will most certainly be made by the opposing sides to co-opt (or repudiate) the a/e team. As much as possible, they should avoid becoming involved. At times, information may be given to a/e team members in confidence. Discreet attempts should be made to confirm such information through nonconfidential sources. If it cannot be confirmed, it should not be used. The auditor/evaluator must protect the sources of confidential information and must not become a conduit for unverifiable criticism of the project.

12.5   MEASUREMENT

Measurement is an integral part of the a/e process. Many issues of what and how to measure have been discussed in earlier chapters, particularly in Chapter 2. Several aspects of a project that should be measured are obvious and, fortunately, rather easy to measure. For the most part, it is not difficult to know if and when a milestone has been completed. We can directly observe the fact that a building foundation has been poured, that all required materials for a corporate annual report have been collected and delivered to the printer, or that all contracts have been let for the rehabilitation of an apartment complex. At times, of course, milestone completion may not be quite so evident. It may be difficult to tell when a chemical experiment is finished, and it is almost impossible to tell when a complex computer program is finally "bug free." Largely, however, milestone completion can be measured adequately.

Similarly, performance against planned budget and schedule usually poses no major measurement problems. We may be a bit uncertain whether or not a "nine-day" scheduled completion time should include weekend days, but most organizations adopt conventions to ease these minor counting problems. Measuring the actual expenditures against the planned budget is a bit trickier and depends on an in-depth understanding of the procedures used by the accounting department. It is common to imbue cost data with higher levels of reality and precision than is warranted.

When the objectives of a project have been stated in terms of profits, rates of return, or discounted cash flows, as in the financial selection models discussed in Chapter 2, measurement problems may be more obstinate. The problem does not often revolve around the accounting conventions used, though if those conventions have not been clearly established in advance, there may be bitter arguments about what costs are appropriately assigned to the individual project being evaluated. A far more difficult task is the determination of what revenues should be assigned to the project.

Assume, for example, that a drug firm creates a project for the development of a new drug and simultaneously sets up a project to develop and implement a marketing strategy for the potential new drug and two existing allied drugs. Assume further that the entire program is successful and large amounts of revenue are generated. How much revenue should be assigned to the credit of the drug research project? How much to the marketing project? Within the marketing project, how much should go to each of the subprojects for the individual drugs? If the entire program is treated as one project, the problem is less serious; but R & D and marketing are in different functional areas of the parent organization, and each may be evaluated on the basis of its contribution to the parent firm's profitability. The year-end bonuses of divisional managers are determined in part (often in large part) by the profitability of the units they manage. Figure 12-2 illustrates project baseline data established for a new product. This figure shows the use of multiple measures including price, unit sales, market share, development costs, capital expenditures, and other measures of performance.

There is no theoretically acceptable solution to such measurement problems, but there are politically acceptable solutions. All the cost/revenue allocation decisions must be made when the various projects are initiated. If this is done, the battles are fought "up front," and the equity of cost/revenue allocations ceases to be so serious an issue. As long as allocations are made by a formula, major conflict is avoided—or, at least, mitigated.

PRODUCT _____ DATE _____
MARKET _____
DATE OF FIRST SALE: U.S. _____
                     O.U.S. _____

	1ST YEAR			2ND YEAR			3RD YEAR			4TH YEAR			5TH YEAR			TOTAL		
	MIN	B.E.*	MAX	MIN	B.E.	MAX	MIN	B.E.	MAX	MIN	B.E.	MAX	MIN	B.E.	MAX	MIN	B.E.	MAX
1. Total Market Size:																		
2. Expected Market Share:																		
3. Kg. or Units:																		
4. Est. Selling Price:																		
5. Gross Sales:																		
6. Est. COPS %:																		
7. Gross Margin %:																		
8. Est. Marketing Expense %:																		
9. Marketing Margin %:																		
10. Loss on Profit from other Products List:																		
11. Est. Profit:																		
12. Development Expenses:																		
13. Capital Expenditures:																		

*Best estimate.

Figure 12-2 Baseline marketing data for a new product.

If multiobjective scoring models rather than financial models are being used for project selection, measurement problems are somewhat exacerbated. There are more elements to measure, some of which are objective and measured with relative ease. But some elements are subjective and require reasonably standard measurement techniques if the measures are to be reliable. Interview and questionnaire methods for gathering data must be carefully constructed and carried out if the project scores are to be taken seriously. Criteria weights and scoring procedures should be decided at the start of the project.

A Note to the Auditor/Evaluator

A kindly critic and colleague uses what he calls the "rules of engagement" to explain to his students how to schedule interviews, conduct interviews, get copies, limit the scope of activities, and handle the many mundane tasks included in auditing/evaluating projects. While the phrase "rules of engagement" seems a bit warlike to us, we do have some similar advice for the auditor/evaluator.

Above all else, the a/e needs "permission to enter the system." It is difficult to describe precisely what is meant by that phrase, but every experienced auditor or evaluator will know. Senior management can assign an individual to the job of heading an audit/evaluation team, but this does not automatically imply that project personnel will accept that person as a legitimate a/e. There will be several indicators if the a/e is not accepted. Phone calls from the a/e will be returned only at times when the a/e is not available. Requests for information will be politely accepted, but little or no information will be forthcoming—though copious, sincere apologies and semibelievable excuses will be. Interviews with project team members will be strangely contentless. Attempts to determine the project's ancillary goals will be unsuccessful, as will attempts to get team members to discuss intrateam conflict. Everyone will be quite pleasant, but somehow promises of cooperation do not turn into fact. Always, there are good excuses and looks of wide-eyed innocence.

If the a/e is reasonably likable and maintains a calm, relaxed attitude, the project team generally begins to extend limited trust. The usual first step is to allow the a/e qualified access to information about the project. Missing information from the official project files is suddenly found. The a/e has then been given tentative permission to enter the system. If the a/e deals gently with this information, neither ignoring nor stressing the project's shortcomings while recognizing and appreciating the project's strengths, trust will be extended, and the permission to enter the system will no longer be tentative.

Trust-building is a slow and delicate process that is easily thwarted. The a/e needs to understand the politics of the project team and the interpersonal relationships among its members, and must deal with this confidential knowledge respectfully. On this base is trust built and meaningful audit/evaluation constructed. There is an almost universal propensity for the a/e to mimic Jack Webb's Sgt. Friday on the old Dragnet TV show—"Just give me the facts, ma'am." It is not that simple, nor are any processes involving human beings that simple.

 SUMMARY

This chapter initiated our discussion of the final part of the text, project termination. A major concluding step in the termination process is the evaluation of the project process and results, otherwise known as an audit. Here we looked at the purposes of evaluation and what it should encompass: the audit process and measurement considerations, the demands placed on the auditor, and the construction and design of the final report.

Specific points made in the chapter were these:

- The purposes of the evaluation are both goal-directed, aiding the project in achieving its objectives, and also aimed at achieving unspecified, sometimes hidden, yet firmly held, ancillary objectives.

- The audit report should contain at least the current status of the project, the expected future status, the status of crucial tasks, a risk assessment, information pertinent to other projects, and any caveats and limitations.

- Audit depth and timing are critical elements of the audit because, for example, it is much more difficult to alter the project based on a late audit than an early audit.

- The difficult responsibility of the auditor is to be honest in fairly presenting the audit results. This may even require data interpretation on occasion.

- The audit life cycle includes audit initiation, project baseline definition, establishing a database, preliminary project analysis, report preparation, and termination.

- Several essential conditions must be met for a credible audit: a credible a/e team, sufficient access to records, and sufficient access to personnel.

- Measurement, particularly of revenues, is a special problem.

In the next chapter, we move into the final state of the project management process, termination. There we will look at when to terminate a project and the various ways to conduct the termination.

 ## GLOSSARY

Audit   A formal inquiry into some issue or aspect of a system.

Baseline   A standard for performance, commonly established early on for later comparisons.

Evaluate   To set a value for or appraise.

Risk Analysis   An evaluation of the likely outcomes of a policy and their probability of occurrence, usually conducted to compare two or more scenarios or policies.

QUESTIONS

Material Review Questions

1. Give some examples of ancillary project objectives.

2. When should an audit be conducted during a project? Is there a "best" time?

3. What occurs in each stage of the audit life cycle?

4. What items should be included in the audit status report?

5. What access is required for an accurate audit?

6. Why is measurement a particular problem in auditing?

7. What is a "baseline"?

8. What is the purpose of a risk analysis?

9. What are the essential conditions of a credible audit?

Class Discussion Questions

10. In a typical project, do you feel frequent brief evaluations or periodic major evaluations are better in establishing control? Why?

11. Do you think that project evaluations cost-justify themselves?

12. What steps can be taken to ease the perceived threat to team members of an external evaluation?

13. What feedback, if any, should the project team get from the evaluation?

14. During the project audit, a tremendous amount of time can be wasted if a systematic method of information handling is not adopted. Briefly explain how this systematic method may be developed.

15. "Evaluation of a project is another means of project control." Comment.

16. Why is it better to rely on several sources of information than just a few?

17. What could be some advantages and disadvantages of the following sources of information: (a) charts, (b) written reports, and (c) firsthand observation?

18. Why is it important to use outside auditors rather than inside auditors who would be more familiar with the company and the project?

19. What kinds of reports might be sent to customers?

20. What would you identify as the ethical responsibilities of an auditor?

21. Given the great variety of items for an auditor to evaluate, what should the PM do given that the project evaluation basis was clearly laid out in the project plan? What about ancillary goals?

Lessons from Auditing 110 Client/Server and Open Systems Projects

22. Which of the four concepts is the most important, in your opinion?

23. Elaborate on item 3.

24. What lessons might you have expected that aren't included?

Management of the Typhoon Project

25. Describe the various cost overruns that this project is facing.

26. Which issues can be traced back to the partnership arrangements that underpin the Typhoon?

INCIDENTS FOR DISCUSSION

Gerkin Pension Services

Dana Lasket was the project manager of a project with the objective of determining the feasibility of moving a significant portion of Gerkin's computing capacity to another geographical location. Project completion was scheduled for 28 weeks. Dana had the project team motivated, and at the end of the twentieth week the project was on schedule.

The next week, during a casual lunch conversation, Dana discovered that the vice-president of finance had serious doubts about the validity of the assumptions the team was using to decide which computers should be relocated.

Dana tried to convince him that he was wrong during two follow-up meetings, with no success. In fact, the more they talked, the more convinced the vice-president became that Dana was wrong. The project was too far along to change any assumptions without causing significant delays. In addition, the vice-president was likely to inherit the responsibility for implementing any approved plans for the new location. For those reasons, Dana felt it was essential to resolve the disagreement before the scheduled completion of the project. Dana requested a project auditor be assigned to audit the project, paying special attention to the assumptions made to identify the computers to be moved.

Questions: Is this a good use of the audit technique? Will it be helpful here? Why or why not?

General Ship Building Company

General Ship Building has a contract with the Department of the Navy to build three new aircraft carriers over the next five years. During the construction of the first ship, the project manager formed an auditing team to audit the construction process for the three ships. After picking the audit team members, he requested that they develop a set of minimum requirements for the projects and use this as a baseline in the audit. While reviewing the contract documents, an auditing team member discovered a discrepancy between the contract minimum requirements and the Navy's minimum requirements. Based on his findings, he has told the project manager that he has decided to contact the local Navy contract office and inform them of the problem.

Questions: If you were the project manager, how would you handle this situation? How can a customer be assured of satisfactory contract completion?

CONTINUING INTEGRATIVE CLASS PROJECT

At this point (or perhaps if a special problem has arisen in the project), the Instructor should have the project audited. Possible auditors include members of the class who have finished their project tasks, the Historian, the Instructor himself or herself, or someone outside the project. Follow the guidelines in the chapter for conducting the audit. An alternative is to show how the Historian's report relates to a full-blown postproject evaluation.

BIBLIOGRAPHY

Baker, B. "In Common." *Project Management Journal*, September 2007.

Bierce, A. *The Devil's Dictionary*. New York: Dell Publishing, 1991.

Corbin, D., R. Cox, R. Hamerly, and K. Knight. "Project Management of Project Reviews," *PM Network*, March 2001.

Meyers, W. R. *The Evaluation Enterprise*. San Francisco: Jossey-Bass, 1981.

Ruskin, A. M., and W. E. Estes. "The Project Management Audit: Its Role and Conduct." *Project Management Journal*, August 1985.

Sangameswaran, A. "A Key to Effective Independent Project Reviews." *PM Network*, April 1995.

Schaefer, A. G., and A. J. Zaller. "The Ethics Audit for Nonprofit Organizations." *PM Network*, April 1998.

Shenhar, A. J., O. Levy, and D. Dvir, "Mapping the Dimensions of Project Success." *Project Management Journal*, June 1997.

Walker, M. G. and R. Bracey. "Independent Auditing As Project Control." *Datamation*, March 1980.

Webster's New Twentieth Century Dictionary, Unabridged, 2nd ed., Wm. Collins Publishers, Inc. USA, 1980.

The following case concerns a multiphase U.S. Army missile development program. The first phase was difficult, and six consecutive flight tests ended in failure, with the contractor paying millions of dollars in fines for the failures. However, the next two tests were successful, and the Pentagon decided to skip a third planned test and move directly to the next phase of the program—Engineering and Manufacturing Development. Before doing so, however, an audit of the program's progress to date was requested of the U. S. Government Accountability Office. The case reports the underlying problems revealed by the audit and the lessons learned by the program managers.

C A S E

THEATER HIGH ALTITUDE AREA DEFENSE (THAAD): FIVE FAILURES AND COUNTING (B)*
Tom Cross, Alan Beckenstein, and Tim Laseter

DEPARTMENT OF THE ARMY
OFFICE OF THE ASSISTANT SECRETARY OF THE ARMY
ACQUISITION LOGISTICS AND TECHNOLOGY
103 ARMY PENTAGON
WASHINGTON DC 20310-0103

It was July 2004. John West and Joy Adams had been through a lot since the THAAD program had begun in 1992. Eleven THAAD flight tests had been conducted in the Program Definition and Risk Reduction (PDRR) Phase. After six initial failures, the first successful missile-to-missile intercept of a ballistic missile target was achieved on June 10, 1999, during Flight Test 10. West and Adams reflected on the contract lessons they had learned.

GAO Study—June 1999

Studies conducted by both Department of Defense and independent sources identified the following underlying problems in the THAAD program:

- The program's compressed flight-test schedule did not allow for adequate ground testing, and as

a result, officials could not detect problems prior to flight tests. The schedule also left insufficient time for preflight testing, post-flight analysis, and corrective action.

- The requirement to be able to quickly deploy an early prototype system diverted the contractor and government project management's attention away from the normal interceptor development process and resulted in interceptors that were not equipped with sufficient instruments to provide optimum test data.

- Quality assurance received insufficient emphasis and resources during the time of component production, resulting in unreliable components.

- The contract for developing the interceptor was a cost-plus-fixed-fee contract, a contract type that placed all of the program's financial risk on the government and did not include provisions that

*Reprinted by permission Copyright by the University of Virginia Darden School foundation, Charlottesville, VA.

could be used to hold the contractor accountable for less than optimum performance.

Flight-test failures had been caused primarily by manufacturing defects rather than problems with advanced technology. These failures prevented the army from demonstrating that it could reliably employ the "hit-to-kill" technology critical to THAAD's success. The restructured program addressed each of the program's four underlying problems. It

- lengthened the flight-test schedule and increased ground testing
- removed the requirement for the deployable, early prototype interceptors
- increased the contractor's quality emphasis, including its commitment, leadership, and quality assurance staffing
- modified the cost-plus-fixed-fee contract to provide performance-based incentives and penalties and introduced a degree of competition into the program.

Despite these changes, the reliability of the remaining flight-test interceptors remained a concern because most components were produced when the contractor's quality assurance system was inadequate.

Contract Performance Lessons Learned

- The THAAD PDRR missiles had not yet demonstrated any military capability. Acquiring a significant number of missiles from the current design to support a contingency deployment concept was unwise. The hardware for the remaining missiles had been built and procured several years before, and only minor changes or upgrades could be made to the existing hardware. Until new hardware was built that incorporated the necessary design changes and improved manufacturing, product assurance, and test processes, there was no reason to expect any significant improvement in the THAAD missile's performance.
- Stable program funding and guidance was essential for program success. That was especially true with a complex "cutting-edge" technology program such as THAAD. Pressures to quickly field a prototype, budget cuts, program restructuring, and the misapplication of the principles of acquisition reform all strongly influenced the programmatic decisions. The Program Management

Office and contractor made tradeoffs that were necessary to meet a budget and a schedule driven by the requirement for early deployment of the User Operational Evaluation System.

- Improved component level design, qualification testing, quality control processes, and product assurance and testing procedures in the manufacturing of the interceptor were needed. Improved component level quality testing to confirm both design and reliability would greatly enhance the reliability and provide increased confidence in the integrated missile subsystems and system.
- More thorough ground and hardware-in-the-loop simulation testing of the THAAD missile assembly, and especially the seeker, needed to be performed. Due to the strong DOT&E influence, the Program Management Office had chartered a team to review the contractor and government hardware-in-the-loop testing capabilities. The team would provide recommendations on where improvements were needed to permit testing of end-to-end integrated missiles and to test critical subsystems (e.g., divert attitude control system, seeker, avionics package, etc.).

Contract Administration Lessons Learned

- A solid teaming environment (Battle Rhythm concept) early in the program life cycle, including all THAAD stakeholders (DCMA, THAAD Program Office (TPO), the prime contractor, and subcontractors) was critical to solving potential problems prior to any major milestone/funding decision points. This resulted in a proactive, solution-oriented business environment, where issues were identified with real-time resolution.
- Prime contractor DCMA Commander needed to participate actively in the Award Fee process, and THAAD stakeholders needed to participate in the Award Fee process, to address the then current program risk factors as determined by the Award Fee Board, to focus contractor risk mitigation efforts to reduce program risk, and to ensure overall mission success.
- Utilization of an electronic data management system to provide all players real-time information of all aspects of the program, from basic contract modifications to IPT minutes to program matrices, which had been paramount to the Battle Rhythm initiative success.

The THAAD program entered the engineering and manufacturing development (EMD) phase in 2000, with the award of a $3.8 billion contract to Lockheed Martin Space Systems Company. West and Adams had used the contract lessons learned and incorporated unique incentives into the EMD contract (Exhibit 1).

Between 2000 and 2003, THAAD engineers reworked the entire system and fixed many of its inherent problems and redundancies. In May 2004, production of 16 flight test missiles began at Lockheed Martin's new production facilities in Pike County, Alabama. Flight testing of the EMD system was scheduled to begin in early 2005 and continue till 2009. The system was expected to enter low-rate production, to support initial operating capability (IOC) in 2007.

Then in the development phase, THAAD was implementing a block development strategy designed to get the THAAD system into the hands of our soldiers as quickly as possible, using the latest technology in the most affordable manner. Each two-year block (Block 2004, 2006, and 2008) built on and integrated with the capabilities of the predecessor block. The program continued to refine and mature the system design to ensure that the element performed to an acceptable standard and could be produced efficiently and maintained. This would be accomplished by continuing current component design and development activities, robust ground tests, and quality assurance programs. Flight-testing would resume in late 2004 at White Sands Missile Range, transitioning to the Pacific Missile Range Facility in Hawaii in 2006 to test against representative threat systems.

Army Acquisition Reform *Newsletter*

**Special Incentives for Successful Flight Tests
in THAAD Award Fee Contract**

The Theater High Altitude Area Defense (THAAD) Engineering and Manufacturing Development (EMD) contract for $3.8 billion was awarded to Lockheed Martin Space Systems Company, Missile and Space Operations (LMSSC/M&SO), Sunnyvale, CA, on June 28, 2000. The THAAD EMD contract is an award fee type contract. The functional performance areas are technical, management, schedule and cost.

Emphasis was placed on the importance of successful flight tests occurring on schedule and within cost by including in the contract an award fee pool with special incentives for successful flight test intercepts for the first two flight attempts at White Sands Missile Range (WSMR) and Kwajalein Missile Range (KMR). If Lockheed Martin achieves a successful intercept within the first two attempts at WSMR, they will receive $25M in award fee. However, if they are unsuccessful after the first attempt, LM will share $15M of the contract cost. If Lockheed Martin achieves a successful intercept within the first two attempts at KMR, they will receive $25M in award fee. However, if they are unsuccessful after the first attempt, LM will share $20M of the contract cost. The clause identifies technical parameters that must be met during each of the first two flight tests at both ranges.

The use of the alpha contracting process for development of the scope of work (SOW) and the integrated Master Plan and Master Schedule as well as proposal preparation/evaluation provided the government with a best value contract. The Integrated Master Plan (IMP) provides the process narratives, events and criteria for the EMD program. The Integrated Master Schedule (IMS) provides the detail tasks and schedule for implementing the IMP. Both of these documents were developed during the alpha contracting process, substantially reducing the normal negotiation time and promoting a better understanding of the EMD requirements and the contractor-proposed approach to meeting these requirements.

EXHIBIT 1 Army Acquisition Reform Newsletter.

QUESTIONS

1. Do you think this was a financial audit, a project audit, or a management audit? Why?

2. Was the purpose of the audit to exert cybernetic control, go/no-go control, or postproject control? Explain.

3. Given the comments in the case, do you surmise that the reason for the audit was to improve future projects or to ascertain the reasons for not meeting the project's goals, and if the latter, its direct goals or ancillary goals?

4. Do you think the GAO was the best choice for an audit team? Would it have the trust of the project personnel?

5. Given the minimal elements of a project audit present in Section 12.2, which element(s) would have been primary to the audit team? Why? Which section would have contained the "underlying problems" reported in the case?

The following reading shows that project audits and evaluations help further knowledge concerning good project practice and improving the understanding of those in the organization about neighboring functions. However, most current audits/evaluations appear to be shallow, based on naive assumptions, and remedies for project difficulties tend to be superficial. Yet audits and evaluations were important learning experiences and are undervalued in organizations in terms of the insights they can provide about good project management.

DIRECTED READING

AN ASSESSMENT OF POSTPROJECT REVIEWS*
J. S. Busby

Potential Benefits

Many organizations set out to do postproject reviews, and for some compelling reasons:

- People do not automatically learn from their own experience, even as isolated individuals. They have to test new experiences against their existing knowledge and revise that knowledge in order to learn. A good example is learning about people. You can encounter a person on several occasions, but you do not learn from these occasions in any profound sense until you make a decision about the person (Eraut, 1994). It is at this point that you assemble the different experiences you have had and draw some coherent conclusions. The upshot is that, if you want to learn from experience, you consciously have to reflect on it.

- The knowledge of what occurred is usually dispersed among several people. We do many things, especially in organizations, where outcomes are

not directly observable. (We might not know, for instance, how readily users of our new product design adapt to the demands made on them.) Therefore, we need to consult other people to know the outcomes of our performance.

- The knowledge needed to diagnose outcomes is similarly dispersed among several people. For instance, people commonly make wrong assumptions about why others fail in their duties, and these misconceptions need to be corrected if reasonable remedies are to be identified for such failings. So, again, if we want to learn from experience, we must do so collectively.

- Dissemination matters, often critically. Organizations are rarely so specialized that every task of type X always goes to individual A. Some organizations seem to arrange things in such a way that tasks always go to the people least qualified to do them. Therefore, what one person learns from doing a project needs to be disseminated to others who might fill similar roles in the future. And, of course, this dissemination does not happen as a matter of course. Repeated errors are a characteristic of organizational life. Learning from experience within an organization has to be a public, recorded activity.

In some organizations, retrospective reviews are a natural and integral part of their operations; these include organizations that are highly regarded, such as military air forces (Lipshitz, Popper, & Oz, 1996).

Potential Drawbacks

The reality is, however, that postproject reviews are often curtailed and sometimes fall into complete disuse. Even when they are enthusiastically conducted, their outcomes are poorly disseminated. The reasons for this neglect include:

- They take time. This is especially a problem in project-oriented firms since project managers want to minimize costs allocated to their projects (particularly toward the end), and the beneficiaries of postproject reviews are future projects, not current ones.

- Reviews involve looking back over events that project participants are likely to feel cynical or embarrassed about. Looking forward to new work is more appealing.

- Maintaining social relationships typically matters more to most people than accurate diagnoses of isolated events. People can be reluctant to engage in activity that might lead to blame, criticism or recrimination (Argyris, 1977).

- Many people think that experience is a necessary and sufficient teacher in its own right. According to this point of view, if you have an experience you will necessarily learn from it, and if you have not had the experience you will not learn from someone else who has. We tried to suggest above this is not so, but many people believe it is and are predisposed against postproject reviews. So the question is, given cogent reasons on both sides, should we conduct postproject reviews? And how should we conduct them?

The Study

Four postproject review meetings were studied in three companies. All the projects involved in the study had values of several hundred thousand to a few million dollars, and all involved extensive engineering design and development activity. All three companies supplied capital equipment to industrial users, although they came from different sectors: one in electrical equipment, one in a coating plant, and one in precision product machinery. One of the companies had a policy of always running postproject reviews, but the other two did so only intermittently.

Discourse analyses of the postproject review meetings were performed (Stubbs, 1983). This kind of analysis involves a detailed inspection of what took place in the meetings. It means dividing up the transcripts into small speech units—typically sentences—and working out the structure of the conversation that these sentences comprise in general rather than particular terms. The advantage of discourse analysis is that it gives a detailed and comprehensive picture of what actually takes place, and generates fairly clear evidence for any conclusions you draw. The drawback is that it is very time-consuming and one cannot cover very many situations. Therefore, the observations we discuss later in the paper are based on clear evidence, but we cannot claim you would see the same thing in postproject reviews in other organizations.

How Did People Learn?

The first thing of interest was how people, collectively, went about learning from project reviews.

Dialectic Argument. First, the participants commonly resorted to a dialectic form of argument. One person would voice an explanation of something, another would come back with a contradictory explanation, and someone would find a third explanation that incorporated both the previous ones, i.e., a case of thesis, antithesis, and synthesis. For instance, in one case the participants were trying to explain why a handover meeting had been missed. One person thought another party had simply ignored a request to participate, the other party argued that it had received inadequate notice of the meeting, and the synthesis was simply that the two parties had insufficient knowledge of the others' time constraints. This kind of argument reflects the common fact that there are several sides to an event, and no one person alone has enough information to consider all sides of the argument. One person can argue one case, another can argue the opposite, and the meeting can reach a conclusion about where the best explanation lies.

Event Rehearsal. Second, a lot of mental rehearsal, or replay, of event sequences occurred. For example, a common case involved participants recalling their interactions with clients about successive changes to design requirements. This kind of replay is a natural process because one of the tests of whether A caused B is whether it preceded it, and building up a picture of event sequences therefore helps us infer why things happened the way they did. That said, there are two caveats. The first is that, despite the importance of time and deadlines during the projects, the review participants verbally rehearsed event sequences but did not put times against those events. (There were a couple of exceptions to this.) And second, precedence is only a partial indication of causality and people are susceptible to inferring causality when none exists (Tversky & Kahneman, 1982).

Mental Simulation. The third thing that was observed was that a kind of mental simulation was very common. This simulation almost always took the form of working out what would have happened had people's practices been different. For instance, in one case, the review participants reasoned about how the outcome would have been different had they used a different supplier. This kind of simulation used the informal, mental models that the participants had about how one event caused another. So, in the case of reasoning about the use of a different supplier, one participant would make a statement about how using the alternative supplier would have meant a greater need for coordinating effort. And another participant then argued that this would have led to a missed deadline since there were no available staff to provide this effort.

Simulation is somewhat similar to replay, except that it involved hypothetical events rather than actual ones. The extent of this simulation is significant in several ways. For a start, working forward from doing something to its result, called *causal reasoning*, is something we know that people instinctively prefer to the opposite, *diagnostic reasoning* (Tversky & Kahneman, 1982). Diagnostic reasoning involves working back from some result to the action that caused it. People generally have less facility with diagnostic reasoning than with causal reasoning. Causal reasoning can also be more acceptable socially because it avoids the question of who did what, concentrating instead on what would happen if someone did something else. The result of this, unfortunately, is a lack of deep diagnosis. Instead of tracing back the chain, or network, of causes and effects, people jump to possible remedies and work forward to simulate their results.

It would be wrong to paint simulation as a wholly misguided strategy, however. In particular, there is a side-benefit, in that it can help you learn from very few examples. If you have very small numbers of experiences from which to reason, maybe just one, it is hard to draw dependable conclusions. By simulating what would have happened had things been a little different you can effectively broaden the sample of experiences from which to draw conclusions (March, Sproull, & Tamuz, 1991).

Review Structure. The reviews that were observed differed in their general structure. In the two firms for which reviews were new, the structure of the review matched the structure of the project. The chairmen divided up the project into roughly chronological stages, asked people to say how successful the outcomes were, and encouraged them to work out why the less successful ones turned out so. In the firm that had had experience with running reviews, the chairman asked people to compile individual lists of good and bad things they had observed about the project, and then encouraged the participants to group these under a set of common headings. This structure had been adopted because the organization had found with the chronological approach that the reviews lasted too long. In

our observations, the discussion processes that took place, and the effectiveness of the reviews, seemed to be unrelated to the overall structure. The successes and failings seemed to be common to the different structures. It was also observed that the intended structure of the reviews was easily sidetracked. Events are so densely interconnected that participants often had to move from one topic to another to reconstruct what happened because they realized in examining the first topic that another was more important.

The one characteristic that differentiated the reviews, in a way that seemed to matter, was the presence of outsiders. The chairman of one review had invited managers of new projects to attend the review, which was an important way of disseminating the results. There was no apparent evidence that the presence of outsiders inhibited the working of the review, but it did mean that the outsiders obtained quite a profound understanding of what had succeeded and failed on the project under review. They not only saw the headlines but also saw the reasoning that led up to the review's conclusions and got a sense of the context in which the project had taken place. Such a sense of context is usually vital in gaining a meaningful understanding of how things succeed or fail.

Historical References. Our next observation is concerned with how review participants referred to history. In principle, historical references should be central to the diagnostic process. You cannot know whether an event on a single project (like an earthquake or a bankruptcy) is unique, frequent, or systemic unless you examine other completed projects. In fact, there were few historical references; only six were made in 12 hours of review meetings. Those that were had three different functions:

1. Using historical events as evidence for some explanation of events.

2. Demonstrating that there had been some change in the firm by contrasting recent events with historical ones.

3. Explaining people's behavior. (For example, people historically had become used to working in a particular way and carried on working in that way even when it became less appropriate.)

There were *no* historical references that simply helped people understand whether events on the project being reviewed were systemic. You could therefore argue that, as a means of learning from a specific experience, the postproject reviews failed to draw effectively on broader experience.

What Did People Learn?

As might be expected, some of the learning that took place involved disseminating knowledge of both successful and unsuccessful practices. For example, in one review, the project managers of new projects were able to hear about the consequences of having a single individual exercising both technical and managerial roles. It was evidently a poor practice. It is impossible to know, of course, if these managers of new projects would actually reproduce those practices in similar circumstances. So we can only say that there has been dissemination of what is called "propositional" knowledge, knowledge that, essentially, you can articulate but not necessarily practice.

Some of the knowledge that was learned was not so much task knowledge as knowledge that helped social relationships. For example, people would find out how hard others' jobs were, understand how severe were the constraints others operated under, and how hard it could be for others to be helpful. Knowing other people's points of view is an important kind of knowledge for effective members of organizations, and evidently it is not always learned during normal working activity.

Another important kind of knowledge was complexity. For example, there were several instances where individual participants had thought they had known why some event had happened, but in the reviews found out the explanation was far more clouded. The case of a late handover meeting illustrated this: everyone had had different ideas about why it had been late, but all turned out to be oversimplified. Individuals had each attributed the delay to a single cause, whereas the reality turned out to be a complex combination of several causes. Although this kind of learning, or really *unlearning*, is as good as any other, people feel less happy about it. It makes their models of their world less definite and more complicated. And it usually means that, contrary to what they might have thought, many problems do not have straightforward remedies.

How Well Did People Learn?

The next question addressed in the analysis was how well the learning process went in the reviews. Although it might seem unfair to do so, our approach was to look for flaws and limitations in the reasoning process that took place. It is unfair in that it might wrongly give the impression that the general level of learning was poor. We did it because it is easier to identify problems than successes. It also gives clues to how the reviews can be improved.

Attribution Problems. First, the reviews demonstrated *attribution bias*. One manifestation of attribution bias is that the participants in a process tend to overemphasize the role of the environment and underemphasize their own involvement when explaining results. You could expect review meetings to tend to blame factors beyond the participants' control and parties not represented at the reviews for problems during the project. Our observations indicated a strong tendency to explain problems by referring to other parties. On only two occasions did an individual admit an error or a need to change a way of working. This said,

occasionally a participant would say something like "Okay, the customer was the problem, but was there anything we could have done?" It is characteristic of most successful individuals and firms to have an "internal locus of control"; that is, to believe that events are within their control, for then they devote effort to exerting control. It is therefore important to ask what could have been done to remedy a problem, even if you believe it had external causes.

Excessive Concreteness. It is hard to provide objective evidence but the analysis at least suggested that review participants were too narrowly specific in their diagnoses. For instance, locating a piece of equipment in a place where it was hard to install and maintain was diagnosed as a slip. No attempt was made to determine whether it reflected a more general difficulty with visualizing installation and maintenance problems during equipment design. Too much specificity means missing bigger problems, tackling intermediate rather than basic causes, and implementing remedies that are too elaborate. There were very few examples of generalization during the review—very few occasions when participants asked something like "Is this a case of a bigger problem?" or "Are we missing something bigger?"

Overall, review participants were therefore too concrete in their diagnoses. The inevitable result is strictly *incremental learning:* learning by small revisions to current knowledge rather than wholesale replacements of it. The result of persistently incremental learning is an inability to react to large changes in the environment. We had no indication that any of the firms currently faced such large changes, but most organizations face them at some time and becoming habituated to incremental learning means they will be ill-placed to cope with large changes.

Shallow Diagnosis. Another characteristic of the reviews was an absence of deep diagnosis. It was mentioned in the previous section that the participants preferred causal reasoning (reasoning forward from cause to effect) to diagnostic reasoning (effect to cause). They were also very reluctant to ask others for diagnoses. No one, during the course of the reviews, asked a diagnostic "why"; they only asked clarifying "whys," as in "why was it poor?" meaning "in what way was it poor?" rather than "what were the causes of it being poor?" The explanation in the last section for the absence of diagnosis was cognitive, involving the preferred styles with which individuals reason. One could probably add social convention. Participants could well have been reluctant to ask others why they had done something because they were reluctant to sour their relationships with them. Sacrificing the truth about a single event that is now beyond correction may be necessary in order to maintain good relationships with a person you might have to work with in the future.

Organizations like the ones studied here also strongly promote the norm of being constructive: managers prefer people who "come to them with solutions, not problems," and it is virtually an automatic response when asked about the value of criticism to say it is important "provided it is constructive." This norm means that people will draw back from exploring the causation behind a problem unless they know they can provide a solution; not so much because they are intrinsically reluctant to criticize but because they know it does not look good to others in the organization to criticize gratuitously.

Lack of Data. A further issue that emerged from the analysis was the lack of reference to objective outcome data, especially costs and time scales that would not have been hard to collect from the firms' records. In some cases participants spent much time trying to recall when things in fact happened. In other cases, there was obvious uncertainty about how well the project had performed financially. Both conditions could have been answered easily by a little research into the record. Given that these outcomes are so central to most people's ideas about project success, it could be argued that such outcomes should be central to the review process. There was one occasion in which costs were available and were an important part of the review. This involved remediation costs: that is, the costs needed to put right errors or problems in preceding parts of the project. Even there, though, the figures were not clear-cut because the accounting basis that underlay them was unknown to the participants. In one sense, accounting conventions are irrelevant to diagnoses of project problems, but, when one does not know what they are, it is hard to know how big were the problems one actually encountered.

In fact, far more references were made during the reviews to practices than to outcomes. Instead of examining how far, say, costs deviated from budget and working out why, most of the time people examined how they worked and whether they could have done better. This seems to be putting the cart before the horse, and one could put this down to the mainly technical participants showing too little concern with business matters. But there are reasons to be concerned more with practices than outcomes. First, outcomes such as financial performance are determined jointly by project members' activities and the environment they work in. This means that poor financial performance does not necessarily indicate poor practices. It also means that the thing project members have most direct control over is their practices, not project outcomes. Thus, they have a natural incentive to examine practices rather than outcomes. Second, global outcomes of complex undertakings like projects generally provide poor feedback when they are composed of many different kinds of activities. It is like trying to learn a complex skill such as driving by being told only how long your complete journey took. For the review participants, project costs and timings were not especially helpful indicators of how well they performed their tasks (even if they are obviously informative to senior project managers).

Interpretation Errors. Even when outcomes were referred to, people sometimes appeared to make interpretation errors. For instance, in one case it turned out that the siting of a piece of equipment was poor because it made maintenance of the equipment difficult. The equipment was small, of low value, and needed relatively little maintenance, so the problem was dismissed as being very minor and led to no further discussion. We would say, however, that this easy dismissal makes the error of assuming that minor outcomes reflect minor causes. The question of maintainability is important for customers in industrial plant industries, sometimes critical. This interpretative error suggested that the organization's engineers had too little awareness of the issue, perhaps through a lack of training, a lack of formal process, or a lack of knowledge transfer among different engineers. None of this was explored. Naturally, organizations with limited time and resources pay most attention to big outcomes, not small ones. The danger of doing so in an unthinking way is that one misses big issues simply because, on isolated occasions, they happen not to have big outcomes. However, later the outcome might be major and adverse; good learning stimulated by a minor adverse outcome could pay big dividends in the future.

How Worthwhile Was It?

After the reviews had taken place, participants were interviewed, for about 10 minutes each, and the researcher spoke informally to members of the other reviews immediately after they had finished. None of the participants dismissed them as worthless, but none gave the reviews unqualified support. There was skepticism, in particular, about any prospect that the reviews would actually make a difference. Part of this skepticism undoubtedly lay in people's cynicism about organizations, conditioned by long experience of managerial activities that led to no obvious improvement. But part of it lay in the unconvincing nature of the remedies that were explored in the reviews. Two of the reviews were distinctly hurried toward the end, so remedies received only superficial treatment. Yet, even in the others, remedies were not analyzed, only proposed and briefly contested. Side-effects were not explored and implementation was not planned. At best, there was only an acknowledgment in one of the reviews that someone would have to go away and plan the remedies in more detail. Given that organizational interventions invariably have unfavorable side effects, and that their implementation is generally protracted and messy, people will naturally be skeptical about remedies that receive only glancing attention.

In all then, a number of limitations in the learning process existed during the course of the reviews. In previous sections the neglect of history, the lack of generalization, and the lack of any profound diagnosis was mentioned. The superficial treatment given to remedies has just been mentioned. However, it was also evident from the analyses that these reviews had a number of important functions:

- They gave people a chance to demonstrate their concern with the organization's objectives.

- They helped people correct misconceptions they had learned in the course of normal project activity.

- They gave people the chance to explain and justify their actions in a way that was not always open to them during the project.

- They suggested available practices that had not been realized by those who might have used them.

- They promoted collective remedies and engendered feelings of commitment to them. Remedies were sometimes dismissed for their superficiality, as explained, but at least they were voiced collectively.

- The reviews had an important disseminating function, although this requires sharing the review results with outsiders. Most review participants who have worked on the project under the microscope say things like "I already knew *X*." But typically it does not occur to them to go around other projects telling people about *X*—maybe because they do not realize *X* matters to others, did not know they knew *X* until it was pointed out, or were just too busy to think about anything to do with *X*. Whatever the case, postproject reviews (provided you invite along outsiders) helped *X* get out. We found, however, that people generally underestimated the dissemination function of postproject reviews.

What Should You Do?

The Shortfalls. The three greatest shortfalls in the reviews that were studied were that people were overspecific, ahistorical, and undiagnostic. Being too specific in your learning actually refers to two different things. One way to be too specific is to have too narrow a view of the process you are learning about. If you think of an engineering project just in terms of what the project manager can affect, for instance, you will not question whether there is something to be learned about, say, the process of assigning project managers. The other way to be too specific is to view what you are learning about too literally. If it turns out that a product fails because a wall thickness of a designed part was insufficient, you could diagnose this as a failure to specify adequate wall thickness. You could go on to add something to your codes of practice that says all wall thickness should be checked with the chief engineer. But you could go to a more general level and diagnose this as a failure among designers to understand the extremes of operating duty that their products have to meet. You might then think of remedies to do with giving designers greater exposure to customers using their products. Both types of overspecificity cause

learning to be less effective than it should be. Therefore, the messages are try to learn about the bigger system, not just day-to-day activities, and try to think of particular failings as examples of more general types of failing.

How much do people think about history? The answer seems to be "not much," since only six references of any kind to historical experience occurred throughout the reviews. The big problem of *not* referring to history is that you will not learn what types of problems are unique and what types are characteristic or systemic. Also, you will have an excessive confidence in any remedies you plan. But, having said this, the way you use history is not clear cut. There are two common aphorisms about learning from history that seem to contradict each other: one is "There is nothing new under the sun" and the other is "History never repeats itself." The first suggests that knowing history is essential because the future will resemble it. The second suggests that knowing history is dangerous because you can be trapped into believing that the future will be the same as the past. The important point is to look at history at the right level of generality. Your next product development will be unique because in all its detail it will differ in many respects from previous developments. At the same time, you simply would not be able to do it if it were wholly unique. You still have to go through very similar processes, deal with very similar *kinds* of objects, and so on.

Finally, true diagnosis was mostly absent. Why, given the extent to which people are encouraged to adopt cause-effect analysis, fishbone diagrams, problem-solving devices, and so on, do they not practice causal diagnosis? As with other matters, you can take your explanation either from individual psychology or from organizational behavior. The psychological explanation has to do with the distinction between causal reasoning and diagnostic reasoning that was mentioned earlier. Individuals simply seem to find it easier to reason from cause to effect than vice versa. The organizational explanation is that most people regard it as a social requirement to avoid direct criticism of one another, especially if they have to maintain some kind of long-term relationship. Most people are not going to sacrifice good long-term relationships for the sake of one or two accurate diagnoses of events that cannot be undone. And they have probably reached their own, private diagnosis of events anyway, and do not see a need for a collective diagnosis. The fact that the collective diagnosis could be better than their private one may not even occur to them. Moreover, it is a social norm to be constructive—emphasizing the search for better ways rather than the diagnosis of a bad way. Unfortunately, the consequence of all this very reasonable avoidance of deep diagnosis is shallow understanding and, most likely, wrong remedies that treat symptoms rather than causes. Ineffective post mortems, like ineffectual people, avoid conflict in the name of long-term ends, but ultimately sacrifice long-term ends for short-term comfort. Getting an organization to do the opposite (pursue long-term ends and endure a lack of short-term comfort) is ultimately a test of leadership, of moral courage, persuasiveness, and will.

Recommendations. We would recommend the following "watchwords" for review chairpersons:

1. Encourage deep diagnosis. Use cause-effect diagrams if they are likely to help.

2. Encourage attention to history. Ask whether similar things have occurred historically.

3. Encourage the examination of the bigger system beyond the immediate confines of the project.

4. Discourage glib categorization. There is little that cannot be put down to "communications problems" in complex projects, but categorizing something this way is only a starting point to the diagnosis, not a finishing point. It is easy to put down as a communications problem, for example, two people making different assumptions about who has responsibility for a particular action. A proper diagnosis would examine how different assumptions arise and why they persist even when they lead to errors.

5. Plan remedies properly by examining side effects and thinking through the implementation. If this has to be the subject of a second meeting, then so be it. Chairpeople need to have the maturity to realize that suggested but unplanned remedies will simply deepen review participants' cynicism.

6. Invite key outsiders to postproject reviews to assist in dissemination. In one of the reviews we studied, managers of new projects were invited, and this was probably far more effective at dissemination than written summaries would have been. Written summaries tend to be written from one person's standpoint, so one often does not know how contentious certain issues were. And these summaries often lack the detail that adopting a new practice depends on.

Most people would probably count such practices as common sense. It is therefore important to be aware that such practices often failed to materialize—even among the highly intelligent, knowledgeable, and thoughtful people who ran the reviews we studied.

Summary

Overall, in the light of this study, we would come out strongly in favor of postproject reviews (provided you do not call them "post mortems"). We could spot flaws in the ones we saw, but they were still valuable. And most of the organizations we worked with had not run them before, so judging them by the first-of-kind would not be reasonable. This study, while limited, points the direction for additional research in this important area of project management.

References

Argyris, C. (1977, September–October). Double loop learning in organizations. *Harvard Business Review*, 115–125.

Eraut, M. (1994). *Developing Professional Knowledge and Competence* (p. 51). London: Falmer Press.

Lipshitz, R., Popper, M., and Oz, S. (1996). Building learning organizations: The design and implementation of organizational learning mechanisms. *Journal of Applied Behavioral Science*, 32 (3), 292–305.

March, J. G., Sproull, L. S., and Tamuz, M. (1991). Learning from samples of one or fewer. *Organization Science*, 2 (1), 1–13.

Stubbs, M. (1983). *Discourse Analysis*. Oxford: Basil Blackwell.

Tversky, A., and Kahneman, D. (1982). Causal schemas in judgments under uncertainty. In D. Kahneman, P. Slovic, & A. Tversky (Eds.), *Judgment under Uncertainty: Heuristics and Biases* (pp. 117–128). Cambridge University Press.

Questions

1. Why do you think organizations tend to ignore postproject evaluations?

2. How could the concept of making such evaluations mandatory be implemented?

3. Evaluate their advice for conducting postproject evaluations.

4. How does an understanding of how people learn affect project audits and evaluations?

5. How can an auditor/evaluator avoid the shortfalls described in the article?

6. Summarize the author's recommendations.

13

Project Termination

As it must to all things, termination comes to every project. At times, project death is quick and clean, but more often it is a long process; and there are times when it is practically impossible to establish that death has occurred. The skill with which termination, or a condition we might call "near termination," is managed has a great deal to do with the quality of life after the project. The termination stage of the project rarely has much impact on technical success or failure, but it has a great deal to do with residual attitudes toward the project—the "taste left in the mouth" of the client, senior management, and the project team. It also has a great deal to do with learning about the things that lead to success—or failure.

At this point, the joy of discovery is past. Problems have been solved, bypassed, lived with, or ignored. Implementation plans have been carried out. The client is delighted, angry, or reasonably satisfied. In construction-type projects where the project cadre remains intact, the termination issue is eased because the team moves on to another challenge. For non-recurring projects, the issue is far more akin to the breakup of a family. While the members of the family may be on the best of terms, they must now separate, go their individual ways, divide or dispose of the family property, and make plans for individual survival. Unless the project life was only a few weeks or a few months, the change is stressful. For projects organized as weak matrices, there will be only a few individuals, perhaps only the project manager, who "belong" to the project. This may represent an even more stressful situation than the breakup of a large project family because there is little or no peer group for support.

The process of termination is never easy, always complicated, and, as much as we might wish to avoid it, almost always inevitable. The problem is how to accomplish one of the several levels of what is meant by project termination with a minimum of trouble and administrative dislocation.

In this chapter, we examine the variety of conditions that may be generally referred to as *project termination*. We then view some decision-aiding models that can assist an organization in making the termination decision. This requires us to return to the subject of evaluation and discuss indicators of success and failure in projects. We also discuss some procedures that decrease the pain of termination, and others that reduce the administrative problems that often arise after projects have been terminated. We look into the typical causes of termination, and finally note that the preparation of a project history is an integral part of the termination process.

13.1 THE VARIETIES OF PROJECT TERMINATION

For our purposes, a project can be said to be terminated when work on the substance of the project has ceased or slowed to the point that further progress on the project is no longer possible, when the project has been indefinitely delayed, when its resources have been deployed to other projects, or when project personnel (especially the PM) become *personae non gratae* with senior management and in the company lunchroom. There may seem to be a spark of life left, but resuscitation to a healthy state is most unlikely. On rare occasions, projects are reborn to a new, glorious existence (Baker, 1997). But such rebirth is not expected, and project team members who "hang on to the bitter end" have allowed optimism to overcome wisdom. The PM must understand that the ancient naval tradition that the captain should go down with the ship does not serve the best interests of the Navy, the crew, the ship, and most certainly not the captain.

On the other hand, the captain must not, ratlike, flee the "ship" at the first sign of trouble. In the next section of this chapter, we note many of the signs and signals that indicate that the project may be in real trouble. At this point, it is appropriate to consider the ways in which a project can be terminated. There are four fundamentally different ways to close out a project: extinction, addition, integration, and starvation.

Termination by Extinction

The project is stopped. It may end because it has been successful and achieved its goals: The new product has been developed and handed over to the client, or the software has been installed and is running.

The project may also be stopped because it is unsuccessful or has been superseded: The new drug failed its efficacy tests; there are better/faster/cheaper/prettier alternatives available; or it will cost too much and take too long to get the desired performance. Changes in the external environment can kill projects, too. The explosion of the Challenger stopped a number of space shuttle projects overnight. More recently, extraordinary cost escalation in the technology and materials associated with automotive racing caused the ruling bodies of both Formula 1 and Indy-car racing to stop (and even repeal) specific technological changes in their respective venues.

A special case of termination by extinction is "termination by murder."* There are all sorts of murders. They range from political assassination to accidental projecticide. When senior executives vie for promotion, projects for which the loser is champion are apt to suffer. Corporate mergers often make certain projects redundant or irrelevant. NCR was forced to cancel several projects following its merger into AT&T, and probably several more when NCR was more recently unmerged.

Two important characteristics of termination by murder, premeditated or not, are the suddenness of project demise and the lack of obvious signals that death is imminent.

---

*The authors thank Professor Emeritus Samuel G. Taylor (University of Wyoming) for noting this special case of termination by extinction.

When a decision is made to terminate a project by extinction, the most noticeable event is that all activity on the *substance* of the project ceases. A great deal of organizational activity, however, remains to be done. Arrangements must be made for the orderly release of project team members and their reassignment to other activities if they are to remain in the parent organization. The property, equipment, and materials belonging to the project must be disbursed according to the dictates of the project contract or in accord with the established procedures of the parent organization. Finally, the Project Final Report, also known as the *project history*, must be prepared. These subjects will be covered in greater detail later in this chapter.

Termination by Addition

Most projects are "in-house," that is, carried out by the project team for use in the parent organization. If a project is a major success, it may be terminated by institutionalizing it as a formal part of the parent organization. NCR Corporation (prior to its merger and demerger with AT&T), for example, used this method of transforming a project into a division of the firm and then, if real economic stability seems assured, into an independent subsidiary. Essentially the same process occurs when a university creates an academic department out of what originally was a few courses in an existing department. For example, most software engineering and/or information systems departments began by reorganizing an engineering or business school "subspecialty" into a full-fledged department.

When the project is made a more or less full-fledged member of the parent, it lives its first years in a protected status—carrying less than an "adult" share of overhead cost. As the years pass, however, the child is expected gradually to assume the economic responsibilities of full adulthood.

When project success results in termination by addition, the transition is strikingly different from termination by extinction. In both cases the project ceases to exist, but there the similarity stops. Project personnel, property, and equipment are often simply transferred from the dying project to the newly born division. The metamorphosis from project to department, to division, and even to subsidiary is accompanied by budgets and administrative practices that conform to standard procedure in the parent firm, by demands for contribution profits, by the probable decline of political protection from the project's corporate "champion," indeed by a greater exposure to all the usual stresses and strains of regular, routine, day-to-day operations.

It is not uncommon, however, for some of the more adventurous members of the project team to request transfers to other projects or to seek the chance to start new projects. Project life is exciting, and some team members are uncomfortable with what they perceive to be the staid, regulated existence of the parent organization. The change from project to division brings with it a sharply diminished sense of freedom.

This transition poses a difficult time for the PM, who must see to it that the shift is made smoothly. In Part I of this book, and especially in Chapter 3, we referred repeatedly to the indispensable requirement of political sensitivity in the PM. The transition from project to division demands a superior level of political sensitivity for successful accomplishment. Projects lead a sheltered life, for all the risks they run. The regular operating divisions of a firm are subjected to the daily infighting that seems, in most firms, to be a normal result of competition between executives.

Termination by Integration

This method of terminating a project is the most common way of dealing with successful projects, and the most complex. The property, equipment, material, personnel, and functions

Project Management in Practice
Project Termination Practices in Indian Industry

Project termination phase, the last phase of the project life cycle, plays a vital role in successful completion of a project. The process of project termination is not an easy task. It has to be planned, budgeted and scheduled like any other phase of the project life cycle. Sometimes special termination managers are put to complete the termination process. Though project termination constitutes a significant part in the total project, it is often overlooked by project managers. A case study was conducted to analyse the problems faced by project managers while terminating projects in India.

The case study revealed that project managers loosen their grip of monitoring the time-bound projects as soon as the installed plants or services start functioning. The last few defects continue to get rectified for long periods in the process of handing over the projects to clients. By the time these defects are rectified, new problems crop up which require further time to stabilize. It has been observed that plants are formally handed over with preliminary acceptance certificate, pending rectification of last few problems. This becomes a vicious cycle before obtaining the final acceptance certificate from the client. Due to non-realization of the last contractual amount, project organizations face shortage of funds, particularly when they are

engaged in multiple projects. For example, a company manufacturing material-handling equipment ran a coal-handling plant for a power project of a leading power generating firm for almost 10 years before it could successfully terminate the project due to the project manager's inability to meet the performance guarantee tests. Another difficult aspect is the identification of the beginning of the termination phase of a project. Project managers use their perception and judgement to identify the starting of termination phase after completion of execution, commissioning, and testing activities.

An analysis of the case study data revealed that the following problems are considered most significant by Indian industry during the project termination phase:

- Negotiating claims with clients.
- Compliance of statutory requirements.
- Receipt of the final instalment of payment.
- Performance guarantee tests.
- Handling claims of suppliers.

Source: De. P.K. Project Termination Practices in Indian Industry: A Statistical Review, *International Journal of Project Management*, Volume 19, Issue 2, pp. 119–126, February 2001. Reproduced by permission of Elsevier.

of the project are distributed among the existing elements of the parent organization. The output of the project becomes a standard part of the operating systems of the parent, or client.

In some cases, the problems of integration are relatively minor. The project team that installed a new piece of software, instructed the client in its operation and maintenance, and then departed, probably left only minor problems behind it, problems familiar to experienced managers. If the installation was a server complete with multiple terminals and many different pieces of software, then the complexities of integration are apt to be more severe. In general, the problems of integration are inversely related to the level of experience that the parent organization (or client) has had with: (1) the technology being integrated and (2) the successful integration of other projects, regardless of technology.

Most problems of termination by addition are also present when the project is integrated. In the case of integration, the project may not be viewed as a competitive interloper, but the project personnel being moved into established units of the parent organization will be so viewed. Also, the project, which flourished so well in its protected existence as a project, may not be quite so healthy in the chill atmosphere of the "real world." The individuals who nurtured the project may have returned to their respective organizational divisions, and may have new responsibilities. They tend to lose their fervid interest in the "old" project.

Following is a list of a few of the more important aspects of the transition from project to integrated operation that must be considered when the project functions are distributed.

1. *Personnel*   Where will the project team go? Will it remain a team? If the functions that the team performed are still needed, who will do them? If ex-team members are assigned to a new project, under what conditions or circumstances might they be temporarily available for help on the old project?

2. *Manufacturing*   Is training complete? Are input materials and the required facilities available? Does the production system layout have to be replanned? Did the change create new bottlenecks or line-of-balance problems? Are new operating or control procedures needed? Is the new operation integrated into the firm's computer systems?

3. *Accounting/Finance*   Have the project accounts been closed and audited? Do the new department budgets include the additional work needed by the project? Have the new accounts been created and account numbers been distributed? Has all project property and equipment been distributed according to the contract or established agreements?

4. *Engineering*   Are all drawings complete and on file? Are operating manuals and change procedures understood? Have training programs been altered appropriately for new employees? Have maintenance schedules been adjusted for the change? Do we have a proper level of "spares" in stock?

5. *Information Systems/Software*   Has the new system been thoroughly tested? Is the software properly documented and are "comments" complete? Is the new system fully integrated with current systems? Have the potential users been properly trained to use the new system?

6. *Marketing*   Is the sales department aware of the change? Is marketing in agreement about lead times? Is marketing comfortable with the new line? Is the marketing strategy ready for implementation?

7. *Purchasing, Distribution, Legal, etc.*   Are all these and other functional areas aware of the change? Has each made sure that the transition from project to standard operation has been accomplished within standard organizational guidelines and that standard administrative procedures have been installed?

8. *Risk Identification and Management*   Most of the questions and conditions noted in items 1–7 represent risks for successful integration. They should be handled like any other risks the project has faced, subjected to analysis, and dealt with accordingly.

Termination by Starvation

There is a fourth type of project termination, although strictly speaking, it is not a "termination" at all. It is "slow starvation by budget decrement." Almost anyone who has been involved with projects over a sufficient period of time to have covered a business recession has had to cope with budget cuts. Budget cuts, or decrements, are not rare. Because they are common, they are sometimes used to mask a project termination.

Project Management in Practice
Pulling the Plug: Projects in a Risky World

Projects can operate on the brink of what is realistically achievable. Being in this precarious position it is possible for the project team to experience the dramatic highs of a success as well as the stresses of a project doomed to failure. Perhaps the arena where we can see this most clearly is in creative projects; such as making a movie.

Lost in Mancha tells the behind-the-scenes story of Terry Gilliam's movie *The Man Who Killed Don Quixote*. Gilliam had previously directed several critically and commercially successful films including *Time Bandits, The Fisher King* and *Twelve Monkeys*. However, his attempts to turn his vision to bring the epic story of Don Quixote to the big screen resulted in frustration and, ultimately, failure.

The mishaps that beset this project cover almost every dimension of the risk kaleidoscope. In the area of "team work," creative tensions between the cast, the director and the crew simmered for a lot of the production. In the area of the "technical operations" the filming schedule was severely disrupted when air force fighter planes thundered across the sky. Also, torrential rainstorms during the initial weeks of filming resulted in a dramatic change to the landscape. The colours of the cliffs changed dramatically as dormant plants grew on a previously barren landscape. Finally, the leading actor had to leave the set due to a serious hernia. This initially disrupted the filming schedule which would have created some cost and time overrun. However, after many weeks the actor had not returned and the films investors filed an insurance claim to recover their losses. As part of this claim, the work done so far on the script, props and filming was passed to the insurance company. Gilliam had lost control of the project and it was terminated.

This case illustrates some of the pressures that projects can face. As well as technical risks (e.g., being able to shoot the film to schedule) there are risks associated to the environment and to the team processes. Ultimately, the cumulative impact of these risks resulted in the project sponsors (the financers) cutting their losses.

A post-script to the story of *Lost in Mancha*: In 2009 Gilliam had re-acquired the rights for the film and was rewriting the script. Initially, casting had been undertaken with Robert Duvall and Ewan MacGregor taking on the lead roles. However, once again the project collapsed after the finance was withdrawn during the summer of 2010. Gilliam's ambitions of retelling this tale to a new audience remain frustrated.

Sources: BBC (2010) "Terry Gilliam loses Don Quixote backers" http://www.bbc.co.uk/news/entertainment-arts-11212328 downloaded on 25th May 2011.

Fulton, K. & Pepe, L. (2002) "Lost in Mancha" Optimum Home Releasing.

Mitchell, E. (31st January 2003) An Impossible Dream: Making "Don Quixote" New York Times http://www.nytimes.com/2003/01/31/movies/film-review-an-impossible-dream-making-don-quixote.html?src=pm downloaded on 25th May 2011.

There may be a number of reasons why senior management does not wish to terminate an unsuccessful or obsolete project. In some firms, for example, it is politically dangerous to admit that one has championed a failure, and terminating a project that has not accomplished its goals is an admission of failure. In such a case, the project budget might receive a deep cut—or a series of small cuts—large enough to prevent further progress on the project and to force the reassignment of many project team members. In effect, the project is terminated, but the project still exists as a legal entity complete with sufficient staff to maintain some sort of presence, such as a secretary who issues a project "no-progress" report each year. In general, it is considered bad manners to inquire into such projects or to ask why they are still "on the books."

13.2   WHEN TO TERMINATE A PROJECT

The decision to terminate a project early, by whatever method, is difficult. As we emphasized in Chapter 4, projects tend to develop a life of their own—a life seemingly independent of whether or not the project is successful. In an early article on the subject of terminating R & D projects, Buell (1967) suspected that the main reason so little information was available on the subject was that it was hard to spell out specific guidelines and standards for the decision. He expressed strong doubts about the ability to "wrap everything up in a neat set of quantitative mathematical expressions," and then went on to develop an extensive set of questions that, if answered, should lead management to a decision. While these questions were aimed at R & D projects, they have wide, general applicability. Paraphrased and slightly modified to broaden and extend them beyond R&D projects, they are:

- Is the project still consistent with organizational goals?
- Is it practical? Useful?
- Is management sufficiently enthusiastic about the project to support its implementation?
- Is the scope of the project consistent with the organization's financial strength?
- Is the project consistent with the notion of a "balanced" program in all areas of the organization's technical interests? In "age"? In cost?
- Does the project have the support of all the departments (e.g., finance, manufacturing, marketing, IT, legal, etc.) needed to implement it?
- Is organizational project support being spread too thin?
- Is support of this individual project sufficient for success?
- Does this project represent too great an advance over current technology? Too small an advance?
- Is the project team still innovative, or has it gone stale?
- Can the new knowledge be protected by patent, copyright, or trade secret?
- Could the project be farmed out without loss of quality?
- Is the current project team properly qualified to continue the project?
- Does the organization have the required skills to achieve full implementation or exploitation of the project?
- Has the subject area of the project already been "thoroughly plowed"?
- Has the project lost its key person or champion?
- Is the project team enthusiastic about success?
- Can the potential results be purchased or subcontracted more efficiently than developed in-house?
- Does it seem likely that the project will achieve the minimum goals set for it? Is it still profitable? Timely?

We could add many other such questions to Buell's list. For instance:

- Has the project been obviated by technical advances or new products/services developed elsewhere?
- Is the output of the product still cost effective? Has its risk level changed significantly?
- Is it time to integrate or add the project as a part of the regular, ongoing operation of the parent organization?

- Would we support the project if it were proposed today at the time and cost required to complete it?
- Are there better alternative uses for the funds, time, and personnel devoted to the project?
- Has a change in the environment altered the need for the project's output?

Such questions clearly overlap, and the list could easily be extended further. Dean (1968) reports that the probabilities of technical and/or commercial failure are the two most important reasons for terminating projects before their completion (see Table 13-1), according to the executives he surveyed. Compared to the great level of research and thought concerning the project selection decision before the 1980s (see also Chapter 2), there has been relatively little research published on the termination decision. But even this bit was more than the work devoted to defining project success. As interest in project termination increased in the mid-1980s, interest in understanding project success also rose. Pinto et al. (1987, 1988) surveyed experienced PMs and found 10 factors that the managers felt to be critical to successful project implementation (see Table 13-2). Jiang et al. (1996) surveyed information system "business professionals" on the relative importance of the Pinto et al. critical success factors and came to roughly similar conclusions. Baker et al. (1983) looked at similar factors associated with R & D project success and failure.

A particularly important finding of Baker et al. is that the *factors associated with project success are different for different industries.* Baker's work was restricted to R & D projects, but the Pinto et al. studies covered many different types of projects. They found that the success-related factors differed between fundamentally different types of projects—between R&D and construction projects, for example. At the very least, the factors and their relative importance are idiosyncratic to the industry, to the project type, and, we suggest, possibly to the firm.

Out of this work came some models that could be used to predict project success or failure, based on certain project characteristics or practices. Pinto et al. (1990), using Pinto's

Table 13-1 Rank Order of Importance Factors Considered in Premature Terminations of R&D Projects (36 companies)

Factors	No. of Companies Reporting the Factor as Being Important
Technical	
Low probability of achieving technical objectives or commercializing results	34
Technical or manufacturing problems cannot be solved with available R&D skills	11
Higher priority of other projects requiring R&D labor or funds	10
Economic	
Low profitability or return on investment	23
Too costly to develop as individual product	18
Market	
Low market potential	16
Change in competitive factors or market needs	10
Others	
Too long a time required to achieve commercial results	6
Negative effects on other projects or products	3
Patent problems	1

Source: Dean (1968).

Table 13-2   Critical Success Factors in Order of Importance

1. *Project Mission*—Initial clearly defined goals and general directions.
2. *Top-Management Support*—Willingness of top management to provide the necessary resources and authority/power for project success.
3. *Project Schedule/Plan*—A detailed specification of the individual action steps for project implementation.
4. *Client Consultation*—Communication, consultation, and active listening to all impacted parties.
5. *Personnel*—Recruitment, selection, and training of the necessary personnel for the project team.
6. *Technical Tasks*—Availability of the required technology and expertise to accomplish the specific technical action steps.
7. *Client Acceptance*—The act of "selling" the final project to its ultimate intended users.
8. *Monitoring and Feedback*—Timely provision of comprehensive control information at each stage in the implementation process.
9. *Communication*—The provision of an appropriate network and necessary data to all key actors in the project implementation.
10. *Trouble-shooting*—Ability to handle unexpected crises and deviations from plan.

Source: Pinto et al. (1987).

work cited above, reported on factors that were associated with project failure. The factors differed for the type of project involved (R&D vs. construction), for the project's position in the life cycle, as well as for the precise way in which "failure" was defined. Green et al. (1993) found that a poor fit with the firm's existing technological expertise and/or with its existing marketing area and channels was a good early predictor of project termination. Kloppenborg et al. (1991) described precursors to success and failure for projects intended to implement expert systems, and Beale et al. (1991) modeled project success, differentiating between factors exogenous and endogenous to the project and the project team.

In the face of this diversity of success factors, it is interesting to note that there are relatively few fundamental reasons why some projects fail to produce satisfactory answers to Buell's questions about early terminations of projects.

1. ***A Project Organization Is Not Required***   The use of the project form of organization was inappropriate for this particular task or in this particular environment. The parent organization must understand the conditions that require instituting a project.

2. ***Insufficient Support from Senior Management***   Projects invariably develop needs for resources that were not originally allocated. Arguments between functional departments over the command of such resources are very common. Without the direct support of a champion in senior management, the project is almost certain to lose the resource battle.

3. ***Naming the Wrong Person as Project Manager***   This book is testimony to the importance of the PM. A common mistake is to appoint as PM an individual with excellent technical skills but weak managerial skills or training.

4. ***Poor Planning***   This is a very common cause of project failure. In the rush to get the substance of the project under way, competent planning is neglected. In such cases, crisis management becomes a way of life, difficulties and errors are compounded, and the project slowly gets farther behind schedule and over budget. Indeed, careful planning is associated with success in almost all empirical research on project success—Tom Peter's "Ready, Fire, Aim" to the contrary notwithstanding. Not only is proper planning often cited as a *success factor*, lack of planning is cited as a *cause of failure* (Black, 1996).

These, and a few other reasons, are the base causes of most project failures. The specific causes of failure, for the most part, derive from these fundamental items. For example,

- No use was made of earlier project Final Reports that contained a number of recommendations for operating projects in the future.

- Time/cost estimates were not prepared by those who had responsibility for doing the work.

- Starting late, the PM jumped into the tasks without adequate planning.

- Project personnel were moved without adjusting the schedule, or were reassigned during slow periods and then were unavailable when needed.

- Project auditors/evaluators were reluctant to conduct careful, detailed meaningful evaluations.

- The project was allowed to continue in existence long after it had ceased to make cost-effective progress.

- Evaluations failed to determine why problems were arising during the early phases of the project life cycle due to inadequate, or no, risk assessment and management.

All these causes of failure underline the need for careful evaluation at all stages of the project. But at the same time, it is most important to note that the lion's share of the attention given to the termination issue is focused on the failing project. It is equally or more important to terminate successful projects at the right time and by proper methods. One rarely mentioned problem affecting many organizations is the inability or unwillingness of successful project managers working on successful projects to "let their projects go." This is a particularly difficult problem for in-house projects. The PM (and team) simply will not release the project to the tender care of the client department. An outstanding technical specialist and manager conducting communications projects was released from employment simply because she insisted on maintaining semipermanent control of projects that had essentially been completed, but which were not released to the users because they "needed further testing" or "fine-tuning."

Also, little consideration has been given to *how* the termination decision is made and *who* makes it. We feel that a broadly based committee of reasonably senior executives is probably best. The broad organizational base of the committee is needed to diffuse and withstand the political pressure that accompanies all terminations—successes and failures alike. To the extent possible, the criteria used by the termination committee should be written and explained in some detail. It is, however, important to write the criteria in such a way that the committee is not frozen into a mechanistic approach to a decision. There are times when hunches should be followed (or rejected) and blind faith should be respected (or ignored). It depends on whose hunches and faith are under consideration (Baker, 1997).

A reviewer of this book noted that we had covered a great many "technical" reasons for terminating projects, but had not said that many projects are terminated for "nontechnical" reasons. There are several nontechnical reasons why projects are terminated, but almost always these terminations seem to be associated with conflict, even when the conflict is anticipated at the beginning of the project.

Political terminations   We mentioned this type of project demise when discussing termination by murder. These terminations are typically the result of conflict between senior managers, one of whom may be terminated along with the project.

Cross-cultural terminations   Multinational projects sometimes fail because the different cultural groups do not/cannot communicate well, or because their working styles do not/cannot mesh. See Chapter 3 for other examples. The conflicts arise when poor communication or diverse working styles cause the different cultures to compete for ascendancy or to engage in win/lose negotiations. The same cross-cultural forces operate when different disciplines, e.g., marketing and engineering, develop precisely the same problems.

Project Management in Practice
Terminating the Superconducting Super Collider Project

When the U.S. Congress pulled the plug on the Superconducting Super Collider (SSC) project, it ended 11 years of work costing over $2 billion and threw 2,000 people out of work. The objective of the planned $11 billion SSC was to accelerate subatomic particles within a 54-mile underground circular chamber to almost the speed of light and smash them together at energies of 40 trillion electronic volts. The benefits to society of these experiments were unclear, some maintaining they could have been enormous, but others, including congressmen, were less sure.

The project also suffered from an identity crisis. It was not clear if this was to be a U.S. "first" in basic science or a "world" science project, funded in its early stages by a $1 billion commitment from other nations. Although the costs of the SSC had ballooned, the main reason it was terminated was that it lost its political support.* Although the SSC scientists and backers had rallied goodwill among universities, schools, and scientific meetings, the potential benefits of the project never reached the Clinton administration, where it only enjoyed lukewarm support at best. When a $4 trillion budget deficit appeared likely, the SSC project was sacrificed.

Source: B. Baker and R. Menon, "Politics and Project Performance: The Fourth Dimension of Project Management," *PM Network*, Vol. 9.

*The authors of this book believe that the loss of political support was because Texas was the only state that would directly gain from the project.

The gigantic tunnels for the super collider are prepared first.

Senescence terminations   There are projects that pass away simply because senior managers, the project champion, the PM, and even key project workers lose interest in the project. The project has neither failed nor succeeded. It simply exists. Meanwhile, other new exciting ideas are being projectized. The organization's attention (and resources) is being directed elsewhere. The conflict between the old and the new may not be active. The senescent project simply gives way to the new.

13.3   THE TERMINATION PROCESS

The termination process has two distinct parts. First is the decision whether or not to terminate. Second, if the decision is to terminate the project, the decision must be carried out.

The Decision Process

Decision-aiding models for the termination decision fall into three generic categories. First, there are models that base the decision on the degree to which the project qualifies against a set of factors generally held to be associated with successful (or failed) projects. Second, there are models that base the decision on the degree to which the project meets the goals and objectives set for it. Third, there are projects that have fallen far enough behind their schedules and planned progress that the cost to complete them is no longer justifiable.

Balachandra et al. (1980; see also Raelin et al., 1985) state that project selection models are not appropriate for the project termination decision. Kumar et al. (1996, p. 277) agree. The argument is that the data requirements for selection models are too large and costly. They also argue that the evaluation of factors in project selection models may change as projects are evaluated at different stages in their life cycles. They note that the probability of technical success of a project is usually estimated to be close to 1.0 early in the life cycle, but lower during later stages when the technical problems are known. This, they say, would bias decisions in favor of new projects and against ongoing ones.

Lee et al. (1986) think that the first argument is generally untrue of those selection models actually being used, which are typically of modest size. As we have remarked elsewhere in this book, the uncertainty associated with most projects is not concerned with whether or not the project objective is technically achievable, but rather with the time and cost required to achieve it. The fact that selection criteria may change between the time that the project is started and the time it is judged for possible termination is not a relevant criticism of the use of a selection model. Indeed, whatever the source of the criteria for termination, they should be determined by the organization's policy at the time the decision is made—not judged by the policy of some prior time.

Adopting the position that sunk costs are not relevant to current investment decisions, we hold that the primary criterion for project continuance or termination is *whether or not the organization is willing to invest the estimated time and cost required to complete the project, given the project's current status and current expected outcome.* We emphasize that this criterion can be applied to any project.

Shafer et al. (1989) developed a project termination decision support system (DSS) based on a constrained weighted factor scoring model (see Chapter 2). The capabilities of most popular spreadsheets allow direct modeling of the scoring model, allow customized menus, and allow decision makers to adapt and enhance the model as they gain experience in the use of the DSS. The decision criteria, constraints, weights, and environmental data are unique to each organization, as are the specifics of using this (or any) decision model. A detailed discussion of various potential decision rules that might be useful with such a model can be found in Shafer et al. (1989). Figure 13-1 illustrates the structure of this model.

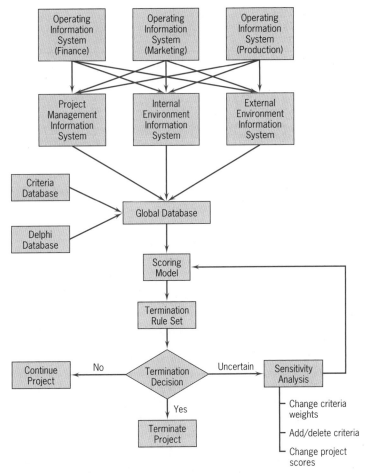

Figure 13-1   DSS structure for a project termination decision. *Source:* Shafer et al. (1989).

The Implementation Process

Once it has been decided to terminate a project, the process by which it will be terminated must be implemented. The actual termination can be planned and orderly, or a simple hatchet job. The former is apt to have significantly better results, and so we suggest that the termination process be planned, budgeted, and scheduled just as is done for any other phase of the project life cycle. Such a project is illustrated in Figure 13-2. Archibald (1992) has prepared an extensive checklist of items covering the closeout of both the administrative and substantive parts of the project (see Figures 13-3a and b).

In some organizations, the processing of the project closeout is conducted under the direct supervision of the PM, but this often raises dilemmas. For many PMs, termination signals the end of their reign as project leader. If the PM has another project to lead, the issue may not be serious; but if there is no other project and if the PM faces a return to a staid life in a functional division, there may be a great temptation to stretch out the termination process.

An examination of Figures 13-2 and 13-3a and 13-3b shows that implementing termination is a complex process. Note that in Figure 13-3b such items as A-4, B-4, C-3, and G-2, among many others, are actually small projects. It is all too easy, at this final stage of the game, to give this mountain of paperwork a "lick and a promise"—easy, but foolish. Someone must

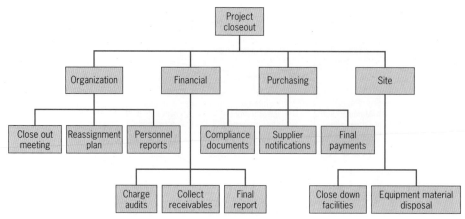

Figure 13-2   Design for project termination.

PROJECT TITLE _____   COMPLETION DATE _____

CONTRACT NO. _____   COST TYPE _____

CUSTOMER _____   PROJECT MGR. _____

The project close-out check lists are designed for use in the following manner:

Column I—Item No.: Each task listed is identified by a specific number and grouped into categories. Categories are based on functions, not on organizations or equipment.

Column II—Task Description: Task descriptions are brief tasks that could apply to more than one category but are listed only in the most appropriate category.

Column III—Required, Yes or No: Check whether the item listed applies to the project.

Column IV—Date Required: Insert the required date for accomplishment of the task.

Column V—Assigned Responsibility: Insert the name of the person responsible to see that the task is accomplished on schedule. This may be a member of the Project Office or an individual within a functional department.

Column VI—Priority (PR): A priority system established by the Project Manager may be used here; e.g., Priority #1 may be all tasks that must be accomplished before the contractual completion date, Priority #2 within 2 weeks after the completion date, etc.

Column VII—Notes, Reference: Refer in this column to any applicable Procedures, a government specification that may apply to that task, etc.

Figure 13-3a   Instructions for project termination checklist. *Source:* Archibald (1992).

handle all the bureaucratic tasks, and if the PM leaves many loose ends, he or she will rapidly get a reputation for being slipshod, a characterization not associated with career success.

The PM also has another option, to ignore the termination process entirely. The evaluation has already been conducted and praise or censure has been delivered. Rather than deal with termination, the PM may let the project administrator handle things. Project team members may well have similar feelings and reactions, and may seek new jobs or affiliations before the project actually ends, thereby dragging out some final tasks interminably.

Special *termination managers* are sometimes useful in completing the long and involved process of shutting down a project. In such cases, the PM is transferred to another project or reassigned to a functional "home." The termination manager does not have to deal with substantive project tasks and therefore may be a person familiar with the administrative

Item No.	Task Description	Required Yes	Required No	Required Date	Assigned Responsibility	PR.	Notes Reference
A.	*Project office (PO) and Project Team (PT) Organization*						
1.	Conduct project close-out meeting						
2.	Establish PO and PT release and reassignment plan						
3.	Carry out necessary personnel actions						
4.	Prepare personal performance evaluation on each PO and PT member						
B.	*Instructions and Procedures issue instructions for:*						
1.	Termination of PO and PT						
2.	Close-out of all work orders and contracts						
3.	Termination of reporting procedures						
4.	Preparation of final report(s)						
5.	Completion and disposition of project file						
C.	*Financial*						
1.	Close out financial documents and records						
2.	Audit final charges and costs						
3.	Prepare final project financial report(s)						
4.	Collect receivables						
D.	*Project Definition*						
1.	Document final approved project scope						
2.	Prepare final project breakdown structure and enter into project file						
E.	*Plans, Budgets, and Schedules*						
1.	Document actual delivery dates of all contractual deliverable end items						
2.	Document actual completion dates of all other contractual obligations						
3.	Prepare final project and task status reports						
F.	*Work Authorization and Control*						
1.	Close out all work orders and contracts						
G.	*Project Evaluation and Control*						
1.	Assure completion of all action assignments						
2.	Prepare final evaluation report(s)						
3.	Conduct final review meeting						
4.	Terminate financial, manpower, and progress reporting procedures						
H.	*Management and Customer Reporting*						
1.	Submit final report to customer						
2.	Submit final report to management						
I.	*Marketing and Contract Administration*						
1.	Compile all final contract documents with revision, waivers, and related correspondence						
2.	Verify and document compliance with all contractual terms						
3.	Compile required proof of shipment and customer acceptance documents						
4.	Officially notify customer of contract completion						
5.	Initiate and pursue any claims against customer						
6.	Prepare and conduct defense against claims by customer						
7.	Initiate public relations announcements re. contract completion						
8.	Prepare final contract status report						
J.	*Extension-New Business*						
1.	Document possibilities for project or contract extensions, or other related new business						
2.	Obtain commitment for extension						
K.	*Project Records Control*						
1.	Complete project file and transmit to designated manager						
2.	Dispose of other project records as required by established procedures						
L.	*Purchasing and Subcontracting*						
	For each Purchase Order and Subcontract:						
1.	Document compliance and completion						
2.	Verify final payment and proper accounting to project						
3.	Notify vendor/contractor of final completion						
M.	*Engineering Documentation*						
1.	Compile and store all engineering documentation						
2.	Prepare final technical report						
N.	*Site Operations*						
1.	Close down site operations						
2.	Dispose of equipment and material						

Figure 13-3b Checklist for project termination. *Source:* Archibald (1992).

requirements of termination and the environment within which the project will be operating (if it continues to live). If personnel performance evaluations are required, and they usually are, they must be prepared by the PM or whoever supervised the work of each individual team member, not by a specially appointed termination manager.

If technical knowledge is required during the termination process, a member of the project team may be upgraded and assigned responsibility for the termination. This "promotion" is often a motivator and will provide development experience for the team member.

The primary duties of the termination manager are encompassed in the following nine general tasks:

1. Ensure completion of the work, including tasks performed by subcontractors.
2. Notify the client of project completion and ensure that delivery (and installation) is accomplished. Acceptance of the project must be acknowledged by the client.
3. Ensure that documentation is complete, including a terminal evaluation of the project deliverables and preparation of the project's Final Report.
4. Clear for final billings and oversee preparation of the final invoices sent to the client.
5. Redistribute personnel, materials, equipment, and any other resources to the appropriate places.
6. Clear project with legal counsel or consultant. File for patents if appropriate. Record and archive all "nondisclosure" documents.
7. Determine what records (manuals, reports, and other paperwork) to keep. Ensure that such documents are stored in the proper places and that responsibility for document retention is turned over to the parent organization's archivist.
8. Ascertain any product support requirements (e.g., spares, service), decide how such support will be delivered, and assign responsibility.
9. Oversee the closing of the project's books.

It is likely that tasks 1 to 3 will be handled by the regular PM immediately before the project termination process is started. If the termination manager must handle these tasks, technical support will almost certainly be needed. Of course, many of the tasks on this list will be quite simple if the project is not large, but even with small- or medium-sized projects, the PM should make sure all items are covered. For routine projects, e.g., maintenance, simplified checklists are helpful.

Item 5 on this list deserves some amplification. The PM can do a great deal to reduce the problems of termination by dealing with these issues well before the actual termination process begins. As we noted in Chapter 2, arrangements for the distribution and disposal of property and equipment belonging to the project should be included in the charter and/or in the contract with the client. Obviously, this does not stop all arguments, but it does soften the conflicts. Dealing with project personnel is more difficult.

Most PMs delay the personnel reassignment/release issue as long as possible for three main reasons: a strong reluctance to face the interpersonal conflicts that might arise when new assignments and layoffs are announced; worry that people will lose interest and stop work on the project as soon as it becomes known that termination is being considered; or concern—particularly in the case of a standalone project organization—that team members will try to avoid death by stretching out the work as far as possible.

As long as the PM has access to the functional managers' ears, any team member who "quits work" before the project is completed or stalls by stretching out tasks or creating task extensions would be subject to the usual sanctions of the workplace. The PM should make it quite clear that retirement while still on-the-job, and tenure-for-life are equally unacceptable.

The first problem results when project leadership is held by a managerially weak PM. The height of weakness is demonstrated when the PM posts a written list of reassignments and layoffs on the project's bulletin board late Friday afternoon and then leaves for a long weekend. A more useful course of action is to speak with project members individually or in small groups, let them know about plans for termination, and offer to consult with each in order to aid in the reassignment process or to assist in finding new work. If layoffs are involved, the use of an outplacement organization is very helpful. (A preliminary announcement to the entire project team is in order because the interviews may cover several weeks or months.) It is almost impossible to keep termination plans a secret, and to confront the matter immediately tends to minimize rumors.

In a large project, of course, the PM will not be able to conduct personal interviews except with a few senior assistants. The project's personnel officer, or a representative from the parent firm's personnel department, can serve instead. This may seem like an unnecessary service to the team members, but a reputation of "taking care of one's people" is an invaluable aid to the PM when recruiting for the next project.

Termination by murder makes it very difficult to follow these suggestions about dealing with project personnel. The project's death often occurs with so little warning that the PM learns of the fact at the same time as the project team—or, as sometimes happens, learns about it from a member of the project team.

There is little the PM can do in such a case except to try to minimize the damage. The team should be assembled as rapidly as possible and informed, to the best of the PM's ability, about what has happened. At this point the PM should start the reassignment/release process.

Items 6 and 7 on our list, and several items in Figure 13-3b (cf. particularly sections I, K, L, and M) concern retention of project-related documents in the parent organization's archives. There are several reasons why document retention may be critically important. Following the completion of the project, the project's parent organization and the client may differ in their recollection of precisely what was promised as output—recall that agreements about the deliverables, including all change orders, must be in writing and signed off by all affected parties. They may differ in their recollection of precisely how nondisclosure agreements were worded.

The problem can be avoided by ensuring the documents retained do not include material previously identified as being "confidential." Most nondisclosure agreements require that confidential material be so labeled. If the inclusion of confidential information in project documents is mandatory for clarity or other pertinent reasons, it is sometimes possible to include it with the prior written permission of the discloser, usually conditioned that the project documents not be disclosed to a competitor, or pursuant to a court order, without immediate notice to the discloser so it can get a suitable court order protecting the confidential information. Finally, the parent organization and client may differ in their understanding of precisely what was approved or not approved at various stages of the project's life. Indeed, maintenance of sign-off records at each of the phase-gates of a project life cycle are critical for the parent organization because it relies on the approval of the current stage before investing the resources required to work on the next stage.* We strongly advise that the organization's attorney be consulted on matters of document retention.

---

*We thank T. D. Mantel, Esq., an attorney familiar with the legalities of document retention, for portions of this paragraph.

Project Management in Practice
When You Have to Kill a Project

It takes courage to kill a project, but sometimes you know it has to be done. Some common symptoms of a failing project are ill-defined initial requirements, constant changes in scope, excessive changes in resources and personnel, and extreme stress/tension over anticipated changes. Yet, a project may have followed the "book" and done everything right, but still need to be terminated. This was the case with a project in the U.K. where the client was highly committed to the project, contributing time, resources, and prompt decisions. The scope was clear, completion criteria agreed upon, the budget and timeframe acceptable to all. Early on, however, an unavoidable scope change had to be made, requiring a 20 percent increase in time and a 10 percent increase in cost, agreed to by the client.

As the project approached the end of the first phase, it was clear that the quality and schedule were both deteriorating, as indicated in progress reports to both the client and senior management. A quick review showed that the results were not going to be acceptable. With

the agreement of the PM, an outside Expert was called in to review the effort to date and make a recommendation. Then a joint meeting was held with the Expert, the PM, the Program Manager, and the primary contractor where it was decided that the best thing to do was to work together to complete phase one and then terminate the project, with a clean handover to another team to tackle phase two.

Although disappointing to everyone, the close and frequent communications of both progress and concerns throughout the project with upper management and the client, offered in timely, digestible amounts, reduced their expectations and protected the client from a surprise at the end. Honest, consistent communication throughout the project life cycle resulted in improved trust, integrity, and confidence in the vendor and their team.

Source: S. Somani, "Anatomy of a Failed Project," *PM Network,* Vol. 24.

13.4   THE FINAL REPORT—A PROJECT HISTORY

PMBOK Guide
2.4.3

Good project management systems have a memory, the Organization Process Assets. A key element of this memory is the Project Final Report. The final report is not another evaluation, though it may be an input to such, and/or for postproject control; rather, it is the history of the project. It is a chronicle of the life and times of the project, a compendium of what went right and what went wrong, of who served the project in what capacity, of what was done to create the substance of the project, of how it was managed. We learn from experience only if the experience is preserved and studied (Whitten, 1999). The fourth edition of PMBOK (Project Management Institute, 2008) emphasizes the importance of keeping and reviewing past experience as prelude to new experience.

The elements that should be covered in the final report are listed below. When considering these elements it is also beneficial to consider where the source materials can be found. For the most part, the required information is contained in the project master plan, a document that includes the charter, the WBS, all budgets, schedules, change orders, and updates of the above. In addition to the master plan, all project audits and evaluations also contain required input data. Almost everything else required by the final report is reflective, based on the thoughts of the PM and others involved in the project. There is little problem in knowing where the needed documents should be kept—in the project's files. Making sure that they are, in fact, there and that they are, in fact, up to date is a serious concern.

The precise organization of the final report is not a matter of great concern; the content is. Some are organized chronologically, while others feature sections on the technical and administrative aspects of the project. Some are written in a narrative style and some contain copies of all project reports strung together with short commentaries. What matters is that several subjects should be addressed, one way or another, in the final report.

1. *Project Performance*   A key element of the report is a comparison of what the project achieved (the terminal evaluation) with what the project tried to achieve (the project proposal). This comparison may be quite extensive and should include explanations of all significant deviations of actual from plan. A final earned value discussion can also be helpful. Because the final report is not a formal evaluation, it can reflect the best judgment of the PM on why the triumphs and failures occurred. This comparison should be followed with a set of recommendations for future projects dealing with like or similar technical matters.

2. *Administrative Performance*   The substantive side of the project usually gets a great deal of attention, while the administrative side is often ignored until administrative problems occur. There is also a strong tendency on the part of almost everyone to treat the "pencil pushers" with grudging tolerance, at best. The administration of a project cannot solve technical problems, but it can enable good technology to be implemented (or prevent it). Administrative practices should be reviewed, and those that worked particularly well or poorly should be highlighted. It is important, when possible, to report the reasons why some specific practice was effective or ineffective. If poor administration is to be avoided and good practices adopted, it is necessary to understand why some things work well and others do not in the environment of a particular organization. This becomes the basis for the recommendations that accompany the discussion.

3. *Organizational Structure*   Each of the organizational forms used for projects has its own unique set of advantages and disadvantages. The final report should include comments on the ways the structure aided or impeded the progress of the project. If it appears that a modification to the accepted form of project organization—or a change to a different basic organizational form—might be helpful for project management, such a recommendation should be made. Obviously, recommendations should be accompanied by detailed explanations and rationales.

4. *Project and Administrative Teams*   On occasion, individuals who are competent and likable as individuals do not perform well as members of a team when a high level of interpersonal communication and cooperation is required. A confidential section of the final report may be directed to a senior personnel officer of the parent organization, recommending that such individuals not be assigned to future projects. Similarly, the PM may recommend that individuals or groups who are particularly effective when operating as a team be kept together on future projects or when reassigned to the firm's regular operations.

5. *Techniques of Project Management*   The outcome of the project is so dependent on the skill with which the forecasting, planning, budgeting, scheduling, resource allocation, risk management, and control are handled that attention must be given to checking on the way these tasks were accomplished. If the forecasts, budgets, and schedules were not reasonably accurate, recommendations for improved methods should be made. The techniques used for planning, control, and risk management should also be subject to scrutiny.

For each element covered in the final report, recommendations for changing current practice should be made and defended. Insofar as is possible, the implications of each potential change should be noted. Commonly ignored, but equally important, are comments and recommendations about those aspects of the project that worked unusually well. Most projects, project teams, and PMs develop informal procedures that speed budget preparation, ease the tasks of scheduling, improve forecasts, and the like. The final report is an appropriate repository for such knowledge. Once reported, they can be tested and, if generally useful, can be added to the parent organization's list of approved project management methods.

The fundamental purpose of the final report is to improve future projects, hence its value in postproject control. It is ultimately focused on the project itself and on the process by which the project was conducted. Data on the project and its outcomes are available in the many interim reports, audits, and evaluations conducted during the project's life. But data on the process come largely from the PM's recollections. To ensure that significant issues are included, the PM should keep a diary. The PM's diary is not an official project document, but rather an informal collection of thoughts, reflections, and commentaries on project happenings. Such a diary tends to be a rich source of unconventional wisdom when written by a thoughtful PM. It may also be a great source of learning for a young, aspiring PM. Above all, it keeps ideas from "getting lost" amid the welter of activity on the project.

Occasionally, the project diary serves a purpose not originally intended. A PM working for a Minnesota highway construction company made a habit of keeping a project diary, mostly for his own interest and amusement. The firm was sued as the result of an accident on a road under construction. The plaintiff alleged that the highway shoulder was not complete nor was it marked "Under Construction" at the time of the accident. The PM's diary noted daily progress on the road, and it showed that the relevant piece of the road had been completed several days prior to the accident. The company successfully defended its position. All company PMs keep diaries now. A vice president of the firm mentioned that they are the same type of diary his high-school-aged daughter uses.

13.5   AFTERWORD

It is common for students to ask, "Does anybody really use this stuff?"—sometimes in less-polite language. Over the years there has been considerable academic research devoted to answering that question; see, for example, Ibbs and Kwak (2000). As we noted in this chapter, there has also been much research on understanding the causes of project success and failure. Comparatively little work has investigated the degree to which specific project management practices are associated with project success. Research helping to close that gap in knowledge has been conducted by Papke-Shields and her coauthors (2010). The remainder of this section reports on their work.

A survey was conducted with responses from 142 active project managers. The frequency of use of each project management practice associated with each PMBOK knowledge area was scored on a five-point scale (never, seldom, sometimes, frequently, always). The use of time management techniques was highest with a score of 4.03 for the average of seven time-related practices (project schedule and updates, baseline schedule, PERT/Gantt charts, activity lists, duration estimates, and updates). Risk had the lowest average score with an average of 2.79 for the six related practices (risk management plan, contingency plan, risk register, quantitative risk analysis, register updates, and preplanned responses).

In addition to time and risk, the other PMBOK knowledge areas surveyed were: integration, scope, cost, quality, human resources, communication, procurement, and status review. All knowledge areas had average practice-usage levels above the level reported for risk.

Project success was measured across three levels, low, moderate, and high. For all project management practice areas, the average use was higher in the high success group than in the low success group. Taken as a group, the practices had a significant impact on the difference between high and low success ratings. Further, the practices in each of the knowledge areas account for the differences in success.

The answer to the question at the beginning of this section is: Yes, the management practices are being used.

Respondents reported that PM practices associated with time, scope, and cost were widely used; practices associated with integration, HR, and procurement were used somewhat less; and finally, practices related to communication, quality, and risk tend to be used least frequently. (Papke-Shields et al. 2010, p. 659).

An unasked, but implied question follows the first question, "So what?" The answer is that "the use of practices across all knowledge areas varied significantly between the 'low' and 'high' success groups." (Op. cit.)
Project managers do use this stuff, and it helps.

 ## SUMMARY

At last, we come to the completion of our project—termination. In this chapter we looked at the ways in which projects can be terminated, how to decide if a project should be terminated, the termination process, and the preparation of the Project Final Report.

Specific points made in the chapter were these:

- A project can be terminated in one of four ways: by extinction, addition, integration, or starvation.

- Making a decision to terminate a project before its completion is difficult, but a number of factors can be of help in reaching a conclusion.

- Most projects fail because of one or more of the following reasons:
  — Inappropriate use of the project form of organization
  — Insufficient top-management support
  — Naming the wrong project manager
  — Poor planning

- Studies have shown that the factors associated with project success are different for different industries and the various types of projects.

- Success-related factors, or any factors management wishes, can be used in termination decision models.

- Special termination managers are often used, and needed, for closing out projects. This task, consisting of eight major duties, is a project in itself.

- The Project Final Report incorporates the process knowledge gained from the project. In addition to preservation of project records, the Final Report embodies the experience from which we learn. It should include:
  — Project performance comments
  — Administrative performance comments
  — Organizational structure comments
  — Personnel suggestions, possibly a confidential section

GLOSSARY

Termination by Addition   Bringing the project into the organization as a separate, ongoing entity.

Budget Decrement   A reduction in the amount of funds for an activity.

Termination by Extinction   The end of all activity on a project without extending it in some form, such as by inclusion or integration.

Termination by Integration Bringing the project activities into the organization and distributing them among existing functions.

Termination by Murder Terminating a project suddenly and without warning, usually for a cause not related to the project's purpose.

Termination by Starvation Cutting a project's budget sufficiently to stop progress without actually killing the project.

Termination Manager An administrator responsible for wrapping up the administrative details of a project.

QUESTIONS

Material Review Questions

1. List and briefly describe the ways projects may be terminated.

2. What problems may occur if the project manager does not have a follow-on project when the current project nears termination?

3. What are the primary duties of a termination manager?

4. On termination of a project, what happens to the information gathered throughout the course of the project?

Class Discussion Questions

10. Discuss the impact, both positive and negative, of termination on the project team members. How might the negative impact be lessened?

11. If the actual termination of a project becomes a project in itself, what are the characteristics of this project? How is it different from other projects?

12. Discuss some reasons why a Project Final Report, when completed, should be permanently retained by the firm.

13. What elements of the termination process may be responsible for making a project unsuccessful?

14. How is discriminant analysis used in project management?

15. What are some characteristics of a good termination manager?

16. How might one choose which termination method to use?

17. Why might a failing project not be terminated?

18. How can termination for reasons other than achievement of project goals be avoided?

19. What must the project manager do in planning, scheduling, monitoring, and closing out the project?

20. Which of the four major types of terminations are Political? Cross-Cultural? Senescence?

21. Would you suspect that most projects are terminated for "non-technical" reasons? Why or why not?

5. What is a budget decrement?

6. Identify the four reasons for project termination.

7. What does the Project Final Report include?

8. What factors are considered most important in the decision to terminate a project?

9. What issues should be considered when using the termination-by-integration method?

Project Termination Practices in Indian Industry

22. Why is the project termination phase important?

23. What is the significance of the project manager's role during the project termination phase?

24. What are the important factors to consider during a project termination phase?

Pulling the Plug: Projects in a Risky World

25. Is making a movie a project? If so, what techniques from project management could be drawn into the practice of making a movie?

26. What risks challenged this project?

Terminating the Superconducting Super Collider Project

27. Which of the various forms of termination was this?

28. The authors of this article maintain that politics is an important element of project implementation. Do you agree? Was this project terminated through "political" means?

When You Have to Kill a Project

29. What are your thoughts about doing everything right and the project still failing?

30. Does the admonition "Never surprise the boss!" now make more sense? Why?

31. Do you think the scope change at the beginning was the problem here, or was there going to be a problem anyway?

INCIDENTS FOR DISCUSSION

Electrical Broom and Supply Co.

IMSCO began manufacturing and distributing electrical brooms to industrial customers 43 years ago. Mr. Bretting, president of IMSCO, has been toying with the idea of using IMSCO's manufacturing and distribution expertise to begin making and selling consumer products. He has already decided that he cannot sell any of his current products to consumers. Also, if IMSCO is going to go to the trouble of developing consumer markets, Mr. Bretting feels very strongly that their first product should be something new and innovative that will help establish their reputation. He thinks that the expertise required to develop a new product exists within the company, but no one has any real experience in organizing or managing such a project. Fortunately, Mr. Bretting is familiar with a local consulting firm that has a good reputation and track record of leading companies through projects such as this, so he contacted them.

Three months into the project, Mr. Bretting contacted the program manager/consultant and mentioned that he was worried about the amount of risk involved in trying to introduce such an innovative consumer product with his current organization. He was worried that the project was oriented too strongly toward R&D and did not consider related business problems in enough depth. (This was a complete about-face from his feelings three months earlier, when he had approved the first plan submitted with no changes.)

Mr. Bretting suggested that the consultant modify the existing project to include the introduction of a "me-too" consumer product before IMSCO's new product was defined and tested. Mr. Bretting thought that some experience with a "me-too" product would provide IMSCO management with valuable experience and would improve later performance with the new product. He allowed the R&D portion of the project to continue concurrently, but the "me-too" phase would have top priority as far as resources were concerned. The consultant said she would think about it and contact him next week.

Questions: If you were the consultant, what would you recommend to Mr. Bretting? Would you continue the relationship?

Excel Electronics

Excel Electronics is nearing completion of a three-year project to develop and produce a new pocket Phone-Fax-Internet device (PFI). The PFI is no larger than a cigarette pack but has all the power and features of full-sized devices. The assembly line and all the production facilities will be completed in six months and the first units will begin production in seven months. The plant manager believes it is time to begin winding the project down. He has three methods in mind for terminating the project: extinction, addition, and integration, but he is not sure which method would be best.

Question: Which of the three methods would you recommend, and why?

CONTINUING INTEGRATIVE CLASS PROJECT

It is time to terminate the project. Decide what form of termination will be appropriate for this project and what the termination duties should include. (Perhaps a party?) How should the project results be distributed? Where will the project workers go next?

BIBLIOGRAPHY

Archibald, R. D. *Managing High Technology Programs and Projects*, 4th ed. New York: Wiley, 1992.

Baker, B. "Great Expectations." *PM Network*, May 1997.

Baker, N. R., S. G. Green, A. S. Bean, W. Blank, and S. K. Tadisina. "Sources of First Suggestion and Project Success/Failure in Industrial Research." *Proceedings, Conference on the Management of Technological Innovation*, Washington, D.C., 1983.

Balachandra, R., and A. J. Raelin. "How to Decide When to Abandon a Project." *Research Management*, July 1980.

Beale, P., and M. Freeman. "Successful Project Execution: A Model." *Project Management Journal*, December 1991.

Black, K. "Causes of Project Failure: A Survey of Professional Engineers." *PM Network*, November 1996.

Buell, C. K. When to Terminate a Research and Development Project. *Research Management*, July 1967.

Dean, B.V. *Evaluating, Selecting, & Controlling R&D Projects*. New York: American Management Association, 1968.

Green, S. G., M. A. Welsh, and G. E. Dehler. "Red Flags at Dawn or Predicting Project Terminations at Start Up." *Research-Technology Management*, May–June 1993.

Hussain, R., and S. Wearne. "Problems and Needs of Project Management in the Process and Other Industries." *Transactions of the Institution of Chemical Engineers, Part A*, April 2005.

Ibbs, C., and Y. Kwak, "Assessing Project Management Maturity: An Empirical Assessment." *Project Management Journal*, 2000.

Jiang, J. J., G. Klein, and J. Balloun. "Ranking of System Implementation Success Factors." *Project Management Journal*, December 1996.

Kloppenborg, T. J., and D. A. Plath. "Effective Project Management Practices during Expert Systems Implementation." *Project Management Journal*, December 1991.

Kumar, V., A. N. S. Persaud, and U. Kumar. "To Terminate or Not—An Ongoing R&D Project: A Managerial Dilemma." *IEEE Transactions on Engineering Management*, August 1996.

Lee, W., and S. J. Mantel, Jr. "An Expert System for Project Termination." *Proceedings, First International Conference on Engineering Management*, Arlington, VA, September 1986.

Papke-Shields, K. E., C. Beise, and J. Quan. "Do Project Managers Practice What They Preach, and Does it Matter to Project Success?" *International Journal of Project Management*, 2010.

Pinto, J. K., and S. J. Mantel, Jr. "The Causes of Project Failure." *IEEE Transactions on Engineering Management*, November 1990.

Pinto, J. K., and D. P. Slevin. "Critical Factors in Successful Project Implementation." *IEEE Transactions on Engineering Management*, February 1987.

Pinto, J. K., and D. P. Slevin. "Project Success: Definitions and Measurement Techniques." *Project Management Journal*, February 1988.

Project Management Institute, *A Guide to the Project Management Body of Knowledge* (PMBOK®), *4th ed.*, Newtown Square, PA: Project Management Institute, 2008.

Raelin, J. A., and R. Balachandra. "R&D Project Termination in High-Tech Industries." *IEEE Transactions on Engineering Management*, February 1985.

Shafer, S. M., and S. J. Mantel, Jr. "A Decision Support System for the Project Termination Decision." *Project Management Journal*, June 1989.

Whitten, N. "Are You Learning from Project to Project?" *PM Network*, March 1999.

Photo and Copyright Credits

Photos:

Chapter 1: *Page 12:* egd/Shutterstock. *Page 14:* stoonn/Shutterstock. *Page 15:* Courtesy Australian Department of Foreign Trade and Affairs. *Page 21:* Neirfly/Shutterstock. **Chapter 2:** *Page 50:* Lim Chew How/Shutterstock. *Page 55:* Jacob Wackerhausen/ iStockphoto. *Page 66:* Courtesy of Decor Cabinet Company. **Chapter 3:** *Page 107:* Jozef Sedmak/Shutterstock. *Page 109:* Ted Denson/Shutterstock. *Page 116:* Thomé de Gamond's 1856 plan for a cross-Channel link. Public domain image. **Chapter 4:** *Page 147:* africa924/ Shutterstock. *Page 158:* Andy Dean Photography/Shutterstock. **Chapter 5:** *Page 187:* AVAVA/Shutterstock. *Page 199:* Adam Gregor/Shutterstock. *Page 205:* ©Media Bakery. **Chapter 6:** *Page 222:* AFP PHOTO/ESA/Illustration by Medialab/NewsCom. *Page 225:* Popperfoto/Getty Images. *Page 227:* edella/Shutterstock. *Page 230:* Richard Hutchings/Photo Researchers. *Page 244:* Owen Franken/Corbis Images. *Page 246:* ssuaphotos/Shutterstock. *Page 250:* Losevsky Pavel/Shutterstock. *Page 255:* ©U.S. Coast Guard/ZUMAPRESS.com. **Chapter 7:** *Page 285:* Courtesy NASA. *Page 288:* Niar/ Shutterstock. **Chapter 8:** *Page 347:* ©Xinhua/ZUMA Press. **Chapter 9:** *Page 384:* David Butow/SABA/Corbis. *Page 393:* World Pictures/Photoshot. *Page 395:* Chicago Sun-Times, Al Podgorski/©AP/Wide World Photos. **Chapter 10:** *Page 455:* Gl0ck/Shutterstock. **Chapter 11:** *Page 474:* Credit: Lawrence Livermore National Laboratory. *Page 488:* Courtesy Australian Consulate. **Chapter 13:** *Page 557:* John Bird Photography.

Copyrights:

Page 30: © 1995 Indiana University Kelly School of Business
Page 82: © 1993 Darden Graduate Business School Foundation, Charlottesville, VA
Page 90: © 1999 Elsevier Science Publishers
Page 134: © 1984 Darden Graduate Business School Foundation, Charlottesville, VA
Page 140: © 1987 Project Management Institute
Page 168: © 1969 International Personnel Management Association
Page 213: © 1997 Project Management Institute

Name Index

Subject Index

Green entry numbers (W...) indicate those items that are located in the appendix section, which can be found on this book's Web site at http://www.wiley.com/go/global/meredith. The suffix "n" following a page number indicates a reference to a footnote.

*entries concern the nature of the PMI, or references to specific materials authored by the PMI.

Table A-1. Cumulative (Single Tail) Probabilities of the Normal Probability Distribution (Areas under the Normal Curve from $-\infty$ to Z)

Example: the area to the left of $Z = 1.34$ is found by following the left Z column down to 1.3 and moving right to the .04 column. At the intersection read .9099. The area to the right of $Z = 1.34$ is $1 - .9099 = .0901$. The area between the mean (center line) and $Z = 1.34$ is $.9099 - .5 = .4099$.

z	00	.01	.02	.03	.04	.05	.06	.07	.08	.09
.0	.5000	.5040	.5080	.5120	.5160	.5199	.5239	.5279	.5319	.5359
.1	.5398	.5438	.5478	.5517	.5557	.5596	.5636	.5675	.5714	.5753
.2	.5793	.5832	.5871	.5910	.5948	.5987	.6026	.6064	.6103	.6141
.3	.6179	.6217	.6255	.6293	.6331	.6368	.6406	.6443	.6480	.6517
.4	.6554	.6591	.6628	.6664	.6700	.6736	.6772	.6808	.6844	.6879
.5	.6915	.6950	.6985	.7019	.7054	.7088	.7123	.7157	.7190	.7224
.6	.7257	.7291	.7324	.7357	.7389	.7422	.7454	.7486	.7517	.7549
.7	.7580	.7611	.7642	.7673	.7704	.7734	.7764	.7794	.7823	.7852
.8	.7881	.7910	.7939	.7967	.7995	.8023	.8051	.8078	.8106	.8133
.9	.8159	.8186	.8212	.8238	.8264	.8289	.8315	.8340	.8365	.8389
1.0	.8413	.8438	.8461	.8485	.8508	.8531	.8554	.8577	.8599	.8621
1.1	.8643	.8665	.8686	.8708	.8729	.8749	.8770	.8790	.8810	.8880
1.2	.8849	.8869	.8888	.8907	.8925	.8944	.8962	.8980	.8997	.9015
1.3	.9032	.9049	.9066	.9082	.9099	.9115	.9131	.9147	.9162	.9177
1.4	.9192	.9207	.9222	.9236	.9251	.9265	.9279	.9292	.9306	.9319
1.5	.9332	.9345	.9357	.9370	.9382	.9394	.9406	.9418	.9429	.9441
1.6	.9452	.9463	.9474	.9484	.9495	.9505	.9515	.9525	.9535	.9545
1.7	.9554	.9564	.9573	.9582	.9591	.9599	.9608	.9616	.9625	.9633
1.8	.9641	.9649	.9656	.9664	.9671	.9678	.9686	.9693	.9699	.9706
1.9	.9713	.9719	.9726	.9732	.9738	.9744	.9750	.9756	.9761	.9767
2.0	.9772	.9778	.9783	.9788	.9793	.9798	.9803	.9808	.9812	.9817
2.1	.9821	.9826	.9830	.9834	.9838	.9842	.9846	.9850	.9854	.9857
2.2	.9861	.9864	.9868	.9871	.9875	.9878	.9881	.9884	.9887	.9890
2.3	.9893	.9896	.9898	.9901	.9904	.9906	.9909	.9911	.9913	.9916
2.4	.9918	.9920	.9932	.9925	.9927	.9929	.9931	.9932	.9934	.9936
2.5	.9938	.9940	.9941	.9943	.9945	.9946	.9948	.9949	.9951	.9952
2.6	.9953	.9955	.9956	.9957	.9959	.9960	.9961	.9962	.9963	.9964
2.7	.9965	.9966	.9967	.9968	.9969	.9970	.9971	.9972	.9973	.9974
2.8	.9974	.9975	.9976	.9977	.9977	.9978	.9979	.9979	.9980	.9981
2.9	.9981	.9982	.9982	.9983	.9984	.9984	.9985	.9985	.9986	.9986
3.0	.9987	.9987	.9987	.9988	.9988	.9989	.9989	.9989	.9990	.9990
3.1	.9990	.9991	.9991	.9991	.9992	.9992	.9992	.9992	.9993	.9993
3.2	.9993	.9993	.9994	.9994	.9994	.9994	.9994	.9995	.9995	.9995
3.3	.9995	.9995	.9995	.9996	.9996	.9996	.9996	.9996	.9996	.9997
3.4	.9997	.9997	.9997	.9997	.9997	.9997	.9997	.9997	.9997	.9998